The Animal D̶ ̶ ̶ ̶ rs

EVIDENCE OF ABUSE OF ANIMALS IN THE COMMERCIAL TRADE, 1952-1997

Edited by Mary Ellen Drayer

Introduction by Christine Stevens

With chapters by Jason Black,
Mary Ellen Drayer, Jim Flasch,
Ruth Fox, Peter Knights,
Jessica Speart, and Clifford Warwick

Animal Welfare Institute
PO Box 3650
Washington, DC 20007

Contents

Contributors

Jason Black, former Communications Director with the World Society for the Protection of Animals, personally participated in the revelations about Mexican cats provided to U.S. biological supply houses.

Mary Ellen Drayer, the book's editor, also researched and wrote the chapters on the random source dealer trade. She is Associate Editor with the Animal Welfare Institute.

Jim Flasch was the journalist responsible for bringing attention to the terrible mistreatment of animals on the premises of dog dealer Ervin Stebane. A hard-hitting series of articles in the *Appleton Post Crescent* shocked the public into realization of the unrelenting cruelty suffered by the dogs.

Ruth Fox, former Publications Coordinator for the Progressive Animal Welfare Society (PAWS) in Washington state, took part in highly effective investigation and law enforcement, including enactment of legislation requiring photographs of each dog purchased from dealers by Washington state scientific institutions.

Peter Knights is a brilliant undercover investigator with a special interest in wild birds, working with the Environmental Investigation Agency and now the Investigative Network.

Jessica Speart is a frequent contributor to magazines and newspapers. She worked closely with Shirley McGreal, head of the International Primate Protection League, in the preparation of the chapter on the primate trade.

Clifford Warwick heads the Reptile Protection Trust in England.

Additional research and writing by Valerie Stanley, Doris Vidigal and Victoria Fox
Layout and design by Patrick Nolan

Introduction

by Christine Stevens

Animal dealers have made ever-increasing amounts of money from their trade in recent years. Efforts to regulate commerce in dogs and cats for use in laboratories have fallen far short of the goal set by Congress in 1966. The importation of primates for experimentation and tests has brought huge profits to dealers even now, though the number of wild primates exported from Africa, Asia and South America has shrunk due to intense exploitation. The dealers take advantage of the scarcity to increase cost per animal.

The pet trade relies on animal dealers to supply them with exotic species, unwilling captives taken roughly and often painfully from their homes in the wild. Mothers and other family members are routinely killed to obtain infant primates.

Passage of the Wild Bird Conservation Act, prosecution of major bird dealers, and the airline ban on transport of wild- caught birds have dampened the enthusiasm that caused an explosion of activity in the trade in the 70s and 80s, when the United States imported 500,000 or more wild-caught birds every year. Traders have turned to exotic reptiles and amphibians, replacing some of their lost sales of wild birds. There are few laws to protect the frogs, toads, turtles and snakes now favored by the pet trade, except for the Lacey Act and the Endangered Species Act, which is under intense pressure from the Congress to repeal its basic provisions. These creatures are subjected to confinement so close that many are dead when the crates are finally opened. Clifford Warwick's chapter on the reptile trade vividly describes the problems.

The Animal Welfare Institute has documented dealer mistreatment of animals for many years. In 1952, Dorothy Dyce, AWI's Laboratory Animal Consultant, gave testimony in a trial before a Tennessee jury that landed an interstate laboratory dog dealer in jail. She showed photographs of the starving dogs forced by hunger to scavenge their fellows who had already succumbed. They fought each other for water from the hose she turned on in the dog dealer's absence. Pictures in the photo section show the acquisition of dogs at the Ripley, Mississippi trade day before transport to the dealer's holding pens in the Tennessee hills and then on to medical schools in Chicago. Despite this successful legal action, the Hargrove family remains in business. This family dog dealership is no exception to the rule. Numerous examples of dog dealer businesses handed on from father to son appear in U.S. Department of Agriculture (USDA) inspection reports of dog dealers throughout the country.

Random source dealers charge laboratories hundreds of dollars per animal if the animal is "conditioned," that is, fed to a normal weight, free of external and internal parasites and easy to handle. According to USDA, there are now less than 40 "random source dealers" (called "Class B dealers" in USDA regulations under the Animal Welfare Act) who sell dogs and cats to laboratories. Some have become millionaires as a result of their trafficking, and guard their turf zealously.

Acquisition of dogs came under Congressional scrutiny in 1965 when a Pennsylvania dealer filled an order for Dalmatians for a New York laboratory, and a hospitalized owner saw a photograph of his Dalmatian, Pepper, among 18 dogs and a goat seized by the local humane society and pictured in the local paper. The dealer and his load of animals were allowed to proceed the following morning. Members of the family who owned Pepper made a long, fruitless journey to a New York dog dealer after the Pennsylvania dealer falsely stated he had taken Pepper there. When the State Police questioned him, he admitted he had delivered Pepper to Montefiore Hospital in New York. Unfortunately, the Dalmatian had been experimented on, killed and incinerated by the time she was tracked down.

Chapter One records a televised interview with a large Midwest dog dealer's employee who decided to quit his job after he saw a pile of dog collars being burned and his own dog was stolen.

The Department of Agriculture has been severely criticized for weak enforcement of the Animal Welfare Act. Veterinary inspectors, who are in charge of visiting and reporting on research facilities, and lay inspectors responsible for the treatment of animals by dealers, have often complained over the years that their recommendations have not been followed by upper-level USDA personnel.

Undue influence by commercial and academic institutions has frustrated the men and women in the field who see with their own eyes the animals and the conditions they are forced to endure. There can be little doubt that the best of the inspectors, given the opportunity to pursue strict enforcement of the law, would have achieved much greater reduction of animal suffering, as intended by the Congress when it passed the Laboratory Animal Welfare Act (later renamed the Animal Welfare Act) and its four subsequent amendments. The best inspectors have, nevertheless, achieved important improvements for great numbers of animals. They have access to every animal room in institutions that use warm-blooded animals for experimentation and testing. The only exceptions are mice, rats and birds, animals who are not included in the inspection and animal welfare requirements that have so far been promulgated by the Secretary of Agriculture, although he has the authority to include them. A lawsuit calling for their inclusion succeeded but was lost in the Court of Appeals because of the intensive intervention of the National Association for Biomedical Research (NABR).

Within the last few years, USDA has stepped up enforcement and filed complaints against approximately 20 random source (Class B) dealers for violating the Animal Welfare Act. Despite this increased enforcement, the problem persists. "Bunchers," unlicensed dealers who supply random source dealers with animals, present insurmountable obstacles to USDA inspectors. Limited funding makes the needed "tracebacks" of B dealers' records exceedingly unreliable. When records are checked, a substantial proportion of the alleged sources prove to be either nonexistent or false. The dogs and cats, meanwhile, have disappeared into oblivion. Not, however, without having suffered fear, pain, thirst and hunger at the whim of the different dealers through whose hands they pass in networks extending beyond state lines and sometimes clear across the country. Once, in a visit to a laboratory, Dorothy Dyce actually found a dog still wearing his identification tag and restored him to his loving family. The elimination of random source dealers who sell to laboratories would go far to raising American standards for the treatment of companion animals. It would also eliminate the substantial cost of the thankless effort to bring these dealers into compliance with the Animal Welfare Act. In 1993 alone, USDA spent nearly a million dollars in an attempt to regulate random source dealers.

As the American conscience continues to expand, the abuses inherent in the commercial animal trade become more and more intolerable. Undercover investigations have revealed the collusion and conspiracy indulged in by big dealers in wild-caught exotic birds who have smuggled African grey parrots from countries whose laws prohibit any export of these remarkably intelligent and talkative birds. The U.S. Fish and Wildlife Service's "Operation Renegade" took years to reveal the true nature of the pet trade's chicanery and greed as they sacrificed great numbers of valuable birds to cut shipping costs. Not until nearly every airline in the world swore off the transport of wild-caught birds did the appalling mortality figures begin to drop. Without intense public outcry and hard, dangerous work by government employees, the wild-caught bird industry would have steamed along with business-as-usual, including such startling figures as 10,606 birds dead on arrival in a single huge shipment.

In 1981, Clark Bavin, the outstanding Chief of the FWS Law Enforcement Division, began a powerful sting operation against the criminals who were importing a great variety of exotic reptiles. Dubbed "Snakescam," the division sent agents on a 14-state sweep to arrest 25 suspects and seize more than 1,000 illegally traded animals. That was just the beginning. A total of 96 individuals were subsequently convicted and sentenced to prison and/or ordered to pay fines in federal court.

The demand from private collectors was the major cause of the illegal reptile trade 15 years ago, but the desire by ordinary citizens to own an exotic animal has greatly increased.

The pet trade feeds on the deep-seated human desire to procure a creature of another species. Some native peoples will nurse a puppy and a child at the same time, and a large variety of different cultures keep birds in cages. Some engage in singing contests with their captives. Turtles and tortoises are the animals of choice in other parts of the world.

Great writers and public figures have made their own pets famous. Verlaine's cat; Lord Byron's Newfoundland dog, Bos'un; President Roosevelt's dog, Fala; Samuel Johnson's cat, Hodge; Queen Victoria's dog, Sharp; Gilbert White's tortoise, Timothy, are all well-known to readers.

John Keats mourned, "I had a dove, and the sweet dove died, and I have thought it died of grieving." George Sand released her doves as a child when she found they were anxious to fly away. Leonardo da Vinci went to the markets where wild birds were sold, bought them and then released them.

The heartfelt individual protest of this great genius against the commercialization of wild birds for pets set an example that nations of the world have been slow to follow. But the very excesses of the modern pet trade, grown to huge proportions in industrialized countries, have led to the necessity for curbs on its overwhelming greed.

Commerce in animals sold to laboratories for experiments and tests is similarly massive and lucrative. It requires effective law enforcement and determined government intervention to protect the animals who have no other recourse from willful persecution and abject neglect.

I hope this book will help its readers to visualize the pain and sorrow of each animal and to demand that they be fairly and justly treated.

Acknowledgments

The Animal Welfare Institute is grateful for the assistance provided by many advocates for animals who have tried to protect animals from the cruelty and greed of animal dealers since the founding of AWI in 1951 right up to the present moment.

Our courageous investigator Dorothy Dyce laid the foundation for our campaign, and kept at it until her death in 1982.

Stan Wayman's heart-rending photos of dogs in dealers' premises, one of them with Mrs. Dyce, contributed greatly to the awareness of both Congress and the public about the trade in "random source" dogs for sale to laboratories. These influential pictures appeared in the old *Life* magazine, whose publisher was Henry Luce. It was his decision to feature this trade in a devastating eight-page documentary article. Though some *Life* staffers whispered that "the old man had lost his marbles," the magazine received more mail on this story than any other article, including those on the Vietnam war. We took a copy to every Member of Congress.

Without Congressional action, it would have been impossible to achieve any restriction on animal dealers. With respect to "random source" dog and cat dealers, major action in Congress began when Sara Ehrman, assistant to Senator Joseph Clark, alerted AWI to the theft of "Pepper," leading to the introduction of the Laboratory Animal Welfare Act by Congressman Joseph Resnick. Chairman W.R. Poage held hearings and got the bill through the House of Representatives. Senator Warren Magnuson introduced a similar bill, and Senator Mike Monroney effectively strengthened it. After hearings in which two brave doctors — Bennett Derby of Veterans Hospital and Nicholas Gimbel of Wayne State Medical School — testified in opposition to the National Institutes of Health, which tried to take over the implementation of the proposed law even before it was passed. But the Senators wisely decided to vest enforcement authorization in the U.S. Department of Agriculture, whose Veterinary Services comprised the largest group of veterinarians in the world.

The law gives USDA inspectors access to the premises of both dealers and the laboratories they sell to. We are indebted to the many USDA inspectors whose dedication to their greatly needed work deserves high praise. It has been an uphill struggle, with the National Society for Medical Research and subsequently the National Association for Biomedical Research working assiduously every step of the way to undermine the law's effectiveness.

Veterinarians Frank Mulhern and Earl Jones actually had to enforce the law for the first year without funding because of the antagonism of the Chairman of the Appropriations Committee — whose congressional district included the grounds of the notorious Ripley, Mississippi trade day where out-of-state dealers came to pack their big trucks with dogs and cats.

Space does not permit us to list the names of all the men and women who have done so much to reduce animal suffering through their insistence on enforcing the law's standards. Among the most outstanding: John Atwell, Richard Rissler, Cecilia Sanz, Janet Payeur, and Dale Schwindaman.

Fay Brisk was a pioneer in the long struggle. She first investigated Dierolf Farms and Zartman's auction, and brought their misdeeds to light. She started an animalport to help animals in transit. She even wrote a novel about animal dealing.

Mary Warner shares her passion for justice. She founded Action 81, named for the highway near her Virginia farm, a route where interstate traffic in random source dogs has long flourished. Action 81 receives and disseminates reports of missing dogs and tabulates and publishes its findings.

Cathy Liss, who is now Executive Director of AWI, has dedicated herself to the prevention of cruelty to animals. As a college student, she chased a hostile dog dealer's truck hundreds of miles, across state lines, until she ran out of gas, and has continued the pursuit of violators of the Animal Welfare Act, working with USDA to increase the effectiveness of enforcement of the law. She has overseen the work of Doris Vidigal, Victoria Fox and other contributors to this book. Her knowledge of this painful subject is unchallengeable. She has recently been invited to address the American Association for Laboratory Animal Science, a massive organization representing the industry. It has often shown intense hostility to the Animal Welfare Institute.

We are grateful to Shirley McGreal, head of the International Primate Protection League, for her determined and often dangerous fight against dishonest primate dealers who have caused extreme suffering to monkeys and apes.

We are grateful to the late Clark Bavin, whose name is memorialized in the Clark Bavin Awards, presented for outstanding wildlife law enforcement at Convention on International Trade in Endangered Species of Wild Fauna and Flora (CITES) conferences. He initiated undercover investigations, including Project Renegade, which brought down the biggest dealers in exotic birds imported from foreign nations. Without his dedicated and determined leadership of the Law Enforcement Division of the U.S. Fish and Wildlife Service (USFWS), the suffering and death of millions more of wild-caught birds would still continue.

Sue Lieberman, USFWS's CITES Policy Specialist, has carried on the Bavin tradition.

We are grateful, too, to former Congressman Gerry Studds for achieving enactment of the Wild Bird Conservation Act, which has curbed the smuggling and severe overcrowding of crates that resulted in the deaths of thousands of birds, a practice that has long characterized the international bird trade.

Greta Nilsson's scholarly tabulation of bird shipments as reported by the U.S. Department of Agriculture and Interior provided documentation that supported legislative action.

Dr. Gerard Bertrand, President of the Massachusetts Audubon Society, lent great strength to the campaign and gave masterful testimony in Congress for all the groups who fought for a strong law.

Mary Ellen Drayer, who holds a law degree from the University of Virginia, painstakingly edited the book in its entirety and brought to completion an effort to which AWI has devoted years of campaigning, investigation and reporting.

— Christine Stevens
Washington, D.C.
September 12, 1997

Chapter 1

Inside the Dog Dealing Business: Dogs, Dollars, and Deceit

"If you get that USDA number, you got it made," remarked a former commercial dog trade employee in the Midwest. "With that, they could make their own rules." The employee, who claimed to have maintained records and conducted sales for a dog dealer, granted a reporter with KSDK-TV in St. Louis an interview on the condition that his identity not be revealed.

"I'm kinda sick of it... I've seen enough of it," he said of the theft, fraud and abuse inherent in commercial dog dealing. The financial returns are enormous: around 5,000 dollars a week from dog sales at one particular operation. "It's so much, I don't know how it could be legal," he reflects. "I kept the records and I kept my mouth shut." Asked how he was paid, he answered, "In cash, paid in cash all the time, or drugs, it didn't matter, whatever you want."

He painted a grim picture of dog collars being burned to prevent identification of animals, dogs subjected to subzero temperatures and starvation; falsified names and addresses used on business transactions; and the common practice of shooting dogs in the head if they were "uncooperative." He said the dealer he worked for could find out when a USDA inspection of his kennel is going to take place, at least "two days" beforehand, and, to avoid being cited for overcrowding "we'd have to move them out, get rid of them, hide some in a barn somewheres till they came and left."

———

Q: Why don't you tell us first of all what your role was with this dealer?

A: I was a record keeper, and I went along on the buys and was a buyer at the sales and private sales.

Q: Who'd you buy from and where did those dogs come from?

A: From individual people and at first, I thought they were all legitimate dogs 'till I figured it out after a while that hey, nobody could have that many dogs every week, raising them on their own.

Q: So they were stolen?

A: Yes, we'd get them and I would keep records by having the people — the sellers would be there and they would make up fictitious names to write down and ask me if I knew any names we could write down for the dogs they could sell, 'cause without a license, they couldn't sell as many dogs as there were.

Q: And you would claim those people were where they got the dogs from?

A: Yes, and they'd have to have them for a certain amount of time and they didn't. They'd just have them for a day or two and they'd take the dogs, load them on a truck and take their collars and put them on a pile and set them on fire, the collars to the dogs.

Q: So there was no evidence then that they were possibly pets?

A: No, different town and different name and no phone number, and that was it. No address.

Q: What was your route? What towns did you go through?

A: Uh, down southern Missouri, Joplin, Kansas City, St. Louis, Rutledge, all around Missouri, and into Kansas and Arkansas too, Illinois.

Q: What kind of dogs?

A: Mostly hounds, gentle animals, house dogs, or pets. Y'know, something that wouldn't bite you.

Q: And you could tell that they were actually someone's pet at one time?

A: Oh sure, they had collars with their name on them.

Q: They went into their yards, how did they get the dogs?

A: They come up to you. I never seen anybody steal them but we know they were stolen when you know their name and they put different names down for the dogs. Why would you do that?

Q: How much money are we talking? You would then go back to your boss and what would you do with the dogs?

A: We'd take them and tag them and medicate them and supposed to keep them five days or so by regulation, and then we'd sell them to the hospitals up in St. Louis, Kansas City.

Q: St. Louis University?

A: We sold them there and at Tyson Research, for Washington University, and then Kansas City, St. Luke's or St. Jude's, I can't remember.

Q: Could any of those dogs that you sold to St. Louis University or Tyson, could any of those be my pet or my neighbor's pet?

A: Probably 75 out of 100 percent chance that it could've been.

Q: And in turn your boss is making how much money?

A: He bought the dog for 25 dollars and sell it for 100 in five days time, maybe have five dollars invested in a dog besides buying it, for medicine.

Q: What about the treatment from the time you pick up the animal to the time it's sold to research; how were those dogs treated?

A: Not very well. Beat if they didn't respond right, jerked around, choked with a choker, and then sometimes when it was uncooperative, they shot him in the head and drove off right then and took their tag off, used it on another dog.

Q: You actually saw dogs killed if they didn't cooperate?

A: Yes.

Q: How many?

A: I don't know... five a week maybe.

Q: And why would you kill them?

A: Just didn't want to fool with them. They were unruly. They all have to be gentle for the hospital, for the students and stuff. They can't bite you.

Q: Could they also have been tattooed? Would he kill them if he recognized that there was a tattoo?

A: Yes.

Q: And there would be proof that it was a pet?

A: Yeah. We always checked in ears and stuff to make sure. Usually if they were stolen, the dogs would come from 150 or 200 miles and if you take them on to St. Louis, that would be 300 miles from where we'd got them. So by then, not much trail of a stolen animal. If you're in another town, you're basically home free right then, once the collar's gone.

Q: You said you were also in charge of the records. How much was this dealer making or how much can he make in a year?

A: I'd say probably he could make $4,000 or $5,000 dollars a week and pay $700 or $800 dollars to buy them and make $4,000 or $5,000 off of one set of dogs, the same dogs he'd pick up.

Q: And off of someone's pet?

A: Yes.

Q: Why are you talking to us?

A: Well, I've had my dog stolen. I'm kinda sick of it too, I've seen enough of it. People's dogs gone, and a lot of them they don't even use. Now that's a bad thing to invest that much money and feed into having one, and to be treated like that. For somebody else to make ten times as much money as they should on something.

Q: And it's just not the money and food, there's a lot of love.

A: Yeah. That's why, that's the dogs they want, that's the only dogs they can use, that the doctors, students and stuff can use, nurses, whatever.

Q: Do you think those doctors and students realize what's going on?

A: No, I don't really think they do.

Q: Why?

A: Because they're wanting to get that test over with so they can make the money and go on so they don't have to fool with another animal again, except their own, but then if it got stolen they'd come crying then.

Q: You've seen some pretty bad things with these dogs.

A: Yeah. With the dogs that weighed too much at the time, starving them and leaving the chain, putting the chain tag on them, on a long-haired dog, and not fooling with it for a month other than somebody coming by and feeding them water and then when the dog just gets bigger, and the chain gets tightened around its neck, I've seen where they had to pull a chain out of the skin and stuff. Now that's not right either.

Q: And then other times you would just shoot them?

A: If it wasn't something I really didn't want to take no time, just shoot it in the head, burn it.

Q: How many dogs would he keep on his property at one time?

A: 200 to 250 altogether. And I could always tell, too, if it was a good-looking dog that might be a hunting dog. And before, whenever I had to buy dogs that nobody could use, y'know, from different dog dealers, but then some that I could tell were stolen, we'd go out and take them out in the field, and see if they'd hunt. If they was good, he didn't want to sell them for just a hundred dollars. He would turn them around and sell them to somebody else for 500 if they were a good dog. If they were beagles, they'd take them out and shoot a gun, and if they weren't gun shy, then he'd try to train them so he could make more money over than letting research have them.

Q: And you could tell that maybe somebody else had worked with that animal?

A: Yeah, you could. That's when I started to be able to tell that a lot of them were stolen. Had to be.

Q: And they were in too good a shape too.

A: Yeah.

Q: And what kinds — I'm thinking retrievers and other kinds — what kinds of house pets?

A: Foxhounds. They're not really house pets but they're farm pets and for general people, and, uh, beagle dogs and collies, and German shepherds, they can use them. And Dobermans are used a lot because they have short hair. Those are all house pets, or, y'know, family pets is what I call them.

Q: In terms of your work you were paid a lot of money, I guess.

A: Yeah, I took care of them real well, 'cause I kept the records and kept my mouth shut and went home.

Q: In exchange for keeping your mouth shut and doing the records, you would make how much and how would you be treated?

A: In cash, paid in cash all the time, or drugs, it didn't matter, whatever you want.

Q: How do you feel right now when you look back at what you were involved in and what people are going through?

A: I'll say I guess I got my just deserts because I had my dog stolen, so I know what it feels like now and it's not a very good feeling, about like losing a person to me if you've been with a dog that long for years.

Q: What do you think should be done with these dealers like the one you worked for?

A: I think the USDA or government or something should step in and watch them a lot closer.

Q: It's kind of a joke with the regulations, isn't it?

A: It is now. If you get that USDA number you got it made. There's nobody hardly touch you, they know everything that's going on.

Q: What do you mean if they get the number and they know what's going on?

A: Well, they get that USDA number where they can sell, and all it does take is money to find out everything else, when inspectors are coming in, check on your treatment, how it's a clean place and stuff.

Q: You can get enough warning?

A: Oh yeah, two days at least.

Q: How would it be if the inspectors were coming as opposed to if they weren't coming?

A: Pardon me?

Q: How would you compare the conditions that the dogs live in, typically, and then if you found out an inspector would be coming. Want to talk about that?

A: Oh, they'd be kept six or seven in a little pen about, uh, six feet by three feet by three feet. They'd have six or seven, they're only s'posed to have two in them I think, I'm not for sure. But we'd have to move them out, get rid of them, hide some in a barn somewheres till they came and left.

Q: Cages probably weren't cleaned out?

A: No.

Q: Food?

A: They had plenty of food and water, but they lived in a mess, y'know, subzero weather out in a little screen with no roof or nothing on this, the screen.

Q: All for money?

A: Yeah. For a lot of money, lots of money on somebody else. It's so much I don't know how it could be legal.

Q: Anything you want to add?

A: I can't think of nothing right now, I don't know.

Q: Did you get another dog?

A: No. Never have got another one.

Q: What do you do now?

A: Work in Jeff City.

Q: I was just curious because you seem to be doing well, you seem like a real together guy.

A: Thank you.

Q: You don't need that garbage.

A: I know there was people that didn't even think there was nothing bad to it. I didn't either for a long time, 'till I seen that day, I seen them burning the dog collars. That's the day I knew they'd stole them. Or you'd keep them, or you'd keep them.

Q: Just that last part you were talking about. Um, they're in such horrid conditions and then you mentioned that it's hard to believe that it's legal. You were talking about the money, lots of money, and how they, the dogs, were treated, combined with the money, and I think you said it was hard to believe that it was legal.

A: The only way that it was legal is they had that USDA number. If they didn't have that, they wouldn't have nothing. But with that, they even make their own rules on them with the dogs. That's the sad part about it, that there are no regulations hardly, or there is I guess, but they don't watch, and they should watch more because there's not that many people around the area that has USDA numbers.

Q: Then what they're doing is legal?

A: Yeah, it's legal. But nobody can prove it because they have a dog come up and say somebody come out and see their dog and they say that's my dog; no, look out here in this record. Joe Smith and so-and-so bought it. If you want to go track him down and say it's your dog, you talk to him.

Q: And there really isn't a Joe Smith?

A: And once you leave, that dog will be gone the next day. You'll never see it again.

Q: And Joe Smith is a name they just made up.

A: Yeah, just any name you want to make up that looks like somebody.

Q: Thank you.

Chapter 2

The Ervin Stebane Case

by Jim Flasch

Introduction

Dogs crowded into small, filthy cages, eating maggot-infested food. A dog castrated without anesthesia and then left to bleed to death. Unwanted puppies dumped alive into garbage cans or thrown against barn walls. Dogs killed and sold as food. Starving dogs cannibalizing their cagemates. These are just a few of the shocking images relayed through United States Department of Agriculture (USDA) inspection reports, newspaper stories and interviews with individuals who visited Ervin Stebane's Circle S Ranch outside Kakauna, Wisconsin.

Reports of inhumane treatment at Circle S, which supplied dogs, cats and other animals to research labs, persisted for close to three decades. Stebane continued a brisk business despite much negative media attention. The University of Wisconsin-Madison, the Medical College of Wisconsin in Milwaukee, Madison Area Technical College and the Appleton Medical Center all maintained their purchasing agreements with Stebane and kept him in business supplying dogs and cats for their experimental laboratories.

USDA was inordinately slow to take action. Despite continuing reports by its own inspectors of what appeared to be serious violations of Animal Welfare Act (AWA) regulations, USDA renewed Stebane's dealer license each year for more than 25 years. Stebane had been mistreating animals for decades, but it was the killing of a single dog that finally stopped him.

The Sunday Feature Assignment

In 19 years of professional reporting, I never had a story quite like the one I was assigned to write in the summer of 1985.

It began as a simple human interest story about a Wisconsin woman scheduled to undergo open-heart surgery. But it would be nearly a year before I wrote word one. By that time, the story was no longer about the woman and her heart problem. I had uncovered a much bigger story, a story about horrendous animal abuse and violations of federal law at a USDA-licensed animal dealer's facility.

Lorraine Stebane was scheduled to be the patient of Appleton Medical Center surgeons who had been trained on dogs supplied by her husband, Ervin Stebane. My editor felt this would be a great feature story, a twist, a case of dogkind helping humankind.

When I called Stebane and requested an interview, he thundered, "No!" He would not elaborate on his refusal. My reporter's curiosity was further piqued when officials at Appleton Medical Center (AMC) denied ever having dogs on their premises. Undaunted, I sought information on AMC through the federal Freedom of Information Act (FOIA). The story was stalled for a year while I waited for a response to my request. I conducted further research, including three additional FOIA requests and countless telephone calls, before all 280 pages of USDA records on Stebane arrived at my desk.

My first stories about the unspeakable conditions at Circle S, published in July, 1986, jolted the reading public into an outrage the likes of which this sleepy little community rarely sees. Phones in the newsroom didn't stop ringing for days, as the public demanded more investigation by state and federal agencies and the *Post Crescent*.

USDA records and inspection reports from 1980 through 1986 showed Stebane to be in serious and repeated apparent violation of the AWA. During the six years covered, USDA cited Stebane 27 times for improper and inadequate housing, 17 times for not providing palatable food and water and 11 times for inadequate sanitation and waste disposal.

According to the USDA reports, inspectors found dogs and cats kept in outside cages winter and summer without any protection from freezing temperatures, snow, rain or sun. On one occasion, kittens were left outside, tied in a feed sack.

Whole, dead calves and chunks of black, decomposing meat with ground-up bones often were thrown into dog pens as food.

Food and water were not provided daily. If there was any water at all, it was either frozen or contaminated with old food and feces.

Dead animals were left in pens or cages with live ones. Dogs were infested with parasites. Old, sick, wounded, diseased, pregnant or nursing animals were not separated from other animals, and the sick or injured did not receive veterinary care.

Animals were not properly identified, and records indicating where animals were obtained or how they were disposed of were not complete.

Two people who had worked for Stebane in 1978 provided me with a personal glimpse into the facts outlined in the USDA reports. As caretakers, they witnessed dogs so hungry they cannibalized each other. "You'd go to feed the dogs and there would be big 50-pound chunks of meat that you'd throw into a kennel with 15 or 20 dogs inside. The dogs would fight over whatever you'd put in there—meat, water, anything... they were so hungry," said one of the former employees.

They described watching helplessly as Stebane slammed a sheep in the head with a hammer and beat a goat with a shovel. On another occasion, Stebane castrated a dog with his pocket knife and then tied the animal to a stake in the front yard. The employees quoted Stebane as telling them an anesthetic wasn't needed. "See, you don't need to waste your money on no anesthetic. Just chop it off," he allegedly told them.

"There was blood all over the place, and [the dog] was whimpering real bad, but [Stebane] didn't do anything for it at all," said one of the employees. After five hours without any medical attention, the dog died, still tied in Stebane's yard.

Stebane allegedly disposed of puppies in a similarly heartless manner. "He just walked up, reached in and grabbed this pup, then he threw it into a garbage can, slammed the cover and walked away," said one of the workers.

They also noted the highly unsanitary conditions at Circle S. "[There were] maggots everywhere in the cages," said one of the employees. They claimed the smell of urine was so overpowering in one of the dog buildings they had to quickly retreat outside to catch their breath.

Past Is Prelude: Life on the Old Farm

After my series ran in the paper I was contacted by a woman who knew about earlier atrocities at Circle S. The woman, who I will call Betty, tipped me off to four stories that ran in our sister newspaper, the *Twin Cities News Record*. A March, 1960 article entitled "Shocking Filth, Frozen Death Found At Nearby Dog Farm" described the inhumane conditions at Stebane's farm. The article quoted observers, who reported "piles of dead puppies, half-gnawed carcasses of Holstein calves, and shocking filth."

On March 5, 1960, Wisconsin Agriculture Department investigators, along with Calumet County sheriff's deputies, converged on Stebane's farm with a search warrant. Betty, who was a member of the local humane organization, Animal Welfare, Inc., was an eyewitness to the raid. "It was just a horror camp," she recounted in our interview. Her eyes still reflected shock and disgust at what she had seen all those years ago.

"There were two very nice hunting dogs staked out in a corn crib. They had to stand in slime from animal entrails up to the first joint in their legs," she said. "They couldn't even lie down unless they were to lie down in that filth. Near one enclosed pig pen, in which there was the half-eaten body of a cat, were two piles of dead puppies whose frozen bodies were covered with snow, but had been uncovered in a recent thaw. Two smaller dogs were shut in an open pen in the field at the rear of the barn. On top of the cages in that section were the frozen bodies of three raccoons."

The doghouses outside the kennels were drifted shut with hard-packed snow, which kept the dogs, who were chained to the houses, from getting back inside for shelter. According to the *News Record* article, Stebane encouraged neighboring farmers to bring him dead cattle to feed the dogs. The article also reported that children of Stebane's tenant farmer had watched Stebane kill "sluggish" puppies by beating them against the barn. The article stated that when the winter snows melted, there were piles of dead dogs and puppies "lying about the barnyard and near the house."

As a result of the investigation, the Agriculture Department suspended Stebane's state milk permit for three days. The Department took no further action to rectify conditions at Circle S, nor did the county sheriff.

Members of the Outagamie County Humane Society had been working to put an end to Stebane's dog dealing since 1958. I interviewed an Appleton woman who had made three trips to Stebane's farm over the years. During one visit, Stebane physically threatened her. She recalled another visit, when she and another humane investigator "opened a grain bin, and here was a dead cat practically rotted away. And there were dead dogs all over. We saw dogs with such pitiful eyes, and I was horrified to learn that we could do nothing about it."

Two decades later, the scene at Circle S had not changed, nor had the official response. In 1982, animal welfare activist Debi Gasper wrote to Dr. Alva R. McLaughlin, the USDA veterinarian-in-charge for Wisconsin. She described a visit to Circle S to search for a missing dog:

> I was not prepared for the terrible conditions of the animals nor the filth of the buildings and cages.... Some of the cages had over 30 animals in them.... None of the pens had food or water.... The troughs were full, thick, and stagnant. All the animals were extremely thin, the ribs were protruding. A lot of them were lame, some never rose. The bodies of the dogs appeared to have mange, fleas, and many had open wounds.... In one of the pens that was full of coonhounds, a small calf carcass had been thrown in and the dogs were fighting over it.... I would appreciate any help that you could offer in cleaning up this situation. We are all willing to help you in any way we can and hope you will contact us soon.

In response, USDA sent an inspector to Circle S. The inspector later called Debi and confirmed her observations. During their conversation, he listed a number of AWA violations he had noted while at Circle S. But USDA's official inspection report, filed the same day, did not mention any of the items related in the telephone conversation, and USDA took no action against Stebane.

Back to the Present: Official Denials, Allegations of Theft

As the stories about Stebane unfolded on the front page of the *Appleton Post Crescent* every day, the phone lines got busier and busier with more witnesses, former employees, next door neighbors, and others calling me with more information.

One of the most interesting leads came from a woman in a nearby city who alleged Stebane had stolen her dog. In a letter to me she described hearing her dog barking one night and going outside only in time to see what appeared to be Stebane's truck disappearing down the street. Her dog, who had been taken from a chain in the yard, could be heard barking from the back of the covered pickup.

Enraged, the woman called the local police department and reported her dog stolen. She sent me a copy of the initial police report along with her letter. According to the woman, the police did nothing to help her retrieve her dog from Stebane's farm.

I wrote the story, leaving out mention of the police report. After the story ran, our publisher came to see me, demanding to know what was going on. His close personal friend, the police chief of that city, had come to his house the night before to protest the story and allegations that the department knew about the theft of the dog, yet refused to take action.

It was a simple matter of belief, I told the publisher. For one thing, I had the police report showing the woman had indeed reported the dog stolen by Stebane. Besides, I said, who are you going to believe, the police chief, who is your friend, or this poor woman who had her dog stolen from under her nose? As for me, I said, I'd have to believe the woman.

"Why's that?" the publisher demanded.

"Because you see," I said, "She's a nun, and that dog was stolen from the convent."

Red-faced, the publisher left my desk and never mentioned the Stebane series to me again.

As I learned later, that incident was just one of many involving police officials from Calumet County who denied knowledge of inhumane conditions at Stebane's farm, and some who even denied ever having heard of the dog dealer's operation. Calumet County Sheriff Dan Gillis, an 18-year veteran of that department, said he'd never had any problems with Stebane and had never heard of anything amiss at Circle S. Gillis said the Sheriff's Department was always aware Stebane was licensed as a dog dealer, but reported no complaints of inhumane treatment of animals. When my articles were first published, Gillis questioned why the complainants had not gone to law enforcement first. "We've been asking why people haven't come to us with these complaints since the first day the articles appeared," Gillis said. "We think maybe they have the cart before the horse."

Calumet County residents claimed they had, in fact, gone to the Sheriff's Department with complaints but that the Department had never acted on those complaints. The Department apparently had close ties to Stebane: according to a USDA inspection report, Stebane functioned as the county's dog catcher until 1986.

Allegations of pet theft had followed Stebane's controversial career since early on. Chester Wilson, a former investigator with the Calumet County Sheriff's Department, said Stebane was investigated at least four separate times on stolen dog complaints. "People from Appleton, Little Chute, Menasha and some others were missing their dogs and then they found them out there," Wilson said during one interview. "But we could never prove anything on him."

There were also allegations of pet theft made in USDA inspection records. Dr. Robert Taylor, a teacher with the Madison Area Technical College (MATC), which regularly bought dogs from Stebane, informed the USDA in Madison he believed Stebane was stealing dogs. One inspection report noted, "Stebane—stealing dogs, sells them to MATC for $18 for small, $35 for medium and $50 each for large dogs." In subsequent interviews, however, Dr. Taylor recanted ever having said he thought Stebane dealt in stolen dogs.

Recordkeeping wasn't the only thing MATC questioned when Stebane delivered dogs to them. According to USDA reports, Dr. Taylor noted Stebane's dogs were not fit for his students to work on. He said Stebane's dogs were "really sick, mange, parvovirus, tick-infested, external and internal parasites, malnutritioned [sic]. Cats with chronic respiratory problems. Severe malnourishment in all animals.... Unsanitary property. Six dogs and cats every month—everything's unhealthy."

Inspector General Investigates and Charges Are Filed

Soon after my first stories about Stebane were published, U.S. Congressman Toby Roth sent a letter to the U.S. Office of the Inspector General requesting an investigation into the conditions at Circle S Ranch. Roth also called for a "complete investigation" into whether or not USDA had compromised its position in dealing with Stebane. USDA records released during 1986 indicated that on one occasion, a USDA inspector left a report for Stebane to fill out himself and return by mail because there was no one at the farm to allow an inspection.

Roth's letter stated that although USDA was aware of Stebane's situation, it had never taken enforcement action.

"In most instances, the USDA either looks the other way, notifies Mr. Stebane in advance of upcoming investigations, or merely slaps Mr. Stebane with a simple fine, and the inhumane conditions continue," wrote Roth. "Mr. Stebane, who is a licensed USDA dog vendor, has had no problems renewing his license with your agency even though he has had repeated violations of the Animal Welfare Act."

One month after the Inspector General's probe began, USDA filed a complaint against Stebane alleging 16 separate violations of the AWA, including failure to provide adequate housing or lighting, failure to remove waste and failure to provide adequate records. Stebane was also charged with refusing to allow an inspection of his premises and refusing access to his records, a common complaint in inspection reports made during the previous six years.

The ink had hardly dried on USDA's civil complaint against Stebane when Congressman Roth upped the ante against the USDA and their own in-house investigation into the conditions at Circle S:

Roth called for a new investigation.

The Second Probe

In a September, 1986 letter to USDA, Roth charged the agency with conducting a "limited and cursory investigation" and issuing an "incomplete report" of conditions at Stebane's ranch. "It seems to me that in this particular case, and perhaps in others, there has been willful negligence in enforcing the law. Inspectors evidently have been told not to enforce the provisions of the Animal Welfare Act," wrote Roth. "Does it take pressure from a member of Congress before action is finally instituted that might result in the lifting of the license of someone who has treated the Animal Welfare Act as if it were a minor inconvenience?"

A Day in Dog Court

In November of 1986, USDA held an administrative hearing on the charges brought against Stebane. Former USDA inspector Kathryn McGlumphy, who inspected Stebane's ranch several times, testified that pens and cages were filthy and that "animals had to urinate and defecate on their bedding because there was no litter facility." McGlumphy also testified she had observed large accumulations of feces outside the pens. "The minute I got out of the vehicle, all I could smell was dog manure. There were very large piles of it," said McGlumphy. "By the amount and the smell, I could tell it was there for a long time."

McGlumphy stated that during one inspection, she discovered a freezer full of meat in one of the animal barns. Both the freezer and the meat were covered with dried blood, and the bottom shelf of the freezer was coated with film and slime.

She also stated that on one occasion she was unable to conduct an inspection because Stebane had become verbally abusive, shaking a hammer at her as he spoke.

The judge issued his decision in the case on March 2, 1987.

Despite his acknowledgment of Stebane's "recurring non-compliance" with AWA regulations, he ordered Stebane to pay a mere $1,500 fine and suspended his USDA license for 20 days, which prohibited him from buying or selling animals during that time but allowed him to keep the animals he already had. Both USDA and Stebane filed appeals. USDA attorney John Griffith said the agency appealed because it felt the penalty wasn't severe enough. Both Stebane's and USDA's appeals were rejected, and Stebane ultimately paid the fine and underwent the inconsequential 20-day suspension.

Despite the judge's conclusion that Stebane had violated the AWA, both the University of Wisconsin at Madison and the Madison Area Technical College announced they would still buy dogs and cats from Stebane as long as he was licensed by USDA. Dr. Ellis Seavey, director of the animal care unit at UW-Madison, said the school was not a regulatory agency and had no responsibility to inquire about the conditions at Stebane's farm. Seavey said the school relied solely on the integrity of the USDA to inspect and license dealers and to alert buyers of any problems.

The judge's decision to fine Stebane and suspend his license came just 11 days after USDA inspector Dr. Richard Bertz had reinspected Circle S and noted nine different deficiencies on his report. Stebane's 20-day license suspension began on September 6, 1993, the same day Dr. Bertz conducted another inspection of Circle S and reported another three deficiencies. After the license suspension was lifted, Stebane was back in business, and he continued to run his operation just as he had in the past. USDA records from 1987 to 1993 documented chronic apparent violations of the AWA. Inspectors noted the same deficiencies time after time, but USDA took no further action against Stebane, and continued to renew his dealer license.

The Sting

The tide began to turn in the spring of 1993, when a member of an animal welfare group in Fox River Valley (WI) contacted a number of people outside Wisconsin to set up a "sting" operation.

Chris DeRose, a longtime animal activist with Last Chance For Animals, planned an undercover investigation at Circle S. DeRose's idea was to send a couple to Circle S to purchase a dog for meat and ask to have the animal butchered on the premises.

Stebane was believed to have been selling dogs for human consumption for some time.

A March 18, 1991 USDA report referred to a conversation between an unnamed woman and USDA inspectors about Stebane selling dogs for food. According to the report, the woman stated "she believes [Circle S is] a meat processing plant for animals (dogs, cats, etc.).... also states that she believes from information she has, that this is a dog ring taking dogs from other areas and selling them for $20.00 each."

On May 26, 1993, DeRose's undercover investigators entered the Circle S kennels with Stebane. One of the investigators wore a fake cast on his arm that concealed a small video camera. The recording mechanism was hidden in a fanny pack. The investigators chose a dog and videotaped Stebane as he shot the dog in the head. Stebane pulled out a knife, slit the dog's throat and began butchering the animal into quarters. "This knife ain't sharp enough," he quipped as he struggled with the dull knife.

The footage was later televised, drawing nationwide public outrage. When the local district attorney saw the videotape, he immediately swore out a warrant for Stebane's arrest. Stebane was charged with cruelty to animals and violating a Wisconsin law requiring anyone processing meat for human consumption to be licensed. Deputies removed 159 dogs from Circle S and placed them in protective custody at 12 humane society shelters throughout Wisconsin.

When Judge Donald Poppy learned DeRose had paid the investigators $1000 (and $400 for expenses) to purchase the dog and film Stebane butchering it, he dismissed both charges against Stebane, citing a Wisconsin law allowing individuals to kill their own animals and sell the remains for food. Judge Poppy also cited an entrapment approach to DeRose's methods of getting Stebane to sell and butcher the dog.

Judge Poppy ordered the return of the confiscated dogs to Stebane, but before the sheriff could make the rounds to all the shelters, the dogs began disappearing. Forty-seven dogs housed at seven different sites were reported stolen to law enforcement officials in six different jurisdictions. The rest of the dogs were returned, and Stebane was in business once again.

The Final Outcome

In May of 1993, Congressman Roth wrote a letter to USDA acting Inspector General Charles Gillun, requesting USDA to suspend Stebane's license. He also appealed to USDA Secretary Mike Espy, asking for "specific recommendations" on how the Animal Welfare Act could be strengthened legislatively "to ensure that operations such as Mr. Stebane's are not allowed to operate in the future."

USDA took an uncharacteristically bold step. On June 30, 1993, it suspended Stebane's license for 21 days and filed a formal complaint requesting "additional penalties," including permanent revocation of Stebane's license. According to the complaint, Stebane had "willfully violated the Animal Welfare Act" between November 1, 1991 and May 25, 1993, the day before DeRose's undercover investigation. Stebane was charged with failing to maintain complete records of who sold him dogs and cats and failing to identify "numerous dogs and cats" as required. Stebane had the right to schedule an oral hearing but opted not to, thus avoiding a public hearing of the case.

According to USDA public relations specialist Margaret Webb, the complaint was amended later to include "more recordkeeping charges, as well as violations of veterinary care, sanitation, housing and food regulations." The amended complaint charged Stebane with failure to hold dogs or cats for the required five days after purchase; failure to provide uncontaminated, wholesome and palatable food; failure to house dogs in compatible groups; and housing dogs in an old school bus that had accumulations of excreta and rust. Inspectors had been reporting similar violations virtually since Stebane first obtained his USDA license in 1966.

The amended charges and continuing battle with animal welfare groups was apparently too much for Stebane. On March 14, 1994, he signed a consent agreement—neither admitting nor denying USDA's charges—and permanently relinquished his Class B license. He agreed to dispose of the 160 animals still on his premises by April 14, 1994, and cease and desist from selling, acquiring or holding any more dogs or cats.

Chapter 3

Regulation of Class B Animal Dealers Selling Dogs and Cats For Research

---

by Mary Ellen Drayer

Licensing and Inspection

The Animal Welfare Act requires animal dealers to be licensed and authorizes the U.S. Department of Agriculture (USDA) to set forth minimum standards of care and recordkeeping requirements for the handling, purchase, and sale of animals by dealers and research facilities. USDA is also charged with inspecting dealer facilities to enforce compliance with the law. USDA licenses two different types of dealers. Class A dealers breed the animals they sell, and Class B dealers purchase animals from various sources and then resell them. Although there are more than one thousand Class B dealers, less than 40 of them are "random source" dealers who sell animals for research.

When the Animal Welfare Act was first enacted in 1966, licensing and inspection of dealers was assigned to USDA's Veterinary Services department, an existing 50-state network of 1,200 veterinarians. But in 1988, during reorganization of the Animal and Plant Health Inspection Service (APHIS), a subdivision of USDA, enforcement of the Animal Welfare Act was moved from Veterinary Services to a new body, Regulatory Enforcement and Animal Care (REAC). Touted for its increased "visibility" and theoretical dedication to animal welfare, REAC was assigned enforcement of the AWA. Abruptly, the ability to call upon a Veterinary Inspector close to a particular dealer's compound or a research facility was lost. Instead, the enormously reduced number of inspectors frequently had to drive long distances to inspect the premises of a dealer who, as often as not, was away from home, so the planned inspection could not take place. As the number of licensed dealers and research facilities continued to grow, the number of inspectors dwindled. By 1996, APHIS had just 71 field inspectors to ensure that the 2,506 research facility sites, 4,265 dealer sites, 2,453 exhibitor sites, 417 intransit handler sites and 725 intransit carrier sites licensed by USDA were complying with AWA requirements. In 1996, the average number of inspections was 1.22 per facility.

In October 1996, APHIS reorganized its Animal Care (AC) program. REAC was dissolved, and all regulatory enforcement activites were moved to a new unit, Investigative and Enforcement Services (IES). AC retained responsibility for licensing, registration, inspection and investigation of complaints from members of the public. The AC program is admistered through regional offices in Annapolis, Maryland; Fort Worth, Texas; and Sacramento, California (See "USDA-APHIS-AC Regional Offices"). APHIS plans to eventually maintain just two regional offices, one in Colorado and one in North Carolina.

Enforcement of the Animal Welfare Act

When an inspector documents violations of animal care or record-keeping standards at an animal dealer's facility, APHIS has the option of issuing a warning notice, suspending the dealer's license for up to 21 days, offering the dealer the opportunity to pay a monetary "stipulation" or fine in lieu of administrative proceedings, or referring the case to USDA's Office of General Counsel (OGC) for formal administrative action. Many dealers have long histories of violating the Animal Welfare Act, and USDA has frequently been criticized for being slow to take action against even the worst offenders. Some dealers have remained in business for decades despite serious, recurrent violations. USDA has permanently revoked the licenses of only a few random source dealers. In many cases where USDA has revoked or suspended a dealer's license, a family member, friend or employee of the dealer steps forward and obtains a license in his or her own name. The business continues uninterrupted, and the new licensee often carries on the same illegal activity that the original licensee engaged in.

A 1995 Office of Inspector General (OIG) report concluded that APHIS was not aggressive enough in using its enforcement powers to discourage violation of the Act.[1] For instance, the report noted that although the Act allows APHIS to assess up to $2,500 per violation, most stipulations were limited to $300 or less. The report referred to an April 1994 APHIS memorandum recommending that stipulations range from $100 and $200 per violation. The report also stated that APHIS did not aggressively pursue collection of stipulations and had, in some instances, arbitrarily reduced the amount of stipulations.[2] In addition, the OIG report noted that APHIS "generally accommodated facility operators who routinely refused APHIS inspectors access to their facilities, instead of issuing suspensions or taking other available enforcement actions." The report concluded that APHIS's enforcement policy offered little incentive for dealers to comply with the Act. "We identified several instances in which facilities continued to commit violations even after the violations had been identified by APHIS.... We visited six facilities where APHIS had previously levied stipulations, and found that five of them had continued to commit violations of the Act," the report stated.[3]

Formal administrative actions against violators can take up to three years or longer, during which time the individual can remain in business and even continue violating the Act. One example is a case USDA referred to OGC in 1991. The dealer involved, a random source dealer in Indiana, had failed to maintain accurate acquisition records and was suspected of operating an unregistered facility. The case was with OGC for almost three years before any action was taken. During this time, the dealer refused an APHIS inspector access to his facility on 29 separate occasions. On the few occasions when the inspector was able to conduct inspections, he documented continuing recordkeeping and animal care violations. Finally, in June 1994, USDA filed a complaint against the dealer. During the same month, the agency confiscated 29 dogs from the dealer's facility. Many of the dogs were so ill they had to be euthanized. A hearing on the 1994 complaint did not take place until May 1996, nearly two years later. In December 1996, an administrative law judge fined the dealer $15,000 and permanently revoked his license. Even though USDA announced that it had "shut down" the dealer, the dealer requested and was granted additional time to appeal the decision, which meant he could stay in business while his appeal was pending. In February 1997, USDA filed yet another complaint against the dealer charging him with 1) failure to allow inspection of his facility; 2) failure to make records of acquisition and disposition available to APHIS; 3) failure to have any health certificates or pound certificates for dogs; 4) failure to identify dogs; 5) failure to provide adequate veterinary care for dogs; and 6) failure to ensure that primary enclosures were constructed and maintained so as to have no sharp points that could injure the animals contained therein. The dealer never appealed Judge Palmer's decision, and it finally went into effect in May 1997. This dealer remained in business for six years after APHIS inspectors first began documenting serious problems at his facility.

Recordkeeping Requirements

One of the ways USDA attempts to prevent the theft of dogs and cats for sale to research is by permitting random source dealers to obtain dogs and cats only from 1) other dealers licensed by USDA, 2) municipal or contract pounds, and 3) individuals who have bred and raised the animals themselves. To ensure that the animals dealers resell to research facilities have been obtained legally, USDA requires dealers to record the name, address, vehicle license number and driver's license number of the person from whom each animal is acquired. USDA audits of dealer records have revealed serious and widespread disregard of this simple requirement. In fact, USDA investigators have uncovered numerous instances of dealers falsifying the identities of their suppliers. One individual, who regularly sold animals to several licensed Class B dealers and who was himself briefly licensed as a B dealer, admitted selling animals he had not bred and raised and providing the dealer he sold them to with false names to be recorded on the dealer's acquisition sheet. USDA never took any action against him. (See Appendix D, "Affidavit of Mark Yardley")

Random source dealers frequently acquire animals from unlicensed individuals like the one described above. These individuals are known as "bunchers." Bunchers collect dogs and cats from various sources and are oftentimes involved in fraudulent activities, even theft. Some obtain animals by responding to newspaper advertisements offering animals "Free to a Good Home" or "adopt" them from shelters or pounds. Others steal dogs and cats from their owners' backyards. Bunchers deliver animals directly to the dealers' facilities, arrange clandestine exchanges, or sell them to dealers at dog auctions, otherwise known as "trade days." Many licensed dealers make regular trips to dog auctions, frequently travelling to auctions in other states. These events are usually part of a larger swap meet or flea market, where clothing, tools, furniture and other household items are offered for sale. Hunters bring their dogs, guns and other hunting supplies to trade or auction off. They can sell unwanted dogs to the dealers, who pay between $15 and $35 per dog. Monthly dog auctions take place in several states, but two of the largest are in Rutledge, Missouri and Ripley, Mississippi.

Whether purchased at dog auctions, pounds or from individuals, many dogs and cats destined for sale to research are transferred from dealer to dealer, often moving across state lines several times. This makes it virtually impossible for pet owners to track down their missing pets and seriously impedes USDA's ability to trace the sources of animals to make sure they are legitimate.

USDA attempted to strengthen its regulations relating to acquisition of random source animals in 1987. The proposed regulations, published on March 31, 1987, included a prohibition on the purchase, sale, use or transportation of stolen animals (Section 2.60); a requirement that dealers record the vehicle license number and state and driver's license number and state for every individual from whom a dog or cat is purchased (Section 2.75); and a requirement that all operators of auction sales be licensed as Class B dealers (Section 2.1). USDA also proposed to add a new section to the regulations permitting Class B dealers to obtain cats and dogs only from state, county or city owned and operated pounds or shelters or from individuals who have bred and raised the animals on their own premises (Section 2.132).

In setting forth the proposed regulation, USDA explained the obvious necessity for a limitation on the sources of dogs and cats sold to research by class B dealers:

In the past few years there have been several instances of licensed dealers obtaining dogs and cats by fraudulent means and apparently knowingly purchasing stolen animals. These dealers were all class "B" dealers who buy and sell animals and the dogs and cats were all random source type animals, that is, they were not purchased from the persons who bred and raised the animals. The Department has also noted an increase in licensed dealers buying dogs and cats at flea markets or trade-day type sales. These animals are purchased from anyone and are usually purchased one, two, or three dogs or cats at a time. Many times the sellers have just recently acquired the dogs or cats and they are not what one would consider a family pet and have not been bred and raised by the persons who sold them. The net effect of the above types of activity is to encourage animal theft for profit. The theft of dogs and cats to supply the needs of research facilities is one of the basic reasons that the original Animal Welfare Act was passed. The above type of activity is, therefore, not in keeping with the original intent of Congress to protect animal owners from the theft of their pets.[4]

USDA stated that another intention of the proposed regulation "was to eliminate the indiscriminate impoundment of 'lost' animals by contract pound operators who are also licensed dealers":

In the past several years, we have learned of increasing numbers of complaints and allegations that contract private animal pounds that are also licensed dealers under the Act have been overzealous in impounding dogs and cats. There are allegations that the impounded dogs and cats are not always stray or lost animals. In addition, the Agency has become aware of several instances where licensed dealers obtained stolen dogs and cats, or obtained dogs and cats under false pretenses or misrepresentation.[5]

The National Association for Biomedical Research and its allies attacked USDA's proposals during the public comment period following publication of the proposed regulations. In a March 15, 1989 request for additional comments, USDA noted: "We received 377 comments (352 from the research community) stating that proposed Section 2.60 [prohibiting the sale, purchase and use of stolen animals] should either be deleted from the regulations entirely or that it should be limited to persons 'knowingly and willfully' engaging in activities using stolen animals." And even though USDA stated it had received 2,865 comments from the general public supporting proposed Section 2.132, it also stated that it received 167 comments from "members of the research community," who claimed such a limitation on the sources of dogs and cats "would limit the availability of animals for use by research facilities, and/or would increase the cost of animals to research facilities." In response to the researchers' complaints, USDA weakened the proposal, removing the provision prohibiting dealers from obtaining dogs and cats from nongovernment pounds and shelters. Dealers would be allowed to buy dogs and cats from private or contract pounds, "but with certain restrictions in order to better ascertain how, where, from whom, and when the dogs and cats were obtained by the pound."[6] Any licensee who also operated a private or contract pound or shelter would be required to maintain two separate facilities, one for the pound and one for the dealer facility, and also comply with the 10-day holding period set forth in Section 2.101 (requiring any dog or cat acquired by a dealer from a contract or private pound to be held 10 full days). Despite the researchers' objections, USDA retained 1) the prohibition on dealers obtaining random source dogs and cats from individuals who have not bred and raised them on their own premises; 2) Section 2.60, prohibiting the sale, purchase or use of stolen dogs and cats; 3) the proposed recordkeeping requirements under Section 2.75; and 4) the requirement that auction operators be licensed under Section 2.1. USDA published the final rules in August 1989.

The Traceback Investigations

The gross failure of many dealers to keep accurate records of the source of dogs and cats that they acquire prompted USDA to conduct two traceback investigations in the early 1990's: the "Midwest Dog Theft Task Force" and the "Random Source Traceback Project." In response to allegations from members of the public and animal welfare groups that dealers, primarily in Missouri and Arkansas, were selling stolen dogs to research institutions, USDA launched the Midwest Dog Theft Task Force in 1990. The Task Force audited the records of nine Class B dealers: Bruce Barnfield, Don Davis, Raymond Eldridge, Randall Huffstutler, Dairal Caruthers, Wilbert Gruenefeld, Dale Hammond, Glenn Johnston and William Walker. The Task Force also monitored activities at five flea markets where licensed dealers were known to trade dogs. The investigation was overseen by then APHIS Administrator Dr. James W. Glosser, a former researcher for the Centers for Disease Control in Atlanta, Georgia.

Despite the Task Force's discovery of serious discrepancies in dealer records, USDA announced in July 1990 that "nearly all" the dealers investigated had complied with federal regulations on keeping accurate records. Even though dealers had provided long lists of sources who could not be located at all, Dr. Glosser acknowledged only that "two dealers may have falsified records." He concluded, "No evidence was found to indicate dealers were knowingly buying stolen animals."

Dr. Glosser and his deputy, Dr. Joan Arnoldi, took the position that education would solve the problems associated with poor recordkeeping and mistreatment of animals by dealers and laboratories. Thus, despite a considerable expenditure of time and scarce funds, the Task Force essentially assured the public that dealers were only recording false or fictitious names so that their bunchers would not have to become licensed under the Animal Welfare Act. A very light slap on the wrist was administered when USDA issued "Warning Notices" to unlicensed dealers and dealers who failed to keep required records of the dogs and cats they purchased. University administrators and chief executive officers of commercial laboratories breathed a sigh of relief as Dr. Glosser's remarks served to clear them of all responsibility for using animals obtained by fraud or theft. The final task force report was suppressed, with only a limited number of copies finding their way outside USDA.

Three years later, USDA conducted another investigation of dealer records. In November 1993, then REAC Deputy Administrator Dale Schwindaman initiated the Random Source Traceback Project. REAC officers conducted random checks of the records of nine Class B dealers. Four dealers targeted by the Midwest Stolen Dog Task Force were revisited by the traceback teams: Barnfield, Eldridge, Gruenefeld, and Huffstutler. Audits of dealer Jerry Vance's records pursuant to an in-depth investigation yielded traceback audits of five of his major suppliers: William Hargrove, Jr., Jeffery Hodges, Jack Stowers, C.C. Baird, and the Hardeman County Animal Shelter, Indiana.

Of the 216 random source suppliers the project attempted to trace, 50 could not be located using the information provided on dealer records. In addition, "five incorrect names were listed in the records; 18 incorrect driver's licenses or social security numbers were listed; 26 incorrect street or town addresses were listed; 14 persons indicated as suppliers in the records had never sold animals to the dealers; and 15 discrepancies existed in the number of animal acquisitions which were listed in the dealer records compared to the number of animals claimed to have been sold by the supplier." Fifty-seven of the suppliers who were contacted stated the dogs they sold to the dealers were not born and raised on their property, as required by law.

The traceback report also noted that county pounds and shelters were selling dogs to dealers and that it was often unclear whether such sales were legal. The report stated: "These facilities appear to be the source of a significant number of the licensed dealers' random source dogs and offer a great opportunity for them to obtain dogs laundered through unregulated sources." As a result of the Traceback Project's findings, USDA issued 16 warning notices to random source suppliers and 49 Letters of Information to individuals suspected of dealing dogs without licenses.

The Pet Protection Act of 1990

In April 1988, before USDA's proposed regulations had been approved, Kentucky Senator Wendell Ford introduced the Pet Theft Act. The purpose of the Act was, in Ford's words, "to protect pet owners from the theft of their animals, and to prevent the sale or use of stolen animals." Two decades after passage of the AWA, pet theft was still a nationwide problem. Increasingly frequent media reports of missing pets ending up in research laboratories had outraged the public. Senator Ford's files were filled with newspaper articles documenting the theft of cats and dogs throughout the country.

In his testimony during the House of Representatives hearing on the Pet Theft Act, Senator Ford stated:

> It's difficult sometimes for a father to see a son who loses a pet that is the son of a three-time field champion. This son and that dog had become quite great companions, and every afternoon at two o'clock the dog would go to the corner and wait for the boy to come home from school. The last time that dog was seen, it was being thrown in the back end of a panel truck with an out-of-state license on it. When you hug your son and he quivers, it's a little tough.
>
> I see what's going on in eastern Kentucky where trucks go through the countryside, men stand there with all kinds of dogs, they throw them in a truck and they take them to Pennsylvania and other places. I think, Mr. Chairman, that we should try the best we can to prevent the theft of pets.[7]

Undercover investigations by humane officers revealed a complex network of unlicensed and illegal dog dealing. In 1988, a Cole County, Missouri humane agent posed as a dealer looking for "clean" dogs. One buncher told the agent he expected to be paid handsomely, because to get "clean" dogs, he'd have to go into "people's backyards."[8] Before his three-month investigation was over, the agent was approached by 15 individuals offering to sell him dogs. He regularly purchased dogs from three bunchers in particular, who pointed out the "hot" dogs in each lot so the agent could sell them first. Only once did any of the bunchers express any reservations. "People know we're getting dogs and we're afraid there'll be a lynching if we steal any of their dogs," one of them said when the agent put in an order for coonhounds.[9]

In 1987, Senator Ford had heard from angry citizens after an out-of-state dealer had come to Kentucky to buy allegedly stray dogs at an auction sale. Many of the animals he bought turned out to be stolen pets. "Public reaction in Kentucky against this episode was loud and strong, as it had been everywhere that cherished animals are suddenly missing in large numbers," said Ford.

"I can show you place after place, time after time, where so-called auction sales — we have documentary proof — induce the theft of pets," Ford told Congress. In her testimony in favor of the Pet Theft Act, Martha Armstrong, the former manager of an animal shelter in Memphis, Tennessee, stated: "It was always easy for us to know when the trade days were taking place. Our calls from frantic pet owners whose dog or cat had disappeared increased by 50 percent on the day before and the day of the event. If owners called prior to trade day, we would inform them to drive... [there] to look for their pet."[10]

Humane groups had long fought to outlaw auction sales, where animals are subjected to abuse and housed and transported under appalling conditions. Humane Society of Missouri investigator David Garcia testified: "I have personally witnessed the exchange of animals and money at public dog auctions without any regard for USDA regulations.... These animals, both initially with the buncher, and subsequently with the Class 'B' dealers, are handled and transported in deplorable conditions that appear to be far below USDA standards. There is never any consideration given for the health, welfare or comfort of any animal."[11]

"It was the problem of stolen pets that caused the enactment of the Animal Welfare Act in August of 1966," stated Senator Ford. "Yet here we are 22 years later with the exact same problem, except that it is now being perpetrated through a loophole in the Act. It is that loophole — the auction sale, that I am trying to close." Ford felt the Pet Theft Act would close this loophole that had allowed bunchers and dealers to continue funneling stolen cats and dogs into the research animal trade. The Act would have prohibited Class B dealers from obtaining dogs and cats from a source other than a state, county, or city owned shelter or pound, or a private shelter under government contract that already released animals for research.

The Act would also have required pounds and shelters to hold dogs and cats for a period of seven days before releasing them to dealers in order to allow sufficient time for animals to be recovered by their original owners or adopted. The longer holding period would prevent dealers from "raiding" pounds as soon as animals arrived. These raids were often prearranged with pound or shelter officials, some of whom gave dealers their own keys to the pounds. The bill also set forth stringent requirements for documentation of dealer purchases and sales. Dealers would be prohibited from selling any random source animals that were not accompanied by a valid certification containing, among other things, the name and address of the person , pound or shelter from whom the dealer acquired the animal, a complete description of the animal, and a statement by the pound or shelter that the holding period requirement had been met.

The bill passed the Senate by a unanimous vote on August 10, 1988. Not surprisingly, the research industry mounted a fierce campaign against the legislation in the House. The National Association for Biomedical Research (NABR), whose president had assured Ford prior to the Senate hearings that the organization would not oppose the Act, now claimed the bill would cut off the supply of animals to laboratories and "inhibit" research. "Over the past two years I have tried to get at pet theft from several angles, and have been opposed by the NABR at every angle," stated Ford in his testimony at the House hearing.[12] "It was only when I hit upon the present formula, which has the strong support of so many in the medical research community, that I was able to obtain a letter from J. Richard Gaintner, President of the NABR, saying that the organization would not oppose my bill.... On the basis of this letter I thought I had an agreement with the NABR.... That is why I was taken aback when the NABR's objections began to surface after S. 2353 passed the Senate."[13]

Representatives of the research industry who testified in the House hearings skirted the issue of pet theft, focusing instead on advancements in health care brought about by the use of random source animals in research. They announced they would support the Act only if two "minor" modifications were made: the prohibition on auction sales and the seven-day holding period requirement would have to be eliminated. As Ford responded, the industry's recommended amendment would "do no less than gut" the bill entirely.

APHIS Administrator James Glosser also testified against the Act, claiming it would "erode" the discretion of the Secretary of Agriculture, hampering USDA's ability "to direct and modify the Animal Welfare Program as circumstances require."[14] He agreed with the industry's position that the Act's restriction on the sources of dogs and cats was too limiting and claimed the requirement that documentation on all sales be maintained for at least 1 year was "unnecessary."

Ford's bill died in the House in 1989. It wasn't until November 1990 that a watered-down version of the Pet Theft Act passed in the House. This bill, entitled the Pet Protection Act, gave the research industry exactly what it had asked for. Gone was the prohibition on auction sales, and pounds and shelters would be required to hold animals for only five days rather than seven. (Note: The holding period under most state and local laws was already at least five days.) The aim of Ford's legislation — to prevent dealers from acquiring dogs and cats from sources most likely to be laundering stolen pets—had been frustrated. The new legislation did, however, incorporate the certification requirements of Ford's original bill. USDA finalized regulations implementing the Pet Protection Act in July 1993. The regulations added the requirement that the five-day holding period include a Saturday. In addition, the regulations require dealers to provide valid certification to anyone purchasing random source dogs and cats from them. The certification must include a detailed description of the dog or cat, an assurance that the dealer informed the person, pound or shelter that the animal provided might be used for research, and a statement by the pound or shelter that it met the holding period requirement. Research facilities must keep dealer certification on file for three years, and dealers must keep a copy of the certification for one year. Dealers found guilty of violating the Act may have their licenses temporarily suspended and be subject to a fine of up to $2,500 for each violation or imprisonment for up to 1 year. Dealers who violate the Act more than once may be fined up to $5,000 per dog or cat acquired or sold, and those who violate the Act three or more times may have their licenses permanently revoked.

Within a few months after USDA had issued its new regulations, Congressman George Brown, one of the authors of the Animal Welfare Act, sent a petition to then Agriculture Secretary Mike Espy, expressing concern about reports that USDA was not properly enforcing the pet theft provisions of the Animal Welfare Act. The petition, co-signed by 28 members of Congress, stated: "Credible evidence has come forth that USDA-licensed animal dealers routinely buy and sell stolen family pets. Moreover, there are charges that USDA inspectors have knowingly ignored repeated violations of federal laws, including the falsification of records of animal origins, the only way to ensure that stolen animals are not entering he research animal trade." The petition urged USDA "to act with decisiveness and forcefulness.... The law must be enforced so that pets and pet-owners are protected from the actions of those people who profit from this unconscionable trade."

The following month, Wisconsin Senator Russell Feingold sent Secretary Espy a letter requesting a review of Animal Welfare Act enforcement. Feingold suggested that USDA "reconsider the initial process for awarding a Class B license, how it deals with repeat offenders, and the length of time a license may be suspended relative to the period of time required for adjudication of a dispute."

In his response to the Brown petition, Secretary Espy wrote: "My colleagues at USDA and I are deeply concerned about increasing reports of pet thefts in some states, and we are committed to taking appropriate action against any of our 1,106 Class B licensees who may be contributing to the problem by dealing in stolen animals.... Please be assured we are committed to administering the AWA to the fullest extent of our authority to prevent pet theft." Espy also indicated USDA was considering making changes to AWA regulations, namely, to strengthen penalties for violations of the Act and improve procedures for reviewing dealer records.

USDA never formally proposed any changes regarding penalties or review of dealer records, but in 1996 it announced that it was working on proposed amendments to the Animal Welfare Act. One of the proposed provisions would phase out Class B dealers as a source of cats and dogs for research over a period of several years. USDA has yet to introduce such legislation. In May 1996, Representative Charles Canady of Florida introduced the "Pet Safety and Protection Act of 1996" (H.R. 3398). This legislation proposed the elimination of Class B random source dealers. Senator Daniel Akaka of Hawaii introduced a companion bill, S. 2114, in the Senate. Under H.R. 3398 and S. 2114, the only legitimate sources of animals for research would be licensed Class A dealers, publicly owned and operated pounds, individual donors who have bred or raised the animals or who have owned them at least one year prior to donation, and other research facilities. The bill also required any pounds providing animals for research to be registered with USDA and comply with the five-day holding requirement and the recordkeeping requirements currently in place for Class B dealers.

Representative John Fox of Pennsylvania introduced a similar bill in the House, "The Family Pet Protection Act" (H.R. 3393), which also proposed elimination of random source dealers and set forth additional requirements for all pounds providing dogs and cats for research. One key difference between H.R. 3393 and H.R. 3398 was that H.R. 3398 would permit only municipally owned and publicly operated pounds registered with USDA to supply dogs and cats for research, whereas H.R. 3393 would permit both public and private (contract) pounds to provide dogs and cats to research, allowing contract pound operators who were also licensed Class B dealers to sell dogs and cats to research facilities.

A hearing on both bills was held August 1, 1996 before the House Subcommittee on Livestock, Dairy and Poultry. USDA's Assistant Secretary for Marketing and Regulatory Programs, Michael Dunn, testified that USDA supported the intent of the proposed legislation and discussed the problems his department has regulating Class B dealers, particularly the difficulty in determining the sources of animals acquired by dealers.

He stated that a USDA traceback project revealed recordkeeping inaccuracies with 52% of the animals traced. "Recordkeeping inaccuracies severely preclude complete tracebacks of animals and consume a large share of our inspection resources," said Dunn.[15] When asked by Representative George Brown, a cosponsor of H.R. 3398, if eliminating Class B dealers "would both save [USDA] money... and eliminate one level of regulation," Dunn responded, "It would eliminate one heck of a headache for us in some areas. There are those people that are falsifying records, as I indicated. It's very tough to traceback those. Every time we develop a new way to look for something, they develop a new way to hide it." Dunn also pointed to unlicensed dealers as another enormous regulatory problem for USDA. "Last year we did about 1,800 searches. That is, going out looking for folks who are dealing but aren't licensed. And that is a whole other problem out there. There is a very, very dirty dealing group of people out there that would stoop to stealing animals, pets, and market them for profit without regard to the impact that it has on the family," said Dunn.

Former USDA Assistant Secretary for Marketing and Regulatory Programs Patricia Jensen also testified at the hearing, stating that despite the fact that Class B random source dealers represent less than one percent of all the entities regulated by USDA, they require "an inordinately large amount of resources in order to adequately regulate them."[16] She stated that while USDA had initiated procedures to target the recurrent problems associated with Class B dealers, "meaningful reform... needs legislation such as that before you today." Jensen stated that the proposed legislation "would correct one of the most egregious problems in research — the introduction of stolen and fraudulently acquired pets into the process."

In a statement supporting the proposed legislation, Representative Bob Goodlatte, a co-sponsor of H.R. 3398, stated, "My congressional district along the Interstate 81 corridor southwest of here is known for being one of the prime areas where a lot of pet owners lose their pets," said Goodlatte. "I have had a number of constituents who have contacted me about this very problem, and sometimes with very substantial evidence that these pets have been hijacked, kidnapped, whatever, and found their way into the stream of commerce for research facilities.... I think this legislation is necessary to deal with that problem and to address this issue in a way that will lead to, I think, much more fair handling of providing animals to research facilities."[17]

Representatives from NABR testified against the proposed legislation, just as they had during hearings on the Pet Theft Act. Using a familiar tactic, they avoided the issue of pet theft almost entirely, focusing instead on their explanations of the necessity for using dogs and cats in medical research. One of NABR's representatives who testified against the legislation is a professor at Wayne State University, a facility that purchases animals from three different Michigan Class B dealers. Each of the three Class B dealers in Michigan who supply animals to laboratories have been cited repeatedly by USDA for apparent violations of Animal Welfare Act regulations. In May 1996, one of those dealers was fined $16,000 for failure to provide adequate veterinary care and failure to maintain adequate records. Ironically, in her testimony in support of H.R. 3398, Dr. Barbara Orlans cited passages from a 1994 USDA inspection report of this same dealer's facility, which reported a number of sick and emaciated animals.

The Congressional session ended soon after the August 1 hearing and before further action was taken. On February 5, 1997, Representative Canady reintroduced his bill as the "Pet Safety and Protection Act of 1997" (H.R. 594).

Notes

1. Office of Inspector General, USDA, "Enforcement of the Animal Welfare Act," 5 January 1995.

2. Ibid.

3. Ibid.

4. USDA-APHIS, Proposed Rules, Federal Register, Vol. 52, No. 61, 31 March 1987.

5. Ibid.

6. USDA-APHIS, Proposed Rules, Federal Register, Vol. 54, No. 49, 15 March 1989.

7. Senator Wendell H. Ford, in testimony before the Subcommittee on Department Operations, Research, and Foreign Agriculture, Committee on Agriculture, U.S. House of Representatives, 28 September 1988.

8. "Report on Dog Theft Operation," Humane Society of Missouri, 1989.

9. Ibid.

10. Martha Armstrong, Massachusetts Society for the Prevention of Cruelty to Animals, in a statement submitted to the Subcommittee on Department Operations, Research and Foreign Agriculture, Committee on Agriculture, U.S. House of Representatives, 28 September 1988.

11. David Garcia, Investigator, Humane Society of Missouri, in a letter to Representative George Brown, Chairman of the Subcommittee on Department Operations, Research & Foreign Agriculture of the Committee of Agriculture, 19 September 1988.

12. Senator Wendell H. Ford, in testimony prepared for the Subcommittee on Department Operations, Research, and Foreign Agriculture, Committee on Agriculture, U.S. House of Representatives, 28 September 1988.

13. Ibid.

14. James W. Glosser, Administrator, Animal and Plant Health Inspection Service, U.S. Department of Agriculture, in testimony before the Subcommittee on Department Operations, Research, and Foreign Agriculture, Committee on Agriculture, U.S. House of Representatives, 28 September 1988.

15. Michael Dunn, Assistant Secretary for Marketing and Regulatory Programs, USDA-APHIS, in testimony before the Subcommittee on Livestock, Dairy, and Poultry, U.S. House of Representatives, 1 August 1996.

16. Patricia Jensen, in testimony before the Subcommittee on Livestock, Dairy and Poultry, Committee on Agriculture, U.S. House of Representatives, 1 August 1996.

17. Representative Bob Goodlatte, in a statement before the Subcommittee on Livestock, Dairy and Poultry, Committee on Agriculture, U.S. House of Representatives, 1 August 1996.

Chapter 4

Class B Dealers Selling Random Source Dogs and Cats for Research

---

BAIRD, C.C. (MARTIN CREEK KENNEL). Williford, Arkansas. USDA license #71-B-108 (1997).

C.C. Baird is one of the largest licensed random source animal dealers, selling approximately 3,500 dogs a year to more than 50 laboratories in the United States and abroad. His clients have included Cedars-Sinai, the University of Missouri, the University of Mississippi, Colorado State University, the University of Arkansas (UA), the University of Arkansas Medical Center and the University of Texas.[1] He reportedly began selling dogs to the University of Wisconsin* and Madison Area Technical College after they stopped buying from Ervin Stebane, and he is believed to have taken over Holco's customers after Don Davis's death.[2] According to USDA, he earns more than $100,000 a year in gross sales.[3] Baird acquires the animals he sells from pounds, from people who drop animals off at his facility and at trade days. Baird has purchased animals from approximately 1,156 different people.[4] In 1997, an administrative law judge found Baird guilty of violating the Animal Welfare Act and fined him $5,000.

In 1991, reports that missing pets were turning up at Martin Creek Kennel prompted a four-part investigative report by KARK-TV, Channel 4 in Little Rock. At that time, Baird allowed pet owners to check his kennel for missing dogs if he believed the people were "legitimate" and not "just troublemakers." Joyce Bogard Hillard, director of investigations for Arkansans for Animals, says a few people did recover their dogs from Baird's kennel. According to Hillard, whenever someone called Baird to ask if he might have his or her missing dog, he always said he didn't, but the dog was back in the person's yard by the next morning. But "now, Baird will only check his computer records with the dog's description and will not allow actual inspections," said Hillard.[5] According to an October 10, 1996 newspaper article, one of Baird's suppliers, Jerry Turner, was arrested on charges of dog theft in 1991.[6] Although Turner claimed he had purchased the dog at an auction, the dog didn't disappear until several days after the day of the

---

* The University of Wisconsin at Madison now has a policy against purchasing animals from Class B dealers.

auction. He was found guilty and fined $200.

USDA audited Baird's acquisition and sales records during its B-dealer traceback project in 1993. Out of more than 88 individuals listed on Baird's records as having supplied him with dogs, 23 of them could not be located using the addresses Baird had listed (some of the addresses didn't exist). In some cases, USDA investigators could not even find any records of drivers licenses that matched the license numbers listed on Baird's records. Two other persons listed had died, one of them having died before he purportedly sold dogs to Baird.[7] Seven of the listed individuals were identified by incorrect driver's license or social security numbers.[8] Investigators discovered that another listed source, Dustin Roach, was a "fugitive from justice" who apparently traded dogs using an assumed name.[9] In 1994, one of Baird's suppliers, an unlicensed dealer in Missouri, signed an affidavit stating he had sold Baird dogs and cats that he had not bred and raised and that he had also provided Baird with false names to be recorded on his acquisition records.[10]

USDA inspectors have documented deficiencies in recordkeeping, sanitation, veterinary care and housing during their routine inspections of Baird's facility:

2-20-91: (258 dogs, 19 cats) "There are 26 outdoor pens that do not have adequate shade and shelters. One or two pens have 6-8 dogs in pens that... have adequate shelter for only 3-4 dogs. There are 5 pens that do not have shelters at all.... The cat litter pans were in need of cleaning and shall be cleaned of waste more often. The northernmost outdoor pens on the west end of the facility have an accumulation of waste in the first couple pens that needs to be cleaned more frequently."

During reinspection on 4-10-91, the inspector noted that the shelter and sanitation deficiencies documented on 2-20-91 had not been corrected: "[Sixteen] of the outdoor pens still do not have sufficient shade. [One] pen with 8 dogs each measuring about 27" long have a shelter that is 46" x 28." This shelter is too small to accommodate these dogs and the pen shall be thinned.... All the outdoor pens need cleaning of waste, and the cat litter pans are too full of feces."

On 6-5-91, the inspector noted that while the previously noncompliant items had been corrected, there were new deficiencies in veterinary care and sanitation: "Dog #914 appears extremely sick with a discharge from both eyes and the nose. There is crusty exudate around the eyes and nose that in my professional opinion, may indicate canine distemper.... A dog was chained inside a dirt isolation barn in unsanitary conditions. This dog, number 620, has a large swelling along both sides of the ventral neck. Other 'sick' dogs were also present in this isolation barn. Dogs that are sick shall not be moved into isolation facilities that are less sanitary than the enclosures they had previously been housed in."

"Dog number 840 was noted in a dirt isolation pen that had rusted metal cages within it and unsealed wood. The owner stated the dog was sick and was to be euthanized that day. On close examination it was determined that the dog was actually dead. Six other dogs were housed in the same pen with the dead dog.... The veterinary care program for this facility shall be reevaluated because there are significant health care problems that are not being adequately addressed. Your veterinarian shall make a site visit to this facility within 48 hours to get these health problems addressed.... The floor of the cat facility is dirty and covered with dead flies. Clutter, paint, used soda cans were also present in the cat room." The inspector also reported that vehicle license numbers were not being recorded for individuals selling dogs to Baird.

On 1-7-92, inspectors reported: "One-hundred and sixty-two dogs are housed in enclosures that have insufficient protection from the cold. The dog houses for these dogs shall have front walls provided — they currently are three-sided with an open front.... Many of the dogs were passing diarrhea. Adequate control of the diarrhea shall be established within 48 hours after consultation with the attending veterinarian.... Dog #2442 has a head wound that shall be adequately treated within 24 hours. Cats #786 and 861 have eye problems that shall be examined by your veterinarian and appropriately treated. Three or four dogs were observed with lameness. Any lame dog shall be examined, treated if necessary or isolated from other dogs."

A 3-25-92 inspection report noted that the shelter deficiency had been corrected. However, subsequent inspections of Baird's facilities and shipments of animals revealed continuing deficiencies in veterinary care and housing:

6-24-93: (Transportation inspection — Professional Labs & Research Services, Suffolk, VA) "Seven large dogs were observed to not have sufficient space to stand, sit or turn around in the affixed enclosures"; 7-7-93: (Sharp Co.) "Dogs housed with contagious diseases such as sarcoptic mange shall not be housed in cages that allow fence line contact with non-infected dogs. To be corrected by 7/9/93"; 7-13-93: (Transportation inspection — University of Texas at San Antonio) "Enclosures do not provide adequate height. Dogs were not able to sit/stand erect as back and head hit top of enclosures"; 3-1-94: (Sharp Co.) "There were two dogs that were in poor condition. These dogs were in need of veterinary care or they should be euthanized. The licensee elected to euthanize the two dogs."

In March of 1994, Baird transported 56 dogs and 6 cats to the University of Mississippi Medical Center. When the truck reached the Center, 42 of the dogs were dead. The cause of the deaths remains a mystery, and USDA never filed any charges against Baird.[11]

On February 17, 1995, USDA filed a complaint against Baird, charging him with failing to maintain complete records showing the acquisition, disposition and identification of animals and acquiring random source dogs in violation of the AWA. The complaint also charged Baird with handling an animal in a manner that caused trauma, behavioral stress, physical harm and unnecessary discomfort to the animal; failing to keep interior surfaces of housing facilities and surfaces that come in contact with dogs free of excessive rust; failing to maintain housing facility surfaces on a regular basis; and failing to make provisions for the regular and frequent collection, removal and disposal of water in a manner that minimizes contamination and disease risks.

A hearing on the charges was held on October 1 and 2, 1996 in Memphis, Tennessee. Administrative Law Judge James Hunt filed his decision in the case on April 9, 1997. In it he concluded that Baird's failure to verify the information given to him by his suppliers — by looking at the person's driver's license — amounted to failure to maintain his records fully and correctly. He also found that Baird had purchased random source animals from unauthorized sources, citing the purchase of animals from unlicensed dealer Mark Yardley and noting that Baird had been in the business long enough to be familiar with the practice among people in the area to sell dogs to dealers that they had acquired through trades or drop-offs. He stated that Baird had the responsibility to guard against this by asking sellers whether they had bred and raised the animals. Judge Hunt went on to state that USDA had failed to show that the rust and chewed wood found at Baird's facility by a USDA inspector was so excessive so as to prevent cleaning or sanitization or affect structural strength.

Although USDA had requested a $50,000 fine and permanent revocation of Baird's license, Judge Hunt imposed only a $5,000 fine and refused to revoke or even suspend Baird's license. He stated that he based his decision on the fact that Baird "had not committed any previous violations." Despite the deficiencies in veterinary care repeatedly reported by USDA inspectors and USDA's charge that Baird had handled an animal in a manner that caused trauma and physical harm, Judge Hunt also concluded that "there is no evidence that the animals at his kennel are provided with less than humane care."[12] Finally, Judge Hunt reasoned that a higher penalty was not warranted because although it was conceivable that some of the animals Baird acquired were stolen, "there [was] no evidence... that any of the animals handled by Baird, whether random source or not, had been stolen 'family pets.'"

Baird is reportedly working on plans to start a Class A business with Farrell Byers, who has set up a kennel on an unused hog farm near Baird's property and has been attempting to obtain a Class A license from USDA.[13] Baird has agreed to let Byers dispose of waste from the facility on his property.[14] Byers currently houses about 120 dogs and plans to add an additional 1,500. In March 1997, the Arkansas Department of Pollution Control and Ecology investigated Byers's kennel in response to public complaints that the facility's waste holding pond was overflowing.[15] The investigator found that the waste holding pond was full and appeared to be leaking in two separate places. The investigator also noted that dead animals were being stored on the site rather than being disposed of properly.[16]

BALL, ANDY, JR. (KISER LAKE KENNELS). Saint Paris, Ohio. USDA license #31-B-001 (1997).

Kiser Lake Kennels was licensed by USDA in 1967 under Paul Anthony's ownership. Anthony had been in the dog business since 1949. Andy Ball, who was one of Anthony's drivers in the 1960s, later became co-licensee with Anthony before becoming the sole owner in 1977. Ball sells approximately 4,700 animals a year, grossing close to $924,000.[17] Kiser Lake has sold animals to Ohio State University, Wright State University, the University of Cincinnati and the University of Pittsburgh. Ball acquires most of his animals from municipal pounds. In 1990, USDA suspended Ball's license for 21 days and fined him $20,000.

On April 5, 1966, Ball and another Kiser Lake Kennels driver, Donald E. Chamberlain, were driving a truckload of dogs out of Lexington, Kentucky when they were stopped by local law enforcement officers. The officers claimed the truck was "crammed" full of dogs. Ball and Chamberlain were arrested and charged with failure to vaccinate a dog against rabies, possession of unlicensed dogs and driving an unlettered livestock truck. The dogs were en route to dealer Michael Kredovski in Pennsylvania (see also: Kredovski, Michael (BioMedical Associates) in this chapter).[18]

The incident was covered by *Newsweek* magazine, which described 159 dogs packed into an 8' x 6' space. "It was the whimpering that first attracted the cop's attention. Approaching, he got a whiff of the truck that almost made him sick." The dogs were confiscated by the local humane society. According to *Newsweek*, one dog was dead; some were so weak they had to be carried into the shelter. All were thirsty and hungry. The dogs were impounded by local dog wardens and returned after Anthony's attorney presented legal proof of purchase and ownership to the police. Ball and Chamberlain were found guilty of cruelty to animals and fined $100 each.[19,20]

Anthony claimed he bought an estimated 200 dogs every other week in Kentucky, primarily from dog wardens in smaller counties. One of his suppliers was Joe Herndon, the Spencer County (Kentucky) dog warden; Anthony reportedly paid him between $2 and $3 per dog. He told the Lexington *Herald* that he felt he was "doing the animals a favor" by buying them because his work "served to save the canines from an almost certain death at the hands of the authorities" who impounded them.[21]

In 1968, Frank McMahon, field services director for the Humane Society of the United States, termed Ohio "the worst state in the Union for dog law violations." At that time (1967-1968), Anthony was collecting dogs from pounds in 19 Ohio counties.

In 1969, the Ohio Humane Federation lost a three-year battle in Ohio's Second District Court to stop Anthony's dog dealing. The suit, filed in July of 1965, sought to revoke Anthony's kennel license and order Champaign County officials to collect license and impoundment fees from kennel licensees, which it apparently had not been doing. Ohio Humane Federation office manager William Green said that a favorable court ruling would make dealing in dogs too expensive for dealers to stay in business. The court decided Anthony's licensing qualifications were not at issue and ruled against the Ohio Humane Federation.[22]

On May 16, 1969, Anthony and dealer Michael Kredovski shipped 150 dogs and 4 cats in cramped crates. USDA filed charges against them in July 1970, but the case was resolved when Anthony voluntarily surrendered his license. Kredovski agreed to a cease-and-desist order and a seven-day license suspension.

At one time, four sites were registered under Ball's license: the Ford Road and Trestle Road sites in Ohio, run by Ball himself; and the Elkfork and Morgantown sites in Kentucky, run by his brother, Clifford, and Barbara Findley, respectively. The Kentucky sites functioned as holding facilities for Ball's dogs. Conditions at all four sites were documented as deficient on USDA inspection reports.

Clifford Ball and Findley received their own USDA licenses in 1991, and both continued supplying animals to Ball. However, Findley's license has since been terminated. Leona Adkins of Adkins Kennels in Ohio and Douglas Grubb of Skyline Kennels in Kentucky are also two of Ball's known suppliers.

APHIS inspectors described Kiser Lake Kennels as a facility with a chronic lack of proper veterinary care for its animals.[23] Inspections of the Ford Road and Trestle Hill sites have revealed deficiencies in veterinary care, housing and sanitation:

8-13-87: Ford Road site, Ohio (372 dogs) "Veterinary care.... Two dogs in new facility are sick and in cage 12 are two sick pups showing distemper signs.... These two pups have been vaccinated 2 or 3 times for distemper. This may be a continuing problem.... Two dogs presently chained to dog houses have no shade other than the dog house.... One pen located outside of fenced-in area... contains eight weaned puppies that require 4608 sq. inches. The pen measures... 3840 sq. inches. A pen this size should house only six pups that size"; 7-26-88 (382 dogs) "Veterinary care.... Dogs in pens 7, 51, 52, 75... presently appear to be sick and in need of vet care... Dog in south end cage appears sick." Other deficiencies were cited. "Meal stored in trash containers is infested with insects.... Pen 2 and 72 contain bitches with pups. The wire mesh flooring outside the box is big enough for the pups' feet and legs to go through causing possible injury. Also some of the smaller dogs in other pens appear to have sore feet from walking on the large wire mesh flooring.... Pens nos. 42, 50 and 79 had too many dogs for the space available."

7-26-88: Trestle Road site, Ohio (220 dogs and 35 cats) "Several pens of dogs are being fed caked, moldy feed.... Several water pans have green slime and need sanitation.... Vet. Care.... Pen 8 in barn, one dog has sores on nose and ears. Cat in end cat pen in 2nd room appears sick."

On April 25, 1989, USDA issued Ball a warning notice for failure to identify all dogs and clean and sanitize pens properly. During a 7-27-89 inspection of the Ford Road site, the inspector observed a thin, drooling, depressed, very ill dog:

> I pointed this out to Mr. Ball and he said he would euthanize the dog. I asked him if he needed any help, but he said no, he would handle it himself.... I heard the dog yelping and whining. I walked over to observe. The dog was still alive and whining. Apparently, the dog had struggled and some of the T-61 (euthanasia agent) had gone outside the vein. Mr. Ball then gave more T-61 and the dog eventually died.... It is my professional opinion that animals at Kiser Lake Kennels are not properly observed for signs of illness and, in some cases, do not receive prompt and proper veterinary treatment or euthanasia.... I do not think he (Ball) is properly trained to administer T-61, nor is he taking the time to properly restrain animals for euthanasia.

In an affidavit dated September 5, 1989, the inspector gave a sobering evaluation of conditions at Ball's facilities:

> Despite repeated documentation of inadequate veterinary care, some sick animals continue to be neglected and do not receive prompt and proper treatment. Mr. Ball claims that this is not true, that all animals receive proper care. He claims that the dogs and cats I cited "probably got sick overnight." While sick animals are to be expected at this type of facility, the animals I cited had been ill far

longer than "overnight," judged by the severity of their condition. While he did indeed treat some of these animals... no attention was given to the fact that many of these animals were dehydrated and/or emaciated and needed fluids and supportive care or euthanasia.

The inspector summarized the conditions she'd documented on the 3-13-89, 4-5-89, 8-3-89, and 9-5-89 inspections of the Ohio sites:

> Previous inspections... also showed a lack of proper veterinary treatment and neglect of seriously ill animals. A log of veterinary treatments was requested due to the repetitive nature of serious health problems at this facility and the questionable methods employed for deciding which animals should be treated.

As deficient as conditions were at Ball's facilities in 1989, they became notably more severe in 1990. In his affidavit describing the 7-10-90 inspection of Ball's premises, an APHIS veterinary inspector noted:

> There was a gross lack of proper veterinary care. We observed many sick dogs, dead and dying puppies, and moribund animals.... It was clear that employees did not keep accurate records or notes of sick animals for the attending veterinarian to examine, and that the veterinarian did not systematically and thoroughly inspect the entire facility for dogs and cats needing immediate veterinary care on his visits. Many den boxes were filthy with caked manure and hair; one contained maggots. Many water containers had moss growing along the sides.

No routine schedule of cleaning had been established at Kiser Lake Kennels. In fact, there were no records indicating that cleaning had ever been done.[24] The kennel's three employees were also responsible for two other sites. The records were, as the veterinary inspector noted:

> grossly inadequate and far below minimum standards set by the law. Well over 75% of the names and addresses for sources of dogs and cats were incomplete, lacking a street address, a town, a zip code, and many even lacking a state. It was impossible to determine which dogs had been trucked to Kentucky holding facilities for conditioning.

Another inspector, also present at the 7-10-90 inspection, described the condition of the animals at Kiser Lake Kennels:

> [I] observed several dogs and cats which were either dead, dying or extremely ill. Among these were four litters of puppies. Almost all of the puppies were very dehydrated, thin and weak. One puppy was dead and several were near death. I observed one adult Beagle (#17054) that was moribund, emaciated.... A white cat (#17939) was dehydrated, weak and very ill. Several other animals

were observed that required veterinary care.... I observed two cages with large amounts of feces.... One of these was infested with maggots. The general level of cleanliness was poor with encrusted feces in cages and pens throughout the facility. Many feeders were filthy with caked, molding food.... There were maggots in at least one dog feeder. Many water bowls were dirty and had algae growth in them.

The inspector's reinspection on 7-12-90 revealed that none of the deficiencies had been corrected: "Ten puppies were observed that had not received adequate treatment. Two of these were dying.... The white cat (#17939) was dehydrated—no fluids had been given. New observations included one dead dog.... Many feeders and water bowls were still filthy.... Many feces and maggots still present.... Mr. Ball was not present during either inspection."

The inspector cited the chronic lack of veterinary care at Ball's facility: "Ten of the last twelve inspections documented inadequate veterinary care. As a result of this neglect, animals are suffering and dying needlessly." Records were cited as "potentially serious.... Preliminary audits of Mr. Ball's records show inconsistencies with records obtained from another licensed dealer. Sources of large numbers of animals are unclear."

The poor veterinary care at Kiser Lake was investigated. USDA investigators interviewed Dr. James T. Stockstill, Ball's attending veterinarian, about the events of the week leading up to July 14, 1990. Stockstill testified that he had not been contacted about any health problems by anyone at the kennels, nor did anyone mention any problems during a routine visit on July 12. But later that day, Ball's wife called him about some problems with some dogs. Stockstill reported that by the time he got to the kennel, the dogs had been euthanized.

USDA suspended Ball's license for 21 days and issued a complaint against him, alleging 18 violations of Animal Welfare Act regulations and standards noted on the inspections of 3-13-89, 4-5-89, 7-29-89, 8-3-89, 1-9-90, 5-10-90, and 7-10-90. Among the allegations were 1) failure to establish and maintain programs of disease control and prevention, euthanasia, and adequate veterinary care under the supervision of a veterinarian, 2) failure to maintain records of the acquisition, disposition, description, and identification of animals, as required, 3) failure to maintain housing facilities for dogs and cats in a structurally sound condition and in good repair and 4) failure to keep the premises clean and in good repair and free of accumulations of trash. USDA also cited Ball for failing to correct previously cited deficiencies noted on the 7-12-90 reinspection.

Ball neither admitted nor denied the allegations. A Consent Decision and Order was entered on 7-26-90, and Ball was fined $20,000 and given a 30-day license suspension. $7,500 of the fine was suspended on the condition that Ball comply with Animal Welfare Act standards and regulations. The order provided that the suspension would be lifted if and when Ball demonstrated he was in full compliance with the Act. The order required Ball to have a licensed veterinarian examine all dogs and cats at his facilities and to have the veterinarian send a written report of his actions to USDA. Ball was also ordered to assist APHIS personnel in conducting a complete inventory of animals at all four of his facilities.

After learning of Ball's license suspension, Madison County, Ohio Commissioners informed him they would be terminating their kennel service with him on the advice of their legal counsel, Madison County prosecutor R. David Picken.[25] Ball's suspension drew coverage from local television stations and newspapers, and inquiries from community organizations and agencies.[26]

Under the terms of the order, Ball was allowed to sell any dogs and cats under his control on the effective date of the order, with prior written consent from APHIS. Ball carried out 43 shipments containing 798 dogs with APHIS's consent between 7-31-90 and 9-24-90. Ball's suspension was lifted on October 1, 1990.

During an inspection of Ball's Morgantown, Kentucky site on 8-28-90 (59 dogs), inspectors noted "Two down from the red feed building has a hole in the box endangering the safety of the animals.... Water buckets are rusty, makes it impossible to clean and sanitize.... Already evidence of rats is present. Fresh drops present, one full hill behind primary enclosure."

Inspectors visiting the Ford Road, Ohio site on 11-20-91 (300 dogs, 69 cats) reported: "Thirty-six (36) individual cages in cat building had no resting boards for cats. Resting boards need to be installed in all cages housing cats... the dealer does not have any health certificates for dogs that he transported within the state of Ohio. The regulation does not provide an exemption for the health certificate requirement if animals are transported within the boundaries of a state.... The facility does not have a written [exercise] plan."

USDA cited deficiencies in recordkeeping and housing at Ball's Laurel Fork Kennel in Elkfork, Kentucky. An APHIS inspector reported that when he and another inspector tried to inspect the facility on 8-3-90, Clifford Ball called his brother, Andy, who then discussed denying USDA access to his facilities:

> During my conversation with Mr. Andy Ball, he adamantly stated that we were not supposed to inspect his facilities without permission from him. I replied that he could refuse us entry, in which case we would leave. After many heated remarks, he asked us to wait

while he consulted his attorney. In a few minutes, the attorney called me back. His opinion too was that we were to have notified them before coming to the premises, and that they would prefer that we not inspect under these conditions. He (Andy) finally agreed that we could inspect the facility, but only if we did not inspect the records. I replied that we would indeed inspect the record of dogs on hand, plus descriptions and identification tags. He replied no deal. We left at that point.

After Clifford Ball obtained his own Class B license in 1991, USDA inspectors continued to document incomplete or inaccurate records during inspections of Laurel Fork Kennels. Inspectors also noted repeated deficiencies at Barbara Findley's DN Kennels (USDA license #61-B-111) in Morgantown, Kentucky, including inadequate identification of animals, failure to observe the required holding period and inadequate sanitation:

7-8-92: Morgantown, Kentucky (23 dogs) "Feces covering the ground under pens #1, 2, 4, 5, 7, 8, 10, 11.... The floor of Pen #2 has a half-dollar size hole.... Some water buckets were slimy and had green moss growing.... Transportation truck needs ventilation on adjacent-opposite sides. Presently, only ventilation is at the back."

Douglas Grubb of Skyline Kennels, in London, Kentucky (USDA #61-B-102), who also sells to Andy Ball, has an annual volume of 1,427 dogs according to 1994 USDA figures. USDA inspectors have cited deficiencies in sanitation and recordkeeping at Grubb's facility:

7-9-92: (78 dogs) "Feces must be raked often enough to prevent accumulation and fly problems. Sawdust was placed on top of feces, and fly problem persists"; 2-18-93: (73 dogs) "Den boxes sheltering dogs need more bedding to provide warmth and protection.... Nine dogs were not wearing permanent identification, but chain and tag were on top of cage. One dog did not have, or we could not find, its identification.... Dogs on hand show 93 dogs; premises is only housing 73 dogs today.... A copy of health certificate does not accompany records of dogs transported across state lines.... Dog #570 in cage 31 had a non-healing toe. Dog #3281 in cage 7 was thin and sick, and dog #3364 was thin with matted eyes."

6-30-93: (86 dogs) "Four dogs euthanized since last inspection.... Deficiencies found on last inspection and again on this inspection: Records. Number of dogs in kennel are 86; number of dogs present on [USDA Form] 7005 are 95. Records need to reflect accurate census in facility."

In 1993, inspectors once again noted serious deficiencies in veterinary care at Kiser Lake Kennels. During an inspection of the Ford Road site on 5-4-93 (337 dogs, 55 cats), the inspector reported: "It is evident that adequate veterinary care is not being maintained at this facility. There seems to be a lack of training of daily employees to properly identify sick animals and report in writing a daily observation of eating, drinking, behavior and to assess their health and monitor the progress of prescribed drugs.... Dogs #12074 and 12070 were in same pen on 5-4-93 — Floyd and Dr. Harlan observed diarrhea and vomiting. The employee did not record the illness.... No fecals were done as per program of veterinary care and no record of how long the diarrhea and vomiting had occurred.... One cat #12296 was weak, dehydrated and lethargic with a nasal and ocular discharge and sneezing. Cat was showing signs of tenderness in abdomen. This cat has no program notes by attending veterinarian and additional veterinary care was needed."

On 3-1-95 (Trestle Road site, 62 dogs), an inspector reported: "It is apparent that cages/runs have not been sanitized as per 3.11(b) (3). Pens 1-10 and 11-15 have varying degrees of build-up of fecal and dirt and debris — sticky brown organic matter on galvanized metal inside enclosures and between metal bar enclosures. Employee indicates cages are being disinfected once a month. All cages need to be sanitized every 2 weeks and frequently if needed." The inspector also noted deficiencies in sanitation at the Ford Road site: "Slab 3 has a large accumulation of debris/fecal, contaminated bedding around outside of enclosures and at doorway of denboxes. The chain link has accumulation of feces, bedding and debris."

The sanitation deficiencies were still uncorrected on 5-3-95: "Slab 1, Slab 2 and Slab 3 have large accumulations of sawdust, feces, hair, debris and food waste underneath the dog dens and trapped in chain link fence underneath dog den area. It needs more frequent cleaning and more thorough cleaning."

DAVIS, BETTY (CIRCLE D KENNELS). Myrtle Creek, Oregon. USDA license #92-B-183 (1997).

Betty Davis, who was first licensed in 1994, sells approximately 268 dogs a year, grossing $121,800.[27] Davis has sold animals to several research facilities in California, including Cedars Sinai Medical Center, the Veterans Administration Wadsworth Facility, and the University of Southern California, which sold 200 dogs purchased from Davis to Good Samaritan Hospital. In 1996, USDA began investigating reports that Davis was buying dogs from individuals who had "adopted" them from shelters and through "Free To Good Home" ads. The U.S. District Court in Oregon issued USDA a warrant to search and seize records as evidence in the investigation. Federal and local law enforcement officials raided Davis's kennel on February 6, 1996 and confiscated her acquisition records for review. USDA's Robert Willems began tracing the previous owners of 29 dogs found at Davis's kennel.[28] Investigators also recovered at least six dogs from facilities in Los Angeles and returned them to their owners in Oregon. According to USDA, the U.S. Attorney's Office is currently reviewing the case to determine whether or not to file any charges against Davis.[29] USDA will consider administrative action against Davis following action by the U.S. Attorney's Office and the Oregon Attorney General. Davis will remain licensed until conclusion of the legal proceedings.

ELDRIDGE, RAYMOND (ANTECH, INC.). Barnhart, Missouri. USDA license #43-B-063 (last licensed as a Class B dealer in 1996).

Ray Eldridge sold approximately 1,314 animals a year, grossing $458,183.[30] His customers have included the University of Chicago, Kansas City Veterans Hospital, the University of Missouri and Cleveland Veterans Hospital. He operated two sites in Missouri, holding between 130 and 250 dogs at a time at site #1 in Jefferson County and between 275 and 650 dogs (and occasionally rabbits) at site #2 in Washington County. Eldridge is now licensed as a Class A dealer (license #43-A-2556). According to USDA, Eldridge is under investigation for alleged violations committed during the time he was a random source dealer.[31]

USDA's Midwest Stolen Dog Task Force audit of Eldridge's acquisition records in 1990 revealed that Eldridge had obtained dogs from at least three unlicensed dealers, including former Class B licensee Al Willard (Codit, MO, license #43-B-013). USDA had terminated Willard's license in April 1989 due to his failure to file an annual report and pay licensing fees, but Willard continued selling dogs to Eldridge for five months after his license termination. In his investigation report, USDA senior investigator Harry Dawson recommended that Willard not be penalized because he evidently "did not fully understand his license termination." USDA closed the case without further action.[32] Wilbert Gruenefeld (Jonesburg, MO, license #43-B-064) — another one of Eldridge's suppliers — was also a subject of the Task Force investigation. According to the Task Force findings, Gruenefeld had also been acquiring dogs from unlicensed dealers.

Eldridge also obtained dogs from Class B dealer Ralph Bezler (Fulton, MO), investigated by both USDA and the Missouri State's Attorney's Office for acquiring dogs under false pretenses through giveaway ads.[33,34]

USDA inspection reports have documented deficiencies in transport, housing and recordkeeping regulations at Eldridge's facilities:

1-15-92: Site #2, Washington County (530 dogs — 130 adults, 400 puppies). "Several pens in building #2 with more than one dog need larger resting surfaces.... In puppy building several portable enclosures housing

2 pups with total of 7.5 sq ft floor space — need at least 12.5 sq ft for 2 pups that are 24" long. These dogs need additional space. Also portable cages in puppy building with 12 sq ft total, housing 3 pups that need at least 16 sq ft need to have additional space provided."

7-6-92: Site #2 (439 dogs — 289 dogs, 150 pups). "2 fronts of houses... have metal that has rusted away leaving a jagged edge across bottom of door.... Outdoor runs between buildings... housing older puppies need additional shade provided that is large enough to cover all occupants in the enclosure. Also, west end... needs to have additional shade.... Several dogs do not have the minimum space provided for those particular dogs.... Dogs housed individually that do not have 200% of the minimum floor space provided are not being given opportunity for exercise."

8-10-92: Site #1 (137 dogs, 26 rabbits). "Several larger dogs (larger than 36") do not have the minimum space provided that is required for those dogs"; 2-4-93: Site #2 (496 dogs — 296 dogs, 200 puppies). "Adequate records showing date of, and persons dogs were acquired from, need to be kept for all dogs that are on hand. Some information is recorded but all required information needs to be kept."

4-29-93: Transportation inspection, Mount Sinai Hospital, Pearlman Research, Miami Beach (6 dogs). "The information accompanying dogs did not contain all of the information required.... On two dogs examined, the accompanying records did not record significant distinctive markings... Dog #431AH/12193 had a tattoo ('HOBAB') in right ear that was not recorded by dealer. Dog #4C280 had the tattoo 'HOBAB' in right ear; this tattoo was not recorded in the dealer records."

8-17-93: Site #2 (372 dogs — 222 adults, 150 puppies). "In building #4, several litters of puppies are on wire that allow the pups' feet and legs to pass thru the openings — smaller wire needs [to be] installed."

GARNER, DICK (COUNTY CANINES, INC.). Osceola, Iowa. USDA license #42-B-031 (1997).

Dick Garner's clients have included the University of Minnesota, the Mayo Clinic, the University of Iowa and several research facilities in Florida. He acquires dogs from pounds, various individuals and at trade days. Garner sells approximately 154 dogs a year, grossing $8,448.[35]

USDA inspectors have documented deficiencies in sanitation, housing and waste removal at Garner's facility:

8-10-83 (50 dogs): "North side behind north facility there is a manure buildup outside the primary enclosures. Manure shall be removed and properly disposed of.... Three of the primary outdoor enclosures are overcrowded and dog numbers are to be reduced." On 1-5-87 (170 dogs), an inspector noted, "The accumulation of manure piles behind the north dog facility must be removed and disposed of properly. Also the six dead dogs laying behind the east building must be disposed of in a proper manner..."

In June 1987, USDA received an animal welfare complaint concerning Garner's facility. The complaint, made by an undisclosed source, alleged "overcrowding, mistreated dogs, dogs roaming freely, trash around premises — place is a mess."[36]

Inspectors continued to document overcrowding and unsanitary conditions:

6-15-87: (250 dogs) "The dog cages behind the south building need to have the dog excreta cleaned out from underneath them."

7-2-87: (125 dogs) "Provisions shall be made for the removal of animal waste. This was listed on the previous inspection of 6-15-87. An attempt was made to remove the dog waste from the back of the north dog facility but not all could be removed.... Garner has agreed to put in a septic tank... to correct this deficiency [by 7-17-87].... The outdoor cage on the west side of the kennel area has too many dogs in it."

On September 13, 1987, Garner purchased 40 dogs at the Rutledge, Missouri Dog and Gun Auction, prompting another animal welfare complaint. According to the complainant, the cages on Garner's truck "were 'stuffed' with dogs." USDA assigned inspector Dan Hart to investigate the complaint.[37] Hart visited Garner the following day to question him. In his report to Area Veterinarian in Charge for Iowa, Dr. Bernard Zecha, Hart wrote:

> Dick Garner stated to me that these dogs were not overcrowded when transported.... It appears that since no USDA personnel visually observed the specific load of dogs reported to be in violation, there is no way of determining whether Dick Garner was in compliance with the Animal Welfare transportation standards.

Subsequent inspections of Garner's facility revealed continuing serious deficiencies in sanitation and housing:

12-16-87: (150 dogs) "There are three dead dogs next to the main kennel building that need to be properly disposed of. Also the outdoor pens on the East side need to have the excreta removed from underneath them"; 4-1-88: (250 dogs) "The one outdoor pen on legs... needs to have the excreta removed from inside."

5-19-88: (155 dogs) "There are large accumulations of fecal material behind the north kennel building and underneath the wire outside cages that needs to be removed.... Also dead dogs are to be buried as a means of disposal. At least two dogs were noticed uncovered, but were covered with dirt during this inspection."

6-9-88: (164 dogs) "Disposal of dead dogs has been changed to burning. Further inspection of burial grounds revealed one partial remains of dog uncovered."

5-31-90: Attempted inspection. No one was present at the time of the inspection.

6-1-90: "Algae in water buckets. [Water] needs to be changed more often."

11-17-92: (134 dogs, 7 puppies) "Shelters for dogs do not have 4 sides. Many only have 3 sides. Shelters with four sides do not have wind or rain breaks.... All wooden structures that come in contact with the dogs (boxes, houses, pens) are worn and scratched and are not impervious to moisture.... Shelters do not allow all dogs to sit, lie, or stand in normal manner. More shelter needs to be added.... Cement runs have excreta buildup on floors and need to be cleaned."

There was no veterinarian-approved written dog exercise plan on file, and puppies were housed outdoors without approval from the attending veterinarian. "One pen contained mother dog and four new pups with another adult female (not the mother or surrogate). " Records were deficient. "1) No vehicle license numbers. 2) Missing complete addresses. 3) Number of dogs on inventory sheet doesn't equal number of dogs on premise."

In 1993, Garner paid a $500.00 stipulation fine to USDA for record-keeping and housekeeping violations. Garner paid another stipulation fine in 1995, but information on the amount was not available from USDA.

GRAVITT, MAX (BAUX MT. BEAGLE FARM). Germantown, North Carolina. USDA license #55-B-033 (1997).

USDA inspectors have documented deficiencies in housing, sanitation, identification of animals and recordkeeping at Max Gravitt's facility:

3-19-92: (4 dogs, 1 cat) "Enclosures next to creek have accumulations of metal and wood adjacent to animal enclosures (dogs).... Animals moved/transported in back of open pickup w/metal enclosure which is rusty and in air transport kennels. During inclement weather, only protection from rain, snow, wind is covering of burlap.... 4 dogs, 1 cat on premises. Only 1 dog and 1 cat tagged and tag is affixed to enclosure and not on collar on animal.... 1 personal dog in facility enclosure not identified by tags or records. 2 dogs not identified by tags or records."

12-4-92: (6 dogs, 3 cats) "Two dog enclosures lack any form of wind break at entrance to den box. Cat enclosures do not have any form of wind break at entrance of den boxes. No bedding available for cats.... Litter pan of cats overloaded with feces.... Of the 24 individual sources of dogs and cats since 9-1-92, only one (1) individual has both driver's license number and vehicle tag number. Twenty-three (23) individuals have driver's license number only.... No records available for acquisition of swine purchased for resale to research."

12-16-92: (5 dogs, 3 cats) "Two dog shelters still lack wind breaks on dens. Cat enclosures lack any form of wind break at entrance.... Litter pans overloaded with fecal debris.... Records still lack vehicle tag numbers"; 2-17-93: (3 dogs, 0 cats) "Enclosure has excessive fecal debris on concrete slab.... Two of the three dog enclosures in use lack any form of windbreak."

On 5-27-93, USDA collected a $100.00 stipulation fine from Gravitt.

8-3-93: (0 dogs, 0 cats) "Approximately one-third of sources for dogs and cats do not have a vehicle license number available"; 12-9-93: (0 dogs, 0 cats) "Five dogs acquired 6-14-93 and disposed of 8-27-93 as listed on USDA Form 18-5 (Record of dogs and cats on hand). However, no dogs were present at facility during 8-3-93 inspection by Dr. D.J. Kelley with Mr. Max Gravitt present. Records are not accurate and do not meet USDA regulations."

1-13-94: (0 dogs) "Inadequate records. Dates for acquisition and disposition of five dogs not correct as described on 12-9-93 inspection form. Record check with North Carolina-Department of Motor Vehicles indicate three of the recorded six numbers (vehicle tag and driver's license numbers) did not agree with Mr. Gravitt's recorded name and address for animal source.... Inaccurate application for license renewal dated 12-6-93. Mr. Gravitt has grossly under-reported the number of animals sold to research facilities during his prior business year."

On 8-29-94, Gravitt paid USDA a $200.00 stipulation fine for the recordkeeping violations documented on 8-3-93, 12-9-93 and 1-13-94.

In 1995, Gravitt informed a USDA inspector that he no longer sold dogs and cats and would from then on sell only swine and goats for research.

HARGROVE, JOHNNIE (U.S. RESEARCH FARM). Medina, Tennessee. USDA license #63-B-101 (1997).

The Hargrove family started selling animals for research in the 1950s. The family business has been passed down through four generations, from Roy Hargrove to William Hargrove Sr. (Roy's son), and from William Hargrove, Jr. to Johnnie Hargrove, the most current licensee. U.S. Research Farm remained in business despite a 1966 cruelty conviction and numerous noncompliant items noted in USDA reports over the years. According to 1994 USDA figures, William Hargrove, Jr. had an annual volume of 466 dogs. In 1993, he paid a $100 stipulation fine for recordkeeping violations. In 1996, Hargrove signed a consent decision agreeing to a 5-year license suspension and a civil penalty of $1,000. Hargrove has since died, and his son, Johnnie, has taken over the business.

William Hargrove was once a major supplier of dogs and cats to research facilities, including Washington University at St. Louis, Northwestern University Medical School and Presbyterian-St. Luke's Hospital in Chicago, and the University of Illinois. He reportedly acquired animals in Mississippi, Indiana, Kentucky, Tennessee and Illinois, and frequented Ripley Trade Day in Mississippi. At one time, the Hargroves had a site in Cicero, Illinois in addition to the Medina, Tennessee site.[38,39]

William Hargrove was also a supplier to Mississippi Class B dealer Jerry Vance (see: Vance, Jerry in "Investigations Into the Acquisition of Animals by Class B Dealers").

The June 9, 1959 edition of the Jackson *Sun* reported that the Hargroves were keeping dogs without food or water and that the dogs were unvaccinated.[40] On September 9, 1959, the Tennessee Office of Public Health wrote to the University of Illinois requesting the school to apply pressure on the Hargroves to vaccinate their dogs against rabies. A rabies epidemic was raging in Tennessee, and the random source animals the Hargroves collected posed a public health danger. The University demurred, stating "it [a rabies vaccination] interfered with some experimental procedures," and "it increases the cost of the dog to us."[41]

In 1966, William Hargrove Sr. was convicted of cruelty to animals by a Gibson County Circuit Court jury. Charges of cruelty were brought by the Animal Welfare Institute's Laboratory Animal Consultant, Dorothy Dyce, after her October, 1965 visits to the Hargrove's dog farm in Medina, Tennessee.[42]

Photographs of the premises and of the starving animals Dyce discovered (see photo section) played an important part in the circuit court's findings, as did the testimony of one of the Hargrove's neighbors, Mrs. Joe Smith. She testified she had seen the Hargroves "for some 20 years mistreat dogs," and had seen them "take a stick and punch the dogs when they were loading them in their big truck."[43]

The jury recommended that William Hargrove Sr. and his father, Roy, be fined $150 each and receive 30-day jail sentences. The Hargroves lost their appeal for a new trial and began serving the 30-day sentences on

December 26, 1966.[44]

USDA inspection reports reveal U.S. Research Farm's record of noncompliance with Animal Welfare Act regulations and standards:

2-11-87: "Not complete [on] dates of acquisition. Number[s] of cats and dogs on hand don't correlate with no. on VS Form 18-5"; 8-12-87: "Dates of purchase not entered and dates removed.... Cat litter pans need cleaning and [to be] replenished with new litter." 8-26-87: "Seven cats on premise. None listed on 18-5.... Cat litter pans need cleaning and [to be] replenished with new litter." 5-2-89: "The entire kennel was filled with junk... covered with old newspapers, dirt and rodent droppings"; 10-11-89: "We need to explain why there is a difference in the inventory versus number of dogs seen on premises — these should match."

3-27-90: (73 dogs) "A bitch with pups was chained to a decrepit dog house outside the main kennel building. The puppies had no protection from predators.... Inventory records are incomplete. Description of animals, from whom acquired plus address, driver's license and vehicle ID is not being provided. This must be corrected immediately. All new records must be complete and accurate. This is a serious deficiency.... Apparently Mr. Hargrove has been using the wrong ID number for a number of years."

"The food storage room is dirty.... Floors have accumulated dried feces.... The ground adjacent to the kennel building is riddled with rat dens and covered with rat feces.... #61990 was suffering from fight wounds."

5-3-90: "The south end of the barn still has lots of rat feces"; 5-31-90: "Mr. Hargrove needs to work still more on pest control."

11-3-92: (Medina site. 60 dogs) "The concrete floors of the outside exercise runs... are badly broken in many places.... The metal dividers [in drainage portion, outside runs] have sharp points.... A bitch with four nursing puppies were tied to a trailer outside the dog compound. There is no perimeter fence, and no shelter as such. The animals are able to retreat under the trailer, but there is no other shelter, and no protection from predators, etc."

3-30-93: (Medina site.) "An enclosure in the hallway has a 2x4 which has been gnawed almost in two. The platform in this enclosure has deteriorated to the point that it is unsafe as a resting board.... A section of wire near the gate... has been damaged to the point that an opening has resulted, with two sharp exposed bits of wire."

On 7-12-93 Hargrove paid a $100 stipulation fine to USDA.

8-12-93: (Medina site. 47 dogs) "The metal sheets used as wall dividers in sick pen have sharp edges.... Also cement blocks used to form back wall of all outside runs has missing mortar, cracks and chips, and various degrees of deterioration, making it impossible to clean and sanitize correctly.... On acquisition sheets 18-5 or 7005, the following was noted: A. several names were lacking complete address, including street or P.O. Box and route, and zip code. All is required. B. sheets were not page-numbered in block 4, upper right-hand corner, making it difficult to put purchases chronologically.... Last Program of Vet Care is dated 1991. This form must be renewed annually."

10-2-93: (Ripley Trade Day, Mississippi. 35 dogs) "The trailer contained 21 enclosures and 35 dogs.... The back of the truck beds enclosure has protruding wire that could cause injury to the dogs.... [Seven primary enclosure] doors are rusting and cannot be properly cleaned and sanitized.... Primary enclosures B5, B4, T3, B3, T2 and right rear upper case and right rear lower cage have inadequate bedding.... The right front bottom lower cage has broken, protruding and rusting wires.... Primary shipping enclosures L3, center front, B2, T2 and right front bottom cage contain dogs that are overcrowded. These dogs cannot stand, sit or lie in a natural position."

3-22-94: (Medina site. 11 dogs) "Dog #65546 was present in kennel, but not recorded on acquisition sheet 7005.... 26 pages of 7005 taken to xerox; will return by certified mail.... Left pound certification info with this report."

4-30-94: (Ripley Trade Day, Mississippi. 8 dogs) "The inside doors of the primary enclosures have sharp metal edges that could cause injury to the dogs.... The wire inside the primary enclosures is rusting and must be repaired or replaced.... Three dogs were not identified by an official USDA tag when purchased.... The dogs purchased were not tagged in sequential order.... The vehicle license number and state registered is not being recorded on the dogs purchased today.... No official Health Certificate on the three dogs transported from Tenn. to Mississippi."

USDA issued a complaint against Hargrove on April 11, 1995, charging him with failing to maintain complete records showing the acquisition of dogs; failing to acquire dogs from an appropriate source; failing to obtain proper health certificates; failing to maintain a programs of disease control and adequate veterinary care under the supervision of a veterinarian; failing to maintain interior dog housing facility surfaces that were free of jagged edges and sharp points; and failing to construct surfaces with materials that allow them to be readily cleaned and sanitized. In the Fall of 1996, Hargrove signed a consent decision and order neither admitting nor denying USDA's charges. He agreed to a 5-year license suspension and a civil penalty of $1,000. The civil penalty was suspended on the condition that he not violate the Animal Welfare Act. Hargrove died following the license suspension, and his son Johnnie took over the business under the same license number. USDA determined that William's license suspension does not apply to Johnnie's business.

HILL, MONA (MONA HILL'S KENNEL). Huntington, West Virginia. USDA license #54-B-002 (1997).

Mona Hill sells between 1,000 and 2,000 dogs a year to other Class B dealers, including Mike Kredovski, one of the largest dealers in the country (see Kredovski, Mike in this chapter). She earns approximately $158,093 a year in gross sales.[45] Hill purchases animals at trade days and from individuals in West Virginia, Kentucky and Ohio. USDA inspections of Hill's kennel have revealed chronic deficiencies in veterinary care, housing, record-keeping and sanitation:

5-23-90: (17 dogs) "Records lack zip code.... 'No dealer shall transport in commerce any dog unless the dog is accompanied by a health certificate executed and issued by a licensed veterinarian.' Correct by 5-24-90." 6-25-90: (65 dogs) "Four dogs were on chains, varying in length from 68" - 82". Dogs were about 32" - 34" in length [chains must be at least 3 times the length of the dog].... One dog (pit bull/coonhound cross) on a chain had wounds on ear tips from flies. No treatment had been given.... It is unclear how some out-of-state dogs arrived at premises; whether they were transported by dealer or delivered. It should be made clear what party transported dogs across state lines as health certificates are required for interstate transport. No health certificates are present for some dogs (Dealer says these were purchased at trade days or delivered)."

10-29-91: (7 dogs) "Roof of sheltered facility has weak areas with evidence of heavy leak. Ceiling has dropped and is separated on interior and is not structurally sound.... Numerous sharp wires exposed in sheltered facility and on outdoor dog runs.... Water bowls are not being disinfected between groups of animals. Pen 1 did not have potable water in water bowl.... All dog boxes and food and water receptacles in the outdoor facilities must be cleaned and sanitized between different groups of dogs.... Pens 1 - 8 have excessive build-up of fecal material.... Sheltered facility animal areas have excessive build-up of dust, hair, debris.... Transport vehicle has contaminated bedding."

2-19-92: (12 dogs) "Noncompliant items previously identified that have not been corrected.... All dog boxes, dens in the outdoor facility must be cleaned and sanitized... at least once every 2 weeks.... Records on hand today reveal that no vehicle license number was recorded for the following [6] people: 1. Sammy Baisden, 2. Gene Blaire, 3. Jack Copeley, 4. Judy Hall, 5. Lonnie Hannah, 6. Carley Walters."

11-16-92: (55 dogs) "Two dogs had lost their tags and were not found during inspection.... These animals were not retagged by the dealer... and were shipped to Biomedical [Kredovski] on 11-17-92 without identification."

6-30-93: (49 dogs) "Records do not state the specific breed or type of dog, or approximate age. The records are lacking for colors and distinctive markings of dogs.... Note: Records were taken from Mrs. Mona Hill. Originals will be kept by USDA until further information is obtained. Veterinary care.... Dr. John S. Godfrey was contacted on 06-30-93. He stated that he had not completed a P.V.C. [Program of Veterinary Care] for 1992. Dr. Godfrey stated that he does not dispense Benza-Pen to Mona Hill. He also stated that he does not vaccinate any dogs for rabies or give any medications (deworming). P.V.C. appears to be completed by Mona Hill. Mona Hill stated that Benza-Pen is sent by [information not disclosed by USDA].... Mike Kredovski... also sends rabies vaccine to Mona Hill for vaccinations of the dogs.... It is apparent that the dealer has no program of veterinary care. The dogs had live ticks and were not dipped on 6-30-93 and 7-1-93. Mona Hill does not have enough tick-dip for the dogs. Dr. Godfrey stated he does not supply any tick medications. A new program of vet care... is needed for above."

During reinspection on 7-20-93, inspectors noted that the deficiencies documented on 6-30-93 had been corrected. However, inspectors continued to note deficiencies throughout 1994 and 1995:

5-4-94: (54 dogs) "Dog #7502 was guarding the feed box and was very aggressive toward other dogs in pen when they tried to eat.... I had Mrs. Hill bring additional feed to demonstrate that other dogs were not being allowed access to feed bin. One dog was so thin; he came up and ate voraciously for several minutes after I removed #7502 from enclosure.... 'Description shall include approximate age, color, and distinctive markings'. Records lack following description.... Dog #7471 lacks full description of distinctive markings and good color description.... #7510 has left blue eye and was not recorded on identification. #7503 is black and tan with distinctive [markings].... Dogs from Ohio and some outside states are transported by private vehicle and owners to Mona Hill's property. She does not record the name of driver or owner of vehicle on 18-5.... There needs to be clarification of who delivered dogs in records.... Two walker hounds are coughing.... One additional hound has purulent green discharge from left nostril. Currently, Mona Hill is not recording any treatments for any sick dogs. A notebook must be kept of all dogs treated, how long... and what medication was given.... Dogs from Ohio from private dog owners do not have health certificates. Certificates are required for interstate transport of dogs."

6-6-94: (46 dogs) The inspector noted that previously deficient items had been corrected but that there were new deficiencies in veterinary care. "Dog no. 7591 has severe dog bite or trauma bite injury to left foot.... No treatment has been given to this dog and no emergency preparations have been prescribed by Dr. Motycha.... There should be emergency care given to this dog by Dr. Motycha within 24 hours."

3-20-95: (33 dogs) "Dog No. 8304 has pit bull predominant breed type; dealer has as cur. This is unacceptable identification for this dog.... Dog #8308 has "heeler" cross head and black tinge on hair ends.... It is identified as cur by dealer. Distinguishing color marks are not in records.... Dog #8328 has very characteristic, distinguishing marks of left brown eye and ear and right eye has brown dapples and little spots over ear.... Dealer did not put distinguishing marks on 18-5."

On May 25, 1995, USDA filed a complaint against Hill, alleging that from June 1993 through December 1994 she failed to: maintain programs of disease control and prevention, euthanasia and adequate veterinary care under the supervision of a veterinarian; maintain complete records showing the acquisition, disposition and identification of animals; properly acquire dogs; house compatible dogs in the same primary enclosure; develop, document and follow an appropriate plan to provide dogs with the opportunity for exercise; possess health certificates issued by a licensed veterinarian for transporting dogs; keep primary dog enclosures clean; and keep housing facilities used for storing food and bedding free of accumulations of trash, waste material, junk and other discarded material. A hearing on the charges is still pending.

HODGINS, FRED (HODGINS KENNEL, INC.). Howell, Michigan. USDA license #34-B-002 (1997).

Fred Hodgins, who began selling animals for experimentation in 1960, has been licensed as a Class B dealer since passage of the Animal Welfare Act in 1966. He obtains dogs and cats from city and county animal shelters and sells to research institutions, biological supply houses and other dealers. In 1994, he reported selling 4,795 animals, grossing $458,966.[46] In 1995, he was fined $16,000 for violations of the Animal Welfare Act.

Hodgins's daughter, Tammi Longhi, has managed Hodgins Kennel for ten years. She attempted to obtain her own license several times, intending to use part of her parents' facility to establish a breeding business. USDA denied each of her applications because the facility was already being operated under the Hodgins Kennel license. In 1995, she formed a partnership with her mother, Janice Hodgins, and filed a new application for a license to operate a kennel at one of the Hodgins' facilities, doing business as L & H Associates. USDA denied her application once again. She requested a hearing, and on October 18-19 and November 28, 1995, an administrative law judge affirmed USDA's denial of the application. USDA argued that it was APHIS policy to issue only one license to a person to operate as a dealer. Since Janice Hodgins was already licensed by virtue of her part ownership of Hodgins Kennel, Longhi and L & H Associates were not eligible to receive a license.

During a USDA inspection of Hodgins's facility on 3-28-88 (274 dogs, 69 cats, 150 rats), the inspector reported: "At time of this inspection buildings and pens were not clean — large amount of fecal waste in kennels. Some kennels were extremely wet from urine.... Mr. Hodgins now dealing in the raising and selling of rats for biological research. This business is written under the name Great Lakes Biological."

On 1-5-89 (355 dogs, 30 cats), the inspector reported: "The buildings all displayed a general need to be cleaned. Ledges are dusty, cobwebs and hair are present, floors need to be swept and mopped — and everything needs to be washed."

On January 13, 1992, USDA issued Hodgins an official warning for alleged violations documented on 10-9-91, 10-28-91, and 10-29-91. The alleged violations included 1) failure to provide adequate veterinary care, 2) failure to provide adequate housing requirements for cats, 3) failure to maintain the primary enclosure in good repair, 4) failure to keep interior surfaces in good repair, 5) failure to keep housing facility structurally sound, 6) failure to provide minimum floor space for dogs, 7) failure to keep premises free of accumulation of trash, 8) failure to keep transport vehicle in good repair, and 9) failure to develop, document and follow exercise program for dogs.

USDA did not inspect Hodgins's facility again until November 1993. On November 16 (124 dogs. 41 cats.), inspectors reported: "Building #4 was in need of some major housekeeping efforts. The walls were spattered with debris and appeared moldy.... The records are not being kept updated. The animals on hand form for dogs showed approximately 273 dogs — nearly 50 dogs over those actually present.... Dog #4134 was obtained today without any assurance that the dog was obtained from an individual who had bred and raised the dog.... Many sick animals were not reported or being treated.... Black male dog with left eye problem.... 32391 (Dog) Shaking head excessively — needs ears examined.... Cat #424551 both eyes stuck shut with copious ocular discharge. Cat was to be euthanized last Thursday but still living and not responding to treatment." During reinspection on 1-18-94 (233 dogs, 22 cats), inspectors noted continuing problems with veterinary care: "Numerous animals were found ill or injured and not receiving adequate veterinary care. The main building: Pen #7 contained a beagle with extensive skin lesions along his back. There was not a treatment card on his cage.... In pen #3 dog #41747 has an eye injury... which is not being treated.... Many, many dogs were noted to be unresponsive and shaking with cold."

Inspectors continued to report serious deficiencies in veterinary care:

4-5-94: (237 dogs, 35 cats) "Dog #45197 was emaciated and very depressed. #45142 black lab was very thin and very depressed.... 41939 and 41956 (2 dogs housed together) had bloody diarrhea which was not detected or treated.... Cat #12171 had ear mites, greatly enlarged lymph nodes, and was non-weightbearing on right front leg. Cat 35851 was depressed, emaciated, dehydrated and severely ataxic. This cat was only getting an antibiotic. Cat #42083 had a swollen shut left eye with a discharge—not being treated for the eye problem."

5-10-94: (217 dogs, 44 cats) "Dog #45375 was found with a bloody nasal discharge. This dog was not detected as being abnormal.... Dog #45425 was extremely depressed and unresponsive, approximately 10% dehydrated and had a purulent nasal discharge. This dog was only on sulfas.... Cat #49922 was extremely thin with a distended abdomen (pregnant?) and had a previous extensive hair loss condition. This cat needs to be isolated, examined and carefully observed.... Dog #45438 was found down, lying in its own urine, refusing to move. When examined, this dog had a bloody injury which was not detected—even though morning treatments were completed. This dog was euthanized during the inspection."

6-23-94: (215 dogs, 31 cats.) "Dog #45606 was recumbent until forced to stand when a left rear non-weightbearing lameness was found by the inspection team. This dog was not detected by the animal caretakers. Dog #45583 was unresponsive, dehydrated, weak, coughing and had a copious nasal discharge which had soiled his front legs."

11-22-94: (189 dogs, 21 cats.) "Veterinary care is still in noncompliance at this facility.... Dog #46222 was hunched up, coughing, thin, depressed and currently getting sulfas only.... Dog 46236 had a profuse nasal discharge, was very thin and depressed, appeared weak and was hunched up. This dog needs to be isolated, worked up and treated appropriately by the vet. Dog 46214 was reluctant to move—when examined he had a swollen left front leg which was not noticed or treated by the animal caretakers.... Cat 49838 had severe diarrhea which was not noticed by or treated by the caretakers."

On March 22, 1995, USDA filed a complaint against Hodgins alleging USDA inspectors had discovered willful violations of the Animal Welfare Act during inspections on 11/16/93, 1/18/94, 3/1/94, 4/5/94, 5/

10/94, 6/23/94, 9/13/94 and 11/22/94. Among the alleged violations were Hodgins's 1) failure to maintain programs of disease control, euthanasia and veterinary care under the supervision of a doctor of veterinary medicine; 2) failure to provide veterinary care to animals in need of care; 3) failure to individually identify dogs and maintain complete records showing the acquisition, disposition and identification of animals; 4) failure to keep interior surfaces of housing facilities and surfaces that come in contact with dogs and cats free of excessive rust; 5) failure to keep the walls and floors of indoor housing facilities impervious to moisture; 6) failure to maintain housing facilities in good repair and provide sufficient ventilation or heat for animals; 7) failure to keep premises clean; 8) failure to provide adequate resting surfaces for cats; 9) failure to maintain surfaces of primary enclosures on a regular basis and 10) failure to provide for regular and frequent collection of animal waste, debris and garbage.

A hearing was held September 27 through October 4 and October 18 and 19, 1995. The administrative law judge hearing the case found Hodgins guilty of all the violations alleged by USDA in its complaint except for failure to keep interior surfaces free of excessive rust, failure to keep floors and walls impervious to moisture, failure to provide adequate resting surfaces and failure to maintain surfaces of housing facilities on a regular basis. Even though USDA had requested a $45,000 civil penalty and a license suspension, the judge only imposed a penalty of $16,000 and no license suspension. Hodgins filed an appeal and a review of the judge's decision is still pending.

HUFFSTUTLER, RANDALL B. (OZARK RESEARCH SUPPLIER). Vienna, Missouri. USDA license #43-B-047 (license suspended in 1996).

Randy Huffstutler inherited his business from his father, Woodrow "Woody" Huffstutler. The family's Class B license was registered in the name of Woody's wife, Mary, until the late 1980s, when Randy applied for a license of his own. Huffstutler sold close to 1,600 dogs a year, grossing $75,000.[47] He supplied animals to Washington University and the University of Missouri (Columbia), and bought dogs at the Rutledge, Missouri auction. In 1996, USDA fined him $7,000 and suspended his license for ten years.

Questions about whether or not the Huffstutlers were acquiring all of their dogs in accordance with USDA regulations arose in April 1987, when USDA Assistant Area Veterinarian in Charge for Missouri David Vogt sent a memo to Dr. Robert Leach requesting an investigation of a "complaint concerning Woody Huffstutler."[48] The complainant reported that while visiting Huffstutler's facility to look for her two missing dogs she observed a "horse trailer containing 10-15 dogs." She stated she had seen "the animals unloaded at [Huffstutler's] and put in his cages."[49] A report of the telephone conservation with the woman noted: "(Ran [license] plate, [name deleted by USDA] Bland, MO). [Name deleted by USDA] has criminal record, stolen property. [Name deleted by USDA] also saw crowded cages containing 5 dogs, large piles of animal waste under cages two feet high, cages too small for the dogs' height etc."[50]

USDA audited Huffstutler's records in 1990 when it assembled the Midwest Stolen Dog Theft Task Force and again in 1993 as part of the B-Dealer Traceback project. The 1990 audit revealed several recordkeeping violations, including failure to record driver's license numbers and vehicle numbers for purchases from other than licensed dealers. Investigators also discovered that some of the names recorded on Huffstutler's acquisition forms were fictitious. Thirteen of 24 listed suppliers could not be located, and investigators determined they were nonexistent after telephone directory, post office and police record searches. Six of Huffstutler's suppliers were located, but only one went on record about the source of the dogs in question. In another case, a man who was listed as having sold Huffstutler 19 dogs told investigators he had only sold 5 dogs. He claimed it wasn't the first time his name had popped up—wrongly—on a dealer's acquisition records.

According to the Task Force investigation report, Huffstutler claimed he'd had no contact with USDA since he took the business over from his parents. The report noted that "records show the last inspection conducted on the kennel was 11-3-88." Huffstutler also claimed he could not recall being notified of the new regulations (effective 11-1-89). The report concluded that "due to the fact Randall Huffstutler may not have had prior knowledge of the revised regulations, it was decided to serve him an Official Notification and Warning of Violation of Federal Regulations." Huffstutler received a warning in April of 1990, and the case was closed.

Of the 15 listed suppliers targeted during the Random Source Traceback Project in 1993, one could not be located and one denied having sold any dogs to Huffstutler. Investigators also documented one incorrect name, two incorrect driver's license numbers and one discrepancy in the number of animals listed as sold to Huffstutler.

USDA inspections of Huffstutler's facility have revealed, in addition to recordkeeping problems, deficiencies in housing, veterinary care and sanitation:

5-16-90: (75 dogs) "A few vehicle license numbers and driver's license numbers need to be included on record on hand for purchases.... Three dog hutches with beagles have wire floors [with] too much gap between wires — Dogs cannot comfortably walk on wire without feet going through floor.... One dog and pup are located in dog house that has drainage problems around it and is inadequate to keep dogs dry and clean.... A buildup of fecal material was observed under hutches and needs to be removed."

11-2-92: (135 dogs, 19 cats) "Outdoor enclosure housing cats needs to have additional shelter provided for cats. Needs enough shelter for all cats in enclosure.... Two small enclosures housing cats need an elevated resting surface provided.... Accumulation of waste under dog enclosures needs to be removed"; 1-12-93 (83 dogs, 8 cats) "Numerous 7005's (acquisition of dogs and cats) do not have complete names and addresses for individuals dogs were acquired from. Several dogs are shown on records as not being sold or removed but are not found on the premises during the inventory."

9-29-93: (160 dogs — 151 adults, 9 puppies, 11 cats) "11 (eleven) cats on premises are not identified. All animals need to be identified with tags or tattoos; 12-27-93 (142 dogs — 141 adults, 1 puppy) "Clean dry bedding needs to be provided for all outdoor enclosures housing dogs"; 5-5-94 (130 dogs — 122 adults, 8 puppies) "Several enclosures housing dogs do not provide the required 6" of head space. All dogs need at least 6" of head space from top of head to top of cage when dog is at a normal standing position. 2 dogs are on chains and need a 6' perimeter fence around dogs or move dogs to enclosures."

On April 11, 1995, USDA filed a complaint against Huffstutler, charging him with acquiring random source dogs and failing to maintain complete records showing the acquisition, disposition and identification of animals. The complaint also charged Huffstutler with failing to: maintain programs of disease control and prevention, euthanasia and adequate veterinary care under the supervision of a veterinarian; store food supplies in a manner that protects them from spoilage, contamination and vermin manifestation; remove excreta and food waste from dog enclosures; and construct primary dog enclosures so that they provide sufficient space to allow each animal to turn about freely; to stand, sit and lie in a comfortable, normal position; and to walk in a normal position. Huffstutler signed a Consent Decision and Order agreeing to a civil penalty of $7,000 and a license suspension of ten years.

KNIGHT, DAVE. Eatonville, Washington. USDA license #91-B-043 (license suspended in 1996).

Dave Knight was first licensed as a Class B dealer in 1989. He sold close to 350 dogs a year, earning $105,860 in gross sales.[51] He was the

University of Washington's (UW) primary source of dogs for several years. UW continued to buy dogs from Knight despite knowledge of his documented Animal Welfare Act violations. In 1992, USDA fined Knight $1,200 for violating the Act. In 1996, it suspended his Class B license for a period of two years.

Knight obtains most of the dogs he sells from friends and acquaintances. He also acquires animals at field trials for hunting dogs, buying the dogs that don't work out or are untrainable. Suppliers to Knight are believed to include Joye Dart (USDA license #91-B-045) of Eatonville and Gary Lavine, Windy River Kennels (USDA license #91-B-036) of Lyle, both in Washington.

USDA inspectors have documented deficiencies in veterinary care, feeding and watering, recordkeeping, identification, cleaning, sanitation and housing at Knight's facility. On 11-2-89 (107 dogs), inspectors reported: "Dogs not provided with safe primary enclosures (chained to bumper of old pickup truck, chained to overturned and unstable pickup bed rack, chained to utility trailer, old chicken coop w/loose wire and nails protruding into enclosure, protruding wire in doorway of doghouse).... 13 of 14 dogs chained inside barn are on chains that are too short.... All water receptacles show sediment such that water does not appear potable.... Roughly 50% of dogs have lost their tags or are not yet identified."

During an inspection on 12-12-89 (122 dogs), inspectors reported: "Majority of dogs' shelters show accumulation of mud on floors such that dogs are not assured of dry resting area during wet weather conditions.... Female hound with nursing pups in pen with a stack of wire and wheels at one end, some of which are falling over as red male hound jumps up and around them; risk of injury to male hound as well as pups; pups allowed to roam at will out of area where female is chained; potential risk of injury by other dogs, machinery, vehicles."

"The vast majority of shelters... do not provide enough room for the dogs to comfortably stand, sit or turn around.... Pile of bread shows substantial degree of mold contamination.... Old animal bones (some with meat scraps still attached) are scattered about floors of pens and shelters and badly contaminated with mud and excreta.... Female lab/retriever cross housed with 4 hounds shows evidence of fight wounds.... Female lab/retriever cross should receive medical attention by or on 12-13-89; older, newly received black hound shows evidence of dermatitis and needs veterinary attention on or by 12-18-89."

Subsequent inspections revealed continuing noncompliance with housing, sanitation, recordkeeping and veterinary care regulations:

4-24-90: (127 dogs) "Dogs housed in outside area chained to doghouses or in open pens to be moved into renovated barn by or on 6/1/90....

Most food receptacles show evidence of dirt and bedding material in them.... All water receptacles show excessive soiling and most are empty of water.... Excessive accumulation of fecal material; frequency of cleaning and removal of excreta to be increased as necessary by or on 4/26/90.... Vehicle and driver license numbers and state of issue not recorded for all incoming dogs from non-USDA licensed or registered sources — 18 dogs and two unidentified puppies received as strays last night."

8-30-90: (123 dogs) "Remodelling of barn not yet completed and dogs (36 total) are still chained to doghouses outside and exposed to elements of sunlight, wind, rain, snow and cold.... Approximately 2/3 of these 36 dogs have doghouses that do not provide enough interior space for dog to make normal postural adjustments."

1-28-91 (161 dogs) "Veterinary care.... Dog has swelling on right body wall.... Dog has wound on cheek below right eye; dog is depressed, lethargic and dehydrated.... evidence of diarrhea in one or more dogs.... 16 dogs not identified; dogs acquired for other licensed dealers are being retagged but tag numbers from original dealer not being readily cross-referenced with new tag numbers.... Official tags worn by dogs acquired from other licensed dealers are being removed and disposed of upon arrival"

4-4-91 (Records review only) "Complete information pertaining to sources of dogs not properly recorded as follows: — vehicle license number and state of issue not recorded for 17 separate suppliers; — state of issue for drivers and/or vehicle license not recorded for 26 separate suppliers; — driver's license number not recorded for 3 separate suppliers."

10-3-91: (233 dogs) "No commercial dog feed is currently available on premises; 'day old' (and older) bread is being fed to adult breeding females; much of the bread is observed to be stale and all is seen to be haphazardly scattered around dog houses.... Many food and water receptacles visibly contaminated with dirt, debris, feces, urine, dead insects.... Cleaning — not adequately corrected since previous inspection — excessive accumulations of feces are seen in many areas where dogs are housed outside.... Veterinary care not adequately corrected since previous inspection.... Female hound #0464 very thin and appears emaciated.... Female hound #1373 is limping noticeably on badly swollen left front paw.... Female hound #470 is thin (appears emaciated), lethargic, apparently anorectic and has open wounds on right hip and on right mammary."

"Identification — not adequately corrected since last inspection — at least 30 dogs seen with no identification and many dogs identified with unofficial tags. Proprietor not on premises during inspection, therefore records, vet care program and medical log not available for review."

During reinspection on 10-11-91 (200 dogs), inspectors noted "Proprietor is again not on premises during inspection.... Veterinary care not adequately corrected since previous inspection.... Attending veterinarian has not visited premises in some months and overall program for the provision of veterinary care under the supervision of the attending veterinarian is inadequate for an operation of this size and type.... Identification not adequately corrected since previous inspection; 35 dogs are seen to be unidentified."

Inspectors continued to document inadequate veterinary care and poor recordkeeping:

12-2-91:(157 dogs) "Written program [of veterinary care] not yet completed.... 31 dogs not identified.... Driver's license and state of issue not recorded for 1 supplier; vehicle license and state of issue not recorded for 9 suppliers; vehicle and driver license and states of issue not recorded for 9 suppliers; address and vehicle and driver license and state of issue not recorded for 11 suppliers"; 4-13-92: (110 dogs) "27 dogs not properly identified.... Complete records not provided for 29 suppliers who have supplied dogs to licensee since last inspection"; 8-24-92: (118 dogs) "One unidentified hound is observed limping on injured right front foot.... 23 dogs not properly identified.... Complete records not readily available for review for 18 suppliers."

In 1992, Knight was fined $1,200 for various Animal Welfare Act violations, including improper drainage and waste disposal; improper shelter for puppies; failure to maintain clean surfaces; inadequate housekeeping and removal of waste; failure to provide an adequate program of veterinary care and inadequate records.

In August, 1993, the Progressive Animal Welfare Society (PAWS) conducted an investigation of Washington state dealers that was aired on KING-TV's "Our Times." Knight was featured as a local dealer. PAWS conducted tracebacks of Knight's suppliers from his records and found that only 19 names checked out. Of those, several were hunters selling rejected hunting dogs; others were breeders with surplus stock. Three people insisted they had not given permission to Knight to sell their dogs to research institutions.

One of those people was Claudia Milbradt. Her dog Roxie, a boisterous puppy, wasn't responding to obedience training. On a relative's suggestion, Claudia called Knight, who agreed to train Roxie as a hunting dog. He reassured Claudia that if Roxie failed as a hunting dog, he'd keep her as a pet for his kids.

Claudia and her family were not allowed to visit Roxie at Knight's home because he warned that it might "disrupt her training." The Milbradts never saw Roxie again. In March 1991, Knight sold Roxie to the University of Washington for $200. The Milbradts didn't find out what had happened to Roxie until PAWS contacted them in 1993. "If we had the slightest idea that he would even consider selling her for research, we would have taken her home immediately," said Milbradt. "We wanted her to have a good home. That was the most important thing to us."[52]

USDA continued to report deficiencies at Knight's facility in 1993 and 1994:

3-2-93: (84 dogs) "Six dogs not wearing identification tags.... Complete records not available for review for 24 suppliers of dogs since last inspection"; 7-6-93: (86 dogs) "Eleven dogs observed without identification tags this inspection.... Complete records not available for review for 7 new suppliers of dogs (since last inspection). Record for dog #2290 does not correspond with true breed of dog. No record available for small black terrier cross"; 5-2-94: (29 dogs) "Three dogs are observed without official identification tags.... Complete records for three new suppliers (since last inspection), dogs #2704, 2694 and two unidentified dogs, not available."

On April 6, 1995, USDA filed a complaint against Knight charging him with failure to provide adequate veterinary care; failure to maintain complete records showing the acquisition and disposition of animals; failure to identify dogs; failure to provide primary enclosures for dogs that were structurally sound and maintained in good repair; failure to construct surfaces of housing facilities in a manner that allowed them to be readily cleaned and sanitized; and failure to equip housing facilities with disposal facilities and drainage systems that were constructed and operated so that animal waste and water were rapidly eliminated and animals stayed dry. On June 12, 1996, Knight signed a consent decision, neither admitting nor denying the charges set forth in USDA's complaint. The order suspended Knight's Class B license for a period of two years and assessed a civil penalty of $20,000. The fine was suspended on the condition that Knight comply with the Animal Welfare Act.

KREDOVSKI, MICHAEL (BIO-MEDICAL ASSOCIATES, INC.). Friedensburg, Pennsylvania. USDA license #23-B-006 (1997).

Kredovski, who has been licensed as a Class B dealer since 1967, sells approximately 3,084 animals a year, earning $899,929 in gross sales.[53] Kredovski's customers have included the National Institutes of Health, Walter Reed Army Medical Center, the Massachusetts Institute of Technology, Harvard and Johns Hopkins University.

In the 1960s, Kredovski's business network included Paul Anthony and Andy Ball (Ohio), Fuzz Shipman (Kansas), and George Gowen (Tennessee). Gowen, who acquired dogs in Georgia and Alabama and reportedly processed between 100 and 200 dogs and cats a week, was convicted of cruelty to animals in July of 1965. According to the Humane Society of the United States, Anthony sold dogs to Kredovski and apparently operated his facility as a "holding station" for Kredovski's dogs.

On April 5, 1966, police in Lexington, Kentucky stopped an unlettered livestock truck crammed with 100 dogs. The driver was Andy Ball, who was then working for Paul Anthony. The dogs were en route to Anthony's facility in Ohio and were destined for sale to Kredovski in Pennsylvania. The police arrested Ball and his assistant, Donald Chamberlain, and charged them with failure to vaccinate a dog against rabies, possession of unlicensed dogs and driving an unlettered livestock truck.[54] The dogs were later released to Anthony and shipped to Kredovski's kennel. The Animal Rescue League of Berks County, Pennsylvania managed to obtain two of the dogs from Kredovski and offered them for adoption, claiming they "seemed most likely to have been pets."[55] In July 1970, USDA charged both Kredovski and Anthony with having transported 150 dogs and 4 cats in cramped crates on May 16, 1969. Anthony voluntarily surrendered his dealer's license, and Kredovski agreed to a 7-day license suspension.[56]

Four USDA licensed dealers who have sold animals to Kredovski are Eugene Peachey (USDA license #23-B-013) of Huntingdon, Pennsylvania, Mona Hill (USDA license #54-B-002) of Huntington, West Virginia (see Hill, Mona in this chapter), Robert Seekman (USDA license #54-B-019) of Omega, West Virginia and Jack Stowers (USDA license #32-B-097) of Frankfort, Indiana (see Stowers, Jack in "Dealers Who Have Lost or Relinquished Their Licenses").

Inspectors have documented deficiencies in veterinary care and recordkeeping at Kredovski's facility:

1-28-92: (470 dogs, 331 cats) "Must still obtain complete mailing addresses when dogs and cats are acquired especially from private individuals. Must also obtain driver's license number and vehicle license numbers of unlicensed individuals.... Must put dates of acquisition.... Records of some beagles did not have dates."

9-23-92: (596 dogs, 131 cats) "Records on hand for beagles purchased did not have the vehicle license number and state and the driver's license number and state of the person from whom the beagles were purchased. This recordkeeping problem was addressed in the inspection report of January 28, 1992.... In cat building #3 cat #1776 had severe swelling of the upper and lower palpebral conjunctiva such that the globe of the eye could not be visualized. Medical records indicate that this animal is being treated with vitamin c every other day and oral antibiotic 'as needed.' More aggressive therapy is indicated. The following animals were being treated with tetracycline three times daily, and had all been vaccinated and wormed. No record of additional treatment was present: Dog #5046 was emaciated and had moderate to severe dehydration. This dog also had bilateral purulent eye discharge, bilateral purulent nasal discharge with blood and exhibited increased respiratory effort. More aggressive therapy is indicated.... Dog #4933 was severely depressed and very weak. The dog's mucous membranes were very pale. This dog also had a one inch wound on its left flank fold, abrasions on its left rear leg and swelling of its left foreleg. More aggressive therapy or euthanasia is indicated."

11-10-92: (520 dogs, 113 cats) "Records on hand for (4) purchases of beagles since 9-23-92 did not have driver's license number and state of person acquired from.... Dog #5501 housed in pen #5 of room was noted to have facial swelling, hair loss and scabbing under its left eye and narrowing of the left palpebral fissure.... No record of observation or treatment of this problem is present.... Dog #4943 housed in run #6 of building B and dogs #5240 (Pen #1) and 5184 (Pen #2) housed in building D were all noted to be very thin and be moderately dehydrated."

12-16-92: (569 dogs, 121 cats) "At least 44 shelters in outdoor area did not provide sufficient protection from wind and rain.... Incomplete records were again noted on dog transactions since inspection report of 11/12/92.... In the outdoor pens dog #A18738 had a draining wound on its left ear and also had a wound, marked swelling and bruising on its left rear leg. Additionally this dog had bruising on its scrotum and cried out when its left ear was touched.... In dog building D, dog #A16158 was noted to have a deep corneal ulcer in its left eye. Additionally this dog was extremely thin and severely dehydrated.... This dog was euthanized at the time of this inspection.... Animals newly in need of veterinary attention are not being identified in a timely manner. Additionally... the therapy given is sometimes inadequate for the severity of the animal's condition."

3-17-93:(426 dogs, 96 cats) "Cat #5687.... was noted to have an open wound on the palmar aspect of its left front foot. This cat is currently being treated with 100 mg chloramphenicol three times weekly. More aggressive therapy is indicated."

6-7-93: (479 dogs, 37 cats) "Incomplete records were again noted.... The following transactions did not have driver's license or vehicle license number of the persons dogs were obtained from: a) April 18, 1993, (9) dogs were purchased with no driver's license number recorded. b) April 18, 1993, (5) dogs were purchased with no vehicle number recorded. c) April 24, 1993, (3) dogs were purchased with no vehicle number recorded, d) April 26, 1993, a total of (28) dogs were purchased during seven transactions and no vehicle license number was recorded."

3-15-94: (352 dogs, 137 cats) The inspector noted once again that driver's license and vehicle license numbers had not been recorded for a number of cats and dogs.

6-20-94: (335 dogs, 128 cats) "Lab female with tag number A19207 arrived on 3-14-94 and was placed in a group pen of (6) dogs. Facility personnel report dog had to be euthanized on 3-15-94 due to severe fight wounds inflicted overnight. Dogs must be housed in compatible groups."

On April 11, 1995, USDA filed a complaint against Kredovski alleging he failed to keep complete records showing acquisition of dogs; acquired random source dogs in violation of section 2.132 of AWA regulations; and housed incompatible dogs in the same primary enclosure.

During an inspection of Kredovski's facility on 9-19-95 (402 dogs, 119 cats), the inspector reported: "Dealers cannot make available pound dogs unless the pound certificates contain complete information, including the breed or type (for mixed breeds, estimate the two dominant breeds or types). Four dogs were accepted on 9-12-95 from licensed dealer 32-B-097. Dogs ID tag's numbers 9223, 9233, 9230, 9228 were listed as XX [crosses] for breed type. The two dominant breeds were not listed."

USDA filed an amended complaint against Kredovski in September of 1996. In addition to reiterating the charges set forth in the 1995 complaint, the new complaint charged Kredovski with 1) failing to make provisions for the regular collection, removal and disposal of animal and food wastes, bedding, debris, garbage, water, other fluids, and dead animals, in a manner that minimizes contamination and disease risks; 2) failing to provide primary enclosures for dogs that were structurally sound and in good repair and to construct and maintain the floors of primary enclosures for dogs so that the floors protect the animals' feet and legs from injury; 3) failing to establish and maintain an effective program for the control of pests so as to promote the health and well-being of the animals and reduce contamination by pests in animal area; 4) failing to maintain complete and accurate records showing the acquisition, disposition and identification of cats; and 5) failing to provide certification containing a description of dogs, including the species and breed or type, when making available random source dogs. A hearing on the charges is still pending.

MILLER, LEM R. (MILLER'S KENNEL). Estillfork, Alabama. License #64-B-053 (1997).

Lem Miller worked for Class B dealer Jerry Vance before applying for his own license in 1993 (see Vance, Jerry in "Investigations Into the

Acquisition of Animals by Class B Dealers"). According to USDA, Miller sells approximately 450 animals a year, primarily to other Class B dealers.

On May 21, 1994, a USDA inspector who checked Miller's acquisition records at the Collinsville, Alabama Trade Day reported: "Complete records are not being maintained on the dogs purchased today. Dogs ID 290, 291, 292, 293 and 294 had the owner's name but no address, drivers license number or vehicle tag number. Mr. Miller said he had all this information at home on his master record sheets. All information must be recorded at time dogs are purchased." On July 6, 1995, the inspector reported again that Miller's records were incomplete: "The following dogs' acquisition records cannot be located: 1175, 1046, 1121, 1055, 1125, 1052, 1007, 1051, 1053, 1095, 1087 and 1038."

According to information provided by USDA in April 1997, Miller is currently under investigation. [57]

PERRY, BOB (SOUTHEASTERN LABORATORY ANIMAL FARM). Raleigh, North Carolina. License #55-B-076 (1997).

Southeastern Laboratory Animal Farm supplies both dogs and cats to research institutions and biological supply houses, including Carolina Biological Supply. Bob Perry sells approximately 1,195 animals a year, grossing $54,895.[58] USDA inspectors have documented deficiencies in veterinary care, housing and recordkeeping at Perry's facility:

1-3-89: (30 dogs, 120 cats) "Several areas of protruding wires at top of partition wall. Potential for injury to enclosed animals.... Several cats appear to be affected with eye disease or injury. All cats should be treated or humanely disposed of by January 18, 1989."

6-5-89: (40 dogs, 150 cats) "The main cat room has excessive humidity and/or odors present.... Fresh air must be provided all animals at all times.... Several broken wires observed 1-3-89 were not in compliance. These are still not in compliance on this date because of failure to adequately repair enclosures." The same day, inspector David Kelley filed an alleged violation report charging Perry with failing to fix the broken and protruding wires.

7-20-89: (45 dogs, 150 cats) "Approximately 8 kittens in S.E. corner room of large cat building have crusted eyes. These cats must be examined by the consulting veterinarian and treated or humanely euthanized."

5-28-91: (36 dogs, 65 cats) "Four kittens in back building have injured and/or infected eyes.... All animals must be examined and treated by attending vet."

Inspectors were repeatedly unable to conduct inspections:

5-24-91: Attempted inspection. "No one present at facility."

12-12-91: Attempted inspection. "No one present at facility."

6-24-92: Attempted inspection. "No one at facility."

6-25-92: Attempted inspection. "No one present at facility to allow APHIS inspection."

An inspector filed an alleged violation report on June 25. Rather than initiate an administrative proceeding, USDA requested written assurance from Perry that the violation would not recur. Despite Perry's assurance that the problem would be corrected and would "remain so in the future,"[59] inspectors had difficulty gaining access to the facility again in 1994, 1995 and 1996:

5-19-94: "No one at facility."

6-2-95: "No one at facility at time of attempted inspection."

12-21-95: "No one at facility — each dealer must make facility and records available for USDA inspection during normal business hours."

12-2-96: "No one present at facility. Noncompliance items noted 7-16-96 could not be determined to have been corrected or not. Original correction date remains."

PESNELL, MARLIN (PESNELL KENNELS). Arab, Alabama. USDA license #64-B-044 (1997).

Marlin Pesnell sells approximately 1,000 dogs a year to other dealers, grossing $45,300.[60] At one time Pesnell sold dogs to former Class B licensee Robert Motsinger (St. Joseph, Illinois, license #33-B-055) USDA inspection reports indicate recurrent deficiencies in housing, sanitation, veterinary care and recordkeeping at Pesnell Kennels:

9-4-91: (45 dogs listed, 65 dogs on site) "11 dogs had no tags.... Records are incomplete. All dogs are not accounted for"; 10-8-91: (37 dogs listed, 39 dogs on site) "3 dogs inventoried were not in kennel.... 1 dog in the kennel was not on the record.... Several addresses were incomplete insofar as acquisition concerned."

11-12-91: (54 dogs listed, 62 dogs on site) "[M]any dogs are not identified. Several dogs in the kennel (those without ID) are not listed on VS 11-5"; 8-16-93: (44 dogs) "Gates in kennels have damaged wire.... Feed buckets rusty, one has broken rim.... Compartments not tall enough for at least 1 dog.... Six dogs in large compartment. No more than 4 allowed...."

Primary conveyance not suitable for transport at temp. above 85°F. No auxiliary ventilation. Conveyance cannot be used at temperatures above 85°F or below 45°F until modified.... Some records of acquired dogs incomplete.... Incomplete medical records."

8-28-93: (Collinsville, Alabama Trade Day, 23 dogs) "Dogs are being put into boxes and records are being kept, but dogs are not tagged until they reach facility at Arab.... Records are at the Home facility. Correct by 8-29-93.... No Program of Veterinary Care available—it is at Home facility.... The dog boxes are 23" tall. Large dogs cannot stand erect."

An amendment to the 8-28-93 inspection report stated: "Eight (8) dogs were brought from the Home Facility in Arab, AL to be sold at Collinsville Trade Day. All 8 dogs' USDA tags had been removed from the dogs and the dogs were not individually identified. Mr. Pesnell said he had removed the USDA tags from these 8 dogs because no one would buy a dog with a USDA tag attached to its collar.... No records were available for inspection on the eight (8) dogs transported for sale at Collinsville Alabama Trade Day from the Home Facility in Arab AL.... No food or water receptacles inside the primary enclosure."

A 10-3-93 inspection report (Ripley Trade Day, Mississippi, 8 dogs) noted continuing deficiencies in identification and recordkeeping: "4 dogs purchased today were not identified by official USDA tags.... Tags applied to the 4 purchased dogs were not used in sequence.... The information for the people the dogs were purchased from was incomplete. Lacking complete address, vehicle tag number, and driver's license.... 4 dogs belonging to the Licensee's son were transported from Alabama to Miss. without a health certificate.... Dogs purchased in Mississippi today need to have health certificates to be transported to the home site at Arab, Alabama."

On 10-4-93 (27 dogs), inspectors reported: "Incomplete medical records.... Wire or boards must be placed over all openings on the primary enclosures inside the transport trailer so dogs cannot put any part of its body outside the primary enclosures.... Holding Period. From 8-24-93 to 10-4-93, 42 dogs were not held 5 complete days. They were held two to four days.... A new Program of Veterinary Care needs to be on file.... Licensee also euthanizes dogs on the premises. This method should be reviewed and approved by the attending veterinarian.... Procurement of random source dogs. From July 25, 1993 to 10-4-93, (38) thirty-eight dogs were purchased from Dallas L. Polk, Route 3, Waynesboro, Tenn. A class 'B' dealer shall not obtain live random source dogs from individuals who have not bred and raised the dogs on their own premises.... Acquisition records checked today for dogs acquired after 8-16-93 revealed four sources and twenty-seven (27) dogs with incomplete information."

On 1-27-94 (32 dogs), inspectors noted that several noncompliant items previously identified on 10-4-93 had not been corrected. "Pens number 1 and 7 gates in kennels have damaged wire.... Wire or boards must be placed over all openings (near top and on doors) on the primary enclosures inside the transport trailer.... Acquisition and Disposition Records checked today for dogs acquired and sold after 10-4-93 revealed several sources and many dogs with incomplete information.... From 10-4-93 to 1-27-94 four (4) dogs were not held 5 complete days. They were held three to four days.... Health certificates should indicate and state that the dogs appear to the licensed veterinarian to be free of any infectious disease or physical abnormality."

During an inspection on 11-16-94 (24 dogs), the inspector noted that Pesnell had purchased 44 dogs from an individual who had not bred and raised the animals on his own property.

During an inspection at the Collinsville, Alabama trade day on 6-10-95 (10 dogs), the inspector reported: "Four dogs are chained to the trees for resale. The USDA tags have been removed and placed in individual dog boxes. The USDA tags must remain on the dogs at all times.... Mr. John Pesnell placed the tags on the dogs. Corrected today."

On 10-25-95 (36 dogs), the inspector noted: "Nineteen (19) dogs have discrepancy in the disposition records and 8 dogs acquired today have incomplete records.... The 8 dogs acquired today now have complete records."

The inspector reported that dogs were not properly identified on 11-18-96 (39 dogs): "The 39 dogs do not have any official USDA tag affixed to the dogs' necks. All dogs must be immediately identified when purchased."

PEUSCHEL, WALTER AND HILDEGARD. Mequon, Wisconsin. USDA license #35-B-008 (1997).

The Peuschels, who also operate a contract pound for the Thiensville, Wisconsin area, sell approximately 100 dogs a year.[61]

USDA inspectors have documented deficiencies in recordkeeping and sanitation at the Peuschel's facility on a number of occasions:

1-7-88: (3 dogs) "Form 18-5 has duplicate ID numbers.... 24 acquired dates have not been entered since last inspection... on 24 animals from a list of 45 animals total.... Dog was brought into cage on 12-14-87 and cage not sanitized since."

5-16-88: (2 dogs) "A number of dead cats obtained from an in-state rendering company and re-sold to NASCO (North American Scientific

Company) in Fort Atkinson , WI were never entered into the facility records as far as date, purchaser, seller, description of the animals, etc.... This deficiency has been corrected as of 5-16-88 as Mr. Peuschel now understands he needs to keep such records on dead cats as well. He will no longer be dealing in dead cats."

On June 17, 1988, APHIS Area Veterinarian In Charge G.S. Jacobsen issued the Peuschel's a warning for failing to "1. keep records of dead cats sold to Nasco, Inc., Fort Atkinson, Wisconsin; 2. record into records all dogs received by pound when transferred to [Class B] facilities ; and 3. hold dogs a full five days after they were transferred to animal welfare facilities."

On 3-13-89, inspectors reported: "10 dogs and cats acquired between 9-7-88 and 3-13-89 were identified as the source as merely Ozaukee Co. or Ozaukee Co Stray or Stray Ozaukee (6) with nothing in the records as to the location [where] the animal was picked up."

On May 24, 1989, APHIS issued the Peuschels an Official Notification and Warning of Violation of Federal Regulations for their failure to provide complete addresses of pound dogs or dogs picked up at the request of local police departments (as noted on a 3-13-89 inspection).

During an inspection on 12-15-93 (0 dogs), inspectors reported: "Some dogs acquired from a contract pound by the licensee have not been held for 10 full days."

On 3-28-94 (0 dogs), the inspector noted: "The contract pound operated by this licensed dealer is located on the same property that the dealer operation is on. Correct by 4-28-94.... Cats #10244 and 10245 with disposition of 3-15-94 have an incomplete certification. Information on the pound where dealer acquired is incomplete and no signed statement from the pound is present in the record."

ROTZ, BRUCE. Shippensburg, Pennsylvania. USDA license #23-B-004 (1997).

Bruce Rotz sells approximately 200 dogs and cats a year.[62] USDA inspectors have documented noncompliance with recordkeeping and housing regulations at Rotz's facility:

1-21-91: (26 dogs, 53 cats) "The indoor/outdoor building must be provided with heat so that temperature cannot fall below 50 degrees inside.... At time of inspection (21) puppies were not identified. Collars were hanging on door at time. Must keep puppies identified once they are separated from dam."

7-9-91: (24 dogs, 4 cats) "Must provide additional ventilation in cat buildings. Windows were closed and no auxiliary ventilation such as fans were present.... Must replace or repair (6) outdoor enclosures. Floors and sides were noted to have holes and gaps between boards.... At time of inspection (18) puppies were not wearing official tags."

3-1-93: (13 dogs, 6 cats) "Need to obtain the vehicle license number and state and the driver's license number and state of whom cats and dogs were obtained from. Records indicate only vehicle license number or driver's license number are being obtained."

10-20-93: (19 dogs, 22 cats) "Still need to obtain the vehicle license number and the driver's license number and state of the person(s) dogs and cats were obtained from."

12-21-94: (12 dogs, 31 cats) "Three dead cats, tags numbered 657, 659 and 660, were observed on ground outside of cat facility. Dead animals need to be properly disposed of. Dead animals cannot be left on the ground."

3-30-95: (16 dogs, 19 cats) "Facility needs to record treatment for animals with health problems or signs of illness. Medical records shall include observations and dates, treatments administered and dates, diagnosis and resolution of the problem.... The new slips used to acquire dogs and cats currently state 'I hereby certify that I have raised the following dog(s) and or cat(s) listed below.' The words 'and bred' should be added to slips."

9-27-95: (9 dogs) "The second freestanding pen housing two hound cross dogs had hole in wire flooring approximately 8 inches by 7 inches. Need to replace/repair wire.... Not all records of dogs on hand or acquired since previous inspection were available at time of inspection. All records need to be available during inspection."

According to information provided by USDA in April 1997, Rotz is currently under investigation.[63]

SCHACHTELE, DANNY (MIDDLEFORK KENNELS). Salisbury, Missouri. USDA license #43-B-032 (1997).

Danny Schachtele applied for a Class B license in 1987 when he and his brother, Johnny, started the Schachtele Dog Auction. Danny later became sole owner and renamed the business Middlefork Kennels. He purchases dogs and cats from various individuals and at trade days, including the Rutledge Gun and Dog Auction. He sells about 3,000 animals a year, grossing close to $200,000.[64] His customers have included the Alton Oschner Medical Foundation of Louisiana, Louisiana State University Medical Center, the Kirksville College of Osteopathic Medicine of Missouri, the University of Oklahoma Health Science Center, and the Oklahoma City Veterans Administration Hospital. USDA fined him $625 in 1995.

During a 3-30-88 inspection of the Schachtele Dog Auction, inspectors reported, "All cats are in poor condition physically. One cat was dead in the box. Cats should be attended to by veterinarian or disposed of. No more cats shall be kept until a different approved facility is provided... Pen with 15 dogs must have a minimum of 3 dogs removed.... 4 cats... must have a surface elevated of adequate size to comfortably hold all occupants."

Subsequent inspections of both Schachtele Dog Auction and Middlefork Kennels revealed continuing noncompliance with veterinary care and sanitation standards:

4-20-88: (55 dogs) "Pen with hound with pups must be cleaned and sanitized.... It has an accumulation of waste beneath the pen and on the wire and brace boards. The box is dirty and has a dead pup within it. This must be attended to immediately"; 9-11-90: "Dead dog and cat carcass need removal.... Cat house has feces on floor.... Dog with pussy or snotty eyes. Dog with chewed ear."

1-27-92: (170 dogs, 30 cats) "All dogs must be able to remain dry and clean — 6 runs on South side are very wet and muddy.... Cat units must have resting surfaces large enough to hold all cats in primary enclosures, also enough clean litter pans.... Dogs on chains — chains must be 3 times the length of dog.... All [dog houses] need to be cleaned and sanitized at least every 2 weeks. Dogs on chain must have waste picked up daily. All cat enclosures shall be cleaned and sanitized at least every 2 weeks.... Cats must be identified by tag collar or tattoos."

During reinspection on 4-29-92 (126 dogs, 33 cats), inspectors reported that some of the deficiencies noted on previous inspections had not been corrected: "Both dog and cat enclosures must be cleaned and sanitized at least every 2 weeks or as often as necessary to keep animals clean.... Cats are still not identified." The inspectors also noted that "dog 6683 has 4 inch piece of skin torn from left hind leg... this dog must have vet care within 24 hours."

On 4-12-93 (132 dogs, 9 cats), inspectors reported, "Cat enclosures showing more than 24 hours accumulation [of feces] this morning.... Inventory of animals on hand need to reflect an accurate identification and accurate inventory count of dogs within the facility at any point in time.... Noncompliant items from previous inspection not corrected: Found 2 out of 12 pens to be overcrowded this morning.... 17 dogs [had] 85 square feet available (need 198 square feet)... first pen on northeast to west with 20 dogs with 85 square feet available (need 200 square feet).... Exercise plan not found to be in files."

On 3-9-94 (158 dogs, 29 cats), inspectors reported: "Two sick dogs pointed out to son needed to be seen by kennel vet — also note that these dogs were extremely thin, in need of isolation, medications, diet changes.... Cat enclosure... showed excess of 24 hours fecal accumulation.... Over one-half of total enclosures were above twelve dogs in number today.... There is no provision for overflow at this point in time.... Approximately twelve or so adult cats were without ID tags.... Dog needing vet care did not have proper ID tag.... Bring inventory of dogs and cats up to date and maintain on current basis."

During an inspection on 9-8-94 (265 dogs, 20 cats), inspectors reported: "The majority of enclosures were found to be crowded today. A few of the new facility enclosures were near or above 30 in number.... Fecal accumulation under wire runs north of office has not been removed — found maggots to be active today. Brush boxes, clean runs and enclosures daily."

In 1995, USDA charged Schachtele with failing to adequately sanitize underneath wire runs and provide adequate floor space for cats. Schachtele signed a stipulation agreement in April 1995, agreeing to pay a $625 civil penalty in settlement of the matter.

During an 11-2-95 inspection of Schachtele's facility, the inspector reported: "Dogs #3480-4500 are in facility today and dog #4486 died — these dogs were singled out as needing prompt vet care on 8-31-95.... It is noted today by Dr. Jones... that there are still dogs within the facility that are in need of vet care. It is asked that Dr. Smith be called to the premises and care for any and all dogs in need within 24 hours."

SCHERBRING, ELMER. Earlville, Iowa. USDA license #42-B-054 (1997).

Scherbring operates his facility as both a contract pound and a Class B dealership. On his 1989-1990 annual report, he reported selling 96 dogs.[65] USDA inspection reports reveal a history of noncompliance with AWA regulations:

3-3-87: (8 dogs) "Feeding pans... [and] watering pans need to be cleaned and sanitized.... Had one dog that was not identified with tag. Dog had collar off, it was in the pen."

3-25-87: (7 dogs) "3:30 PM... Mr. Scherbring has sold some cats to research center in Iowa City.... [He] stated that these were his personal cats. Mr. Scherbring was told not to sell any more cats to research... as he does not have an approved facility for the buying and selling of cats."

In a 3-25-87 memo to APHIS Area Veterinarian in Charge Dr.

Bernard Zecha, a veterinary inspector questioned Scherbring's sale of cats he claimed were his own. "Due to Mr. Scherbring's past history this may or may not be true. Also, a review of Mr. Scherbring's file will reveal a history of non-compliance."

Inspectors were often unable to gain access to Scherbring's facility to conduct inspections:

2-25-87: attempted inspection. "No one home. Went there twice— 0900 and 1415.... Will contact Mr. Scherbring by phone to check and see if his hours at home have changed"; 12-13-87: Attempted inspection. "No one home"; 1-26-88: Attempted inspection. "No one home"; 8-25-88: Attempted inspection. "Two trips. 1st trip no one home.... 2nd trip no one home"; 10-31-88: Attempted inspection. "No one home."

When inspectors were able to conduct inspections, they continued to report deficiencies in sanitation, recordkeeping and adherence to holding period requirements:

2-23-88: (5 dogs) "North facility needs a good general cleaning, excess amount of excreta—needs clean bedding, and debris accumulation around primary enclosures. South facility is no longer used to house dogs. Owner has sheep in the building at the present time"; 8-1-88: (5 dogs) "Both East and South housing facilities need to have animal and food waste removed and bedding removed and replaced. Food receptacles... and watering receptacles need to be cleaned and sanitized. Primary enclosures need to have excess amount excreta removed. East building needs a good cleaning."

9-27-88: (La Crosse Vet Clinic. 5 dogs) "Of 5 dogs in this shipment, only 3 tags were presented and only one of these was affixed to the dog. Two tags were presented loose. The two dogs without any tag affixed or presented were not assigned a tag number on the form 18-6." On October 12, 1988, a USDA inspector filed an alleged violation report citing failure to identify all dogs.

During an inspection on 6-20-90 (9 dogs), the inspector reported: "Barn floors where dogs are kept must be cleaned of bedding, feces and debris more frequently.... Fresh water must be presented to each animal each day, and receptacles should be kept clean and free of dirt, algae and other contaminants." The inspector also noted that Scherbring had not been recording complete names on his acquisition records.

On 1-28-91, USDA sent Scherbring a warning notice charging him with failure to record USDA license numbers, vehicle license numbers and driver's license numbers on his acquisition forms during the period of 3-5-90 through 12-17-90.

Inspectors continued to document deficiencies at Scherbring's facility:

10-13-92: (3 dogs) "Feces and food waste must be removed from primary kennels daily.... 1) The Animal Pound facility must be physically separated from the licensed facility where the research dogs are kept. 2) Accurate and complete records shall be separately maintained by the licensee. 3) The facility must hold the research dogs at least 10 full days."

11-12-93: (9 dogs) "Moderate accumulation of dirt/debris on walls.... Spider webs accumulated in buildings.... Several dirty bowls in kennels.... Water bowls need to be cleaned.... Water bowls need to be cleaned.... Moderate accumulation of feces and dirty straw, needs to be cleaned"; 3-18-94: (15 dogs) "Walls in kennel need to be cleaned on regular basis. Moderate accumulation of dirt/debris on walls.... Several dirty bowls with old feed present.... Water bowls need to be cleaned. Dirt buildup in pans.... Moderate accumulation of feces and dirty straw present." The inspector discussed with Scherbring the requirement that a contract pound/shelter must be physically separate from a Class B facility.

In 1996, USDA filed a complaint against Scherbring, alleging that from 1993 through 1994, he failed to 1) obtain certifications for random source dog purchases; 2) provide certifications to buyers when selling random source dogs; 3) hold random source dogs for 5 days before delivering them to the purchaser; 4) make and maintain accurate records of three random source dogs that were rejected by the purchaser and 5) immediately identify a dog with an official identification tag. USDA also charged Scherbring with falsifying his records by participating in the forgery of purported certification for at least 52 random source dogs and reusing official identification tags. A hearing on the charges is pending.

SCHROEDER, KENNETH (HILLSIDE KENNELS). Wells, Minnesota. USDA license #41-B-017 (1997).

According to information he provided to USDA, Kenneth Schroeder sells approximately 1,304 animals a year, earning $88,052.[66] He acquires animals from individuals and at trade days and has sold dogs to the University of Wisconsin (the University of Wisconsin at Madison stopped purchasing animals from Class B dealers five years ago).

USDA inspectors have cited recordkeeping and housing deficiencies at Schroeder's facility:

3-30-88: (105 dogs listed, 96 dogs on site; 20 cats listed, 18 cats on site) "Few lost tags—or slipped collars.... Roofs on some of the outside dog houses need to be inspected or replaced.... Feed and water pans need to be checked over and replace ones with sharp edges and chewed edges."

4-14-88: (122 dogs listed, 113 dogs on site; 11 cats listed, 16 cats on site) "Few lost tags on cats.... Roofs on some of the houses... need to be repaired or replaced. Was given until 4-29-88."

5-23-89: (138 dogs listed, 145 dogs on site; 5 cats) "On this date, an older female in big pen in barn had a missing toe nail. Blue tick hound in granary had a lump under its jaw. These animals had not been treated or seen by veterinarian at time of inspection. Treat by May 24, 1989.... Indoor housing shall be ventilated so as to minimize drafts and odors. On this date, the cattery had an odor build-up."

10-11-90: (109 dogs listed, 105 dogs on site; 0 cats listed, 134 cats on site) "A Chesapeake Bay retriever had no dog house — shelter needs to be provided.... Almost all pens in barn, loft, and also some tethered animals had a manure build-up — manure needs to be removed.... Loft has open slat sides and is not adequate protection from cold weather. Walls need to be fixed to provide adequate protection."

3-24-92: (70 dogs, 11 cats) "General all around cleaning must be done to remove dirt on walls, cobwebs, hair, etc. from barns.... Cattery. Excess odor in house. Additional ventilation must be provided.... Excessive amount of excreta in some pens in barn and also corn crib.... Need to add street address on dogs purchased."

3-9-94: (41 dogs, 41 cats.) "Cat facility has an excess accumulation of excreta and food waste on floor and in primary enclosures.... Acquisition records do not all contain the complete address and/or driver's license and car license plate of the persons from whom the dogs were obtained."

USDA investigated Schroeder's allegedly inaccurate recordkeeping in 1989 but never filed any charges against him.

SILCOX, DENNIS (REGENCY RESEARCH ENTERPRISES). Lexington, Kentucky. USDA license #61-B-105 (1997).

Dennis Silcox sells approximately 350 animals a year, grossing $50,775.[67] USDA inspectors have been unable to gain access to Silcox's facility on many occasions. When they have been able to inspect the facility, they have documented chronic deficiencies in recordkeeping and sanitation:

9-21-88: Reinspection. "Records not available for review"; 11-7-88: Attempted inspection. "No one home — no inspection made"; 12-8-88: Attempted inspection. "No one home — no inspection done"; 2-1-89: Attempted inspection. "No one home. No inspection made"; 7-11-89: Attempted inspection. "Not home — no inspection done. This is the third time since

January 1989 that I have driven to your facility and found no one present."

7-18-89: (29 cats) "One cat untagged—no official ID."

11-2-89: (44 cats) "5 cages with 2 cats in each cage so minimum space requirement not met.... Water pans in recently cleaned cages had old food floating and on bottom.... Two cats per transport enclosure. Regulations require 1 cat/enclosure.... Some records do not include full address. Point of the Act and records is to be able to trace animal origin."

7-3-90: (38 cats) "Veterinarian must visit premises at least every month, and more as needed. To correct from this day forward."

1-7-91: Attempted inspection. "Licensee was not at facility during stated business hours. Called licensee. Licensee's wife stated licensee was on his way; we waited another 1 hour, 20 minutes—no show.... Licensee obviously does not take Hours of Business seriously."

2-5-91: (55 cats) "Cages do not appear to be properly sanitized at least once every 2 weeks.... Form 18-6 shows 18 cats transported at one time. Licensee needs to show me that 18 cages can fit into transport vehicle. Any cat over 6 mo. old must be transported singly in a transport enclosure."

6-25-91: "Note: Discussed Pet Theft Protection Act. New regs in effect Aug. 14, 1991"; 10-24-91: (94 cats) "Middle room of facility is very dim; not all cats have access to sufficient light.... Disposition sheets 18-6 are missing Buyer/Receiver USDA license/registration number. Form must be accurate and complete"; 5-21-92: Attempted inspection. "Came by at 11:00 A.M. on Thursday, May 21, 1992. Licensee's business hours are 10 A.M.-2 P.M. Licensee is responsible to have someone present at facility to allow inspection."

6-24-92: (107 cats) "On Form 18-6 dated 6-11-92 going to the University of Louisville all cats checked back to acquisition records. Out of 28 cats, 8 were lacking arrival dates to the facility, and 19 were missing removal dates. Accurate acquisition and disposition records must be maintained to correct this day forward.... Holding period, Cat #8493 shows up on record acquired from pound on 6-4-92 and shipped 6-11-92. Holding period requirement for pound animals is 10 days not including the day of transport.... Health certificates must accompany out-of-state shipments."

4-14-93: (79 cats) "Records reflecting sales to Pennyville Animal Clinic were missing and no dogs are shown on acquisition index cards. A record of all animals must be kept for USDA inspection for at least one year."

10-24-95: (95 cats) "7006 disposition records were lacking registration numbers of buyer.... And boxes 9-13 regarding transportation were left blank. One 7006 disposition form listed seven cats, but only six cats were noted in boxes 15 and 17 and no reason given for rejection of seventh animal. All 7006 disposition forms need to be completed and accurate."

STEPHENS, KELLIE (TEAYS RIVER VALLEY RANCH, INC.). Marion, Indiana. USDA license #32-B-094 (license suspended in 1997).

Kellie Stephens has supplied dogs to St. Luke's Medical Center, Chicago University, and Loyola University (all located in Illinois), and acquires dogs from pounds in Michigan and trade days in Kentucky. Stephens sells approximately 200 dogs a year, grossing $37,440.[68] She also sells goats, mini pigs, sheep, cattle and a number of exotic species including ostriches, emus and Brazilian opossums.

USDA inspections of Teays River Valley Ranch have revealed repeated noncompliance with AWA regulations:

1-24-90: (41 dogs, 14 cats) "There is no record of vehicle lic. no. or state or driver's license no. and state when dogs purchased from non-licensed individuals."

12-6-90: (47 dogs, 3 cats, 1 cougar, 3 goats, 18 Barbados sheep, 5 fallow deer) "Records are not current at this time. Dispositions have not been entered on 18-5s or in the computer.... Holding period cannot be verified in all cases because records are not current. Correct by 1-21-91."

4-10-91: (78 dogs, 9 cats, 1 cougar, 40 assorted Barbados sheep and goats, 7 fallow deer) "Dispositions [records] have not been entered on computer since 1-15-91. For at least one dog, #3574, the record of disposition or date of death is unavailable. Inspector spent 7 hours cross-referencing 18-6 disposition sheets with computer print-out of acquisition and completed an inspection of only approx. 25% of the records. In at least 9 instances of those records inspected [9 tag numbers listed], there is record of disposition but no record of acquisition.... Holding period cannot be verified in all cases because records are not current nor are they complete.... Dog #3639, left front leg badly chewed and swollen. Dog is most submissive in enclosure. Dog shall be moved to enclosure by itself.... Dog #3410, left ear infected, shaking head badly, ear ends lacerated. Correct (seek adequate veterinary care) by 4-12-91."

7-7-91: (95 dogs listed, 83 dogs on site; 7 cats listed, 42 cats on site; 1 cougar, 16 fallow deer, 50 assorted sheep and goats) "On the following animals there was no record of disposition available: [12 tag numbers listed]; On the following animals there was no record of acquisition: [7 tag numbers listed]. In one instance there was no address or driver's license no/vehicle license no. available on individual from whom a dog was acquired. In 4 instances there was no driver's license no./vehicle license no. available from individuals from which a dog was acquired.... In [9] instances animals were acquired from a private or contract pound and held an insufficient period of time (less than ten days)."

7-22-92: (126 dogs, 29 cats, 1 cougar) Noncompliant items uncorrected from previous inspections (12-6-90, 4-11-91, 7-17- 91): "Records. In 3 instances there was no record of driver's license no. and vehicle license no. from individual from whom a dog/cat was acquired. In 9 instances there was an incomplete address available."

11-18-92: (75 dogs, 2 cats, 1 cougar, 245 mini-pigs) "Weaned puppy less than 16 weeks old does not have official ID.... Dog #5599, a pit bull has chain collar which is too tight and is cutting into skin (abrasion).... In 3 instances dogs and cats were transported interstate without health certificate. Also dogs are being transported from Michigan to facility without health certificates.... In 2 instances from previous inspection there is evidence that dogs/cats were obtained from individuals who did not breed or raise them on their own property.... Also, it has been explained that a social security number is not adequate identification for random sources that are not USDA licensed unless it coincides with driver's license number."

3-17-93: (Partial records inspection at licensee's attorney's office, Muncie, Indiana) "It cannot be verified at this partial records inspection that individuals from whom dogs/cats were acquired bred and raised them on their own property.... Noncompliant standards newly identified.... In 3 cases, there is no address or driver's license no./vehicle license no. available on individuals from whom dogs/cats were acquired. In 6 cases there was an incomplete address available on individuals from whom dogs/cats were acquired.... In records of acquisition of dogs acquired from an out-of-state county dog pound from 6-5-92 to 10-23-92 there were 75 dogs listed on licensee's records, whereas the records obtained from the pounds list 67 dogs as having been acquired. Correct by 3-18-93."

1-6-94: (45 dogs) Uncorrected noncompliant item from 11-18- 92, 3-17-93, 9-16-93 inspections: "Dogs that are transported from Michigan to facility are accompanied by health certificate, except that there is not a correlation between these certificates and actual shipments." Noncompliant items documented on 3-17-93 inspection which could not be verified: "Acquisition information on dogs from out-of-state county dog pounds cannot be verified without further investigation of pound records."

On January 30, 1996, USDA filed a complaint against Stephens charging her with failure to provide necessary veterinary care to animals in need of such care, destruction of animals by gunshot, and falsification of acquisition records. The complaint alleged that Stephens claimed to have acquired more animals from a municipal pound than she actually did and falsely reported acquiring a total of 357 dogs from an apparently nonexistent pound. In 1997, Stephens signed a consent decision and order neither admitting nor denying USDA's charges. She agreed to a 10-

year license suspension and a $20,000 civil penalty. The $20,000 penalty was suspended on the condition that there be no further violations for 15 years.

ULRICH, MARY d/b/a CHERI-HILL KENNEL. Stanwood, Michigan. USDA license #34-B-006, #34-R-004 (1997).

Mary Ulrich has both a Class B dealer license and a research facility license. She sells approximately 590 animals a year, grossing $101,860.[69] She has sold animals to the Buckshire Corporation in Pennsylvania (see Wrigley, Glenn and the Buckshire Corporation in "Class B Dealers Selling Non-Random Source Dogs and Cats for Research"). In 1993, Ulrich paid USDA two $750 stipulation fines.

USDA inspection reports have documented deficiencies in housing, veterinary care and recordkeeping at Cheri-Hill Kennel. On 1-22-91 (244 dogs listed, 194 dogs on site; 192 cats listed, 143 cats on site), an inspector reported: "The new cat enclosures in the cat building do not have solid resting surfaces.... None of the animals being treated for illness had a medical record — or any other mechanism providing information on problems of animal health.... 35 Beagles and 24 cats were not on the record at the time of inspection."

During an inspection on 10-24-91, inspectors noted "[Two] cats in the boarding room have broken resting boards.... The cat boarding room had holes in the walls.... Dogs in the middle building on wire did not have resting boards.... Many dogs were improperly identified by noting the tags on the enclosure.... This facility has not followed their exercise plan. Dog #2556 was housed singly in a 30 x 34" enclosure. It measured 31 inches. 31 + 6 = 37, 37 x 37 = 1,369, 30 x 34 = 1,020. The plan stated that dogs housed singly will have 200% of space required. "[Enclosure with 4 dogs] 4699" required... 3196" provided.... [Enclosure with 1 dog] 1369 required... 1020 provided.... [Enclosure with 3 dogs] 4133 required... 3842 provided."

Several noncompliant items remained uncorrected from a 1-22-91 inspection: "Cat #1574 was sneezing, #1530 had a swollen eye, dog #2686 was coughing, dog #4016 had diarrhea. None of these animals were noted in the treatment logs as having medical problems or as receiving medical care.... The records reflected 339 dogs and 301 cats. Total dogs on hand were 285, cats 167."

Later inspections revealed continuing deficiencies in veterinary care:

5-5-92: (171 dogs, 106 cats) "Dog #4646 had a bilateral eye discharge.

Dog #4651 was very thin.... Dog #4730 had a right front leg lameness, dog #4725 was very thin, #4712 was very thin and dog #4715 was coughing... dog #4645 had a nasal discharge and was depressed. None of these dogs were noted as abnormal nor were they on the treatment records; 1-28-93 (CHK Research and Development site. USDA registration #34-R-004. 63 dogs, 6 cats, 29 rabbits) "Dog #3921 in South building A appeared depressed, thin, dehydrated and nonresponsive and was not getting fluids or the proper dosage of antibiotics. He was getting cephalexin SID [once a day] instead of QID [four times a day] as per instructions. Dog #3935 was to be treated with durapen and gentacin but was being treated with cephalexin SID [once a day] instead. The medical Standard Operating Procedures designed by the attending vet were not being closely followed and some dogs were not getting adequate care."

During an inspection of Cheri-Hill Kennel the same day (179 dogs, 117 cats), inspectors reported, "Dog #3909, cage #19. A female Lab cross had severe diarrhea and was not receiving any treatment. Dog #3954 Collie not on treatment list for coughing, thin, depressed; [Doberman] #3966 not being treated for copious nasal discharge and cough; Spaniel cross not on treatment list for severe malaise; cat #2224 not being treated for diarrhea. Cat #2260 was getting cephalexin only SID [once a day] instead of QID [four times a day] as indicated. Sick and injured animals need to be detected, and given proper medical attention as quickly as possible."

On 3-15-93 (Cheri-Hill Kennel, 137 dogs, 64 cats), inspectors noted many noncompliant items that were uncorrected since the previous inspection: "Cat #31554 had a reddened left eye with a watery discharge. This problem was not noted nor was the condition being treated. Dog #3562 in Bldg 1 had sores on both front feet. Sores not noted nor treated. Dog #5072 in Bldg 1 was coughing but was not noted... the health record stated that the dog was 'doing fine.' Dog #3929 had a nickel-size crusted lesion on his nose, hair loss on an ear and severe hair loss on hind legs and tail. Dog was biting and excessively scratching. This dog was treated for fleas days ago and 'NTR' (Nothing to Report) was entered on his health chart. Dog #3444 (Bldg 1) was noticeably limping on the left front leg. The limp was not recorded, nor was the dog getting treated. A puppy #5242 had bilateral eye discharge, was listless, straining and had a bloated abdomen. This dog was not being treated." An inspection of Ulrich's Research and Development site the same day also revealed deficiencies in veterinary care: "Dog #3271 in South Building of the Research building had open, raised, weeping sores on his right rear foot. This condition was not reported nor was the dog being treated. Animals must receive prompt and adequate care for problems of health."

On June 18, 1993, Ulrich paid two $750 stipulation fines for record-keeping and animal care violations.

WISE, EVA AND JOHN H. (HILLSIDE KENNEL). Four Oaks, North Carolina. USDA license #55-B-081 (1996).

According to information they provided to USDA, Eva and John Wise sell about 3,000 cats a year, grossing $37,422.[70] Another member of the Wise family, John D. Wise, also operates a Class B business (Carolina Kennel, selling approximately 4,000 cats a year to laboratories and biological supply companies and earning $46,368 in gross sales[71] (see also Wise, Alman in "Class B Dealers Who Have Lost or Relinquished Their Licenses").

USDA inspectors have reported deficiencies in housing, record-keeping and sanitation at Hillside Kennel:

10-15-90: (10 cats) "Excreta, hair, etc. in empty enclosures.... Approximately 20% of records have social security numbers instead of driver's license number and vehicle tag number"; 10-24-90: (96 cats) "Excessive odors, moisture, etc. in animal building. Animals must be provided fresh air at all times.... Water, urine and other fluids standing over 20% of enclosure floor of one occupied enclosure. Animals are being contaminated from wastes.... Excessive fecal, urinary and food debris in litter pans and floor."

1-26-91: (76 cats) "Four of the sixteen total sources... do not have driver's license and/or vehicle tag numbers.... Twenty-nine of cats on location do not have dates of acquisition listed on records." 6-17-91: (48 cats) "Two newly born kittens in enclosure with 9 adult cats. Kittens less than four months of age can only be housed with their dams.... Five collars in and under enclosures (not on animals).... Approximately 15-20% of sources have only social security numbers and not a driver's license number and/or vehicle tag number as specified in regulations."

On June 22, an inspector filed an alleged violation report charging Wise with failure to identify individual cats and maintain adequate acquisition records. On 10-17-91 (60 cats), the inspector reported: "Both pens have excessive accumulation of fecal wastes. One pan has approximately one inch of urine wastes.... Three of the total fourteen individuals (sources of animals) do not have complete driver's license number and/or vehicle tag number.... Two newly born kittens in enclosure with twelve adult cats.... Animals must be housed in compatible groups at all times." The inspector filed another alleged violation report on October 18, again charging Wise with inadequate recordkeeping. On October 30, Southeast Sector Supervisor Joseph Walker requested an investigation of the alleged violations.

In early 1991, USDA's Animal Care staff had issued three letters of clarification regarding the information dealers were required to obtain from individuals from whom they acquired animals. The letters stated that the agency would accept a social security number in lieu of a driver's license number and vehicle tag number. In addition to a social security number, a complete address, telephone number and directions to the premise (source) would be required. In January 1992, Walker sent a memo to senior investigator Page Eppele recommending that the case against Wise be closed administratively. "The use of Social Security numbers as identification has clearly been sanctioned," wrote Walker.

During an inspection of Wise's facility on 2-24-92, the inspector reported that although four of seven listed sources of animals included social security numbers and mailing addresses, there were no telephone numbers or directions to the premises.

Wise was also cited repeatedly for failure to allow inspectors access to his facilities:

10-20-92: Attempted inspection. "Mr. and Mrs. John H. Wise not present at site. Daughter of Wise's did not have key to animal facility and was not willing to sign USDA form 7008"; 10-26-93: Attempted inspection. "No one present at facility to allow inspection of facility, records, transport vehicles, etc. Facility must be available during normal business hours"; 10-27-93: Attempted inspection. "No one available at facility to allow USDA access to records, facility, etc."

When inspectors finally gained access to the facility, they again reported deficiencies in veterinary care, housing and sanitation:

12-1-93: (9 cats inspected) "Cat identified as 55-B-081-14076 (gray tiger striped) has infected and/or injured left eye. Cat must be examined by attending veterinarian, treated or euthanized as need.... All enclosures must meet USDA Minimum Standards for height, etc."

1-19-94: (0 cats) "Sheltered facility does not have fuel tank available for heating system.... No live animals can be housed until adequate heat is provided or weather improves.... Approximately 25% of primary enclosures have worn paint and/or rusted wire."

10-27-94: (37 cats) "Four cats... have severely injured and/or infected right eyes. All four cats must be examined by attending veterinarian and provided appropriate vet care."

2-6-96: (0 cats) "Excessive fecal debris in primary enclosures. Enclosures must be cleaned of fecal debris prior to use."

WOUDENBERG, JAMES AND ROBERTA (R & R RESEARCH). Howard City, Michigan. USDA license #34-B-001 (1997).

R & R Research, licensed since 1969, is owned and operated by James and Roberta Woudenberg. The Woudenbergs have an annual volume of

1,640 animals and earn approximately $172,200 a year in gross sales.[72] They acquire animals from individuals and pounds. At one time, they obtained unwanted and stray dogs and cats from the Wyoming-Grandville, Michigan dog warden. According to a March 22, 1973 newspaper article, the Woudenbergs arranged to purchase cats through the pound, offering "50 cents per cat when pound personnel compile[d] the list of animals to be picked up at local homes and $1 for each unwanted cat received at the animal shelter."[73] A local humane society objected to the arrangement, arguing that it encouraged cat stealing. The Woudenbergs have sold animals to the University of Iowa. In June 1994, the Woudenbergs paid USDA a $2,000 stipulation fine.

Between 1983 and 1988, USDA inspectors attempted inspections of R & R on six occasions but were unable to gain access. The few times they were able to conduct inspections, they reported deficiencies in housing, recordkeeping, sanitation and veterinary care:

3-1-83: (27 dogs and 31 cats inspected) "One primary enclosure contains 18 cats and another contains 13. Both are in excess of the minimum allowed of 12 cats per enclosure."

9-10-84: (46 dogs and 24 cats inspected) "Kennel runs on North side of facility are not adequately separated between runs. Some dogs can jump on to separating wall or over separating fence.... Excessive number of flies in dog facility."

4-1-87: "One female dog had puppies while in a pen with two other dogs. All pups died. This pregnant dog should have been placed in a separate whelping pen. Another dog in the pen has live pups. The third is pregnant. Better care and separation should be provided for these pregnant animals.... A large barrel appears to be used for euthanasia by CO_2. The barrel is rusty and in need of paint. A dead dog was found in it. This animal should be properly disposed of.... None of the cats had tags on."

2-9-89: (44 dogs, 13 cats) "The dog facility is a large converted barn which does not have a furnace. The building was so cold that the water was frozen.... The ambient temperature shall not be allowed to fall below 50 degrees for dogs and cats."

In a March 7, 1989 letter to APHIS, James Woudenberg wrote:

This letter is in regards to an inspection error which has reclassified one portion of my facility. On February 9, 1989, my facility was inspected by your agent... [a USDA inspector]. This was the first time... [the inspector] has inspected this operation. In the inspection report issued to me the dog housing operation was improperly classified as an 'indoor facility.' In order to clarify this discrepancy I would like to explain the architectural design and historical record of inspections for this building as it relates to its classification. The dog housing facility is a converted barn....

In the late 1970s this building was converted under the guidance of your organization to a housing facility for dogs. Throughout the years this building has been continuously upgraded.... In reviewing the records of past inspections you will find that this area of operation has never been cited for gross construction deficiencies. In keeping with the guidelines and design of this building it is apparent that this facility is properly classified as' an 'outdoor facility.' To convert such a structure into an 'indoor facility,' is by design impractical and certainly not cost effective.

On March 23, 1989, Dr. A.E. Hall, Acting Sector Supervisor of Veterinary Services, responded:

This letter is in regard to the 'inspection error' for your dog facility that disturbed you. Random source dogs are, as a rule house dogs, and not conditioned for outdoor facilities. Putting house dogs in an outdoor facility environment can be cruel and inhumane for many of these animals.... We support [the inspector's] findings in her inspection of your facility. It makes no difference whether an indoor or outdoor facility, there were animals that were suffering. That cannot be excused away by an administrative definition of what type of housing the animals were in at the time.

On 2-12-92, the inspector again cited the Woudenbergs for insufficient heating: "The temperature in the barn was measured at 23°F on my thermometer and the one in the facility. All of the dogs there were random source and non-acclimated. Water in the water bowls was frozen indicating that the temperature was below freezing and below 45° for more than four hours. Many short haired dogs... were noticeably shaking from the cold. The temp. must not fall below 45° for more than 4 hours for non-acclimated dogs, sick, injured, young or short haired dogs."

Between 1993 and 1995, the inspector noted deficiencies in record-keeping and holding period requirements:

3-5-93: (83 dogs, 14 cats) "Many animals are not being held the required 5 full days"; 9-28-93: "This facility is not obtaining health certificates for animals being delivered out of state"; 6-14-94: "Out of 587 dogs and cats through this facility since the last inspection of 3-21-94, 4 dogs (in two shipments) were sold on day 5 of the holding period"; 8-29-94: "Since the last inspection of 6-14-94, two cats have been sold on the fifth day of their holding period"; 12-12-95: "The records show some discrepancies. Three animals were shown on the records to be euthanized before they were received. D6023 was in on 6/7 but euthanized on 6/6, D6024 in on 6/7 and euthanized on 6/6, and D6027 was in on 6/8 and euthanized on 6/6.... Two animals were not held for 5 full days."

On June 24, 1994, James Woudenberg paid USDA a stipulation fine of $2,000.

Notes

1. John Raughter, "Dealer Faces USDA Hearing," Columbia, MO: *The Missourian*, 26 May 1995 and USDA-APHIS inspection reports for Martin Creek Kennels, 1993 and 1994.

2. The Animal Lobby, "Stebane's License Jerked," *The Animal Hot-Line*, Summer 1994.

3. USDA-APHIS, Annual Sales Of Currently Licensed Class B Dealers Providing Random Source Dogs And Cats To Research Facilities, 1996.

4. Decision and Order, In re: C.C. Baird, d/b/a Martin Creek Kennel, Respondent, 9 April 1997.

5. Joyce Bogard Hillard, "Animal Dealing in Arkansas," 29 December 1993.

6. Angela Roberts, "Canine Broker's Motto: 'Don't ask, Don't Tell,' " Salem, AR: *The News*, 10 October 1996.

7. Decision and Order, In re: C.C. Baird, d/b/a Martin Creek Kennel, Respondent, 9 April 1997.

8. Ibid.

9. Ibid.

10. Mark Yardley, in an affidavit dated 8 November 1994.

11. Angela Roberts, "Canine Broker's Motto: 'Don't Ask, Don't Tell,' " Salem, AR: *The News*, 10 October 1996.

12. Decision and Order, In re: C.C. Baird, d/b/a Martin Creek Kennel, Respondent, 9 April 1997.

13. Joyce B. Hillard, Arkansans For Animals, in a letter to Animal Welfare Institute President Christine Stevens, 2 June 1997.

14. Land use contract between Farrell Byers and C.C. Baird, executed 16 December 1996.

15. Dale Washam, Inspector Supervisor, Water Division, Arkansas Department of Pollution Control and Ecology, in a letter to Farrell Byers, 7 March 1997.

16. Ibid.

17. USDA-APHIS, Annual Sales of Currently Licensed Class B Dealers Providing Random Source Dogs and Cats To Research Facilities, 1996.

18. Philip S. Bacon, "100 Dogs Found Jammed Into Back of Truck Here," Lexington, KY: *The Lexington Herald*, 6 April 1966.

19. Jim Ennis, "Impounded Dogs Released To Kennel Owner, Are Trucked Away," Lexington, KY: *The Lexington Herald*, 7 April 1966.

20. National Affairs—Crime: "The Dognappers," *Newsweek*, 16 May 1966.

21. Philip S. Bacon, "100 Dogs Found Jammed Into Back of Truck Here," Lexington, KY: *The Lexington Herald*, 6 April 1966.

22. William W. Barringer, "Suit Falters In Try to Halt Dog-Dealing," Ohio: *Journal*

Herald, 12 February 1969.

23. USDA-APHIS veterinary inspector, commentary on Kiser Lake Kennels inspection dated 12 July 1990.

24. USDA-APHIS veterinary inspector, in an affidavit dated 16 July 1990.

25. Madison County Commissioners, in a letter dated 2 August 1990, to Andy Ball.

26. Dr. Valencia D. Colleton, Northeast Sector Supervisor, Regulatory Enforcement and Animal Care, in a memo dated 6 August 1990, to Dr. John Kolpanen, Acting Assistant Deputy Administrator, Animal Care. "Ball's suspension promoted a lot of media coverage and inquiries: Allison Ash, Channel 4, Tome Kurtznab, Channel 5, Rob Russel, Director of Animal Welfare League, St. Paris, OH, Robert Edwards, Madison County Commissioner, Cathy Fox, Erbano *Daily Citizen*, and Jim Thompson, Special Investigator for Ohio Vet. Medical Board."

27. USDA-APHIS, Annual Sales of Currently Licensed Class B Dealers Providing Random Source Dogs and Cats To Research Facilities, 1996.

28. Michael Dunn, Assistant Secretary, Marketing and Regulatory Programs, USDA-APHIS, in a letter to Last Chance for Animals Executive Director David Meyer, 8 May 1997.

29. "New Trends Emerge In Pet Theft," *Animal People*, May 1996.

30. USDA-APHIS, Random Source Class B Dealers, 1997.

31. USDA-APHIS, Annual Sales Of Currently Licensed Class B Dealers Providing Random Source Dogs And Cats To Research Facilities, 1996.

32. USDA Animal Welfare Task Force Findings on Al Willard, 27 April 1990. Willard apparently believed that his license would expire in September 1989, not April 1989. A review of Eldridge's records showed no purchases from Willard after September 1989.

33. "USDA Checking Dog Sales," Fulton, MO: *Missouri Sun Fulton*, 21 September 1986.

34. Columbia, MO: *Columbia Daily Tribune*, 28 September 1986.

35. USDA-APHIS, Annual Sales Of Currently Licensed Class B Dealers Providing Random Source Dogs and Cats To Research Facilities, 1996.

36. Dr. Bernard Zecha, Area Veterinarian in Charge for Iowa, USDA, Animal Welfare Complaint Form, 11 June 1987.

37. Dr. Bernard Zecha, Report of Telephone Conversation with Dr. Strating, 14 September

38. Kay Pittman, "Dog Auction Sale in Mississippi Shocks Animal-Loving Reporter," Memphis, TN: *Memphis Press-Scimitar*, 9 March 1966.

39. Animal Welfare Institute, memorandum on Class B Dealers, 14 August 1967.

40. "Dog Pack Found Caged in Madison," Jackson, TN: *The Jackson Sun*, 9 June 1959.

41. William C. Dolowy, Animal Hospital Administrator, University of Illinois, in a letter to Dr. Luther E. Fredrickson, Public Health Veterinarian, Tennessee Office of Public Health, 15 September 1959.

42. William Way, "Dog Farm Operator, Father Convicted at Humboldt," Tennessee: *The Commercial Appeal*, 3 September 1966.

43. Memphis, TN: *The Memphis Press-Scimitar*, 2 September 1966.

44. Memphis, TN: *The Memphis Press-Scimitar*, 28 December 1966.

45. USDA-APHIS, Annual Sales Of Currently Licensed Class B Dealers Providing Random Source Dogs And Cats To Research Facilities, 1996.

46. Fred Hodgins, USDA-APHIS Application For License, April 1995.

47. USDA-APHIS, Annual Sales of Currently Licensed Class B Dealers Providing Random Source Dogs and Cats To Research Facilities, 1996.

48. David A. Vogt, Assistant Area Veterinarian in Charge for Missouri, USDA, in a memo to Dr. Robert Leech, 6 April 1987.

49. M. Westrut, USDA, Report of Telephone Conversation, (name of complainant blocked out), 2 April 1987.

50. M. Westrut, USDA, Report of Telephone Conversation, (name of complainant blocked out), 2 April 1987.

51. USDA-APHIS, Annual Sales Of Currently Licensed Class B Dealers Providing Random Source Dogs and Cats To Research Facilities, 1996.

52. Progressive Animal Welfare Society, *PAWS News*, Autumn 1993.

53. USDA-APHIS, Annual Sales of Currently Licensed Class B Dealers Providing Random Source Dogs and Cats to Research Facilities, 1996.

54. Jim Ennis, "Impounded Dogs, Released To Kennel Owner, Are Trucked Away," Lexington, KY: *The Lexington Herald*, 7 April 1966.

55. "Basset - And Friend - Create Howl," Reading, PA: *Reading Times*, 29 April 1966.

56. USDA-APHIS, "Prosecutions For Animal Welfare Violations 1968-1980."

57. USDA-APHIS, Random Source Class B Dealers, 1997.

58. USDA-APHIS, Annual Sales Of Currently Licensed Class B Dealers Providing Random Source Dogs and Cats To Research Facilities, 1996.

59. Bob Perry, in a letter to Joseph A. Walker, Southeast Sector Supervisor - Animal Care, USDA, 16 July 1992.

60. USDA-APHIS, Annual Sales of Currently Licensed Class B Dealers Providing Random Source Dogs and Cats To Research Facilities, 1996.

61. USDA-APHIS, Application For License Renewal, submitted by Walter and Hildegard Peuschel, 13 May 1992.

62. USDA-APHIS, Annual Sales of Currently Licensed Class B Dealers Providing Random Source Dog and Cats To Research Facilities, 1996.

63. USDA-APHIS, Random Source Class B Dealers, 1997.

64. USDA-APHIS, Annual Sales Of Currently Licensed Class B Dealers Providing Random Source Dogs and Cats To Research Facilities, 1996.

65. Elmer Scherbring, USDA Application For License Or Annual Report, 18 April 1990.

66. USDA-APHIS, Annual Sales Of Currently Licensed Class B Dealers Providing Random Source Dogs and Cats To Research Facilities, 1996.

67. Ibid.

68. Ibid.

69. Ibid.

70. Ibid.

71. Ibid.

72. Ibid.

73. "Humane Society Advocates County Cat Control Laws," Wyoming, MI: *News-Advocate,* 22 March 1973.

Chapter 5

Investigations Into The Acquisition Of Animals By Class B Dealers

BEZLER, RALPH. Fulton, Missouri. USDA license #43-B-018 (last licensed in 1987).

Ralph Bezler reportedly acquired dogs by "adopting" them through giveaway ads. He then sold them to major USDA-licensed dealers such as Ray Eldridge of Antech, Inc. (USDA license #43-B-063) in Barnhart, Missouri (see also: Eldridge, Raymond in "Class B Dealers Selling Random Source Dogs and Cats for Research").

According to Jim Ward, USDA Veterinarian-in-Charge for Missouri, "[USDA] inspector Mark Westrich discovered Bezler had obtained dogs from people in the Columbia trade area through newspaper advertisements. [Bezler] kept the dogs he bought for less than the five days required by the federal Animal Welfare Act."[1] USDA found evidence that Bezler had altered purchase dates at least three times in order to bypass the required five-day waiting period. Inspector Westrich said USDA's case for punishing Bezler was "strong... because Bezler often obtained dogs under false pretenses."[2]

The Missouri State Attorney General's Office reported that as many as 11 people filed complaints against Bezler alleging he "promised to give their pets good homes and offered no indication that he planned to sell the dogs for research." However, Westrich's tracebacks of Bezler's records resulted in the recovery of only two dogs, both Labrador retrievers.[3]

One of the first people to file a complaint against Bezler was Columbia resident Robin Kramer, whose 7-year-old dog Merlin was "adopted" by Bezler and killed in an experiment before he could be rescued. Bezler told Kramer that Merlin had "run away." Kramer alleged that Bezler never told her that her dog would be used for research.[4]

After a two-week investigation, Missouri agricultural officials recommended that Bezler temporarily lose his dealer's license. The state later determined that he had not violated a Missouri trade-fraud law because no money was exchanged in the transfers of the dogs. Although USDA officials initially announced that the dealer could face stiff penalties for alleged poor recordkeeping and for not keeping dogs for the mandatory holding period, the agency never brought charges against Bezler.

DAVIS, DON AND GLADYS (HOLCO, INC.) West Fork, Arkansas. USDA license #71-A-105 (last licensed in 1993).

The Davises supplied dogs to the University of Arkansas, Yazwinski's Parasitological Research and Stanton Animal Hospital in Arkansas; the University of Chicago, Carlson Research, Reese Medical Center, St. Francis Hospital, and Loyola University in Illinois; Theracon in Kansas; the Louisiana State Medical Center; the University of Missouri Department of Laboratory Animal Medicine; Oklahoma College of Osteopathic Medicine, the University of Oklahoma City Health Sciences Center and Oklahoma Medical Research Facility; St. Joseph's Hospital, the Texas College of Osteopathic Medicine, Shriner's Hospital and the University of Texas Medical Branch in Texas.

According to the Coalition of Municipalities to Ban Animal Trafficking (COMBAT), which obtained Holco's acquisition and sale records from January, 1987 to April, 1989, Holco handled between 1,500 and 2,000 dogs and cats a year and maintained a network of suppliers (406 cited) covering a six-state area.[5] REAC investigators audited Holco's records during the Stolen Dog Task Force investigation in 1990. Of the 35 individuals Davis listed as having sold dogs to Holco, 14 could not be located with the information provided in the records, 7 denied selling any dogs to Holco and one had died four years prior to the traceback. In addition, the records listed four incorrect or falsified names and driver's license numbers.

Attention was focused on Holco after a series of Northwest Arkansas Times articles reported that Washington County, Arkansas deputy sheriff Jerry Yaeger allegedly sold dogs to Holco after "adopting" them from area pounds and shelters and through giveaway ads. Yaeger apparently promised owners he would find good homes for their animals. One woman was able to identify Yaeger as the person who had responded to a giveaway ad she had placed for cats.

Yaeger's ex-wife spoke with a local reporter about her former husband's relationship with Holco, claiming Yaeger made approximately $1000 a month from his bunching activities and had at one time talked of leaving the sheriff's department and working for Holco full-time.[6]

Arkansas state police launched an investigation of Yaeger in January of 1989. The State Prosecutor's Office subpoenaed Holco's records as part of the investigation; Yaeger's name appeared in Holco's 1987 acquisition records 17 times. In his statement to police, Yaeger claimed he had been dealing with Holco for many years:

> I sold about 30 or 40 dogs total to Holco over the years.... I got the dogs I sold by buying them from other people or having other people give them to me. I also used some of the hounds that I got that I could not train.

Yaeger underwent three polygraph tests, which indicated he was telling the truth when he denied stealing any of the dogs he sold to Holco. He was never questioned about obtaining dogs under false pretenses. The state determined there was insufficient evidence to file charges against Yaeger and closed the case.[7] Yaeger remained in his position as sheriff's deputy.

In 1990, members of the USDA Midwest Stolen Dog Task Force contacted an Arkansas state investigator to question him about Yaeger's activities. The investigator stated that he felt there was no evidence to indicate Yaeger was dealing in stolen dogs.

Following the Task Force investigation, USDA suspended Davis's license for falsification of records. Davis died before the license suspension was lifted. His wife Gladys was listed as licensee on subsequent USDA records. In September, 1993, Davis was fined a civil penalty of $5,000, ordered to cease and desist from further violations of the Animal Welfare Act, and disqualified for 5 years from obtaining licensing under the Act. She was charged with falsifying and failing to maintain complete and accurate records of the acquisition, disposition, description, identification, and source of animals. She was also charged with obtaining random-source dogs from individuals who did not breed and raise the dogs on their own premises.

USDA Midwest Stolen Dog Task Force Investigation of Holco, Inc. Records

The following suppliers' names, addresses, and number of dogs sold were recorded in Holco's 18-5 Forms. USDA enforcement action and/or remarks on each case are provided.

Name	Address	Dogs Sold	Disposition of Case/Remarks
Bob Hall	Ava, MO	12 dogs	USDA could not locate "Bob Hall" through P.O. or phone books in area. Vehicle license number registered to a Marvin Wilcox of Springfield, MO, who did not sell dogs. Case closed on 5-9-90.
Fred Jump	Mansfield, MO	14 dogs	USDA could not locate "Fred Jump" or his vehicle license number through P.O., phone, or motor vehicle records. Case closed on 5-12-90.
Gary Hutchinson	Carthage, MO	5 dogs	USDA could not locate "Gary Hutchinson" through phone or motor vehicle records; someone else lives at address provided by "Hutchinson." Case closed on 5-12-90.

Name	Address	Dogs Sold	Disposition of Case/Remarks
June Deardruff	Peggs, OK	9 dogs	License tag did not belong to subject, whose actual address is Hulbert, OK. Case closed for insufficient evidence on 4-24-90.
Alvin Rankins	Wagoner, OK	7 dogs	License tag did not belong to subject. USDA could not locate "Alvin Rankins." Case closed for insufficient evidence on 4-24-90.
Frank Rankins	Wagoner, OK	8 dogs	License tag incorrectly recorded. Subject told USDA that he never sold to Holco, but had sold some pups to Class B dealer Lambriar in Kansas. USDA ruled that subject did not violate Act. Case closed on 4-24-90.
Sonny Stewart	Wagoner, OK	10 dogs	License tag belongs to another person. USDA could not locate "Sonny Stewart." Case closed on 4-24-90.
George Drywate	Wagoner, OK	7 dogs	License tag not on record. USDA could not locate "George Drywate." Case closed on 4-24-90.
LeRoy Denton	Wagoner, OK	6 dogs	Subject's address and license tag incorrect. Subject told USDA he owns beagles and trades dogs with a Homer Steeley, but never sold dogs to Holco; believes that Steeley used his name. USDA ruled that subject did not violate Act. Case closed on 4-24-90.
Ed Montgomery	Coweta, OK	8 dogs	Subject refused to come to the door when USDA called on him. Two license tags were recorded incorrectly. Six dogs were sold under the name of LeRoy Denton, who told USDA he was the subject's friend. USDA ruled he did not violate Act. Case closed on 4-24-90.
Junior Broomfield	Coweta, OK	11 dogs	License tag not on record. USDA could not locate "Junior Broomfield." Case closed on 4-24-90.
Fred Sours	Coweta, OK	9 dogs	USDA could not locate "Fred Sours." Case closed on 4-24-90.
Jim Williams	Wagoner, OK	10 dogs	License tag not on record. USDA could not locate "Jim Williams." Case closed on 4-24-90.
Donald Webster	Locust Grove, OK	15 dogs	License tag did not belong to subject. USDA could not locate "Donald Webster." Case closed on 4-24-90.
David Farrell	Pryor, OK	10 dogs	License tag not on record. USDA could not locate "David Farrell." Case closed on 4-24-90.
Kenneth Dry	Haskell, OK	15 dogs	Subject stated to USDA that he did not sell dogs to Holco. License tag written on sales form did not belong to subject's vehicle. Subject claimed to know a Homer Steeley, who traded hunting dogs (see LeRoy Denton entry). USDA ruled that subject did not violate Act. Case closed on 4-24-90.
Walter Dry	Haskell, OK	14 dogs	Subject was the deceased brother of Kenneth Dry; died in 1986. USDA ruled that no violation had occurred. Case closed on 4-24-90.
Red Saunders	Muskogee, OK	7 dogs	License tag registered to another person. Case closed for insufficient evidence on 4-24-90.
Mike Blackmon	Muskogee, OK	18 dogs	License tag registered to another person. USDA could not locate "Mike Blackmon." Case closed for insufficient evidence on 4-24-90.

Name	Address	Dogs Sold	Disposition of Case/Remarks
Mike Blackman	Haskell, OK	18 dogs	License tag registered to another person. USDA could not locate "Mike Blackman." Case closed for insufficient evidence on 4-24-90.
Jim Owens	Muskogee, OK	8 dogs	Two "Jim Owens" were located by USDA; neither sold or traded dogs. License tag registered to another person. Case closed for insufficient evidence on 4-24-90.
Clyde Taylor	Sallisaw, OK	8 dogs	Subject stated to USDA that he never sold dogs to Holco, but claimed to know a Homer Steeley (see LeRoy Denton, Kenneth Dry entries). License tag not on record. Subject's hometown was Vian, not Sallisaw. Case closed for insufficient evidence on 4-24-90.
Gene Beeks	Prairie Grove, AR	9 dogs	Subject sells no more than four dogs a year. USDA notified him that licensing was required on future sales. Case closed on 5-7-90.
Ray Meyers	Seymour, MO	12 dogs	USDA could not locate "Ray Meyers" through police, motor vehicle, or utility records. "It appears that Mr. D.J. Davis recorded a fictitious name and license number." Case closed 5-7-90, but USDA would use this info to develop a case against Holco.
A.J. Pritchard	Gravette, AR	20 dogs	Subject stated to USDA that he sells or trades hunting dogs and sold 20 dogs to Holco due to an injury which made him unable to care for his dogs. USDA notified subject that licensing would be required on future sales. Case closed on 5-9-90.
Francis McNalley	Bentonville, AR	8 dogs	Subject stated to USDA that he raises dogs for fox hunting, trades and sells rejects. USDA notified him that licensing would be required on future sales. Case closed on 5-9-90.
Archie McNalley	Pea Ridge, AR	12 dogs	USDA did not locate subject, but spoke with subject's brother, who told USDA that he sells hunting dog rejects to Holco. Case closed with no further action on 5-9-90.
Bill Wilkerson	Garfield, AR	11 dogs	Subject stated he raises "running dogs" and sells rejects to Holco. USDA notified him that licensing was required on future sales. Case closed with no further action on 5-9-90.
Harley McCutcheon	Valley Springs AR	5 dogs	Subject denied to USDA that he sold dogs to Holco. Case closed on 5-9-90. "McCutcheon's sworn statement to be used in a pending violation case involving Holco."
Ed Johns	Ozark, MO	10 dogs	USDA could not locate "Ed Johns" through P.O. or police; concluded that it was an "incorrect name." Case closed on 5-10-90.
Ronald Coleman	Springdale, AR	6 dogs	Subject told USDA that he never sold dogs to Holco. License tag was not on file. "It appears that Mr. D.J. Davis recorded a fictitious name and license number for the 6 dogs." Case closed on 5-8-90, but USDA would use info in a "case being developed against D.J. Davis."
Leroy Coulter	Mulberry, KS	14 dogs	Subject's wife said he was out of town. Case closed for lack of evidence on 5-22-90.

Name	Address	Dogs Sold	Disposition of Case/Remarks
Randy Coulter	Mulberry, KS	8 dogs	Subject told USDA that someone else was using his name; he was not in dog business, owned only four hunting dogs. Case closed on 5-22-90.
Dale Lee	Howard, KS	9 dogs	Subject told USDA that he did not sell dogs to Holco; sold to a Jim Felkins of Carl Junction, MO. Case closed on 5-22-90.
Dean Rion	McCune, KS	10 dogs	Subject moved away from area sometime in 1987. USDA could not locate "Dean Rion." Case closed on 5-29-90.
Joe Ebby	West Mineral, KS	11 dogs	USDA could not locate "Joe Ebby." Case closed on 5-29-90.

GRUENEFELD, WILBERT AND JUNE. Jonesburg, Missouri. USDA license #43-B-064 (1995).

Wilbert Gruenefeld and one of his suppliers, Class B dealer Raymond Eldridge (see also: Eldridge, Raymond in "Class B Dealers Who Have Lost or Relinquished Their Licenses"), were two of the dealers investigated by the USDA Midwest Stolen Dog Task Force in 1990. USDA cited five of Gruenefeld's fifteen unlicensed suppliers for selling random-source dogs without a license; the remaining ten were not penalized by USDA because their transactions were below the number for which a license is required by law.

USDA Midwest Stolen Dog Task Force Investigation of Gruenefeld's Records

The following suppliers' names, addresses, and number of dogs sold were recorded in Gruenefeld's 18-5 forms. USDA enforcement action and/or remarks on each case are provided.

Name	Address	Dogs Sold	Disposition of Case/Remarks
Donald Johnson	Urbana, MO	17 dogs	Subject stated to USDA that he raises coonhounds. USDA advised him on licensing requirements and restrictions. Case closed on 5-10-90.
Delmar H. Collins	W.Plains, MO	11 dogs	Subject stated to USDA that he was not aware of Animal Welfare Act regulations. USDA issued him an Official Notification and Warning of Violation of Federal Regulations on 4-11-90.
Howard Faulkner	St. James, MO	—	Subject stated to USDA that he was not aware of Animal Welfare Act regulations. USDA issued him an Official Notification and Warning of Violation of Federal Regulations on 4-8-90.
Billy D. Eades	Truxton, MO	5 dogs	Subject was a minor; subject's father stated that he was not aware of son's activity. Dogs sold were acquired by subject in a trade with friend. Case closed on 4-27-90 with no further action.

Name	Address	Dogs Sold	Disposition of Case/Remarks
Billy & Lisa Miller	Salem, MO	13 dogs	Subjects told USDA that the dogs sold were born and raised on their premises. USDA ruled that the subjects were exempt from licensing.
Gerald & Marilynn Milliam	Robertsville, MO	9 dogs	Subjects told USDA that dogs sold were born and raised on their premises. USDA ruled that subjects were exempt from licensing. Case closed on 4-26-90 due to lack of evidence to document a violation.
Robert D. Collins	Warrenton, MO	7 dogs	Subject stated to USDA that he sold 25 to 30 dogs to Gruenefeld in 1989. USDA issued him an Official Notification and Warning of Violation of Federal Regulations on 4-11-90.
Jack Collins	West Plains, MO	1 dogs	USDA could not locate "Jack Collins" through P.O. or phone records. Case closed on 5-9-90 with no further action.
Willie Miller	West Plains, MO	1 dogs	USDA could not locate "Willie Miller" through P.O. or phone records. Case closed on 5-9-90 with no further action.
Dale Collins	Pomona, MO	22 dogs	Subject stated to USDA that dogs sold were born and raised on premises; forced to sell due to inability to afford their care. USDA advised him that licensing would be required on future sales. Case closed on 5-9-90.
Jack Jones	Bowling Green,MO	4 dogs	Subject stated to USDA that dogs sold were born and raised on premises. USDA ruled that subject was exempt from licensing. Case closed on 4-27-90 due to lack of evidence to document a violation.
Uriah Williams	Robertsville, MO	2 dogs	Subject stated to USDA that dogs sold were born and raised on premises. USDA ruled that subject was exempt from licensing. Case closed on 4-27-90 due to lack of evidence to document a violation.
Larry Todd	Steelville, MO	5 dogs	Subject stated to USDA that dogs sold were born and raised on premises. USDA ruled that subject was exempt from licensing. Case closed on 4-26-90 due to lack of evidence to document a violation.
Clifford Todd	Steelville, MO	2 dogs	Subject stated to USDA that dogs sold were born and raised on premises. USDA ruled that subject was exempt from licensing. Case closed on 4-26-90 due to lack of evidence to document a violation.
Herbert Otterman	Cuba, MO	18 dogs	Subject stated to USDA that half of the dogs sold were born and raised on premises; the others were obtained in trades or purchases with hunters and friends. Subject also delivered friends' dogs to Gruenefeld. USDA issued him a verbal warning in lieu of Official Notification and Warning of Violation of Federal Regulations form. Case closed 4-26-90.

HICKEY, JAMES W., (S & S FARMS AND S.S. FARMS, LINN COUNTY, INC.) Lebanon, Oregon. USDA license #92-B-50 (last licensed in 1990).

James W. Hickey was one of the West Coast's largest suppliers of dogs and cats for use in research, selling an estimated 700 animals a year. His clients included University of California at Los Angeles Medical Center, Stanford University, Oregon State University, Oregon Health Sciences University and Class B dealer Henry Knudsen. In addition to selling animals for research, Hickey was a rye grass farmer, cattle rancher, and owner of the Lebanon Bag Company. His kennel served as the Linn County Dog Shelter in 1973 while the county built its own facility.

Almost immediately after Hickey received his first USDA license in 1977, inspectors began documenting serious deficiencies in recordkeeping, identification and sanitation at S & S Farms, deficiencies that would recur throughout the next ten years. There were also concerns by the public about how Hickey acquired the dogs he sold. A local newspaper revealed that in August, 1977, Hickey purchased ten dogs from the Lane Humane Society after signing an "adoption" contract that prohibited him from selling the animals or allowing them to be used for experimentation. A reporter who visited Hickey's kennel soon after the story broke claimed the facility was overcrowded and dirty.[8]

During the same month, USDA conducted one of its first inspections of S & S Farms: "No 18-5's are made out on the dogs presently on hand," wrote the inspector. "I have explained the necessity of keeping these records, and Mr. Hickey agrees to fill out these records as soon as possible." On 11-11-77, an inspector reported: "Water containers need to be cleaned to remove algae growth.... There is a large accumulation of feces in the runs – this must be cleaned more often.... 18-5's are incomplete at this time – He has assured me that these will be completed by 11-14-77.... Animals aren't being held the required time – this must be done."

On 5-19-78, the inspector noted again: "Water containers must be thoroughly cleaned and disinfected as algae is growing in the containers.... Dog runs are extremely dirty with feces – this must be cleaned as soon as possible and disinfected at the same time.... Records of inventory are still not being made out for dogs on hand."

During the next several years, inspectors continued to report alleged violations of recordkeeping and sanitation regulations. Although Hickey would often correct the deficiencies, his efforts were only temporary – the same deficiencies would turn up during later inspections.

USDA finally sent Hickey a Letter of Warning in 1983, charging him with failure to identify dogs, maintain proper records, hold dogs the required length of time and provide lighting and ventilation as required for cats. In 1984, Area Veterinarian in Charge W.D. Prichard submitted an alleged violation report to Robert D. Whiting, Chief Veterinarian, Interstate Inspection and Compliance. "The records show that Mr. Hickey is chronically in non-compliance of the Animal Welfare Act," wrote Prichard. "He corrects deficiencies when given deadlines, but does not continue to maintain the standards."

Rather than initiating legal action against Hickey, USDA sent him two more warning letters. The warnings alleged that inspectors had documented lack of proper identification of dogs; overcrowding; unsanitary water receptacles; accumulation of fecal material in primary enclosures; mingling of sick and healthy dogs; and incomplete and inaccurate record-keeping. On November 14, 1984, two days before USDA sent Hickey the second warning letter, an inspector visiting S & S Farms reported: "There is not presently adequate disposal of animal wastes and food wastes. There are decaying cow limbs, bones, intestinal tracts, lungs and other offal. These are not wholesome food and must be removed.... There were large accumulations of feces around six individual dogs that were chained out.... There are four dogs with health problems.... These dogs need attention to specific health problems of lacerated ear, lacerated foot, mange, conjunctivitis and depression."

W.D. Prichard sent Whiting another alleged violation report in February, again citing unsanitary conditions, inadequate veterinary care and inadequate recordkeeping at S & S Farms. In a March 21, 1985 letter to Whiting, Prichard expressed his concern about Hickey's failure to identify dogs and to make inspectors aware of all the dogs he housed:

> At the time of his inspection on July 24, 1984, Mr. Hickey had approximately 40 dogs at an unusual location on his premises. These dogs were unidentified and were not kept in a facility that met the requirements of the Animal Welfare Act.... It appears that Mr. Hickey is presenting some dogs for inspection, but there are some dogs which he prefers that we did not know about.... Considering that the purpose of the Animal Welfare Act is to prevent improper acquisition of pets by dealers, we are concerned by the presence of undisclosed or unidentified dogs at Mr. Hickey's premise and by his failure to permit unannounced inspections. We have repeatedly tried to gain compliance from Mr. Hickey, but it appears that he wishes to operate outside the regulations.

Despite the second alleged violation report, USDA took no formal action against Hickey.

As an April 3, 1985 letter from Melvin Crane, Interstate Inspection and Compliance, to USDA Assistant General Counsel J.C. Chernauskas indicates, the agency was also well aware of questions surrounding Hickey's acquisition of dogs: "Recently, Mr. Hickey's operations were suspected of close ties with dog thefts and misrepresentation of the source and disposition of his animals." In fact, during the spring and summer of 1985, several stolen dogs were recovered from S & S Farms. The first was an eight-year-old Airedale named Kena, who belonged to Jo Lynn Smith. On April 28, Smith had reported Kena stolen to the Corvallis Police Department. During her search for Kena, Smith was advised to contact Hickey. When she called Hickey and described her dog, he claimed he didn't have any Airedales but would call her if one came in. Hickey never called Smith, even though his records indicated her dog was on his premises when she called. During an inspection of S & S Farms on May 15, USDA inspectors observed three Airedales. Smith identified one of them as Kena. Hickey's records didn't state where he had acquired Kena, and when questioned by the inspectors, he claimed he had purchased her from Linn County Dog Control. However, dog control director John Adair signed an affidavit stating that no Airedale was sold or given to Hickey between April 20, 1985 and May 20, 1985.

On May 16, a Benton County sheriff's officer arrested Scott Nolan and charged him with the theft of Smith's dog. Nolan admitted stealing the dog and selling her to Hickey for $25.00.

Hickey was also arrested in connection with the theft and charged with possessing a stolen dog.

The second dog to be recovered, a collie mix named Fritz, belonged to Corvallis resident Linda Griffith. On June 11, a detective with the Benton County Sheriff's Department arrested Mark Breeden, who had admitted taking Fritz from Griffith's yard and selling him to Hickey the same day. Later that month, two USDA investigators visiting the Linn County Dog Pound were approached by a Lebanon resident who stated his four-month-old labrador puppy had been stolen the previous day. He said that during his search for the dog, he was told to look at S & S Farms. He found his dog there, and Hickey returned the animal to him after requesting him to sign the back of a receipt. The man claimed the name "John Henry" appeared on the front of the receipt. When investigators questioned Hickey about the receipt in July, "he could not or would not produce the document for... review."[9]

On July 8, 1985, the Benton County Sheriff's Department received a call from a local humane society regarding a possible theft by deception case involving a golden retriever who had been given away through a newspaper advertisement. The dog's owner, Linda Satra, stated that the man who had taken Lucky promised to give him a good home. In a photo lineup, Satra identified Mark Breeden as the person who had taken her dog. Breeden was placed under arrest for first-degree theft. Hickey admitted purchasing a golden retriever from Breeden on May 22, and claimed he had sold the animal to a research facility a week later. He would not tell investigators where the dog had been sent. USDA finally found Lucky at UCLA, and he was returned to Satra.

On December 9, 1985, Hickey pled no contest to second-degree theft of Jo Lynn Smith's dog Kena. Two other theft charges against Hickey were dismissed in exchange for the no contest plea. Hickey was fined $200.

USDA filed a formal complaint against Hickey in January 1986, charging him with 71 violations of the Animal Welfare Act, including failure to keep and maintain records that fully and correctly disclosed necessary information concerning dogs purchased; failure to properly identify dogs; refusal of access to and inspection of records; and violation of regulations relating to the humane handling, care, treatment and transportation of dogs and cats. USDA also charged Hickey with falsely reporting the dollar amount of his sales on his annual license renewal report.

While Hickey was awaiting a hearing date, another stolen dog was discovered at his facility. Hickey returned the dog, a border collie named Bell, to Raymond Michaelis, who had reported seeing a suspicious looking vehicle parked in his driveway just before Bell disappeared. Police arrested Kevin Terwilliger in connection with the theft, who admitted selling the dog to Hickey. Hickey maintained that he hadn't known the dog was stolen.

A hearing on USDA's charges against Hickey was finally set for August 26. Soon after the date was set, Hickey's attorney filed a motion to postpone the hearing until after November 1, claiming that Hickey "wasn't feeling well" and had been advised by his doctor to "avoid stress in the immediate future."[10] The administrative law judge granted the motion, and after several more months of delays, he finally set the hearing for March 1987. USDA had renewed Hickey's Class B license in July, allowing him to stay in business, and, as inspections in the fall of 1986 revealed, continue violating the Animal Welfare Act. In a October 14, 1986 alleged violation report, compliance officer Lisa Halop wrote: "This report will show that James Hickey does not maintain his facility in accordance with minimum levels pursuant to the Animal Welfare Standards.... In addition, it will show that Mr. Hickey did not make corrections of substandard conditions by specific deadlines given to bring his facility into compliance." Halop cited recurrent deficiencies in sanitation, veterinary care and separation: "Dogs are constantly housed together that are incompatible (fighting) and injured dogs are not being treated by a veterinarian or euthanized until these problems are brought to Mr. Hickey's attention by the USDA inspector."

Hickey's hearing was held in March as scheduled, and the judge issued his decision on June 17, 1987. He found Hickey guilty of keeping inaccurate records concerning his purchase of dogs from the Yamhill/McMinnville and Linn County dog pounds; refusing access to and inspection of his records by USDA officials concerning a stolen black Labrador puppy found on his premises; falsely reporting the dollar amount of sales on his annual license report as $9,460, when in fact the sales for that period exceeded $37,000; and failure to keep records concerning the descriptions and identification numbers of all animals in his possession. The judge also found Hickey guilty of housing dogs in enclosures that were not structurally sound and that did not protect them from predators or possible injury; failing to properly sanitize food and water receptacles; failing to house dogs in compatible groups; failing to keep primary enclosures free of excessive buildup of excreta; and failing to keep facility free of scattered trash, broken glass and contaminated dead animal parts.

In his decision, the judge stated:

> There is evidence that Mr. Hickey's deceptive and false records facilitated his acquisition of stolen and fraudulently obtained pets found on his premises.... On one occasion, his records for the purchase of two dogs with specified tag numbers and a seller's name matched hearsay evidence presented by Deputy Sheriff John Strong, who testified that two thieves he arrested told him that they sold two dogs they had stolen to Hickey for $30.00 who told them: "I don't care if the dogs are hot; I just don't want the cops out here."

In sentencing Hickey, the judge concluded, "Mr. Hickey... has violated [the humane care and treatment]... provisions of the Animal Welfare Act, deliberately, willfully, and cruelly for personal gain and profit." He ordered Hickey to cease and desist from violating the Act, fined him $40,000 and suspended his Class B license for 25 years. The decision was upheld on appeal in May 1988. Hickey then appealed to the U.S. Court of Appeals, which affirmed the original decision on November 16, 1989. Hickey was allowed to stay in business throughout the appeal process.

HICKEY, JAMES JOSEPH (S & H SUPPLY) Lebanon, Oregon. USDA license #92-B-145 (last licensed 1991) (see also: Hickey, James W. and Stephens, David and Tracy in this chapter).

James "Joe" Hickey agreed to carry on the family business following USDA's suspension of his father's Class B license. After his father's administrative hearing, Joe told a newspaper reporter that he was willing to take over S & S Supply "but would want to rely on his father's expertise in running it."[11] The elder Hickey certainly passed his own brand of "expertise" on to his son — Joe ran the business in much the same way his father had.

Since the Hickey name had become so well known, Joe's fiancee, Shannon Hanson, applied for and was granted a license to operate the business, which she and Hickey renamed S & H Supply. USDA reissued the license in Joe's name in June 1988. Although Joe officially took the business over, his father remained licensed for several more years while he appealed the USDA's suspension. In fact, he was still licensed as late as 1990, and it is likely that he remained active in the business throughout that time.

By September 1988, there were new reports that missing and stolen dogs and cats were being discovered at S & H Supply. Those who found their pets at Hickey's facility claimed the animals had either been stolen or had been given away to someone who promised to give them a good home. At least five people were charged with selling stolen pets to S & H Supply.[12] Hickey himself was never implicated in the thefts, and according to USDA's Richard Overton, Hickey was "acquiring the animals legally.... He [was]... not intentionally doing anything wrong."[13] USDA reiterated this determination in response to Oregon Senator Mark Hatfield, who contacted the agency after receiving a letter from a constituent who felt USDA was not responding to allegations that Hickey was soliciting and receiving stolen pets:

> A dealer will not necessarily know that an animal is stolen when it is presented for sale. APHIS doesn't have a violation against the dealer, if he enters the source and complies with all the requirements of the Animal Welfare Act. Veterinary Services is allowed to monitor records but does not empower them to retrieve stolen animals. That authority is given to legally constituted law enforcement agencies.[14]

In addition to maintaining his father's facility in Lebanon, Oregon, Hickey opened a "cat facility" in Albany. USDA inspections of both facilities revealed many apparent violations of the Animal Welfare Act:

7-14-88: (Lebanon site, 85 dogs) "Repair the drain system and clean the feces around the fence (buildup due to inability to clean up hair etc. stuck to the fence and grass).... The 18-5's (sale of dogs) are not complete. The 18-6's (inventory sheet) are not complete.... It is impossible to determine if the dogs [purchased from Mr. Jim Hickey] are held 5 working days." 7-18-88: (80 dogs) "Dogs must be provided with additional shade to protect them from overheating. There is no shade at present"; 8-25-88: (Albany site, 62 cats) "8 cats with no I.D. Records not at site for inspection.... Almost all food receptacles were empty.... None of the cats have water.... Water was supplied to the cats during the inspection at the request of inspectors. Cats were very thirsty.... There are no records available at the time of inspection. Impossible to determine holding time or length of ownership."

The inspectors also discovered that Hickey was holding cats at the Lebanon Bag Company, an unapproved site: "The Lebanon Bag Plant is not an approved site – cats were being held at this facility without the knowledge or approval of Veterinary Services.... One cat is held in a burlap bag –

inadequate ventilation—other cats are held in cages inside the plant—the doors are closed and locked.... [Nineteen] cats were without water and water containers were dirty.... There is no identification on any cats.... There are no records available for these cats.... It is impossible to determine the length of time these cats have been held."

During an inspection of the Lebanon site the same day, inspectors reported: "Cats are being held in red onion sacks, wired shut at top of bag, lying on ground for approximately one hour. Employee David Stephens was directed to put cats in proper sized cages based on size of animal.... Records not available for inspection. Records will be kept on site for inspection at all times."

Inspectors continued to document deficiencies in recordkeeping and identification of animals at Hickey's facilities:

8-26-88: (Albany site, 88 cats) "There are 67 cats that are not properly identified"; 9-16-88: (Albany site) "Records were unavailable both at Hwy. 20 and at the Gold Farm Rd. premises... because records were not available, we could not determine acquisition of animals and holding periods"; 10-6-88: (Lebanon site, 69 dogs) "Records indicate 70 dogs on premise—official count 69."

On October 6, USDA suspended Hickey's license for 21 days, charging him with failure to identify animals and provide proper records and sufficient food, water and facilities for dogs and cats. USDA also charged him with interfering with inspection of his facilities.

During an inspection of the Lebanon site on 10-28-88, inspectors noted: "There were 50 dogs on the premises and only 47 dogs on the records. This is a reoccurring deficiency and is a violation."

USDA filed a formal complaint against Hickey, his wife and his parents on November 7, 1988. The complaint alleged 57 violations of the Animal Welfare Act, the most serious involving irregularities in record-keeping. Hickey remained in business while awaiting a hearing on the charges.

Meanwhile, inspectors continued to report apparent violations of the Animal Welfare Act at Hickey's facilities:

2-14-89: (Lebanon site, 54 dogs) "Dead dogs are buried in pit at back of property. Some... bodies have been left uncovered in pit.... Bodies in pit should be covered immediately.... Great Dane #A985 has bloody diarrhea and large open wound... joint swollen and appears infected. Mr. Hickey says that dog will be euthanized today. German Shepherd-type dog #A935 has lameness in left front leg. Scheduled to be brought to vet today"; 4-18-89: (Lebanon site, 87 dogs) "A maximum of one live dog shall be transported in a primary enclosure. There was one primary enclosure in the transport vehicle with 4 dogs in it. There were two other primary enclosures with two dogs each in them. All dogs were adults.... Corrected at time of inspection.... The open burial pit at the rear of the facility contains dog carcasses that are unburied and in various states of decay. There are several carcasses floating in a pool of water at the bottom of the pit. This standard was not in compliance at the last inspection of 2-14-89 and is not in compliance at this inspection of 4-18-89."

A hearing on the charges against the Hickeys was not held until October 31, 1989, almost a year after USDA had filed its complaint. Evidence presented at the hearing showed that between August 8, 1988 and September 12, 1988, Joe Hickey acquired 54 dogs from the Jefferson County, Oregon pound, but only recorded acquiring 18 dogs. Hickey testified that he hadn't recorded the additional dogs because he intended to destroy them, not sell them. On one occasion, the pound gave him twenty-three unweaned puppies in addition to the four adult dogs he purchased. He transported the puppies in a box to the Lebanon facility, where he shot and buried them. The administrative law judge found that "the number of animals Hickey shot and buried as part of his deal with the pound operator... [was] startling."[15] He concluded that "to avoid those cases where subterfuge is used to thwart efforts to locate missing pets," the recordkeeping requirement should apply to all dogs and cats acquired, not just to those intended for resale."[16]

The judge also determined that Hickey was guilty of housing 28 cats in a facility not designed for animals and without adequate ventilation or lighting. Despite Hickey's testimony that he was not aware his employees were holding cats in onion sacks, the judge concluded:

> I have found Mr. Hickey's testimony to lack credibility. I infer that the use of onion sacks was a customary practice of his employees and that Mr. Hickey knew about it and condoned it. By his testimony, Mr. Hickey demonstrated a complete lack of compassion for animals. I have no doubt that because he believed the sacking of cats could facilitate his business operation, he had no qualms about his employee doing so.

He also found Hickey guilty of failing to provide records at each facility inspected; failing to tag or otherwise identify animals; failing to provide adequate veterinary care; verbally abusing and threatening a USDA inspector; and denying inspectors access to his Lebanon site. In imposing sanctions against Hickey, the judge stated,

> Mr. Hickey's compliance with APHIS's requirements has at best been begrudging. His concern for the animals he buys and sells seems limited to how acceptable their appearance is to customers. I doubt he would follow APHIS's humane care standards except to protect his license.... In sum, I have concluded that Mr. Hickey

committed many recurrent violations of the utmost gravity, and that his conduct and testimony show he did not act in good faith.

He ordered Hickey and his wife to cease and desist from violating the Animal Welfare Act, assessed a civil penalty of $10,000 and suspended Hickey's license for one year. Prior to the judge's decision, Hickey's parents had entered into a consent decision in which they agreed not to engage in the animal business in any way during the elder Hickey's 25-year license suspension. They also agreed to abide by the cease and desist order imposed on them previously.

Joe Hickey was able to continue his business activities while he appealed the administrative law judge's decision.

Less than a month after the judge's decision, on 2-7-90, USDA inspectors reported more apparent deficiencies at Hickey's Lebanon facility: "Provision shall be made to properly dispose of dead animals. There were three partially uncovered, and rotting dog carcasses exposed in the burial pit at the back of the facility..... The bedding in the shelter in pen #6... contained bedding soiled with feces.... No program of veterinary care has been submitted.... A young dog... showed obvious lameness in the left rear leg. This has not been attended to."

In a February 13 letter to Dr. Ron DeHaven, USDA's Western Sector Supervisor, Hickey's attorney, Andrew Ositis, claimed that the deficiencies documented on the 2-7-90 inspection report were "deliberate fabrication[s]":

> This complaint is directed to you as it is my client's belief that these inspectors are using their official positions and the inspection process for wrongful and improper purposes. In the past Mr. Hickey proceeded on the naive assumption that inspections were a means by which your agency assisted dealers in complying with the statute and regulations. Instead it is being used as a means of accumulating deliberate fabrications and distortions which are in turn to be eventually used as a basis of punitive action against the licensee.... He requests that the inspection report be corrected in writing so that the fabrications and distortions of that report be removed officially.[17]

In his response, Dr. DeHaven stated that after a review of Hickey's allegations and the inspectors' statements regarding their observations, he had concluded that the inspectors acted within the scope of their employment and in accordance with USDA policies: "It is my opinion that the inspection report accurately reflects the condition of Mr. Hickey's facility at the time of the inspection. No changes will be made to this report as it was originally written."[18]

In April 1994, USDA filed another complaint against Hickey, this time charging him with purchasing 46 random source dogs and cats from an unlicensed dealer; failing to maintain complete records showing the acquisition, identification and disposition of animals; failing to maintain programs of disease control and prevention and provide adequate veterinary care to animals in need of such care; failing to provide provisions for the removal and disposal of animal wastes; failing to provide primary enclosures for dogs that were structurally sound; failing to sanitize primary enclosures as required; failing to give inspectors access to records; and interfering with inspection of facilities through verbal abuse and threats. Hickey failed to file an answer to the complaint, and on August 23, 1994, an administrative law judge entered a default judgement against him. The judge's order disqualified him from becoming licensed under the Act for ten years and assessed him a civil penalty of $10,000.

HIPPERT, DONALD A. AND SHIRLEY, (LAKE SHORE KENNELS), Mapleton, Minnesota. USDA license #41-B-166 (last licensed in 1995 as Lake Shore Acres).

Donald and Shirley Hippert were first licensed in 1967, calling their business "Hill View Farms." Because Dodge County, Minnesota had no pound of its own, county authorities reportedly gave Hippert permission to collect and house stray dogs and cats. Although the Hipperts stopped selling dogs and cats in 1990, they later applied for another Class B license and now buy and resell pigs and geese for research (see also: Hippert, Morris E. in "Class B Dealers Who Have Lost or Relinquished Their Licenses").

Between December 1983 and January 1984, the Mower County, Minnesota Sheriff's Department received 11 reports of stolen dogs. The dogs had been unchained, snatched from their yards, even removed from locked kennels. Some of the missing animals were recovered from the Mayo Clinic's Institute Hills Research Center in Rochester, Minnesota. A spokesperson for the Center told Deputy Sheriff D.K. Russell that the Center had purchased all of the dogs from Don Hippert, with whom they had done business for many years.

One of the first dogs to disappear belonged to Ella Erie of LeRoy, Minnesota. When Erie returned home from a funeral on the afternoon of January 5th, she was not greeted by the familiar barking of her ten-year-old border collie, Rex. She searched the garage where Rex had been chained, but found only the strange tire tracks of a vehicle that had backed up to the door.

Five miles away, Wayne and Bonnie Siskow and their children were combing their farm for Sheba—a two-year-old miniature collie who had vanished from inside a barn. Two years had passed since another one of the Siskow's dogs had mysteriously disappeared, and a year before that, Wayne's brother had lost a dog in a similar manner.

Norburt Rud's red retriever, Dennis Hammeister's blue tick coon hound and Jim Boe's Scottish collie would also be taken from their owners' Stewartville residences on the same day.

After taking the dogs from their homes, "buncher" Greg Green trucked them to his home in Dexter, Minnesota, 20 miles north of LeRoy. Neighbors would later recall the incessant barking that had emanated from Green's property. On January 6, Green sold four of the dogs to Hippert for $10.

On Sunday, January 8th, Julie and Randy Tapp and their three children left their Austin, Minnesota home for approximately one hour. When they returned, they found only a very frightened cocker spaniel — one of their two dogs. Their missing dog, a shepherd-collie mix, had never wandered. The Tapps would spend the next seven days searching for him on a snowmobile.

At around 5:00 p.m. on January 9, Don and Kathy Adams of LeRoy discovered that their St. Bernard was missing. Smokey was one of the five animals Green sold Hippert for $12 that afternoon.

Austin residents Dave and Mary Grignon left their two dogs locked inside a pen near their garage on January 12th. When they returned from work that day, the kennel door was ajar, and their basset hound sat nervously on the farmhouse steps. That afternoon, Green sold the Grignons' black Labrador, Isaac, to Hippert, along with two other dogs — one of whom Green had allegedly "adopted" from a local animal organization. Hippert sent 16 dogs from Green, together with 53 from other sources, to the Mayo Clinic's Institute Hills Research Center and the University of Minnesota.

In their search for Isaac, the Grignons contacted both the University of Minnesota and the Mayo Clinic. Isaac had injured his foot a week before, and at the time he was stolen, a fresh white scar with stitches was visible on his foreleg. The Grignons felt confident that the scar would serve to identify him. "We were lucky that way," explained Dave. "We felt that he couldn't be missed or mistaken."

The University of Minnesota claimed it hadn't admitted any dogs fitting Isaac's description. A Mayo Clinic staff member promised to look for Isaac and assured Mary that she would be contacted if he turned up. Mary never heard from the Clinic.

On January 19th, a deputy sheriff suggested that the Grignons conduct their own inspection of Institute Hills Farm — the Mayo Clinic's laboratory animal facility. Dave rushed to Rochester — to the building where roughly 500 dogs were housed. He entered the first of nine rooms, and, as he later explained, "Boom! Isaac was right there." The dog had contracted a serious respiratory infection. In a letter to USDA, the Grignons described the heart-wrenching ordeal of having their dog stolen and sold to a laboratory:

> After confronting the research facility with the fact that they were holding our stolen dog, David was told that the dog had been sold to the research facility by the local USDA dog dealer — a Mr. Hippert. David contacted Mr. Hippert by telephone from the research center. Mr. Hippert refused to give us any information about where he got our dog....
>
> To see our dog in that state, for no other reason than for someone to earn a few dollars by selling him to be cut up for research sickened us.[19]

After recovering Isaac, the Grignons phoned friend Carol Kough, who had been searching tirelessly for Isaac, and neighbor Julie Tapp, whose dog had been missing for nearly two weeks. Kough and Tapp then contacted a number of individuals who had advertised their lost pets in area newspapers, and arranged to meet at Institute Hills Farm the following afternoon.

"I had no idea we were going to find one dog, let alone several," said Carol Kough. Of eight families who went to Institute Hills on January 20th, five recovered their pets. Ella Erie, Julie Tapp, and Kathy Adams were among those who found their dogs that afternoon.

Thanks to television and newspaper coverage of the incident, another 15 stolen dogs were identified at Institute Hills within a week of Isaac's recovery. The stolen dogs were recovered between two and 16 days after delivery to the research center. Because Mayo Clinic policy required all new dogs to be "conditioned" for 21 days prior to use in experimentation, none of the animals had been used in research.

Unfortunately, the owners of two of the 16 stolen dogs found at Institute Hills were never located, and the animals were later used in research projects. Two more shepherds from the same lot of stolen dogs turned up at the University of Minnesota. One of these animals died of unknown causes, and the other had already been used in an experiment.

The Grignons, whose dog lost upwards of 40 pounds during his week-long ordeal, spent a great deal of time and money at the veterinarian's after recovering Isaac. "Part of it was that he had dropped weight, but actually... he had developed some kind of bug plus kennel cough.... The vet was going to put him on IVs if at one point in time he didn't get better," explained Mary.

As for Rex, the Border Collie, Ella Erie called his condition "awful": "There wasn't much to him. He was starved, and when I got him home here, I started giving him water, and I thought he was going to kill himself drinking water. I had a 5-quart pail filled two-thirds of the way with water, and he left just the littlest bit in the bottom. He'd drink and then he'd turn and walk around a little bit, and then he'd go right back to drink."

Mayo employees "questioned us because they weren't sure it was our dog," said Erie. "Then we took Rex's picture out. When he saw that, he couldn't say much more you know.... There was a guy that kind of rubbed up on my shoulder and he said, 'Are you going to write me a check?'" Asked how long it took Rex to get back to normal, his owner answered, "He really isn't back to normal yet.... He isn't the dog he was. He can't run anything like he did when they took him. I'll tell you, I think that deal took a lot of years out of his life."

The Adamses' dog, Smokey, was also in poor condition when they recovered him: "All he did when I saw him in the kennel was lift his paw when I got in there.... He's got St. Bernard in him and they can look so sad, and he just didn't even look like the same dog. He had lost a lot of weight. I brought him home, and he came to life a little when he seen the kids. But then he just lay down and he didn't hardly move. So we took him to the vet, who said that he had a hundred and five temperature, his lungs were congested, and he had a cough. She sent me home with a bunch of antibiotics.... He was very, very dehydrated. He drank a 5-quart pail of water and half of another one. Just non-stop.... It took him about a month to recover."

Another dog, Mr. Cool, apparently had been beaten. His owner said: "When we got him back from over there, our opinion of his condition was that he was beaten. His sides were sore. Somebody had kicked him. When you touched his sides, he'd yelp.... He was very thirsty. He drank an ice cream bucket full of water, and he was hungry. He was coughing."

Mayo personnel gave some of the dog owners a hard time. One man said, "They were trying to make Rex's owners pay.... I think the vet over there changed his attitude towards me and Carol when he saw Randy.... He was giving us grief and then when Randy came in, he just shut his mouth and took us back there." Randy said, "There was a short, fat, stocky guy who had a bad attitude. That's the one that asked Ella how much she would give them to get their dog back."

The Mower County Sheriff's Department initiated an investigation. Hippert claimed he hadn't known the dogs were stolen, that he had in fact warned Green that he didn't want any stolen dogs. Hippert's purchase records corresponded to the descriptions of the dogs reported stolen, and investigators discovered that all of the names and addresses of people Green supposedly obtained the dogs from were fictitious. Sheriff's deputies arrested Green and charged him with felony theft of 13 dogs. The felony theft charge was dismissed in exchange for Green's plea of guilty to three misdemeanor theft charges. His sentence amounted to 30 days in county jail — 10 days for each count of theft.

In August 1984, USDA filed a complaint against Green charging him with operating as a dealer without a license. Green denied the charges and requested an oral hearing before an administrative law judge. The judge fined him a civil penalty of $18,000 and ordered him to cease and desist from further violations of the Animal Welfare Act. Hippert was never charged in connection with the thefts.

On July 31, 1990, the Hipperts notified USDA that they were no longer dealing in dogs and cats and requested that the agency stop sending them letters regarding lost pets. The Hipperts ceased operating Hill View Farms in 1990. In September, 1992, USDA granted them a new class B license to buy and resell pigs and geese under the name of Lake Shore Acres.

KNUDSEN, HENRY, "BUD" (KNUDSEN'S ANIMAL LABORATORY SERVICE). Lathrop, California. USDA license #93HK (last licensed in 1984).

Bud Knudsen, who started his business in 1959, was one of USDA's first licensed animal dealers. His customers included the Syntex Corporation, Cutter Laboratories, the U.S. Public Health Service, Stanford University, UCLA, the University of California in Davis and San Diego's Naval Regional Medical Center. He purchased dogs from city and county pounds, bunchers and other dealers, most notably James Hickey. In 1983, he spent $13,970 buying dogs from Hickey (see also: Hickey, James Joseph in this chapter).

Like Hickey, Knudsen remained licensed for decades despite evidence that he was violating the Animal Welfare Act. Reports of cruelty from his former employees and repeated discovery of stolen dogs on his property were apparently not enough to prompt action from USDA. According to USDA attorneys, the agency did not have sufficient evidence to bring a case against him. The unavailability of evidence may have had something to do with the infrequency of inspections: USDA inspected Knudsen's kennel only once in 1984.[20]

In July 1983, San Joaquin County sheriff's deputies arrested Knudsen and four other men and charged them with allegedly obtaining dogs under false pretenses. Knudsen's co-defendants, who had obtained dogs through "free to good home" ads and then sold them to Knudsen, eventually pled guilty to misdemeanor charges and served jail sentences ranging from 90 to 180 days. After a two-day jury trial, Knudsen was acquitted on one count of receiving stolen property. "It was our contention that Bud (Knudsen) had knowledge the four were going out at night and picking up strays, and during the day obtaining dogs from ads under false pretenses," said sheriff's investigator Larry Mills. "But the jury didn't buy the story... and he was acquitted."[21] While investigating the theft charges against Knudsen, law enforcement authorities obtained statements from Knudsen's employees "indicating they had been ordered to use inhumane measures to destroy sick animals. Instead of deadly injections, dogs were shot and cats were slaughtered on bricks with a rubber mallet. In at least one instance, an employee said he was instructed to tie up the feet of several cats and drown them in a 55-gallon drum."[22]

After Knudsen's acquittal, the county returned the 74 animals who had been removed from his kennel during his arrest on the condition that he provide adequate care for them.

On November 1, 1984, sheriff's deputies and animal control officers visited Knudsen's property in response to neighbors' complaints of "noise and stench." They found the decomposed and partially eaten carcasses of 18 dogs and 18 cats, most showing signs of having starved to death. They also found 88 live animals, all of whom were emaciated and dehydrated. One sheriff's deputy described the scene as "one of the most completely disgusting situations" he had ever seen.[23] A number of dogs were found dead in their feeding troughs, their pens soiled with feces "piled more than an inch thick."[24]

The dogs found alive were without food, and some were without water. Many of them were feeding on the carcasses of the dead dogs. "The stronger dogs were jealously guarding the dead and partially consumed bodies of fallen comrades from other animals," stated one deputy. "Other dogs... were so weak they could not stand. The rib cages of most of the animals still alive were pushing against their skins."[25] A veterinarian who examined the animals stated some may have gone without food for more than a month.

According to the Humane Society of the United States, several of the surviving dogs were reunited with their human companions:

> [some of the dogs were identified] as having been given away through "Free to Good Homes" advertisements.... One dog named "Sunshine" was identified by its owner when the Peninsula Humane Society ran pictures of the animals on television. The dog had been stolen from the back yard of the owner's home in Ukiah [Oregon] over a year ago.[26]

A couple from Brush Prairie, Washington discovered that their dog, Tyke, had also ended up at Knudsen's kennel. They had given the dog to a man who answered their giveaway ad in a local newspaper.

Local authorities charged Knudsen with 124 counts of misdemeanor cruelty to animals. USDA immediately suspended his dealer's license and filed a complaint charging him with 124 Animal Welfare Act violations. After a January 31, 1985 administrative hearing on the USDA's charges, Knudsen signed a consent decree admitting he had cruelly neglected the 124 animals housed at his facility. Under the consent decree, Knudsen agreed to permanently forfeit his federal dealer's license and pay a $10,000 fine. An additional $114,000 fine was suspended on the condition that he not engage in any business regulated by the Animal Welfare Act.

A trial on the state criminal charges against Knudsen was not held until April 4. Prosecutors reduced the charges to four counts of cruelty, and Knudsen changed his plea from not guilty to no contest. He was fined $2,000, sentenced to six months in jail and given three years' probation.[27]

LUDLOW, GREG (GTL KENNELS). Goodyear, Arizona. USDA license #86-B-044 (last licensed in 1995).

Greg Ludlow, at one time one of the largest suppliers of animals to research facilities in the Los Angeles area, was charged with obtaining dogs under false pretenses on three separate occasions. His clients included Cedars-Sinai Hospital, the University of the Pacific, the University of California at Los Angeles, the University of California at Davis, the Letterman Institute, the University of Arizona, and several Arizona laboratories.

Ludlow held two USDA licenses under his own name and for several years did business under a third license belonging to Robert F. Hockensmith (Animal Enterprises of Phoenix, #86-B-044). From 1988 to 1990, Ludlow operated as Greg Ludlow & Associates (#86-B-20). He sold animals under Hockensmith's license from 1990 until 1993, when he obtained a new USDA license and renamed his business GTL Kennels (#86-B-044).

Before he gave up his first USDA license, Ludlow had been linked to more than one sale of fraudulently obtained dogs for research. Greyhound owners initiated a civil suit against him after he sold 112 greyhounds to Letterman Army Institute in San Francisco, which was then conducting bone-grafting experiments for 3M Corporation. The Greyhound owners had not known their dogs would be used for research. As a result of the greyhound owners' lawsuit, Congress withdrew $700,000 of support from 3M Corporation in 1989.

In 1990, Ludlow sold 20 greyhounds to Cedars-Sinai without the knowledge or consent of the dogs' owners. The owners' attorneys attempted to contact Cedars-Sinai several times to resolve the case but received no response. After USDA initiated an investigation of the incident, Ludlow surrendered his license. However, he continued to sell greyhounds under Robert Hockensmith's license, and USDA issued Ludlow a new Class B license in early 1993.

In February, 1994, Ludlow obtained 12 more greyhounds on fraudulent grounds and sold them to the University of Arizona. After being tracked down to determine ownership, the dogs' owners told the Greyhound Protection League they thought the dogs were going to be adopted and had not given permission for them to be experimented on.

Dr. Susan Wilson-Sanders, Director of Animal Care at the University of Arizona, stated the University had double-checked Ludlow's credentials because of his past troubles but went ahead with the greyhound purchase in February, believing Ludlow "had cleaned up his act, that his paperwork was in good shape."[28]

According to USDA, the greyhounds were the legal property of the University of Arizona, which was under no obligation to return them. However, the University expressed a "moral obligation" to give the dogs up, later releasing them to two greyhound adoption programs.

On March 31, 1995, USDA filed a complaint against Ludlow, charging him with failure to maintain complete records showing the acquisition of dogs between February 1993 and February 1994. The complaint also charged him with acquiring random source dogs in violation of the Animal Welfare Act. On May 19, 1995, he signed a Consent Decision and Order assessing him a $500 penalty and suspending his Class B license for ten years.

RUGGIERO, BARBARA AND FREDERICK J. SPERO (BIOSPHERE, INC.), Los Angeles, California. USDA license #93-B-166 (last licensed in 1991).

Barbara Ruggiero used her two boarding kennels — Budget Boarding and Comfy Kennel — as holding facilities for the dogs and cats she later sold to research facilities. She and her business partner, Frederick Spero, obtained animals through "free to good home" ads, from her buncher, Ralph Jacobsen, and from other dealers, including David Stephens of Lebanon, Oregon, who in 1993 pled guilty to charges of purchasing dogs obtained under false pretenses (see also: Stephens, David and Tracy in this chapter).

Ruggiero and Spero set up Biosphere in October 1987. By mid-January 1988, they had acquired some 150 cats and dogs, 64 of whom had already died in laboratories. They sold the animals to Cedars-Sinai Medical Center in Los Angeles, Loma Linda University School of Medicine and the Veterans Hospital in Sepulveda, California, charging $100 for cats and between $150 and $500 for dogs, depending on weight. Ruggiero sometimes took in as much as $17,500 a month.[29]

Biosphere often sold strays, animals "adopted" from shelters, and animals collected by Ruggiero's ex-boyfriend, Ralf Jacobsen, who earned $10 for each cat and $20 for each dog he brought in. Using false names and playing the roles of newlyweds or parents, Ruggiero and Jacobsen obtained dogs and cats from people who had advertised them for giveaway in local newspapers. They promised to give the animals wonderful homes.

"He was a clean-cut, all-American, super-nice guy who wanted to give my dog a good home on his 10-acre ranch," said one of the people whose dog was "adopted" by Jacobsen, or "Mike Johnson," as he often identified himself.[30]

Norman Flint thought he had found the perfect home for his two Labrador mixes, Wiggles and Bear. He had picked Ralf Jacobsen after interviewing nearly twenty potential adopters. Jacobsen told Flint he was a lawyer and that the dogs would be living in a big house and have a fenced yard to play in. He even told Flint he could come visit the dogs anytime he wanted. But two weeks later, when Flint tried to call Jacobsen to find out how the dogs were doing, he got a wrong number. When he decided to drive by the address Jacobsen had given him, he discovered no such address existed. Flint found out later that Ruggiero sold Bear to Cedars-Sinai Medical Center, where he was killed in a heart attack experiment. Flint eventually recovered Wiggles, who was one of the animals animal control officers confiscated from Budget Boarding after Ruggiero's scam was finally uncovered.

One of the women who gave her dog to Jacobsen became alarmed after discovering that the telephone number he gave her was disconnected. She began calling others who had placed "free to good home" ads. She soon found five other people who had given their animals to a man fitting Jacobsen's description. He told all of them the same story: he was a pilot and a law student, and the animals would live with him on his 10-acre ranch. The woman contacted Last Chance for Animals (LCA), an animal rights organization based in California. LCA began checking all of the "free to a good home ads" and discovered that a woman was also responding to them. Coincidence led LCA to Ruggiero.

While an LCA staff member was on the phone with an advertiser who was 'seeking homes for three cats' to warn her about "Mike Johnson" and "Barbara," the girlfriend Jacobsen had frequently spoken of, a woman calling herself Barbara rang the advertiser's doorbell to inquire about the cats. When cross-questioned, she grew flustered but agreed to leave an address where the animals could be delivered the next day.[31]

LCA learned that a van parked at that address was registered to Ruggiero, who owned both Budget Boarding Kennel in Sun Valley and

Comfy Kennel. They also discovered Ruggiero had a USDA Class B license. Activists and anguished pet owners gathered outside the kennels to keep watch. The woman who had first called LCA jumped a fence at Comfy Kennel to search for her dog. She found him in a pen with three other dogs. After her discovery, angry pet owners broke into the kennel to look for their dogs and cats. Some found their animals; others found only collars and tags.

LCA and local activists contacted the three research facilities that had purchased animals from Biosphere. Cedars-Sinai Medical Center, which bought 31 dogs, initially denied having any of animals. Guards blocked the way when pet owners sought entry. When LCA president Chris DeRose went in to negotiate, he was forcefully ejected — sustaining injuries to add to those inflicted earlier by Ruggiero, who had attempted to run him down in her van.

Cedars-Sinai finally agreed to let a third party into the laboratory to see if any of the missing dogs were there, only to renege later, offering instead to allow people to examine photos of the dogs. However, after extensive media coverage of the story, the medical center agreed to release all six of the dogs who had not yet been killed in experiments.[32] Three of the dogs were immediately reclaimed. In the meantime, the 55 animals remaining in Ruggiero's kennels were released, and many of them were reunited with their owners.

Prosecutors charged Ruggiero, Jacobsen and Spero with 73 counts of misdemeanor theft and conspiracy to obtain property by false pretenses and promises. They also charged Ruggiero with one added count of theft for accepting a $35 placement fee to find a good home for a dog she subsequently sold to Cedars-Sinai. Prosecutor Jim Hahn described the defendants as "three very cold-blooded people who were given pets because they promised to give them good homes and then sentenced them to death by selling them for medical research."

In his sentencing remarks in court on September 9, 1991, Judge David Schacter spared no words in his description of Ruggiero: "Miss Ruggiero is a conniving, manipulative individual who has no morals or ethics when it comes to achieving a desired goal. In her dealings with vulnerable pet owners and with animals, she is the personification of evil." Of Ruggiero and her associates, Judge Schacter stated, "Nothing the Court has seen would indicate that these defendants are remorseful for their past conduct."[33]

Judge Schacter sentenced Ruggiero to 6 years and 2 months imprisonment, Spero to 5 years, and Jacobsen to 3 years. On May 9, 1994, the convictions of Barbara Ruggiero and Frederick Spero were overturned and vacated on a legal technicality. The case against Ruggiero and Spero was dismissed in December, 1994 for failure of the court to notify the parties as to a retrial within the prescribed sixty-day period. After she was released from prison, Ruggiero reportedly was back in business, operating under someone else's Class B license.

STEPHENS, DAVID AND TRACY (D & T KENNELS), Lebanon, Oregon. License #92-B-159 (last licensed in 1992).

USDA's role in uncovering a scam that went on for more than a year—in which pet owners unwittingly relinquished their animals to a buncher working with David Stephens—was as exemplary as its handling of the Hickey and Knudsen cases was disappointing. The Stephenses undoubtedly would still be in business if it weren't for the persistence of two USDA employees.

Before starting his own Class B business, Stephens worked as a caretaker for Joe Hickey at S & H Supply, where he discovered that selling dogs and cats for research was "real lucrative."[34] By all accounts, D & T was a profitable business. Stephens supplied animals to Barbara Ruggiero and many of Hickey's former customers, claiming to sell between 25 and 30 animals a month to research facilities in California and Nevada and earning between $70,000 to $80,000 per year.[35] In 1991, he earned approximately $96,000.[36]

As a combined investigation by USDA, the Oregon Department of Agriculture and the Oregon Department of Motor Vehicles would later reveal, the Stephenses' main supplier was Brenda Linville, another USDA-licensed dealer (USDA license #92-B-169). Evidently, Linville had been acquiring and selling dogs and cats for research long before she applied for a dealer's license. In 1991, after receiving information that she was selling animals to Stephens, USDA sent Linville two warning notices informing her that she was required to be licensed if she was selling animals covered by the Animal Welfare Act. She applied for and received a license, but as USDA inspectors reported, whenever they attempted to inspect her premises she told them she wasn't in business yet.

Linville acquired dogs and cats through "free to good home" ads, posing as someone wanting "a family pet," "a stock dog," "a protection dog," "an inside animal," "a pet for son" or "a farm dog." In a little over a year's time, Linville acquired 567 dogs and 117 cats through newspaper advertisements.[37] She sold them to Stephens, who in turn sold them to Cedars-Sinai Medical Center, the VA hospitals in Sepulveda and Wadsworth, California, Oregon Health Science University or the University of Nevada.

In May 1991, Linville responded to an ad Kimberly Williams placed in the Corvallis *Times Gazette* offering to give her two cocker spaniels,

Tramper and Frederica, free to a good home. Williams's ad specified that the dogs were "not to be used for research." Linville told Williams she wanted both dogs as pets and took them the same day. She then sold the dogs to Stephens, giving him the name "Kelly Crocker" to list as the dogs' owner. The Stephenses entered Crocker's name and address in their acquisition records, and on May 22, they sold the two dogs to the University of Nevada in Reno. The dogs were later killed in research projects.

Similarly, the Stephenses listed Doris Cox's dog, Chelsea, as "Bertha L. Schackmann's" dog. Lyny Pheyffer's two dogs, Zeke and Casey, became "William Pickle's" dogs, and Mike and Wendy Kirk's golden retriever, Bo, became "Paul Youngblood's" dog. The Stephenses sold all of the dogs to research facilities.

Linville also answered Irene Clemmer's giveaway ad for her two dogs, Penny and Charlie. Clemmer gave the dogs to Linville, who told her she wanted Penny for her family and that her husband wanted Charlie, an Australian shepherd mix, for a stock dog. A few weeks later, the Stephenses sold Charlie to the Sepulveda Research Corporation and Penny to the Veterans Administration Research Center in Los Angeles.

Clemmer contacted USDA Veterinary Medical Officer Robert Willems after she found out the dogs were no longer in Linville's possession. While reviewing records at D & T Kennels, Willems and investigator Gregg Nelson discovered that two dogs matching the descriptions of Clemmer's dogs were listed as having been sold to D & T by Deborah Ford. When located and questioned, Ford told Willems and Nelson that she hadn't sold dogs to anyone and had never heard of either the Stephenses or Linville.

Willems and Nelson found that the other individuals listed as having sold dogs to the Stephenses hadn't given or sold dogs to anyone. They also discovered that all of the listed individuals had renewed their driver's licenses a few days before the recorded dog sales. Nelson obtained a search warrant from the Linn county sheriff's department and visited D & T Kennels, where he found Oregon Department of Motor Vehicles (DMV) transaction slips. As the Stephenses would later reveal, Linville, who often helped her father with his job as a janitor at the DMV, removed the transaction slips from DMV trash and gave them to David Stephens for use in filling out his acquisition records. Willems and Nelson's investigation revealed that the Stephenses falsely recorded the names of at least 60 people as having sold more than 150 dogs to D & T kennels. Linn County Deputy Sheriff Dennis Cole raided D & T on April 2, 1992 and arrested the Stephenses.

USDA confiscated 22 dogs and 4 cats from D & T and placed them in the custody of the Oregon Humane Society (OHS). One of the rescued dogs was Bo, Mike and Wendy Kirk's golden retriever mix. The Stephenses had already sold many other animals to research facilities. Since the sources of these animals were uncertain, OHS was able to persuade several facilities to relinquish dogs purchased from D & T Kennels. The VA hospital in Los Angeles returned seventeen dogs and the University of Nevada in Reno sent back three.[38]

Irene Clemmer asked OHS to help her reclaim Charlie and Penny, who were tracked down by Willems and Nelson through D & T's records. Sadly, Penny had already been killed in the course of a research project. Charlie was still alive but was being used in an ulcer study; his body had been surgically altered for the five-year project. According to OHS, "the facility was reluctant to part with Charlie, preferring to purchase or euthanize him."[39] After two weeks of negotiation, the hospital agreed to let an outside veterinarian examine the dog. A veterinary surgeon offered to donate his services, and after two surgeries to reverse what the researchers had done to him, Charlie was on the road to recovery. He was later returned to Oregon and reunited with Irene Clemmer.

The Stephenses and Linville were initially charged with first-degree theft by deception under Oregon's 1991 law making pet theft a felony, but the state charges were dropped when the U.S. Attorney's Office requested the case. On August 12, 1992, the U.S. government filed a three-count indictment against the Stephenses and Linville, charging them with conspiracy to defraud USDA; knowingly and willfully falsifying, concealing and covering up material facts required by USDA; and making false entries and statements on USDA records. On August 14, David Stephens requested cancellation of his Class B license.

In November, the dealers pled guilty to the conspiracy charge in exchange for the government's dismissal of the second and third counts of the indictment. In its sentencing memorandum, the U.S. Attorney's Office recommended that each of the defendants receive the maximum incarceration allowed under the guidelines:

> The actions of these three defendants have brought a great deal of pain to many people. Certainly the dog owners mentioned in the indictment have suffered immensely. Many other dog owners victimized by these defendants do not know that their beloved animal(s) was obtained from them by fraudulent means, only to be sold for profit and utilized for experimental research.... Certainly those who suffered the most, however, are Rusty, Tramper, Fredrica, Penny, Chelsea, Boots, Zeke, Casey and the many other unknown dogs who were obtained fraudulently from their owners, only to pay the ultimate price after their bodies had been utilized for research purposes.[40]

Attached to the sentencing memo were statements from eight dog owners and others who had been affected by the defendants' actions. Mike and Wendy Kirk wrote: "We thought we had chosen the perfect family to adopt Bo. Brenda told us everything we wanted to hear about what kind of life Bo would have. This was all a lie. She took him directly to the kennels to be sold. Luckily when the kennel was raided he was still there alive."[41]

Kimberly Williams's statement echoed the feelings of guilt and betrayal of many of the people whose beloved animal companions had passed through the defendants' hands:

> I trusted Brenda Linville, and even went to see her "lovely house and pasture" where my dogs would supposedly be running free.... There isn't a day that goes by that I don't think of my dogs.... I grew up with them.... I would tell [Brenda Linville] that I would have been better off if she would have killed me instead of my dogs. At least then I wouldn't have to suffer a life full of pain and knowing.[42]

Also attached to the sentencing memo was a petition signed by more than 130 individuals asking that the defendants receive the "strongest possible sentence... that the law allows."

The U.S. District Court in Eugene, Oregon pronounced sentencing on February 22, 1993. David Stephens was sentenced to 12 months confinement, 10 months of which was to be served in prison, followed by two months of home detention. Brenda Linville was sentenced to 10 months incarceration—eight months in prison and two months home detention. Tracy Stephens was sentenced to three years probation, including one year of home detention. Both Linville and David Stephens appealed. The appellate court threw out Linville's original eight-month sentence after concluding that even though her two USDA warning notices for selling dogs to research without a license placed her in a higher sentencing category, the warnings alone were not sufficient to justify additional prison time.[43]

TONEY, JULIAN J. Lamoni, Iowa. USDA license #42-B-067 (1995).

Julian Toney and his wife, Anita, sold between 1,000 and 1,500 dogs and cats a year to the University of Minnesota (UM) and the University of Iowa (UI). They employed several unlicensed "part-time buyers" who acquired animals throughout Iowa, Missouri and Nebraska. In 1991, USDA sent at least two of these buyers warning notices for selling dogs without a license. The Toneys also purchased dogs at their monthly gun and dog auction, the "Terre Haute Trading Post, Ltd.," later renamed "Rendezvous."

The Toneys became licensed as auction operators in 1983, but it was not until 1986 that they applied for and received a dealer's license. USDA inspection reports indicate the Toneys had difficulty complying with Animal Welfare Act requirements soon after they became licensed as dealers. On January 22, 1987, an inspector reported, "Dogs are in need of more floor space.... Many dog facilities... in need of fecal material removal and sanitation." On September 24, 1987, an inspector noted, "Wire floors that have been broken need to be repaired.... Feces need to be beat down through the wire and feces cleaned off the solid floors.... Feeding receptacles need to have the rust removed.... Sick dog needs to have veterinary care."

Inspectors also discovered serious deficiencies in the Toneys' acquisition and disposition records. An audit of records on all dogs and cats handled by the Toneys between 1-1-90 and 11-19-91 revealed that 1) driver's license numbers and vehicle numbers for unlicensed sellers were not being recorded as required, 2) USDA license numbers were not being recorded, 3) dates animals were acquired were not recorded, 4) some of the names the Toneys listed as sources for the dogs were false, and 5) the Toneys were acquiring dogs from unlicensed dealers. The records also showed the purchase of 50 dogs from various Missouri pounds and 90 dogs from nine individuals living in Missouri. When asked by USDA to confirm the sales, investigator Mark Westrich discovered that none of the pounds identified actually sold dogs to the Toneys. An attempt was made to find the nine individual sellers through their social security numbers and motor vehicle records, but none of them could be located.

Investigator Richard Gunderson included the results of the audit in a June 21, 1991 alleged violation report. The report also noted that the Toneys sold a total of 1,598 animals to the University of Minnesota and the University of Iowa between June 1, 1989 and June 1, 1990 and that they received $104,419 for these animals, not the $39,592 they reported on their license renewal. "This investigation has shown that Julian and Anita Toney have been dealing in random source dogs and have not kept complete records, that their records are not accurate and are in fact sometimes false," concluded Gunderson. "It is also evident that Julian and Anita Toney made false statements on [their] license renewal.... There is evidence... that Julian Toney has attempted to interfere with this report by contacting witnesses and by attempting to intimidate USDA investigators."

USDA didn't file a complaint against the Toneys until September 28, 1992. It charged them with failing to keep complete records on the acquisition of dogs and cats by falsely claiming to have acquired 131 dogs from pounds in Missouri and 112 dogs from various individuals; failing to record the date of acquisition of at least 720 dogs and cats; and failure to record the address, driver's license number and vehicle tag number of the person from whom the animal was acquired for at least 1,600 dogs and cats. The complaint also charged them with failure to hold at least 100 dogs and cats for the required five days after acquisition. The Toneys were permitted to remain in business pending a hearing on the charges.

One month later, USDA sent the Toneys a warning notice for alleg-edly housing dogs on broken wire flooring, failing to provide dogs protec-tion from the elements, housing puppies outdoors without veterinary approval and housing three cats in a cage providing inadequate space. They were also charged with failing to have a written exercise plan and failing to identify all dogs. In 1993, the Toneys received another warning notice, this time alleging Animal Welfare violations documented during inspections on 12-7-90, 11-25-91, 11-17-92, 11-25-92, and 2-11-93, including failure to pro-vide animals with shelter from the elements.

In May 1994, before a hearing on the initial charges had been held, USDA filed another complaint against the Toneys, this time charging them with willfully maintaining false and incomplete acquisition records; selling at least 44 random source dogs to research facilities accompanied by forged documents purporting to be certificates from a municipal pound; failing to individually identify dogs; and failing to provide appropriate animal care and facilities.

Administrative Law Judge Dorothea Baker consolidated the 1992 and 1994 complaints in May, and an oral hearing was held in June. Cliff Waterbury, one of the Toneys' "part-time buyers," testified that he acquired dogs from various pounds and also at dog auctions, mainly the Rutledge Gun and Dog Auction. He also stated that he purchased unwanted hunting dogs from acquaintances or friends of his son Terry, a Class B dealer in Missouri (Waterbury Kennel, license #43-B-108). Red Silkwood and dealer Elmer Scherbring (Earlville, Iowa, license #42-B-054) also sold the Toneys dogs acquired from pounds and other individuals. According to testimony by both Scherbring and Jim Knaack, an animal control officer for the city of Vinton, Missouri, Scherbring had Knaack sign blank certification forms used to show that a dog or cat had been acquired from a pound and that the holding period requirement had been met. Additional evidence indicated that Scherbring made duplicates of the signed forms and that Anita Toney filled in the descriptions and identification numbers of the animals after receiving them from Scherbring.

Rather than listing in their acquisition records the names of the people from whom they actually purchased animals, the Toneys recorded the pounds where the dogs allegedly originated. When questioned about the Toneys' failure to accurately identify sources of animals, USDA investigator Mark Westrich stated: "Tracing is not possible, and also... [it is] possible to hide unlicensed dealers.... The persons that are truly selling those dogs, their names aren't reflected in those records."

USDA next called investigator Marshall Smith to the witness stand. Smith had attempted to trace some of the individuals the Toneys listed as suppliers. When he was unable to locate them through local telephone books, he gave the Missouri Highway Patrol a list of names and social security numbers. "There was no match for the names and social security numbers that I had furnished to them," testified Smith. "[A Highway Patrol] officer told me that one of the social security numbers he ran had been assigned to a person living in Puerto Rico."

USDA also presented evidence that the Toneys were violating regulations governing animal care. Inspector Grant Wease testified that during his inspection of the Toneys' facility he "found a number of dog enclosures that had an accumulation of feces and hair on the wire flooring." Wease stated that debris—including metal pipes, dead animals, wood scrap and a barrel full of trash—was scattered throughout the premises: "We found an entire deteriorating cow carcass of several days duration with evidence of loose dogs that were eating various parts of the carcass.... And there was also underneath one of the dog enclosures... two immature dogs, believed to be puppies... which were... in advanced stages of decomposition." Dr. Wease also testified that he discovered "a number of dog enclosures with broken wire on floors and the walls" and that "a number of enclosures were deteriorating... which allowed dog appendages and heads to protrude to the outside portions of the pens."

In her April 29, 1995 decision, Judge Baker wrote: "The record, as a whole, supports [USDA's] allegations as to numerous violations of the Act and the applicable regulations. These have been repeated, flagrant and willful. Such disregard by Respondents reflects a situation where the purposes of the Act are thwarted and render its objectives a nullity." She stated that USDA had "set forth at least one hundred instances or more of false and incorrect entries as to the source of... dogs." "Completely apart from falsified entries and incidental errors, the Respondents' system fails to fully disclose the specified information such as addresses, license plate numbers, driver's license numbers, the name and address of the person from whom a dog or cat is acquired, their vehicle plate and state, and driver's license number and state," wrote Judge Baker. She also found that the Toneys had failed to individually identify dogs and hold at least 190 dogs and cats for the required five-day holding period. "There is substantial evidence to indicate that the Respondents altered their records to conceal violation of the holding periods," she stated. "It appears that there are transactions where the dates are altered in the notebooks." The judge permanently revoked the Toneys' Class B license and fined them $200,000, the largest civil penalty ever assessed against a Class B dealer.

VANCE, JERRY. Eupora, Mississippi. USDA license #65-B-008 (1994).

By contracting with various Mississippi towns and counties to pick up and dispose of stray or abandoned dogs and cats, Jerry Vance secured a cheap and readily accessible supply of animals for his Class B business. If the animals he picked up were not claimed within ten days, he moved them to his own kennel for sale to laboratories. Vance also acquired animals from the Hardeman County Animal Shelter in Indiana and other Class B dealers, including William Hargrove, Jr. (Tennessee), Jeffery Hodges (Mississippi), Jack Stowers (Indiana), and CC Baird (Arkansas)[44] (see also: Baird, C.C. and Hargrove, William in "Class B Dealers Selling Random Source Dogs and Cats for Research"; and Hodges, Jeffery and Stowers, Jack in "Class B Dealers Who Have Lost or Relinquished Their Licenses").

Vance was a large dealer, selling at least 2,500 animals a year. In 1991, he reported selling 3,400 animals, grossing $384,000.[45] His clients included the Veterans Administration Medical Center in Sepulveda, California; the University of Southern California in Los Angeles; the University of Mississippi Medical Center in Jackson; Mississippi State University Veterinary School; the University of Tennessee and Texas A & M University.

In addition to a "home" site in Eupora, Mississippi, Vance operated two other sites: one in Newton, Mississippi, owned by Wayne Clanton, and one in Estillfork, Alabama, owned by Lem R. Miller. Both Clanton and Miller acted as Vance's employees, acquiring animals for him on a regular basis. In 1992, after USDA cited him for buying and selling animals without a dealer's license, Miller applied for and received his own license (#64-B-053).

USDA inspectors who visited Vance's facilities documented deficiencies in housing, sanitation and veterinary care; however, the most serious and chronic deficiency noted was inadequate recordkeeping:

5-17-90: (Home site, 159 dogs, 20 cats) "Addresses not recorded." A notation by the reviewer, Dr. Richard Overton, appeared at the bottom of the inspector's report: "I have discussed with Dr. Wood the requirements that correct IDs be applied on all records and [that] this should be a category three deficiency."

1-12-93: (Estillfork site, 39 dogs) "Records must include purchased from USDA license number or vehicle license number and driver's [license] number and complete address with date of purchase. Correct with next purchase."

1-13-93: (Home site, 374 dogs) "Incomplete address on one entry.... 253 dogs are not on premises... have no record of disposition. 23 dogs have dates of disposition but no destination. 6 animals tagged and in pens but not on records. 5 animals tagged and in pens have been recorded as sold.... Correct records within 30 days."

Following inspections of Vance's Estillfork site on January 13 and 16, Dr. Elizabeth Goldentyer prepared an alleged violation report charging Vance with maintaining incomplete and inadequate records and obtaining a dog under false pretenses. On the same day, Southeast Sector Supervisor for Animal Care Dr. Joseph Walker sent a memo to Mario Morales of Regulatory Enforcement requesting an investigation of the alleged violations. Walker also requested an investigation of "stolen dog reports and contract pound arrangements."[46] Attached to the request were complaints from individuals who alleged they had found their missing dogs at Vance's kennel. The complaints also alleged Vance was picking up pets and refusing to return them and that he housed animals in poor conditions.[47]

Mississippi Senator Thad Cochran had also contacted USDA about Vance, claiming to have received complaints from his constituents regarding the dealer's activities. In response to Cochran, USDA Acting Administrator Lonnie King wrote: "Our Animal Care inspectors carefully reviewed Mr. Vance's records and found numerous discrepancies. As a result, we will be forwarding this case to our Regulatory Enforcement staff, who will conduct a formal investigation."[48]

USDA initiated an investigation on February 5. Investigator Aldean Valentine obtained affidavits from the individuals who had found their dogs at Vance's kennel and from USDA's Elizabeth Goldentyer, who had received several phone calls from an individual who claimed her dog had been stolen and that she had found him at Vance's kennel. Despite the dog owners' claims that their animals had been stolen, Valentine couldn't find any proof that Vance was involved in dog theft.

Frustrated by Vance's refusal to allow people to look for their missing pets in his kennel, In Defense of Animals (IDA) and a group of local residents organized a protest outside the dealer's home on March 3, 1993.[49,50,51] The event drew 35 dog owners who demanded access to the kennel. Although the protesters were unsuccessful in gaining entrance to the kennel, the demonstration prompted two CBS news programs – "Eye to Eye with Connie Chung" and "60 Minutes" – to run stories about Vance. Both programs reported pet owners had found their missing dogs at Vance's kennel.

Vance denied ever knowingly purchasing stolen pets. "I don't have anything to hide.... They have no proof. We don't steal dogs," Vance told the Jackson, Mississippi Clarion-Ledger.[52] In his interview on "Eye to Eye," Vance was asked how he knew whether or not a pet was stolen. "How can you make sure the pets aren't stolen, Mr. Vance? What do you do to make sure that it's legal?" "Get proper information like the USDA says to do," he replied.

But getting the proper information was clearly not what Vance was doing. During an inspection of Vance's Eupora site on May 5, the inspector reported: "Records do not fully and correctly disclose: (1) Full address of individuals from whom dog or cat was acquired. (2) Incorrect sex recorded on 15 dogs. (3) Incorrect color or markings on several dogs. (4) 3 dogs in kennels were recorded as 'died.' (5) 5 dogs not in kennels with no record of disposition."

On May 19, Dr. Walker sent Morales a memorandum requesting a trace back audit of five of Vance's major suppliers: Hargrove, Hodges, Stowers, Baird and the Hardeman County Animal Shelter. "Mr. Jerry Vance has been accused of dealing in stolen dogs," wrote Dr. Walker. "Our inspection and investigation of this facility discloses noncompliance of recordkeeping.... Based upon our review of the records and the complaints received against this facility we are requesting an in-depth investigation." Walker also suggested that investigator Valentine do a call-back search to validate the source of 58 dogs listed in Vance's inventory.[53]

In his preliminary violation report, Valentine stated that the records audit had revealed Vance was not keeping adequate acquisition and disposition records and that he had acquired random source dogs from individuals who had not bred and raised the animals on their own premises. He also stated there was substantial proof that Vance had falsified records of approximately 80 dogs allegedly sold to Mississippi State University (MSU) in late 1992 and early 1993.[54] Valentine obtained affidavits from four MSU employees who stated Vance had asked one of them to help him with a problem he had concerning some dogs. According to one of the affidavits, "Vance wanted the employee to disclose on the records that MSU had received the dogs when, in fact, they had not."[55] The employee agreed to Vance's request and falsified the records. Shortly after learning of the incident, MSU officials announced they would no longer purchase dogs from Vance.

Investigator Valentine filed his final alleged violation report with Dr. Walker on August 12, 1993. He stated that while the claim that Vance was dealing with stolen dogs could not be confirmed, his investigation did reveal that Vance had not maintained complete and accurate records of the animals he bought and sold. The report noted that the original sources of dogs purchased by Vance from C.C. Baird and Jack Stowers could not be validated.

Meanwhile, inspectors continued to report serious problems with Vance's recordkeeping. During a 9-16-93 inspection of a shipment of dogs received by Texas A & M University, an inspector noted: "Records shall contain name, address of [individual] from whom the dog was obtained. Twelve dogs on this shipment are identified by USDA tags; however, no source of origin is available on these dogs.... Corrected during inspection."

USDA filed a complaint against Vance on September 2, 1993, charging him with failure to maintain complete and accurate records of the acquisition and disposition of at least 442 dogs and preparing records purporting to show the sale of 84 dogs to a research facility when in fact he did not know the actual disposition of the animals. In November, Valentine sent Morales the results of his traceback of the sources of 58 dogs listed on Vance's May 6 records. Valentine reported that the addresses given for sources were inadequate, making the tracing process especially difficult. More than half of the individuals contacted stated they had not raised the animals they sold to Vance on their own premises.[56]

In an amended complaint filed on November 30, USDA additionally charged Vance with failing to maintain complete records showing the acquisition of dogs by making false entries as to the identities of the individuals from whom the animals were acquired. The amended complaint also charged Vance with failing to individually identify dogs; failing to maintain a program of adequate veterinary care; failing to provide dogs with housing facilities that were structurally sound and maintained in good repair; and failing to provide housing facilities for cats that were sufficiently ventilated.

USDA filed a second amended complaint in December, adding another charge of making false entries as to the identities of individuals from whom he acquired animals. In July 1994, Vance signed a Consent Decision and Order, in which he neither admitted nor denied the USDA's charges but agreed to cease and desist from violating the Act. He was permanently disqualified from holding a USDA dealer license and fined $25,000, $20,000 of which is suspended on the condition he does not violate the Animal Welfare Act for 20 years.

VRANA, HELEN AND RUDOLF (VRANA RESEARCH ANIMALS), Millville, New Jersey. USDA license #22-B-21 (last licensed in 1988).

Vrana, once a major dealer in Pennsylvania, Virginia and New Jersey, sold animals to Mt. Sinai Hospital, Columbia University, and Einstein College of Medicine in New York, and U.S. Surgical Corporation (USSC) in Norwalk, Connecticut. He acquired animals from other dealers and at auctions, including the Gilbertsville auction in Pennsylvania.

Vrana's dog sales to USSC, which manufactures surgical staples, received widespread public attention. USSC uses live dogs to train sales-men—who have no medical training—in surgical stapling techniques. USDA documents show that in the first ten months of 1981 alone, USSC used and then euthanized 922 dogs in training exercises.[57,58] According to a USDA investigative report on USSC's dog sources, USSC stopped purchasing dogs from the Vranas in September 1981 "due to the bad publicity they received [after] newspaper reports said Vrana was unlicensed."[59]

Although claims that Vrana was involved in pet theft were never substantiated, Vrana was charged with receiving stolen property: a dog he purchased from a buncher.[60] In a note on a 2-16-84 USDA inspection report, Area Veterinarian in Charge Dr. Irwin Huff wrote, "Review records each inspection.... Petnapping continues to be reported from that area where Vrana is located. We need to have assurances that Vrana's records are kept in the correct manner so that he will not become involved with stolen pets and can verify the source and disposition of each."

In 1983, humane investigators charged Vrana with cruelty to animals twice within a two-week period. On February 28, Charles Gerofsky, president of the New Jersey Society for the Prevention of Cruelty to Animals, stopped Vrana en route to several laboratories in the New York area. Gerofsky described Vrana's truck, which held approximately 30 dogs, 21 cats, and 39 rabbits, as "packed right to the roof."[61] The animals, crammed into small wire cages and chicken crates, were unable to stand or turn around. Most of the animals "were in very poor condition."[62] Many of them were ill, and some were bleeding or foaming at the mouth. "There was no ventilation in the van, and the animals were hungry, nervous and soaking wet," said Gerofsky. "They were packed on top of one another and so tight in the crates they couldn't avoid being urinated on by each other."[63] Gerofsky seized the animals and charged Vrana with 20 counts of cruelty to animals.

Comparing the conditions on Vrana's truck to "the concentration camps of Nazi Germany," a municipal court judge found the dealer guilty of 12 counts of animal cruelty.[64] Vrana paid his $4,980 fine in cash.

Twelve of the animals Gerofsky confiscated from Vrana died as a result of illness or infection. Five of the remaining animals were released to people who identified them as their missing pets. According to Gerofsky, the SPCA received hundreds of phone calls from people—some as far away as Ohio and Pennsylvania—who were looking for missing animals.

Following the municipal court judge's decision, USDA suspended Vrana's Class B license for 21 days. The suspension was based on both the SPCA charges and the results of a USDA inspection of Vrana's facility on February 24, which uncovered deficiencies in veterinary care, sanitation, identification and recordkeeping.

Gerofsky stopped Vrana's truck again on March 14 because he saw a rabbit cage leaning at a bad angle. Gerofsky claimed Vrana was extremely uncooperative and would not give him a clear view into the truck. In an attempt to flee, Vrana kicked Gerofsky in the stomach and shoved him away. A back-up humane officer attempted to get Vrana's truck keys by reaching for them through the driver's side, but Vrana rolled up the window, pinning the officer's arm. He started to drive away with the officer still pinned to the window.[65] After a scuffle, Vrana was arrested and charged with eluding a law enforcement officer, assault and battery of law enforcement officers and six counts of cruelty to animals.

In May, USDA charged Vrana with violating transportation, sanitation and recordkeeping requirements on five occasions during February and March 1983. The charges were based on the February 28 and March 14 incidents and Vrana's failure to keep adequate records. An administrative judge fined Vrana $3,000, ordered him to cease and desist from violating the Animal Welfare Act and suspended his Class B license for 30 days. The Vranas continued in business until 1988, when they voluntarily surrendered their USDA license and moved out of the state.

Sources indicate the Vranas may still maintain connections in the dog dealing business years after relinquishing their license. USDA officials reportedly sighted between 70 and 80 dogs on property purchased under the name of Vrana's son near Sparta, North Carolina.[66,67]

Notes

1. Lamar D. Graham, "Federal Officials Find Discrepancies in Dog Dealer's Records," Columbia, MO: *The Columbia Daily Tribune*, 28 September 1986.

2. Ibid.

3. Ibid. The two Labrador Retrievers were owned by Cheryl Tiddwell of Columbia, Missouri.

4. "USDA Checking Dog Sales Stories," Fulton, MO: *The Missouri Sun*, 21 September 1986. Kramer's case was also covered in *The Columbia Daily Tribune* of 28 September, 1986.

5. COMBAT (Coalition of Municipalities to Ban Animal Trafficking), in "COMBAT Gets Dealer's Records," *Network News*, Fall 1990.

6. COMBAT, "Deputy Buncher," *Network News*, Fall 1990.

7. Coalition of Municipalities to Ban Animal Trafficking (COMBAT), *COMBAT NEWS*, v. 2, n. 1, Fall 1990. COMBAT gives a complete account of the Yaeger case from newspaper accounts and other documents. During the polygraphs of Yaeger, police focused on two questions: "Did you steal any of the dogs that you sold to Holco?" and "Did you steal even one of the dogs that you sold to Holco?" Yaeger was not asked if he obtained dogs under false pretenses through "free to good home" ads.

8. Rick Bella, "Humane Society Sold Dogs for Research, " Springfield, OR: *Springfield News*, 8 October 1977.

9. David G, Williams, USDA Area Compliance Officer, in a Compliance Officer Report, 22 July 1985.

10. James W. Hickey, in an affidavit in support of a motion for continuance, 4 August 1986.

11. Hunter Jameson, "Court Hearing Ends on Charges Against Linn Kennel Owner," Albany, OR: *Albany Democrat-Herald*, 28 March 1987.

12. Gary Whitehouse, "Man Charged in Cat Theft Case," Albany, OR: *Albany Democrat Herald*, 30 November 1988.

13. Gary Whitehouse, "Missing Pets Ending Up at Animal Dealer," Albany, OR: *Albany Democrat Herald*, 8 September 1988.

14. W.D. Pritchard, USDA Veterinarian in Charge, in a letter dated 12 October 1988, to W.D. Stewart, USDA Chief Staff Veterinarian. The response given was suggested by Dr. Richard Crawford, USDA.

15. Chief Administrative Law Judge Victor W. Palmer, in his Decision and Order in re: S.S. Farms Linn County, Inc., James W. Hickey, Marie Hickey, James Joseph Hickey and Shannon Hansen, 22 January 1990.

16. Ibid.

17. Andrew P. Ositis, in a letter to Ron DeHaven, USDA Western Sector Supervisor, 13 February 1990.

18. Dr. Ron DeHaven, USDA Western Sector Supervisor, in a letter to Andrew P. Ositis, 26 March 1990.

19. David and Mary Grignon, in a letter to USDA, 3 April 1985.

20. Andrew Ross, "How Could Pet Horror Happen in Stockton?" *San Francisco Examiner*, 11 November 1984.

21. Ibid.

22. Ibid.

23. "36 Dogs, Cats Found Dead—Lab Owner Faces 124 Charges," Stockton, CA: *The Stockton Record*, 1 November 1984.

24. Ibid.

25. Marjorie Flaherty and Ben Remington, "Animal Lab Scene of Horror," Stockton, CA: *The Stockton Record*, 2 November 1984.

26. "Research Animal Dealer Arrested, Charged with Cruelty to Animals," West Coast Regional Office Report, The Humane Society of the United States, Spring 1985.

27. Judy Keen, "Kennel Owner Gets Six Months in Jail," Stockton, CA: *The Stockton Record*, 5 April 1985.

28. Carla McClain, "Group 'Rescues' 12 Greyhounds," Tucson, AZ: *Tuscon Citizen*, 5 March 1994.

29. Judith Reitman, *Stolen for Profit*.

30. "Three Charged in Callous Pets-for-Research Scam," *The Animal Welfare Institute Quarterly*, v. 37, n. 3 &4, Fall/Winter 1988/89.

31. *The Animal Welfare Institute Quarterly*, Fall/Winter 1988/89.

32. Ibid.

33. Ibid.

34. Marilyn Montgomery, "Imprisoned for Dog Fraud, Ex-Dealer Reflects on His Business," Albany, OR: Albany Democrat Herald, 29 March 1994.

35. Portland: OR: KOIN-TV Interview, 3 April 1992.

36. APHIS press release, May 1993.

37. Judith Reitman, *Stolen for Profit*.

38. The Oregon Humane Society, "Some Lucky Dogs and How They Got That Way," *Oregon Humane Society News*, Summer 1992.

39. Ibid.

40. Government's Sentencing Memorandum, United States v. Brenda Arlene Linville, David Harold Stephens, Tracy Lynn Stephens (D. Ore. 1993).

41. Wendy and Mike Kirk, Victim Impact Statement, United States v. Brenda Linville, David Stephens and Tracy Stephens.

42. Kimberly Williams, Victim Impact Statement, United States v. Brenda Linville, David Stephens and Tracy Stephens.

43. Marilyn Montgomery, "Ex-Animal Dealers Sentenced," Albany, OR: *The Albany Democrat Herald*, 11 January 1994.

44. United States Department of Agriculture, USDA Records Audit Pursuant to Investigation of Jerry Vance, 19 May 1993. A review of Vance's records, along with public complaints, prompted USDA audits of five of Vance's major suppliers.

45. Jerry Vance, APHIS Form 7003, Application for License, 1992.

46. Dr. Joseph Walker, Southeast Sector Supervisor-Animal Care, in memo to Mario Morales, Southeast Sector Supervisor-Regulatory Enforcement, 2 February 1993.

47. O. Aldean Valentine, Senior Investigator-RE, Investigator's Report of Alleged Violations of the Animal Welfare Act, 12 August 1993.

48. Lonnie King, USDA Acting Administrator, in a letter to Senator Thad Cochran, 10 February 1993.

49. Terri Ferguson, "IDA Offers Rewards," Grenada, MS: *The Daily Sentinel Star*, 1 April 1993.

50. J. Lee Howard, "Pet Owners Converge On Animal Dealer's Kennel," Jackson, MS: *The Clarion-Ledger*, 8 March 1993.

51. Terri Ferguson, "Protestors Ask to View Caged Dogs on Calhoun County Dealer's Land," Mississippi: *The Daily Sentinel-Star*, 8 March 1993.

52. Dan Fost, "Animal Rights Group Rescues Hound Dogs," *The Independent Journal*, June 1993. Vance's comment from *The Clarion-Ledger* was quoted in the *Independent Journal* article.

53. Dr. Joseph Walker, Southeast Sector Supervisor-Animal Care, in a memorandum to Mario Morales, Southeast Sector Supervisor-Regulatory Enforcement, 19 May 1993.

54. Aldean Valentine, REAC Senior Investigator, Preliminary Report of Alleged Violations of the Animal Welfare Act, 4 June 1993.

55. Ibid.

56. Aldean Valentine, REAC Senior Investigator, in a memorandum to Mario Morales, Southeast Sector Supervisor-Regulatory Enforcement, 15 November 1993.

57. Lisa Pagliarulo, USSC spokesperson, stated that 900 dogs were destroyed in a one-year period at USSC in an interview with *The Morning Call*, 25 February 1982.

58. Alleged Violation of 9 CFR, Subchapter A, Animal Welfare, Section 2.28 by USSC on 6 February 1980: Dr. A.E. Decoteau in a memo dated 22 October 1981 to Dr. Gerald J. Fichtner, Regional Director, Northern Veterinary Services, with attachments showing disposition and source sheets of USSC's animals. Disposition sheets showed USSC euthanized 922 dogs between January and October 22, 1981.

59. Alan Christian, USDA Compliance Officer, in a memo dated 29 January 1982 to Dr. A.E. Decoteau, in reference to USSC Investigation #82-83.

60. "Animal Dealers Given Jail Sentences in Local Violations," Associated Humane Societies, *Humane News*, November/December 1987.

61. Andrew Maykuth, "N.J. Laboratory Supplier Charged with Cruel Transport of Animals," *Philadelphia Inquirer*, 1 March 1983.

62. Ibid.

63. Gail C. Lerner, "Animals Packed Into Van; Driver Accused of Cruelty," Burlington

County, NJ: *The Burlington County Times*, 1 March 1983.

64. Frank Herrick, "Pet Cruelty Costs $4,980," Trenton, NJ: *The Trentonian*, 11 March 1983.

65. Charles Gerofsky, President of the New Jersey Society for the Prevention of Cruelty to Animals, in a personal communication to the Animal Welfare Institute.

66. Action 81, Berryville, VA: *Action 81 News*, December 1988.

67. Judith Reitman, "The Dog Mafia," *Penthouse*, February 1991.

Chapter 6

Class B Dealers Selling Non-Random Source Cats and Dogs for Research

CHARLES RIVER LABORATORIES, INC. Wilmington, Massachusetts. USDA license #14-B-013 (1997).

Charles River is the largest commercial research animal dealer in the United States, leading the industry as the major supplier of primates. The company breeds and sells animals through its subsidiaries in Japan, Germany, Italy, France and Great Britain. In 1982, USDA fined Charles River $3,500 for violating transport regulations. In 1984, Bausch & Lomb bought Charles River for $108 million. Bausch & Lomb is the tenth largest producer of scientific and photographic equipment in the U.S., with sales of $1.88 billion in 1993.[1,2]

Charles River sells rodents, dogs, cats, primates (colony-raised rhesus monkeys and imported wild-caught primates) and pigs. The company's colony-raised rhesus monkeys in Key Lois, Florida are descendants of a colony of rhesus monkeys captured in the Himalayas in 1972 by Charles River founder Dr. Henry Foster.[3]

The most recent figures show that Charles River had the following shares in various research animal markets: 48 percent of mice; 49 percent of rats; 48 percent of guinea pigs; and 50 percent of hamsters and gerbils. The company also had 42 percent of the colony-raised rhesus monkey and 41 percent of the imported primate markets.[4]

In addition to selling animals to private companies, Charles River derives a percentage of its sales from contracts with government agencies such as the National Institutes of Health (NIH). Thirty percent of its sales are from overseas accounts.

The growth of the biotechnology field has increased sales of mice and rats for new diagnostic and therapeutic products, and has led to greater demand for surgically altered animals. Charles River sells animals with pituitary or adrenal glands removed before delivery and an inbred, germ-free mouse that costs the equivalent of $750 a pound.[5]

In a speech before the New York Society of Security Analysts in 1979, Dr. Foster expressed his enthusiasm over the projected increase in toxicological testing on animals and what that would mean for the future of Charles River:

> If you read the papers, everything seems to have carcinogenic effects. But that means more animal testing, which means growth for Charles River... the use of more animals, and we believe, the use of more Charles River animals....

> Just let me take a few minutes and read you a list that rather excites us. It's a partial list of people who are building substantial facilities for laboratory animals.... A lot of those names are probably familiar to you, and probably surprise you as users of laboratory animals.

The list read by Dr. Foster included Lederle, Procter & Gamble, Shell Chemical, Exxon and Monsanto.

In fact, Charles River's growth fulfilled Dr. Foster's 1979 projections. Net sales in 1978 were $24.4 million; four years later, in 1982, net sales were $40.9 million. By 1989, sales were $75 million: $61.8 million from rats and mice; $5.5 million from guinea pigs; $1.3 million from hamsters and gerbils; $2.5 million from colony-raised rhesus monkeys; $1.5 million from imported primates; $1.7 million from miniature swine; $0.7 million from domestic swine.[6]

As of 1994, the Charles River empire consisted of the following sites:

Charles River, Wilmington, MA (Site #1)

Charles River Kingston, Stone Ridge, NY (Site #2)

Charles River Lakeview, Newfield, NJ (Site #3)

Charles River Portage, Portage, MI [Shaver Rd.] (Site #4)

Charles River Key Lois, Summerland Key, FL (Site #5)

Charles River Raccoon Island, Summerland Key, FL (Site #6)

Charles River Maine, Windham, ME (Site #7)

Charles River Pittsfield, Pittsfield, NH (Site #8)

Charles River Houston, Houston, TX (Site #12)

Barton's West End Farms, Oxford, NJ (Site #14)

Tufts University School of Veterinary Medicine, N. Grafton, MA (Site #15)

Charles River Portage, Portage, MI [Portage Rd.] (Site #16)

Mannheimer Primatological Foundation, Homestead, FL (Site #17)

University of Miami, Miami, FL (Site #18)

Sasco Oregon, Oregon, WI (Site #19)

Sasco Omaha, Omaha, NE (Site #20)

In 1982, Charles River admitted that for more than a year it had mistakenly filled orders for an inbred strain of mice (BALB/c) with mice of different genetic backgrounds. This "mix-up" came on the heels of a previous problem with genetically impure rats supplied to several customers, including Georgetown University in Washington, D.C.

Several research studies using the mixed BALB/c strain were invalidated, involving an estimated 1,000 experiments. The National Institutes of Health had to scrap four months of research and subsequently banned receipt of Charles River mice for several months.

The University of Wisconsin and Dr. Brenda Kahan sued Charles River for fraudulent misrepresentation. Kahan's nine months of work at the University using the BALB/c strain were invalidated. Charles River settled with the University of Wisconsin in 1984 by establishing a research fund of $40,000. The terms of its settlement with Kahan were not disclosed.[7]

USDA inspection reports have documented widespread non-compliance with Animal Welfare Act standards, particularly in transport of animals, cleanliness and safety of animal enclosures, and proper maintenance of facilities. Deficiencies commonly cited at Charles River's facilities are frequently due to inadequate maintenance of premises and insufficient numbers of employees necessary to maintain a regular schedule of cleaning and sanitation, particularly at the Summerland Key (Florida) monkey island sites.

Transport Deficiencies

Inspectors reported that a 6-8-74 shipment of monkeys from New York to Meloy Labs, Inc. in Springfield, Virginia held "No water container. 5 monkeys in one crate." On 9-16-74, while inspecting a shipment from New York to Microbiological Associates, inspectors reported: "monkeys in crate with little ventilation. Bottom fell out of crate. Patched up."

Several crates were cited for being in substandard condition in a 10-2-74 shipment of monkeys from New York to Flow Laboratories in Rockville, Maryland. The inspector noted: "Crates [were] falling apart. Metal strips coming off. No way to water."

On January 18, 1982, USDA issued Yale University a warning for a 7-22-81 shipment to Flow Laboratories in McLean, Virginia. The container

was deficient in several transportation standards of the Animal Welfare Act.... Ventilation... no ventilation openings located in the lower one-half of the container... lack[s] adequate handholds or lifting devices.... The cage utilized by Yale University in this alleged violation was obtained from Charles River Research Primates. This primate dealer has a number of alleged violations concerning the shipping standards for primates pending against them.

On December 10, 1982, Charles River was fined $3,500 for improperly transporting primates between July 10, 1979 and November 24, 1981. The shipments originated in New York with destinations in Southboro and Boston, Massachusetts; Buffalo and Albany, New York; and Cedar Rapids, Iowa.

USDA noted that "[The] crates... were too small and others... weren't sturdy. Loose wire and the size of wire mesh permitted the fingers and tails of the monkeys to protrude, allowing possible injury to both the monkeys and to persons who might come into close contact." Charles River accepted the penalties without admitting or denying the charges, advising USDA that it would "make a concerted effort to educate their employees in proper handling and care of monkeys."

On February 7, 1985, three squirrel monkeys died from exposure to extremely cold temperatures either before or during a flight from New York to the University of California in San Francisco. On the same day, a pigtail macaque was delivered to the University of Michigan, also dead of exposure to extreme cold, his body covered with frostbite.[8] The carrier in both cases was Emery Worldwide.

None of the parties involved—Charles River, Emery Worldwide or the University of California—notified USDA of the apparent Animal Welfare Act violations. The University of California merely asked Charles River to replace the dead monkeys; Charles River, in turn, demanded $1,250 in compensation from Emery Worldwide.[9]

The incident came to light when a whistleblowing Emery employee informed the Animal Welfare Institute that "Emery (at least at NYC-JFK) is not equipped to handle live animal shipments nor are personnel trained to see to the animals' health and safety.... Animals left unattended on a loading dock in subzero temperatures were almost certain to die."

The Emery employee enclosed copies of supporting documentation pertaining to the shipment. A letter dated February 20, 1985 from Dr. Daniel T. Lau, Clinical Veterinarian at the University of California, to Charles River confirmed the monkeys' cause of death:

> This... is in regards to the three squirrel monkeys (*Saimiri sciureus*) that were found dead on arrival in our facility on February 8, 1985.... Upon post mortem examination, all the dead animals had congested mucous membranes.... In my opinion they died due to

exposure to extreme cold temperature (Hypothermia). We are therefore requesting to obtain a replacement of these three animals from you as soon as possible.

On 3-31-92, inspectors reported: "A pig was shipped from Boston to Philadelphia with no written food and water instructions attached to the enclosure.... Written instructions should include when the animal is to be fed and watered and the appropriate diet."

A 9-2-93 inspection of an air shipment from Los Angeles (on Burlington Air Express) revealed: "One crate containing 2 pigs had no water container. Animals in transit since 10:00 on 9-1-93 (per notation on crate). Driver could not ascertain when animals last watered. Did not water at time of pickup."

Site Deficiencies

Inspections revealed deficiencies in housing, sanitation and veterinary care at Charles River facilities:

9-9-92: Site #1, Wilmington, Massachusetts (7,153 guinea pigs, 271 primates, 200 gerbils, 10 pigs, 32,552 mice and 45,206 rats) "Certain primates must be provided special attention regarding enhancement of their environment. 2 primates exhibiting abnormal behavior in primate room should be addressed in environmental enhancement plan along with any others showing such behavior even though enhancement efforts are undertaken." The housekeeping in the receiving area, guinea pig barrier room, and packing room was noted as inadequate."

11-15-93: Site #1, Wilmington, Massachusetts (540 guinea pigs, 53 pigs, 270 gerbils, 10,750 mice, and 18,920 rats) "Pig #2989 very thin condition. Pig #3508 has very generalized red/purple skin. Several pigs in facility have thickened dark, dry crusty skin. Pig #3393 has several scratches/wounds on rear end—no notations in records of cause and/or treatment."

The report also described dirty and damaged animal enclosure areas. "Pig area—severely damaged ceiling panels from leakage of water from ventilation (roof). Area 101 (Barrier facility guinea pigs). Several areas of damaged concrete visible from viewing area... [and] ceiling ductwork vents have buildup of dirt/dust on and around vent openings... [and have] standing water on floor next to animal enclosure rack."

Inspections of Site #2 in Stone Ridge, New York on 3-3-92 and 6-6-92 revealed space requirement deficiencies, and during an inspection of that same facility on 11-9-92, inspectors noted, "The primary enclosures for the guinea pigs in area 84 were excessively soiled with fecal material and the caretaker informed us that it had been approximately one month since they [had] been sanitized." Several noncompliant items were cited as uncorrected from a previous inspection. "One primary enclosure in area 84 was checked and it contained 13 guinea pigs weighing less than 350 grams... [in] 690 sq in of space. This provided each guinea pig 53.1 sq in of space. Guinea pigs weighing less than 350 grams must be provided at least 60 sq in."

On 12-21-93 and 12-22-93 (9,240 guinea pigs, 1,700 hamsters), inspectors wrote, "Approximately 40 primary enclosures containing hamsters were noted to have an accumulation of urine scale along the outside edge.... The autoclave room containing feed and shavings was noted to have mud on the floor, an accumulation of food pellets and excreta on the floor... and a buildup of old shavings on the areas protruding from the wall."

Inspectors noted sanitation deficiencies during a 6-8-92 inspection of Site #4, Portage, Michigan. (8,500 guinea pigs): "The floor is chipping leaving an unsealed surface which traps fecal material.... Many flies were seen in both guinea pig rooms.... The guinea pig enclosures are being sanitized only once every 3 to 4 weeks, instead of the required once every 2 weeks." On 2-9-94, the inspector noted that, "All of the rooms at this facility are barrier rooms and therefore were inspected through windows only."

During a 12-9-92 inspection of Site #5 in Key Lois, Florida (1,200 primates), inspectors reported: "The field cages have an unusually strong odor. They are not being raked and spot cleaned at sufficiently frequent intervals.... The cages' furnishings are soiled, and need upgraded surface cleaning, and worn surface maintenance.... Some of the buildings and structures are not in good repair.... These structures present hazards to the free roaming population, and must be <u>completely repaired</u> or <u>completely removed</u> .... Areas of noncompliance noted today appear to be related to an insufficient number of employees to maintain standards on this island" (underlined in original).

During inspections of Site #5 on 3-30-94 and 3-31-94 (1,240 primates), inspectors noted: "Singly housed juveniles require additional environmental enhancement. Cages are only provided perches placed at a level of the lower 1/3 of the cage. No toys or devices are provided.... Several PVC feeding tubes were dirty in the field cages.... The treatments for the primate in cage #20 are recorded on the blackboard, but are not being documented on the daily reporting sheets, which are then forwarded to the veterinarian." Noted as uncorrected from the 12-9-92 inspection, "Open bags of feed were again observed in cooler.... Old compound (compound 3) in free roaming area still present and in disrepair."

Inspectors also found deficiencies at Site #6, Raccoon Island, Florida (2,200 primates) during a 12-9-92 inspection: "Despite specific attention noted, the old grand cage is in continuous deterioration; stacks of old, stored rigid 'foam' is providing harborage for rodents; and the feeding platforms are deteriorating. These items should be completely repaired, or completely removed.... Areas of noncompliance noted today appear to be related to an insufficient number of employees." On 3-30-94 and 3-31-94, inspectors reported, "Veterinary care. No records were available to document the actual treatments for [monkey in cage number] F519.... Singly housed juveniles require additional environmental enrichment. Cages are only provided perches.... No toys or devices provided.... Numerous water valves were leaking inside the old feeding stations, creating large puddles of water underneath these stations. In addition, numerous puddles of green slimy water are around the entrances to these stations. The primates must pass through these puddles to gain entrance.... All old wooden feeders... have an accumulation of old fecal material and food wastes. These areas require more frequent cleanings." There were also items uncorrected from the previous inspection: "The feed shed roof is in disrepair. The roof is water stained and moldy. The... floors are not steady, and several metal poles have rusted through."

During an inspection of the Stone Ridge, New York site on 1-18-95 (15,285 guinea pigs, 12,116 hamsters), the inspector reported: "Many of the cages in room 84 containing approximately 7,000 guinea pigs had not been sanitized since December 20, 1994 and there was a buildup of excreta on the sides.... Many of the shoe boxes containing breeder hamsters had a buildup of urine scale on them. These enclosures need to be cleaned more thoroughly to remove scale."

HAZLETON RESEARCH PRODUCTS, INC. Denver, Pennsylvania. USDA license #23-B-053 (1997).

With over $65 million in sales, Hazleton is the third largest supplier of research animals in the United States. Hazleton buys and sells animals throughout the United States and abroad and maintains facilities in Denver and Robesonia, Pennsylvania; Cumberland, Virginia; Alice, Texas; and Kalamazoo, Michigan.

Hazleton sells guinea pigs; rabbits (conventional and specific pathogen free); dogs (purebred beagles and purpose-bred mongrels); and primates (colony-raised rhesus monkeys, crab-eating macaques, and African green monkeys). In business year 1993-1994, Hazleton reported selling 127, 632 animals.[10]

Hazleton's major competitor in the primate market is Charles River Laboratories. Hazleton sells 42 percent of its rhesus monkeys to the pharmaceutical industry, 40 percent to government and academia and the remainder to other companies in the health care industry. Hazleton's customers include Dow Chemical, Eli Lilly, Pfizer, Upjohn, Abbott Laboratories, and 3M.[11]

USDA inspectors have reported deficiencies in housing, sanitation and veterinary care at Hazleton's facilities. During an inspection on 8-24-88 (Cumberland, Virginia site. 10,096 dogs), inspectors reported, "Several cages had wooden dog houses that were too small for two large mongrel dogs to rest in comfortably. On 5-10-89 (Robesonia, Pennsylvania site), inspectors reported approximately 80 percent of the dogs were overcrowded. "There is still overcrowding in the shelter boxes used in the wire cages.... Drainage... is an ongoing problem with this facility."

In 1988, Hazleton purchased Laboratory Research Enterprises (LRE), one of the world's largest breeders of beagles for use in research. When Hazleton purchased LRE, it assumed the terms of a January 12, 1988 Consent Decision that stemmed from allegations by USDA that LRE failed to provide dogs with sufficient space. In the Consent Decision, LRE agreed to "renovate its existing facilities... so as to provide sufficient space in its primary enclosures for all dogs... within two years of the effective date of this order." LRE had not completed the renovations by the time Hazleton took over, and USDA granted Hazleton an extension, giving the company until 1-12-91 to come into compliance.[12]

Inspections of the Hazleton-LRE facility revealed chronic non-compliance not only with space requirements but with housing, sanitation and veterinary care standards:

7-13-89: (8,507 dogs, 24 cats) "The wire mesh on the floors of the enclosures are wide enough to allow some of the paw to be unsupported. This is causing, in some cases, severe injury to the interdigital areas of the paws. The older, heavier dogs are most affected. Approximately 40-50% of dogs in this age/weight category show signs of foot pathology. The young puppies cannot walk on the wires normally — many were observed having one or two legs fallen through and struggling to get back on their feet.... Dust and hair accumulations were found on most surfaces. Walls, doors, sink areas, and cabinets were noted to be splashed with hair, excreta, feed & grime.... Many dogs had been found to be in need of veterinary care that had not been reported by the animal care staff. More frequent and knowledgeable observation of animals is in order."

10-26-89: (4,746 dogs) "The wire mesh on the bottom of the enclosures is too wide. Portions of the paws slip through the mesh and become injured.... Although sanitation of enclosures and rooms is more frequent [it] is still not being done once every two weeks.... The housekeeping had improved — but still needs much more time and effort to bring the facility into compliance. Every room had splashed feces, hair, and food on the walls and doors."

1-17-90: (8,883 dogs) "Portions of the paws (or with puppies' entire legs) slip through the wire mesh on the enclosure bottoms and the paws become injured.... Some of the buildings... housed too many dogs per enclosure even though many cages were empty.... The enclosures are not being sanitized often enough—enclosures shall be sanitized at least once every 2 weeks."

4-5-90: (3,337 dogs) "Several dogs were noted to have injuries or symptoms of disease: Dog BB039 with a lesion on left front paw; Dog AVJ29 with a cyst lesion on the right rear paw; Dog DMAKT with a left eye discharge; Dog DMAKE with a left eye 'cherry eye.' And Dog DMBMC with a bilateral eye discharge.... A very strong odor was noted in Buildings 11, 8, 15 and 9. Odors can be minimized by increasing cleaning frequency or increasing fresh air flow.... The enclosure floor mesh openings are so large that portions of the paws are unsupported and the area between the toes becomes injured.... The primary enclosures are not being cleaned frequently enough to meet compliance."

Inspectors also reported deficiencies in veterinary care, housing and sanitation at Hazleton's other facilities:

5-25-90: Strasburg, Pennsylvania site (1,000 rabbits) "Observed two moribund rabbits. Caretaker had no means to humanely dispose of these animals. A method of euthanasia must be established at this site. To be corrected by May 30, 1990."

7-10-90: Cumberland, Virginia site (10,700 dogs) "One cage containing 3 mongrel dogs was measured. Cage = 3,240 sq. inches. Dogs require 4,184 sq. inches.... Enclosures were noted during this inspection to contain an excessive accumulation of feces and hair."

In a June 2, 1992 letter to USDA investigator Renee Clavin, Hazleton president David Valerio stated that the company renovated the old LRE buildings in 1989 and 1990 with the exception of Building 14, which was scheduled for re-caging later in 1992.[13] Despite the renovations, inspectors continued to report deficiencies in housing, sanitation and veterinary care:

1-9-91: (7,439 dogs) "The enclosure flooring has a mesh that is too large for small pups to walk normally without falling through.... Many dogs were found to be housed in enclosures which provide inadequate space per dog.... The primary enclosures are not being cleaned and sanitized frequently enough to be in compliance.... The run floors... were noted to be so slick that several dogs slipped and fell during the inspection. When asked, the caretaker said that falling injuries had been documented resulting from the slick flooring.... Bldg. 12... was in the process of being cleaned. Although the dogs were removed from the enclosure, it was found that they and other dogs were still getting wet from the hose spray. Adequate measures shall be taken to protect the animals from being contaminated with waste."

"When filling out health certificates and forms to send dogs interstate, required information was not included, such as adequate descriptions, driver's license #, USDA registration and if it was a sale, trade or donation.... Several dogs were noted to have abnormalities which were not noted on the medical records of the facility.... A mechanism of direct and frequent communication is required so that timely information on problems of animal health is conveyed to the veterinarian."

10-9-91: (1,194 dogs) "The enclosure floors have a mesh that is too large for the small pups to walk normally without falling through.... Many dogs were found to be housed in enclosures which provided inadequate space per dog.... The facility is not cleaning and sanitizing enclosures at least once every two weeks as per regulations. Urine scale is not being effectively removed in Buildings 3, 9, and 14.... Several dogs were found to have health problems which had not been found and recorded. Example: Dog JEX 8 RT eye problem, SR 65-RR limp and head shaking, RT 98 LF non-use of leg.... Building #3, 9, 14 had standing water/urine/feces in the troughs."

On the same day, a USDA inspector filed an alleged violation report, charging Hazleton with nine different violations, including failure to provide adequate veterinary care (on 10-9-91; 1-9-91; and 4-5-90); failure to provide adequate space for dogs (on 10-9-91; 1-9-91; 4-5-90; 1-17-90; and 10-26-89), and failure to provide proper sanitation, cleaning and housekeeping (10-9-91; 1-9-91; 4-5-90; 1-17-90; and 10-26-89).

In November, Assistant Northeast Sector Supervisor for Animal Care Jerry Dienhart requested an investigation into the alleged violations at the Hazleton-LRE facility. In his memo to John Kinsella of Regulatory Enforcement, Dr. Dienhart stated, "I am leaning toward a case, pending RE investigation."[14]

In December 1992, Hazleton accepted a stipulation offer from USDA in resolution of alleged violations cited between 1989 and 1992. Hazleton paid the $700.00 fine in 1993.

In June 1993, three Hazleton employees contacted People for the Ethical Treatment of Animals (PETA) after making unsuccessful reports to their supervisors about abuse of animals at the Kalamazoo facility. The three whistleblowers alleged that a lab technician had beaten, maimed and killed rabbits he was responsible for caring for at Hazleton.[15] Steven Stahr allegedly beat the rabbits if they scratched or struggled as he packed them for shipment. One employee stated he had seen Stahr throw rabbits against the wall and beat them with his fists. 'If one of them scratched him, it was dead,' the employee said. 'If he was mad at someone, he'd take it out on the animals."[16]

Three bodies of allegedly abused rabbits were taken to veterinarians in the Kalamazoo area and Michigan State University (MSU) to determine the causes of death. The MSU necropsy revealed the force of the blows sustained by one rabbit was so massive that the animal's liver had been "fractured."[17]

On August 31, PETA sent an 11-page letter of complaint to USDA, citing 26 alleged violations of the Animal Welfare Act. The alleged violations included causing trauma or unnecessary discomfort to animals, physical abuse in handling and not euthanizing diseased and/or injured animals who were beyond treatment. After interviewing Hazleton employees and obtaining documentation of several instances of abuse, the Kalamazoo County sheriff charged both Stahr and Hazleton with violating Michigan's anti-cruelty law.[18]

On June 9, 1994, Stahr pleaded no contest to the cruelty charges. He was fined $1,360, sentenced to two years of probation and ordered to seek counseling for his "violence and anger." His sentence also consisted of 250 hours of community service. Stahr was further barred from working or volunteering in positions involving contact with animals. In exchange for Stahr's no contest plea, the Kalamazoo County Prosecutor's Office dropped the charges against Hazleton. According to a deposition filed by Stahr, Hazleton fired him the day before he was sentenced but gave him $10,000, provided him with three months of health insurance and paid his legal fees. Stahr claimed he had planned to plead not guilty until Hazleton offered him the money.[19]

During an inspection of Hazleton's Denver, Pennsylvania site on 11-14-94, the inspector reported: "During inspection employee in room #2 of guinea pig area was noted to be tossing guinea pigs .... Animals shall not be handled in a manner that causes trauma, stress, harm or unnecessary discomfort."

USDA filed a complaint against Hazleton in June 1995, alleging that the company's employees handled animals in a manner that caused trauma, behavioral stress, physical harm and unnecessary discomfort. The complaint also charged Hazleton with failure to provide veterinary care to animals in need of care; failure to construct and maintain primary enclosures for animals so as to provide sufficient space to allow each animal to make normal postural adjustments; failure to keep food receptacles for animals clean and sanitized; failure to keep primary enclosures for dogs clean and sanitized; and failure to construct primary enclosures for dogs so that the opening in the wires of the cages prevented the dogs' legs from passing through. On November 8, 1995, Hazleton signed a consent decision and order agreeing to pay a $25,000 fine and to cease and desist from violating the Animal Welfare Act.

WRIGLEY, GLEN G. d/b/a BUCKSHIRE CORPORATION. Perkasie, Pennsylvania. USDA license #23-B-002 (1997).

Owned by Glen Wrigley and his wife Sharon Hursh, Buckshire Corporation was first licensed by USDA in 1967 as a Class A dealer. Now a Class B dealer, the company is a major supplier of animals used in research. In 1986, Buckshire signed a consent decision and order agreeing to pay a $450 penalty in settlement of USDA's charge that it had violated the Animal Welfare Act. Buckshire signed a second consent decision and order in 1994, agreeing to pay a $2,000 penalty in settlement of charges filed by USDA in a 1993 complaint. USDA filed another complaint against Buckshire in 1996. A hearing on the charges included in that complaint is still pending.

Buckshire operates three sites in Pennsylvania: the Lab Rab rabbit breeding facility in Westfield, the Hemlock holding facility at Columbia Crossroad, and the Perkasie facility. A fourth site is located in Miami, Florida.

The company markets dogs (beagles and purpose-bred mongrels), advertising its "Buckshire mongrels" as having short hair and a "large chest" and notes that all mongrel puppies are "tail docked at three days of age." Buckshire also sells pigs (miniature and domestic swine), primates (imported and colony-raised rhesus macaques, marmosets and chimpanzees); sheep, goats and cats. Rabbits, however, are their top-selling animals.

In 1989, Buckshire had a 9.0 percent share of the rabbit market; 14.5 percent of the cat market; 9.0 percent of the colony-raised rhesus monkey market; 8.0 percent of the imported primate market; 32.0 percent of miniature pig and 2.5 percent of domestic pig market. In 1987, Buckshire sold 21,734 animals, grossing $1,044,176.[20]

Buckshire's customers have included Alcon Laboratories, Humana Hospital and Lackland Air Force Base (Texas); Amira, Harvard Medical School, Massachusetts Eye and Ear Infirmary, Massachusetts General Hospital, the Massachusetts Institute of Technology, Tufts Medical Center and the Veterans Administration Medical Center (Massachusetts); the University of Maryland in Baltimore; Boys Town National Research Hospital (Nebraska); Eli Lilly (Indiana), the University of California at San Francisco and SRI International (California); Yale University and the University of Connecticut (Connecticut); Bush Boake Allen, Quest International, Schering-Plough Research Institute and Dragsco (New Jersey); Dartmouth Medical School (New Hampshire); Rockefeller University (New York); Allegheny General Hospital, Biosearch, Thomas Jefferson University and the University of Pittsburgh (Pennsylvania); SC Johnson Wax (Wisconsin); Louisiana State Medical Center; the University of Alabama and the Schepens Eye Research Institute.

Buckshire also does business with licensed Class B dealer Mary Ulrich of Cheri-Hill Kennel in Michigan.[21]

Inspection reports show chronically substandard conditions and numerous deficiencies at Buckshire's facilities, including untreated, sick and/or injured cats and dogs; incompatible pairing of animals; overcrowding and lack of protection from rain, wind and sun.

During a 1-16-85 inspection of the Perkasie facility, inspectors reported, "Several primary enclosures were observed in the puppy areas which do not have sufficient space for the dogs housed in them."

On 7-2-85 at the Hemlock Creek Farm site, lack of shelter from the elements was cited as a major deficiency: "Whelping area—there is no adequate way of controlling the temperature in this building.... These housing facilities provide very little if any shade from direct sunlight. Majority of these housing facilities are out in the yards with no means of shade—artificial or natural.... Back kennel—this will become a problem during the fall and winter months. These kennels are open in the front with no shelter from the cold wind and rain." Buckshire stated it would stop using this area after 8/24/86.

On 5-22-85, the inspector noted: "25 rabbits are in cages lacking sufficient space; 6 lb. rabbits are in cage with space 180 square inches; 10 lb. rabbits are in cage with 288 square inches instead of 540 square inches." Insufficient space for 25 large rabbits was cited again on the 5-24-85 inspection. At its "Lab Rab" facility, on 9-30-85, the report cited "21 rabbits deficient in space by 108 inches."

In 1986, Buckshire paid a $450 civil penalty without admitting or denying USDA allegations that it provided substandard, poorly ventilated, unsanitary housing for approximately 219 dogs held at its Hemlock Creek Farm in Pennsylvania between February 27, 1985 and April 23, 1985.

Subsequent inspections revealed continuing deficiencies in housing, veterinary care and sanitation:

3-18-86: (500 dogs) "Dogs housed in outdoor runs need additional shelter to protect them from cold weather"; 6-17-86: "Dogs housed in outdoor areas will need additional shelter to protect them from cold weather when cold weather returns"; 6-9-87: "Puppy IXA3 observed to be weak and dehydrated. This pup should be moved to another kennel (isolated) and treated and/or euthanized." On the next inspection of 1-6-88, it was noted that the puppy had died at a clinic following treatment.

On 12-20-88, inspectors discovered three dogs in need of veterinary care, including a beagle with "severe corneal ulcers in both eyes," a dog with conjunctivitis in one eye, and a white lab with bleeding from the ear "due to trauma inflicted by another dog." "A bitch currently delivering a litter has

3 wounds on the upper left leg.... 1 wound is open and raw."

The inspectors also cited gross fecal contamination of dogs and their surroundings: "Feeder without lid has feces in it.... The dogs in many of the runs have feces all over them because the feces are hosed out of the runs and the dogs dance in the residue. The runs are not squeegeed and remain wet hours after cleaning."

On 12-28-88, inspectors reported, "Many of the water dishes have feces in them and the dogs are drinking the water."

During a 3-22-90 inspection of Buckshire's Hemlock Creek Farm, inspectors noted, "Presently several [drains] are plugged and waste from food and the animals is running out on top of the ground." In barn 2, several dog cages were overcrowded; all the adult dogs were housed in cages which were only two-thirds of regulation size. In the whelping barn, several cages with broken floor supports allowed puppies to escape and become caught between the floor and cage door.

A 4-24-90 inspection of Buckshire's Miami primate facility revealed noncompliance with housing regulations: "At least 3 large adult macaques were in lab type cages that were too small for the comfort of these individuals.... Many animals are now housed in several rows of steel... cages.... The rows of single cages extend all way to the edge of the open-ended barn. Thus, animals in the end cages would not be properly sheltered from blowing rain."

On 5-19-92, inspectors reported numerous deficiencies in housing and veterinary care at the Perkasie facility (221 dogs, 275 cats, 800 rabbits, 259 primates). Primates situated in four rooms were "in need of dental care, tartar build-up on teeth. Attending veterinarian should develop dental care program within current program of veterinary care.... Primates in rooms A-7, Cage 25 appeared withdrawn, depressed" with evidence of "hair loss due to overgrooming.... Primate plan should address steps taken to enrich environment of particular species, by providing noninjurious species-typical activities and documenting process.... In Rm. B-26, primary enclosures housing 3 cats had resting surface... only allowing 2 cats to rest comfortably.... Observed 2 queens without resting surface in primary enclosure [in rm. B-21]. Each cat over weaning age must be provided a resting board."

Inspectors reported continuing deficiencies in veterinary care at the Perkasie site during a 1-26-93 inspection: "4 kittens in Runs 13, 10 and 9 showing signs of an upper respiratory condition, such as labored breathing, crusty eyes, and runny noses. Presently animals are receiving airborne treatment, but affected animals are not isolated from the rest of the colony.... Primate medical records need to clarify what type treatments, observations made pertaining to psychological wellbeing, and clearly document what's actually being done. Mechanisms must be in place to accurately [report] problems of animal health, behavior and general wellbeing to attending veterinarian."

In November 1993, USDA charged Buckshire with violating several sections of the Animal Welfare Act between January and August 1992. Alleged violations included failure to provide adequate veterinary care; failure to provide uncontaminated and accessible food; failure to provide regular and frequent food and animal waste disposal; failure to maintain a prescribed level of husbandry; failure to maintain a dog exercise program; failure to provide sufficient space and failure to control pests. On March 25, 1994, Buckshire signed a consent decision and order agreeing to pay a $2,000 fine and to cease and desist from violating the Animal Welfare Act.

In April 1996, USDA filed another complaint against Buckshire, charging the company with failure to maintain complete records showing the acquisition and disposition of animals; failure to individually identify cats; failure to provide adequate veterinary care; failure to provide for the regular and frequent collection, removal and disposal of animal and food wastes; failure to provide sufficient lighting in indoor housing facilities for nonhuman primates; failure to maintain structurally sound primary enclosures for cats; failure to construct and maintain primary enclosures for cats so as to provide sufficient space; failure to keep water receptacles for dogs clean and sanitized; failure to keep the premises in good repair and clean and free of trash and waste; failure to provide dogs in outdoor facilities with adequate protection from the elements; and failure to adequately ventilate facility for nonhuman primates to provide for the health and comfort of the animals at all times. A hearing on the charges is still pending.

Notes

1. Ellen Benoit, "Through a Glass Slowly,"*Financial World*, v. 158, n. 24, 28 November 1989.

2. Robert Famighetti, editor, *The World Almanac and Book of Facts 1995* (New Jersey: Funk & Wagnalls, 1994).

3. Allan T. Demaree, "Henry Foster's Primately-for-Profit Business," *Fortune*, 10 April 1978.

4. Theta Corporation, Research Animal Markets, Report No. 982 (Middlefield, CT: Theta Corporation, September 1989).

5. Allan T. Demaree, "Henry Foster's Primately-for-Profit Business."

6. Theta Corporation, Research Animal Markets, Report No. 982.

7. The Animal Welfare Institute, *The Animal Welfare Institute Quarterly*, v. 32, n. 3, Fall 1983.

8. Richard A. Lyons, Treasurer of Charles River, in a letter dated 4 March 1985 to Walter Szumilo, Emery Worldwide, New York. "We hereby make claim for the following shipments.... 2 Squirrel Monkeys @ $350.00 each, 1 Pigtail Monkey @ $200.00 each."

9. Ibid.

10. Hazleton Research Products, Inc., USDA-APHIS Application for License, 5 July 1995.

11. People for the Ethical Treatment of Animals, *Research and Investigations Annual Review for*

1993, (Washington, D.C.: People for the Ethical Treatment of Animals, 1993).

12. Dr. Valencia D. Colleton, Northeast Sector Supervisor for REAC, in a letter to Russell D. Robinson, Director, Hazleton Research Products, Inc., 13 July 1990.

13. David A. Valerio, President, Hazleton Research Products, in a letter to Renee S. Calvin, Investigator, USDA, 2 June 1992.

14. Gerald B. Dienhart, Assistant Sector Supervisor, Northeast Sector-AC, in a memo to John Kinsella, Sector Supervisor, Northeast Sector-RE, 21 November 1991.

15. People for the Ethical Treatment of Animals, "Workers Blow the Whistle at Hazleton," *PETA News*, Winter 1993.

16. Michael D. Evans, "Plant Worker Faces Animal Cruelty Charges," Kalamazoo, MI: *Kalamazoo Gazette*, 27 October 1993.

17. "Workers Blow the Whistle at Hazleton," *PETA News*, Winter 1993.

18. Michael Evans, "Plant Worker Faces Animal Cruelty Charges," Kalamazoo, MI: *Kalamazoo Gazette*, 27 October 1993.

19. Kelley Quinn, "Animal Rights Group Protests Corning Inc. Subsidiary," Corning, NY: *Corning Leader*, 28 July 1994.

20. Theta Corporation, Research Animal Markets, Report No. 982.

21. PETA Factsheet: Buckshire Corporation.

Chapter 7

Class B Dealers Who Have Lost or Relinquished their Licenses

ADKINS, LEONA J. (ADKINS KENNEL). Caldwell, Ohio. USDA license #31-B-020 (last licensed in 1996).

Adkins supplied dogs to Class B dealer Andy Ball and had an annual volume of 500 dogs, according to USDA's 1994 report on annual sales of Class B dealers. USDA inspections revealed deficiencies in housing, sanitation, veterinary care, recordkeeping and adherence to holding period requirements at Adkins's facility:

7-9-91: (39 dogs) "The dogs are not kept 10 days excluding day of acquisition and the day of disposition."

8-14-91: (46 dogs listed, 41 dogs on site) "Tether dog #128 had food container that was unprotected from rain. Tether dog nos. 121 and 62 had unprotected food containers. One container was a used paint roller pan (bent) and the other was a hubcap. These are not appropriate food containers for dogs.... Tethered dogs' water receptacle were rusted coffee cans. This cannot be properly sanitized. Tethered dogs 128 and 62 had no water. At the request of the inspector, water was provided and these dogs drank vigorously.... Need to have complete records on all dogs. The following dogs #55, 73, 209, 212 and 113 records of disposition were missing.... Dealers must develop, <u>document</u> and follow an appropriate plan to provide dogs with the opportunity for exercise" (underlined in original).

4-1-92: (14 dogs) "No supplemental heat was provided inside the sheltered kennel. Inside temperature was 45°F and outside temperature was 40°F. Additional supplemental heating must be provided when temperature goes below 45°F." Noncompliant items uncorrected from previous inspection: "Dog #473 which arrived on 1-23-92 did not have a record of disposition.... There is no written plan provided for exercise. This plan has not been written and approved by the attending veterinarian."

1-28-93: (29 dogs) "Underneath all pens (1-16) there is excessive fecal buildup.... Pen 2 had fecal material in nestbox shavings."

1-13-94: (23 dogs) No Program of Veterinary Care was found on inspection. Other deficiencies were noted: "All water receptacles have excessive rust... and have not been maintained.... The amount of rust is excessive and must be repaired for all enclosures.... No supplemental heat was provided inside sheltered kennels. Inside temperature taken by inspector was 37° F. Outside temp is 32°F.... Water receptacles do not contain potable water. Two water receptacles were felt by hand and had thick scum, black and brownish in color. Water is very murky and tinged grey with particles of food.... There are numerous fresh rodent tracks in the snow with many fresh rodent trails worn slick from activity around the end of facility and numerous large rodent holes surround this building.... More aggressive rodent control is needed.... Acquisition records from Dogtown pound and dealer disposition records do not contain adequate identification records for each dog."

Noncompliant items not corrected from the previous inspection: "Pens 1-16 have excessive feces buildup. Uncorrected. Pound certificates do not identify dogs by color and type or distinguishing marks.... There was one blue tick cross with Aussie and no description of dog. This dog was not reidentified by Adkins Kennel before being sold."

2-17-94: (23 dogs) "Program of veterinary care is incomplete and lacks the emergency veterinarian's address and emergency telephone number.... One dog #1320 has right front leg injury and tendons are exposed (3/4 of limb). Dog is to be euthanized by emergency vet.... Daily observations of all dogs must be done.... No record of this injury in file and no treatments."

Documentation of dogs acquired from pounds was insufficient in many respects. "Pound certificates lack address of Noble County pound [and] lack address of Adkins Kennel and signature of dealer (Mrs. Adkins).... [Also] lack complete description of 'cur'. There is no color and distinct markings or scars if present. Markings must indicate right or left side of animal.... Pound certificates lack age of dog as accurate as possible.... Pound certificate must have statement that dog might be used for research or education."

3-15-94: (25 dogs) "Pound certificates lack address of Noble Co. Pound.... Pound certificates lack address and USDA no. and signature of dealer Andy Ball... [and] Statement that dog will be used for research."

5-9-95: (30 dogs) " (1) Dog #22055 has mucous thickened in eyes. (2) Dog #22045 has thick mucous in both eyes and has a dry-rasp cough indicating some respiratory problems. (3) Dog #22009 has pale mucous membranes with greyish tinge. Skin turgor indicates dehydration. Dog is weak, very thin and has gaunt look and unstable gait from weakness.... These dogs need evaluation by dealer and attending veterinarian.... There is no reporting system in place for sick animals to be discussed with attending veterinarian. There are <u>no</u> veterinary medical records kept for sick or ill animals."

1-2-96: (23 dogs) "Pen 16 has excessive piles of feces in outdoor floor screen area.... Pens 5, 6 and 8 also have inside shelter compartment with excessive feces in floor area. It is so excessive that dogs must walk in feces to come to drink or eat from food receptacle.... Primary enclosures of pen 16, pen 5, and 8 have excessive fecal buildup.... Pens 5, 6, 8 and 16 have outdoor and indoor area of shelter with excessive feces accumulation. All feces must be removed daily. This has not been done."

In 1996, Adkins requested USDA to terminate her license.

BARNFIELD, BRUCE, (BAR WAN FARMS). Iberia, Missouri. USDA license #43-B-060 (last licensed in 1993).

The Barnfield family held both a Class A and a Class B license for three decades. Bruce Barnfield was formerly listed with his parents, Lester and Wanda Barnfield, as a co-owner under their Class A license (#43-A-517). Both "A" and "B" licensed sites were located on the same premises. In 1990, USDA charged Barnfield with violating the Animal Welfare Act and suspended his Class B license for one year.

Barnfield reported on his 1986 USDA annual report that he grossed $101,000 from the sale of 650 animals. His customers included Monsanto, 3M Corporation, Searle Pharmaceuticals, Wyeth-Ayerst, Medtronic, Merrell Dow, American Critical Care and the University of Iowa.[1] Barnfield bought dogs at the Rutledge, Missouri auction. USDA's 1990 Midwest Stolen Dog Task Force cited Barnfield for keeping inadequate records and recording false or fictitious names and vehicle identification numbers for his suppliers. Investigators discovered that Class B dealer Henry Lee Cooper (C and C Kennels, Wewoka, Oklahoma, license #73-B-130) sold six dogs to Barnfield in 1990 even though he was unlicensed at the time.

During a prelicensing inspection (prior to transfer of Wanda Barnfield's Class B license to Bruce) on 10-29-85, inspectors reported: "Need better waste removal system than just covering fecal material with gravel.... No individual identification on any dog or cat on premises.... No record on any dog or cat present.... Many of the dogs were wet and shivering and no bedding was present in the shelter. The temperature was 45 degrees Fahrenheit and dropping."

In 1985, Lester and Wanda Barnfield consented to an administrative law judge's order to pay a $15,000 civil penalty. USDA had charged the Barnfields with selling dogs without a proper license and failing to file the required reports on their volume of business.

Subsequent inspections revealed continuing deficiencies in veterinary care, housing and sanitation:

6-22-87: (505 dogs) "Veterinary care: One dog is lying prostrate and the owner says it is having a reaction to a worm shot.... All the primary enclosures are of older, hutch-type outdoor construction using wood and wire. There are 400 in use at this time. About 30 percent need work done on frames, wire flooring, or roofing at this time.... Water bowls dirty and need cleaning.... There is not sufficient space for some of the dogs to maintain normal postural positions. About 20 dogs could not stand straight legged without their backs touching the tops of the cages.... There were about 20 larger dogs that had sore feet from standing on a wire bottom cage.... Records did not have name and address of seller."

8-19-87: (555 dogs) "There is not sufficient space for some of the dogs to maintain normal postural position. Dogs could not stand straight legged without their backs touching the top of the cages. Many of the pens have excess waste under them causing unsanitary buildup.... Dogs that had sore feet from standing on a wire bottom cage... Feed pans were dirty and rusty."

9-24-87: (455 dogs, 85 puppies) "Several of the pens (about 20% of over 400) still have an excess waste under them, causing unsanitary buildup... Pans either dirty or rusty and need cleaning or replacement." Among other uncorrected deficiencies, USDA noted "eight individual dogs who could not stand normally and 23 other pens where the dogs were too tall for their enclosures." Inspectors noted that transportation enclosures were too small for the dogs: "With dogs as high as 35" the postural movement requirements cannot be met if they are shipped in the available enclosures which measure 19" high and 23" high in the vehicles seen."

1-28-88: "Continual violation of space [requirements] with too tall dogs in too short of kennel.... Continual violations in record keeping.... Records did not match the dogs in the pen or USDA tag number in 3 out of 4 dogs sampled by Dr. Allen."

3-7-90: "When buying from licensed dealers, be sure to write seller's license or registration number on records. If seller is not licensed under the [Animal Welfare] Act, the vehicle license number and state, and the driver's license number and state of seller must be recorded on your records. Also be sure to put the year of dates recorded on your records. To be corrected immediately and on all future purchases."

USDA filed a complaint against Barnfield on June 29, 1990, charging him with failing to maintain housing facilities for dogs in a structurally sound condition and in good repair; failing to make provisions for the removal and disposal of animal wastes; failing to provide dogs kept outdoors with shelter from rain or snow; failing to provide sufficient space for dogs in primary enclosures; failing to keep food and water receptacles clean and sanitized; failing to keep premises clean; failing to individually identify animals; and failing to maintain records of the acquisition, disposition, description and identification of animals, as required. On March 29, 1991, Barnfield signed a consent decision and order suspending his Class B license for one year.

Throughout 1992 and 1993, inspectors continued to document deficiencies in recordkeeping and housing:

5-7-92: (81 dogs) "All outdoor hutch type enclosures housing dogs need a front wall added to the dog box.... 3 water buckets... have been chewed and have jagged edges and sharp edges. These buckets need replacing.... Owner needs a new written program for veterinary care. Correct by 6-7-92.... Dog #4025 was in a pen that did not allow enough height for the dog to stand in a normal manner."

1-13-93: (77 dogs) "Several dogs are not tagged. Tags need to be placed on the animals. 4-month and 9-month old puppies also need to be identified.... Inventory of dogs and cats forms — Several individuals that dogs were obtained from do not have complete addresses given. Complete addresses, drivers license and license plate numbers need to be recorded"; 6-9-93: (12 dogs) "Several cages need repair, i.e., chewed front of dog houses.... Several cages need accumulation of waste underneath pens removed."

USDA terminated Barnfield's license in 1994 after he failed to submit a renewal application and pay the required license fee.

BEISE, GARY M. (BEISE KENNELS). Jordan, Minnesota. USDA license #41-B-142 (last licensed in 1994).

At one time, both Delores and Melvin Beise held Class B licenses. They operated two sites—one in Hastings, Minnesota and the other in Jordan. Their son, Gary, became sole licensee in 1988. Beise sold between 700 and 900 animals a year.

In the 1960s, advertisements for Beise Kennels stated: "Don't dump your dogs or cats off on highways. Bring them to Beise Kennels, Hastings. No charge. They have feelings, too. We find new homes for them."[2] The fact that the Beises sold animals for research was not mentioned.

Dorothy Dyce, laboratory animal specialist with the Animal Welfare Institute, visited Beise Kennels (Hastings site) in July of 1965. "Conditions here on my visit in summer of 1965 were equally as bad as they are in Jordan Kennel," wrote Dyce. "Both kennels are run by the same family. Both sell to

University of Minnesota." Dyce also visited the Jordan site: "On visit to this dealer in January of this year found puppies and other animals housed in unheated building. The temperature was 18 below zero the night before. Water in their water dishes was frozen solid."

In February 1989 an APHIS veterinary inspector received a letter from an individual who visited Beise Kennels and was distressed by the seemingly poor condition of the dogs and allegedly suspicious business practices:

> On 17 February 1989 four adults went to Beise Kennel and were refused admittance to the barn — Gary said "My inspector told me not to admit anybody".... They asked to adopt some animals so three dogs were presented; white shep cross, Bernese mountain dog & shep-Lab. cross — from which [Gary] removed the U.S.D.A. Tags.... He charged.... Gave no receipt for their cash payment.... While there the animals in barn were fighting violently — screams, whining. All such noises as accompany an animal fight.

Someone in the group saw a young Collie and asked to buy her. Beise told them to come back on February 21, but when they returned, Beise refused to give the dog up. "He said she was sick," the letter stated. "He admitted she was hurt in a fight." The writer claimed the dog had puncture wounds on her head and bleeding eyes and nose. According to the letter, Beise again refused to give her up several days later, claiming her wounds had not healed.[3]

During an inspection of Beise Kennels on 12-26-89 (16 dogs listed, 57 dogs on site, 8 cats listed, 10 cats on site), inspectors reported: "There were 4 pups in single cages. These animals are overcrowded. Animals should be moved to larger quarters or separated and placed into individual cages... Cat litter boxes needed to be cleaned.... Some puppies did not have identification on their necks but on the cages.... There are dogs in the kennel not listed on the records."

On November 11, 1990, USDA received a phone call from a veterinary technician who had gone to Beise's kennels to purchase a dog:

> [The caller] Went to purchase dog. Red bone coon hound. 8 months old. 20 lbs., no muscle control — couldn't stand up.... Told that the dog was underweight because he was in a pen with many dogs and didn't get enough food. Caller said he offered to take the dog and put it out of its misery. Was told the research people would be there on Thursday and take the dog and pay [amount not disclosed] for it.[4]

On 3-7-91, more than one year after USDA had last visited Beise Kennels, inspectors noted: "Noncompliant regulations that were identified on last inspection, but unable to determine if corrected this inspection....

Records not available for review.... South side far west run has sheet metal pulled away from wall exposing jagged edges.... All dog runs had areas of peeling paint or areas of scratched or chewed paint causing a surface which is not impervious to moisture."

On June 13, USDA's Richard Watkins filed an alleged violation report against Beise, charging him with failure to maintain premises free of debris and failure to maintain surfaces that were impervious to moisture. On the first page of the report Watkins wrote: "Mr. Beise has completely redone the outside of the building and is now working on the inside. Half of the kennels (west side) have just been repainted. I would like to go with only a warning letter and check back in 60-90 days."

In a September 19, 1991 letter to Beise, Dr. Jerry Diemer, USDA Supervisor for Animal Care, wrote: "On the last USDA inspection of your facility conducted June 13, 1991... there were several noncompliant items documented which also appeared on the previous inspection of December 26, 1989 and March 7, 1991." Diemer went on to state that current USDA policy was "to encourage compliance through education and cooperation rather than legal action" and that no further action would be taken at that time in reference to the apparent violations. Diemer warned Beise that "if similar problems are documented on subsequent inspections, we will be forced to take appropriate legal action against you."

During an inspection on July 15, 1992, the inspector documented additional deficiencies: "Dog runs on north side of kennels have areas of scratched and peeling paint.... Excreta should be removed underneath cages as often as necessary to prevent accumulation of waste.... The litter pan under the end cat cage had an excess of feces and hair.... Several cats did not have ID tags on collars around their necks and were not tattooed."

Dr. Diemer sent Beise another warning letter on April 23, 1993, again citing failure to maintain surfaces that were impervious to moisture and again stating that no further action would be taken on account of USDA's policy "to encourage compliance through education and cooperation rather than legal action."

USDA terminated Beise's license in 1995 after he failed to submit a renewal application and pay the required license fee.

CLAXON, RON (TRI-STATE BIOMEDICAL). Garrison, Kentucky. USDA license #61-B-110 (last licensed in 1995).

Claxon sold approximately 1000 animals a year to research facilities and other Class B dealers, including LBL Kennels (Indiana), South Jersey

Biological Farm (Pennsylvania), Meridia Huron Hospital (Ohio), Mt. Sinai Medical Center (Ohio) and Ohio State University. In 1993, Claxon paid a $600 stipulation fine after USDA charged him with violating the Animal Welfare Act. USDA inspection reports revealed Claxon's chronic noncompliance with recordkeeping, sanitation and veterinary care regulations.

On 1-11-91, just a few months after Claxon first became licensed as a dealer, an APHIS inspector reported: "A) USDA tags are not being used in numerical order. B) Drivers license number and vehicle tag numbers were not obtained. C) Form 18-6 not completed — needs to include buyer's name, address and license number. D) Dog # USDA tag 427 was not recorded in records.... All transport primary enclosures need to allow for normal postural adjustments. Health certificates required for interstate movement." On 2-6-91, the inspector, accompanied by Regulatory Enforcement investigator Mike Nottingham, took photographs of Claxon's premises and made photocopies of his records. On his inspection report, the inspector noted, "Records — some names are not accompanied with vehicle tag number. Licensee should not buy dog until full information can be obtained. Holding period — some records were without acquisition date."

The inspector submitted an alleged violation report on 2-25-91. Noting he had given Claxon explicit instructions on recordkeeping requirements (even leaving filled-out forms for him to use as models) during the final prelicensing inspection of 11-6-90, the inspector stated Claxon was not providing complete information on dog acquisition and disposition records:

> I took the time again to explain the importance of accurate recordkeeping to Ron Claxon. The week preceding my last inspection of 2-5-91, I received numerous public and licensee complaints concerning Ron Claxon's Trade Day activities, transporting methods, and health certificates. This prompted my inspection on 2-5-91. Records were again noted as deficient, and we xeroxed all records from 12-21-90 through 2-5-91. I became suspicious that the acquisition records were fabricated. I mailed official letters to 17 people Ron Claxon had obtained dogs from as recorded on his 18-5s. To this date, I have received 5 back stamped "insufficient address" or "no such address."[5]

Soon after the inspector filed his report, USDA requested a formal investigation of Claxon. In June, investigator Nottingham sent a report of his findings to Dr. Richard Overton: "It appears Mr. Claxon used fraudulent names and addresses on official documents VS Form (18-5), which is in violation of the Animal Welfare Act."[6] Attached to the report were affidavits of two of the five listed suppliers whose envelopes were returned to the inspector. They both confirmed their sales of puppies to Claxon. In his own affidavit, Claxon attributed his poor recordkeeping to lack of time. "In my haste of purchasing dogs, I failed to get some of the information," he stated.

"I was shown the 5 returned envelopes marked insufficient address. I know all these people and did buy dogs from them. I will try to get the correct address of the 5 people."[7]

On 7-8-91, USDA sent Claxon an Official Notification and Warning for his "failure to make, keep and maintain records or forms which fully and correctly disclose information as required" by federal regulation for the period between 1-1-90 and 2-2-91.

During an inspection of Claxon's facility on 10-1-91, the inspector reported: "Records show licensee shipped 41 dogs at one time, yet only 8 transport cages were inspected. I have serious doubts that 41 dogs can be transported and hold to minimum space requirements.... Acquisition of dogs and cats form not complete. Many dogs sold but not recorded as such. Records show many more dogs on premises than were present.... Noncompliant standards addressed 7-9-91 and still not corrected: Acquisition records were missing city, state, and zip codes for some sellers and missing zip codes on others. On form 18-6, buyer's or receiver's license numbers not recorded."

On 2-20-92, the inspector noted: "Licensee feeding raw human garbage along with regular pelleted feed.... Four living dogs and one dead dog with no identification or tag.... Holding period not met with dogs 1738, 1692, 1693, 1694. Also, bottom portions of 18-6 Disposition Forms not filled out.... 18 dogs in facility — 28 on record — [Form] 18-6 does not match inventory.... One dead dog found on premises. All dogs need proper vet care or humane euthanasia.... Licensee not home when called during business hours. Licensee must allow full inspection."

On 6-3-92, the inspector reported: "Excessive feces accumulation underneath wire cages.... Form 7006 Disposition of dogs is not completely filled out. Some are missing buyer's USDA # and some have boxes 9-13 left blank.... Also number of dogs listed on form 7006 does not match number of dogs on health certificates.... Noncompliant standards found on 2-20-92 and still not corrected this date.... Dogs on premises are not receiving adequate veterinary care. Dogs #2001, 2143, 2239, 2197 and 2221 need immediate veterinary care.... Also number of dogs listed on 18-5 (35) does not match number of dogs inspected."

Inspectors filed four separate alleged violation reports against Claxon on 6-3-92, citing failure to provide health certificates for animals shipped out of state; failure to provide adequate veterinary care and veterinary care records; and failure to hold dogs the required length of time. On 6-18-92, an inspector sent Richard Overton copies of the alleged violation reports regarding Claxon's health certificate violations. "Ron Claxon already has received a [warning notice] since he was issued a license in November 1990," wrote the inspector in a memo to Overton. "[Inspection reports] show chronic recordkeeping problems, holding period violations, and a blatant disregard for accurate interstate health certificates and adequate veterinary care. There are sixteen documented violations of interstate health certificates, one count of holding period and one count of access [to] property and records.... I recommend a stipulation based on a cumulative addition of all counts."[8]

Dr. Walker requested a full investigation of Claxon on June 25. Investigator Nottingham sought information on Claxon's shipment of dogs into Indiana, Ohio and Pennsylvania from investigators Kent Permentier (IN), Don Castner (OH) and William Swartz (PA). In his requests for information, Nottingham noted there had been reports that animals coming from Claxon's facility were not accompanied by health certificates and that some of the animals were in poor condition.[9] Nottingham asked the investigators to obtain affidavits from Claxon's customers, including LBL Kennels in Indiana, Mt. Sinai Medical Center in Cleveland and Gregory Fedechko of South Jersey Biological Farm in Pennsylvania.

In his signed affidavit, Mark D. Lynch of LBL Kennels stated that of 101 dogs sold to him by Claxon during a four month period, 28 had not been accompanied by health certificates.[10] Gregory Fedechko signed an affidavit stating: "At times the identification listed in the APHIS form 7006 or VS Form 18-6 does not correspond with the identification listed on the health certificates."[11]

In his own affidavit, Claxon explained that the reason some of the dogs he transported lacked health certificates was that after taking a group of dogs to his veterinarian to obtain the certificates he occasionally returned home and loaded more dogs onto his truck before driving across state lines.[12]

An inspector filed another alleged violation report on 7-15-92. "Surfaces were found dirty and in need of maintenance," he wrote. "[Inspection report] dated 6-3-92 gives correction date of June 27, 1992. As of 7-14-92, this was not done.... On [inspection report] dated 6-3-92, it states dogs must receive adequate vet care, and treatment records and record of euthanasia must be made available to the USDA vet. Three dogs had died on licensee's premises between 6-3-92 and 7-11-92."

On September 9, investigator Nottingham sent Dr. Walker a complete report of his investigation, in which he stated:

> It appears that Mr. Claxon has continuously violated the Animal Welfare Act. Mr. Claxon was issued a VS Form 3-60 July 8, 1991 for failure to make, keep and maintain records or forms which fully [and] correctly disclose information as required by Part 2.75. Since the issuance of the VS Form 3-60 Mr. Claxon has shown total disregard [for] the Animal Welfare Act in the fact that he has continued to violate the regulations.... Mr. Claxon has violated the

holding period for the dogs, has had inadequate veterinary care, inadequate recordkeeping, inadequate identification [and] missing and improper health certificates.

In an October 19 letter, USDA charged Claxon with the violations Nottingham listed in his report and failure to properly clean and sanitize primary enclosures. Claxon waived a hearing on the charges and agreed to pay a $600 stipulation fine to settle the case. Claxon paid the fine, and USDA renewed his Class B license in November.

Inspectors continued to document deficiencies at Claxon's facility:

1-12-93: "Licensee was called during regular business hours to meet at facility—no response.... Dr. Richard Overton accompanied me on this attempted inspection.... Both dog pens, holding 11 dogs, had no food. Feed bins were upside down and dirty.... Both dog pens... had no water. Water buckets were tipped over and water pans were empty.... Numerous piles of feces littered the dirt floors of both pens, far in excess of proper sanitation."

1-13-93: "All dogs still without feed. Feed buckets are still upside down in enclosure.... All dogs still without water. Dr. Overton offered to water the dogs—they exhibited thirsty behavior by gulping water and competing for space around the bucket.... Dogs had dug holes in dirt floor and were attempting to drink from rain accumulation.... Dr. Richard Overton accompanied me on inspection and took photographs of the above noncompliant items.... Large accumulation of fecal piles still on dirt floor of dog pens."

2-24-93: "Since Mr. Claxon's facility is not at his home address, our arrangements have been to call him from Garrison, KY, then meet him at his facility.... Mr. Claxon's phone has been disconnected and we have no way to reach him to conduct an inspection."

6-17-93: (41 dogs) "Document by new attending vet Kelly Carver not on file or in records.... Fly problem exists around dogs and pens.... Piles of debris around pens #13-16 due to storm damage.... Identification. One coonhound in pen #13 does not have tag. One terrier-cross dog in pen #14 does not have tag." Uncorrected items from last inspection: "Acquisition sheets show 46 dogs on premises, but only 41 were present.... USDA has only inspected one transport truck, and it would not hold numbers of animals that licensee is shipping—30 on 5-12-93, 34 on 4-21-93, 50 on 3-12-93, 43 on 3-10-93, 47 on 1-23-93, 33 on 4-28-93, 42 on 10-20-92, 52 on 1-30-92.... Dog #3422 in cage #2 has matted eyes and coughing. Records show one treatment of streptocillin on 5-24-93—incomplete and inadequate. Current Vet Care Program not on file.... Cats sold to Mt. Sinai Hospital, but no vet care records and no cat housing facilities on premises. Access to all records—did not have access to vet care forms and dog exercise program."

On April 11, 1995, USDA filed a complaint against Claxon, charging him with failure to: individually identify dogs; maintain complete records showing the acquisition, disposition and identification of animals; maintain programs of disease control and prevention, euthanasia and adequate veterinary care under the supervision and assistance of a veterinarian; develop, document and follow an appropriate plan approved by the attending veterinarian to provide dogs with the opportunity for exercise; keep premises in good repair, clean and free of trash, junk, waste and discarded matter; establish and maintain an effective pest control program; feed dogs at least once a day; offer water to dogs at least twice a day; and remove excreta and food waste from primary enclosures daily so as to prevent soiling of the dogs and reduce hazards, insects, pests and odors. An administrative hearing was held in April 1997. A decision is still pending.

ESPOSITO, SAMUEL D/B/A QUAKER FARM KENNELS.
Quakertown, Pennsylvania. USDA license #23BJ (last licensed in 1989).

Samuel Esposito was one of the largest and most successful dealers in the country, earning millions of dollars a year selling dogs and other animals acquired through an extensive network of suppliers along the east coast and throughout the Midwest. On his 1984-1985 annual report, he reported selling 6,458 dogs and 4,399 cats, grossing $1, 188,468.03.[13] He is believed to have acquired dogs from auctions and bunchers in Pennsylvania, Missouri, Kentucky, Illinois, Tennessee, and Indiana, as well as from numerous pounds in Virginia and West Virginia. A Wythe County, Virginia warden reportedly supplied Esposito with close to 80 dogs a month and even gave Esposito's driver his own keys to the pound.[14] Esposito's "purchasing agents" parked their pickup trucks at county stock markets, in shopping centers and outside restaurants, offering between three and five dollars for cats and $25 or more for dogs. Reports indicate that Esposito also purchased animals from a number of unlicensed dealers. Charles Hazzard of Hazzard Kennels reportedly sold dogs to both Esposito and Russell Hutton. Hazzard was found guilty of cruelty to animals and operating without a license in 1978.[15] Hazzard finally obtained a license in 1984 (#23-A-24).

In addition to dogs and cats, Esposito sold rabbits, chickens, sheep, pigs and goats. His clients included the National Institutes of Health, the Johns Hopkins University, Sloan Kettering Cancer Institute, U.S. Surgical and Yale University.

On February 24, 1976, one of Esposito's drivers was arrested in

Martinsburg, West Virginia and charged with cruelty to animals. State trooper Ron Jones noticed a pickup truck stopped on the side of Interstate 81, its driver asleep and 101 dogs "packed like sardines" into the back. The dogs had less that a square foot of space each. Esposito's driver pleaded guilty and paid a $63 fine. Esposito dispatched two trucks from Pennsylvania to pick up the dogs.[16,17] Some of the dogs were injured, and several were dead by the time the replacement truck reached Esposito's kennel in Pennsylvania.

USDA charged Esposito with failure to transport dogs in compatible groups, failure to transport them in containers that were large enough for natural movement, failure to maintain proper identification and records, and shipping dogs in a mechanically unsound vehicle. The administrative law judge who heard the case concluded there was insufficient evidence to support the allegations that Esposito had failed to maintain proper records and had shipped the dogs in a mechanically unsound vehicle. He did, however, find Esposito guilty of transporting dogs in overcrowded conditions and of housing them in incompatible groups. He suspended Esposito's Class B license for two weeks. Esposito appealed, but an appellate judge upheld the decision. "The flagrant violation involved in this case reveals a callous disregard for the welfare of the animals being transported and warrants a severe sanction," the judge concluded. He also ordered Esposito to cease and desist from future violations of the Animal Welfare Act.

On April 11, 1980, Esposito and his driver were jailed in Huntington, West Virginia for transporting dogs without health certificates. Marijuana and $2,000 in cash were allegedly found in their truck. Esposito was fined $75 and sentenced to five days in jail, but the case was dismissed on appeal. Drug charges were dismissed based on delayed submission of evidence. Esposito's driver, Harry Floyd, pleaded not guilty to health certificate violations but was found guilty on April 28, 1980 and fined $100.[18,19,20]

On July 18, 1980, two of Esposito's drivers were arrested in West Virginia for health certificate violations and felony possession of a lockblade knife. The 19 dogs they were transporting were confiscated. They were fined $400, but since this was a first offense, they did not receive jail time.[21]

Esposito was arrested and charged with three counts of cruelty to animals on June 18, 1983 by the Phelps County Sheriff's Department in Missouri. Esposito was stopped near Dean Martin's Dog and Gun Auction, between Rolla and St. James, with approximately 100 dogs crowded into his truck. He pleaded not guilty to the charges of overcrowding and failure to provide adequate food and water.[22] The case was later dismissed after witnesses for USDA testified that Esposito had not violated the Animal Welfare Act.[23]

Samuel Esposito died in 1988. On June 2, 1989, Dorothy Esposito wrote to APHIS to advise that she would not be renewing the Class B license.

Quaker Farms made its last delivery of animals on May 17, 1989.

FEDECHKO, GREGORY (SOUTH JERSEY BIOLOGICAL FARM, INC.). Friedensburg, Pennsylvania. USDA license #23-B-024 (last licensed in 1996).

Fedechko sold approximately 2,000 dogs a year. In 1983, USDA charged him with violating the Animal Welfare Act. According to USDA inspectors, Fedechko shipped ten dogs under overcrowded conditions from his kennel to a research facility in Bloomfield, N.J. He signed a consent decision and order agreeing to pay a $1,000 civil penalty. USDA filed another complaint against Fedechko in April 1995, alleging numerous violations of the Act. He signed a consent decision in March 1996, agreeing to permanently relinquish his Class B license and pay a $5,000 civil penalty.

USDA inspectors repeatedly documented deficiencies in housing, recordkeeping and veterinary care at South Jersey Biological Farm:

2-11-87: "Cats and pigeons cannot be housed in same primary enclosure"; 10-22-87: "One pen was observed to be housing nineteen dogs. Cannot house more than 12 dogs in a primary enclosure/ shed area housing dogs does not meet the Animal Welfare Act requirements for interior surfaces.... Dogs must be moved to new location or facility must be renovated. Cat facility must be equipped with resting boards and litter pans."

2-9-89: (124 dogs, 55 cats) "Temperature was recorded to be 33 degrees F in dog building. Also trailer number 3 for dogs was recorded to be 28 degrees F and trailer number two was... 31 degrees F. There was no heat present in these three areas. Temperature must not be allowed to fall below 50 degrees F in dog indoor facilities"; 7-21-89: (139 dogs and 93 cats) "Additional shade must be provided over new outdoor enclosures to properly protect these animals during hot weather months"; 1-25-90: (258 dogs and 132 cats) "Records — Must obtain a complete mailing address when dogs and cats are acquired. Must obtain the vehicle license number and state and the driver's license number and state of unlicensed dealers animals were obtained from. Must put date on records of when animals were obtained."

10-10-90: (180 dogs, 127 cats) "Building #1 housing 46 cats was observed to have a strong ammonia smell.... Cats were sneezing during inspection. Additional ventilation is needed in this area.... Could not check records to see if standard was corrected. Records were not available. Owner was not present." 6-19-91: (262 dogs and 52 cats) "One black/tan female hound in shed area was noted to have open sore on lower right side approximately 1 inch in diameter.... She was housed with 5 other adult dogs. At the request of USDA, dog was removed and isolated.... Facility did begin treatment at time of inspection.... Building one for cats was not sufficiently ventilated.... New building for dogs was noted to have strong ammonia smell.

"Noted excessive accumulations of excrement on wire surfaces. In some areas excrement was 1 to 3 inches thick.... Again observed water in cat building number one to be dirty and discolored."

7-18-91: (221 dogs, 38 cats) "Dog number 14579 had a left front leg injury. Animals were limping at time of inspection. Dog number 14586 had dark pink/red areas around both eyes, muzzle and right side of neck. Right lateral front leg also was injured. Area was bleeding at time of inspection. Dog number 35886 had left eye inflammation."

On July 26, 1991, USDA issued Fedechko a warning notice for failure to properly store food and keep water receptacles and premises clean. On 9-3-91 (201 dogs and 84 cats), inspectors noted, "Program of veterinary care still does not appear adequate.... Observed male Beagle tag 128845 to be under distress.... Dog was lame in front right leg and was being reinjured with other dogs in enclosure.... There was no record of dog... being treated.... Water receptacles in hill area (4), yard area (1) and building (5) for dogs were noted to have dirty water receptacles. Water was discolored, not potable."

During a 10-21-91 inspection (334 dogs listed, 200 dogs on site; 199 cats listed, 90 cats on site), several animals were observed to have inadequate veterinary care: "(a) Cat building one: cat 102783 and cat 127077 were dead in their cages. Bodies were stiff at 11:10 a.m. Cat 127660 was emaciated, dehydrated with nasal exudate. Cat 127072 (black) was emaciated, dehydrated with severe crusty nasal exudate.... More intensive care is needed.... Dog 129682, husky, was emaciated, depressed, weak with severe nasal and ocular discharges. This animal was housed with other apparently healthy dogs.... More intensive treatment or euthanasia is needed.... Dog number 3745 walker hound... had hind leg weakness. Dog could not walk normally. Right rear leg was swollen from hock down."

"In reviewing dog records from July 1991 through October 21, 1991 the records showed 334 dogs still present. Only 200 dogs were observed on premises. In reviewing cat records from May 4, 1991 through October 21, 1991, the records showed 199 cats still present. Only 90 cats were observed on premises.... Water receptacles were again noted not to be clean and sanitary.... Again observed (26) dogs in area 3 and 5 with no official tags."

Subsequent inspections revealed continuing deficiencies in veterinary care:

1-22-92: (171 dogs, 145 cats) "Dog #16759 was observed to have discharge and corneal edema with vascularization in right eye. No record of examination or treatment was available.... Dog #16458 was observed to be emaciated. Last recorded treatment for this dog was on 12-19-91 with antibiotics.... Cats 128001, 128220, 128223 were observed to have... discharge (nasal). Cats are currently being treated with 50 mg. of amoxicillin.... These cats are not separated from other cats in the room to prevent further exposure.... Cat building two... Gray tiger (no tag) and... black (no tag) had severe encrustation of eyes and nostrils.... These cats require nursing care to remove dried exudate."

4-9-92: (159 dogs and 76 cats) "Number of dogs were affected with respiratory problems, i.e. coughing, sneezing and eye discharge. Air was stagnant at time of inspection.... The following animals were observed to have inadequate veterinary care at time of inspection.... Cat #3843 had bilateral ocular and nasal discharge with cat litter adhered to nasal discharge. Additionally this cat was thin and dehydrated. This cat is currently on antibiotic therapy and dietary supplementation, but more aggressive monitoring, therapy and nursing care is required.... Dog #6117 was depressed, very thin and had bilateral nasal discharge and increased respiratory effort.... Dog #1981 has nasal discharge, blue discoloration of the right cornea, and is very thin and slightly dehydrated... (with) soft swelling over the left carpus (wrist) and is reluctant to put weight on right front leg.... Dog #2046 had wounds on both right rear leg and left rear foot. Additionally this dog is depressed, thin and shows increased respiratory effort and reluctance to bear weight on left rear leg.... More aggressive therapy is indicated... Dog #129312 was lame in the right front leg and had wounds on the digital pad on the same leg. Animal is currently on no medications. Dog should be examined and treated by veterinarian."

On 11-10-92, Fedechko paid a stipulation fine of $1,500 to USDA. USDA filed a formal complaint against Fedechko on April 11, 1995, alleging that from December 1992 through December 1994, he failed to: maintain programs of disease control and prevention, euthanasia, and adequate veterinary care under the supervision and assistance of a veterinarian; individually identify dogs; store food and bedding supplies in a manner that protects them from spoilage, contamination and vermin infestation; maintain primary dog enclosures that were structurally sound and in good repair; provide cats with sufficient space; make provisions for the regular and frequent collection, removal and disposal of animal and food wastes, bedding, debris, garbage, water, other fluids and wastes, and dead animals; provide dogs in outdoor facilities with adequate protection from the elements; keep dog water receptacles and potable water clean and sanitized; remove excreta and food waste daily from primary enclosures; provide sufficient lighting in indoor cat housing facilities; and maintain complete records showing the acquisition, disposition, and identification of animals. The complaint alleged that on five separate occasions the Fedechkos had falsely claimed to have acquired a total of 35 dogs from individuals they had not acquired them from.

On March 12, 1996, Fedechko signed a Consent Decision and Order in which he agreed to permanently relinquish his Class B license. The Order also assessed a $10,000 civil penalty, $5,000 of which was suspended on the condition that he not violate the Animal Welfare Act between the date of the Order and surrender of his license on August 1, 1996.

FINCH, KATHERINE (Pineland Farm Kennel). Raynham, Massachusetts. USDA license #14-B-002 (last licensed in 1995).

Katherine Finch sold approximately 500 dogs a year. USDA inspectors documented chronic noncompliance with recordkeeping, housing, sanitation and veterinary care standards at Finch's facility:

7-14-93: (124 dogs) "No [veterinary] records are being kept at this time. This practice must be followed to ensure adequate veterinary care is being provided to the animals.... The third building had 4 outdoor runs presently being used. These runs are in total disrepair. All pipes/bars are rusty, [and] there was a 4'x 8' panel of fencing within one run to separate the two runs due to the fact that the cement block wall was deteriorating.... Several of the long-haired dogs.... had extremely matted coats.... Pomeranian #066 had bite wounds to left front paw, and right shoulder had a skin lesion. Skin lesions along the neck were [also] observed.... One black cocker had a creamy, thick discharge from its eyes. It was severely matted and had opened sores, skin lesions on rear end."

"During today's inspection approximately 22 dogs were not identified by tags.... Mrs. Finch admits to buying dogs from people who have not breed [sic] the animals on the property. But the animals were obtained as puppies and are no longer wanted by the seller supposedly.... At least 32 dogs were sold to research in June and July of 1993 that were recorded as raised on the premise[s]. No birth dates were noted, and the dogs were usually identified shortly before going to research. There is no way to verify that the dogs were raised at the kennel and not obtained from other sources."

10-26-93: (146 dogs) The inspector noted that although Finch had started keeping veterinary records and that the previously documented deficiencies in veterinary care had been corrected, other deficiencies remained uncorrected. He also reported several new deficiencies: "The third building had 4 runs presently being used. These runs are in total disrepair.... During today's inspection 7 dogs were without tags.... Boston Terrier — third building — 4th run down on the left had an ulcerated cornea of the right eye. Across from the Boston Terrier enclosure there is a Vari-Kennel being used to house one old Pekingese, which was shivering and lethargic. The enclosure had no food or water present and was fairly dirty with wet/soiled bedding."

2-22-94: (130 dogs) "Due to a snow storm on 3-11-94, there was snow accumulation in all of the outside runs. Some of the runs containing smaller breed dogs had hard packed snow, making it difficult for the dogs to walk freely. Most of the runs with large breed dogs had excessive accumulations of feces, and there was no outside area available to these animals so as to allow them to avoid contact with excreta.... It is apparent from the buildup of cob webs/sawdust and debris on the components that make up the inside primary enclosures... that routine sanitizing is not being done at least once every two weeks as specified in the standards."

3-21-94: (126 dogs) "Boston Terrier with enucleated right eye and blind in the left eye was being housed in a pen behind the main house. The pen had an accumulation of broken glass and other debris. These items may cause injury to the animal (corrected 3/24/94).... All buildings had an accumulation of cobwebs and sawdust debris.... There appears to continually be a rodent problem as evidenced by the rodent droppings along the sink and the holes in boxes of biscuits within the food storage area. The cabinets above the sink are cluttered and should be reorganized to eliminate nesting areas.... Run #1E — pit bull cross female had runny eyes and appeared thin.... Run #1J — sheepdog had excessive amount of mats. This dog was identified on the last inspection and still has not been groomed.... Run #1K — 2 Yorkies — both excessively matted.... Run #2D — black & white Akita pup being housed with adult female and 2 littermates appears thin.... Run #4I — terrier — no USDA tag # — had sores on all four legs."

9-6-94: (132 dogs) "Entire kennel, all four buildings, had a strong odor of urine and feces even though doors to hallways and guillotine doors in dog runs were all open.... Water receptacles, within the buildings, had an accumulation of dead flies in several of them. Water receptacles outdoors — all had an accumulation of slime, algae, dirt, leaves and other debris. All receptacles need to be cleaned and potable water offered to these animals.... As indicated by this and previous inspection reports, this facility's employees are not performing to minimum standards nor are they being appropriately supervised."

"During today's inspection of all paperwork, the following discrepancies were found: tan [crossbreed] — USDA tag #7636 was on the premises; however, records of 'animals on hand' show that the animal was sold and transfer papers (18-6) also show the transaction.... [Tag] #7606 was found on a sheltie. However, according to [the] records, this tag was assigned to a black mongrel that was sold to research.... Dogs continue to be inadequately identified on records. For example, a Dalmation was being recorded as a black and white mongrel....132 dogs were seen on the property. Only 104 were found in the records. And 53 dogs were seen on the premise without tags. There appears to be a major discrepancy [between] the records and what is actually on the premise."

The inspector also reported continuing and serious deficiencies in housing, sanitation and veterinary care: "General overall condition of facility had an accumulation of trash, debris, tools, food and water receptacles, fencing, chemicals, insecticides, etc.... All runs had an accumulation of feces. One run with 2 large dogs had over 20 piles of feces within it. A run with 3 miniature pinschers had over 30 piles of feces within it.... Animals continue to be housed in the pens behind the house which still contain glass and other harmful material.... There continues to be a pest problem. On today's inspection there was a tremendous.... [Number] of flies in all buildings and outside pens.... Used needles and syringes were found within a dog's primary enclosure.... Since May 1994 there [have] been no entries made in the medical records.... 1 long-haired dachshund in left side of building #1 had excessive hair loss.... Last run of building #4 had shepherd with limp (hind) and thin.... Red Akita in building #3 was thin, prominent ribs.... Many dogs had loose stool and must be checked."

11-7-94: (100 dogs) "During today's inspection it is apparent that excreta and food waste are not being removed daily.... Several of the outside runs had an accumulation of feces. [A run with] 2 dachshunds had 12 piles of feces in it, [and another with] 2 Boston terriers had 25 piles of feces in it.... Animals continue to be housed in pens with glass in them. Most dogs have been removed. However, one dog pen containing 2 Pomeranians still had glass in the back corner.... No tags on shep [crossbreed] pup in run #3 of building #1 and 2 Jack Russells in run #13 of building #1, and no tags were on any of the dogs behind the house."

4-6-95: (129 dogs) "Five outdoor puppy enclosures which contain 14 puppies had no additional bedding or mats within their shelters. Temperatures were below 32 last night and not above 50 today. Clean bedding that is dry must be provided for the animals.... Boston terrier being housed with collie/Sheltie was observed to be shivering and in distress. Vet records indicate that the last exam was Feb. 9, 1995. The dog had several abrasions and lacerations.... The following animals were thin: 1 hound in building #4, 2 dobie [crossbreeds] in building #4, dachshund [in] building #7.... 9 dogs in the kennel did not have tags on them, and the tattoos are illegible."

On each report, the inspector wrote, "This facility is not in compliance with standards or regulations as evident by the number of noncompliant items documented on this and previous inspections." But it was not until April, 1995 that USDA filed a formal complaint against Finch. The complaint charged Finch with failure to: maintain programs of disease control and prevention, euthanasia, and adequate veterinary care; maintain complete records showing the acquisition, disposition, and identification of animals;

individually identify dogs; maintain primary enclosures, buildings and surrounding grounds in good repair; establish and maintain an effective pest control program; store supplies of food and bedding in a manner that protected them from spoilage, contamination and vermin infestation; remove excreta and food waste from primary enclosures daily; provide transported animals with health certificates; and keep primary enclosures and watering receptacles clean and sanitized as required. A hearing on the charges against Finch is still pending.

FOW, BETTY (HILLTOP KENNELS). LaGrange, Kentucky. USDA license #61-B-193 (last licensed in 1991).

Hilltop Kennels, first licensed in 1977 under Lee R. Smith's name, sold both rabbits and dogs. In 1986, Smith closed his rabbit facility, and Betty Fow assumed sole ownership of the business soon after. Fow sold between 100 and 200 animals a year. Like so many other Class B dealer facilities, Hilltop Kennel functioned as a holding facility for area pounds. During the time Fow was licensed as a dealer, USDA inspectors cited her for missing inspections, threatening an APHIS official, and using gunshot and drowning as means of destroying animals.

9-21-89: (23 dogs) Attempted inspection. "You are required to be open for unannounced inspections. You were in violation of the law by not being available for inspection. I am initiating a case against you that will result in one or all of the following: a warning, a fine, a suspension, revoke of license."

10-11-89: Attempted inspection. "No one home—No inspection made."

10-25-89: (23 dogs listed, 25 on site) "Resting boards made of wood in indoor pens at back of facility on left are chewed and not impervious to water.... 27 dogs were on list 18-5; only 25 dogs were in facility. Dog #17060... was never recorded on the official form 18-5."

11-29-89: Attempted inspection. "You are in violation of the Animal Welfare Act — must be accessible for unannounced inspections."

On 4-20-90, USDA issued Fow an official warning charging her with "failure to make premise and facilities available for inspection."

On 5-29-90 (24 dogs listed, 52 dogs on site), inspectors noted, "County pounds leave dogs in 2 front holding pens to be destroyed.... Two front holding pens need a constant water source for dogs. Water pans were knocked over and dogs did not have access to water.... Water bucket in side pen is chewed, exposing rough edges."

On 8-10-90 (0 dogs listed, 19 dogs on site), inspectors reported, "Nine of sixteen dog runs had protruding wires that could be injurious to animals.... Water bucket of east pen was dirty with growth of moss or algae.... An alternative to gunshot to the head should be found immediately. Drowning of pups is not an acceptable method of euthanasia. This problem needs to be addressed immediately to avoid a violation.... 9 dogs in kennel runs are not USDA tagged. All animals should be tagged at all times except those left by the pound to be destroyed.... 9 dogs in kennels are not reflected in records."

In an 8-12-90 memo to Dr. James Sharp, Hilltop's attending veterinarian, an APHIS inspector discussed "acceptable euthanasia procedures" in response to Dr. Sharp's question about USDA's policy on euthanasia. "No policy memo by the USDA has been written," wrote the inspector. "It is our interpretation of the American Veterinary Medical Association (AVMA) guidelines that gunshot to the head should only be used when there is no other alternative, or the animal is dangerous.... Alternate methods that are less traumatic are recommended. Drowning of pups is not acceptable."

During an inspection on 10-19-90 (12 dogs), the inspector reported that Fow had not corrected deficiencies noted during the 8-10-90 inspection: "Dogs are euthanized by gunshot to head, which is against AVMA guidelines. This situation has been going on since July 9, 1990, and is long overdue to be resolved.... Discussed proper pest control and processing of new animals, including vaccinations, dip, weight, worming. Also discussed license termination procedures and went over proper way to fill out annual reports. Discussed 2nd vet to perform euthanasia."

Later the same day, the inspector contacted Dr. Sharp about Hilltop's euthanasia program. He reported that Dr. Sharp "was not comfortable dispensing Class III drugs to Hilltop Kennels, and did not have time to perform weekly euthanasias on site."[24] According to Fow's daughter Tammy, Hilltop "had contacted another vet about euthanizing their dogs" but that he was too expensive. A few days later, Dr. Sharp, who was also director of animal care at the University of Louisville, resigned as Hilltop's attending veterinarian.

By November, Hilltop Kennels still had not contracted the services of a veterinarian. In a 11-7-90 memo to Fow, the inspector wrote: "Your facility cannot operate without an attending veterinarian. Dr. James Sharp resigned. You may either replace him immediately or turn in your license. If I have not received your vet care program by Nov. 14, your license will be terminated."

On 11-19-90 (Attempted inspection), the inspector reported, "No one at facility. Gate locked. Hours of business state 9 AM-12 noon, Mon-Fri. Licensee has already been penalized once for careless attitude concerning availability of facility to USDA veterinarian. Called Mrs. Betty Fow on phone in Campbellsburg, Kentucky. She stated she plans on turning in her license this week, then stated she'd filed a discrimination suit and hung up."

On January 3, 1991, the inspector filed an alleged violation report against Fow. "Mrs. Fow's facility has been without an attending veterinarian since 10-23-90. I spoke with her numerous times to resolve the matter. Mrs. Fow became belligerent, padlocked her facility, and is not keeping business hours." USDA issued Fow an official warning notice on January 22, charging her with failure to have an attending veterinarian and threatening an APHIS official.

The inspector attempted another inspection of Hilltop Kennel on 2-11-91. "Facility padlocked and empty," he wrote. "License renewal due 2-17-91.... As discussed with Dr. [Richard] Overton, if Mrs. Fow renews her license we will instigate a case. If her license lapses and is terminated, the [warning] issued 1-22-91 will suffice."

Fow failed to renew her license before its expiration date, and on February 18, 1991, USDA informed her that her license had been officially terminated.

FOX, EARL, JR. (TOAD). Forest City, Iowa. USDA license #42-B-030 (last licensed in 1994).

Fox, whose facility functioned as both a contract dog pound and Class B dealership, was first licensed by USDA in 1984. He sold between 200 and 300 animals a year. USDA inspectors repeatedly cited Fox for noncompliance with recordkeeping and identification requirements.

On 2-28-84, inspectors reported: "The five dogs observed in the kennel building were not tagged and identified as required.... Please be advised that upon reinspection of this kennel all records of dogs purchased and sold will be checked back to January 1, 1984."

Subsequent inspections revealed inadequate recordkeeping:

1-24-90: "No proof of purchase present at this inspection.... Cannot prove that animals are not stolen!.... Since owner receives animals from pounds, police stations, private drop-offs, etc., particular attention must be paid to the records of each animal (source, disposition, etc.) and individual identification. Without these records it would be difficult to prove that animals were obtained legally."

9-19-90: "All animals must be identified via tag or tattoo while on owner's premises. Only has records of sales, not acquisitions.... Several pens not in use require cleaning (and waste removal)."

3-25-91: "All dogs must be identified individually.... Still has excessive amounts of dirty bedding and excessive clutter."

In an April 4 memo to the inspector responsible for Fox's facility, USDA's Dr. Ellen Magid wrote: "Dr. Bellis told me that Mr. Fox has only one facility. Dealer and "pound" must be physically separated.... If Fox operates as a contract pound he needs two separated facilities and should have been written up for this. If this is the case, I suggest a reinspection of Mr. Fox to address this issue fairly soon."

On May 20, 1991, Dr. Jerry Diemer, Acting Supervisor of Animal Care for REAC's North Central Sector, sent a warning letter to Fox regarding noncompliant items noted on previous inspections. The violations included failure to maintain surfaces that were impervious to moisture and failure to maintain primary enclosures that were clean and free of excessive clutter. There was no mention of the requirement that pound and dealer facilities must be physically separate. He advised Fox that continued noncompliance would result in "appropriate legal action."

On 1-27-92, the inspector noted that Fox was still not identifying all dogs immediately upon arrival. Beard also documented "inadequate records on where dogs came from — auction or random source" and instructed Fox that random-source animals had to be kept separate from pound animals.

On 3-26-92, the inspector reported, "Animals still not identified by official tag and number.... Dealer still not keeping records where obtained dog from.... Still doesn't have separate holding facility for random source animals." Dr. Magid filed an alleged violation report against Fox the same day, charging him with failure to maintain surfaces that were impervious to moisture; failure to individually identify dogs; failure to maintain records of acquisition of dogs; failure to maintain facility free of excessive amounts of dirt and debris; and failure to maintain separate, nonadjacent facilities for the contract pound and Class B dealership.

On May 15, 1992, USDA issued Fox an official notification and warning covering the alleged violations, which stated that no further legal action was anticipated but that further violations would "justify a more severe penalty."

On 9-3-92 (12 dogs), inspectors noted, "Holding facility. Still doesn't have a separate facility for random source dogs."

USDA was unable to inspect Fox's facility on two occasions:

11-10-92: (Attempted inspection) "Reinspection. On 11-10-92 at 10:45-11:15 AM licensee Earl Fox failed to have a responsible party available to conduct an animal welfare inspection. This is an alleged violation of CFR Part 9, Section 2.126."

4-13-93: (Attempted inspection) "Not home. [Licensee] selling dogs in Geneva, Minnesota.... Licensee failed to have a responsible party present to conduct an animal welfare inspection."

USDA terminated Fox's license in January 1994 after he failed to file a renewal application and pay the required license fee.

HIPPERT, MORRIS E. (HIPPERT'S KENNEL). New Ulm, Minnesota. USDA license #41-B-104 (last licensed in 1990).

Morris Hippert, the brother of dealer Donald Hippert (See Hippert, Donald and Shirley in "Investigations Into the Acquisition of Animals by Class B Dealers), sold between 100 and 300 animals a year. He purchased dogs from Nicollet County dogcatcher Bob Boys for 20 years, buying an average of 15 to 20 animals a year. According to Boys, he pocketed the money he made selling dogs and kept no record of the sales.[25]

Despite repeated warnings, Hippert never complied with Animal Welfare requirements for establishing and submitting a written program of veterinary care:

1-4-82: (2 dogs) "None" was listed under the name of Hippert's veterinarian and there was no veterinary care program submitted to USDA; 3-24-82: (3 dogs) "None" was listed under the name of the veterinarian and there was no veterinary care program. The inspector noted, "No heat in building. Ice formed on floor."

Inspectors also reported deficiencies in housing, sanitation and recordkeeping at Hippert's Kennel:

2-17-83: (5 dogs) "Pens must be cleaned before new dogs are put into building. Primary enclosure not large enough to handle dogs being taken to Donald Hippert"; 8-12-83: "One white poodle in the barn not tagged.... [Hippert] did not have all records on hand, claimed dogs destroyed some records."

Hippert continued his business for several more years without implementing a veterinary care program:

5-21-84: "None" was listed under the name of Hippert's veterinarian. The inspector reported, "One white terrier dog without a collar or tag.... It appears three numbers were reused."

Hippert listed the name of a veterinarian on an 11-9-84 Program of Veterinary Care form but signed the veterinarian's name himself. USDA sent Hippert another blank veterinary care form with a note stating, "This form requires the signature of a veterinarian and not signed by you," In 1988, Hippert wrote on his annual report that he did not have a consulting veterinarian.

Hippert still hadn't hired a consulting veterinarian by 1989. On 6-22-89, the inspector reported, "No agreement (of vet care) has been signed. The veterinarians in town do not want to handle it." On 9-25-89, the inspector wrote: "Mr. Hippert stated that he doesn't keep the dogs around long enough to need a veterinarian. He also stated that the vets in town do not want to sign an agreement due to the controversial nature of his business with the Humane Society. He said that if he needed vet care he could take an animal to a clinic in town if needed.... Prior to introduction of dogs into empty primary enclosures previously occupied, such enclosures shall be sanitized."

In October 1989, Hippert submitted a program of veterinary care form to USDA in which he wrote "doin' my own vet" in the space where a veterinarian's name is required. On his 1989 annual report, Hippert once again indicated he did not have a consulting veterinarian. Hippert still had not implemented a program of veterinary care by June 1990.

On November 14, 1990, USDA terminated Hippert's license for failure to file a renewal application and pay the required license fee. Hippert later notified USDA that the land he rented for his dealer facility had been sold and he no longer had any dogs.

HODGES, JEFFERY (DIXIE KENNELS and BOGASHA KENNELS). Vaiden, Mississippi. USDA license #65-B-105 (last licensed in 1994).

Jeffery Hodges, an animal control officer for the City of Winona, Mississippi, had both a Class B and a Class A license (USDA license #65-A-202, site located in Kosciusko, Mississippi). He was a supplier to Class B dealer Jerry Vance; USDA investigated his records in 1993 as part of a traceback of Vance's records. Of three licensed research dealers in Mississippi, two—Hodges and Vance—were under USDA investigation throughout 1993 and 1994. In 1993, In Defense of Animals (IDA), a California-based animal rights group, asked Winona city officials to examine the legality of Hodges's position as dog warden. IDA alleged he was violating Mississippi state conflict-of-interest laws by using his position as a public employee for private gain.[26,27] Hodges sold approximately 1,200 animals a year.

On June 24, 1994, Hodges agreed to the issuance of a consent decision and order in settlement of a USDA complaint charging him with numerous alleged violations of Animal Welfare Act regulations and standards between February and September 1993. USDA had charged Hodges with failing to: construct and maintain sound and safe housing for animals that were structurally sound and in good repair; individually identify dogs; maintain complete records showing the acquisition, disposition and identification of animals; maintain programs of disease control and prevention, euthanasia and adequate veterinary care; hold dogs for a period of not less than 5 business days after acquisition; keep buildings and grounds free of trash, junk, waste, discarded matter, weeds, grasses, bushes; provide dogs with adequate protection from elements; provide regular maintenance to housing facility surfaces; clean and sanitize dog water receptacles and cat food receptacles; maintain food and storage areas that are free of toxic substances; and properly transport the permitted number of animals in the same cages. USDA fined Hodges $10,000, although the entire amount was suspended on the condition that he not operate as a dealer during a period of one year from the date of the order. Hodges also received a one-year license suspension.

HUTTON, RUSSELL (MOUNTAINSIDE KENNEL). St. Thomas, Pennsylvania. USDA license #23-B-003 (last licensed in 1991).

Russell Hutton, in business as a dealer for 24 years, traversed Ohio, Virginia, West Virginia, Kansas, Oklahoma, and Pennsylvania in several trucks, making the rounds of auctions, pounds, and dealers. Hutton reportedly did business with Noel Leach (Virginia), Charles Hazzard (Pennsylvania), Joe Self (Oklahoma), and Haycock Kennels (Pennsylvania), all licensed Class B dealers. On his 1989-1990 annual report, Hutton reported selling 2460 animals, grossing $149,250.[28] In 1988, USDA fined Hutton $2,000.

Hutton is one of the Pennsylvania dealers associated with Pepper, a five-year-old Dalmatian whose disappearance in June of 1965 from an 80-acre farm provided the impetus behind the introduction of the federal Laboratory Animal Welfare Act. Within the span of nine days, Pepper was reported as missing, transported across state lines, handled by four dealers, detained by a local humane society and sold to a research hospital. Hutton was one of three dealers in the supply chain that "processed" the dog before her final destination: Montefiore Hospital's experimental laboratory in New York.

According to a New York Times report, Easton, Pennsylvania police stopped William R. Miller of Broken Arrow Kennels in McConnellsburg, Pennsylvania for overloading his truck with animals. The Easton Animal Shelter confiscated the animals while Miller acquired a better transport vehicle. A published photograph of the dogs held at the shelter caught the attention of the Lakavage family, who recognized Pepper among the 17 other dogs and 2 goats pictured.

By that time, Miller had sold Pepper and five other dogs to Montefiore Hospital. He later stated that he had purchased Pepper from Russell Hutton, who acquired her from Jack Clark of Everett, Pennsylvania, who claimed he had acquired the dog from a dealer in Altoona, Pennsylvania.[29,30]

On July 3, 1965, Fay Brisk, a long-term campaigner for reform of the big Pennsylvania dog dealers, called the Animal Welfare Institute for help in trying to get Pepper back to the Lakavage family. Mrs. Lakavage and her three young children set off on a 240-mile long odyssey in pursuit of Pepper after police were misinformed (by Miller) that the dog had been taken to a dealer named Nersessian of High Falls, New York. When the exhausted family arrived, Nersessian refused them entry.

Senator Clark of Pennsylvania, a well-established fighter for animal protection and the chief sponsor of pending legislation to require humane treatment of experimental animals, was out of town, but his legislative assistant, Sara Ehrmann, responded to the Animal Welfare Institute's call for help. She telephoned Congressman Joseph Resnick of the House Agricultural Committee, in whose congressional district Nersessian's dog farm was located. But even Congressional intercession failed. Pressure by the state police brought an admission from Miller that he had taken his load not to Nersessian, as he first had said, but directly to Montefiore Hospital in New York. Immediately, Fay Brisk telephoned the hospital and could hear the rattling of dog tags at the other end of the phone line. Then, she was given the bad news: the dog had died on the operating table the day before and had already been incinerated.

Congressman Resnick, angered by the dealer's high-handed refusal to admit the family to search for their missing pet, decided to introduce a bill that later became known as the Laboratory Animal Welfare Act. The Act was designed to prevent family pets like Pepper from ending up in laboratories.

Conditions on Hutton's premises were described in 1984 by a humane investigator who was searching for a missing dog.[31] The investigator observed approximately 300 hunting dogs tied to short metal chains:

> The dogs were extremely thin. Their backbones and ribs could be seen distinctly. No dog had water. The temperature was 88 degrees. The feeding pans... were covered with flies.... Approximately fifteen of the hounds were too weak or ill to stand.

In a shed behind the hounds were 60 to 80 dogs in pens with "room only for the dogs to stand or lie down. There was no food or water in any pen." One dog was "stuffed" into a cage measuring 12 inches high and two feet long. "There was not enough space for the dog to stand. It was crouched on its chest with his four legs bent. There was no food or water in the cage." The investigator was told to leave the property when she was recognized by one of Hutton's employees.

USDA inspectors noted serious deficiencies in housing and sanitation at Mountainside Kennel:

10-1-84: (150 dogs) "Area that is used for sick dogs — the chains on the dogs are not the required length.... There are five buildings that are used to confine dogs. The primary enclosures and runs need to be cleaned and sanitized"; 10-31-84: (165 dogs) "Dog is too big for primary enclosure. Several chains on beagles do not meet length requirements. Approx. 8 chains were measured. Again I explain this to R. Hutton and workers. Two housing facilities were not cleaned; bedding needed [to be] replaced"; 11-27-84: (173 dogs) "Two dogs.... Chains were too short."

5-16-85: (165 dogs) "Dog boxes need to have an extended shelter roof added. Old fecal matter, bones, etc., must be removed.... Pen and back building showed evidence of not being cleaned for some time (2-3 weeks)"; 6-20-85: (225 dogs) "Both of these enclosures have the maximum amount of dogs allowed under the Animal Welfare Act, so therefore need to be cleaned more often"; 11-21-85: (145 dogs) "11:30 AM.... (Sick bay area.) Approximately 20 dogs in this area had no water and had not been watered since previous evening. The workers were raking leaves and would water the dogs when they finished."

5-14-86: "Two pens called 'heat pens' need [to be] cleaned and sanitized. Those two pens have not been cleaned in the last week.... Three dogs need attention or to be disposed of"; 10-9-86: (200 dogs) "Those primary enclosures that are not directly protected by the trees from the elements need to have an extended shelter attached to the primary enclosure.... Buildup of excreta, old bedding." 12-12-86: (165 dogs) "Approximately 10 enclosures need additional bedding.... One dog needed attention immediately, bad cough, heavy breathing. Dog was put down at time of inspection."

In May of 1988, Hutton paid a $2,000 civil penalty and consented to a cease-and-desist order, neither admitting nor denying USDA charges that he failed to provide adequate care and treatment of dogs. USDA alleged that between October 1, 1984 and November 21, 1985, Hutton failed to 1) sanitize primary enclosures for dogs often enough to prevent an accumulation of excreta and debris, 2) properly store animal food supplies, 3) provide sufficient and clean bedding material for dogs kept in outdoor shelters, 4) keep water receptacles clean and 5) provide potable water for dogs held at his facility. USDA originally sought a license suspension against Hutton.[32]

Inspectors continued to report deficiencies in housing and sanitation:

6-6-89: (250 dogs) "Must do a better job of cleaning enclosures (pens). Some of the pens were noted to be wet and have accumulations of excrement"; 6-6-90: (250 dogs) "All bedding needs [to be] removed from group pen — packed and dirty. Needs to be done more frequently."

In a 1984 WJLA-TV investigative report, reporter Scott Klug (now a U.S. Representative from Wisconsin) interviewed a Manassas, Virginia man who went to Hutton's facility to look for his missing hunting dog, Jip. He didn't find Jip, but he did find another dog who had disappeared from Manassas around the same time as Jip. Even though Hutton told both the man and Klug that he didn't buy dogs from Virginia, Klug showed Hutton documents tying him to an unlicensed dealer in Virginia. Hutton claimed he didn't know the dealer was unlicensed.

During the interview, the WJLA-TV cameramen filmed several very thin dogs and the makeshift shelters Hutton used to house the dogs. Klug remarked that Hutton's employees rushed to feed and water the animals shortly after the WJLA-TV crew arrived at the facility.

USDA inspectors also reported noncompliance with veterinary care, storage and recordkeeping standards at Hutton's facility:

3-7-91: (187 dogs) "The use of outdated or unknown drugs does NOT constitute adequate veterinary care under the Animal Welfare Act.... Several drug containers—1 unknown; 1 penicillin were in the refrigerator with needles stuck into the tops. This is not an acceptable method of storage of injectable drugs.... The following items are not being adequately recorded for all dogs received and disposed of: 1) Date animal received—approximately 20% of the animals listed on the records reviewed did not have this date listed. 2) License number of the dealers they are purchasing animals from. This is NOT being recorded with the animals purchased. 3) On 18-6 they are not recording their license number (USDA) or the USDA license or registration number of the purchaser.... With the number of animals whose acquisition date was not recorded the extent of this problem (noncompliance with 5 day holding period) is difficult to determine."

4-23-91: "Records and storage facilities only were inspected." The inspector listed new requirements for storage of food and bedding; prohibition of keeping sick, infirm or aged dogs outside when temperatures were below 50°; new requirements for outdoor facility shelters; new cleaning requirements; and, the requirement of a plan for dog exercise by August 15, 1991. After writing all of these out, the inspector then noted, "Mr. Hutton has expressed an interest in surrendering his license which expires on May 13, 1991. He would like to have approval to continue selling dogs until June 15, 1991."

USDA received the following handwritten letter from Hutton on April 29, 1991:

I am going to get out of Research Dogs and will not be renewing my License but would ask for an extension until June 15-1991 to dispose of the dogs I have on hand if it would be possible.

USDA granted the extension on the condition that Hutton not purchase any more animals after expiration of his license on May 13. On May 31, USDA sent Hutton official notification that his license had been terminated.

During a 6-7-91 inspection (68 dogs), inspectors noted: "Must clean excrement from around dog enclosures daily. Noticed several piles of excrement on hill in isolation area.... No more than 4 dogs can be housed in transport enclosure.... These dogs were in enclosures that did not provide sufficient cage height. Cannot use this vehicle to transport.... At time of inspection records were not being kept on dogs that were euthanized. Three dogs rejected on the May 15, 1991 shipment could not be located in the records or on premises. Dogs number 2239, 2066, and 1955 had no disposition records or medical records from University of Pittsburgh."

LEACH, NOEL (LEACH KENNELS). Chase City, Virginia. USDA license #52-B-044 (last licensed in 1994).

Leach's strong influence in the southeast was maintained through an extensive network of bunchers, dealers, pounds, auctions, and dog wardens throughout a five-state area. In 1982, it was rumored that he had as many as 42 vehicles on the road making pickups and deliveries. At one time, Leach's kennel functioned as the Mecklenburg County, Virginia pound.[33] On his 1976-1977 annual report, Leach reported selling approximately 12,000 animals and grossing $130,316.[34] However, by the late 1980s, Leach was selling between 1,000 and 5,000 animals a year.

Among Leach's customers were A. H. Robbins, the Medical College of Virginia, George Washington University, Georgetown University, Howard University, Washington Hospital Center, Children's Hospital of Washington, D.C., the Carolina Biological Supply Company, the University of Virginia and Eastern Virginia Medical Academy.

Leach regularly purchased animals from several North Carolina pounds. Paul Bernhardt located his missing dog at Leach's kennels in 1977. A local dog warden had sold Bernhardt's dog to Leach less than 48 hours after picking him up. According to Bernhardt, he found his dog in a truck parked in a mud hole on Leach's property:

> The pet was in a small cage compartment exposed to the weather; one of our infrequent snow storms was in progress and the temperature was well below freezing. The compartment was so small the dog could not stand up and was filthy with dog waste. When the dog was removed he found it difficult to stand up. As soon as the dog was returned to Salisbury we noticed he was in bad shape

and immediately took him to Dr. Hill for treatment. The cost of getting the dog well was some one hundred dollars.[35]

In 1982, the Caldwell County, North Carolina pound sold Sue Ellenburg's dog to Leach just a few hours after the pound picked the dog up. Ellenburg drove to Chase City to retrieve her dog, arriving there just before Leach was to send two trucks—one carrying her dog—back on the road. Ellenburg claimed that when her dog was pulled from one of the trucks, "he fell to the ground and was very disoriented. He did not seem to know us at first.... He was starved. I believe that he had very little if any food or water during the five-day period. He appeared to be dehydrated. Upon examining him at home we found a portion of his left ear torn away, a tooth knocked out, filth and excrement on his body and numerous bald spots in his hair."[36]

During that same year, Caldwell County, North Carolina commissioners met to discuss the appropriateness of sales of pound animals to Leach and investigate allegations by the Western Piedmont Humane Society that Leach transported animals in crowded conditions for long periods of time without adequate food, water, ventilation, or sanitation.[37] They invited Leach to make a presentation. "I'm at your service to help you and help our fellow man," he told them. He admitted to not being in compliance with Animal Welfare Act transport regulations limiting one dog per enclosure. "I am not abiding by the law. That may sound like a bold and crazy thing to say.... Those compartments have a capacity for 5, 6, 7 medium-size dogs."[38]

Four North Carolina counties had already banned pound sales to Leach—Catawba, Davidson, Cabarrus, and Guilford. The University of North Carolina (UNC) and Duke University ceased buying dogs from Leach due to the poor condition of the animals upon receipt. UNC officials described Leach's truck as "very unsanitary and filthy."[39] Animals Leach sold to Georgetown University were described as "pitifully thin, dirty, and in some cases clearly suffering from infectious diseases."[40] The Caldwell Commissioners eventually placed a 60-day moratorium on sales of animals to Leach.

On January 27, 1983, USDA charged Leach with numerous alleged violations of the Animal Welfare Act regulations and standards, including failure to properly clean and sanitize transport cages; failure to provide enclosures that were large enough to allow each animal to stand, sit and lie in a normal position; failure to house animals in compatible groups; and failure to individually identify all animals. The charges stemmed from an inspection of one of Leach's trucks by two North Carolina humane investigators in May 1982.

At the June 29, 1983 oral hearing, a former USDA compliance officer who was for several years the assigned inspector of Leach's facility testified that based on photographs taken by the humane investigators, it was his opinion that the animals had not been overcrowded. As to the other charges, he stressed the subjectivity involved in applying regulatory standards and implied that it wasn't clear whether Leach had violated the Act. Administrative Law Judge Dorothea Baker found his testimony more persuasive than that of the two humane investigators. She was also unconvinced by the testimony of the North Carolina USDA inspector who initiated the complaint after seeing the humane investigators' photographs of Leach's truck. Judge Baker found Leach guilty of only one violation: failure to remove dogs from their cages while the cages were being hosed down. She ordered Leach to cease and desist from failing to comply with the Animal Welfare Act.

USDA inspectors continued to report deficiencies at Leach's facility. During a 7-1-83 inspection, inspectors noted: "In the walls and ceiling were dust, hair, cobwebs, dead animals, fecal material.... Some dogs were observed with mucopurulent discharges from nose and eyes.... Some with ticks should be provided with immediate veterinary care.... Per Mr. Leach's statement as well as the primary enclosure we saw (chicken crates), showed us that he was not in compliance with the transportation standards.... Rodent feces were observed in the storage area."

In 1987, Leach requested a letter from USDA stating that he was in compliance with Animal Welfare Act regulations. He received the following response from Dr. Terry Taylor:

> During the period January, 1984 through January, 1986 you have been inspected by us a total of twenty-four (24) times.... A total of twenty (20) deficiencies were noted... [This] is not acceptable. The average animal dealer with no deficiencies in Virginia was inspected only six (6) times in the past three (3) years.... I would like to be able to say you are in compliance, but in fact **yours is a marginal facility which requires an excessive amount of USDA input.** According to our records, at least eight (8) of the twenty-four (24) inspections were a result of complaints to our office by the public. This is not acceptable.

In May of that year, the Montgomery County, Virginia Board of Supervisors denied a request by a local humane society to stop sales of pound animals to Leach. The society had expressed concern that Leach was selling lost pets and questioned whether the animals were treated humanely during transport to and from Leach's kennel. The society presented the board with a petition—signed by almost 3,500 people—asking that the sales be stopped. After questioning Leach and visiting his kennel, the board voted to deny the request, claiming the charges against Leach could not be proved to its satisfaction.[41]

During an inspection of Leach's facility on 3-22-88, an APHIS inspector ordered "[The] treatment or removal of sick animal(s)." On 6-19-89 (80 dogs, 61 cats), inspectors noted: "Noncompliant standards newly identified on this inspection... The transportation enclosures for cats are chicken crates. These do not meet the listed standards.... The complete name and address of the person from whom the dogs and cats were acquired was not complete in the records."

Subsequent inspections revealed serious deficiencies in veterinary care, handling of animals, housing, food storage, sanitation and recordkeeping:

3-12-90: (68 dogs, 55 cats) "3 dogs require immediate veterinary care or euthanasia. 30898 male blue tick hound, left ear infection pen #4. 30661 male white Lab X, Dermatitis, pen #10. No ID Hunting Dog, bilateral conjunctivitis. 75% of the cats demonstrated upper respiratory symptoms of illness with nasal and ocular discharges, sneezing and malaise. Several pens had piles of diarrhetic feces. 2 cats in pen #2 had numerous fight wounds on the face, ears and head.... A wild and vicious cat was handled by Mr. Leach by use of a catch pole. The animal exhibited signs of distress from choking while observation of the identification tag was conducted."

"The euthanasia chamber was located in a brick shed. The brick walls contained numerous cracks and separated mortar which allowed buckling at the walls outward. This is an extremely dangerous location for the gas tank and chamber. This chamber is used for dogs and cats.... At the cat barn the storage container had 4 dead mice in the bottom.... Rat holes and feces were evident in the dog barn feed storage shed. Rat holes and a dead rat were evident at the perimeter of the dog barn. "

"The hunting dog shed had an excessive accumulation of feces in all the pens.... At the cat barn, the floor contained an excessive accumulation of litter, feces and dirt.... The premises around the cat barn contained numerous fallen branches, a three-fourths full bucket of used vaccine vials and syringes, a motor, metal scraps and discarded and unused items."

"Transport enclosures.... The space between the bars are large enough to allow injury to the animal when a paw is put through them. These crates do not meet the standards.... Records.... Items not listed properly in forms include... complete description of animal acquired... date of acquisition... incomplete source name and address... animals acquired from other licensed dealers are not listed in Form 18-5... Incomplete address of sites of disposition... Holding period.... The records showed dogs and cats held at the facility less than 10 days. Numerous animals were removed from the facility within 4 days of acquisition.... Animals acquired from other dealers do not show the date of disposition. Therefore, the holding period cannot be determined."

During reinspection on 6-21-90 (48 dogs listed, 36 dogs on site; 16 cats listed, 25 cats on site), inspectors noted that while some of the previous deficiencies had been corrected, others had not: "Uncorrected non-compliant standards: Transport enclosures.... The chicken crates used for transporting cats do not meet the standards. Records.... The following information is not being maintained as required... complete address of buyer or receiver when sold, USDA license number if licensed of buyer or receiver, driver's license number and state of person from whom acquired if not USDA licensed or registered, vehicle license number and state of person from whom acquired if not USDA licensed. Holding period: All animals are not being held the prescribed number of days as specified."

In September 1990, the group Friends of Animals (FoA) released a videotape purporting to document "horrific conditions" at Leach Kennels. The tape showed a burial pit containing uncovered dog carcasses and piles of used vaccine vials and syringes in the surrounding woods.[42]

A USDA Veterinary Medical Officer viewed the videotape to determine whether it was actually filmed on Leach's premises. In her affidavit, she stated that she did recognize some of the buildings and barns on the tape from previous inspections. She said the fact that she didn't recognize all of the locations led her to believe Leach may have had an additional holding facility and a burial site that USDA was unaware of.[43] Two other USDA investigators later confirmed that the areas the Veterinary Medical Officer had been unable to recognize were located on Leach's property. As part of its investigation of FoA's allegations, USDA showed the videotape to Mr. and Mrs. Leach. The Leaches suggested that the decomposed animals shown on the tape had been dug up by the makers of the videotape. They also questioned the source of the vaccine vials and syringes, claiming they disposed of all vials and syringes in the burial site or in county trash containers. USDA promptly closed the investigation, concluding: "No violations were found to exist that had not been previously documented."[44]

The following month, USDA received a letter from a concerned bystander who had seen one of Leach's truckloads of dogs being unloaded on a hot day in August. The witness described the conditions in detail:

> [The dogs] were encaged in an unmarked yellow van... with no visible ventilation.... The interior appeared filthy dirty with an odor of ammonia and feces; the animals had no water and were panting vigorously. They distinctly appeared hot, exhausted, and fatigued.... [The driver] was unconcerned for the welfare of the dogs when I mentioned the heat factor and perhaps they needed some water and or air. In fact, his reply was, "they don't need any."

After an investigation of the complaint, USDA concluded that "the transport vehicle used by Leach Kennels does have adequate ventilation and is normally maintained in a clean manner. No violations of the transportation standards were established."[45]

That same month, USDA inspectors noted continuing violation of Animal Welfare Act requirements at Leach's facility:

10-17-90: (54 dogs listed, 57 dogs on site; 38 cats listed, 34 cats on site) "This facility has a chronic history of noncompliance in numerous sections of the USDA regulations and standards. Specific items of noncompliance have been noted on previous inspections.... Additional or different deficiencies have been noted under the same regulation or standard upon subsequent inspections. Therefore, the following deficiencies noted during this inspection are listed as uncorrected non-compliant standards.... Structural strength: The dog barn and hunting dog facility have numerous problem areas of wood rot and weather decay.... Flies were evident on the feed.... Waste Disposal. The burial pit has some exposed bones (mandible, tibia, femur and other small bones). All carcasses and bones must be covered sufficiently to minimize disease hazards."

"Veterinary care. The following animals were noted on this inspection needing veterinary attention. Pen #12 #33166 Male Rottweiler — has bite wounds on the left ear and over the left eye. These areas are swollen. Pen #6 #33160 Female collie cross — has an open and draining wound on the left ear. The ear is swollen. The carbon monoxide euthanasia chamber door has a hinge which is not secure... Some blood and leaves in the lower rear left corner."

"Identification. One 3-4 month old hound puppy in pen #1 of the hunting dog facility does not have any identification. 12 animals were examined for proper identification. The description of the animals as documented in the records does not match 5 animals examined.... Improper disposal of tags. Numerous identification tags were found in a 50-gallon drum along with other items of trash.... Records. The records of acquisition have the complete address missing on 10% of the listed sources. The vehicle number and state is not listed for 75% of the unlicensed sources. The driver's license number and state is missing on 10% of the listed sources.... It was discussed with Mr. Leach that when animals are acquired by him and his employees, they are to identify themselves as a licensed USDA animal dealer."

A November 1990 USDA Facility Report by Dr. Richard Overton concluded there was "no way to determine [from Leach's records] if the animals are being legally acquired."[46] Although it was explained to Leach that this was "a serious violation of the Animal Welfare Act," he resisted a request to provide the required information:

When Mr. Leach was asked to list complete addresses, license vehicle tags and driver license numbers for a group of individuals he balked. Mr. Leach's wife was also resistant and claimed that if we were to locate the people that some of them would probably be liars.

At this time we discovered that a Jimmy Lyles had sold a large number of cats and dogs to Mr. Leach and that he was really an employee of Mr. Leach, and that instead of listing the correct owner of these animals, Mr. Leach just used Mr. Lyle's name.

In the report, Dr. Overton stated that during a review of dealers in North Carolina, he had noted "incomplete or incorrect acquisition and sales records for transactions involving" Leach and other dealers. He had also noted that health certificates were not being made for dogs and cats transported by Leach from dealers in North Carolina.

On September 5, 1991, USDA filed a complaint against Leach alleging violations found during inspections on 10-19-90, 6-21-90, 3-12-90, and 6-19-89. The alleged violations included: failure to provide adequate veterinary care; failure to maintain complete records showing the acquisition, disposition, and identification of animals; failure to individually identify dogs and cats; failure to maintain housing facilities for dogs that were structurally sound and in good repair; failure to provide for the removal and disposal of animal wastes; failure to keep primary enclosures clean and sanitized as required; failure to keep buildings and grounds clean and in good repair and free of accumulations of trash; failure to keep dogs in compatible groups; failure to keep food receptacles for dogs clean and sanitized; failure to establish and maintain programs of disease control and prevention, euthanasia, and adequate veterinary care under the supervision and assistance of a veterinarian; and failure to construct and maintain primary enclosures for cats so as provide sufficient space to allow each animal to turn about freely and to easily stand, sit and lie in a comfortable normal position.

On November 24, 1992, Leach signed a Consent Decision and Order, neither admitting nor denying the charges against him. He was ordered to relinquish his license permanently and was assessed a $10,000 penalty, which was suspended on the condition that he not violate the Animal Welfare Act.

STEBANE, ERVIN d/b/a CIRCLE S RANCH. Kaukana, Wisconsin. USDA license #35-B-009 (1994).

Ervin Stebane sold between 1,000 and 2,000 dogs a year (see Chapter 2, "The Ervin Stebane Case").

On March 2, 1987, Administrative Law Judge John Campbell fined Stebane $1,500 and suspended his dealer license for 20 days. The judge commented that his order was consistent with USDA's "severe sanction policy," and that such sanctions were "appropriate, reasonable and necessary to achieve the remedial purpose of the Act, and to deter respondent and others from similar violations." Some of the violations that formed the basis of this sanction were as follows:

February 15 and 22, 1985 and March 6, 1985: improper storage of food, subjecting it to contamination or vermin infestation; failure to maintain interior of three building surfaces so they were impervious to moisture; failure to keep wire fencing between outdoor runs in good repair.

May 2, 1985: failure to provide adequate lighting in an indoor animal housing facility; failure to provide litter boxes for cats.

August 2, 1985: failure to provide a suitable method to rapidly eliminate excess water; failure to provide clean watering receptacles and remove an accumulation of excreta from primary enclosures.

October 7, 1985: failure to provide a litter box in a primary enclosure for cats; failure to provide adequate space, clean food and watering receptacles for cats; failure to furnish records.

November 7, 1985: Stebane invited a USDA inspector to conduct an inspection, but told the inspector to stop harassing him, made disparaging remarks about the inspector's conduct and questioned her use of common sense in carrying out previous inspections, all of which constituted a refusal to permit the inspection.

The judge noted that although deficiencies were found to be corrected on subsequent inspections, new violations were identified on those reinspections.

Inspection reports revealed inadequate recordkeeping, housing, sanitation and veterinary care at Circle S ranch:

11-12-87: (75 dogs, 7 cats) "1 cat... does not have an official USDA I.D. (tag).... 4 tags are hanging on the cat primary enclosure from cats sold — none of these animals have a record of dispersal (date, name, address, description of animal, etc.)."

8-5-88: (158 dogs) Six adult dogs and seven puppies were observed "with no ID tags.... One dog... was not entered into the records." Ten deficiencies were observed during this inspection.

These included two pens containing seven dogs "with no other supplementary shade nor protection from the elements.... Galvanized dog crate has no lower catch pan (has a wire bottom) to catch feces/urine.... Old box crate used as a cat transport enclosure doesn't have a solid bottom to catch feces/urine."

9-6-88: (111 dogs, 8 cats) "Middle building northwest pen now contains 5 small dogs (25 lbs. or smaller) with an approximately 3′ x 3′ foot dog house just able to contain all dogs at one time to stand or lay down with not enough room for 'normal postural movements.'"

5-5-89: (163 dogs, 9 cats) "5 of 9 cats appear to have moderate to severe upper respiratory disease—ocular & nasal discharge—with some severe conjunctivitis. No treatment is evident.... Litter pans in cat building—very soiled, also walls & rest boards dirty.... Outdoor cat pen—accumulated mud, bones, feathers—coming up through floor of pen—cannot be cleaned.... In cat building—1 pan of wet cat chow outside without shelter—inside a whole chicken.... Urine and feces in several water dishes and food bowls.... Frozen pans of ground meat [for dogs] are stored outside in an open water tank with a piece of canvas on top."

9-28-89: (170 dogs) "Building #1 indoor pen.... 4,094 sq. inches available. There are 8 dogs in pen... Necessary space = 9,248 inches.... 17 dogs were tagged with tag numbers which had no entry on Form 18-5.... 4 dogs had no tags and no tags were attached to the appropriate pen. 6 dogs had tag numbers which did not match the entry on Form 18-5. Entry indicated that the dog had been sold or was of a different breed."

12-9-89: (110 dogs) "4 dogs had tag numbers which did not match the entry on Form 18-5; 2 dogs had no tags; 8 dogs had tag numbers which had no entry on 18-5 Forms; 6 tags were hanging on pens and did not appear to match untagged dogs.... 5 dogs had registration papers and proper records but were not identified in pen.... Mr. Stebane has been operating as a contract pound for area towns in the past. With the advent of new regulations he is no longer acting in this capacity and has no plans to do so in the near future."

12-27-90: "Frozen chunks of meat piled up outside building.... Primary enclosure measures 23"x30"x10" and contained 9 adult cats. Space available to house only 2 cats.... [Feeding] food on floor.... Pens #7, 6, 5, 1 frozen meat on floor.... Many of enclosures appeared to have more than acceptable level of accumulation of waste (excreta).... 10+ dogs on records not found on premises.... 1 dog... Tag had been used previously.... 5 dogs untagged—were tagged in our presence.... 9 cats acquired last night were untagged."

9-3-92: Attempted inspection. "Licensee failed to have a responsible party available to conduct an animal welfare inspection."

Stebane's license was suspended for 21 days on June 30, 1993. On March 14, 1994, Stebane signed a consent decree permanently revoking his USDA license.

STOWERS, JACK (SUGAR CREEK KENNELS). Frankfort, Indiana. USDA license #32-B-097 (1997).

Jack Stowers supplied dogs to the Cleveland Clinic in Ohio and other Class B dealers, including Michael Kredovski (see Kredovski, Michael in "Class B Dealers Selling Random source Dogs and Cats for Research"). Stowers acquired the animals he sold from individuals and from pounds and trade days in Michigan, Tennessee and Kentucky. According to information he provided to USDA, he sold approximately 1,238 animals a year, grossing $43,000.[47] However, during an administrative hearing on charges of violating the Animal Welfare Act brought against him by USDA, Stowers testified that he sold dogs to research facilities for between $120 to $130 apiece, earning a gross profit of between $100,000 and $130,000 per year.[48] This testimony not only refutes the $43,000 figure but also his testimony during the same hearing that he earned only $20,000 to $25,000 a year.[49] Between the time he was first licensed in 1988 and his hearing in 1996, Stowers handled close to 10,000 dogs.

In June 1994, USDA suspended Stowers's license for 21 days and confiscated 29 dogs from his kennel. In December 1996, an administrative law judge fined him $15,000, ordered him to cease and desist from violating the Animal Welfare Act and revoked his license. USDA filed a new complaint against Stowers in February 1997, charging him with many of the same violations he was found guilty of in 1996.

Between 1990 and 1994, Stowers failed to allow a USDA inspector access to his facility on 29 separate occasions. A January 1995 USDA Office of Inspector General Report noted that "APHIS inspectors generally called ahead to schedule appointments because of [Stowers's] repeated refusal to cooperate in allowing inspections."[50] The report stated that despite the fact that the inspectors called in advance, in most cases they were "either refused admittance outright, or could not get in because the owner was gone." On two occasions when inspectors had made appointments and were allowed to enter the facility, they could not locate any animals.

When inspectors were able to conduct inspections, they documented serious deficiencies in sanitation, recordkeeping and housing:

2-20-90: (59 dogs) "Excessively strong ammonia smell.... 3 weaned pups without identification.... Records are not kept at facility at this time.... Holding period – Cannot be verified because records are unavailable"; 6-27-90: (25 dogs) "Dogs in Run #6 – 10 have no shade outside of dog house.... No records of to whom dogs were sold available this inspection."

1-3-91: (13 dogs) "Several dogs are doubled in (transport) enclosure and do not have adequate space to lift head in order to stand erect.... Dogs in transporting vehicle are not tagged or otherwise identified.... Some 18-6s were available for inspection... but there are no records of acquisition on the dogs being transported.... Holding period cannot be verified because records are inadequate."

6-10-91: Records inspection only. "Noncompliant standards documented on previous inspections that are not corrected this inspection: 1) Animals No.'s 2922 to 2930 appear twice on the VS Form 18-5 with different acquisition dates. 2) In [4] animals, there is a discrepancy between the date of sale on the VS Form 18-5 and the VS Form 18-6.... #2189... was a hound and not an alley cat as listed on VS Form 18-5. 3) With [5] animals a double tag number was used with no record of acquisition for one of them... 4) There is no information on acquisition for [11] animals... 5) There is no information on the disposition of [5] animals... 6) [7] animals were listed as 'Lost Tag' in the records, and there is no record of acquisition or date of acquisition... 7) [4] animals were listed as having been `shot' on the VS Form 18-5, but were actually sold on another date.... 8) Animal #2553 (mentioned in the VS Form 18-8 dated 1-3-91), appears on a VS Form 18-6 (which was not available at the time of inspection of 1-3-91), as having been donated to C. Alexander on 12-18-90, and then reappears on another VS Form 18-6 as having been sold to a research facility on 12-18-90."

On 8-6-92, the inspector noted: "This is the 3rd attempted inspection during the hours listed on the most recent Hours of Inspection dated 5-19-92.... I arrived at 3:00 pm, checked with Chester Stowers, the neighbor, who called Jack Stowers's home and it was reported he was not at home and they did not know when he would be home." More than a year had passed since the last inspection of 6-10-91.

In October 1992, Dr. Jerry Diemer, Supervisor of the North Central Sector Office, requested Regulatory Enforcement to take "expedited action" in Stowers's case, one of several submitted to the Office of General Counsel for review:

> [Stowers's] Violations include incomplete records, being unavailable for inspections, and not holding animals for required time. Last complete inspection was June 27, 1990; since then, there have been seven attempted inspections. Local humane organizations allege that Mr. Stowers deals in stolen animals. As we have not been able to inspect premises or records since June 21, 1991, we cannot document movement and or care of animals. Therefore, we feel this is a very high priority case.[51]

On 3-30-93, the inspector reported: "Noncompliant standards documented on previous inspections (6-27-90, 1-3-91, 6-10-91) that are not corrected: "In the case of [12] dogs/cats the same tag number was used to identify two (2) animals, with no record of acquisition for one of them.... In the case of #5440, the same tag number was used twice with no record of acquisition or date of acquisition for either of them; in the case of animals #4063, 4135, 4179, the same tag number was used twice with no record of date of acquisition. [15] dogs/cats were listed on the records as 'LOST' or 'LOST TAGS' but were actually sold or offered for sale. Therefore, there is no record of acquisition, description, or date of acquisition.... [15] dogs/cats were either sold or rejected for sale on 2-16-93 and there is no description, date of acquisition, or record of acquisition. [3] dogs/cats were sold 3-10-93 and there is no description, dates of acquisition, or record of acquisition."

Other noncompliant standards documented from previous inspections (1-3-91, 6-10-91) that remained uncorrected included the sale of 37 animals before the required holding period had been met. Use of the same tag numbers to identify more than one animal was noted as uncorrected from the 6-10-91 inspection. Inspectors also noted: "There are no copies of health certificates available on interstate transportation of dogs/cats from Kentucky to Indiana, and Indiana to Mississippi."

On June 16, 1994, USDA filed a complaint against Stowers alleging he 1) failed to maintain complete and accurate records of the acquisition, disposition and identification of dogs, 2) failed to hold dogs for the required period of time, 3) failed to identify dogs as required, 4) failed to allow USDA officials to inspect his premises on 22 separate occasions, 5) offered dogs for transportation in enclosures that did not conform to structural requirements and 6) obtained random source dogs from individuals who had not bred and raised the dogs on their own premises. On June 17, Kent Permentier, an APHIS senior investigator, delivered a 21-day license suspension notice to Stowers. Stowers refused to allow an inspection at that time and threatened to harm the APHIS inspector if he returned and attempted to inspect the premises at a later time.

On June 28, two USDA inspectors, two U.S. Marshals and a county sheriff went to Stowers's facility to photograph the dogs covered under the 21-day suspension. Many of the dogs were excessively thin and ill. Stowers was instructed in writing and orally through his wife Cindy to obtain veterinary diagnosis and treatment for the sick animals within 24 hours. The following day, investigator Permentier and the inspector returned and discovered that Stowers had not provided the dogs with veterinary care. They confiscated all 29 dogs housed in the facility. Many of the dogs were in such poor physical condition they had to be euthanized. Others were placed in homes by a local humane society.

On 6-30-94, Stowers allowed an APHIS inspector to conduct an announced records inspection. The inspector reported: "Of the approximately 1490 dogs/cats listed in the records as having been obtained since 5-8-93, approximately 1162 have both an incomplete address and no driver's license number / vehicle license number on the individual from whom these dogs/cats were acquired.... Another 36 animals have an incomplete address on individuals from whom they were obtained.... Another 119 animals have no driver's license number on individuals from whom they were obtained.... For the following tag numbers there is no record of disposition: [total of 59 animals].... [5] were listed in the records as 'shot' but were actually sold at a later date.... 18 dogs/cats were not held a sufficient number of days.... In the following dogs/cats the same tag number was used to identify more than one animal: [15 tag numbers listed].... There are no pound certificates available for pound-derived dogs/cats that were acquired after 8-23-93."

On 10-12-94, the inspector reported: "There were 8 dogs where there was no date of acquisition available.... There are no pound certificates available for the 89 pound derived dogs acquired since last inspection (Note: Mr. Stowers has acquired blank pound certificates)."

USDA filed an amended complaint on October 28, 1994, charging Stowers with additional violations of the AWA, including failure to provide adequate veterinary care to dogs; provide health certificates for transported dogs; and construct and maintain primary enclosures for dogs so as to protect them from injury and contain them securely.

In July 1995, Pennsylvania state dog wardens stopped Stowers as he was returning to Indiana after delivering a truckload of dogs to Mike Kredovski. Most of the cages in the truck were empty, except for two sick dogs Kredovski had refused to accept. Stowers admitted transporting 28 dogs from Indiana the previous day without food or water. The dog wardens and officials from the local SPCA charged Stowers with transporting dogs without an out-of-state kennel license; failure to provide records or bills of sale and cruelty to animals, including overcrowding and failure to provide food, water and veterinary care. Stowers never answered the charges against him, and there is still an outstanding warrant for his arrest.

On May 2 and 3, 1996, almost two years after it had filed a complaint against Stowers, USDA held an administrative hearing in Indianapolis, Indiana. USDA investigators testified that when they had attempted to trace back individuals listed as supplying dogs to Stowers, they were unable to locate many of the people based on the information in Stowers's records. Other listed suppliers who were located stated they did not know Stowers and had never sold him any dogs. Although Stowers argued that USDA failed to prove he purchased dogs from individuals who hadn't bred and raised the animals on their own property, he testified that he suspected that about sixty percent of the dogs he buys are not raised on the sellers' premises.

In his December 23, 1996 decision, Chief Administrative Law Judge Victor Palmer wrote: "Mr. Stowers has proven himself unwilling to submit to statutorily required government regulation. His claims of showing good faith are negated by his admitted threats against APHIS inspectors and his routine refusal to allow the inspection of his facility."[52] Judge Palmer noted that because Stowers had committed 33 violations, a fine of as much as $82,000 could have been assessed. "Considering the extent of Respondent's noncompliance, the $20,000 penalty requested by Complainant is not inappropriate." Because Judge Palmer had dismissed three of the recordkeeping allegations based on the government's failure to present substantiating evidence, he reduced the fine to $15,000. He also ordered permanent revocation of Stowers's license and issuance of a cease and desist order. Although the decision gave Stowers 30 days to appeal the decision, he requested and was granted a two and a half month extension to file an appeal. He never did file an appeal, and, in May 1997, Judge Palmer's decision became effective. USDA filed another complaint against Stowers in February 1997, charging him with 1) failure to allow inspection of his facility; 2) failure to make records of acquisition and disposition available to APHIS; 3) failure to have any health certificates or pound certificates for dogs; 4) failure to identify dogs; 5) failure to provide adequate veterinary care for dogs; and 6) failure to ensure that primary enclosures were constructed and maintained so as to have no sharp points that could injure the animals contained therein. It is not known whether USDA will take any action on the complaint.

THORSEN, GEORGE (THORSEN BREEDING LABS). Enosburg Falls, Vermont. USDA license #13-B-004 (last licensed in 1993).

George Thorsen sold both purpose bred and random source dogs and cats to Yale, Harvard, and Brown universities.[53] In the late 1970s, Thorsen and another Vermont Class B dealer, Rosaire Paradis, purchased as many as 2,000 animals a year from Canadian pounds in south Quebec. Thorsen later rented Paradis's kennels in order to expand his own operation.[54,55] He continued to acquire animals in Canada until 1993, when USDA informed him that purchasing animals from dealers and pounds in Canada would no longer be permitted. In 1991, Thorsen reported selling 583 animals, earning $68,698 in gross sales.[56]

Inspections of Thorsen's facility revealed deficiencies in identification of animals, veterinary care, housing and sanitation:

6-11-87: (Goff Farm, Westboro, MA, 43 cats) "No facility veterinarian exists, no written program therefore. An agreement with a veterinarian must be established.... There was a strong odor of ammonia upon entering.... An inadequate employee situation still exists, as evidenced by the lack of work accomplished – UNCORRECTED REPEAT DEFICIENCY.... The transport vehicle was inspected and found dirty with no apparent ventilation, and no way to secure the cages to the vehicle floor"; 12-18-87: "There are two cats in a travel carrier that are 11 x 18. Cats need a minimum floor space of 2 1/2 square feet. There are two cages 27" x 24" that have 2 small cats which also need 2 1/2 sq. ft. of floor space."

12-6-88: Attempted inspection. "Mr. Thorsen was not available today. Therefore, records could not be inspected, [and] the matter of health certificates couldn't be discussed."

9-11-90: (142 cats) "Indoor facility does not provide ample lighting so as to provide for inspection and cleaning.... An attempt must be made to identify cats.... None of the cats have identification affixed to them.... Dealer would not provide access to complete names and addresses of sources of cats.... [Determination of whether cats were being held the number of days required] could not be checked due to dealer not allowing USDA access to cat source."

11-6-90: (107 cats) "Strong odor noted in both downstairs and upstairs.... Records do not contain the complete name, address, vehicle license number, or driver's license number."

5-30-91: (95 cats) "Noncompliant standards documented on 11-6-90, 9-11-90 that are not corrected: Eight cats noted from one source the address, vehicle license number are not indicated."

In May, 1991, Thorsen notified USDA that he had rented Rosaire Paradis's kennels in Berkshire, Vermont: "We are continuing to prepare and also breed cats for research but are also providing dogs for research on a very limited scale using Mr. Paradis's kennel.... The updating [of the facility] will include the addition of more lighting, insulating of inside perimeter walls, addition of cleaning and preparation stations, painting and additional ventilation which will all lead to an excellent facility for Lab Animals before shipment to the community."[57]

Despite Thorsen's assurances, inspections of the new site revealed deficiencies in sanitation and veterinary care:

6-10-91: (16 dogs, 51 cats) "The cages for cats have strong fecal, urine odors.... Some areas of the kennel had to be inspected with a flashlight. Lighting must be provided."

3-25-92: (19 dogs, 69 cats) "The indoor facility noted with strong ammonia odor.... Ventilation must be provided at all times so as to provide for the health and well being of the animals.... Second cat section... noted not sufficiently lit so as to provide for proper inspection.... Cat #3159 noted to be severely matted; this cat needs to be bathed and groomed. Cat #3222 noted with right eye closed and some drainage. Also cat #4089 noted with severe nasal and ocular discharge and also coughing. Cat #4015 noted with tail that is necrotic and seeping serum — the above animals need to be seen by the attending veterinarian... (Also three dead puppies were noted)."

4-7-92: (17 dogs, 50 cats) "The dog and cat area noted with a strong ammonia odor. Ventilation must be provided so as to minimize odors and ammonia levels.... The attending veterinarian was not contacted concerning the sick animals noted on 3-25-92.... Cat #4015 was euthanized by the facility and #3222 and 4089 were treated by the facility without being seen by the attending veterinarian.... Cat #4086 noted with wound on right front leg such that the cat is limping and licking at the area. The program of veterinary care stated that the attending veterinarian will visit the facility monthly — The veterinarian has not been to the facility in about 8 months. Also the program states the fecals will be conducted on admission of the animal to the facility — this is not being followed. At present the veterinarian is not included in a regular plan to prevent, control, diagnose and treat diseases and injuries."

Inspectors documented inadequate ventilation again on 9-9-92 and 10-15-92. Thorsen closed the Berkshire site on October 23, and moved all of the animals back to the Vermont facility. In September 1993, USDA terminated Thorsen's license after he failed to submit the required renewal application and license fee.

WISE, ALMAN d/b/a TARHEEL CATTERY. Benson, North Carolina. USDA license #55-B-037 (last licensed in 1990).

Alman Wise, known as "the Catman," supplied cats to Carolina Biological Supply Company in Burlington, North Carolina (USDA license #55-B-010). On his 1988-1989 annual report, he reported selling 13,509 cats, grossing $128, 343.[58] Wise had a long history of noncompliance with the Animal Welfare Act. USDA fined him $1,000 in 1984 and $6,000 in 1986.

Al and Dorothy Wise, John D. Wise, John H. Wise, Faye Wise and Vaden Wise are one of many examples of families that form commercial networks with individually licensed family members located in diverse geographic areas. Faye Wise (#72-B-028) and Vaden Wise (#72-B-13) operated facilities in Louisiana at different times; the remaining Wises operated out of North Carolina. Al Wise's wife, Dorothy, tried unsuccessfully to obtain her own license.

In 1984, Wise signed a consent decision and order fining him $1,000 and ordering him to cease and desist from violating the Animal Welfare Act. The charges against Wise were based on three inspections and an incident in Rocky Mount, North Carolina, where Wise had trapped a number of cats at a mobile home park. Some of the cats were strays, but many of them were pets of park residents. Wise's brother, Kirby, transported the cats in a truck with a faulty exhaust system, so that fumes leaked into the area were the cats were held. As a result, twenty-one of the cats died. On another occasion, USDA inspectors cited Wise for transporting 145 cats in four crates that were not large enough to allow the animals to make normal postural adjustments. Inspectors also discovered that many cats were not held for the required holding period, many were improperly tagged or identified and record-keeping was inadequate. The consent decision ordered Wise to identify all animals immediately upon acquisition, maintain complete records on all animals and observe the required five-day holding period. The decision also ordered that whenever Wise acquired stray animals by capturing them, he was to place conspicuous notices near his property with information on the date of capture of any stray animals, together with his business name, address and telephone number. The notice was to remain posted at least throughout the holding period.

In October 1985, one of Wise's employees, Billy Brock, was convicted on a charge of cruelty to animals. Brock had driven his truck into a woman's driveway in Mebane and asked her if she had any cats she didn't want. The woman said she saw 10 cats in the back of the truck crammed into small cages. "They were packed so closely that the ones that had their backs to me could not turn around," said the woman.[59] None of the cats had any food or water. A judge ordered Brock to pay court costs but did not impose a fine.

USDA filed a complaint against Wise on June 11, 1986, charging that notwithstanding the provisions of the 1984 consent decision and order, Wise had willfully violated the Animal Welfare Act, the regulations and the order. The complaint alleged that 1) on 7-8-85, Wise's employee Billy G. Brock transported cats in an overcrowded cage; 2) on 7-12-85, Wise failed to identify 25 cats and keep a record of names and addresses of the cats' sources; and 3) on 7-12-85 and 10-10-85, Wise failed to provide adequate litter for cats. In October, USDA ordered Wise to cease and desist from violating the Animal Welfare Act and assessed him a $6,000 civil penalty.

A 7-18-90 inspection revealed continuing noncompliance with re-cordkeeping violations. Of the 340 individuals listed as supplying more than 1,200 cats to Wise between May and July, none were noted to have vehicle or driver's license numbers recorded, and 90 percent did not have a complete address listed. "This failure to maintain records is a violation of a cease and desist order of Oct. 28, 1986," wrote the inspector.

The same month, compliance officer Page Eppele and investigator William Groce attempted to trace back some of Wise's suppliers. In his report to Southeast Sector Supervisor Joseph Walker, Groce wrote, "I was unable to locate any person listed on the VS Form 18-5's who had given cat(s) to Al Wise or Tarheel Cattery."[60] After her own investigation of Wise's records, officer Eppele reported:

Several people whose names were listed on the VS Form 18-

5... signed affidavits stating they did not give cats to Al Wise or Tarheel Cattery nor did they know Al Wise or Tarheel Cattery. Other names on form could not be located or were believed fictitious.

Eppele's report also described how, during a delivery to CBSC, Wise had been observed using a metal rod to prod cats into cages before placing them in a gas chamber. A witness swore in an affidavit that:

> At no time during the entire process... did I observe Mr. Wise or any regular CBSC employee make any record of transfer of live cats from dealers to CBSC, either through identification by USDA identification tag or description of individual animal.

On October 22, 1990, ABC-TV's "World News Tonight" aired video footage on CBSC and Wise filmed by People For the Ethical Treatment of Animals (PETA) investigators. The video showed Wise delivering a large number of cats to CBSC. Even though the video clearly depicted the delivery of live cats to the CBSC loading dock, CBSC president Dr. Thomas Powell asserted on camera that the animals CBSC purchased were "always dead" when acquired. The video also showed cats roughly prodded with metal hooks into crates, which were then placed in a gas chamber. Some of the animals were shown still moving when they were taken to the embalming table. Some clenched their jaws as the formaldehyde was injected into their veins.

The footage showed an ABC News producer trying to interview Wise, who responded by attempting to run the producer down in a tractor. As the television crew tried to get away, a second camera filmed Wise ramming the tractor into a ABC-TV News van.[61,62]

USDA Inspector William Groce noted that during a 10-23-90 inspection, Wise discussed giving up his license. "Mr. Wise stated he wasn't able to stand the pressure. The folks at church and his neighbors were saying about him. 'They all think I'm bad and did wrong,' Mr. Wise stated, 'I think I'll give my license up and that way I won't be prosecuted.'... Mr. Wise further stated he would wait a while till things cooled off and reapply for a new license."[63] Wise officially surrendered his license on October 31,1990.

In January 1991, Wise reapplied for a Class B license under a new company name, Double C Ranch. In response to Wise's reapplication, Dr. Richard Overton sent a memo to USDA Assistant Deputy Administrator of Regulatory Enforcement Arthur J. Wilson, which stated:

> In an attempt to avoid prosecution, Mr. Wise has surrendered his license and has reapplied for a new license.... Mr. Wise has a chronic history of noncompliance with the Animal Welfare Act, particularly in the area of acquisition of cats.... Because of the size of his business of $110,506.50... and the total lack of credibility of his

acquisition records, plus the previous history of noncompliance, we recommend that the maximum civil penalty be assessed against Mr. Wise... that Mr. Wise's license be permanently revoked and Mr. Wise be barred as a licensed Dealer under the Animal Welfare Act or have any activity in this area.

USDA denied Wise's license reapplication on January 23, 1991. In 1993, USDA filed a complaint against Wise for violations documented before he relinquished his license. The complaint charged Wise with failing to maintain records of the acquisition, disposition, and identification of cats, failing to establish and maintain a written program of adequate veterinary care and failing to provide sufficient space for cats in primary enclosures. On July 7, 1993 Wise signed a consent decision and order, which disqualified him from becoming licensed under the act for ten years and prohibited him from engaging in any activity for which a license is required under the Act.

ZOOK, HARRY (MAPLE HILL KENNELS). Martinsville, Indiana. USDA license #32-B-2 (last licensed in 1990).

Harry Zook, at one time the Town Marshal for Morgantown, Indiana, was first licensed as a Class B dealer in 1967. He operated his kennel as a contract pound for the City of Morgantown, and his wife was the Morgan County dog warden. Zook also had a contract to accept dogs from the St. Joseph County, Michigan Pound, where he acquired the majority of his dogs. He reported selling 547 dogs in 1988.[64]

USDA inspectors reported deficiencies in recordkeeping, sanitation and housing at Maple Hill Kennels:

3-30-87: (48 dogs inspected) "Wire on outside and inside cages broken and bent.... Several piles of used sawdust and fecal matter piled up in facility.... Inadequate lighting available in indoor facility.... Walls and floor of indoor facility allowing water seepage into pens.... Outside pen has 3 doghouses in bad repair.... Dogs not able to remain dry and clean.... Food receptacles have food buildup.... Water receptacles are dirty.... All pens, indoors, walls, ceilings have buildup of cobwebs, dust, rust, floors covered with thin film of waste.... Dog boxes on vehicles are made of wood; urine and water soak into wood.... Current program of euthanasia is to gas dogs in a box container with exhaust from truck.... 48 dogs on hand. Dogs not [identified] and no records — correct by 4-4-87."

On April 1, 1987, Dr. James Downard, APHIS Area Veterinarian in Charge for Indiana, wrote to Zook expressing his outrage at conditions found at his premises:

I have just reviewed the March 30, 1987 inspection report for your facility. I am appalled at the conditions found by our inspectors. The following actions must be implemented immediately: (1) Any dog that you acquire must be identified immediately upon acquisition and a record made of where acquired, the name of the person from whom acquired and a brief description of the animal.... (2) All sick or injured dogs must be placed in individual kennels and not in a common pen as you have been doing.... (3) Daily sanitation must be implemented.... (6) Euthanasia must be performed in a humane manner. Exhaust fumes from a truck is entirely unsatisfactory.

Although an inspector reported that conditions at the facility had improved somewhat by April 8, subsequent inspections revealed new deficiencies in sanitation and recordkeeping:

9-1-87: (19 dogs, 7 cats) "Indoor kennels have large buildup of cobwebs, dust.... Serious fly problem.... 15 dogs received on 8-31-87 not identified at time of this inspection.... Records from 6-22-87 still present do not disclose sales of dogs obtained. Records from 7-22-87 do not disclose dog acquisition or sales."

9-11-87: (24 dogs, 7 cats) "Cat pen — dusty — buildup of fecal matter — resting boards dirty.... 3 dogs no I.D. — Mr. Zook stated dogs just arrived at facility.... Cats are not identified — must be identified in records and by numbers.... Cats are not included in records."

12-8-88: (35 dogs listed, 55 dogs on site; 10 cats listed, 9 cats on site) "Deficiencies not corrected from previous inspection (11-21-88).... Dogs, cats recently acquired are not identified and not entered on records.... Water receptacles overturned in multiple runs with no other source available. Provide at least 2 feed pans and 2 water pans in each pen due to number of dogs in each pen and size differential between dogs.... Moderate accumulation of fecal material in multiple runs. Increase frequency of cleaning to prevent disease, odor, vermin problem."

In a January 3, 1989 letter to REAC's R.L. Crawford, Dr. Morley Cook, Veterinarian in Charge for Indiana, questioned the legality of Zook's dual function as dealer and pound:

It has been brought to our attention... that Mr. Harry Zook, dba Maple Hill Kennel, 32-B-2, Martinsville, Indiana, is a licensed dealer and is operating a contract city pound for the City of Morgantown and Morgan County.... Mr. Zook's facility does not meet the requirements set forth in The Animal Welfare Manual.... However, the facility has been licensed since May 24, 1967 and has essentially operated as a contract city pound for several years. We are requesting your interpretation of regulation requirements in respect to this type of facility and the recommended course of action to be taken.

Zook eventually constructed a separate facility to hold the Morgan County pound dogs.

In January 1990, the Zooks voluntarily relinquished their license.

Notes

1. Judith Reitman, *Stolen for Profit: How the Medical Establishment Is Funding a National Pet Theft Conspiracy*, (New York: Pharos Books, 1992).

2. Advertising information on Beise Kennels from Animal Welfare Institute file on Beise Kennels, 1965, compiled by Dorothy Dyce, Laboratory Animal Specialist.

3. Letter to Dr. Ellen Magid, Veterinary Inspector, USDA-APHIS-REAC, (signature deleted), 28 February 1989.

4. USDA-APHIS Animal Care Complaint Contact (complainant unidentified), 27 November 1990.

5. USDA-APHIS Veterinary Inspector, Report of Alleged Violation of the Animal Welfare Act, 25 February 1991.

6. Michael K. Nottingham, Investigator, REAC, Report of Investigation of Alleged Violation of the Animal Welfare Act, 4 June 1991.

7. Ron Claxon, in an affidavit dated 3 April 1991.

8. USDA-APHIS Veterinary Inspector, in a memo to Dr. Richard Overton, Animal Care Specialist, USDA-REAC, 18 June 1992.

9. Michael K. Nottingham, Investigator, REAC, in a letter to REAC investigator Kent A. Permentier, 14 August 1992.

10. Affidavit of Mark D. Lynch, 24 August 1992.

11. Affidavit of Gregory Fedechko, 26 August 1992.

12. Ron Claxon, in an affidavit dated 26 August 1992.

13. Samuel Esposito, USDA-APHIS Application for License or Annual Report, 6 May 1985.

14. Action 81, Berryville, VA. Information on dealers who acquired dogs from Virginia; various dates.

15. Ibid.

16. "Truck Carrying Canines to Labs Uncovered by Officials Locally," Martinsburg, WV: *The Martinsburg Journal*, 9 March 1976.

17. "Action 81 Group Formed to Help Stop Dognapping," Martinsburg, WV: *The Martinsburg Journal*, 16 April 1976.

18. Action 81, Berryville, VA. Information on dealers who acquired dogs from Virginia; various dates.

19. Huntington, WV: *The Huntington Herald Dispatch*, 12 April 1980.

20. Circuit Court of Cabell County, WV, Criminal Case Information Sheet, Case No. 80M-860, 28 April 1980.

21. Action 81, Berryville, VA. Information on dealers who acquired dogs from Virginia; various dates.

22. Philadelphia, PA: *The Sunday News*, 10 July 1983.

23. John D. Wiggins, Phelps County Missouri Prosecuting Attorney, in a letter dated 22

August 1983.

24. USDA-APHIS Veterinary Inspector, in a memo to Dr. Joseph Walker, Southeast Sector Supervisor, USDA-REAC, 19 October 1990.

25. Thor Tolo, "No License Means Headache for Local Dogcatcher," St. Peter, MN: *St. Peter Herald*, 18 April 1985.

26. Tommy Wolfe, "Group Asks Winona Aldermen to Review Contract with Dealer," Mississippi: *The Daily Sentinel-Star*, 7 April 1993.

27. "Rewards Target Mississippi Pet Thieves," Memphis, TN: *The Commercial Appeal*, 8 April 1993.

28. Russell Hutton, USDA-APHIS Application for License or Annual Report, 10 April 1990.

29. *The New York Times*, 6 July 1965.

30. Cole Phinizy, "The Lost Pets That Stray to the Labs," *Sports Illustrated*, 29 November 1965.

31. Delmara Baylor, State Humane Investigator, Virginia, in a letter dated 1 September 1984 to Mary Warner, Action 81, Virginia.

32. "Dog Dealer to Pay Fine of $2,000," Harrisburg, PA: *Harrisburg News*, 3 March 1988.

33. Walt Lane, Virginia Federation of Humane Societies, in a letter to Leroy E. Bowan, Jr. DVM, Animal Welfare Officer, Commonwealth of Virginia, dated 5 August 1982.

34. Noel Leach, USDA-APHIS Application for License or Annual Report, 3 May 1977.

35. Paul L. Bernhardt, in a letter dated 28 October 1981.

36. Sue G. Ellenburg, in a letter to the Caldwell County Commissioners dated 30 August 1982.

37. Clarke Morrison, "Animal Dealer Defends Treatment of Dogs, Cats," North Carolina: *The Hickory Daily Record*, 21 September 1982.

38. Clarke Morrison, "Animal Dealer Defends Treatment of Dogs, Cats," Hickory, NC: *Hickory Daily Record*, 21 September 1982.

39. Dr. William Rumpp, University of North Carolina researcher, in an address to the Caldwell County Commission. Unsanitary truck conditions were documented by UNC officials during a 1975 inspection. Hickory, NC: *Hickory Daily Record*, 21 September 1982.

40. The Animal Welfare Institute, statement submitted to Caldwell County Commission, July 1982.

41. Kathy Loan, "County Plans to Keep Selling Dogs," Virginia: *News Messenger*, 12 May 1987.

42. Friends of Animals press release, 14 September 1990.

43. Kay Carter-Corker, Veterinary Medical Officer, USDA-APHIS-REAC, in an affidavit dated 10 October 1990.

44. Worth V. Hash, Investigator, USDA-APHIS-REAC, in an investigation report to Dr. Joseph Walker, Sector Supervisor for Animal Care, USDA-APHIS-REAC, 28 November 1990.

45. Worth V. Hash, Investigator, USDA-APHIS-REAC, in an investigation report to Dr. Joseph Walker, Sector Supervisor for Animal Care, USDA-APHIS-REAC, 27 November 1990.

46. USDA Facility Report on Noel Leach, dated 1 November 1990: Dr. Richard O. Overton, Animal Care Specialist, Southeast Sector, to Dr. Morley H. Cook, Associate Deputy Administrator, Regulatory Enforcement and Animal Care.

47. USDA-APHIS, Annual Sales of Currently Licensed Class B Dealers Providing Random Source Dogs and Cats to Research Facilities, 1996.

48. Decision and Order, In re: Jack D. Stowers, d/b/a Sugar Creek Kennels, Respondent, 23 December 1996.

49. Ibid.

50. USDA Office of Inspector General report on APHIS's enforcement of the Animal Welfare Act, 5 January 1995.

51. Jerry W. Diemer, North Central Sector Supervisor for Animal Care, APHIS-REAC, in a letter to Alan Christian, Staff Director, REAC, 1 October 1992.

52. Decision and Order, In re: Jack D. Stowers, d/b/a Sugar Creek Kennels, Respondent, 23 December 1996.

53. Action 81, 1984 information.

54. David Johnston, "Peddling of Animals Illegal in 8 States, Medical Researchers Turn to Canada," Montreal, Canada: *The Montreal Gazette*, 27 August 1985.

55. Montreal, Canada: TV Channel 12, "As It Is," 2 March 1985.

56. George Thorsen, USDA-APHIS Application for License or Annual Report, 26 August 1991.

57. George and Matt Thorsen, in a 30 May 1991 letter to USDA.

58. Alman Wise, USDA-APHIS Application For License Or Annual Report, 25 July 1989.

59. Mike McQueen, "Man Who Collects Cats for Research Is Found Guilty of Cruelty to Animals," Raleigh, N.C. : *The News And Observer*, 19 October 1985.

60. William T. Groce, Investigator, REAC, in a letter to Dr. Joseph A. Walker, Southeastern Sector Supervisor, REAC, 19 December 1990.

61. The Animal Welfare Institute, *AWI Quarterly*, v. 39, n. 4. Winter 1990-91.

62. In March, 1994, administrative law judge Dorothea Baker ruled there was insufficient evidence to support USDA's charges of animal cruelty against CBSC (for allegedly embalming live cats). Her decision was based on "expert" testimony regarding the videotaped evidence provided by PETA. The tape was viewed by veterinarians representing USDA and CBSC. Of the USDA's two veterinarians, Judge Baker said: "Dr. Dienhart had no experience in embalming and no experience in euthanasia of animals with carbon monoxide.... Although [they] were veterinarians, their training and experience were not of the persuasiveness of the Respondent's highly trained and competent expert witnesses, who held a high degree of skill, experience, and knowledge relating to embalming."

63. Affidavit of William Groce, Regulatory Enforcement, dated 18 January 1991, in reference to a 23 October 1990 interview with Al Wise.

64. Harry Zook, USDA-APHIS Application for License or Annual Report, 5 September 1989.

Chapter 8

Washington State Research Animal Dealers

---

by Ruth Fox

With only a few USDA-licensed research animal dealers, Washington state is a minor player in the business of procuring dogs and cats for laboratory use. But investigations into the dealers and their practices reveal all the basic elements of high drama: theft, greed, deception, and heartbreak.

The Pet Connection

In 1985, Don Johnson rescued Sosha, a young German shepherd/Doberman mix, from an abusive home. Johnson quickly became attached to the dog. But his extended hours away from home, coupled with his landlord's objection to the new housemate, convinced him to find Sosha a new home. He had her spayed and placed a classified ad.

His ad in the Journal America, a daily newspaper that covers Seattle's eastside suburbs, ran for three weeks before Johnson found someone who sounded good enough for Sosha. Don and Judee Peters, a genial retired couple, came to Johnson's home, where they played with Sosha for 45 minutes and described the idyllic life she would have as their companion on a ranch. Johnson took the couple's mailing address and elicited a promise that he could visit as often as he wished. Just before they drove off with Sosha, Johnson hugged and kissed the dog. He told Don Peters that he had feared Sosha might end up in the hands of people who sell animals for research.

When Johnson's letters to the couple's post office address went unanswered and he was unable to obtain their phone number, he became suspicious. Nearly a year later, his worst fears were realized. Johnson's parents came across an article in PAWS NEWS that described the couple and the methods they used to procure dogs. Don and Judee Peters, doing business as The Pet Connection, were USDA Class B research animal dealers.

Johnson immediately called PAWS. Using documents obtained

under the state's Public Disclosure Law, PAWS was able to determine that the Peters sold Sosha to the University of Washington about a week after they took her from Johnson. She had been killed in an experiment.

"When I called the UW to find out what happened to Sosha," Johnson said, "they couldn't have been more callous or uninterested in helping me. When I asked why they didn't suspect Sosha was somebody's pet when they saw her recent spay surgery, they said that where the dogs come from is not their concern."

By pursuing leads from classified ads in back issues of local newspapers PAWS was able to locate other individuals who had been deceived by Peters. PAWS obtained statements from seven of them and prepared extensive documentation, including proof of identification and holding period violations, for submission to the USDA, but the agency took no action.

With the assistance of PAWS, Johnson filed suit against the Peters. By the time the case was heard, their dealer registration had lapsed and they had left the area. In December, 1990, a Snohomish County, Washington, Superior Court ordered the couple to pay Johnson $1,000 for making false statements, $1,000 for breach of contract and $8,000 for causing him severe anxiety and emotional distress. A lien in the amount of $10,000 was attached to the couple's property.

Said Johnson: "I will never forget saying goodbye to Sosha. This can't bring her back, but maybe it will serve as a deterrent to heartless people who wouldn't otherwise hesitate to do this kind of thing." The court ruling has been hailed by animal advocates because it takes into account factors above and beyond the animal's marketplace value in assessing damages.

Sunnydell Kennels

Sequim, Washington, located on the Evergreen State's Olympic Peninsula, is a haven for retirees and a favorite spot of gun enthusiasts who flock to the area to shoot and Chuck Dryke's Sunnydell Shooting Grounds. The "Entering Sequim" sign alongside the highway also proclaims the town as Home of Matt Dryke. Chuck Dryke's son, Matt, holds world records and the 1984 Olympic Gold Medal in skeet shooting. To get to Sunnydell shooting grounds you turn onto Dryke Road. The Shooting Grounds are just down the road from Sunnydell Kennels, where Chuck Dryke kept his research dogs. Since at least 1978 Chuck Dryke was a Class B USDA research animal dealer. The Bob Hope International Heart Institute in Seattle was his sole customer. In 1986 it paid Dryke $18,000 for 223 dogs.

For miles around, Dryke was known as a problem solver when it came to dogs. You could take him litters of pups after you'd picked out the good hunting prospects. You could take him strays or family pets. He'd take them all. It was understood that he'd train some as gun dogs, and the others he'd place as companions: notably, companions for senior citizens. Dryke's research connection was not generally known.

In early 1987 a rash of dog disappearances occurred around normally quiet Sequim. On March 31, Darcel Batchelor's nine-month-old pup Sis disappeared after Darcel's cousin, Bud, and his pals had stopped by. Just the day before, Darcel had picked up Bud and a friend, who were hitchhiking, and the men asked Darcel to stop at Sunnydell so they could get some money from Dryke. They explained that he paid them for bringing him dogs. Bud even joked to Darcel that she shouldn't be surprised if one day her dogs disappeared.

That same evening, the Batchelors' neighbors, Shannon and Donna McCreary, returned home to find Buddy, their laid back black labrador, missing.

By midday on April 1, the Batchelors had made several phone calls to family and friends, one of whom contacted Sunnydell. During the fourth telephone conversation with Sunnydell, Dryke's companion Rosemary Knotek finally said, "We've found your dog." Sis was dropped off at the Batchelors' home that afternoon by a Sunnydell employee.

On April 2, a neighbor of the Batchelors and the McCrearys saw the McCrearys' Lost ad for Buddy and called the Batchelor home to tell them of Buddy's disappearance. Darcel's mother, Becky, called Chuck Dryke and asked if she could come look for the McCreary's dog. Dryke said no. But that night, Becky Batchelor and Shannon McCreary drove to Sunnydell. As somebody watched from the Dryke home, they found Buddy in a kennel and took him home.

Within a week's time, PAWS received four calls from Sequim area residents about Chuck Dryke. The November, 1986 issue of PAWS NEWS that had alerted Don Johnson's parents to the Peters' research sales also listed Chuck Dryke as a research animal dealer. When Judy Nikodym of the Clallam County Humane Society heard about the disappearances that week, she took the magazine to the local sheriff's office. Detective Steve Snover called PAWS for information. He later told PAWS that three men had been involved in the incidents he investigated. One man had admitted to taking two dogs in the nearby towns of Agnew and Port Angeles. In Port Angeles, he had untied a dog from in front of a furniture store after becoming frustrated with his inability to catch a different dog he had been chasing around town. He sold both dogs to Dryke.

Under questioning by Detective Snover and later, PAWS, Dryke admitted to having paid area youths for dogs but denied knowing they were stolen.

Chuck Dryke was no stranger to Judy Nikodym. Ever since she had been director of the Clallam County Humane Society, Dryke had been adopting large numbers of dogs. In 1986 he adopted at least 147 dogs from the shelter, paying $20 rather than the customary $30 fee. The standard neutering deposit was also waived for Dryke. Each time Dryke adopted a dog he signed a form stipulating that the dog would not be used for research. On a few occasions, the shelter delivered dogs to Sunnydell.

Although one shelter employee said it was understood the dogs were being sold for research, Nikodym said she was unaware of this fact. In January 1987, after a PAWS investigation of Dryke had received widespread media coverage, Nikodym informed Dryke he could no longer adopt dogs from the shelter. In the coming months, at least six dogs were adopted by Dryke employees. Nikodym later noted that dogs had started disappearing from area yards around the time she cut Dryke off.

The Hope Heart Institute failed to take any definitive action in response to information about Dryke's methods of acquiring dogs.

In May 1988, Dryke admitted to USDA investigators that "he had not been keeping proper records and that he may not have been holding over dogs for five business days before selling them." He also admitted "he had never really discussed setting up programs of disease control and prevention, euthanasia and adequate veterinary care" with the person he had listed as his consulting veterinarian.

In October 1988, Mark Dulin, the Area Veterinarian in Charge for the USDA, recommended that Dryke be prosecuted for violations of the Animal Welfare Act, including failure to maintain required records, failure to observe the mandatory holding time of five business days before selling dogs for research, failure to perform needed repairs to the kennel facility, and failure to establish a program of veterinary care. USDA investigator Mike McCann wrote: "[Dryke's] policy of buying stray dogs from local youths; keeping no records of the purchases; and not holding the dogs as required was unwise at best, in addition to being in violation of the Animal Welfare Act." Because Dryke had not kept the mandatory acquisition records on the dogs he received, and had even disposed of some records in between USDA visits, possible avenues of further investigation and prosecution were blocked.

Although he received an official warning notice from the USDA, Dryke was never prosecuted.

Dryke first voluntarily switched to an A dealer's license, "to get you guys off my back," as he told PAWS, and started to establish his own breeding colony. A short time later it was reported that he was planning to resume sales of random source dogs. But, before long, his name stopped appearing on the USDA list of research dealers. There is no official indication that he is now involved in selling dogs for research.

Jackson

Kathryn Holl's nine-month-old, 42-pound, neutered poodle/Afghan mix, Jackson, disappeared while tied to a post outside a Port Angeles store in March, 1987. It was almost a year before Holl learned what had happened to Jackson.

"We looked for Jackson intensively for eight weeks and as each week slipped by I became more and more desperate. The search became an obsession for me. I cried many times. Throughout it all, I blamed myself. If only I had been a better pet owner he wouldn't be gone. It never occurred to me that he had been stolen and sold to a research animal dealer for a lousy $25," Holl said later.

In January 1988, while volunteering at the Clallam County Humane Society, Holl had a chance encounter with PAWS director Mitchell Fox, who was in the area to confirm some details about the Dryke investigation. Fox had learned from local law enforcement officials about Bud Batchelor's report that his friend Adam Clark had untied a black, curly-haired dog from a post outside the 8th Street Furniture Store in Port Angeles in March and had sold the dog to Dryke. When Holl described Jackson's disappearance to Fox, he told her of the theft admission. A review of the records at Hope Heart Institute revealed that Dryke sold the facility a black fuzzy male mixed breed on March 25, just four days after Jackson disappeared. Hope Heart Institute logged the dog in as a 45-pound poodle. The dog was killed in an experiment on July 21, 1987.

Holl pursued the matter with law enforcement officials, and charges were filed against the theft suspect, Adam Clark, who was then living in California. The case was never brought to trial.

Said Holl, "Did Jackson grieve for my loss as I did for his? I believe he did, and that's a painful thought I won't ever forget. He didn't deserve to die in a research lab, and I didn't deserve to go through all the mental anguish we felt for the past year. Maybe over time, I won't feel the pain I do now, but I'll never forget Jackson."

The Pet Theft Bill

Working with PAWS, Washington state senator and animal advocate Ray Moore introduced a dramatic bill in January 1988. Senate Bill 6390 prohibited selling dogs and cats from shelters for research and outlawed the sale of all random-source dogs and cats in the state. The bill was killed in committee after heavy lobbying from the University of Washington and other animal consumption-oriented interests, including the Cattlemen's Association. However, Senate Agriculture Committee Chair Scott Barr found the testimony of Kathryn Holl, Don Johnson and other residents compelling. After meeting with them between legislative sessions, he vowed to introduce a more limited bill in 1989.

The bill, Senate Bill 5827, made stealing or fraudulently obtaining pets for research a Class C felony, punishable by five years in jail or a $10,000 fine. The bill also requires research facilities to maintain a file, including a photo and certification of the animal's origin, on each dog or cat obtained by them. These files are open for public inspection. The bill, co-sponsored by Senator Moore, won the unanimous approval of the state legislature and was signed into law in the Spring of 1989. Documentation and testimony about incidents involving the Peters and Chuck Dryke played a crucial role in the bill's passage.

The Aftermath

Washington research facilities continue to obtain cats and dogs from animal dealers in and outside the state (see H.D. Cowan, Marvin and Joye Dart and Dave Knight in "Currently Licensed Class B Dealers Selling Random Source Dogs and Cats for Research"). Although the recordkeeping requirements under Senate Bill 5827 provide some recourse for owners of missing pets, there remains little oversight of research animal dealing by the USDA or law enforcement agencies.

Said PAWS's Mitchell Fox: "Rumors of misdealings by research animal dealers in Washington state persist. We have no reason to believe these allegations are false. Dealers have plenty of room to maneuver, and, with no agency actively and conscientiously monitoring them on a local level, little threat of being caught and punished. It seems that as one unscrupulous dealer closes down, another comes in to take his place. I think it would be a mistake for pet owners and others concerned about animals to think they or their pets can breathe easier."

Chapter 9

The Mexico Connection: The Supply of Feline Dissection Specimens to American Companies

by Jason Black

The investigation began when the office of the World Society for the Protection of Animals (WSPA) in Boston received an emotional letter describing what had become "a city without cats." Shortly thereafter, WSPA learned of a report about a truck carrying 2,000 preserved cat specimens in Mexicali, about ten miles from the U.S. border, allegedly bound for biological supply houses in the United States.

As a result, WSPA conducted an investigation to uncover the roots of this terrible trade, under the auspices of its international Pet Respect campaign. An expert team from WSPA and the Massachusetts SPCA was dispatched in March, 1994, to carry out an undercover investigation in the Mexican states of Baja California and Sinaloa.

The findings suggested that Mexico has become a primary source of dissection animals to American biological supply companies. In the process, cats, many of whom are acquired through theft and deception, are killed inhumanely by drowning. Several cities in Mexico have experienced sharp reductions in local cat populations.

One of the American companies identified during this investigation was Fisher Education Material Division (EMD) of Illinois. Boxes clearly labelled with the Fisher catalogue number for cat specimens were videotaped by the WSPA team. Fisher acquires its cats from Southwestern Scientific in Tuscon, Arizona. According to Fisher EMD, "all cat specimens [from Mexico] are obtained utilizing humane and socially accepted procedures." An Associated Press report published after WSPA's investigation stated that an official from Southwestern Scientific denied that the cats are mistreated. But WSPA's investigation provided evidence to the contrary.

The Biological Supply Industry

In the U.S., there are a number of biological supply companies that together supply preserved animals for dissection to almost every school in the country. According to data analyzed by the Humane Society of the United States, more than six million animals are killed each year to provide dissection "specimens" for high schools and colleges. Of these, an estimated 20,000 to 50,000 are cats. The huge traffic in these animals fuels a multi-million dollar industry.

Biological supply companies are regulated by the Animal Welfare Act, which is intended to prevent theft of animals for use in laboratories. This is the only Federal law that provides any protection for live animals destined for dissection.

Despite the increasing availability of humane alternatives to dissection, including films, videos, and computer assisted models, the biological supply industry continues to thrive, with some companies processing as many as 3,000 orders for specimens a day.

Prelude to the Investigation

According to reports obtained by WSPA, a ramshackle building in Mexicali containing wood and wire cages housed 55 live cats and the bodies of 247 dead cats. The reports indicated that some of these animals were wrapped in plastic bags, while others were strapped on a bench in the process of being preserved.

Local authorities had raided the premises and detained three men — Carlos Salcido Lopez, Gregorio Butimia, who admitted killing the cats, and Marco Antonio Lopez Garcia, the owner of the vehicle apparently used to transport the animals.

Lopez Garcia produced a document authorizing him to collect cats on behalf of Preparation of Animal Material for Scholarly Study (PARMEESA), a biological supply company located in Los Mochis, Sinaloa.

On January 30, 1994, Mexicali police were alerted to suspicious looking individuals moving plastic bags from a pickup to a truck. They discovered that the truck contained the bodies of 2,000 preserved cats in plastic bags. They also discovered that the permit issued in the name of Lopez Garcia only provided for the sale and transport of 1,000 cats to PARMEESA in Sinaloa, not the 2,000 found.

The WSPA Undercover Investigation

On March 12, 1994, the team visited the ramshackle Mexicali facility and observed the remains of equipment used to process the cats before they were sent to Sinaloa. A strong smell of formaldehyde pervaded the compound.

WSPA staff spoke with several residents living near the facility, who confirmed on videotape many of the details provided by driver Lopez Garcia and his nephew. One man said that workers transported hundreds of cats in cages to the facility, and that two pick-up trucks regularly transferred the plastic bags containing the preserved cats to a large truck that was unable to negotiate the narrow dirt road outside the compound.

Another woman told the WSPA team that one of the men approached her house and placed a noose over her cat's neck while the cat was lying in her front yard. She said she ran outside screaming at the man, and that he then released the cat from the noose. She reported that he asked if she would sell the cat to him for US $1. She refused, taking her cat into the house.

The WSPA team then visited PARMEESA's facility in Sinaloa, where they saw numerous boxes stacked on wooden pallets, apparently ready for dispatch. An address label was affixed to each box bearing the name of Fisher EMD and its mailing address. The boxes were clearly marked in Spanish: "Preserved Cats, Made in Mexico." The labels indicated that each box contained four packs referenced as catalogue no. S1806S. There appeared to be 20 boxes on each pallet, and the animals were separated by sex. Ten pallets were observed, for a total of over 1,600 cats. The current Fisher EMD catalogue distributed in the USA identifies this catalogue number as "Large Cat 18, Double $41.20."

Using a guise, the team spoke with employees and established that PARMEESA had been operating for approximately 20 years, providing specimens to biological supply houses in the United States. PARMEESA employees referred the team to an American manager, with whom they agreed to meet.

According to the WSPA team, the manager was initially suspicious, but he soon relaxed and stated that he worked for an American company in Arizona. When the team suggested they might be interested in obtaining specimens directly from the company in Los Mochis, the manager claimed PARMEESA was under exclusive contract to provide Southwestern Scientific with biological specimens.

Early the next morning, the team returned to PARMEESA and recorded a short videotape of the operation. Later that day, WSPA staff met with officials of the Secretariat of Agriculture and Hydraulic Resources (SAHR) at Obregon, where PARMEESA obtains permits to transport preserved cats into the U.S. WSPA staff members then visited a SAHR check point where they confirmed that PARMEESA transports the cats by means of 16-wheel trailer-trucks as often as three times a week. The vehicles carry the specimens from Los Mochis to Southwestern Scientific's facility in Arizona.

Acquisition and Euthanasia of Specimen Cats in Mexicali

WSPA staff visited the home of Lopez Garcia, and, in his absence, spoke with family members. They were told that Garcia had worked for PARMEESA for about eight years. Garcia allegedly employed six men who operated from two trucks. Visiting local areas with a loud speaker attached to one of the vehicles, they offered to pay US $1 for any unwanted cat. The men worked seven days a week, and each truck usually collected 30 to 40 cats a day. These trucks then transported the animals to the Mexicali facility.

The WSPA team made arrangements to meet with Garcia, and recorded an interview with him on hidden camera. He confirmed that he worked for PARMEESA, and alleged that the company was a subsidiary of Southwestern Scientific.

Garcia claimed that when he found a cat on the street, he made an effort to identify the owner. He said he offered US $1.00 for each cat. He claimed that he did not take any cat who was not purchased, but asserted that many cats on the street did not have owners and could be legitimately taken.

When asked how the cats were killed, he said there were a number of ways it could be done but that he preferred drowning. He explained that approximately ten cats were placed in a cloth bag. The bags were submerged two at a time in a 200-liter metal drum filled with water. According to Lopez Garcia, the drowning process "took a few minutes."

The following day, WSPA staff met Jose Molina Orozco, the Sub-Director of the Directorate of Public Security and were permitted to view the files on the case. He assured WSPA that any report of illegal killing of cats would be vigorously pursued by his officers, and appropriate action would be taken. He confirmed that he had received complaints about missing and stolen cats in recent months.

With information obtained from police files, WSPA staff identified and located the person who killed the cats in Mexicali, Carlos Salcido Lopez.

Lopez told the WSPA team that he had been in charge of killing the cats—estimated at about 1,000—and corroborated the information from Lopez Garcia. He said local children would bring many cats to the trucks. He agreed that a large percentage of these cats were probably owned.

According to Salcido Lopez, the animals were removed from the

Above: Substandard housing at an Iowa Class B dealer's facility

Left: A 1986 photograph of a Class B dealer's premises(BOB BAKER)

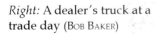

Right: A dealer's truck at a trade day (BOB BAKER)

Right, and below: Cats in a ramshackle Mexicali, Mexican warehouse; they are intended for sale to biological supply companies in the United States to be used in school dissections. (WSPA)

Bottom: A crate of frightened cats at the Mexicali facility (WSPA)

Right: A starving victim of the random source dealer trade, rescued from a Tennessee dealer's facility (BOB BAKER)

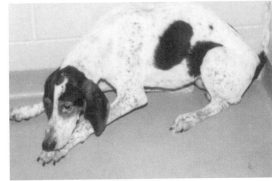

Right: One of 29 dogs confiscated from Jack Stowers's kennel and relinquished to the Indianapolis Humane Society (IHS)

Left: Kitten with an infected eye at a USDA-licensed dealer facility (PETA)

Left: An overcrowded kitten enclosure at a dealer's facility (PETA)

Top left: Smokey was stolen from his Minnesota home, sold by a buncher to Donald Hippert for $12, and then sold to a laboratory. He was rescued before being used in an experiment, but he was seriously ill, and his recovery took many weeks.

Top right: Rex was stolen and sold to Class B dealer Donald Hippert, who sold him to a laboratory. When Rex's owner, Ella Erie, discovered where he was, a laboratory employee tried to make her pay to get him back.

Left: Sheba was taken from inside a barn on her family's farm and sold to Donald Hippert, who sold her to the Mayo Institute. Sheba was lucky enough to be rescued prior to her use in an experiment.

Below: Sign in front of Class B dealer Donald Hippert's facility. Dodge County, Minnesota officials gave Hippert permission to house the county's stray animals.

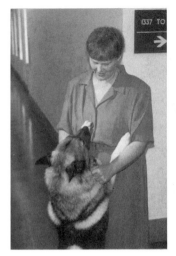

Top left: Karyl Parks and her dog Danny, who was stolen and sold for research. Danny was recovered before he was experimented on. (J.D. BEARY)

Top right: Wiggles and Bear were acquired through deceit by a man responding to a "free to good home" ad. USDA-licensed dealer Barbara Ruggiero sold Bear to Cedars-Sinai Medial Center, where he was killed in a heart attack experiment. Wiggles was recovered one day prior to his shipment to a research facility. (NORMAN FLINT)

Right: Class B dealer Barbara Ruggiero and her business partner, Frederick Spero, after their adoption scam was uncovered. (LAST CHANCE FOR ANIMALS)

Below: At left, Al "the Catman" Wise, who sold cats to Carolina Biological Supply, attempts to run down an ABC-TV reporter who requested an interview. At right, Wise rams an ABC-TV van with his bulldozer.

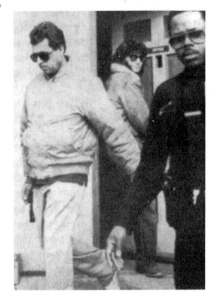

Above left: A dog being loaded onto a Class B dealer's truck (HSUS/GREYHAVENS)
Above right: A box of dog collars, some with identification tags still attached, at a licensed dealer's facility (PETA)
Below: Sosha, age 5 months, with Theresa Johnson, age 10. Posing as a retired couple eager to find a dog to live with them on their ranch, Class B dealers Don and Judee Peters adopted Sosha through a "free to good home" ad. A week later, they sold her to the University of Washington, where she was killed in an experiment.

Above left: A shepherd languishing in the back of a dealer's truck. Canton, Texas trade day, 1966
Above right: Dealer kicking dog. Rome, Georgia dog auction, 1965
Below: An emaciated hound with her puppies. Canton, Texas trade day, Dec. 6, 1965 (MARYBETH VAUGHN, *THE TYLER STAR*, TYLER, TEXAS)

Above: A dealer's truck loaded with animals destined for laboratories. Ripley, Mississippi trade day, Feb. 1966

Left: Two saleable dogs in the trunk of car. Canton, Texas trade day

Left: Class B dealer William Hargrove in front of his three-tiered transport truck. His employees are sorting through burlap bags full of kittens. Ripley, Mississippi trade day

Above: Offal on the floor of pen at a dog dealer's kennel, the only source of food provided
Below: Dog dying of chorea and starvation at Missouri dealer's facility, 1966

Top left: A bird supplier grabs a young parrot by the head and pulls it from a nest in Salta Forestal, Argentina (Currey/EIA)

Top right: A felled tree whose hollow trunk was once a parrot family's home. During the 1980s, 100,000 quebracho trees were chopped down for removal of parrot chicks (Currey/EIA)

Center right: This parrot chick has been over-fed and is dying. (Currey/EIA).

Bottom left: A blue-fronted Amazon parrot chick is force-fed a mixture of maize and water in Argentina. (Currey/EIA).

Bottom right: Choked to death due to rough force-feeding, this parrot chick joins others in dealer's trash can.

Above: Blue-fronted Amazon parrot chicks who were force-fed and nearly choked to death, then shaken violently to clear their lungs. For the moment, they have survived. (EIA)
Right: A black cap unable to free itself from the powerful glue of the limestick, a cruel trapping device commonly used in the trade
(G. MAGNIN)
Below: Typical overcrowded handling of wild-caught birds (EIA)

Above: Up to 2000 finches may be packed in these crates in a dealer's premises in Senegal. (EIA)

Left: Frightened African grey parrots in a Senegalese dealer's aviary. African grey parrots make up 65% of Senegal's bird exports, yet this species does not occur in the wild in Senegal. (CURREY/EIA)

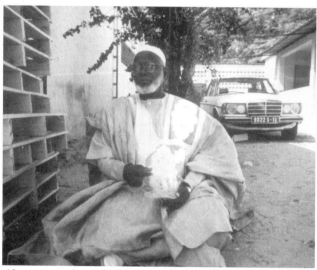

Above: Amadou Diallo, Senegal's biggest bird exporter. In 1990, he earned several million dollars for his sales of African grey parrots.

Above: Chatachuk Sunday Market in Bangkok, November 1988. In the stall are three CITES Appendix I species (*Ara militaris, Ara macao, Probiscer aterrimus*), and six species on Appendix II. (IFAW/David and Alex Dawson)

Right: A bird dying in an exporter's premises in Buenos Aires (CURREY/EIA)

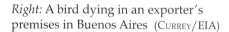

Left: Trapped in a mist net for the exotic wild-caught bird trade

Right: Illegally captured Amazon parrots for sale on the street in Mexico (LINDA TYRELL/AWI)

Below: Hyacinth macaws can be sold for at least $10,000 each. (CURREY/EIA)

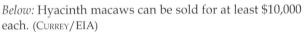

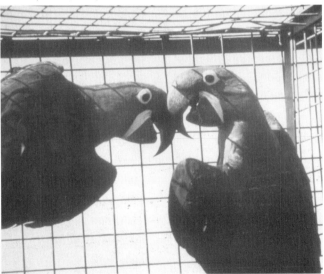

Above: Transported birds found dead on arrival and confiscated by U.S. Customs officers (U.S. CUSTOMS SERVICE)
Below: These parrots, hidden in a car and wrapped in newspapers, had suffocated before being found by Customs officers. (U.S. CUSTOMS SERVICE)

Top: Turtles piled on top of
each other in a shipping box,
destined for the pet trade
Above: Turtles in an overcrowded enclosure at a Belgian
zoo

Left: An endangered stuffed sea
turtle (USFWS, DIVISION OF LAW
ENFORCEMENT)

Above: A rattlesnake handler in Victoria, Texas shows off in front of the crowd. Mishandling is extremely stressful (snakes evolved to travel parallel to the ground, not perpendicular) and can cause muscular and circulatory problems. Rattlesnakes are popular in trade, both as food and as pets. (MIKE KREGER)

Right: Wild-caught adult red-eared sliders. These turtles, not naturally social, are crowded around the periphery of the pen. They are housed in a dry pen, even though the red-eared slider is a water-loving species.

Above: A baby baboon dying in an illegal trap. His mother was killed by the trapper because she was unacceptable to the laboratory animal dealer. (CURREY/EIA)

Below: 29 squirrel monkeys with their tails tied together, shipped from Bolivia to Japan via Lima, Madrid, and London. Six of the monkeys were dead soon after arrival. Iberia Airlines, an IATA member airline, was fined £400 for causing unnecessary suffering (JOHN BROOKLAND/EIA)

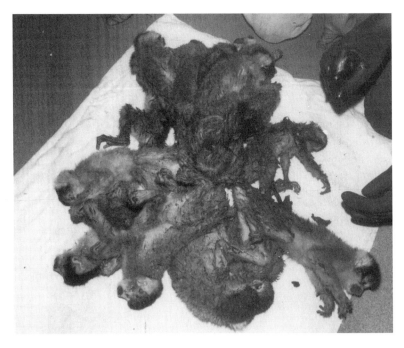

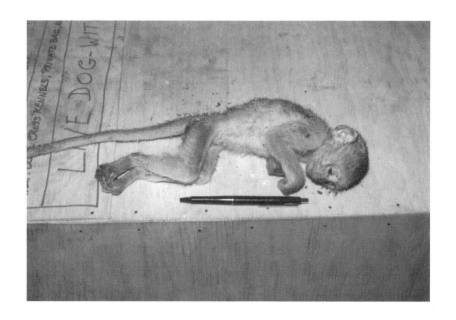

Above: An infant casualty of the commercial primate trade (USDI/FWS)
Below: A monkey for sale at Pramuka Market, Jakarta (IPPL)

Left: Thomas, one of the infant orangutans smuggled internationally by dealer Matthew Block, died from internal injuries caused by being shipped upside-down in a cramped crate. Intensive nursing care failed to save him. (DIANNE TAYLOR-SNOW/IPPL)

Above: Animal dealer Matthew Block tries to cover his face as Miami TV films him.

Above: A chimpanzee confined at a USDA-licensed Class B dealer's facility. (PETA)

barrel after being drowned and placed on their backs on wooden boards. The bodies were secured with two rubber straps, and wooden blocks were placed in the cats' mouths to keep them open. An incision was made in each cat's trachea, and a special needle was inserted into a jugular vein. A mixture of phenol, glycerin and formaldehyde was then pumped into the body.

Finally, the cats were sealed in plastic bags, and carried in a pick-up truck to the transfer point where they were loaded into another truck that took them to Sinaloa. During the interview, Lopez produced some of his equipment, including three metal syringes, scalpels, pliers, plastic bags, and a tin of red liquid latex.

Additional Evidence From Southern Mexico

WSPA obtained further confirmation of the trade in cats involving PARMEESA from Mrs. Blanca Perea Escobar, Councilwoman of Ecology in the State of Oaxaca, who, acting on an anonymous complaint, found a clandestine cat-killing operation in Tehuantepec, Oaxaca. She initiated a formal complaint with the municipal authorities who investigated and found Faustino Bartilote with 500 preserved cats on his premises. Bartilote admitted that the animals were being consigned to PARMEESA. Since Bartilote had no permit to operate, the authorities immediately closed down his facility and placed Bartilote in jail. The Excelsior newspaper of March 10 indicates that Escobar is continuing to press the issue of the inhumane killing of the animals.

When news of this investigation was first reported in The Boston Globe, an executive from Fisher EMD in Illinois acknowledged the company makes no effort to determine how the cats are procured or killed. "I only have the word of the people we deal with," he said.

However, a subsequent news item in the Tucson Citizen quotes a spokesperson from Fisher EMD as saying, "If that is how the cats we obtain are being collected and killed, we will no longer do business with Southwestern Scientific.... They say they collect and process cats in a humane way, and there is a humane way to euthanize animals. But drowning animals is not humane and not acceptable." Because of these reports, Fisher EMD states that it will ask its suppliers, including Southwestern, to "verify how [the] cats are killed."

Second Investigation Prompts New Legislation in Mexico

One year after WSPA exposed the cat-killing operation in Mexicali, the Mexican government made it a violation of federal law to kill a domestic animal, unless the animal is suffering as a result of an accident, disease, physical incapacity or extreme age, or if the animal poses a threat to human health.

Mexico passed the law after WSPA raided another cat-killing facility in Matamoros, just across the border from Brownsville, Texas.

Through an elaborate undercover operation by WSPA, the owners of the Matamoros operation, the Centro de Preparacion Zoologica para Investigacion (CPZI), believed they would be supplying cats to an independent entrepreneur, who wanted to purchase the animals directly, circumventing the U.S. biological supply companies.

On the morning of the raid, an undercover camera crew posing as perspective buyers had entered CPZI and recorded the cat-killing process with a miniature video camera concealed in a pair of eyeglasses. During the raid, the owners tried to deny that they were killing cats, claiming they had stopped doing so in July, 1994. While inside CPZI, the WSPA operative and camera crew saw 15 barrels full of embalmed cats and frogs, and another ten dead cats on the embalming tables. Eventually, CPZI's owners admitted on videotape that they had a contract to supply thousands of cats to a U.S. biological supply company. As the filmed confrontation continued, the CPZI owners finally agreed to stop killing cats.

At the end of the raid, the WSPA team operative found a lone survivor of the killing operation: a small, female kitten, hiding behind barrels full of dead animals. The kitten was weak and hungry. In all likelihood, she witnessed how the other cats, and perhaps her own mother, had been killed. In the end, her small size saved her from a similar fate. She received veterinary care and was soon adopted by a member of the camera crew. CPZI's permit to trade in cats was revoked, and the Mexican Attorney General initiated legal action against the company's owners.

WSPA is currently working with members of the U.S. Congress to add a provision to the Animal Welfare Act that would prohibit the importation of animals into the U.S who were not legally obtained or humanely euthanized.

Chapter 10

Keeping Companion Animals Out of the Hands of Dealers

Theft of pet dogs and cats is a crime under state laws, and, although the Animal Welfare Act does not apply to pet theft, USDA regulations prohibit the sale of stolen animals to research facilities.[1] They also prohibit individuals from obtaining dogs or cats for sale to research by use of false pretenses, misrepresentation or deception.[2] Unfortunately, this has not stopped dealers from selling illegally obtained animals. In cases where missing animals have been found at a dealer's facility, the dealer generally denies knowing the animals were stolen, blaming his suppliers and downplaying his own legal responsibility to obtain complete documentation on the source of each animal. A dealer is not required to scrutinize or cross-examine those supplying him with dogs and cats: his responsibility under the Animal Welfare Act is fulfilled the very moment he writes down a name, address, vehicle license plate number, driver's license number, or, if the supplier is a dealer, a USDA license number.

However, as USDA's own Animal Welfare Task Force findings from 1990 revealed, a street address and vehicle license number on a dealer's acquisition form don't necessarily correspond with a real individual. Within the recordkeeping neverland of incomplete, incorrect and false information, identification of stolen and missing animals can and does become obscured, rendering tracebacks of sources nearly impossible.

Many states have passed legislation making theft of a dog or cat a felony. In 1989, Washington state passed a law prohibiting the sale of a stolen or fraudulently acquired animal to a research facility. The legislation provides for a penalty of up to five years in jail and/or a fine of up to $10,000. It also requires research facilities to maintain a file on each dog or cat that must include a certificate of ownership, a photograph, and a description of the animal.

In 1994, a dog owner won $8,000 in damages after filing a civil lawsuit against a Class B dealer who had engineered a false adoption of the owner's dog and then sold the dog to a university for research [see Johnson and Peters case in "Washington State Animal Dealers"). The court held that the false adoption constituted theft by misrepresentation.

Deterring Theft of Your Dog and Cat: Tags, Tattoos and Microchips

Theft of companion animals will continue as long as USDA continues licensing random source dealers and research facilities continue buying animals from them. Although no dog or cat is really safe as long as a market for random source animals exists, there are some things you can do to reduce the chances of your dog or cat ending up in the hands of a dealer.

Typically, dealers look for healthy, friendly dogs and cats. Hounds, Labrador Retrievers, Beagles, Doberman Pinschers, German Shepherds and Dalmatians are particularly in demand because of their size and physiology. Mixed-breed dogs are also desirable. As one Class B dealer put it, "Don't believe what you read about labs only wanting thoroughbred dogs. They want mongrels because they're more even-tempered."[3] Virtually any medium to large-sized dog is valuable in the commercial trade.

Your goal should be to make theft of an animal as risky and complicated as possible. Since theft is often a crime of opportunity, limiting opportunities for access to an animal is the single most important preventive action an owner can take. Keep dogs and cats inside. Never leave an animal unattended even for a few minutes. It is risky and irresponsible to leave an animal in a car alone, tied to a parking meter or even in the back yard when you are away from home.

Identification of your dog or cat is important: make sure your animal is always wearing a collar with an ID tag bearing your name and telephone number. Rabies vaccination and county license tags are also effective forms of identification; serial numbers can be traced back to the owner's records through the animal clinic or animal control facility that issued the tags. Keep a clear, color photograph of your animal.

Because collars and tags are easily removed, it's prudent to use some form of permanent identification on your animal. A tattoo is an effective means of identification, providing both traceability and proof of ownership. The standard procedure is to tattoo the owner's social security number onto an animal's inner thigh or belly. However, several points must be considered when using tattoos: they fade, are alterable, and can sometimes be difficult to locate without shaving the animal's inner thigh. Moreover, unless the animal's serial number is registered with a reputable national registry with a computerized database, such as the National Dog Registry, it cannot be traced back to the owner. Attempts at locating the owner of any tattooed animal can be hindered by the fact that there is no centralized national data bank on tattooed animals; in addition to NDR, there are at least ten other tattoo registries operating on various levels.

Tattoos are not without risk. While some thieves have been known to release tattooed dogs unharmed at the side of highways or in woods, there are also reports of thieves simply killing tattooed dogs. After conducting an investigation of dog dealers in Missouri, David Garcia of the Missouri Humane Society concluded, "Any dog that bears a tattoo (which means it is traceable) is killed or abandoned by either the buncher or the dealer." Garcia's finding is supported in part by statements made by a former employee of a midwest dog dealer, who revealed in a television interview that tattooed dogs were routinely shot and their collars burned (see: "Inside the Dog Dealing Business: Dogs, Dollars, and Deceit").

Some thieves reportedly cut out or scrape off a dog's tattoo. "Labs regularly report purchasing dogs and cats with missing ears," says Bette Rapoport of the National Dog Registry. Dog thieves resort to "lopping off an ear to keep from being caught in possession of stolen property." For this reason, tattooing an animal's ear is not advisable.[4]

A few research laboratories examine animals for tattoos and will attempt to contact a registry if a tattoo is found. A tattooed German Wirehaired Pointer stolen in Quebec in 1979 was found eight months later at Yale University by a researcher who recognized the dog's Canadian kennel club tattoo. The dog, sold to Yale by Class B dealer Rosaire Paradis of Vermont (USDA license # 13-B-001 in 1990), was returned to his owner by order of USDA.

Awareness about animal identification and registries has been increasing in the research community, thanks to efforts by organizations such as the National Dog Registry, which has tried to overcome the reluctance of laboratory personnel to report tattooed animals.

During the 1991 meeting of the American Association for Laboratory Animal Science, discussions revealed that ignorance about whom to contact, fear of negative publicity and job loss, distrust of animal protection groups and previous negative experiences with registries hindered laboratory workers from reporting a tattooed animal.[5]

The latest innovation in animal identification, the microchip ID, has been lauded as a hi-tech, virtually indestructible form of identification. It is highly effective as a means of establishing the identity (and owner) of an animal, but offers no deterrence against theft and is useless unless an electronic scanner is used to retrieve the encoded information.

The microchip—about the size of a grain of rice—is encoded with information about the animal's identity and is injected into the skin between the animal's shoulder blades. Information can be accessed by passing a hand-held electronic scanner over the animal's back; information is then displayed on a small screen in the scanner.

Three types of microchips are currently in use in the U.S.: AVID (American Veterinary Identification Devices), Destron IDI and Trovan/Infopet. In June 1995, the Amercian Kennel Club launched its nationwide Companion Animal Recovery Program, which promotes identification of animals with a Destron microchip marketed under the name "HomeAgain." The National Dog Registry also registers microchips. Until recently, microchips could be read only by scanners marketed by the same company selling the microchip. But in 1996, AVID and HomeAgain developed a universal scanner capable of reading all pet identification microchips sold in the U.S. The scanner, called the Universal Pocket Reader EX, is distributed to animal shelters free of charge.

A few research facilities reportedly scan incoming animals for microchip ID's. The University of Minnesota (UM), Twin Cities Campus, utilizes both the InfoPet and Destron systems; the Destron scanner has the added feature of signalling the presence of non-Destron microchips but does not read them. It is UM's policy not to use any animals identified by either microchips or tattoos in any research programs until the animal's status is verified.[6,7] In 1995, the University began phasing out all acquisition of dogs and cats from Class B dealers. The University now has a policy against purchasing animals from Class B dealers.[8]

The National Dog Registry

In 1965, David Timrud notified an animal shelter near Princeton, New Jersey that his dog had been stolen from his backyard. The shelter advised him to check with dog dealers in Pennsylvania on the possibility that one of them purchased his missing dog. Not only did the dealers Timrud contacted deny him the opportunity to search for his dog, they told him that even if he found his dog, he could never prove the dog was his.[9]

Timrud was moved to action. He testified in the 1966 congressional hearings in support of proposed federal legislation to ban the theft of dogs for sale to research (the Animal Welfare Act). Soon after, he founded the National Dog Registry (NDR).

NDR registers an animal's tattoo or microchip number for a one-time fee of $35. Tattoo clinics sponsored by animal shelters, animal rescue groups, and research institutions offer a discounted fee of $25. The registration lasts for the owner's lifetime and will protect all of the registrant's animals who have been tattooed or microchip implanted. Registration enables NDR to notify an owner when an animal bearing the NDR-registered number has been found. The Registry maintains a hotline for lost and found pets 24 hours a day, 365 days a year.

Over the past three decades, NDR has absorbed records kept by registries that have gone out of business, thus ensuring the traceback of non-NDR registered animals. In 1992, an American Staffordshire Terrier bearing a tattoo registered with a non-NDR agency was identified at a research facility while she was being shaved for a surgical procedure. The research facility contacted NDR and requested a traceback of the dog's tattoo number. NDR traced the number through several regional registries and found a match within state department agricultural files some 350 miles away from the research facility. The dog's owners reported that she had been missing for three months.[10]

Animals are tattooed and microchipped by veterinarians, handlers, groomers and trainers, or through the auspices of animal shelters, kennel clubs, breed rescue groups, animal clinics and research institutions. When done properly, a tattoo etched onto an animal's inner hind leg usually takes between three and five minutes to apply. If an owner wishes, NDR will register a tattoo other than a Social Security number. However, because of the danger of duplication, owners should think carefully before using other numbers to permanently identify animals.

In 1989, NDR began working with research institutions to train their personnel how to tattoo animals and organize community tattoo clinics. The first clinic sponsored jointly by NDR and the University of Missouri took place in 1989. Since that time the University of Missouri has held clinics twice a year. The Southeast New Mexico American Association of Laboratory Animal Science, the White Sands Research Center of New Mexico and the Veterans Administration Medical Center of Albuquerque have also held tattoo clinics under NDR's auspices.

For more information on tattoos, microchipping and registration, contact: National Dog Registry, 227 Stebbins Road, Carmel, NY 90512. Telephone: 1-800-NDR-DOGS, 1-800-637-3647.

Protecting Companion Animals:
Changing Human and Animal Behavior

Keeping a Watchful Eye: Unsupervised animals are easy targets for thieves who take advantage of an animal owner's false sense of security and subsequent lack of vigilance. Increased vigilance in the form of a neighborhood watch program can benefit animals as well as people. Strange vehicles, people or activity can be monitored and reported to local authorities.

Again, the most effective step you can take to protect your companion animal from theft is to not leave him or her unsupervised. Close supervision works in all but the worst-case scenarios where dogs are stolen from within locked houses or grabbed from an owner while walking on a leash. Cases of dogs being stolen from inside houses were reported in Arkansas in 1989.[11] Virginia theft statistics maintained by Action 81 documented thefts occurring from within homes in a 1982 report: "As nearly as we can estimate, 150-200 cats have been stolen in the last month from inside homes, cars, patios... mostly during daylight hours." Action 81 received individual reports describing animals being stolen from a crate in an owner's bedroom, a dog stolen through a broken window and a dog snatched from within a screened porch that had been sliced open.[12]

Reducing the Urge to Roam: Neutering male animals helps curb the urge to roam that is associated with the search for mates. Wandering dogs are easy targets. The use of females in heat to attract male dogs is a well-known trick employed by thieves. A neutered male's response to a female in heat is certainly decreased, if not completely eliminated.

An Animal Disappears: General Guidelines

A missing animal requires immediate action. Search your neighborhood and surrounding areas promptly. Ask neighbors to keep an eye out for your animal. Take the following steps as soon as you notice your animal is gone:

• Call and visit shelters: Call the local animal shelter or pound (and those within 100 miles of your home) and file a missing animal report. Provide shelter personnel with a complete description of the missing animal and, if possible, a photograph. Don't rely on the telephone - visit the shelter every two days to look for your animal.

• Contact all veterinary hospitals in the area in case your animal was injured and taken to a veterinarian for treatment.

• Talk to people: Neighbors and other people familiar with the immediate area are good sources of information and should be consulted: newspaper carriers, postal carriers, garbage collectors, gas meter readers, joggers.

• Advertise. Newspapers and radio stations sometimes run "lost pet" announcements at no charge. Offering a reward is acceptable. If the reward exceeds what a dealer would offer, a thief may return your animal rather than sell him or her. Posting flyers around the neighborhood for several blocks and in other public places such as grocery stores, pet supply stores, libraries, and animal hospitals is also an effective way to publicize your animal's disappearance. Include a description of the animal and your telephone number in the announcement. You can also post a notice on the World Wide Web. USDA recently made its new Animal Care site on the Web available for advertising missing or found pets. The page lists cats and dogs by state and can display pictures of the animals scanned from photographs.

The Animal Care site address: http://www.aphis.usda.gov/reac.

• Contact the laboratory animal departments of all local universities and teaching hospitals. Give them a description of your animal take a photograph of your animal to the facility and ask to have it posted.

Animals have been found months and sometimes years after disappearing. Given the intricate geographical network of dealers and bunchers, some animals end up thousands of miles away from their homes after changing hands a number of times. In a well-known New York case, a tattooed English Setter taken from his owner's kennel in 1983 was recovered from a research laboratory in Rochester in October, 1986, three years after he had disappeared.[13] The dog, registered with Tattoo-A-Pet, was identified by a laboratory worker who contacted USDA. You may be able to trace your animal by contacting research/medical facilities directly.

If theft is suspected or confirmed, either by eyewitness accounts or evidence of human tampering, file a "stolen property" report with local law enforcement agencies. Alternatively, you can file a "missing property" report if you believe your animal merely wandered away from the yard. Contact local animal protection organizations and the nearest USDA-APHIS-AC Regional Office (see Appendix B). They can provide you with a list of research facilities and dealers in your area.

If there is reason to suspect your animal is at a dealer's facility, contact your local police department or sheriff's office for assistance. USDA regulations authorize law enforcement officers to conduct inspections of a dealer's premises, animals, and records if there is probable cause to suspect a missing animal is on the premises.[14]

By law, a dealer must allow a police search of his premises. An owner cannot enter a dealer's premises to look for a missing animal without permission unless accompanied by a police officer on an official search. In a few cases, dealers have voluntarily allowed owners to look for missing animals on their premises.

Adoption Scams: Another Form of Theft

Numerous cases of false adoptions by dealers and bunchers have been publicized in recent years and have brought attention to this particularly insidious form of theft. Never advertise a dog or cat as "free to a good home." Such an ad is an open invitation to bunchers or laboratory animal dealers pretending to want to adopt a dog or a cat. Releasing an animal to someone, no questions asked, should not be done under any circumstance. Many owners have been devastated to discover the companion animals they gave away died in experimental laboratories. Only in rare cases have animals been retrieved.

Joy Cloninger of Lewiston, Idaho, was one of the lucky ones. She advertised one of her German Shorthaired Pointers for adoption and was delighted when a man who claimed he had two children, a ranch, and a wife who was home all day, called to adopt her dog. Once at her home, he convinced her to give him not one, but two dogs—the dog advertised, and her companion, another German Shorthaired Pointer.

Days later, Joy learned from a friend that the "adopter" was a buncher. She attempted to track down her dogs at the address the buncher had given, but they were not among the 20 or so dogs tied in his front yard. Eventually, after making several inquiries, she discovered that her dogs were on the West Coast. A few days later, her dogs mysteriously reappeared at her house, in poor physical condition, but alive.

Adoption scams have been uncovered in Kansas as well as in Missouri, Oregon, California, and Washington. According to Kansas Humane Society preseident Ellen Querner, bunchers "obtain the animals, free, through deception and make runs to Missouri on a two-week basis and sell the dogs to dealers."[15]

If you must place an animal in another home, screen potential adopters carefully. If you advertise in a newspaper, state that you will charge an adoption fee. Write down the adopter's automobile license number, driver's license number, address and telephone number. Always visit an adopter's home <u>before</u> releasing an animal. Most importantly, don't be afraid to say "no" if you have any reservations about a potential adopter. Remember, your animal friend's future is in your hands.

Notes

1. 9 C.F.R. 2.60

2. 9 C.F.R. 2.132

3. Allentown, PA: *The Morning Call*, 25 February 1982. Class B dealer Marlin Zartman, owner/operator of the auction at Gilbertsville Sales Stables, quoted in an interview.

4. The National Dog Registry, New York: The National Dog Registry, informational brochure, 12 April 1990.

5. Ronald M. McLaughlin, DVM and Mitch Rapoport, "Using Tattoos to Keep Pets out of Research," *Lab Animal*, June 1993.

6. Dr. Wendeline L. Wagner, DVM, University of Minnesota Department of Comparative Medicine, in a letter dated September 1994. Destron-Fehring is a popular system in the Missouri-Arkansas area. Info-Pet is standard among pounds and humane societies in a seven-county area surrounding Minneapolis-St. Paul.

7. The University of Minnesota, "U of M Strengthens Rules on Research Animal Purchases," Minneapolis, MN: University News Service, 22 July 1994. The University of Minnesota instituted the practice of checking animals based on the recommendations of a University task force that evaluated procurement of dogs and cats from Class B dealers in response to "concerns regarding alleged illegal activities on the part of some of the Class B dealers."

8. Richard W. Bianco, Program Director, Cardiovascular Surgical Research Laboratories, Division of Cardiovascular and Thoracic Surgery, University of Minnesota Medical School, in a conversation with Cathy Liss, Executive Director, Animal Welfare Institute, 18 March 1997.

9. Ronald M. McLaughlin, DVM and Mitch Rapoport, "Using Tattoos to Keep Pets out of Research," *Lab Animal*, June 1993.

10. Ibid. Later investigations revealed that the dog had been picked up by animal control and sold to a Class B dealer without being checked for identification. NDR reports the pound was reprimanded for its failure to properly check the dog for identification.

11. Deborah Robinson, "EACE Fights Area Pet Thefts," Fayetteville, AR: *Fayetteville Times*, 1 February 1989 .

12. Action 81, Theft of Dogs and Cats in the United States, 1974-1992 (Berryville, VA: Action 81, 1993).

13. Robin Wilson Glover, "Stolen Dog, Almost Test Animal, Saved," Rochester, NY: *Time-Union*, 17 October 1986.

14. 9 C.F.R. 2.128

15. Ellen Querner, President, Kansas Humane Society of Wichita, in a letter dated 21 September 1988, to Representative George Brown.

Chapter 11

The Primate Trade

by Jessica Speart

Lufthansa Flight 779 began its journey in Jakarta, Indonesia with 22 crates containing 110 crab-eating macaques loaded into cargo. Weighing less than twenty pounds apiece, the small Southeast Asian monkeys are much in demand as subjects for biomedical research throughout the world. The first leg of the journey took them to Singapore and then on to Frankfurt, Germany where they were transferred to Lufthansa Flight 462. On August 20, 1992, Flight 462 landed at Miami International Airport. But as the ground crew unloaded cargo, it was obvious that something had gone terribly wrong. No sound could be heard inside the crates. All 110 macaques were dead. The autopsy report noted severe hemorrhaging in the nose and lungs with probable cause of death listed as irreversible shock, possibly due to heat stroke or asphyxiation. Wrapped in double layers of red plastic and labeled 'medical waste,' all the bodies were burned and the crates destroyed. It was almost as if the incident had never taken place.

The 102 Pygmy slow lorises were discovered inside the men's rest room at Chiang Kai-Shek International Airport in Taiwan. Contained in individual plastic bags, four of the palm-sized nocturnal primates were already dead. Although the Pygmy loris is an endangered species, there was no air waybill, health or export certificate to be found. Taiwanese Customs officers assumed the lorises had been part of an aborted smuggling attempt and had been flown in from Vietnam. Less than 48 hours later, having received no food or water, the 98 remaining lorises were packed inside cages and sent back. No one ever thought to notify Vietnamese officials of the fragile shipment that now sat unattended at Ho Chi Minh Airport for nearly 24 hours before its discovery. Only seven of the Pygmy lorises survived the ordeal.

One of these shipments was legal. The other was part of the escalating illegal trade in wildlife. But when it comes to the primate trade, many times it's hard to tell the difference. Both tend to be secretive businesses involving suffering and death on a scale that has been consistently underestimated. After years of filling the voracious demands of laboratories, circuses, entertainers, private collectors and zoos, many primate species are closer to extinction than ever.

The Legal Trade

The primate trade can be traced back thousands of years. Mesopotamians used monkey bones in the manufacture of drugs, and Egyptians trained baboons to harvest figs. A popular trade item at the height of the Roman Empire, monkeys later became a fashion statement during the days of the French monarchy when they were used as living decorations on women's wigs. In this century, primates have been highly valued for use in research and testing. During the 1950s, more than 1.5 million monkeys were imported by researchers each year in the race to develop a polio vaccine.[1] The United States alone imported 200,000 primates annually.[2] The numbers have dropped significantly in recent years. In 1989, world trade in primates numbered 54,694,[3] of whom ninety-nine percent were wild caught.[4] The United States topped the list of consumers, importing 18,562[5] of the 51,000[6] primates used each year for research, followed by Japan and Great Britain.[7] The United States received more than 39 different species of primates, but crab-eating macaques were by far the largest number imported.[8] Based on U.S. Fish and Wildlife Service (FWS) figures for the first seven months of 1994, the U.S. again led the way, importing 13,603 monkeys.[9] With research labs demanding a continuous supply of primates, there is big money to be made in the monkey business.

The Convention on International Trade in Endangered Species of Wild Fauna and Flora (CITES) was negotiated and ratified in 1973 to regulate trade in threatened or endangered species. Species are listed under one of three appendices depending on the degree of protection provided. Appendix I is comprised of species threatened with extinction and in which commercial trade is banned. Appendix II lists species that may be threatened with extinction unless trade is strictly controlled. Appendix III gives nations the option of listing native species that are already protected within their own borders. It is intended to help CITES members gain cooperation from other nations in enforcing their own wildlife trade regulations. All non-human primates are listed as either Appendix I or Appendix II. According to CITES, international trade now numbers 40,000 primates a year for use in biomedical research.[10]

Rhesus Monkeys

In the 1950s, the rhesus macaque was the monkey of choice for biomedical research due mainly to its physiological and immunological similarity to humans.[1] Found in northern and central India, the Himalayas, Bangladesh, Burma, Indonesia and Afghanistan, rhesus monkeys once populated India in large numbers. An estimated 10 to 20 million lived there at one time.[2] More than 100,000 rhesus were exported from India to Europe and the United States each year throughout the 1950s, mainly for polio, malaria and rabies research.[3] By 1959, the rhesus population of northern India had seriously declined. According to conservative estimates, one in four monkeys died during capture or in transit for every one who reached a lab alive. That alone would account for the loss of six million rhesus monkeys in the wild.[4] In 1973, the export quota was 30,000 monkeys, then selling at prices of $250 to $450 each.[5] Still, by 1976, India feared the population had declined by as much as 80 to 90 percent, to below 200,000 monkeys, a fraction of its former self.[6] The export quota was reduced to 20,000 a year.[7]

In 1977, the International Primate Protection League (IPPL) learned that the U.S. military was using rhesus monkeys in radiation experiments. In one study, monkeys were trained by electric shock to run on treadmills for six hours at a time before being subjected to fatal doses of radiation. Returned to the treadmill, they were forced to continue running until incapacitated by internal bleeding, vomiting, diarrhea, and finally, death. The purpose was to see how well American soldiers would be able to fight after exposure to a neutron bomb. According to figures given by the National Academy of Sciences, 93 percent of rhesus monkeys exported to the U.S. were killed in similar experiments during their first year of arrival.[8]

This news hit India like a neutron bomb. A 1955 agreement between India and the U.S. prohibited the use of exported monkeys for military studies.[9] Armed with this information, Indian Prime Minister Morarji Desai banned all export of rhesus monkeys from India beginning March 31, 1978. The ban quickly became a bone of contention between the two countries as multi-national drug firms put intense pressure on the Indian government to lift the ban. But India held firm, and the ban remains in place to this day.

In March 1977, eight months before India's ban took effect, U.S.-based MOL Enterprises signed an exclusive contract with Bangladesh for the export of 71,500 rhesus monkeys over a ten-year period.[10] Claiming to have done a survey of Bangladeshi monkeys to justify such a high export figure, MOL also arranged to import an unspecified number of endangered gibbons. In return, MOL agreed to give Bangladesh $81.50 per monkey and to establish breeding farms.[11] The Bangladeshi monkeys ended up costing MOL an estimated $200 a piece. At the time, rhesus monkeys were selling for more than $1000 each in the U.S.[12]

It was soon discovered that not only had MOL never bothered to conduct a survey, but that Bangladesh's population of rhesus monkeys couldn't possibly support such an inflated trade.[13] U.S. State Department papers at the time reveal concern that large numbers of rhesus monkeys were being smuggled out of India into Bangladesh to satisfy the demand.[14] In 1978, U.S. primatologist Dr. Ken Green discovered that the Bangladeshi rhesus population was so scarce he requested the U.S. Interior Department to categorize the monkeys as "threatened" under the U.S. Endangered Species Act.[15] Then IPPL revealed that a number of monkeys shipped to the U.S. had been sold to the Armed Forces Radiobiology Research Institute in order to test the effects of atomic weapons and neutron radiation. The contract with MOL specifically banned such use. AWI and IPPL appealed to Bangladesh Ambassador Husain to intervene. In January 1979, after just 1,600 monkeys had been exported, Bangladesh canceled the contract, alleging that MOL had not only violated the agreement by selling monkeys to the U.S. military, but had also failed to set up breeding farms.[16]

Frantic to continue the flow of rhesus monkeys for research, President Ronald Reagan's White House science advisor, Dr. George Keyworth, stepped into the fray. An emergency meeting was called with the Bangladesh ambassador to the U.S. in an effort to stop the ban from taking effect. Former Senator Bob Packwood, then chairman of the U.S. Senate Commerce Committee, added his weight by writing a strong letter to the Bangladesh government asking that the MOL contract be resumed. He stated that his office would inform potential private investors of Bangladesh's failure to honor the contract, jeopardizing future investment in the country. Finally, Senator Howard Baker's office contacted the State Department, adding yet another voice to the rising protest. When Bangladesh refused to budge, the U.S. government threatened to invoke the Hickenlooper Amendment, cutting off all foreign aid to the nation for mistreating a U.S. firm. Aid was never revoked, and, with a ban in effect in both India and Bangladesh, the supply of rhesus monkeys to the U.S. was virtually extinguished.

Crab-Eating Macaques

The U.S. soon began using crab-eating macaques not only for biomedical research but also in chemical and nuclear warfare testing. In 1977, the U.S. imported 10,585 macaques from Malaysia along with another 18,000 in 1978.[1] But in June 1984, Malaysia followed the lead of India and Bangladesh by placing a ban on export of monkeys. With the market tightening up, the Philippines moved in to fill the gap, soon becoming the number one exporter of macaques in Asia. Little publicized was the fact that as early as 1975, the Institute of Laboratory Animal Resources had identified the Philippine population of crab-eating macaques as being in danger of extinction should the massive trade continue.[2] But the demand for crab-eating macaques was on the rise. In the first ten months of 1979, the Philippines sent 4,000 of the monkeys to the U.S. alone.[3] Shortly after, the Philippines raised the quota to 15,000 macaques.[4]

IPPL used the Freedom of Information Act to obtain documents from the US Defnese Department that showed the extent to which Philippine monkeys were being used in studies of potential biological warfare agents. In one experiment, monkeys were placed in aerosol gas chambers into which disease agents were pumped through a series of tubes. The monkeys would fall sick, dying within hours or days.

By March 1985, the Philippines had "rediscovered" that macaques were listed on Appendix II of CITES, and the export quota was dropped to 12,000.[5] In 1989, the export number was reduced to 10,000 macaques a year.[6] Although the Philippines had never taken a census of its monkey population, 83,439 crab-eating macaques were exported during the years 1981 to 1988.[7] By 1990, the excessive shipments that had been allowed under the Marcos regime were curtailed. The Philippine Department of Environment and Natural Resources announced that by 1994, wild caught-monkeys would no longer be exported. They would be replaced with captive-bred macaques.

Indonesia was also supplying the wild-caught macaque trade, exporting an average of 15,000 annually.[8] While both Indonesia and the Philippines set quotas specifying the number of wild-caught animals to be shipped out each year, neither government took into account the suffering and high mortality rates in capture, holding and shipment when setting the quotas. Nor did they include the enormous number of macaques captured to supply the growing number of breeding programs.

Journey to the Lab

A monkey's journey from capture in the jungle to a research lab is brutal at best, with each stage contributing to a wastage of wildlife in vast numbers. Though capture methods vary, often a group of trappers will locate a tree in which a colony of monkeys are asleep, and, in the darkness of night, surround it with large nets. In the morning, with no escape possible, the monkeys descend to be captured. Grabbed by their tails, those who fight back may have their teeth bashed in with stones. Trappers may cram as many as fifteen of the animals together in a small cage. Those who are considered too old, damaged or small for research are clubbed to death or sold onto meat markets. Indonesian exporter C.V. Primaco revealed that of all the animals trapped usually only 25 percent are considered suitable to be sent on to a lab.[1] Once in cages, the monkeys are held until a sufficient number have been caught to warrant a journey to the holding station. Exporter Chuck Darsano estimates that 71 percent of Indonesian monkeys die from stress, malnourishment, exposure or neglect before they are even exported.[2]

Unfortunately, the suffering doesn't end once the monkeys are loaded for export. In September 1979, 485 monkeys out of a shipment of 625 died en route from Indonesia to the State Bacteriological Institute in Sweden.[3] Packed in tiny crates, they suffocated to death. The dead monkeys, who were found with their eyes hanging out of their sockets, had reportedly bitten off their own tongues. Curiously, U.S. Fish and Wildlife Service (FWS) statistics make no distinction between monkeys who arrive dead and those who arrive alive. In August 1992, 110 monkeys who arrived in Miami dead were entered into FWS's computer as "live." Only hunting trophies and wildlife products are entered into the computer system as "dead." It is just one of the ways in which mortality rates in the legal trade are kept a well-hidden secret.

Even those animals who survive capture and shipping aren't guaranteed better treatment once they reach their destination. On March 1, 1989, LACSA Airlines left four plywood crates filled with monkeys unattended overnight at JFK International Airport. Crammed into small cages in which they were unable to stand, and with no food or water, the monkeys were in near freezing temperatures for twelve hours. Eight of them died.[4] In a similar incident at JFK, several crates of monkeys were left unattended and unprotected from freezing temperatures while awaiting shipment.[5]

With this amount of mortality, and as the largest consumer of primates, U.S. labs have begun turning to "recycled" primates. Referred to as a "monkey supermarket," the Primate Supply Information Clearing House (PSIC) provides a replacement service for surplus primates held by U.S. research facilities. PSIC also provides body parts, bones and blood along with dead animals. While such service has helped take some of the pressure off species caught in the wild, it also means some captive primates may be passed from one nightmarish experiment to another, with little relief other than that brought by death, if an institution's IACUC agrees to an exception to the Improved Standards for Laboratory Animals Act's provision that an animal should not be used for more than one painful experiment.

Up until the late 1980s, the fact that wild-caught monkeys can be hotbeds of deadly diseases was rarely considered. Exacerbated by over-crowded shipping conditions and poor sanitation, the situation added up to a disaster just waiting to erupt. In April 1989, an epidemic identified as Simian Hemorrhagic Fever (SHF) broke out at New Mexico State University's Primate Research Lab in Alamagordo. A Centers for Disease Control (CDC) investigation team quickly pinpointed its origin to a group of crab-eating macaques that had been imported from the Philippines to a primate dealer's holding station in Florida before arriving in New Mexico. While over 400 monkeys died, this episode of SHF was just a harbinger of a far worse disease to come.[6]

In October 1989, a shipment of 100 crab-eating macaques from the Philippines was under quarantine at Hazelton Research Products in Reston, Virginia when some of the animals began to hemorrhage and die.[7] Once again, the CDC was called in. This time, what they found frightened them. The disease resembled the deadly Ebola virus. First discovered in 1976 in Zaire, where it killed approximately 500 people, Ebola broke out again in Sudan in 1979. The virus has up to a 21-day incubation period and kills roughly 90 percent of its human victims. While studying tissue samples from some of the monkeys who had died in Reston, scientists at the U.S. Army Medical Research Institute for Infectious Diseases found that although the filovirus looked like Ebola, it wasn't quite the same. Ebola is contagious to those who come in close contact with its victims through blood or other bodily fluids. This virus seemed to be spreading through the air, since monkeys in separate areas became ill. The virus was dubbed Ebola Reston, and the research facility in Virginia was quietly sealed. The surviving monkeys were killed, and the buildings were filled with toxic gas.

A short time later, a second shipment of monkeys held by an importer in Pennsylvania came down with Ebola Reston.[8] Then, in January 1990, four more shipments to Hazelton were found to contain monkeys dying of filovirus infection.[9] In all, more than 500 monkeys were killed in an attempt to stop the spread of the disease.[10] In the meantime, a number of workers who had handled the monkeys were tested. Seven of them were found to carry antibodies to the disease. One of those infected was an employee of the American Society for the Prevention of Cruelty to Animals Animal Hostel at JFK International Airport.

In March 1990, fearing that even more monkeys brought into the U.S. might carry the virus, the New York State Health Department slapped severe restrictions on all primate imports into the state. Up to this point, JFK International Airport had been the entry point for 80 percent of the 16,000 to 20,000 research monkeys imported into the country each year.[11] In effect, a ban was put on rhesus and African green monkeys and crab-eating macaques unless they had been in quarantine for 60 days in their country of origin and were tested for viral infection before export. In addition, imported monkeys were required to remain in quarantine for another 60 days upon arrival and be tested yet again for antibodies to the virus. Since few exporting countries had either quarantine or testing facilities, the flow of monkeys for research came to an abrupt halt.

At the same time, CDC officials made surprise inspections of primate importers' facilities. They discovered that Charles River Primates, Hazelton Research Products and Worldwide Primates in Miami, the three dealers responsible for handling more than 90 percent of U.S. monkey imports, were maintaining inadequate quarantine facilities.[12] Their licenses were immediately revoked. CDC officials charged Worldwide Primates with 46 violations, noting, "In some caging, the monkeys in the top tier were observed to defecate, urinate and drop other wastes through to the cage immediately below."[13] With three-fourths of all drug testing performed on crab-eating macaques, researchers and drug manufacturers were up in arms as they pushed to re-open the trade.

Emergency measures remained in effect for sixteen months. Although CDC eventually re-certified the importers, the cost of research monkeys more than doubled. Crab-eating macaques jumped in price from $400 in 1989 to between $1,500 and $1,600 in 1991.[14] And, while other states slowly lifted their restrictions on primate imports, the New York State requirements remain in effect to this day, almost entirely halting shipment of monkeys into JFK Airport.

Chimpanzees

The legal primate trade also supplies the research industry with chimpanzees. Once abundant in 25 African countries, chimpanzees ranged in the millions. Now they are extinct in four of those countries, with only Zaire, Gabon, Uganda, Rwanda and Tanzania hosting significant numbers today.[1] While chimpanzee population estimates range from 100,000 to 150,000, no one is really sure just how many are left, their numbers having been decimated by habitat destruction and commercial exploitation.[2] That their DNA is approximately 99 percent the same as man's has only helped doom them.

In 1977, Merck Sharp and Dohme Research Laboratories applied to the U.S. Federal Wildlife Permit Office to import 125 wild-caught chimpanzees, at least one year of age, 100 of whom would be female.[3] They were to be used for hepatitis research and then moved to form a breeding colony at the International Center for Environmental Safety at Alamagordo, New Mexico. Listed on Appendix I of CITES, chimpanzees were also categorized as "threatened" on the U.S. Endangered Species List. This meant that authorized signatures would be required from both the importing and exporting countries for trade to take place. The 125 chimps were to be obtained by Franz Sitter, an Austrian expatriate animal dealer operating out of Freetown, Sierra Leone.

Young chimpanzees are captured by killing their mothers along with other group members who fight to protect the infants. It is estimated that five to ten chimps may be lost for each infant taken. To fill an order for 125 infants, 500 to 750 chimpanzees would most likely be killed in the process. In order to fulfill the additional requirement that 100 of the chimps be female, the number of deaths could easily rise to as high as 1,200.[4] Because of Sierra Leone's liberal export permit policy, the country's chimp population was already on the decline. Sierra Leone is bordered by Guinea and Liberia, both of which had banned any export in chimps; however, the three countries' borders are extremely porous. It was suspected that poachers were shooting chimp groups in Liberia and Guinea and then smuggling the infants into Sierra Leone. It was also believed that Sitter was responsible for much of the decimation taking place.[5] Controversy over Merck Sharp and Dohme's request erupted in the U.S., and the export permit application was eventually withdrawn.

In 1982, in order to circumvent problems importing live chimps, the Austrian pharmaceutical firm Immuno sought to establish a lab for hepatitis research in Sierra Leone. Franz Sitter was chosen as the man to be in charge of establishing a breeding colony, which would provide a cheap and steady supply of chimps. At the time, Sitter's facility was described in a *Mail on Sunday* article as a place where a dozen chimpanzees, mostly babies and juveniles "are a pitiful sight. Light hardly enters their jail and they sit in cages chained to the rafters. They are strangely silent and sway neurotically. There is no foliage - just filth."[6]

Immuno ordered 60 to 80 wild-caught chimps to kick off the plan.[7] When international pressure caused the plan to fall through, Immuno imported 20 chimps who had already been procured in Sierra Leone to its facility in Austria, declaring them the company's private property.[8] Furious at the apparent flouting of international regulations, CITES denounced Immuno's actions and reprimanded Austria—a CITES signatory—for permitting the chimps to enter the country.

The discovery of AIDS made chimpanzees even more valuable to the research industry. Since the chimpanzee is the most biochemically and genetically similar species to us, researchers initially thought the animal would be a good model for AIDS research. But they soon discovered that some chimpanzees injected with HIV did not keep the virus alive, and most of those who did become infected had no observable response to it. Years went by before there was any indication that any of the chimps would develop full-blown AIDS. Then, in 1986, a 13-year-old chimp who was infected with the virus in 1985 died after exhibiting AIDS-like symptoms.[9] Even though no other chimps had developed AIDS, a number of researchers continued pushing for the use of chimpanzees to test possible vaccines. Chimpanzees had been listed as "threatened" in the U.S. Endangered Species Act since 1976, but the additional trade pressure prompted primatologists to petition FWS to upgrade wild chimps to "endangered." That would mean permits would be required for all interstate movement of chimpanzees. Fearing opposition from the biomedical community, FWS made a compromise decision. Chimpanzees outside the U.S. would be classified as "endangered," while the captive population in the U.S. would retain their "threatened" status. In March of 1990, wild chimps were formally re-classified as "endangered."

There are about 1,800 captive chimpanzees available for medical research in the U.S., and nearly half of them are in the hands of one man - Dr. Frederick Coulston, chairman of The Coulston Foundation (TCF).[10] Coulston and TCF have a troubling history of apparently negligent animal care, including substandard living conditions and insufficient medical attention resulting in questionable chimpanzee injuries, illnesses and deaths. In 1994, the U.S. Department of Agriculture (USDA) filed a complaint against TCF, charging the Foundation with violating the Animal Welfare Act.[11] The charges stemmed from the deaths of several chimpanzees. In October 1993, three chimps died a grisly death after a heater malfunctioned, causing the temperature in their enclosure to soar to 140 degrees. On December 18, 1994, a caretaker found four chimps either dead or dying in their cages. An autopsy revealed that the chimps had gone without water for at least three days. According to U.S News & World Report, "Although the caretakers were trained to test the animals' automatic waterers every day, they had in fact simply been checking off that task on their daily logs without actually performing the tasks."[12] USDA's complaint also charged TCF with housing 37 chimps in undersized cages. In June 1996, TCF agreed to settle the charges by paying a $40,000 fine.[13]

Coulston has also been critized by his colleagues in the research industry. A behavioral biologist who took part in TCF's testing of a painkiller for the drug manufacturer Glaxo Wellcome severed his ties with Coulston after several chimpanzees died during caesarian sections performed during the study. According to the biologist, the veterinarians Coulston hired to perform the surgery had almost no experience with primates.[14] After touring TCF in 1994, representatives from three NIH subsidiaries prepared a report raising what it called "major concerns" about veterinary staffing and experience and the "minimal number of animal care personnel" at the facility.[15]

Despite the serious questions surrounding the care of animals at TCF, Coulston is in the process of acquiring 100 more chimpanzees from New York University Medical Center's Laboratory for Experimental Medicine (LEMSIP). TCF is also leasing 150 chimps, formerly used in space research, from the U.S. Air Force.[16] Legislation that would have given the Air Force chimps to Coulston was defeated after protest from Dr. Jane Goodall and other animal welfare advocates. Dr. Goodall also objected to the transfer of the LEMSIP chimps to TCF, and asked New York University to require Coulston to correct all Animal Welfare Act violations at its New Mexico facilities before giving TCF any control over the animals.[17] Also opposed to the plan was former LEMSIP director Dr. Jan Moor-Jankowski. In an August 1995 New York Times article, Dr. Moor-Jankowski stated that he was worried not only about the fate of the chimps but also about what Coulston would do with the $705,000 that was supposed to be used to care for the animals once they were no longer useful as research subjects.[18] Moor-Jankowski said that he felt NYU's decision to give the chimps to Coulston was a form of retribution for his having blown the whistle on animal mistreatment at another NYU lab.[19] Soon after announcing the transfer of the LEMSIP chimps to TCF, it fired Moor-Jankowski. He has since filed a lawsuit against NYU charging the university with unfair retaliation.

Ironically, on January 22, 1997, an 11-year old chimp named Jello, recently transferred to TCF from LEMSIP, died after being anesthetized. According to an autopsy report, Jello's trachea was filled with food, which means he had rececently been fed and most likely choked to death on his own vomit.[20] "The most dangerous thing that can done is to anesthetize an animal or a person with food in his stomach because of the danger of vomiting and suffocating," said In Defense of Animals president Dr. Elliot Katz. "The circumstances surrounding Jello's death indicate egregious negligence and irresponsibility."

The Alternative

In 1992, an announcement by the Regional Primate Research Center at the University of Washington caused scientists to believe they had found a viable alternative to using chimpanzees. Preliminary testing at the Center appeared to show that pig-tail macaques could be infected with the AIDS virus. Indigenous to the forests of Indonesia and Malaysia, pig-tail macaques are named for their short, curly tails. Unfortunately for the macaques, scientists saw them as both cheap and abundant. Listed under Appendix II, they are, in truth, "vulnerable," with wild populations slowly shrinking due to habitat destruction and hunting. According to primatologist Ardith Eudey, a buying spree erupted after the Center made its announcement. In 1992, the number of pig-tail macaques imported into the U.S. was 1,198, nearly twice as many as had been reported to CITES by Indonesia and a huge increase from the 200 to 300 imported during the mid-1980s.[1] Shortly after the announcement, the initial tests were proven wrong. Sales of the monkeys immediately flattened.

By 1994, both Indonesia and the Philippines had announced they would no longer export wild-caught monkeys, only captive-bred animals. It was an announcement that many concerned with plummeting populations of wild primates had been waiting to hear for years. But while the captive-bred primate business takes the strain off wild populations, it also fosters the view that monkeys are nothing more than renewable resources.

A number of countries are already involved in the captive- bred primate trade. Since 1988, China has been a major source of captive-bred rhesus monkeys for both the U.S. and Europe. Barbados has the largest monkey colony in the Northern Hemisphere, with a population of 8,000 green monkeys supplying a steady flow for research purposes.[2] The island of Mauritius, with a population of 20,000 to 35,000 crab-eating macaques, exports both wild and captive-bred monkeys.[3] Mauritius still sets a quota on the number of wild-caught monkeys that may be shipped out, but captive breeding provides a way around this problem as well. Pregnant females and females with young are trapped, and their offspring are sold as captive bred. Once the mothers stop breeding, they are sold as wild-caught.[4]

Both the Philippines and Indonesia supply U.S. importers with crab-eating macaques who are officially claimed to be captive bred. But there are many who question whether this is truly the case. One major primate importer in the U.S. confided his suspicions that a number of the "captive-bred" monkeys he receives are actually wild caught. A U.S. wildlife inspector voiced the same concern to Shirley McGreal of IPPL. It is a loophole that even Indonesia's Jakarta Post has reported on, maintaining that many breeding farms simply camouflage the fact that a large number of monkeys are still being removed from the wild.[5]

Vietnam has become the newest export center for captive-bred primates. It is there that the provincial government's "April 18th Company" maintains the Monkey Island breeding center, where it raises rhesus monkeys and crab-eating and pig-tail macaques. Officials at the Ministry of Forestry in Hanoi claim that all primates shipped from the breeding center are captive bred, but an investigation by the U.S.-based Endangered Species Project (ESP) turned up contradictory information. According to the ESP investigators, 50 percent of the monkeys shipped out are wild caught and sent to Hong Kong where they are supplied with false papers.[6] From there the monkeys travel as captive bred to Europe, Great Britain and the U.S. According to an article in Vietnam Business magazine, monkeys on the island are also used to produce brain wine and monkey balm-items used in traditional Chinese medicine. Approximately 50 monkeys are killed every three months for this use. One monkey brain produces about ten bottles of wine. The skin, organs and bones are ground up as ingredients for 'balm,' or powder, which is dissolved in water and taken in liquid form by women who have recently given birth or those who are weak.

The Environmental Investigation Agency (EIA) investigated another Vietnamese captive breeding center in 1994. After visiting the premises of Nafobird outside Ho Chi Minh City, EIA came away equally concerned. Though the Vietnamese government has banned the export of wild macaques, the hunting of endangered primates and other rare animals continues to be a problem. The government passed wildlife legislation in 1992 to curtail illegal trade in endangered and threatened species, but to little avail. In

March 1993, Prime Minister Vo Van Kiet issued a second decree calling for increased law enforcement in an attempt to control the escalating trade.[7] However, it is believed that the country's resources continue to be exploited.

The Illegal Trade

Primate smuggling has become a booming business. A 1990 CITES report to the International Criminal Police Organization (Interpol) estimated that 40,000 primates are traded illegally every year. Annual revenues from the illicit trade in all endangered species is estimated to be in excess of $5 billion.[1]

The shadowy, underground world of animal smuggling is dominated by a network of increasingly powerful dealers and syndicates, often the same people who traffic in drugs and weapons. Wildlife is just one more commodity in which to trade. The advantage is that it requires minimum investment and low risk while reaping maximum rewards. Punishment for violations rarely exceeds more than a fine. A lucrative and loathsome business, it has become the second leading cause of species extinction, surpassed only by the increasingly rapid destruction of habitat.

CITES was designed to regulate trade in wildlife species that could withstand the pressures of commercial exploitation and at the same time protect endangered species. Unfortunately, there are many ways around CITES regulations when the stakes are high enough. The wildlife trade involves literally thousands of species and dozens of major importing and exporting nations. Add to this the hundreds of thousands of wildlife shipments, along with the many avenues by which they can be moved between their points of origin and their final destinations, and it is easy to see the kind of odds CITES is up against. Many countries only create more problems by providing what would seem to be nonexistent enforcement. In its twenty-odd years of existence, CITES has tried with mixed success to monitor and deter illegalities. But the organization is only as strong as the desire of its member nations to save their wildlife. In the end, it all comes down to money, greed and corruption. And there appear to be a number of very weak links in CITES fragile chain.

CITES documents authorizing wildlife trade are often stolen and reused, even though dealers are required to cancel certificates once shipments reach their final destination. Forgery is also commonplace. Species originally listed on documents may be changed along with the number of animals being shipped and their country of origin. Often primates are hidden in boxes that are marked as containing a different species altogether. Terrified gibbons have been found stuffed inside snake crates sealed as tightly as coffins. Orangutans have easily passed from one country into another squeezed in crates labeled "birds." And, if all else fails, there is always the oft-used method of bribing local officials. But CITES itself offers what is perhaps the best loophole: a captive-born species exemption that allows wild-caught animals to enter through the back door and leave by the front as "captive bred."

The Singapore Connection

A major problem for many years has been the use of "laundry countries." Wild animals are smuggled from their country of origin to a country where they are provided with fake captive bred papers. Singapore was exposed as such a center as early as 1975. Although it had virtually no wildlife of its own, it exported protected primates from neighboring countries into the U.S. and Europe. During the 1960s and 1970s, a steady stream of siamangs was smuggled by way of coastal freighters plying the waters between Thailand and Singapore. Gibbons were concealed in false petrol tanks under trucks to make the journey from Thailand via Malaysia. Smugglers rendezvoused with Indonesian fishing boats to collect orangutans who were brought back to Singapore's shores. This route came to be known as "The Singapore Connection."[1] Illicit traffic flourished for years, taking its toll on primates legally protected under their own country's laws. Once inside Singapore, dealers apparently had no problem obtaining health certificates and export documents from government officials. Importing countries accepted the shipments with little hesitation. Under the Wildlife Reservation and Protection Act of 1965, Thailand declared all gibbons protected. Since that time, there have been no officially sanctioned exports of the primates. Yet in 1973, at least 67 siamangs and 43 gibbons entered the U.S. from Singapore.[2] Since gibbons are protected under Appendix I, such trade was in direct violation of both CITES and the U.S. Lacey Act.

Originally passed in 1900, the Lacey Act is America's 'long arm law' and is one of the most effective trade laws ever set forth by a major wildlife-consuming country. It makes importation of animals or animal products taken or exported in violation of another country's laws a federal crime. It also prohibits the import, export, transportation, sale or purchase of any endangered wildlife covered under the Endangered Species Act.

FWS finally banned Singapore's $17 million wildlife trade with the U.S. in September 1986. The ban virtually shut down the country's lucrative $12 million tropical fish trade.[3] Faced with a huge loss of income, Singapore finally capitulated and joined CITES, an action it had been stalling on for years. Though now a member, Singapore still maintains its reputation as a "laundry" country. As late as 1993, Singapore's chairman of the National Council on the Environment declared the country to be a major transshipment center for endangered wildlife smuggling.[4]

Thailand

The Polish and Cambodian Connections

Word spread of the lucrative trade and soon Thailand decided to partake of the easy money to be made. Although the Thai government had joined CITES in 1983, it never bothered to adopt enforcement measures. This, along with aid from corrupt government officials, helped Thailand become the hub of illegal wildlife trade. Since it was seemingly penalty-free even if uncovered by Thai officials, smuggling continued to grow in popularity. In 1990, security guards at Don Muang Airport in Bangkok x-rayed a suitcase on its way to Paris and discovered three tiny bodies moving inside. Upon opening the luggage, the guards found three endangered gibbons wrapped in towels and wedged into a cardboard box. Barely able to move or breathe, the gibbons couldn't have survived the 13-hour flight to France. Customs officials took no action against the passenger responsible for the attempt.[1]

Endangered wildlife has also been found for sale at Chatuchak Park in Bangkok. A massive open-air fairground, Chatuchak is a potpourri of animals not only from Thailand but from Southeast Asian countries including Burma, Laos, Cambodia and Vietnam. A major animal market, it was from here that protected wildlife could be bought and smuggled around the world in oil drums, plastic bags and briefcases, often suffocating in the luggage compartments of airplanes. Two glaring loopholes in Thailand's 1965 Wildlife Protection Act were deemed responsible for allowing the illegal trade to continue. First, animals imported from other countries were not included in the law. And second, traders dealing in Thai-protected species could only be arrested if they were caught in the middle of a transaction.

Aside from gaining notoriety as a prime transshipment center, Thailand also became known as home to the dealers who controlled the trade. While a number of methods were used to smuggle wildlife, a common one was to take animals across the Thai border into Vientiane, the capital of Laos. Unlike Thailand, Laos is not a member of CITES. Once there, dealers obtained documents from the Laotian government as to origin and then shipped the animals back into Thailand and on to world markets.[2]

One of these dealers was Preecha Varavichit, owner of Pimjai Birds in Bangkok. Considered a crucial link in an international ring of animal smugglers operating throughout Southeast Asia, Europe and the U.S, Preecha was one of Thailand's biggest dealers. At the time, Preecha had paid Laotian authorities $5,000 to operate an animal exporting business in the country.[3] He ran a similar trade out of Vietnam (then not a member of CITES), having paid government authorities $10,000 in order to operate there for two years.[4]

When confronted with his actions, Preecha boasted to the Bangkok Post that officials from the Forestry Department — the agency directly responsible for curtailing the illegal wildlife trade in Thailand — supported his trade. He was quoted as saying, "If government officials didn't give their cooperation, I would not be able to do business. Don't blame me alone. They work as a team. If they take legal action against me, I will reveal everything."[5]

But it wasn't until IPPL received a mysterious package of documents that the extent of Preecha's operation was revealed. Working in conjunction with Swedish animal dealer Ingemar Forss, Preecha was shipping protected wildlife from his fraudulent Laotian "Phoudou Zoo" by Laos Aviation's morning flight to Don Muang airport in Bangkok.[6] From there, the shipments would continue on to the next leg of their journey.

Wildlife traffickers rely on countries and zoos that knowingly cooperate in the illegal trade. In the past, a number of Eastern European zoos have been more than willing partners. Such was the case with protected wildlife that Preecha shipped out of Laos. Their destination was to zoos in Poland. Lacking hard currency with which to buy animals, a number of Polish zoos turned to laundering illegally caught wildlife. In return for supplying false certificates, which claimed the animals were captive bred, the participating zoos kept some of the animals for their own collections. This ruse became known as "The Polish Connection." Poland's Wroclaw and Poznan zoos were two such zoos that became involved in Preecha's scam in the 1980s, providing facilities where endangered species could be "quarantined." Freshly laundered, the animals then continued on to zoos in Western nations in what appeared to be legal transactions. Among the animals shipped were orangutans, endangered douc langurs, lorises and tapirs.[7]

However, in October 1987, Preecha was arrested in Laos for falsifying government export documents. He received a three-year jail term and a $150,000 fine, but was pardoned and released after only three months due to diplomatic intervention from Thailand.[8] The argument presented to Laotian officials was that through the nature of his work, Preecha had contributed a large amount of foreign exchange to Laos and therefore should not be severely punished.

Thai dealers next moved their illegal wildlife trade into Cambodia. The most enterprising of the lot was Khun Khampeng Ploentham of the Bangkok Wildlife Company. Working in conjunction with German dealer Marlies Slotta, owner of the animal trading firm Slotta Interzoo, Khampeng sent a number of shipments of protected animals from Cambodia to zoos in Eastern Europe.[9]

In order to legitimize his trade, Khampeng set up a phony zoo in Cambodia that he named "Koh Khong Zoo." In essence, it became his own private permit factory from which he issued captive born certificates signed by himself, as zoo director, on official-looking stationery. In September 1988, "Koh Khong Zoo" shipped two orangutans as "captive born" via Wroclaw Zoo in Poland to the Soviet Union. The orangutans were accompanied by fraudulent export permits. One of the animals died, and the other is currently housed at Russia's St. Petersburg Zoo. Khampeng also shipped twelve white-handed baby gibbons to Wroclaw Zoo. They arrived at the zoo in poor condition, and eleven eventually died. The sole survivor was sent on to Lesna Zoo in Czechoslovakia.[10] In February 1989, two "captive-born" orangutans were exported from "Koh Khong Zoo" to the Film Board of Czechoslovakia where they were used to make a movie about the endangered status of orangutans. Marlies Slotta sent a telex to Khampeng to confirm their arrival, referring to the pair as "big red birds," the smugglers' code name for the species.[11]

While "Koh Khong Zoo" stationery did not include a street address for correspondence, a post office box was listed in Phnom Penh. IPPL contacted a Cambodian representative at the United Nations and learned that not only was Koh Khong Province the scene of intense fighting at the time, but that there were no zoos in Cambodia and certainly no "captive-bred" orangutans. A massive letter writing and publicity campaign forced the closure of the Polish Connection, and, in December 1989, Poland joined CITES. However, it is believed that both Khampeng and "Koh Khong Zoo" are still in operation.[12]

By 1991, having officially recognized Thailand as the foremost laundering center in Asia, CITES called for a worldwide embargo on all wildlife trade with the country. Finally, in 1992, Thailand passed legislation to enforce CITES regulations. By 1993, new laws designed to protect foreign countries' endangered species helped slow the trade. Animal dealers were now forced to turn to other Indochinese countries, such as Vietnam, for re-export of illegal wildlife. But according to Thai sources, much of the country's indigenous protected wildlife can still be found for sale every weekend at Chatuchak Park.[13]

The Trade in Orangutans

Although a CITES signatory, Indonesia has long been recognized as a major center for illegal trade in endangered wildlife. But it is Pramuka Market in the capital city of Jakarta where trade in vanishing species flourishes. Here among the storefronts and stalls, a smuggler may find whatever he desires. Gibbons with large, frightened eyes peer out from inside cardboard boxes as customers from Taiwan, Europe, China and the Middle East openly haggle over their illicit sale. For the right price, export permits that will whisk any species out of the country are easily procured. But the hottest items in demand among those who scour Pramuka's treasure trove of wildlife are the orangutans.

Found only on the islands of Borneo and Sumatra, orangutans number between 20,000 to 30,000 in the wild, down from 70,000 only ten years ago.[1] Their population continues to decline by several hundred each year due to commercial exploitation and habitat loss. Protected by Indonesian law since 1931, orangutans are also listed on Appendix I of CITES. Neither of these protections have succeeded in stopping the trade. Tottering on the verge of extinction has only made orangutans all the more valuable on a booming black market that has grown from a trickle to a torrent over the past 20 years. The voracious demand of entertainers, private collectors and foreign zoos, along with destruction of the species' forest home, have all contributed to what appears to be the last stand of orangutans in the wild.

Orangutan mothers must be killed to capture their babies, and the mortality rate of young orphans is high. It is estimated that for every smuggled baby that survives and arrives at its final destination, five or six have died. While a hunter gets $200 for a baby, the middleman can sell it for $1,000 in Jakarta. From there, orangutans range in price from $5,000 if sold to a family in Taiwan, to $30,000 if purchased by a foreign circus or zoo. When the final destination is the U.S., the price can soar to as much as $50,000.[2] Even dead orangutans garner a profit. A thriving trade exists in Kalimantan, Borneo, where souvenir shops sell orangutan skulls to foreign tourists for $70 apiece. Skulls that have been decorated with tattoo-like markings can fetch up to $200 each.[3] Employees of the Forestry Office, the government agency in charge of inspecting local shops for illegal wildlife items, tend to ignore the trade. The result is that orangutans are under siege in a battle for their very existence.

Money is what fuels the animal trade. Add to that the desire to obtain the ultimate wildlife status symbol, and the demand on a species can be overwhelming. Taiwan was once a frequent destination for smuggled orangutans. It was there that the popular TV show "The Naughty Family," which had a young orangutan as its star, fueled an orangutan fad. The show prompted a craze among the nouveau riche to keep orangutans as pets, and it is estimated that over 1,000 of the animals were smuggled into Taiwan from Borneo aboard logging and fishing boats.[4] It also meant that 5,000 to 7,000 orangutans died to supply the pet trade in Taiwan alone.[5] Taiwan's capital, Taipei, soon ended up with more orangutans per square mile than in the animals' native habitat. A nearby zoo, which houses 40 of the abandoned pets, has found itself with the largest collection in the world. Before long, Taipei earned the nickname "Mad Monkey City."[6]

Infant orangutans grow up quickly, only to have their days as pampered pets in private homes come to an abrupt end. One has only to visit Snake Alley, Taiwan's infamous street bazaar, to discover how orangutans discarded by once loving families are now kept. Exhibited in front of Chinese medicine shops, juvenile orangs are frequently seated on stools, held in place by chains around their necks. Kept as tourist attractions, they are harassed by their owners and teased by passers-by until eventually they are abandoned on street corners, having lost their appeal with age. Not allowed by China to be a CITES member, Taiwan did little to stop the trade until 1989, when the country passed a Wildlife Conservation Law. The law required citizens to register all orangutans that were owned, but only about 300 of the primates were ever reported.[7] As for the rest, those who were not sold to zoos, circuses or shops were abandoned, dumped in forests or recycled on the black market.

While the Orangutan Foundation has repatriated about two dozen orangutans to Indonesia, a new problem has cropped up. A number of discarded orangutans have been found to carry hepatitis B and tuberculosis antibodies, ruling out any chance of their return to the wild. Permanent castoffs, homeless orangutans are being banished to a "shelter" in southern Taiwan to spend the rest of their days in tiny cages, prisoners of a heartless trade.[8]

The Bangkok Six Case

The infamous "Bangkok Six" case provides perhaps the best view into the orangutan trade, revealing just how sophisticated organized wildlife crime has become. It was on February 20, 1990, at Don Muang airport in Bangkok, when cargo handlers first heard cries that sounded like those of human babies coming from three small wooden crates labeled "Birds." Having been off-loaded from Thai Airways flight 414 for Singapore, they were destined for the city of Belgrade in the former Yugoslavia. An X-ray machine revealed that one of the boxes held two siamangs. Stuffed inside the other two crates were six baby orangutans. Starving, with bloated stomachs and covered with feces and vomit, the babies were pale and suffering from dehydration, parasitic infection and pneumonia. Three had been shipped upside down, two of whom were comatose. Eventually four of the infants died.[1]

The orangutans, dubbed "The Bangkok Six," were quickly taken from the airport to Wildlife Fund Thailand, at which point Shirley McGreal of IPPL was contacted. It was McGreal who not only helped break the case wide open but eventually pushed it to its conclusion. The first break came when the Thai Wildlife Department received a letter from Vukosav Bojovic, director of the Belgrade Zoo, requesting that the "monkeys" confiscated from a "Mr. Schafer" be sent to him immediately. "Mr. Schafer" turned out to be Kurt Schafer, a well-known German animal dealer who had been arrested twice previously in Australia for smuggling birds.[2]

According to Schafer's information, along with that provided by FWS and the German Wildlife Department, a prime player in organizing the shipment was Matthew Block, a major Miami dealer and owner of Worldwide Primates. Working in conjunction with Kenny Dekker, an animal dealer from the Netherlands who has since been convicted of bird smuggling, Block arranged the shipment through a Singapore middleman. The original supplier of the animals was rumored to be a notorious Indonesian exporter. Reputed to be the biggest and richest animal dealer in the country, this dealer is also the brother-in-law of a former Indonesian wildlife chief. Taken by boat to Singapore, the animals were delivered to James Lee of Honey Pets, who was later indicted in the U.S. in 1993. The first attempt to move the animals came in November 1989, when they were to be shipped from Singapore directly to Moscow on Aeroflot. The crates were checked in as cargo, while paperwork for boxes actually containing birds was taken to Primary Production (a branch of CITES) for approval. From there, shippers took the crates to the airline, where they switched them with identical boxes containing the orangutans. But there was a hitch: The plane was fully booked and the cargo was refused.

At that point, Kurt Schafer was called upon to organize the shipment. Electing to take an alternate route, Schafer checked the orangutans on a plane to Thailand as his personal luggage. A favorite ploy of animal dealers, checking wildlife as personal luggage avoids the problem of having to obtain an air waybill, which would leave authorities with a paper trail to follow. From there, Schafer and the orangutans were to board a flight for Yugoslavia, where zoo director Bojovic planned to 'launder' the animals by supplying papers declaring them captive born. In return, Bojovic would receive two siamang gibbons. From Belgrade, the orangutans would be sent as cargo to Prodintorg, a state-run trading company in Moscow, where more phony documents would be exchanged to further confuse the orangutans' origin.[3]

In February 1992, Block was indicted on two felony and two misdemeanor counts.[4] But by October of that year, Block and his lawyers had managed to work out a plea bargain with an assistant U.S. attorney that would have left him with only a small fine and no jail time. Before a hearing could be held, IPPL managed to organize a massive letter writing campaign in protest. Block's plea bargain was thrown out in December 1992, and, in January 1993, Block pled guilty to participation in a felony wildlife smuggling conspiracy. In April of 1993, he was sentenced to 13 months in federal prison and fined $30,000 for his role in the most notorious animal smuggling case in history. Free on bond while his case was being appealed, Block continued running his business. His final appeal was denied in September 1995, and on October 18, he was incarcerated at the Jesup Correctional Institute in Georgia.

A legend in the animal business, Block entered the exotic bird trade at the age of thirteen. By the time he was in high school, he was making close to $100,000 a year.[5] In 1986, Bolivian authorities issued a warrant for his arrest, alleging that he tried to smuggle 300 monkeys out of the country.[6] Block ran into more trouble following his 1993 conviction. The U.S. Department of Agriculture moved to suspend his dealer's license, claiming that primates at his holding compound ate spoiled food, were not provided with water as required and were housed in filth. Block settled the case in January 1994 by agreeing to pay a $16,000 fine.[7] However, in August of the same year, FWS permanently revoked Worldwide Primates' license to import and export primates due to Block's conviction.[8] But according to Shirley McGreal, this will have little effect on Block's business. Having established a breeding colony in the U.S., Block stockpiled hundreds of crab-eating macaques before his conviction. FWS' revocation of Worldwide's license does not bar Block from continuing animal dealing as long as it does not involve animals entering or leaving the U.S. In essence, this leaves Worldwide free to sell its renewable supply of macaques to research labs within the U.S. Involved in a captive breeding center in Indonesia as well, Block can continue conducting business as usual around the world.[9]

The other players in the "Bangkok Six" case remain unpunished. A Singapore court charged Kurt Schafer with exporting orangutans without a permit, but only fined him $1,200.[10] Was the case of the Bangkok Six a lesson to those who deal illegally in animals? It's difficult to know. In June 1990, just four months after confiscation of "The Bangkok Six," IPPL received a tip that five more orangutans were on a Thai dealer's premises, four of whom were to be shipped to an unknown destination as "personal baggage." In May 1993, a baby orangutan was confiscated from a freighter traveling from Thailand to Taiwan, and, in 1994 another orangutan was seized off a freighter in Hong Kong harbor, also heading toward Taiwan.[11] With such examples, there is no reason to believe that the orangutan pipeline should not continue running smoothly. The discovery of "The Bangkok Six" was probably a fluke. Just the tip of the iceberg, it popped to the surface for a moment only to drop back down, leaving the world with a tantalizing glimpse of how the illegal trade works and how unprepared governments are to deal with it.

Illegal Trade in Africa

Walter Sensen

While much has been publicized about the illegal trade in Southeast Asia, that is not the only area of the world rich in endangered wildlife. Africa also offers animal dealers the opportunity to make easy money smuggling primates.

One of the first major cases unfolded in January 1987, when three young gorillas were flown out of Douala, Cameroon headed for Taiwan. The first stopover on their journey was Kinshasa, Zaire. There the gorillas were to be transferred to UTA Airlines and flown to South Africa where they would be loaded on a South African Airways flight bound for Taipei. But trouble arose when it was discovered that two of the gorillas had died of asphyxiation on the Douala-Kinshasa leg of the flight. The insurance company that had been contracted to cover the shipment called in Dr. Robert Cooper, a veterinarian working in the African nation of Gabon. Since the gorillas had been insured at $150,000 a piece, the insurance company was already facing a $300,000 loss and was anxious to avoid an additional $150,000 claim.[1] Dr. Cooper was able to save the third gorilla.

As with so many others, this shipment might have gone undiscovered if Dr. Cooper had not contacted IPPL. It was soon revealed that the three gorillas had been shipped illegally from Cameroon accompanied by papers identifying them as "monkeys." Banned from commercial trade due to their listing on Appendix I, lowland gorillas are in great demand by zoos and collectors alike. Moreover, Cameroon is a member of CITES and forbids their export. But it seems that at least one Cameroonian government official protected the shipment, having received $25,000 from German animal dealer Walter Sensen for a permit.[2] As residents of Cameroon, Sensen and his son Bernd had been running their wildlife business out of the country for several years. Working in conjunction with native poachers, Sensen was able to offer a continual supply of both gorillas and chimpanzees to a number of sources. When it came time to ship his "goods" out, government officials in high places always made sure there weren't any problems.

With this information in hand, IPPL contacted the insurance company with proof that the gorilla shipment was illegal. Since contraband cannot be covered, the company refused to pay the $300,000 claim.[3] The surviving gorilla continued on his journey to the Taipei Zoo where he lives alone today.

As a result of the storm over the "Cameroon Three" shipment, Sensen and son were booted out of the country, only to resurface later in Equatorial Guinea. There they managed to obtain a five-year government contract to export wildlife, including gorillas and chimpanzees.[4] During this time, IPPL received information that West Germany had placed Sensen under a professional prohibition forbidding him to deal in wildlife, legally or illegally. In September 1988, the CITES Secretariat put an embargo on all wildlife trading with Equatorial Guinea due to its association with Sensen. Sensen continued trading despite the embargo. He offered gorillas to a Swedish zoo director, and shipped a young female gorilla to Pata Mall in Thailand.[5,6] Although a member of CITES, Thailand didn't bother to confiscate the gorilla on her arrival in the country. Allegedly, a young female gorilla had been shipped to Thailand via Moscow a few years earlier, also bound for Pata Mall. She arrived frozen to death.[7]

In December 1988, Sensen booked a shipment of four baby chimpanzees on an Iberia Airlines flight from Equatorial Guinea to Madrid, where they would be transshipped to Dubai via Istanbul. The young chimps were packed in two 2x2 crates for the 36-hour journey. Sensen arranged the shipment in conjunction with an American in Madrid by the name of Jack Kelly, whose stationery identified him as a "Special Delegate of the President of Equatorial Guinea." It was a clue that animals traveling this route were most likely being sent as "diplomatic baggage," thus avoiding confiscation.[8]

In June 1989, it was discovered that Sensen had shipped two gorillas to the brand new Guadalajara Zoo in Mexico for which his company, "African Animal Export," was paid $130,000.[9] Aside from the fact that the pair had entered Mexico as Sensen's "personal luggage," the Equatorial Guinean export permit for the two gorillas was nearly a year out of date. Learning of the shipment, El Occidental, a Guadalajara newspaper, reported the incident, and a scandal evolved. The director of the Mexico City zoo called the sale "a disgrace to Mexico," and the mayor of Guadalajara announced that the zoo's trustees would be replaced.

Though all of these dealings were illegal, Sensen escaped punishment for years because none of the shipments ever touched West German soil. Animal dealers have been taking advantage of this loophole for years. Countries without a "long arm law" like the Lacey Act are not responsible for any wildlife crimes committed by their nationals on foreign soil. German authorities took no action against Sensen until animal advocates launched several major campaigns in protest, and Sensen's activities could no longer be ignored.

IPPL provided German government representatives with the information it had gathered about Sensen's illegal activities. German officials received a deluge of mail from IPPL members demanding that Sensen be stopped. Finally, in March 1990, Sensen was jailed in Nuremberg, Germany on charges of violating the professional prohibition that had been placed on him previously. His sentence was two years without parole.[10] Once in jail, Sensen immediately appealed the length of his sentence, citing his 'precarious' financial situation. After serving only three months, Sensen was set free by judge Dieter Grafe, who declared that not only had Sensen shown regret about his actions during his last 100 days of detention, but that he could not be regarded as a tormentor of animals since he 'is interested in the survival of the animals.'[11] Although Sensen is apparently no longer involved in the wildlife trade, his son Bernd carries on with his work, having taken over the "African Animal Export" company in Equatorial Guinea.

The Chimp Trade

Perhaps most lucrative is the illicit trade in chimpanzees. For the past 25 years, the capture of infant chimps in developing African countries has proven to be a quick way to make hard cash. But with an estimated loss of five to ten primates for every infant captured, it is a costly transaction for the chimpanzee population.[1] While it is known that chimps exported through Sierra Leone have usually been taken from Liberia and Guinea, other trade routes exist as well. In 1988, authorities uncovered the "Cuba Connection," which involved shipping chimps from Angola to Cuba via Cubana Airlines. From there they were re-exported to the Netherlands as "captive bred," only to be re-exported again, with several shipped off to Japan.[2] Such circuitous itineraries are the norm with illicit wildlife cargo - not only to obtain captive bred papers, but also to avoid certain transit points where a shipment might be intercepted, all the while creating a maze that is impossible for authorities to follow.

Today, chimpanzees are flowing out of ports in Guinea at the rate of six a week. Aeroflot flight 420, which leaves Brazzaville Airport in the Congo Republic every Thursday, has been nicknamed "The Wildlife Express."[3] Stopping at Douala and Malta Airports, its final destination is Russia, where most of the animals are destined to be sold as merchandise in Moscow's booming wild animal markets. It is believed that many wild-caught chimps are intended for research labs in Russia and Eastern Europe.[4]

The first report of Aeroflot's involvement in the animal trade came on December 8, 1994, when an agitated young chimp was spotted in a plastic bag outside the airport in Brazzaville. Agents moved quickly to discover that a Congolese man was intending to smuggle three chimps on board the weekly flight to Moscow. Even though the man carried no CITES documents authorizing the export, airport police blocked all efforts to confiscate the chimps. An international alert was broadcast by both CITES and IPPL as the flight took off for Moscow via Cameroon and Malta. But authorities in Cameroon were prevented from searching the plane — this time by Aeroflot pilots. Continuing on to Malta, the plane was allowed once again to take off without a search since Maltese law does not allow for the confiscation of smuggled wildlife in transit. By the time Flight 420 reached Moscow, it was discovered that the chimps had been off-loaded during one of the stops along the way. However, two weeks later, Congolese authorities seized three chimpanzees, three guenon monkeys, an African grey parrot and a crate of ivory as they were being loaded onto Flight 420.[5] This is the only known seizure, and it is not yet clear whether this means that there has been a change of policy in Congolese law enforcement. With little to halt the trade, The Wildlife Express continues its run every Thursday. The assumption that Flight 420 is an airborne channel for Africa's dwindling supply of endangered species is fortified by reports of chimpanzees for sale at Moscow's notorious bird market.[6]

The Middle East is exploding as the newest marketplace for both chimps and lowland gorillas. A confidential source revealed to IPPL that influential Saudis regularly send chimps smuggled out of Tanzania to Saudi Arabia aboard private flights. No official CITES documents authorize their export. In late 1993, nine wild-caught chimps were illegally shipped from Tanzania to Riyadh, where they sold for $100,000 apiece. Three young chimps were also discovered for sale at the Jeddah Zoo. Meanwhile, pet shops in Faifa, Taif, Riyadh and Jeddah advertise chimps along with other protected species, helping feed a voracious appetite for exotic pets.[7]

Some suspect that Egyptian embassies in Africa are supplying false papers and holding primates before shipping them to countries in the Middle East. A recent smuggling incident involved a one-and-a-half year old female eastern lowland gorilla and a nine-month old female chimp who had been illegally transported from Zaire to Ethiopia before being confiscated at Kigali Airport in Rwanda. Implicated in the plot were an Egyptian animal dealer and an employee of the Egyptian embassy in Rwanda.[8]

Circuses traveling through Africa have also been known to serve as fronts for wildlife smuggling operations. Wanted on charges of animal trafficking in Uganda and Kenya is Akef, owner of the Egyptian Akef Circus.[9] He is suspected of having smuggled between five and eleven chimps out of Kenya during 1994. The Ugandan Wildlife Department recently confiscated four chimps from him while he was performing in that country.[10] Using the circus as a front, Akef sells smuggled chimps in the Mideast for prices as high as $100,000.[11] Having traveled the African continent with his circus for years, Akef went about his activities with little interference due to his political connections within the Egyptian government. Akef's uncle is the Minister of Tourism in Egypt, which has helped provide him with the protection of Egyptian ambassadors in countries throughout Africa.[12]

One area of the trade that appears to have been shut down, at least temporarily, is the market for beach chimps. From the 1970s into the early 1990s, Spain and the Canary Islands were considered two of the safest havens for trade in endangered species. Spain in particular had become a gateway for major European markets as well as a transit point for countries in Asia. But the beaches and resorts of Spain and the Canary Islands were the final destination for hundreds of chimps who were used by itinerant photographers each summer to attract tourists. At one time, more than 200 chimps helped photographers ply their trade.[13] Aged between a few months and five years, the chimps were forced to work 16 hours a day, seven days a week, attracting business along the beaches by day and in smoky bars at night. Squeezed into tight-fitting children's clothes, their feet squashed into human shoes, they were often drugged with tranquilizers to keep them docile. Their teeth were yanked out with pliers to prevent biting. Misbehavior was punished with beatings or cigarette burns. Disoriented and dazed, they were easy fodder for attracting attention. Having received no care or maternal love, they reacted with pathetic tenderness toward anyone willing to show them a moment's affection as a photo was shot, even as the constant flash of the camera destroyed their eyes.[14]

But such a booming business demanded a constant supply of chimps. When infants grew into unruly adolescents, they needed to be replaced. By the time beach chimps reached five years of age, they were at the end of their short, stressful working lives. Some were thrown off cliffs, others were abandoned to starve in the hills, and many more had their throats slit or were drowned.[15]

To keep a steady supply flowing, baby chimps were regularly smuggled into Spain from West Africa. In order to provide 200 infant chimps, at least 1,000 adults were shot. The majority of the captured babies died en route due to illness, malnutrition, dehydration, poor transport conditions or bullet wounds.[16] By journey's end, ten chimps would have died for each one who made it to Spain. Allegedly, a large number of these chimps originated in Equatorial Guinea, where they were reportedly shipped out on Iberia flights and military planes by none other than Walter Sensen and son.

In 1986, Spain joined the European Economic Community and automatically became a signatory of CITES. But Spanish authorities turned a blind eye, and the trade continued. Although a few confiscations took place, many times judges simply returned chimps to the photographers. In one instance, the chimp rather than the photographer was incarcerated for four days.[17] Finally, in 1991, a massive media campaign was launched. Radio, TV, newspapers and magazines throughout Great Britain and Europe covered the story. Not only was the abuse of the chimps publicized, but also the fact that they posed a major health risk by carrying serious infections such as tuberculosis and hepatitis that could easily be transmitted to tourists. Over a number of years, the trade was slowly brought to a halt.

The trade in beach chimps was just one form of exploitation to be found. In 1988, officials in Uganda discovered that an underground trade in chimps had been flourishing for years. On September 10, 1988, five infant chimps passed undetected through Entebbe International Airport bound for Dubai in the United Arab Emirates (UAE).[18] On October 16, authorities seized another infant chimp headed for Dubai. In the process, they uncovered a chimpanzee racket involving top customs and security officials.[19] On January 9, 1989, authorities seized yet another shipment of infant chimps bound for Dubai.[20] On December 6, 1989, two baby chimps were placed on board a Uganda Airlines flight. Squeezed into a poorly ventilated wooden box with no food or water, the pair were seized in Sharijah in UAE and returned to Uganda.[21] Ugandan Chief Game Warden Moses Okua declared that the chimps were being brought in illegally from Zaire, where smugglers were able to obtain false export documentation.[22] But it was discovered that infant chimps were being smuggled out of Uganda's own forests as well.

The trail of corruption in the Ugandan chimpanzee trade reached even higher than customs and security officials. A major scandal erupted in September 1990. It began when the notorious dealer Ingemar Forss, of Polish Connection fame, struck a deal with Ugandan Deputy Minister of Tourism and Wildlife, Dr. Wilson Nadiope. Allegedly, four chimps worth $400,000 on the world market would be exchanged for a pair of Siberian tigers from the Moscow State Circus.[23] The four wild-born chimps were from among a group at Entebbe Zoo who had been smuggled and confiscated once before.[24]

Carrying an export permit signed by Chief Game Warden Okua, which claimed the four chimps had been zoo bred, Forss boarded an Ethiopian Airlines flight bound for Moscow.[25] The chimps were checked in as personal luggage. Once the Entebbe 4 (as they would to become known) reached Moscow, Victor Schulman, an American and owner of the Soviet American Arts and Entertainment Company (SAAEC), took them off Forss' hands. Having paid $34,000 in advance for the chimps, Schulman planned to train them to perform in Sovincirk's "Circus on Ice."[26] It wasn't until Schulman had gathered the chimps and departed that officials discovered the export documents had been falsified. Shortly after that, the Ugandan Minister of Tourism and Wildlife, Samuel Sebagereka, publicly confirmed that the Entebbe 4 were indeed wild-born infants who had been held at Entebbe Zoo. It was also confirmed that the tiger exchange was a fraud. Though Russia is a member of CITES, the authorities there failed to confiscate the Entebbe 4 despite pressure from the CITES Secretariat to do so.

Soon after, both Schulman and the chimps fled the country and eventually turned up in Italy. Local authorities confiscated the chimps in Rome, only to have them returned to Schulman by a local judge. While the Ugandan embassy was appealing the judge's decision, the ice circus disappeared again, this time transporting the chimps out of Italy into Austria. Though both Italy and Austria are members of CITES, the circus passed through each country's borders with no problem. Border guards never bothered to ask Schulman for any legal documentation for the cargo he carried.

Intent on capturing the chimps, CITES officials embarked on a wild chase as they followed the ice circus truck from Austria into Hungary. The

CITES Secretariat had forewarned Austrian and Hungarian frontier stations about the chimps' possible arrival, but the truck made it across the borders once again. The border stations along the Russian Frontier were alerted next as Katalin Rodics of the CITES Management Authority in Hungary followed in hot pursuit. Finally, Rodics intercepted the truck at the Russian border and confiscated the chimps.

After illegally crossing the borders of at least six different countries without ever having been checked for legal documentation, the four endangered chimps were returned to Uganda one year after their export. On October 16, 1991, Uganda became a member of CITES. As for Ingemar Forss, no action was ever taken. Though a member of CITES, Sweden does not have a long arm law. As long as the animals were not brought onto Swedish soil, nothing could be done to punish Forss for his actions.[27] Forss is still working as an animal dealer in Scandinavia. FWS initiated an investigation into Victor Shulman's role in the case, but no charges were ever filed.

The Illegal Trade Today

Uganda's smuggling problems didn't stop there. The country continues to be plagued by illegal wildlife trade. Bordered by Rwanda, Sudan, Zaire, Tanzania and Kenya - countries all rich in wildlife - Uganda remains a major transshipment point. Much of this is due to the fact that the country offers well-built roads along with an international airport providing easy access to Asia, Europe and the Middle East. It was for this very reason that the U.S. chose Uganda as a base for its relief operation during Rwanda's recent civil war, with Entebbe International Airport serving as its headquarters.

In September 1994, yet another major smuggling ring was uncovered in Uganda, linking airport cargo handlers, customs officials, wildlife game officers and Ugandan businessmen to the illegal trafficking of primates, parrots and leopard skins. Their clients included UN relief workers supporting the Rwandan aid effort and foreign diplomats. The ring was discovered when two American investigators from the Endangered Species Project asked a cargo handler at Entebbe International Airport if he handled much wildlife. Investigator Kathi Austin soon found herself surrounded by airport workers who eagerly offered to sell her everything from chimpanzees to reptile skins. Believing the investigators to be UN relief workers, the dealers revealed that chimps were being smuggled from Rwanda and Zaire into Uganda where they were sedated and then shipped as airline cargo to Dubai, Hong Kong or Japan. Austin also learned that chimps were loaded onto trucks bound for Kenya, hidden inside crates filled with bananas. Another dealer spoke of a trader who regularly flew chimps from Kigali, Rwanda into Saudi Arabia via Uganda. However, the easiest way of all to smuggle was if a customer happened to hold a diplomatic passport or had use of cargo planes or military transport.[1]

The investigators revealed what they had learned to both Interpol and Uganda's Criminal Investigations Department, and a sting was quickly arranged. Only the Ugandan Game Department refused to participate. Delivering the first of six promised baby chimps, two of the dealers were arrested. Two more members of the group were arrested the following day, but the ringleader managed to escape. As for the investigators who helped uncover the smuggling ring, both women were called before U.S. military officials in Entebbe. Accused of jeopardizing the Rwandan relief effort in Uganda, the women were pressed to reveal which Ugandan officials they might have embarrassed with the scandal. Informing them that they could be "stepping on somebody's toes," U.S. officials asked the investigators to leave the country, offering to transport them anywhere else they wanted to go.[2]

While it might have been hoped that this would bring a temporary end to the smuggling in Uganda, that, unfortunately, is not the case. In March 1995, four mountain gorillas were speared to death in the Bwindi Impenetrable National Park. The black back male, nursing adult female and two juveniles found slaughtered were part of a group of 18 animals under habituation for scientific research. It is assumed they were killed by poachers during the capture of infant gorillas to be smuggled and sold.[3] Shortly after the discovery, the Director of Uganda National Parks confirmed that two infants were missing.[4]

But the killing didn't stop there. Recently, two more mountain gorillas were found dead in Zaire's Virunga park, their bodies filled with rounds of high-velocity ammunition. They are believed to have been shot by armed refugees for their infants who were most likely sold to a private zoo or collector. Though one infant mountain gorilla was later confiscated and returned successfully to his family group, the fate of the other unfortunate infants remains a mystery. What is known is that no mountain gorilla has ever survived in captivity. With less than 620 mountain gorillas left on earth, any loss to the gene pool is a disaster in the making.[6]

How much smuggling of gorillas is actually going on today? While it is fairly easy to keep track of the deaths of the few remaining mountain gorillas, lowland gorillas are a different matter. They inhabit countries with porous borders, and it is suspected that a number are smuggled out along rivers without a trace, ending up in the Mideast and Asia in private menageries like expensive works of art to be savored in private. For it is only those few failed smuggling attempts that the world ever hears about.

In April 1995, ten primates were confiscated at Manila Airport in the Philippines. Squeezed tightly inside two wooden crates, the animals were loaded onto a Pakistan Airlines flight that originated in Karachi with a stop in Bangkok before continuing on to Manila. The crates were declared to contain "monkey trophies and six love birds." They were opened to reveal a baby male gorilla, two endangered drill monkeys, two patas monkeys, four vervet monkeys and a baboon. Two Pakistani nationals had checked the animals in as "personal luggage." The only document the two men could produce upon request by Philippine officials was one that had been issued for trophies by the Ministry of Agriculture and Natural Resources, Wildlife Management Unit in Kano, Nigeria.[7]

International efforts to halt illegal wildlife trade have not been successful, not least because of the miserly sums dedicated to export and import inspection. In most countries, inspection of wildlife shipments runs from shoddy to non-existent. Even the U.S., which boasts the toughest wildlife laws in the world, falls hopelessly short where inspection is concerned. Due to a lack of manpower and scarcity of money, FWS inspectors appear to be fighting a losing battle. With approximately 90,000 wildlife shipments entering the country each year, the rate of inspection can vary anywhere from twenty-five percent to five percent, and all the way down to zero depending on the port of entry.[8] In 1992-93, convicted felon Matthew Block imported some 60 shipments of primates into Miami without a single one being checked by wildlife inspectors. With the majority of shipments cleared on paper alone, one can only guess what is being smuggled through our ports each and every day. The failure of Congress to appropriate funds for adequate inspection is a tragedy for commercially exploited primates and other wild creatures.[9]

The Latest Market

At present, of all the black holes pushing endangered species towards extinction, there is none worse than that found in Vietnam. As other countries in Southeast Asia tighten their borders against wildlife smuggling, Vietnam has welcomed the trade with open arms, turning itself into the largest endangered species market in the world. Foreign wildlife smuggled across the borders of Laos and Cambodia flows into Cho Cau Mung market in Ho Chi Minh City even as Vietnam's own indigenous species are steadily shipped out.[1]

The rise in the illegal trade can be traced back to 1988 as a direct result of Vietnam's liberalized economic policies. Along with the growth in tourism, an influx of foreign investment helped spur the already burgeoning trade. To a country recovering from both a long war and an embargo, where the annual per capita income is less than US $500, the prices offered by wealthy Asian tourists and traders for protected wildlife must have seemed too good to pass up. Before long, government-owned companies as well as private businesses were involved in the wildlife trade. During a three year investigation that began in 1990, the Endangered Species Project revealed that the government company Naforimax openly traded in Appendix I species such as rare douc langurs and gibbons along with Asian elephants and leopards. Naforimax exported animals by boat and air to Singapore, Taiwan, Thailand, Japan, Hong Kong and Eastern Europe. The company provided a full service approach, even offering forged CITES export documents to expedite shipments.[2]

But where the trade has really taken root is in Ho Chi Minh City. Consisting of 34 stalls, Cho Cau Mung market offers a wide variety of wildlife that often spills out onto the street. The market has become a regular stop for Taiwanese tourists, who can shop for both living and dead souvenirs. Cages filled with slow lorises sit under the hot sun. Squeezed tightly together without any water, they will likely die within a few days. Further down the row of stalls, one can find white-cheeked and black-crested gibbons and rare douc langurs, all trapped behind bars like prisoners awaiting their fate. But perhaps saddest of all are the 20 to 30 terrified macaques that huddle together in a cage barely large enough to hold one of them. They will most likely end up at one of the many local restaurants where the favorite dish on the menu is monkey brains, popular with both tourists and residents.[3] A chef chops off the top of the macaque's skull while the animal is still alive in order to provide gourmet customers with the freshest of monkey brains. The macaques are often gagged so their screams won't be heard in the dining room.[4]

Although the Vietnamese Ministry of Forestry passed a law in 1989 that banned the killing and trade of certain declining species, in 1992 the Ministry found it necessary to issue a second decree aimed at protecting wildlife considered "rare and precious." But according to the Institute of Ecology and Living Creature Resources under the Ministry of Science, Technology and Environment, these laws have had little effect. As of 1994, the number of species traded in Vietnam had climbed to 70, 60 of which are officially protected.[5] In addition, wildlife markets continue to provide enterprising smugglers with an overwhelming abundance of goods. ESP investigators interviewed a Taiwanese man at Cho Cau Mung market who claimed to be involved in the lucrative business of smuggling monkeys from Vietnam to Taiwan by boat. He told investigators he worked for a shipping company and had managed to smuggle 150 monkeys in just three months into the Taiwanese port of Kaohsiung, apparently with little problem from customs. Busy wildlife trading posts along the Vietnamese/Chinese border pose an added problem. Gibbons, small Asian apes famous for their spectacular acrobatics and melodious voices, are considered by many Chinese to be China's rarest animals.[6] They are in great demand not only for the growing pet trade but also for their meat and bones, which are used as ingredients in traditional Chinese medicine.[7,8] Vietnamese poachers have been more than happy to comply by depleting their own forests in order to fill China's rapacious requests.[9] By April 1994, Vietnam had joined the growing rank of CITES members. But without adequate enforcement in place, it remains to be seen if this will be one more membership in name only.

The demand for endangered wildlife rises with each new war that takes place, each country that breaks apart, each trade barrier that falls, each zoo that needs to be refilled and each species that creeps closer to extinction. As long as there is a demand, the trade will continue uninterrupted, filling animal dealers' pockets as it empties our planet of wildlife. As for endangered primates, they have come to be viewed as a commodity as priceless as gold. But unlike gold, their days appear to be numbered, and, once gone, they will never be replaced.

Notes

The Legal Trade

1. Sarah Fitzgerald, "Whose Business Is It?," World Wildlife Fund, 1989.

2. Ibid

3. International Primate Trade, HSUS Report, 1994.

4. *IPPL News*, August 1991.

5. Shirley McGreal, "Primates and Profits," *Animal Welfare Institute Quarterly*, Vol. 40, No. 2, Summer 1991.

6. Steve Sternberg, "Outbreak of Deadly Virus Leads CDC To Limit Imports of Research Monkeys," *The Atlanta Constitution*, 23 March 1990.

7. International Primate Trade, HSUS Report, 1994.

8. *IPPL News*, August 1991.

9. Lemis Species Report.

10. Susan Lieberman, "The Transport of Live Animals," CITES/C&M, 1994.

Rhesus Monkeys

1. Charles Southwick and M. Farooq Siddiqi, "Rhesus Monkey's Fall From Grace," *Natural History*, February 1985.

2. Ibid.

3. Edna Kendall, "Ban on Monkey Exports," *The Observer*, 23 October 1977.

4. Telegram from the American Embassy in New Delhi, India to the Secretary of State, Washington D.C.

5. Charles Southwick and M. Farooq Siddiqi, "Rhesus Monkey's Fall From Grace," Natural History, February 1985.

6. Telegram from the American Embassy in New Delhi, India to the Secretary of State, Washington D.C., 2 December 1977

7. ILAR Report

8. Telegram from the American Embassy in New Delhi, India to the Secretary of State, Washington D.C.

9. *IPPL News*, August 1978.

10. "Monkey Monopoly?," *The AV*, June 1982.

11. Carol Skyrm, "Bangladesh: Pressure to Engage in Monkey Business with U.S.," Interlink/ IPS, 2 April 1982.

12. "'MOL' mauls monkeys," IPPL, 1982.

13. Telegram from the American Embassy in New Delhi, India to the Secretary of State, Washington D.C., May 1978.

14. James Long, "Monkey Dealer Agreeable to Trade Ban Mediation," *Oregon Journal*, 17 March 1982.

15. "Ban on Monkey Exports," Bombay, India: *Economic Times*, Bombay, 23 June 1982.

16. Carol Skyrm, "Bangladesh: Pressure to engage in monkey business with U.S.," Interlink/ IPS, 2 April 1982.

Macaques

1. "Malaysia Bans Monkey Exports," Traffic Bulletin, 8 February 1984.

2. Letter to Clark Bavin, Director of Law Enforcement, U.S Fish and Wildlife Service, from Shirley McGreal, 2 November 1982.

3. Ibid

4. "Monkey Trade Status in the Philippines," The Haribon Foundation for the Conservation of Natural Resources.

5. Perry S. Ong, "A Study on the Karyotypes of Long-Tailed Macaques from Four Major Islands of the Philippines."

6. "Monkey Trade Status in the Philippines," The Haribon Foundation for the Conservation of Natural Resources.

7. "Monkey business is big business for exporters," *The Manila Bulletin*, 1 August 1989.

8. "Don't Monkey Around with Exports," *The Jakarta Post*, 23 April 1987.

Journey to the Lab

1. "Briefing Paper on the International Trade in Primates for Research," British Union for the Abolition of Vivisection (B.U.A.V.), 1992.

2. "Monkey Business: 500 Die in Transit," *IPPL News*, 1979.

3. Letter to the Ambassador of India from the Monitor Consortium, 13 November 1979.

4. *ASPCA News*, 1 March 1989.

5. Letter to IPPL from a Charles River Research Primates Corporation employee, 3 February 1989.

6. CDC Report, 1989.

7. D'Vera Cohn, "Deadly Ebola Virus Found in Va. Laboratory Monkeys," *The Washington Post*, 1 December 1989.

8. Steve Sternberg, "Outbreak of Deadly Virus Leads CDC to Limit Imports of Research Monkey," *The Atlanta Constitution*, 23 March 1990.

9. Letter to Hazelton Research Animals Lab from CDC, 9 March 1990.

10. Letter to Editor of *The Washington Post* from Physicians Committee for Responsible Medicine, 12 December 1989.

11. Steve Sternberg, "Outbreak of Deadly Virus Leads CDC to Limit Imports of Research Monkey," The Atlanta Constitution, 23 March 1990.

12. CDC Reports, 22 March 1990.

13. CDC Report to Matthew Block of Worldwide Primates, 22 March 1990.

14. Christopher Andersen, "Primate Imports Confusion," Nature, Vol. 351, 13 June 1991.

Chimpanzees

1. Dr. Virginia Landau, personal communication.

2. Ibid.

3. Letter to the director of the Wildlife Section of the Forestry Development Authority in Liberia, from Shirley McGreal, 28 January 1978.

4. IPPL News, August 1978.

5. IPPL News, December 1978.

6. Linda Duberley, "The Evil Trade of Dr. Sitter," *The Mail on Sunday*, 3 April 1988.

7. "Austrian Request to Establish a Hepatitis Research Institute," (Paper from Sierra Leone Minister of Agriculture to the Secretary to the President), 20 April 1983.

8. Letter to Sierra Leone's ambassador to the US, Amb. Robert Houdek, from Shirley McGreal, 15 January 1987.

9. David Berreby, "Twists and Turns in Chimp AIDS Research," *The New York Times*, 4 February 1997.

10. Ibid.

11. Ibid.

12. Shannon Brownlee, "The King of the Apes," *U.S. News and World Report*, 14 August 1995.

13. Berreby, "Unneeded Lab Chimps Face Hazy Future."

14. Shannon Brownlee, "The King of the Apes," *U.S. News and World Report*, 14 August 1995.

15. Eric Kleiman, "Space Chimps Confront Greatest Challenge," *National Anti-Vivisection Society (NAVS) Bulletin*, April 1995.

16. Berreby, "Unneeded Lab Chimps Face Hazy Future."

17. Andrew Revkin, "Animal Advocates Protest Plans for a Primate Lab," *New York Times*, 7 August 1995.

18. Ibid.

19. Ibid.

20. In Defense of Animals, "Another Chimpanzee Dies at the Coulston Foundation," News Release, 28 January 1997.

21. Ibid.

The Alternative

1. Carol Ezzell, "Too Much Monkey Business? Pig-tailed Macaques and AIDS Research," *The*

Journal of NIH Research, Vol. 5, June 1993.

2. Jane Gyorgy, "Monkey Business," *The Globe and Mail,* 22 1993.

3. "Briefing Paper on the International Trade in Primates For Research," B.U.A.V. 1992.

4. US primate dealer, personal communication.

5. "Don't Monkey Around With Exports," *The Jakarta Post,* 23 April 1987.

6. Heather Smith, Vietnam Trip Report, Endangered Species Project, January 1994.

7. "Sales of rare animals banned," *Vietnam Investment Review,* 18 April 1993.

The Illegal Trade

1. Press Release from the Endangered Species Project, 20 September 1994.

The Singapore Connection

1. Shirley McGreal, personal communication.

2. Letter to Clark Bavin, Chief of Law Enforcement Division, U.S. Fish and Wildlife Service, from the Natural Resources Defense Council, 11 March 1976.

3. Pat Morrison, "U.S. Imposes Wildlife Ban on Singapore," *Los Angeles Times,* 3 October 1986.

4. Dominic Nathan, "S'pore 'Not a Major Centre for Illegal Wildlife Trade,'" *The Straits Times,* 26 July 1993.

Thailand - The Polish and Cambodian Connections

1. Charles Wallace, "A Wildlife Smuggler's Paradise," *Los Angeles Times,* 20 October 1990.

2. Shirley McGreal, personal communication.

3. Pichai Chuensuksawadi and Supradit Kanwanich, "Wildlife Trader Shrugs off Critics," *Bangkok Post,* 26 August 1990.

4. Ibid.

5. Ibid.

6. Shirley McGreal, personal communication.

7. IPPL News, November 1993.

8. Pichai Chuensuksawadi and Supradit Kanwanich, "Wildlife Trader Shrugs off Critics," *Bangkok Post,* 26 August 1990.

9. "The Ape Trade," BBC Investigative Report (Producers David Perrin and Chris Terrill), 1991.

10. *IPPL News,* November 1993.

11. Shirley McGreal, personal communication.

12. Leonie Vejjajive, personal communication.

13. Ibid.

The Trade in Orangutans

1. Gary Shapiro, The Orangutan Foundation, personal communication.

2. Shirley McGreal, personal communication.

3. Esmond Bradley Martin, "Orangutan Skulls for Sale in Kalimantan," *Swara Magazine*, June 1991.

4. Marcus Phipps, The Orangutan Foundation, personal communication.

5. Ibid.

6. Ibid.

7. Gary Shapiro, personal communication.

8. John Bonner, "Taiwan's Tragic Orangutans," *New Scientist*, 3 December 1994.

The Bangkok Six Case

1. Leonie Vejjajive, personal communication.

2. Shirley McGreal, personal communication.

3. Ibid.

4. U.S. Department of Justice News Release, 20 February 1992.

5. Next Magazine, August 1981.

6. Telegram from American Embassy in Asuncion, Paraguay to Secretary of State, Washington D.C., 30 December 1986; Telegram from American Embassy in La Paz, Bolivia to Secretary of State, Washington D.C., 10 September 1986; U.S.FWS Declaration for Importation of Wildlife, 1 January 1986.

7. *IPPL News*, April 1994.

8. *IPPL News*, December 1994.

9. Worldwide Primates advertisement.

10. Shirley McGreal, personal communication.

11. Ginette Hemley, The World Wildlife Fund, personal communication.

Illegal Trade in Africa - Walter Sensen

1. *IPPL News*, April 1990.

2. Ibid.

3. Ibid.

4. Ibid.

5. Ibid.

6. *IPPL News*, April 1992.

7. Kurt Schafer, personal communication.

8. Shirley McGreal, personal communication.

9. Ibid.

10. IPPL Primate Infraction Report, 1989-1992.

11. Peter van de Bunt, IPPL.

The Chimp Trade

1. *Endangered Species Technical Bulletin*, Vol. XV, No.4, April 1990.

2. Letter to Cleveland Amory from Shirley McGreal, 29 April 1988.

3. Letter to Shirley McGreal from Janis Carter, 7 September 1995.

4. Alex Goldsmith, "The Wildlife Express," *BBC Wildlife*, 8 December 1994.

5. Ibid.

6. Shirley McGreal, personal communication.

7. Confidential letter to Shirley McGreal, 21 March 1994.

8. Pat McGrath, President of Dian Fossey Gorilla Foundation, personal communication.

9. Cites Infractions Report, November 1994.

10. Ilse Mwanza, "Egyptian Circus Probed," *The Zambian Post*, 7 June 1994.

11. Ibid

12. Jason Black, World Society for the Protection of Animals press release, 20 December 1993.

13. Press release from World Wildlife Fund, 1984.

14. *IPPL News*, August 1991.

15. Ibid.

16. *IPPL News*, October 1980.

17. Press release from World Wildlife Fund, 1984.

18. "Chimpanzee Commerce," The Jane Goodall Institute, 1991.

19. Ibid.

20. Ibid.

21. Ibid.

22. Letter to Shirley McGreal from Ugandan Chief Game Warden J.M. Okua, 22 March 1994.

23. Nydakira Amooti, "Minister Linked to Shady Chimps Deal," *New Vision*, 28 September 1990.

24. "Chimpanzee Commerce," The Jane Goodall Institute, 1991.

25. Permit signed by J.M. Okua, 10 January 1991.

26. Invoice from Zoo Forss, 17 September 1990.

27. Letter to IPPL from the Swedish Environmental Protection Agency, 28 November 1990.

The Illegal Trade Today

1. Kathi Austin, personal communication.

2. Ibid.

3. International Gorilla Conservation Program press release, 27 March 1995.

4. Ndyakira Amooti, "The young gorillas disappeared," *New Vision*, 10 April 1995.

5. Shirley McGreal, personal communication.

6. Diane McMeekin, African Wildlife Foundation, personal communication.

7. IPPL News, August 1995.

8. "Crimes Against Nature," Endangered Species Project, November 1994.

9. *IPPL News*, April 1994.

The Latest Market

1. Leonie Vejjajive, personal communication.

2. "The Black Market Trade in Vietnam," Endangered Species Project, 1993.

3. Ian Baird, Doing Business in Vietnam, 1992.

4. Peter Knights, The Investigative Network, personal communication.

5. Timothy Karr, "New Laws May Not Quell Appetite for Rare Wildlife," *Vietnam Investment Review*, 3 July 1994.

6. E.H. Haimoff, X.J. Yang, S.W. He, N. Chen, "Conservation in Gibbons in Yunnan Province, China," Oryx 21, 1987.

7. Shirley McGreal, personal communication.

8. E.H. Haimoff, X.J. Yang, S.W. He, N. Chen, "Conservation in Gibbons in Yunnan Province, China," *Oryx* 21, 1987.

9. "The Black Market Trade in Vietnam," Endangered Species Project, 1993.

Chapter 12

The Bird Dealers

by Peter Knights

Introduction to the Bird Trade

A bird in flight has long been a symbol of freedom. From the tales of Daedalus and Icarus in Greek legend to contemporary movies like "Birdy" and "Brazil," people have sought to shed worldly constraints and to take to the air with the birds. For equally as long, we have jealously clipped their wings and confined them to cages for our amusement, depriving them of their gift of flight. Caged wild birds are kept for their colorful plumage, their song, their mimicry and wit, and their companionship. The reasons differ, but the results for the victims are the same. They are snatched from the wild for a sentence of life imprisonment. Who can say what birds think or feel about this, but as a human I like to walk and sometimes even run. If I were a bird, I think that I would like to fly. It's what birds do.

Behind the capture and imprisonment of wild birds is an international business worth millions of dollars annually to the key players. Some aspects parallel slavery: The birds lose their freedom and are shipped across the world, often in overcrowded and disease-ridden conditions. Complex routes are used to launder smuggled birds into the "legal market" through countries with lax or corrupt authorities, just as drug barons launder illegal cash into legal credit through front companies.

This is a brief account of the widespread abuse that has characterized the wild bird trade. These are my findings, experiences and impressions from five years of investigation and research, from the bush or the forest in the developing world and the exporters' holding premises, to the dealers' premises in Asia, Europe and the United States, and finally to unwary pet owners. Though their activities go largely unreported, and little is known about many traders, I have tried to identify a few of the main dealers in some of the key countries. Between them, these traders have been responsible for life imprisonment or death sentences for literally millions of wild birds every year over the past few decades. Some of these people and their customers are also responsible for the decimation of some of the world's most beautiful and intelligent bird species. As one species has been depleted, the traders have moved to the next. The profiteers cannot lose. The rarer a species becomes, the higher the asking price.

The reality of the business I experienced bears little resemblance to how the rule books state the bird trade should operate or how complacent or sometimes corrupt government officials claim it operates. Instead, the traders leave behind them a catalogue of abuse of laws designed to regulate their business.

A Brief History

The first records of caged birds date from early Egyptian times. References have also been found in ancient Greek and Roman literature. Native peoples kept birds in Central and South America long before Columbus – the world's first transatlantic bird dealer – took parrots back to Spain as one of the wonders of the New World.[1] However, it was technological advance that enabled the trade to expand into a truly global activity. The conversion from sail to steam is said to have increased the volume of trade substantially. Until then, much of the business was localized or involved species that bred readily in captivity, like canaries or budgerigars. Only zoos or the wealthy could afford to import exotics from the wild. But faster, more reliable transport meant dealers could plunder remote rainforests and make species that previously had been unavailable affordable for ordinary birdkeepers and pet owners. But it was not until the 1960s, when air transport became widely available, that the trade really took off.[2] Transport time was reduced from days to hours, which meant there was less mortality, making large commercial shipments more profitable. Recent refusal by most airlines to transport wild birds destined for the pet trade is one of the major factors contributing to a decrease in its current scale.

Increasing consumer affluence and more viable transportation meant the numbers of wild birds in the pet trade probably peaked in the 1970s; however, even now, the levels of trade are not recorded in many cases, so assessments of global trade can only be educated guesses. It is estimated that during the early 1980s, approximately 15 million birds were taken annually from the wild. It was not until the early 1990s that European and U.S. imports declined markedly due to national legislation in importing and exporting countries, airline embargoes and increased breeding in captivity for many species. Levels of trade in the Asian market remain unrecorded in many areas, but it is highly unlikely that the market will have declined to the same extent as those in the West. Indeed, with increasing Asian affluence and lax enforcement of wildlife laws in some Asian countries, numbers of birds in trade could be increasing greatly in this region.

The Threat to Species

Compared to overall global bird populations and bird losses from other factors, such as habitat destruction and use of pesticides, numbers of birds involved in the trade may seem small. But it is the impact on individual species highly prized in the trade, particularly slow-reproducing species like the larger parrots, that has concerned conservationists. As such a species becomes rarer, the price on its head rises, increasing the hunting pressure. On the other hand, if a species is hunted for food, for example, rarity is more likely to lead to substitution with another target species.

Spix's macaw (*Cyanopsitta spixii*) was a scarce species long before it was in demand as a caged bird. However, once its rarity was realized, the remaining population was systematically plundered to supply birdkeepers, who were willing to pay small fortunes to add the species to their collections. There are now 20-25 Spix's macaws known to be in captivity, most of whom were obtained illegally by some of the world's most prominent birdparks and private collectors. Only one Spix's macaw is known to survive in the wild, and another was released in 1995 in hopes that the two will mate. Although little publicized, this is perhaps the rarest species in the world. The last individual has to be guarded day and night from poachers and has been observed trying to mate with a macaw of another species. Meanwhile, squabbling and egocentrism have blocked attempts to bring the remaining captive birds into a collective captive-breeding program. The closely related Lear's macaw (*Anodoryhnchus leari*) is not doing much better, with a known population of around 118 in the wild and an unknown number in captivity. The total population of the world's largest parrot, the bright blue hyacinth macaw (*Anodorynchus hyacinthus*), is thought to be in the low thousands. It is believed there are more in captivity than in the wild. Captive-bred hyacinth macaws are sold for up to $10,000 each.

The fate of the Moluccan cockatoo (*Cacatua moluccensisis*) illustrates the devastating effect trade can have on a population in just a short period of time. Until 1970, this beautiful pale pink cockatoo with a salmon pink crest occurred in relatively large numbers on Ambon and in Western Seram in the Moluccan Islands of Indonesia. It was even described as "abundant" within its limited range. In a 1981 survey, none were found on Ambon or in the Western part of Seram, whereas comparatively large numbers were seen in Eastern Seram. Legal exports of Moluccan cockatoos in 1984, 1985 and 1986 were registered as 7,398, 7,525 and 7,360, respectively.[3] However, when smuggling and loss occurring during trapping and transport are taken into account, the actual number taken from the wild each year was probably between 15,000 and 20,000. Even when the species was found to have experienced a significant decline, Indonesian authorities failed to take action to restrict the trade. By 1985, the species had become extremely rare or even extinct in virtually all its former habitats, with the exception of the virgin rainforests in the Mansuela National Park, a supposedly protected area. In 1987, two British ornithologists, John Bowler and John Taylor, spotted Moluccan cockatoos on only 54 occasions at Mansuela.[4] In all probability, these sightings represented less than 20 individual birds. The endangered status of the species led the European Community to ban imports, but Indonesian authorities ignored the ban. In fact, large capture quotas were set in 1988 (5,000) and 1989 (3,000).[5] According to official records, the annual capture quota of 3,000 in 1989 was exceeded in U.S. imports alone by over 2,000 individuals. U.S. bird importers were buying up as many as they could, conscious that the species would soon be listed as endangered, thus protected from the trade. Flooding of the market even caused the price to drop momentarily. At that time, these cockatoos were being offered for as little as $150 each. Now they fetch $1,000 or more each. Finally, in late 1989, the species was listed on Appendix I of the Convention on International Trade in Endangered Species (CITES), banning all international trade. The species is now thought to be faced with "imminent extinction." In a 1991 survey, not a single Moluccan cockatoo was seen in the Mansuela Park area.[6] A 1992 documentary film, "Bird Traffic," by the Royal Society for the Protection of Birds, showed the merciless exploitation of these endangered birds. Lumber companies destroying habitat negotiate with villagers to ensnare the birds on their roosts and ship them illegally to Singapore and elsewhere in Asia.

What happened to another Indonesian species of parrot demonstrates how quickly trade can be a threat to a population. The red-and-blue lory (*Eos histrio*) was initially only threatened by habitat destruction, with little international trade pressure. One subspecies was considered endangered or critically endangered (less than 2,000). Another subspecies was considered critically endangered or possibly extinct (between 0 and 1,000).[7] In 1990, Indonesia set a capture quota of 1,000, and 140 were reportedly exported. Between 1992 and 1993, an estimated 700 were removed from the largest population, thought to number less than 2,000. More than 500 birds may have been exported since April 1992. In addition, some birds have been seen in domestic trade and some are caught as by-catch from fruit bat trapping. Researchers noted: "Islanders recognized that the capture of Red-and-Blue Lories was illegal and acknowledged that the bird has been trapped beyond the point where it is no longer worth the effort to try and catch further specimens.... Most of the catching now is from the protected forest... which is about the only forested region left in the islands."[8] The report by the trade monitoring group TRAFFIC notes, "The Red-and-Blue Lory is not listed in the 1992 capture quotas. However, at least seven CITES export permits have been issued." 1994 CITES conference listed it on Appendix I. The 1994 *Birds to Watch 2* (Birdlife International) predicts extinction from combined effects of illegal trade and habitat loss.

Sustainable Use of Parrots?

Habitat loss is still the most significant threat to bird species, but, contrary to claims from dealers and proponents of "sustainable use," the wild bird trade has added to this pressure. As habitat has been destroyed, previously inaccessible populations have become available. Some conservationists (and all the bird traders) believe that it is possible to prevent habitat loss by encouraging "sustainable use" of birds for trade. They argue that by giving the birds an economic value, local people will protect the species and the habitat so they can "harvest" the birds in perpetuity at a "sustainable rate."

Provided you have no ethical problem with caging wild birds as pets, "sustainable use" sounds like a great idea: Parrots are preserved forever, and humans "harvest" them each year. However, parrots are not fields of grain, and you only have to look around to see that very few of man's commercial activities are conducted at a "sustainable rate." Fisheries around the world, for example, have been managed and "sustainably used," often to the point of commercial extinction. When elephants were "sustainably used" for the ivory trade in the 1970s and 1980s, their numbers dropped from 1.5 million to 600,000. There are hundreds of examples of consumptive commercialization leading to sharp decline. In a world primarily motivated by short-term gain, major political and sociological changes would be required before sustainability could have even a remote chance of success. "Sustainable use" of parrots in commercial trade has never been demonstrated to work.

Theoretically, it would be possible to create such a "sustainable" system; however, technical, economic and sociological obstacles remain. First, the level of scientific knowledge required to assess a sustainable take is not available for any but the most abundant of species. In most cases we don't know how many animals exist, let alone how removing individuals will affect the population. Second, the take must actually be controlled and limited. This chapter will show that control has not been a characteristic of the wild bird trade at either the producer or consumer end. Protecting vast areas of sparsely populated range from poachers is often impossible. Preventing smuggling and laundering is also difficult. It seems likely that even a sincere attempt at sustainability would fall prey to poachers and smugglers. Third, the economic incentives have always been short-term, not long-term. Fourth, local peoples have never received an adequate share of profits from the trade to be able to afford a long-term approach. They seldom have rights over the "resource" — in this case the birds. If they don't take the birds themselves this year, they reason, someone else will.

As long as the big bird dealers remain central to the trade system and trade is driven by business interests, it seems unlikely these problems can be solved. In other words, there are still many obstacles to "sustainable use" of birds for the international pet trade, let alone use generating enough revenue to replace logging, farming and other activities that cause habitat destruction. Non-consumptive use, such as ecotourism, offers much lower risks, higher potential rewards and a definite incentive to save the species and its habitat in the long term.

The Treatment of Individual Birds in Trade

Even if "sustainable use" was technically possible, the wild bird trade would still raise ethical concerns. The trade supplies what is essentially a luxury market. It is ironic that most wild bird purchasers would doubtless describe themselves as "bird lovers." In some cases, they can be passionately intimate with their birds, kissing and cuddling them and generally doting on them. Yet, some have been only too willing to look the other way when confronted with the cruelty of the wild bird trade. What price in terms of the suffering of individual birds is acceptable to supply a colorful pet?

The appalling conditions and cruelty en route to the consumer have been well documented by environmental organizations, but the long-term behavioral and physical problems that caged wild birds suffer have been less publicized. One consequence of poor conditions in trade is excessive mortality at all stages. A colleague of mine says that anyone purchasing a wild bird should also receive the corpses of the birds who died to bring the survivor to the pet store. Perhaps it would make buyers think again. Awareness among bird owners, at least in the U.S. and Europe, has improved in recent years, and many now condemn any continued take from the wild for the pet trade, asserting that captive breeding is now feasible and greatly to be preferred.

The Bird Sellers

No developed countries allow international pet trade in their native wild birds. They simply consume other countries' wild birds! Interestingly, two champions of "making wildlife pay its own way" through consumptive sustainable use, South Africa and Zimbabwe, do not allow trade in their own native wild birds. They encourage captive breeding instead. When you look at the prospect of monitoring and regulating the wild bird trade properly, it soon becomes clear that it would cost more to enforce than it would generate in revenue. The bird dealers know this and rely on lack of enforcement to bend the rules.

Although most countries prohibit commercial capture of their wild birds for the pet trade, some continue to lose their wild birds to illegal trade, which often operates from countries with weaker laws. The key countries in the "legal" trade have changed as protective legislation has closed some supplies in light of over-exploitation, corruption and cruelty. The dealers themselves have often adapted to these temporary setbacks by moving to neighboring countries with less restrictive laws. Their new homes are often no more than "flags of convenience," with the birds continuing to be poached from the original source. There is evidence of illegal cross-border trafficking in birds from all major bird exporting countries.

Africa has long been a major source of birds for the trade. Though a few species of parrots, including the African grey parrot and the Fischer's lovebird, have been exported in large numbers, the vast majority of birds exported are small, colorful songbirds, such as cordon bleu finches, Red Bishops and wild canaries. Subsaharan Senegal in West Africa reports an annual export rate of over one million birds, the highest number recorded in the world. Some sources believe this is a drastic underestimate of the real number exported.[9] The other francophone countries in the region—Guinea, Côte d'Ivoire, Togo and Mali—have exported much smaller numbers, but much of this business has been controlled by the Senegalese. Cameroon and Zaire have allowed the export of African grey parrots. Botswana and Madagascar have allowed a small-scale export of birds, while Tanzania in East Africa is a large exporter, sending out in excess of 200,000 birds annually, including many larger birds, such as flamingos, touracos and cranes.

Most Latin American countries have now banned exports. For example, Honduras and Bolivia were previously significant exporters, but have now banned the trade. Only Argentina, Peru, Guyana, Surinam and Nicaragua have set quotas for exports of wild birds, predominantly parrots. Thousands of parrots from all over Latin America are also smuggled across the Mexican-U.S. border or via the Caribbean to Europe.

China may now be the largest bird exporting country of all. It has been suggested that up to 3 million birds, mainly songbirds, are exported each year.[10] A recent report entitled "Sold for a Song" documents the trade of millions of birds in local markets in Indonesia, Hong Kong and Singapore.[11] Hong Kong acts as a natural funnel for Chinese birds, and many dealers are based there. Singapore has also been an important center, particularly for "laundering" smuggled birds from all around the world. Indonesia has long been the major exporter of cockatoos. They also have species that are unique to one or two islands. Many of these vulnerable species are threatened by habitat loss and systematic plundering for the trade.

Australia has many unique and colorful species that are particularly attractive to the pet industry. Despite a long-standing export ban on native Australian species, many of these species are very common in the caged-bird industry. The fact that hundreds of thousands of these birds have been bred in countries like Belgium and the Netherlands demonstrates that there is no need to continue taking millions of them from the wild each year. The pet market could be supplied from captive stocks alone.

The Bird Consumers

Aside from Asia, the European Union (EU) is the largest importer of wild birds. According to pet trade sources, in the late 1980s, between one and 3 million birds were imported into the EU each year.[12] France is probably the biggest consumer, importing large numbers of songbirds from West Africa. Germany also has a large market, particularly for the more expensive parrots. The United Kingdom imported more than 185,000 birds a year in the late 1980s.[13] Belgium and the Netherlands are important buyers as well; despite their small sizes, they have long-established birdkeeping traditions and more than their share of international dealers. They act as transit countries for distribution throughout Europe, the U.S. and Asia, and they export tens of thousands of captive-bred and wild birds each year.

In 1984, official U.S. imports peaked at over 913,000 birds.[14] With the recent implementation of the Wild Bird Conservation Act of 1992, it remains to be seen how many wild birds will continue to be imported. In addition to declared U.S. trade, an estimated 50,000-150,000 birds per year are smuggled across the Mexican border in car tires, hidden compartments or on foot by couriers known in thieves' jargon as "mules."

Although little information is available, Japan is thought to be a considerable consumer. South Africa imports a large number of birds, but many are re-exported. Some reports indicate increases in trade into developing countries as affluence grows.

How the Trade Operates

Although an endless stream of licenses, permits and other papers superficially legitimizes the wild bird business, dealers ignore international conventions and break or sidestep national laws and local regulations. Conditions for the birds are so bad that many of them don't survive. All to bring a brightly colored finch or parrot to a cage in someone's living room. When we follow the trail from bush to cage, we see just how many rules it is possible to break.

Trapping: Tree-felling and Nest Robbing

Inhumane treatment begins during the trapping process and persists right through to the consumer. To obtain parrot chicks, some trappers fell ancient hollow trees, destroying scarce nesting sites and threatening the future of the species. Chicks sometimes die or are badly injured when the nesting trees fall. In Argentina, we discovered that overmature trees, often more than 150 years old, are cut down with chain-saws to catch helpless blue-fronted Amazon parrot chicks. Other nests are broken into and all the offspring removed. This is the easiest method of catching birds. Scientists estimate that up to 95% of nests raided are destroyed. Thus the trade is destroying the habitat of the species with short-term profit logic. After a desperate report from Argentine scientists and an Environmental Investigation Agency (EIA) documentary film publicizing the plight of the blue-fronted Amazon around the world, the Argentine government suspended international trade in this parrot for two years. Unfortunately, domestic trade to supply pet parrots for the Argentine market has been allowed to continue unchecked.

Liming

Trappers around the world catch birds with lime, a thick, glue-like extract. The lime is wrapped onto sticks placed strategically among the top branches of a tree as likely looking perches. A live "caller bird," or decoy, is tied to a branch among the lime sticks. The decoy's job is to call to other birds of the same species, luring them to the trap and leading them to believe it is a safe place to perch. The trapper will often hide on a lower limb of the tree with another "teaser" bird of the same species. The trapper tickles, squeezes and prods the teaser bird, inducing it to call out in annoyance. The caller bird replies, and passing birds are lured in, thinking there is a squabble over some avian delicacy. When they land on the convenient perches, they are in for a shock. They soon become firmly stuck, and their frantic attempts to escape only serve to gum up their wings with lime, preventing flight. Few birds escape once they have landed on lime.

The trapper retrieves the lime sticks to the accompaniment of the terrified calls of his prey. He pulls off as much of the lime as he can for re-use, then lobs the disabled birds up to 50 feet down to the ground. There is a crash and a thump as the bird plummets through the undergrowth and hits the ground like a stone. The bird skulks off, if it can, and is later retrieved by the trapper, its primary feathers crudely "clipped" with a machete or, if very lucky, with scissors. The lime is removed from the bird either by plucking contaminated feathers or wiping with a wet cloth, sometimes using petrol as a solvent. Plumage can be totally spoiled, and often the birds must be kept by the trapper until the next moult.

This method of trapping is sometimes indiscriminate, and non-target species are often caught. EIA investigators observed liming on four occasions; twice there was unwanted by-catch. Since they have no commercial value, non-target species will undoubtedly be left to die or be eaten. If they are released, they will have little chance of survival since their flight feathers are usually damaged. In Côte d'Ivoire, EIA investigators filmed a Senegal kingfisher falling victim to a lime trap set for African grey parrots. According to the trapper, older grey parrots are usually too intelligent to fall for lime traps, having seen many of their brothers and sisters come to a sticky end. Younger birds are more easily fooled. The kingfisher was merely a passerby attracted to a convenient perch. Its wings soon became gummed by the lime, and its attempts to escape glued it more firmly. Because its laugh-like, high-pitched distress calls would disturb any parrot in the area, the trapper tortuously pulled it from the lime by its other wing. Eventually it snapped clear like a piece of elastic, and the trapper nonchalantly threw it to the ground 30 feet below.

Nets and Entanglement

In Senegal, West Africa, EIA investigators filmed a trapper preparing a decoy bird, a Senegal parrot, to lure other parrots into a net. A wire noose was tied around the bird's leg. The other end was tied around a stick staked to the ground. The distraught bird managed to escape momentarily by frantically flapping his wings. The trapper quickly recovered the bird and crudely hacked away his flight feathers with a blunt machete, drawing blood. The trapper then retreated to a nearby hide where he could trigger his clap-net. EIA investigators saw one bird crushed to death by the net's wooden stake.

Ornithologist John Taylor described trapping methods in Indonesia:

The traps all involve the use of nylon fishing line. One method is a series of small loops tied along a branch, usually in a roost tree, or where birds are known to feed regularly. As the birds walk up and down the branch their feet become entangled and so they are ensnared. A second method is... far more basic. The nylon line is simply wound loosely around a branch creating a haphazard tangle, again the birds easily become caught up.... The noose method is particularly inhumane. One report states that 10 to 30% of cockatoos caught are designated as 'non commercial' due to the loss of toes, feet and legs from trapping with nooses.[15]

While any form of trapping involves a great deal of stress and some risk of injury for wild birds, the least inhumane method of trapping birds is with a "mist" net, often used by ornithologists when ringing birds. These long nets are strung between trees. Their mesh is so fine as to be literally invisible to the birds. However, these are usually too expensive for trappers and are not appropriate for some types of birds and habitats. When they have been used for the bird trade, in some cases nontarget species have been caught or birds have been left for hours or days struggling in the nets, sometimes dying of dehydration.[16]

Breaking the Trapping Rules

Most exporting countries require bird trappers to be licensed, though this seldom means that authorities have effective control over trapping. In April of 1991, as we followed the journey from bush to pet shop, we discovered a seized shipment of finches and parrots at Gouloumbou in Senegal. The trapper's license had run out two years earlier. A day later, a collector who had a current license was given the birds, and business went on as usual. In Senegal, trappers are licensed to trap for one exporter, who is supposed to be responsible for the trapper's activities. In practice, they will sell to any dealer, and we met a number of unlicensed trappers. The local official responsible for policing the trade told me he thought there were no trappers in the nearby village. We had just filmed one trapping birds in an adjacent field; the trapper kept his birds less than 100 yards from the official's office. We were also told of trapping expeditions to Gambia, a nation that had long banned trapping of its native birds. Other trappers told us some species were protected.

"So you don't catch them?" I asked.

"Oh yes, we do. We just hide those birds," they responded.

Investigators in Tanzania have often found birds in the hands of unlicensed trappers and even National Parks staff. Such trappers often flee when challenged, abandoning the birds.

Breaking Local Regulations

After they have been trapped, the birds are usually assembled together for collection or delivery to the exporter by a middleman or "collector." In Salta province, Argentina, we filmed 425 blue-fronted Amazon parrots en route to Buenos Aires being counted and placed into transport cases by exporter and parrot collector Antonio Chacon. The local wildlife official was unable to inspect the shipment, as he had no means of transport. His records listed only 350 birds in the shipment. Investigation of a few other local parrot collectors revealed that more than 2,500 birds had already left the area. The recorded total, however, was 1,600. The official was not surprised to learn this, but what was he to do? The scam ruined any possibility of an assessment of the numbers of birds taken from the area and enabled the exporter to dodge local taxes. Until recently, Argentina indiscriminately designated all parrot species as pests to justify the export trade. Local officials listed some species as pests in provinces where they did not even occur! Some of the species listed did not even occur in Argentina.

Keeping to Quotas

In theory, quotas or limits on exports are set to avoid overexploitation of species. However, because population, population dynamics, reproduction rates, mortality in trade and numbers caught for illegal trade are unknown, there is seldom any scientific basis for quotas. The figures chosen are often set according to previous trade levels. To make matters worse, even these arbitrary and demand-driven limits are often exceeded. For example, Senegal sets quotas for the number of birds of each species that may be exported annually. The quotas are routinely ignored. In 1990 these quotas were exceeded for 15 species. No action was taken by the authorities against offenders. As the new officer in charge of monitoring the bird trade in Senegal said at an international meeting, "We are at the mercy of the exporters."[17] Senegal stopped releasing export figures after 1990 to prevent further embarrassment.

The same laxity in law enforcement has characterized the Indonesian bird trade. There, capture quotas, not export quotas, are set. Ostensibly this would limit take from the wild, but in practice they are treated as export quotas, and no allowances are made for all the birds that die in the trade process. Again, quotas have not been enforced by Indonesian authorities. In 1989, Indonesian authorities set an annual capture quota of 1,000 birds for the Moluccan cockatoo. However, 5,073 were "legally" imported to the U.S. alone.[18] In 1988, exports recorded by Indonesian authorities exceeded capture quotas for 15 species by 112% to 312%. In 1990, exports exceeded capture quotas for 12 species by 108% to 192%. In 1991, exports exceeded capture quotas by 106% to 127% for four species.[19] These figures do not include domestic consumption or smuggled birds. Quotas give an illusion of control and management, but like any regulation, they are meaningless unless strictly enforced.

Sharing the Pie: Dealer Quotas

Most bird-exporting countries, like Senegal and Tanzania, have attempted to break monopolies in the trade. To distribute revenue from the trade, they allocate quotas among a number of dealers. Allocation of quotas can give a false impression of the true extent of monopolization within the trade. In most exporting countries, there are less than a dozen active bird exporters. Despite quotas intended to divide bird exports between Senegalese dealers, three big exporters — Amadou Diallo, Viv Anim and Boubou Wade — were responsible for over 80% of all the declared exports from Senegal in 1990. As we were told by disgruntled trappers, such market domination gives those dealers much influence, enabling them to keep prices paid to trappers down.

In many countries, traders sell quotas to each other. Some authorized exporters hardly ever see a bird; they merely trade their right to export. In Tanzania, dealers control a number of export companies to increase their quota. In the U.S., ten companies have routinely controlled more than 80% of wild bird imports. Some of these companies are conglomerates of the same dealers, and others work together closely.

Circumventing the Health Regulations

A compulsory pre-export quarantine for wild birds is supposed to prevent the transfer of avian diseases like Newcastle disease, potentially deadly to poultry populations, and psittacosis, which can be passed on to humans. Quarantines are usually carried out by the exporters themselves. Inspections of quarantines are often conducted by private veterinarians and countersigned by government officials who never actually inspect the birds themselves. Exporters want to move birds through as fast as possible to avoid mortality in their hands, reduce holding and feeding costs, and increase cash flow.

An Amazon parrot shipment we followed in Argentina received a health certificate at the airport without anyone inspecting the birds, let alone testing for disease. The Argentine government used to require all bird exports to pass through a government quarantine station, but a spot-check revealed that keys to the "secure" quarantine were in fact held by a trader. Of the 60,000 birds officially noted to be under quarantine, less than 170 were actually there. While posing as potential buyers, we were told by a Senegalese dealer that we could obtain a health certificate for the birds even before we selected them. The Kenyan Society for the Prevention of Cruelty to Animals (KSPCA) noted that some of the dead birds they found in a high mortality shipment from Tanzania were so decomposed that they must have died days before the date on the accompanying "health certificate."[20]

The frequent occurrence of disease in imported wild birds shows that pre-export regulations have been relatively ineffective. Diseases such as salmonellosis and avian influenza continue to be exported in wild birds on a regular basis. Although most importing countries have established quarantines, quarantine periods are seldom long enough to prevent the spread of psittacosis and certain other diseases

Under these quarantines, birds are not supposed to be treated for disease, as this may disguise the presence of diseases quarantine is designed to detect. Sometimes birds are treated illegally with antibiotics, which suppress both the disease and the immune system. When an unwary customer buys a bird and doesn't continue treatment, the bird may succumb to the disease. If the bird dies more than 24 hours after purchase, the seller is usually not liable. Wild birds are a gamble: Customers may pay less for a wild bird than for a captive-bred bird, but risk the bird dying from some latent disease, parasites or stress.

Stealing From Your Neighbor

Bird dealers have little respect for the laws of neighboring countries that have banned wild bird trade. In fact, it is hard to find a wild bird exporting country not implicated in the laundering of wild birds from other countries. Brazil, Bolivia and Paraguay all prohibit the export of wild birds, but birds from these countries have been laundered into the international market via Argentinian "legal" trade. We discovered one well-used route through Bolivia into Argentina which, besides being used to smuggle parrots, is now developing into the new route for cocaine for European and U.S. markets.

Penetrating the Guyanan rainforest is not as easy as taking a boat along the coast to the Orinoco Delta, where illegally trapped Venezuelan birds can be purchased. In the past, many of the birds exported by Guyanese traders actually originated in Venezuela. Later, when the Delta area was trapped out of its valuable macaws, traders turned back to Guyana.

Not content with exporting millions of its own birds, Senegal also trades the protected birds of Gambia. One Senegalese dealer told us on tape that it was a mistake to think all the birds come from Senegal. They come from all the surrounding countries. In fact, at one time, most of the profit from Senegalese bird exports came from African grey parrots (*Psittacus erithacus*), a species that does not exist in the wild in Senegal. Besides constituting international theft, poaching directly undermines the conservation efforts of other countries.

CITES Efforts to Stop Overexploitation

The Convention on International Trade in Endangered Species of Wild Fauna and Flora (CITES) was created in 1973 to combat the increasing threat of overexploitation of animals and plants in international trade. By 1997, there were 129 parties to the CITES treaty. The wild bird trade is one of the main businesses covered by CITES. Except for budgerigars and cockatiels, all of the world's 338 parrot species are listed on the CITES Appendices or lists. Forty-five species are considered endangered and are listed on CITES Appendix I, which prohibits international trade in these species. One species, the ring-necked parakeet (*Psittacula krameri*), is listed on Appendix III, which means trade is monitored. The rest are all listed on CITES Appendix II, which is for species that, though not yet endangered, may become so unless trade is monitored and regulated. These species may only be traded when an independent "Scientific Authority" in the country of origin "has advised that such an export will not be detrimental to the survival of that species."

Unfortunately, like so many other "controls" in the wild bird trade, this requirement was often not worth the paper it was written on. Major exporting countries that actually had the independent Scientific Authority required under the treaty failed to carry out studies to assess the effects of trade on wild bird populations, and trade was allowed to continue. At each CITES meeting, more species were upgraded to Appendix I as a result of overexploitation, indicating that the system was failing. In 1993, CITES finally started a double-checking system on these "non-detriment" findings. As a result, many species that were previously traded in large numbers are being suspended from trade pending scientific studies.

CITES Resolves to Use Captive-Bred Animals for Pets

More than fifteen years ago, CITES passed Resolution 1.6. Recognizing high mortality and the risk of overexploitation in the pet trade, the Resolution urged "that exporting countries endeavor to restrict gradually the collection of wild animals for the pet trade and that all contracting parties encourage the breeding of animals for this purpose, with the objective of eventually limiting the keeping of pets to those species which can be bred in captivity." While many countries like India, Honduras and Bolivia have banned the trade, other CITES parties, such as China, continue to supply very large numbers of wild birds in a virtually unrestricted manner and with no scientific information on the effects. For their part, most importing countries have done very little to encourage captive breeding.

However, private aviculturists have taken up the challenge. Technically speaking, it is now possible to breed all species sold in the commercial pet trade, and breeding for the trade has greatly expanded. In fact, the main restraints on captive breeding are financial ones. Since competing against low-priced imports of wild birds is difficult, the best way to encourage commercial breeding is to end large-scale imports from the wild. When Australia banned its wild exports in 1960, breeders rapidly filled the demand. Australian species are now bred in vast numbers. Budgerigars, cockatiels, rosellas and Australian parakeets are amongst the most common pet birds, and they are all bred in captivity.

Abusing the CITES System

Law enforcement is by far the biggest problem facing CITES today. There have been numerous direct contraventions of CITES regulations. By the time all the facts of the cases have been established, the animals and culprits involved are usually long gone, and many countries do not have adequate legal systems or penalties to deal with them effectively. Traders in Argentina photocopied genuine CITES certificates and used them to cover illegal shipments of birds. Over a dozen phantom companies have been uncovered in Argentina using their own brand of CITES certificates. Another cover used by traders is to change the species or the numbers on original permits. Few perpetrators have ever been prosecuted, and it often takes several years before the forgeries are discovered. They can be quite sophisticated, and the average customs officer charged with nominally enforcing CITES has little chance of recognizing a good forgery. These doctored permits continue to show up around the world.

It is impossible for most officials to identify the hundreds of different species in trade. Of the 338 species of parrots, there are 27 species and many subspecies of Amazon parrots, some of which are highly endangered and most of which are protected. Some species are still legally traded. They are all medium-sized parrots that are predominantly green with small patches of other colors on them. Even for an expert equipped with identification aids, which are often not available, it is very difficult to distinguish species when the birds are crammed into dark shipping crates. As a result, many species are misidentified. Dealers even disguise birds further by removing distinctive feathers or dyeing plumage.

Since it is virtually impossible to count birds when they are moving around inside transport crates, numbers of birds are often underdeclared. Exporters often ship extra birds to compensate for the inevitable mortalities en route. Only a few countries provide official supervision of unpacking of birds at quarantine stations, the only time accurate counts could be made. Even when supervision does occur, inspectors are frequently bribed. A U.S. Department of Agriculture official recently was found guilty of assisting bird dealers in smuggling activities. In exchange for her help, dealers provided her with exotic birds for her own collection. She was sentenced to 18 months imprisonment in February 1994.[21]

Illegally trapped birds can be laundered into the legal trade by routing them through countries that will provide papers with no questions asked. Argentina, Senegal, Côte d'Ivoire and Togo have been implicated in laundering birds. Naive or corrupt officials often provide papers declaring wild birds as captive-bred specimens. In one scam, rare South American wild birds were routed through Singapore to Malta and then to Europe. The exporter claimed he was breeding the birds in Malta, although he had not finished building his "breeding" center.

CITES enforcement by member countries has improved in recent years, but the system still has great weaknesses that are readily exploited by international smugglers. Despite pleas of the CITES Secretariat and non-government organizations, CITES parties still do not give law enforcement the priority it needs. For example, although there is a permanent CITES committee on producing species identification manuals, there is no committee on enforcement.

Avoiding Export and Import Duty

A favorite trick in the bird trade is to underdeclare the value of birds, using a double-invoicing system. Traders save income tax and customs duty and avoid surrendering hard currency. This reduces the revenue exporting countries earn from the trade, concentrating it in the hands of a few dealers. A dealer in Argentina, going by the name of Triantofilo, explained how the double-invoice system works. He staples the real invoice inside the birds' crate so it cannot be seen until the birds have been unpacked. Another, lower-value invoice is shown to customs and the taxman. The blue-fronted Amazon parrots we followed in Argentina were declared at $23 each. Argentinian price lists value the birds at $70 to $100 each.

Another trick to avoid taxes is to arrange part of the payment for birds to a bank in another country. When I was undercover at the premises of one Dutch dealer, I found myself acting as a translator for an exporter from Ghana, who wanted his payment to be made to a bank account in London. One of our Argentine "friends," Carlos Fraga, wanted his payments to be made to a Uruguayan account in the name of a relative.

The Bird Traders

Having outlined some of the ways the trade works, it is now time to introduce some of the main players — the modern day avian slave traders. Despite their shared occupation, their characters vary greatly. Some of them are simple men from a previous era: the old days of unrestricted wildlife trade. Others are calculating, slick businessmen who may be involved in other commercial activities and just see birds as a fast source of cash or even as a cover for other activities, such as drug running. But fortunes can be both made and lost in the bird trade, and many speculators come and go quickly. Some bird traders generate a positively evil aura, while others appear relatively genial. Some are involved because they are themselves interested in birdkeeping. To others, birds are merely products. As the bird trade is being cracked down on, some dealers are switching to trading reptiles, which is still a free-for-all with little regulation and no airline embargoes to slow down business. Some cynically acknowledge that they are involved in a destructive business, but justify it by pointing out that the world is set to self-destruct anyhow, so why shouldn't they make a quick buck in the process? The attitude of one small-time importer sums up the rivalry: "Some of them are the biggest crooks on this earth." Many that I have met believe it is other traders who are creating problems; if only they were all good traders like them, things would be okay. However, this is not usually consistent with their track records when they are available. Another favorite justification for the trade is the claim that native peoples benefit from the wild bird trade. But it is clear from our investigations that most trappers are employed seasonally and get paid just enough to keep them trapping rather than improve their lot. The lion's share of the profits from the wild bird trade are restricted to relatively few large traders.

Senegal

Senegal officially exported more than one million birds annually until recent airline embargoes cut this figure in half. The trade is dominated by the world's largest bird dealer, Amadou Diallo, or "Diallo Pitch," as he is known throughout Senegal ("Pitch" is the local word for small bird). Diallo, who has been described as the "father" of the Senegalese bird trade, started in the bird business some 30 years ago. Diallo claims to have up to 200,000 birds on his premises on occasion. According to the dealers, many birds shipped out of Senegal come from neighboring countries, yet all the species in trade are reportedly abundant in Senegal. Diallo has another bird exporting operation in Mali and still another in Guinea-Bissau. As Amadou has grown older, he has passed most of his business on to his son, Alassane. In 1990, Diallo received over 60% of the value of the Senegalese bird trade.

EIA investigators first met Amadou and Alassane Diallo in 1986 when they claimed to be exporting 800,000 birds a year, though the official records showed only 229,980 birds exported. In 1990, they officially exported more than 180% of their permitted quota. Profits from the bird business have financed a small fishing fleet and a French green bean farming business for the Diallos. Diallo has dealt with most of the large importers in the U.S., exporting vast numbers of finches, such as bright blue cordon bleus, red firefinches, cutthroat finches and weaver birds. He also sells glossy starlings, doves and parrots. He openly admits that his birds come from a number of countries outside Senegal. His biggest money earner, however, is the African grey parrot. In 1990, Diallo grossed several million dollars from his sales of African greys. Overall, 65% of the estimated total value of the Senegalese bird trade was derived from African grey parrots, one of the most valuable species exported. All the birds were re-exports, and most of these had been illegally trapped in countries with commercial export bans, like Zaire or Ghana.

For many years, the African grey parrot (*Psittacus erithacus*) has been the most popular of the larger parrots traded internationally. The bird's popularity is largely due to its intelligence and mimicry ability. It is not very colorful in comparison to other parrot species, being grey with only a flash of red or maroon in its tail feathers. But the grey parrot is probably the most intelligent species of bird. Communication studies carried out at the University of Arizona have found levels of intelligence in a grey parrot previously only thought to occur in chimpanzees and dolphins. Alex, the grey parrot subject of the experiments, expresses himself in English and says "I'm sorry" when he makes a mistake. Alex has more than 71 labels for objects, actions, colors, shapes and materials and is able to put together phrases he knows to communicate his feelings. On an occasion when he was sick, his teacher, Dr. Irene Pepperberg, took him to the veterinarian for an overnight stay, and as she started to leave, he called out: "Come here. I love you. I'm sorry. Wanna go back."[22]

Being smart has not served the grey parrot well. On the contrary, it has led to overexploitation and illegal trade to supply the pet industry. Grey parrots seem to suffer more than their fair share of behavioral problems resulting from captivity. Some never tame and are known as "growlers" because of the low, rasping noise they emit when approached by humans. Others pluck their own feathers out in boredom, loneliness or stress.

The sociable and intelligent grey parrot is often caged alone for years on end. A sanctuary for unwanted parrots I visited in the Netherlands has far more grey parrots than any other species. Most of these have been abandoned because they never tamed or had pulled out their own feathers.

The African grey used to have a wide range throughout West and Central Africa, but populations have been devastated throughout many areas due to habitat loss and commercial exploitation. One scientist told me he used to see 30 to 40 in flight together but now he sees only 2 or 3 in one of the species' main ranges. In other areas, the African grey has been wiped out completely.

There are two subspecies of African grey in trade. The "red-tail" subspecies (*Psittacus erithacus erithacus*) occurs from east Côte d'Ivoire across West Africa to Zaire. It is thought to be no longer present in Togo and much of the rest of its former range. To the west of Côte d'Ivoire as far as Guinea, the less colorful Timneh ("maroon" or "black-tail") subspecies (*Psittacus erithacus timneh*) is found. These are not as popular and fetch a much lower price on the international pet market. They are relatively easy to distinguish, but traders have at times misidentified the subspecies to export red-tails from Timneh range countries. Sometimes this fraud has been detected; undoubtedly on other occasions it hasn't been. Shipments frequently circumvent physical inspection, since officials only review permits and are often unable to distinguish species. Even when they know the difference, it can be hard for customs officers to make out whether the birds, huddled inside dark and inaccessible crates, have red or maroon tails.

To complicate the issue of where parrots in trade are actually coming from, the "red-tail" subspecies is further divided into two races: the "West African," "Ghanaian" or "Ordinary" greys, and the "Central African" or "Congo" greys. As they tend to be larger and healthier, the Congos carry a higher price than the West Africans, though some argue the latter are more intelligent. West African red-tails are found from eastern Côte d'Ivoire to Nigeria, and the Congos are found in Cameroon, Congo, Central African Republic and Zaire.

Diallo dealt in both subspecies and both races, preferring the most valuable Congos. As you may have noticed, the range of the grey parrot does not reach as far as Senegal, but Senegal nevertheless established an export quota of 8,000 grey parrots a year. Even this false quota was ignored and exceeded by Diallo and the other dealers. In the late 1980s, the most common route used by Amadou Diallo to smuggle Congo red-tails was from Zaire to Senegal. Since Zaire did not allow commercial exports of African greys at that time, Diallo would purchase them from middlemen, smuggle them out and buy "legal" permits from other countries to disguise the source. The most expensive part of the transaction was said to be obtaining the paperwork, but there were plenty of officials from various countries ready to oblige. The story was that Amadou Diallo's son, Alassane, arrived in countries with a suitcase full of cash and left with a suitcase full of permits.

The European Union Scientific Working Group, which reviews quotas set on animal exports, noted that Senegal had no African grey parrots and banned exports to the European Union (the U.S. had no legal structure to refuse shipments at that time if an export permit had been issued by the relevant authorities). A game of cat-and-mouse then ensued as the Diallos and others bought permits from one country after the other that either did not have red-tail grey parrots or only had very small populations—Guinea, Sierra Leone, Mali, Côte d'Ivoire, Togo, Benin—and the EU closed them down one after the other. It is strongly suspected that it made little difference what the permits said; the birds were still coming illegally from Zaire. Another West African dealer, Ndaw, explained to U.S. Fish and Wildlife (USFWS) undercover agents that he used to drive from Senegal to Guinea to purchase CITES export permits. However, by 1991, Ndaw was stating that the Guinean CITES authorities had cracked down on granting permits because some of their shipments had been seized. Ndaw reverted to flying to Côte d'Ivoire to get the permits because officials never looked at the birds there.

With the European Union closing down their sources of paperwork as fast as they could find new ones, the Diallos concentrated on supplying the U.S. market. But U.S. Fish and Wildlife undercover agents were onto the scam (see section on U.S. dealers). Though a number of U.S. importers have been successfully prosecuted for their involvement in grey parrot smuggling, the Diallos escaped untouched. Senegalese authorities took no action whatsoever against Diallo for smuggling or violating their national quotas.

In April 1991, I found little had changed in the way the Senegalese trade operated since EIA's previous visit in 1986. The dealers were much more suspicious of cameras after EIA exposed them in the international media, and airline embargoes were encroaching upon their business, but otherwise it was business as usual. I travelled all over the country with a photographer but could find little active trapping. Finally, after driving thousands of kilometers, we discovered most of the birds were being trapped in the most remote and inaccessible region in the southeastern corner of the country, close to the Malian border. The only road to this area was so severely ridged and potholed that we were forced to abandon our rental car for a 4-wheel-drive pickup and travel crammed together with 20 local people. Just like the birds, we were sandwiched in, and I got a feel of what they must go through. Five of the other passengers were physically sick due to the roughness of the journey, and as I was tightly wedged in and couldn't move, one of them vomited down my back. On my other side, a small child kept falling asleep on my arm, due to fatigue from the arduous journey. It was the height of the dry season. The daytime temperature of 110 degrees in the shade only fell to 95 degrees during the night. Birds would finish their journey having been thrown around in boxes, dehydrated, shaken, and covered with dust and the feces of their fellow captives. If they received any water, it would be spilled in the first few minutes of the journey. Up to 2,000 birds would be crammed into one box. During this hellish journey, we discussed why dealers did not fly the birds out rather than putting them through the mangle of this journey. Since dealers claimed all the birds were abundant, we wondered why they didn't trap them in more accessible areas. The answer, I can only presume, is either the birds are not as abundant and widespread as is claimed, or it is simply cheaper. In such a remote area, the dealers pay little for the birds. It must be cheaper to lose birds on the way than to pay for proper transport conditions or to collect them from other regions.

When we arrived, caked in dust and shaken from the bumpy ride, we met a man claiming to be one of Amadou Diallo's sons. He was certainly an employee of the Diallos, as he was driving Diallo's distinctive van, which we had been tailing across Senegal. This van had holes cut into the side to increase ventilation for the birds. Easily recognizable, it is known along the route, and we had been told at various stops along the way that it was a day or so ahead of us. The driver was about to embark on his 400-mile journey back to Dakar, which he made on a bi-weekly basis in the high season. He would be taking some 10,000 birds. The boxes were stacked two high in the back and on the roof of his van. We asked him, in a taped conversation, how many birds he would need to pack in order for 100 to arrive alive in the capital. "For 100 in Dakar, you need to take 150 and even then it is not certain," he replied. He was suggesting that in just one stage of the journey to the pet shop, around a third of the birds might die. Earlier studies of how birds fare on the dealers' premises found that more than 10% die at this stage as they suffer the stress of captivity, come into contact with large numbers of other birds and try to adjust from a wild to a captive diet.

There are ten other registered dealers in Senegal, all of whom are supposed to be allocated part of the official quota. However, the dealers ignore the overall quota and allocations, and trade is really concentrated in a few hands. If official Senegalese statistics for 1990 are to be believed, the three largest dealers were responsible for 81.7% of the exports; the next three dealers shared 13.8%, leaving the remaining six dealers with only 4.5% among them. Estimates of revenue for each dealer are even more skewed, with the Diallos making close to 68% of the trade turnover—a clear monopoly. The top four dealers received over 93% of the revenue between them.

Another interesting character in Senegal is the expatriate French Consul in Kaolack, Léon Masfrand. His company, Afrique Océan, is not one of the top three bird exporters, but he also deals in wild primates for research. His walled compound is located near the Gare Routière in Kaolack, which is close to Gambia, the tiny country that cuts through the middle of Senegal on either side of the River Gambia. Gambian officials have complained that the protected wildlife of Gambia, such as Cape parrots, have been smuggled out and exported from Senegal with ostensibly legal paperwork. In 1986, EIA documented the smuggling of olive baboons from Gambia to Senegal in Masfrand's own vehicle. EIA Director Dave Currey also discovered a large pile of dead adult baboons. Presumably, they had been killed because they were too large for the research industry. When interviewed on camera, Masfrand explained his primate business. He sold the animals to the French nuclear program. "A few medical facilities buy them as well, I'm not sure what for, I think they cut them into little pieces!" he said, laughing. As a child, Masfrand suffered from polio. He still walks with a stick and claims his affliction justifies his illicit business activities in the name of medical research.

When I met him in 1991, he was still in business, though he had reportedly tried to sell his enterprise on several occasions. Even posing as a prospective buyer, I had difficulty getting into his compound. "We had some problems with ecologists," he said, referring to EIA having put his photograph in the newspapers with far from flattering commentary on his dubious primate activities. While we were in his compound, which housed some 10,000 birds, we saw a large aviary housing dozens of shore birds, who cannot be legally exported and are not kept as pets. We were told these were kept "for their beauty alone." I also saw a shipment of glossy starlings arriving from the bush destined for export. Since they peck at each other when confined, many had been blinded in one or both eyes. As so often, I was struck by the beauty of the birds and the horror of their situation.

Ghana and Côte d'Ivoire

In 1992, Ghanaian authorities invited EIA to assist them in tracking down parrot smugglers. The Chief Game and Wildlife Officer in Ghana had been complaining for some time that grey parrots were being smuggled out of Ghana in large numbers to be laundered into the international market with false certificates of origin from Côte d'Ivoire, Togo and other nearby countries. In response, CITES had arranged a brief survey of Ghanaian parrot populations, with the intention of re-opening a legal parrot trade out of Ghana, supposedly to replace the illegal trade. Ghana wanted a second opinion from EIA on the proposed scheme to re-open the trade in addition to help tracking down smuggling. The Ghanaian authorities wanted to re-open the trade only if it could be properly managed. From experience in tracking the ivory trade and wild bird trade in other countries, Dave Currey and I believed that legalizing trade in Ghana could make smuggling even easier and increase the pressure on parrot populations. If we could obtain evidence of smuggling, we could persuade CITES authorities in importing countries to close down the laundered trade from Ghana's neighbors.

Ghana, and perhaps Nigeria (where the parrot population has not yet been surveyed), would appear to have the only significant remaining populations of West African red-tails. Both countries prohibit commercial exports, but recently Ghanaian birds have been flooding out illegally in the thousands via Côte d'Ivoire, Togo and Benin. The United States and South Africa have been the principal markets for these birds.

Ghana had closed down and re-opened the parrot trade several times. Each time, overexploitation or illegal trade had led to resumption of the ban. The ban was last put in place in 1987, and this time many of the Ghanaian parrot dealers had moved to Côte d'Ivoire or other countries, thinking the ban would be permanent. After consulting with the Ghanaian Game and Wildlife Department, we decided to investigate the western smuggling route to Côte d'Ivoire.

The same team that had investigated the parrot trade in Argentina was to work on the project: Dave Currey, cameraman Clive Lonsdale, and myself. As before, Dave was responsible for still photographs, which would later be used to illustrate magazine articles; Clive would cover our activities on film to document the evidence. I was there with the expertise on the trade and birds to bluff our way into the trade and to buy the other two enough time to get their pictures.

We set off for Elubo on the Ivorian border. A short walk across the border and a few casual inquiries as prospective buyers gave us several leads. The hottest was to seek out the palm wine seller, Christian Mark, in a nearby Ghanaian town. We were told he could get us parrots. After a brief tour of the town, we tracked down Mark at his third profession, as a security guard for the Ghanaian National Petroleum Company. We soon convinced him we were genuinely interested in buying parrots to ship abroad, and, while Clive secretly filmed him, he detailed the illegal trade from the area and mentioned many familiar names. "So normally we've been smuggling them out.... At times we give people about four to five hundred." Mark wanted to be our Ghanaian agent and gave us the names of all the Côte d'Ivoire dealers, saying, "They have been coming here each and every one of them." He estimated that thousands of parrots may have been smuggled out of Ghana each year either through Côte d'Ivoire or Togo.

He introduced us to his friend James who worked for Ghanaian Game and Wildlife. James was even more ambitious than Mark. He told us he wanted to be rich like Robert Maxwell (the recently deceased tycoon, who had swindled money from his employees' pension fund). He told us about the possible re-opening of the parrot trade. We asked him about the proposed quota if exports were re-opened and if this would limit the amount of birds exported under a legalized trade. James confirmed our worst fears. "To every rule there is an exception," he said. "Once there is a permit system, there must be a system for everything to go through.... If they lift the ban, it will be easier." Although smuggling was a serious problem, people were very wary inside Ghana. Most people knew it was illegal, and most people took the threat of arrest seriously. To get permits, parrots had to be smuggled to another country. With trade legalized and permits in circulation, it would be virtually impossible to police the internal market. Permits would be re-used or forged, and anyone could move parrots around the country easily and then smuggle them across the borders for illegal export. In many places, crossing the border only involves a 40-yard canoe journey. We did this 20 or more times and never saw a sign of a border patrol.

James was definitely the man to facilitate laundering illegal birds. He promised to try to get a permit for some parrots from Accra, which we could use to get our parrots out. He told us he would say the birds were pets who had been caught years ago and that we could use the same permit many times. We returned to Accra to pass this information on to the authorities. Already they were beginning to see what legalizing the parrot trade would involve. Even their own staff members would be subject to temptation.

Mark and James told us that if we wanted to smuggle parrots, we would need to make some contacts in Abidjan, capital of Côte d'Ivoire. Mark told us they had been doing it for years and gave us the name of a shipping agent in Abidjan, Jean Aman. To find him we had to scout around Abidjan airport. It soon became clear that the smuggling of grey parrots was common knowledge there. An employee of Air Afrique told us to come back the next day: "They get the parrots from Ghana. Aman takes care of it."

In the meantime, we got settled in our hotel and set up what we later dubbed the "Video Box." We invited the Abidjan bird dealers, one by one, to our room to discuss their business activities as the video camera, which Clive had nonchalantly left on the table, recorded. They left us in no doubt as to what was happening. As Jean Aman emphasized on several occasions, "The birds are from Ghana, but we take the permits here, no problem." Although Côte d'Ivoire is thought to have a small population of red-tail parrots, each of the traders we interviewed stated that all red-tails exported from Côte d'Ivoire originated in Ghana. The business had been going on for years, though now the government had come under pressure to curtail it. They also told us the embargoes on carriage of wild birds by most airlines have made smuggling much more difficult. At the time, only Air Afrique would carry wild birds from Côte d'Ivoire. This left only New York and Johannesburg as possible destinations.

Jean Aman proved to be the key figure and kingpin of the operations, the "Mr. Fixit" of smuggling. Genial and friendly, with a taste for extremely bright-colored shirts, Jean soon became our guide to the Abidjan bird scene. He was a Ghanaian and worked for an Abidjan shipping company. He confirmed what Mark had told us, that sultry, humorless Ali was the man who brought the birds from Ghana. Jean described Ali's quarantine as "bad" and suggested that we house the birds somewhere else. He claimed we could get the CITES permit from Guinea if we had problems in Côte d'Ivoire. He knew a veterinarian who could give us a veterinary permit saying the birds came from Guinea even though they would actually be from Ghana.

He also explained it was now much more difficult to get permits from Côte d'Ivoire. The former director of Eaux et Forets (the wildlife department) was not supposed to sign permits; nevertheless, he had done so, allegedly for the highest bidder. The dealers claimed even the director's secretary got into the act and had been forging signatures on permits. This had finally been discovered and a new man, Aman's friend, Cisse Dramane Habout, was now in charge. In addition, importing countries had pointed out to Côte d'Ivoire that although it only had a small number of red-tailed parrots, it was exporting thousands. So it was going to be much harder to get permits. But where there's a will there's a way, and Jean told us we should visit Habout: "If we can't solve this problem, we shall invite him somewhere else.... If he likes a little money, we shall give it to him, then he prepares the certificate for you."

Jean Aman arranged an interview with Dramane, and after a considerable wait outside his office, we were shown in and offered seats. Jean clearly knew the man well. Dramane mentioned that pressure from "ecologists" in the U.S. was a problem. We nodded, "Yes we've had problems with them, too." He explained trapping was not actually legal in Côte d'Ivoire, so allowing exports was at odds with the law. The government was reviewing the situation and trying to encourage exporters to become "breeders," as this was the future for the business. I was almost encouraged by this until Jean explained, "When we talk about breeding, it means that they must be tamed." "Does this mean no trapping from the wild?" I asked. "No, you can capture them.... We have plenty of birds here," answered Dramane. Jean clarified, "We can keep the birds for one or two months, then on the CITES [permit] it will be written they are captive-bred." Dramane reassured us, "If someone comes to us and says, 'I've got 500 parrots to ship that I've bred,' we put 'captive-bred.'" Jean later told us the exporters already had bands supposed to denote captive-bred birds for trappers to slip over the legs of wild parrot chicks. Ghanaian exporter and confidence trickster Sam Quartey later commented to us, "They only want to make the paperwork, just to get official proof they are captive breeding."

Captive breeding is open to abuse by being used as a laundering mechanism for wild birds, particularly when carried out in countries where the species occur naturally in the wild. If it also involves individuals experienced in smuggling and evasion of wildlife regulations, there is considerable risk of abuse. Another Abidjan exporter, K.B. Freduah, was an entrepreneur for whom birds were just another sideline business. We met him in his office behind his African curio store. He had heard about the Wild Bird Conservation Act in the U.S. and was already preparing to circumvent the law. Rather than continuing to bring parrots from Ghana to export, he was going to get into "captive breeding." He proudly showed us plans for his "breeding" complex. He claimed that his friend, Dimitri (identified as Dimitri Chaniotis, based in the U.S.), was planning to invest U.S. $1 million in the scheme. K.B. thought he could be exporting captive-bred birds in around six months, even though he had no experience in breeding and though it often takes parrots several years in captivity before they have settled enough to breed. Naturally, all his "breeding stock" would come from Ghana.

Ghanaian authorities contacted me later to ask if I had any information on Dimitri. Dimitri wanted to set up a captive breeding station for grey parrots in Ghana. His proposed partner was Petersen Nimako-Baah, the man who had told us captive breeding was too expensive and impractical when people could just go and trap chicks from the wild, slip a closed band over their legs and declare them captive-bred. I was able to track down Dimitri's record. He had been prosecuted in the United States for smuggling ostrich eggs.

Jean Aman claimed to work with American importers Gators of Miami, Pet Farms and Alex Perrinelle. Another friend of Jean's was Petersen Nimako-Baah, also a Ghanaian exile. He had moved to Abidjan when the trade was closed down in Ghana. He told us some people were making their own false CITES papers (a shipment had been seized in New York with false papers a few weeks before). Petersen claimed to have used permits from Liberia and Zaire to ship birds from Abidjan. Petersen was adamant that we should not trust the other dealers, who would make lots of promises they could not keep. He also said they packed their birds badly and shipped them straight from the bush, not putting them through proper quarantine. He complained he had been cheated by a South African partner, who had claimed the birds Petersen sent to him were diseased and had died. Petersen had gone to South Africa and found them still alive. In a similar case in Belgium, a bird importer had stored dead birds in his freezer to cheat exporters. He would pull them out, photograph them and pretend they had died in later shipments. He used the dead birds time and time again.

There are countless stories of wild bird dealers cheating each other. Another dealer, Mr. Kaba, was a rough-and-ready type of the old school of animal dealers. He only tolerated our questioning because he badly needed money, and we looked as if we might be an easy source. He alleged that a Chicago-based bird dealer had not paid him for his last shipment. The dealer told him all the birds had died. "There were some Americans who came, they took 3,000 black-tails [Grey parrots] and 500 red-tails... [one of the dealers was] from Chicago.... He owes me a lot of money... he didn't pay." Sometimes importers don't pay exporters because birds arrive with disease or in bad condition; sometimes it's just to make a bigger profit. It is very difficult for the exporters to get the money back, since they are rarely in a position to take importers to court.

Kaba took us to a rundown shed that housed a motley selection of birds. I pointed out a large rat hiding under one of the cages for Clive to film. The 150 Ghanaian red-tailed grey parrots there looked nervous and sick. Many were covered in excrement from the cages above. It was hard to believe that if these cringing and wretched creatures survived, they could end up in people's homes as pets. African greys make a unique sound when the are scared. It is a "growl" rather than the squawks and whistles normally associated with parrots. This growling intensified when we neared the cages, and the resulting din remained unpleasantly loud during our stay. If

I have one overriding memory of my visits to bird dealers' premises around the world, it is the noise: the agitated and alarmed cries of hundreds, sometimes thousands, of birds confined in a crowded and dusty building. In the wild, these birds would be spread out over miles.

Kaba explained it was possible to pick up export permits for birds from a number of countries, including Mali, Togo and Guinea. It did not matter where the birds came from. You simply get the paperwork from the cheapest or most convenient source.

Another dealer, Djibril Diallo (no relation to Amadou), told us how he had been forced to move from country to country as the E.C. closed each down for parrot exports. So far he had been from Mali to Liberia, then Guinea, Sierra Leone, back to Guinea, and finally to Côte d'Ivoire. It can be a very transient life for a wildlife dealer trying to stay one step ahead of the law.

Ghanaian parrots were also shipped out through Togo, where a Frenchman, Fouchard, runs the trade. This smuggling had eased due to general strikes and political unrest in Togo. We were told that when it looked as if the government might fall, Fouchard, who enjoys the protection of the regime, left the country. Togo now says it wants to cooperate with international conservation agreements and will stop all exports of grey parrots, but Fouchard remains active. Sam Quartey is said to be the second largest dealer out of Togo, though others claim he ships very little and specializes in obtaining deposits and then not supplying any animals. Ghanaian birds are generally collected in the town of Kumasi for shipment to Togo. Quartey claims that he can move birds from Kumasi to Togo in four hours.

Sam Quartey was undoubtedly the most interesting character we met in Ghana. He gave us vivid insight into how the West African animal trade works. I first heard of Quartey a few weeks before leaving England for Ghana. Purely by chance, we had received one of his price lists that he circulated in England. He offered to sell red-tails (with permits from Benin) and a variety of reptiles. We called him once we got to Ghana. We posed as British traders, and he soon arranged to meet us. He gave us details of his bank accounts in Germany and other countries and claimed to deal in commodities like palm oil, vegetables, spices and minerals in addition to wildlife. In short, if you want to buy something from Africa, Sam will sell it to you.

He proudly explained his knowledge on manipulating the CITES permit system. Although Quartey was nominally based in Ghana, he claimed to use papers from Togo, Benin, Zaire and Cameroon to export parrots, often using the name of other traders. He also claimed to export a wide variety of live reptiles. Even though much of his work may have involved conning deposits out of would- be importers, what was impressive about Sam was that he was right up-to-date on which countries he could get permits from, which airlines would carry wild birds and which would not, and other technical details of the business. If he did not have information at hand, he would find it out quickly for us. Some of the other Ghanaian dealers alleged Quartey seldom deals in animals, but that he acts like an agent and just arranges the paperwork. One U.S. reptile dealer claimed to have forwarded $6,000 to him for baby royal pythons and had not heard from him since. Although he is not registered as a wildlife exporter, he is definitely known to have been involved in at least one python shipment out of Ghana.

He told us he had shipped birds by declaring them captive-bred. He had been getting his permits from Zaire and Cameroon and suggested transporting the birds via Lagos in Nigeria to get around the airline bans. Of Zaire, he said: "The permits are very expensive. There are only two people who get permits, and one of them is the son of President Mobutu, who is a very good friend of mine." Quartey invited me to go with him to Zaire. He said we could make a boat trip up the river with some friends of his in the military. I politely declined this tempting offer. He also claimed to have an operation in Benin. This was confirmed by a receipt he dropped from Benin CITES authorities. "I have been getting my CITES permits from Douala, Cameroon, then Congo and Zaire, and I have more than enough. They don't give on a quota basis, you come and they give, you come and they give.... Now they want to introduce a quota in Zaire." But this would not stop Sam. "If I want to export thousands, it means I have to use the names of five different people."

Sam was also involved in shipping live reptiles. He claimed that while he was shipping Ghanaian parrots out on Togolese permits, he was shipping Togolese reptiles on Ghanaian permits. He also explained how he could ship rare and protected Angolan pythons by mixing them up with the more common royal pythons. He summed up the situation: "The permit is the business."

When asked about the possibility of Ghana re-opening trade, he was dismissive: "If they are given a quota of 4,500 for all in a year, that's not business." After we met with Sam several times, he was persuaded that we were seriously interested and agreed to arrange for us to see a number of illegally held parrots in Kumasi, Ghana. Meanwhile, we were arranging for Ghanaian Security forces to follow us, and hopefully, seize the birds. For two days we sat in our hotel room waiting for a call. Finally, Sam rang. It was all arranged. We would leave for Kumasi in half an hour. We quickly called our contact in the security forces, who I will call Simon. They would pick us up on the Kumasi road and tail us to the destination. At a given signal, they would swoop and arrest everyone, including us.

Unfortunately, communication in Ghana does not always work as well as it might, and Simon was unable to pick up local backup in Kumasi. While we were cruising around town in our hired car with Quartey and his colleagues, we tried to keep them talking to make sure they did not spot Simon's car. It seems Quartey's agents wanted to try to disorientate us before revealing the location of the hidden stash of illegal parrots they had assembled. So we were taken around the back streets. Luck was with Quartey that day. We were told to follow his colleague's taxi down a closed-off street, but the taxi became stuck while trying to negotiate the road repairs. The whole crew had to get out to lift the car over the barrier, and we were forced to go back the way we had come, passing Simon's car. Quartey had spotted the car earlier, so he took an experimental route to test his pursuers. We feigned confusion and concern. Finally, certain they were being trailed, Quartey and his companion jumped out and disappeared into the crowd. He sent a scout back to question us. Of all things, the scout accused us of being Canadian customs officers. None of us had any doubt that Quartey had intended to take us to see the poached parrots before trying to extract money from us. He knew he couldn't complete the deal until he had. Quartey kept a low profile for a few days, and when we called him, he still seemed unsure of our role. The Ghanaian police later picked him up for questioning. Although they were unable to locate his business records (he claims to have premises in Togo and Benin), they did find a copy of a forged CITES permit when they searched his house. The investigation continues.

Tanzania

In 1991, I was asked by the Wildlife Conservation Society of Tanzania and the Tanzanian National Bank to look into the bird dealers' export declarations. No individuals stand out as dominating the trade in Tanzania as Amadou Diallo does in Senegal or Fouchard does in Togo. In 1991, there were 176 registered wildlife dealers, though only 73 were actively trading. Many of the companies are engaged in activities other than bird trade, ranging from live reptile exports to electronics and mining. Virtually anyone with an eye for a fast buck in Tanzania would request a bird export quota — it could always be sold to another dealer. The quotas for Tanzania had been set per dealer and without any effective limit on the number of dealers. Some people operate more than one company in order to increase their quota. I easily identified one man, Jacob Nyangi Nyakiban, who was Director of three companies. As there are thought to be less than 20 bird-holding premises in Tanzania, I am certain many more were linked by silent partners or relatives. Three companies were so indiscreet they used exactly the same typed invoice layout, just changing the company name at the top. It was also clear that dealers and officials often ignored the quota anyway. "Special permits" to export even protected species were available at a price.

Perhaps the biggest irony is that whenever the trade in Tanzania has been criticized, the immediate response is that it is an important industry for the country as it earns much-needed foreign currency. Under Tanzanian law, traders are supposed to declare all foreign currency to the National Bank of Tanzania. They must deposit the receipts and then are allowed some of the hard currency back. I was asked by the Bank to look into currency declarations they believed were being underdeclared. I spent two weeks wading through invoices and computer records and found it hard to believe how blatant the abuse was. A two-tier fraud became clear. The dealers were using a double invoice system: a real invoice for the customer, and a second, phony one for the government. The second invoice grossly underdeclared the value of the birds. For example, one company would declare a Greater flamingo at $40 on its invoice, but its price list offered them at $250. Although dealers offered discounts, some species were declared at only 10% of their real value. This was repeated across-the-board, with the consequence that the Tanzanian bird trade, which was probably worth well over $3 million a year, was declared at around $750,000. In the second stage of this fraud, traders kept most of the underdeclared money outside the country. Only $290,000 of the $750,000 ever got to the Tanzanian National Bank. The rest was kept in foreign bank accounts.

I was able to ascertain this from comparing the declared invoices with a large number of price lists from Tanzanian dealers that I had received by fax or letter through my "front companies" in the U.K. and the U.S. (Faxes have greatly facilitated the operation of bird dealers. They can instantly transmit price lists, orders and copies of permits to each other, while they used to have to rely on the vagaries of the postal system or coded messages via telex). Even allowing for considerable discounts, the differences were unbelievable.

Five dealers from Tanzania (and no one from the Wildlife Department) turned up to discuss the wild bird trade at an international meeting organized by the World Wildlife Fund. They came because airline embargoes had slowed business. Their representative, Zablon Masiaga, opened the discussion by stating Tanzania had many protected species. He said that although the dealers wanted to trade these protected species, their respect for the law kept them from doing so and that it was unfair to criticize the Tanzanian trade. EIA responded by asking Mr. Masiaga why, if he respected the law, did he advertise these protected species on his price lists? The Tanzanian traders and other trade representatives around the room were furious and stated we could not hold discussions if spurious allegations like these were going to be made. Afterwards, some of the dealers encircled me, angrily demanding to see the evidence. They were quickly silenced with a copy of Masiaga's price list. I later saw him being severely scolded by the other traders. He was not allowed to address the meeting again.

Tanzania sells not only finches, parrots and starlings, but also virtually any other type of bird, including flamingos, pelicans, storks and cranes. There is some confusion over "protected species" in Tanzania. A number of species are not listed on export quotas and are, therefore, presumed to be protected from trade. However, as mentioned before, there appears to be some sort of unofficial system for "special permits." These can be purchased even for protected species. Enforcement agents around the world have been confused as to whether permits are fraudulent or "special" — granted at the apparent whim of officials.

The Tanzanian trade is rife with scandal, from exportation of species that are supposed to be protected (e.g., Kori Bustards) to depletion of endemic species (e.g., Fischer's lovebird (*Agapornis fischeri*)). This brightly colored, small parrot has been traded in the tens of thousands annually, making it one of the most heavily traded parrot species. Ornithologists report it has been wiped out over much of its former range. Trappers poach the birds from protected areas, like the Serengeti National Park. Although Tanzania wished to continue exports of Fischer's lovebird, the Significant Trade Review of CITES suspended all trade as there was no scientific data to justify such high levels of trade. Tanzanian authorities, however, wanted to continue.

There have been numerous cases of extremely high mortality during transport in wild bird shipments from Tanzania. Hundreds of birds are often stuffed into completely inadequate crates and left unfed and unwatered on a tarmac under the blazing African sun. In 1990, before it implemented an embargo on wild bird shipments, Lufthansa transported 8,400 birds from Tanzania via Kenya. Over 100 crates were unloaded and left on the hot tarmac. There was very little food and water, and many crates were overcrowded; 1,270 birds died of starvation, dehydration or asphyxia. In August of 1990, seven out of nine pelicans died on a KLM flight en route to the Netherlands. In 1989, a KLM shipment routed through Amsterdam and London to the U.S. was detained in London; 1,209 birds were found dead. One British newspaper, not permitted by U.K. authorities to photograph the dead birds, ran a photograph of a sticker used on some of the transport crates. The sticker features a photograph of a flamingo with the caption, "I enjoyed my stay at the KLM Animal Hotel." KLM finally agreed to suspend shipping wild birds. In May 1991, a shipment of 4,500 birds on Egyptian Airlines arrived in Brussels, including bustards, storks, flamingos and parrots. More than 1,300 of the birds were dead on arrival.

As if this was not enough, a large-scale abuse of CITES permits had been detected in Tanzania. Twelve companies were named as being involved in the scam. The Dutch authorities questioned some dubious permits. In response, Tanzanian authorities reported permits as "stolen." In other cases, "security stamps" on CITES permits were removed, then stuck onto fake permits. Such fake permits may have been used to ship birds to other countries where law enforcement officers are not so vigilant as the Dutch.

Clearly, vested interests, allegedly reaching as far as the ministerial level, have been at play in the Tanzanian bird trade. Only airline embargoes have reduced the scale of the trade. A project funded by the U.S. Agency for International Development (USAID) was supposed to be reforming the trade. After confirming that the trade was out of control, the project set about establishing an improved management system. The scheme aimed to convert the trade from a low-value, high-volume business to a low-volume, high-value one. The project would have reduced the maximum numbers of birds exported legally each year from 278,900 to 18,700. By introducing a strict minimum declared value system, it hoped to ensure an annual declared value of $1.5 million instead of the $200,000 declared in previous years. It was hoped that the lower volume would improve standards of care for the birds and professionalism among the dealers. The lower quotas were designed to prevent depletion of the species. This would seem like a very good deal for Tanzania — the best of both worlds — less birds, more money. However, it was not a good deal for dealers who had been cheating and defrauding the system, and although the government finally accepted the plan in principle, it has yet to implement it. In 1994, a new policy on bird trade was set in place.[23] It remains to be seen if this new policy will be implemented and any meaningful restraint put on bird exports from Tanzania.

Argentina

Argentina has 24 species of parrots, mostly distributed in the northern part of the country. Argentina used to be the largest supplier of wild-caught parrots in the world, supplying up to 150,000 each year during the past 15 years. Though Argentina did not allow the export of other types of birds, parrots (the most valuable species to the pet trade) were arbitrarily declared as "pests" in order to justify exports for the pet trade. The Tucuman Amazon (*Amazona tucumana*) parrot was still classified as a pest when it was listed on CITES Appendix I in 1989. Its population was thought to number less than 10,000. One parrot species, the monk parakeet (*Myopsitta monachus*), does do significant damage to agriculture in Argentina, but U.S. importers certainly do not need to bring them in from Argentina. Feral monk parakeets already exist in several U.S. states, having escaped their cages. The European Community even lists the U.S. as a country where the species occurs in the wild. The parakeets caused some problems for agriculture and U.S. native species.

You might ask yourself what country would allow the large-scale importation of a declared pest species? The answer is virtually any country in the world, and this is an often forgotten aspect to wild bird importation. In recent times, the export trade has greatly decreased due to reduced quotas imposed by the Argentinian wildlife authority, though some species may still be overexploited for the domestic market, which continues unchecked in some species.

In 1991, EIA carried out an investigation that was used to make a National Geographic film, "Dead on Arrival," which followed the Argentinian trade from tree felling to catch parrot chicks right to Buenos Aires airport. EIA discovered some 20 dealers in Argentina. Three of them deserve special mention— Antonio Chacon, Miguel Angel Lina and Carlos Lazaro Fraga.

Antonio Chacon, one of the major traders, is in his fifties and is a jovial, short, balding man. He exports to the EU, U.S., Taiwan, Japan, China, South Africa, Switzerland and Czechoslovakia and has invested profits made from dealing birds into a large collection of rare protected parrots at Corrientes Loropark. Chacon told us he picked this site, ten kilometers from the Paraguayan border, because of local laws that are favorable to breeders. A conservationist alleged Chacon had bribed local officials to draft a law allowing him to carry out otherwise illegal activities. Whether or not this is true, Chacon had presumably obtained "legal" paperwork for the very rare and protected wild-caught birds in his collection, such as hyacinth, military and Caninde macaws. His wife told us on film the birds had all come from neighboring countries. These countries have all had export bans for a number of years, and the species are protected under Appendix I of the Convention on International Trade in Endangered Species (CITES). Yet Argentinian authorities have taken no action against Chacon.

Of over 1,000 rare birds at his "breeding station," Chacon had bred only 30 birds of two species in four years. His son, who runs the station, could not even identify some of the species in his care. Although Argentina has now cut its export quotas for parrots significantly, Chacon recently represented his country at an international meeting on "sustainable use."

The EIA team met Chacon on three occasions. He cooperated, believing the team members were freelance journalists interested in making easy money on a lightweight story about his work with parrots. He desperately wanted publicity for his parrot park to establish Corrientes as one of the world's "best" collections. We gave him plenty of publicity all right, but not the sort he was hoping for. We first met him after we had filmed his collectors choking six parrots to death as they hurriedly force-fed them. We had just finished filming some of the most horrific scenes documented in the wild bird trade when Chacon appeared. I had to smile and chat with him so we could arrange to meet up later and follow the shipment to the airport. Hundreds of partially fledged chicks are collected together destined for export in dirty and overcrowded conditions where disease can be devastating. In one crate, I filmed the decomposing body of a chick, so long dead its flesh had turned black. The chicks are fed by means of plastic ketchup dispensers containing a thick maize-and-water mix.

As we watched one of the twice-daily feeds, I thought it would be a fairly benign process. The chicks were hungry, and the collector we observed had been in the business for many years. I have seen the delicacy of care that some bird breeders lavish on baby parrots in the U.S. and Europe. To them, every loss of a bird is a personal defeat. The contrast was striking. I witnessed how the mechanics of a commercial business in wildlife work. Because there are so many birds to feed, individual care gives way to callous practicality in what amounts to a parrot production line. Henry Ford would have been proud of the turnover, but shocked by the number of "rejects." Losses are just a cost of business. One by one, the parrots were grabbed by the neck from the shallow crates in which they were normally housed. While holding a chick by the neck, the handler inserted the nozzle of a bottle filled with maize into the chick's mouth and squeezed an amount roughly estimated to constitute a full gizzard. Sometimes the judgment or aim of the nozzle was poor, and the mixture would explode back out, spraying both the chick and the feeder. At least ten birds choked as the food was pumped into their lungs instead of their stomachs. This was obviously a regular occurrence, as the collector's son would take these birds to the trash can and violently shake them to try to clear the lungs. This violent "shaking" usually broke the birds' necks, and the few birds who survived the rescue attempt appeared to be in shock. They would probably die later from pneumonia due to lung contamination.

We watched Chacon count 425 Amazona chicks into crates to be transported more than 1,000 kilometers to the capital of Buenos Aires. They were asked on several occasions to confirm this total, and Chacon did so on camera, saying he had only taken 425 this year. We filmed the official documents for this shipment, which stated that only 350 birds were in the shipment. By doing this, Chacon was able to avoid a small tax on each bird. Later, at Chacon's quarantine station in Buenos Aires, we saw what was left of the shipment; many had already died and others looked precariously close to death. Chacon's vet told the team that birds often came in and out of quarantine at Chacon's holding premises. Chacon claimed that there was a compulsory 30-day quarantine. We even accompanied Chacon to the airport with his first consignment of birds. There he declared the value of the young parrots at $23 each. Price lists from dealers offer the species between $70 and $100 each. The crates in which the birds were shipped on the long journey to Taiwan did not meet the international standards, and although they received a health certificate, they were not inspected.

Another significant Argentinian trader, Miguel Lina, was allegedly involved in a very large permit fraud. His fraudulent permits turned up in a number of countries. Lina traded under the name of Chrismau. Like Jean

Aman in Côte d'Ivoire, he was actually a shipper, not an animal dealer, and was regarded as something of an outsider by the other bird traders. We were told that three other exporters — Pujol, Medone and Sartini — had problems with customs due to their illegal trading and were banned from exporting. They would, therefore, use Lina as their export mechanism or middleman. He nominally bought the birds from these dealers and sold them to their customers, taking his cut for shipping and using his close contacts at Buenos Aires Ezeiza airport to get the animals out.

Lina said that of the 105 CITES permits issued to him in 1988, he had only used 41 and had canceled the rest. However, many of the canceled permits turned up later. Lina used them to export wildlife or wildlife products to Holland, Germany, Spain, Portugal, Japan, Italy, Singapore and Switzerland. It is thought that 30% of Lina's permits for reptile skins and parrots in 1988 were old ones that he had canceled and then used, thus avoiding quotas and CITES control. False CITES certificates started appearing all around the world. The system has now been changed so that all "unused" permits must be returned. Lina was implicated along with customs officials in illegal dealing from Ezeiza International airport in Buenos Aires. Senior customs officers, airline officials and Lina allegedly were involved in avoiding tax and customs checks. They were allegedly able to bring cargoes directly to the plane, avoiding all controls.

Carlos Lazaro Fraga is certainly a character. His main business apparently was trying to obtain deposits from foreign exporters. Fraga's company, "Libra S.A.," also claims to sell firearms, cars, motorbikes and leather goods, although he was registered as a bird exporter with the Argentinian authorities. Fraga would circulate price lists featuring a number of protected and rare species. One of the species listed was a glaucous macaw (*Anodorynchus glaucus*). The bird is thought to be extinct. The last known specimen was seen in a zoo in 1913. The bird closely resembles the Lear's macaw (*Anodoryhnchus leari*), which has fared little better, with a known wild population of around 118, according to the world's leading macaw expert, Dr. Charles Munn. In the same family is a closely related species, the largest of the parrots, the hyacinth macaw (*Anodorynchus hyacinthus*), thought to number less than 5,000 in the wild. Fraga's price list also offered hyacinths.

It is quite possible that a small, undiscovered glaucous macaw population still exists in the wild. There are a number of aviculturists looking for wild populations at present. Some would like to help conserve the birds in the wild, while others would undoubtedly try to become the first to breed the species in captivity.

The ultimate goal of many aviculturists is success with producing numbers of difficult-to-breed and rare species. While this can increase the numbers in captivity, attempts at reintroducing captive-bred specimens of the larger parrots have been unsuccessful. These attempts have been made mainly by scientists using captive-bred birds. Not knowing what to feed on or how to evade predators, the captive-bred specimens have usually not behaved like their wild counterparts. They can also harbor diseases acquired in captivity. Because of this and the cost of reintroduction programs, most ornithologists believe maintaining wild populations should take priority over removing birds for captive breeding efforts.

We sent a journalist working in Buenos Aires on the trail of Carlos Fraga. Our contact tracked down the portly, bearded Fraga at one of his pet shops in Rosario, Argentina. At his palatial home, which was packed with military paraphernalia, our contact was shown a sabre bearing Fraga's name "For Services to the S.I.D." S.I.D was the secret service responsible for the "disappearances" of thousands of innocent people in Argentina. Fraga showed him what he claimed was a photograph of one of the glaucous macaws and explained the birds had sold quickly and had been shipped using Fraga's ex-air-force airline pilot contacts.

A professor hired by bird traders to conduct a population survey in Argentina told me not all bird traders were bad. Some were good, he asserted, and when I asked which ones, he told me Ernesto Boikens was a good example. My only knowledge of Boikens was from a report from Swiss veterinarians.

In January 1989, Swiss officials seized one of Boikens' shipments of blue-fronted Amazon parrots en route to Taiwan. The transport crate was 1 m x .5 m x .4 m and was described as "stuffed" by the Swiss officials. Contrary to regulations, Boikens had sealed the crate so the contents could not be observed. Officials found that 90% of the animals inside were chicks under three months who were incapable of feeding themselves. Two were dead and the rest in very poor condition. Swiss veterinarians were surprised any of the birds survived the journey. Five days later, only five of those who had survived the trip were still alive. This was a shipment by an allegedly "good" exporter!

Guyana

In 1993, a new government in Guyana imposed a moratorium on wildlife trade. The trade is not supposed to reopen until long-overdue population surveys have been carried out and new wildlife legislation is enacted.

Before this moratorium, Guyana was the largest exporter of macaws, the largest and slowest-reproducing parrot species. A number of sources have stated large quantities of macaws exported from Guyana have been taken illegally in neighboring countries, like Brazil and Venezuela. Some areas of the Orinoco Delta in Venezuela appear to have been severely depleted of the larger macaws. Venezuelan authorities have seized shipments of parrots in transit from Guyana on grounds that the birds actually originated in Venezuela. Parrot smugglers from Guyana have even exchanged gunfire with Venezuelan authorities.

In October 1991, an official delegation from EIA and the Royal Society for the Prevention of Cruelty to Animals (RSPCA) was invited by Guyanese authorities to "inspect" the bird trade. Of course, rather than being allowed to drop in on the dealers unannounced, the group was led on a "magical mystery tour" of prearranged meetings. The sanitized official itinerary would have meant spending four days flying over the rainforest and seeing nothing of the real conditions for animals in trade. In the end, some members of the party managed to slip away from the guided tour and discovered some useful information. For example, they discovered parrots allegedly being shipped illegally to Miami. One particular weekly flight was named. It turned out this flight had never been targeted for detailed customs or wildlife inspection. When U.S. Customs checked this flight, they found no birds but did find traces of cocaine, indicating quantities of the drug had been removed from the plane before inspection. This showed that the route was certainly feasible.

EIA's Dave Currey got to meet some of the most prominent Guyanese bird traders, including Lawrence Van Sertima. He is not Guyanese, though he owns a large property in Guyana. When in Guyana, he carries a pistol at his side. He warned Currey not to wander too far from the official itinerary or it could be very dangerous. He said that both Currey and I were listed in his electronic diary as "very bad people."

Kurt Herzog is Swiss and has lived in Guyana for a number of years. He is a tall, burly man with dark hair and a moustache. I met him at a CITES meeting in Switzerland in 1989 when he approached me, unaware of my interest in the trade. He started complaining about fellow dealer and former partner, Louis Martins. He told me about Martins poor treatment of birds and alleged illegal activities. Herzog told Dave Currey his trappers had discovered three pairs of "small blue macaws" in the interior. He believed these to be a previously undiscovered wild population of either Spix's macaw (known population in the wild: one) or Lear's macaw (known population in the wild: 118). He had immediately offered his trappers an outboard motor for capturing any or all of the birds. Luckily, his trappers had left the birds alone, thinking they were too small to be valuable. Herzog intended to capture, for profit, some of the rarest animals in the world, knowing that at the time, Guyanan law would not prevent him from doing so. By the same loophole, some traders kept large numbers of internationally protected Scarlet macaws (*Ara macao*) in their holding premises ready for illegal export.

Ironically, one of the most vocal opponents of the trade in Guyana has been former exporter and convicted smuggler, Jagdeshwar Saddhu Lall. Lall claims to have seen the light, although it is widely alleged he is still up to his old tricks. Lall was convicted of smuggling 27 rare Black Palm Cockatoos (*Probosciger aterimus*) from Papua New Guinea and other parrots from the British Virgin Islands into the U.S. He was also using forged health certificates. Two high-speed boats used for smuggling the birds were seized as evidence. Repeatedly in trouble in the U.S. as well as in Guyana, Lall established a private zoo on the Caribbean island of Grenada. He chose this island because of its proximity to the Latin American mainland and because at the time it was not a member of CITES and so had no laws or authorities controlling the movement of endangered species. Until he was finally closed down, he used the "zoo" as a holding station for wildlife trading. One shipment of macaws went to Hungary on a British Airways flight. Many of the birds later died of psittacosis. Indeed, when Lall's zoo was closed down, many of the animals were found to be very sick, undernourished and otherwise afflicted by the unconscionable treatment at the facility.

Lall was allegedly involved in a shipment of birds containing cocaine that was sent to Beijing, China. Although such cases are often kept quiet for enforcement purposes, drugs have frequently been found in wildlife shipments, particularly in Miami. Dead parrots and live snakes have been found containing drugs. Cocaine has been found disguised as a preservative powder used to ship reptile skins, and bags of liquid cocaine have been found in shipments of tropical fish.

Formerly trading as "Jungle Export," Lall emerged in 1992 under the name of "Guyana Wildlife Trust" and later as "Friends of Wildlife." Describing the trade as "cruel," "primitive and outdated" and "immoral," Lall took the Guyana government to court for violating CITES and destroying the nascent ecotourism industry in Guyana. According to Lall, pressure from him led the new government to uncover "serious fraud in the Wildlife Management Authority Office. Security stamps are missing [used to certify genuine permits] and there is no regard for the national quota [supposed to limit exports]." Lall stated: "The legal trade is just a cover-up for heavy smuggling operations... I suppressed the voice of my very soul to stay in this evil and cruel business for several years in the past. As an act of penance for my part in this sinful trade, I pledge to publicly fight this gruesome business in my country for the rest of my life." Although there is evidence to support many of Lall's allegations, some sources allege he only wants action against the bird trade as revenge.

The United States

The U.S. has long been one of the most lucrative markets for illicit wildlife of all kinds. Wildlife imports are only permitted through designated ports of entry, and the legal bird trade has concentrated itself primarily in Miami and Los Angeles. Even though the European market is larger, the U.S. was the biggest consumer of the rarer and more valuable larger parrots such as macaws and cockatoos until the passage of the Wild Bird Conservation Act in 1992. In an undercover operation extending over the past several years, the U.S. Fish and Wildlife Service (FWS) found many of the largest "legal" dealers were involved in paperwork fraud. FWS also discovered an organized smuggling operation that imported cockatoo eggs from Australia and New Zealand. In addition, large numbers of protected species have routinely been smuggled via the long-underpoliced Mexican border.

Wherever you go in the bird dealing world, "Gators of Miami" is a well-known name. For 35 years it has been run by A.A. "Buzz" Pare. Gators is one of the largest importers of wild birds into the U.S. and consistently has been at the top of tables of shipments with the highest mortality rates. Gators has seven quarantine stations in Miami. Pare was one of the key players in the systematic destruction of Moluccan Cockatoo (*Cacatua moluccensis*) populations in the late 1980s, when dealers bought all they could in antici- pation of the species becoming classified as endangered. Balding and bespectacled, Pare looks innocent enough, but his quarantine mortality records speak for themselves. In a newspaper article,[24] he claims, "We're providing friendship and love to people at a reasonable price." According to Pare, "fewer than 2.3%... [of the birds] died each year." His official records for 1989 stated 9% were either dead on arrival or died in quarantine.[25] He goes on to claim: "If imports are cut off, it will be devastating. There are only a handful of breeders, so you won't be able to buy birds."

On December 21, 1994, Pare was indicted by a Miami Grand Jury for violating the Lacey Act. Charges included:

> • one count of conspiring to illegally smuggle African Grey parrots into the U.S. and defraud the U.S. government by filing false importation documents on 12 separate shipments of parrots;

> • six counts of smuggling approximately 4,702 African Grey parrots; and

> • two counts of making and submitting false records.[26]

In a plea agreement reached in April 1997, Pare pleaded guilty and agreed to pay $300,000 in restitution, the largest sum ever imposed in a federal wildlife smuggling case.[27] Although Pare still faces up to $500,000 in fines and 10 years in prison, sentencing guidelines will probably result in a less severe penalty.

According to the indictment and public documents, Gators of Miami, Inc. was the nation's largest importer of African grey Parrots from 1988 through 1990, having imported approximately 24% of all such birds. Between February 1988 and August 1991, Pare allegedly conspired to smuggle approximately 14 shipments totalling 5,102 "Congo" African grey parrots who had been illegally taken from the wild in Zaire, where commercial trade in this species has been completely banned. Pare reportedly paid $85 for each bird and then resold them in the U.S. for between $600 and $1,000 apiece.[28]

The African grey parrot is listed on Appendix II of the Convention on International Trade in Endangered Species (CITES). The CITES export documents accompanying the parrots claimed they originated in Guinea or the Côte d'Ivoire. Neither country has wild populations of these birds.

Willie Lawson has five registered quarantine stations under the name of "Bird Haven" in Miami. In the August 26, 1991 issue of the Sun newspaper, Lawson is quoted as saying, "I'm doing business according to all the international, federal and state rules." However, although he has yet to be charged, public documents indicate Lawson was involved in another case in which Richard Furzer, a major importer, made illegal imports of African grey parrots from Zaire.[29] Many of Lawson's shipments have been disastrous. In 1990, Lawson had one shipment from Hong Kong in which all 2,804 birds died in transit or in quarantine. Two shipments from Peru suffered over 40% mortality.[30] Between 1985 and 1989, Lawson shipped 244,180 birds, with 15% dying in transit or in quarantine.

Mario Tabraue was based in Medley, Florida and imported wildlife under the name "Zoological Imports Unlimited." When police raided his house, they found an extensive collection of exotic wildlife. A 1987 indictment alleged that Tabraue headed up a drug smuggling ring responsible for killing and dismembering a police informant.[31] The ring was said to have bribed Miami and Key West police and trafficked half a million pounds of marijuana.[32] It was said to have smuggled $95 million of marijuana and cocaine. Tabraue was convicted in a drug racketeering scandal and forfeited $75 million in assets, one of the largest criminal forfeitures in the southern District of Florida.[33] As well as running a bird import company and having a number of exotic birds, he had two leopards and two cheetahs illegally in his possession.[34] He was holding submachine guns both at his home and at his pet store.[35] Although illegal wildlife was found when his premises were raided, no charges were pressed. In 1989, Tabraue's business still imported 2,328 parrots from Honduras in March and June; 24% of these were dead on arrival or died in quarantine.[36] These imports were made after Mr. Tabraue's conviction in February 1989 and prior to his sentencing.

Every year, tens of thousands of baby parrots, mainly Amazon parrot species endemic to Mexico, are smuggled across the U.S.-Mexican border to be sold directly through contacts, newspaper ads or in U.S. pet stores. In

1989, Gregory B. Jones pled guilty to receiving protected wildlife and making false statements to a federal officer when he received 60 baby yellow-naped Amazon parrots.[37] He was sentenced to two years in prison and fined $140,000. His son also pled guilty to a misdemeanor charge of transportation in the same case. The 300 parrots involved, some of them carrying Newcastle disease, reportedly died later.[38] They had been smuggled into the U.S. from Mexico concealed in vehicle panels.

However, this was by no means the end of Jones's career in the bird business. Although he could no longer get a license for a quarantine station, his wife, Phyllis, could. They continued to import large numbers of wild birds with an appalling mortality record. Between 1985 and 1989, they imported 45,234 birds, with 21% of them either dead on arrival or dying in quarantine. One infamous shipment was routed from Tanzania through Amsterdam and London on KLM. Some 2,000 birds were dead on arrival in London and many others died in quarantine.

South-African-born Richard Furzer has three quarantine stations in Los Angeles. According to U.S. Department of Agriculture (USDA) quarantine returns, he imported 484,859 birds between 1985 and 1989, with an 18% mortality rate during transit and quarantine. He regularly ships up to 30,000 birds in one shipment. In 1989, he was the largest bird importer in the U.S., bringing in 82,919 birds and losing 19% en route or in quarantine.[39] In 1993, Furzer pled guilty to five charges of smuggling more than $1 million worth of African grey parrots from Zaire via Senegal, Côte d'Ivoire and Guinea. From intercepted fax and telephone messages, it was clear to U.S. Fish and Wildlife agents that Furzer was well aware of the illegal nature of the transactions. He explained to an undercover agent that "they were smuggled into Senegal and then they get the paperwork from Guinea." In February 1994, Furzer was sentenced to 18 months in prison and fined $75,000 dollars.[40]

Alex Perrinelle is a major U.S. bird importer. He operates six quarantine stations, working with fellow dealer David Mohilef. According to USDA quarantine records, between 1985 and 1989, Perrinelle shipped 372,227 birds, with an overall mortality of 19%. Ivorian bird dealers alleged that Perrinelle has bought African grey parrots from Côte d'Ivoire dealers who were smuggling parrots from Ghana. He has also shipped a large number of grey parrots from Cameroon, where parrot populations are said to have been decimated by over-trapping. I met him at the 1993 CITES Transport Working Group in Dakar, Senegal, where he and Senegalese traders ensured that attempts to reduce mortality by limiting shipment size were blocked. He was very vocal in claiming the airline embargoes had increased mortality due to longer routes. I stated there was no firm evidence to show this. In fact, from U.S. data, as the numbers of birds being shipped had decreased, so had the mortality. There was one notable exception – the largest death toll in one shipment I had ever heard of. Perrinelle was the importer. Someone, probably the Indonesian bird dealers, possibly even the government, had persuaded Garuda Indonesia Airlines to lift its voluntary embargo on wild bird shipments. In March 1991, Perrinelle imported 10,756 birds to his Los Angeles quarantine station. USDA quarantine forms showed that 10,606 birds were dead on arrival, a 99% mortality rate. Perrinelle told me the mortality had been entirely the airline's fault — baggage handlers had stacked mail bags on top of the birds, blocking ventilation. The birds were either asphyxiated or roasted in their own heat. Since then, Garuda has wisely reinstated the embargo on carriage of wild birds.

When confronted with such appalling mortality, bird dealers tend to claim such "accidents" don't really count and most shipments are okay. Unfortunately, these accidents happen only too often. Sometimes a van may have a flat tire and birds are left in the scorching sun. Sometimes a highly infectious disease is unwittingly introduced to a holding station crammed with birds held in unsanitary conditions. Sometimes it's delays, sometimes poor loading, sometimes lack of care en route. The U.S. and U.K. governments, EIA and other groups have suggested shipment sizes be limited to reduce risk of such disasters. The trade has blocked all attempts to do this, since it would affect profitability and volume of trade.

Perrinelle is a director of the Pet Industry Joint Advisory Council (PIJAC), which collects over $1 million a year to represent the pet industry in its various battles, from puppy mills to wild bird imports. Although they are presumably major contributors, bird dealers reflect badly on the whole pet industry, which would do better to concentrate on supplying the public with a far superior "product," namely tame and healthy captive-bred birds. The real money for the industry is in bird feed, cages and accessories, and captive-bred birds. The wild bird trade is a money maker for only a few big importers.

Importer Darrell Alexander spent six months in a Ghana jail after he was arrested on June 6, 1988 while trying to leave the country with 1,500 African grey parrots. He was jailed for conspiracy to commit a crime, committing acts detrimental to the welfare of the sovereign people of Ghana, attempted smuggling, corruption of a public officer and attempting to bribe a public officer. While in jail, he complained he "lost 70 pounds to an inadequate diet" and "suffered a great deal of stress"[41] — conditions pretty similar to those facing wild birds trapped for the trade!

My colleague Ann Michels and I provided technical assistance in an inspection of one shipment of birds into the U.S. The immediate concern to the U.S. Fish and Wildlife Service was that they make a correct identification of the species and an accurate count of the individual birds. Of concern also was compliance with humane transport regulations and USDA importation and quarantine requirements, especially as the birds were being tran-shipped via New York. A large number of birds had previously been lost in a shipment from Tanzania.

At around 6:00 a.m. we watched the shipment of 90 crates of birds arrive at New York's John F. Kennedy Airport on Air Afrique. The shipment included three consignments claimed to originate in Côte d'Ivoire, Cameroon and Guinea. The dealer accompanied the shipment. The crated birds were loaded on three pallets onto an open flat-bed truck. Approximately two-thirds of the crates contained red-tailed African grey parrots (*Psittacus erithacus erithacus*) and maroon-tailed African grey parrots (*Psittacus erithacus timneh*) — the rest were finches, softbills and zoo specimens, like owls, falcons and kingfishers. The crates obviously violated transport standards — most lacked sloping fronts to ensure adequate ventilation, none had suitable water containers and some birds had drowned in the water pots. The majority of parrots could not stand upright in their crates.

Because of dim lighting, the huddling behavior of the birds, and the fact that some of the birds were still juveniles, proper identification was nearly impossible. It made me realize the difficulty of the job for the few FWS inspectors who are sparsely distributed and face thousands of wildlife shipments each year. Identification of the species took over two hours. Meanwhile, not all the crates were secure, and at least two finches escaped as the shipment was being transported out of the cargo area, making something of a mockery of subjecting the rest of the birds to quarantine to prevent introduction of disease to the U.S.

The birds were then loaded onto a privately chartered DC-3. USDA inspectors remarked that the shipment should have been accompanied by USDA personnel to ensure that biosecurity was maintained. Instead, the dealer accompanied the shipment. The flight arrived in Chicago four hours later, and the crates were moved by conveyor belt to a truck. The birds appeared very stressed by the rough unloading and the transfer from the freezing, unheated interior of the plane to the warm, 80-degree air tempera-ture. Debris, including litter, food and droppings from the transport crates blew out of the crates as the truck moved down the highway, again making a mockery of biosecurity measures. The truck pulled up to the side door of the quarantine station, and employees unloaded the cargo. The station was a small warehouse. We attempted to enter the same side door, but were stopped by USDA personnel — they said we could not bring any cameras into the station because they were concerned about biosecurity. Eventually they relented but said we would have to disinfect the cameras before leaving. This seemed ludicrous given the other laxities.

Two ends of the crates containing finches were removed, and light bamboo poles were used to push them out, scattering the finches from inside the boxes. Once the birds were removed from the crates, it was impossible to accurately count them. The birds were constantly in motion and would cluster in the corners of the flights. Hours later, a second crate of finches was unloaded into each flight — many of the birds had no perching space because the flights were so crowded. By the end of the night, 24 hours after we had met the birds in New York, many of these small birds had escaped through holes in the wire mesh of the cages.

Three people began uncrating the African grey parrots, taking the top board of the crate off and reaching inside to pull the parrots out by their necks. It took hours to complete the unpacking. The crates had to be shaken to wrest the unwilling, growling parrots from their grip on the wire. Often the parrots would clamp their beaks to the thick gloves of the unpackers, who would shake the birds off and fling them into the corners of the cages. Unlike the older birds, the baby parrots had little ability to release their grip on the transport cages; this, along with poor capture and holding techniques, resulted in broken legs and torn ligaments. As these younger parrots were unpacked and placed on perches, many thumped to the ground as they lost their grip. One bird was completely unable to stand because of its injured legs. Later, this same bird, taking its last breaths, choked to death on food that was carelessly forced down its lungs.

Many of the parrots were too young to fly or feed themselves. The dealer said that they would learn to eat by example from the others. But by the end of the night, it was obvious that only some parrots had successfully found the soaked corn and were eating. Some of the baby birds huddled together tightly in the corners of the cages. Others seemed to lose any motivation to survive and just lay where they were. A severely ill bird sat on a perch with its head under its wing; this was one we knew would soon be picked up by USDA personnel and thrown into a plastic bag with other "losses."[42]

The dealer discussed the banding of birds in quarantine to prevent fraud. Though birds are required to be banded by the seventh day of quarantine, he told us he waited until a few days before their release to band them. He then removed the bands immediately after release from quarantine. He claimed if birds were banded any sooner, there would be a possibility of a band catching on the wire flight cages. He also claimed some species, such as cockatoos, react violently to being banded, sometimes chewing their own legs off.

The more unusual imported birds, including softbills, waterfowl and raptors, were then uncrated. The dealer personally dealt with the touracos, a bright blue colored pheasant-type bird; he yanked out all of their tail feathers to prevent the birds breaking any of these blood feathers inside the cages and becoming infected. These birds reacted violently to being caged, slipping off the perches and running directly into the sides of the enclosure. Eventually, a white sheet was placed over their cages to calm them.

The most striking birds were tiny electric blue Pygmy kingfishers; only two of the original six birds survived long enough to be uncrated. After being placed in the cage, one immediately fell into the food bowl of live insects. The bird was removed from the dish and propped up. The bird's head fell forward until its bill stuck in the wire bottom of the cage; it obviously wouldn't live long.

Although the dealer was happy that the overall mortality on arrival was low, a crate stuffed with red finch-like seedcrackers (*Pirenestes ostrinus*) suffered very high mortality. As a FWS agent unloaded handfuls of birds from the crate, I could see that close to half of them were dead. The remainder continued to suffer significant mortalities throughout the night. I have two overriding memories of that horrendous night. First was the unbelievable dust and noise. I was lucky enough to wear a mask the entire night, as the air was thick with fine dust from feathers and debris from the crates. Two people that did not wear masks later contracted psittacosis and were seriously ill until treated with antibiotics. The constant noise of more than 10,000 terrified birds left my ears ringing throughout the next day.

"Operation Renegade"

The Special Operations unit of the U.S. Interior Department's Fish and Wildlife Service (FWS) conducted a three- year "sting" resulting in indictments of six men and a woman who allegedly smuggled hundreds of cockatoo eggs worth over $1 million from Australia into the United States. Rose-breasted cockatoos, red-tailed black cockatoos, Major Mitchell cockatoos, and slender-billed cockatoos hatched from the eggs were sold to collectors. Australia strictly prohibits commercial exportation of all native birds and their eggs.

"Operation Renegade" is a continuing investigation into the international nature of the illicit trade in exotic birds. It has resulted in criminal convictions, including that of Richard Furzer, whose guilty plea was mentioned earlier.

Another of the biggest smugglers of African grey parrots, Elias K. Mantas, a/k/a Louie Mantas, was charged with conspiring to transport seven shipments in violation of the Lacey Act. Mantas allegedly smuggled the African Greys from Zaire, a country that strictly bans their export. He conspired with two different African suppliers, and FWS Special Operations obtained copies of the telex traffic, revelations from which are reprinted below.

In November 1988, Mantas telexed: "THE BIRDS ARRIVED LAST

NITE ON LH [Lufthansa]. THEY WERE STUCK IN FRANKFURT. THE BIRDS CAME IN REAL GOOD. (4 DEAD) OUR FAUNA PEOPLE ARE QUESTIONING THE PAPERS FROM U. AT THIS POINT WE DON'T KNOW IF THEY WILL ACCEPT THEM. PLS HV SUSAN FROM ABIDJAN CALL ME SO I CAN EXPLAIN IT TO HER."

In May 1989, Mantas's African supplier telexed: "I'VE JUST AR-RIVED FROM ZAIRE AND BURUNDI TO SEE MY TEAM OVER THERE AND SOLVE ALL PROBLEMS. NOW EVERYTHING IS OK.... I'LL BE ABLE TO SEND BIRDS NOW I THINK THE NEXT SHIPMENT OF 1,000 ZAIRE GREY WILL ABOUT ONE MONTH."

African grey parrots are listed by the Convention on International Trade in Endangered Species, and dealers need papers to make their birds seem to be legal. In August, Mantas telexed: "WHEN U SEND THE ZAIRE GREY, PLS SEND ALL ORIGINAL CITES FROM IVORY COAST WITH THE SHIPMENT. ALONG WITH THE RE EXPORT CITES FROM GUINEA." Later that month, Mantas telexed: "LET'S ONLY SEND 220 ZAIRE GREY TO SEE HOW THEY ACCEPT THE CITES HERE."

In a September telex, Mantas told a supplier: "OUR WILDLIFE AUTHORITIES SAW THE LETTER AND THEY THINK SOMETHING IS GOING ON THAT IS NOT CORRECT... AND THEY ARE CONCERNED THAT THE BIRDS HAVE COME FROM ZAIRE AND PAPERS FROM I. COAST AND SHIPPED FROM GUINEA. THE REASON FOR THEIR CON-CERN IS THAT RECENTLY IN MIAMI OVER 1100 AFRICAN GREY PARROTS WERE CONFISCATED BECAUSE OF THE SAME PROBLEM (AS YOU REMEMBER I WAS TELLING YOU ABOUT IT 2 MONTHS AGO). I DON'T UNDERSTAND WHY YOUR BROTHER SENT THAT LETTER WITH THE SHIPMENT AND MADE REFERENCE TO 'ZAIRE PARROTS.' NOW IT SEEMS WE MAY HAVE PROBLEMS."

Mantas's next telex in October stated: "FOR THE NEXT SHIPMENT WE WOULD NEED 600-700 ZAIRE GREY.... IF YOU SHIP FROM GUINEA MAKE SURE YOU SEND A ORIGINAL CITES FORM I. COAST AS LAST TIME. BUT PLEASE NO LETTERS THIS TIME."[43]

Each count of violations of Title 18, United States Code, is docu-mented for consideration by the judge.

Another major achievement of "Operation Renegade" was the 15-count indictment of Tony Silva, Gila Daoud (Silva's mother), and two other cohorts on charges of conspiracy to violate the provisions of the Convention on International Trade in Endangered Species, the Endangered Species Act, the Lacey Act and several foreign wildlife protective laws. The indictment covered a six-and-a-half year period and the smuggling of many highly endangered psittacine (parrot) species, as well as one count of smuggling elephant ivory. According to FWS, many of the birds — which had allegedly been stuffed into plastic pipes to evade detection—died of suffocation.

In one case, the defendants smuggled 186 hyacinth macaws, valued at over $1.3 million. Wild hyacinth macaws are only found in Bolivia, Brazil, and Paraguay, and no more than 5,000 of the birds are thought to remain in the wild. Capture for the pet trade is a major factor in the collapse of wild populations. It is estimated that 90% of smuggled parrots die between their point of capture and final destination.

Silva, a purported parrot conservationist, has written several books and hundreds of articles on breeding rare parrots. For three years, Silva was Curator of Birds at Loro Parque (Parrot Park) in the Spanish Canary Islands. Meanwhile, his mother allegedly managed the family smuggling operation.

Silva pleaded guilty to the charges in February 1996. He was fined $100,000 and sentenced to 82 months in prison without the possibility of parole. The judge also ordered him to perform 200 hours of community service during a 3-year supervised release program subsequent to his prison term. Gila Daoud was sentenced to 27 months in prison to be followed by a one-year supervised release and 200 hours of community service.

To date, "Operation Renegade" has led to the convictions of 30 individuals on charges of parrot smuggling.[44]

Europe

A lot less information is available on the activities of European bird traders than their U.S. counterparts. This is for a number of reasons. There is no Freedom of Information Act in the European Community. Many countries do not even collect rudimentary data on non-CITES species imported or mortality levels in trade. There is no legislation like the U.S. Lacey Act whereby U.S. nationals can be prosecuted for violating the wildlife laws of other countries. Few European countries have put serious efforts into investigating the illegal activities of bird traders. Sting operations, by far the most effective way of infiltrating smuggling rings, are not used. Most countries do not have special, dedicated enforcement agencies like the U.S. Fish and Wildlife Service Division of Law Enforcement.

A notable exception is the Netherlands. There, the General Inspection Service of the Ministry of Agriculture has conducted a number of detailed investigations into the illegal wild bird trade and has pioneered new techniques, such as the use of DNA fingerprinting, to expose false captive breeding claims. I dubbed one such investigation "The Maltese Parrot." The routes and ruses used in this operation resembled the twists and turns in the plot of the famous film concerning another Maltese bird. Two Dutch traders, Jan Van der Gulik and Peter Koy, had been bringing a number of endangered bird species into the Netherlands, declaring them as "captive-bred" in

Malta. In fact, the Maltese breeding station was no more than a holding facility. Malta was not a member of CITES at that time, and the birds, originating in Paraguay and Papua New Guinea, among other places, were sent to Singapore, then Malta, then into the Netherlands. .

Conclusion

In this chapter I have discussed just a few of the abuses carried out by some of the biggest international bird dealers. These are a few of the individuals who have shaped the nature of the contemporary wild bird trade. Many, many more abuses have undoubtedly gone unreported. Many exporters and importers have not been mentioned due to lack of information, the Europeans and Asians in particular. From my experience, the bird dealers at both ends of the trade are adept at avoiding controls of all sorts. There are strong financial incentives for them to do this, and regulation attempts are always underfunded.

Recently, there have been attempts to reform rather than end the commercial wild bird trade, to make it more "sustainable." The ostensible justification for this is that the trade may be able to generate conservation benefits by giving incentives to conserve species and habitats. I am very skeptical that a wild bird trade could achieve these goals or even be effectively regulated and still be commercially profitable. Even if this were possible, the conservation benefits would also have to outweigh the costs of inhumane treatment, which I believe inevitable in the trade, whether it is cruel trapping methods or the longer-term cruelty of keeping a wild bird caged.

In this sustainable dream, there is no room for the big dealers of the world to take their cut. Their entrepreneurial role introduces the short-term profit motive that leads to overexploitation, overcrowding and other cost-cutting at the expense of the animals. Unfortunately, much of the effort to reform the trade has involved negotiating with traders and accommodating them rather than starting from a conservation perspective. I believe such an approach is doomed to failure and will only perpetuate the problems and cruelty, while generating no conservation benefits.

Europe, the United States, Australia, most of Africa and South and Central America, and most Asian countries have all banned export of their own wild birds for the pet trade. Only a dozen or so countries still have a commercial trade. Hypocritically, the wealthy countries still continue to import from some of the countries least able to regulate a wild bird trade. The trade is highly profitable for a few individuals precisely because they cut corners at every stage. For every rule there is an abuse, and such abuse is widely practiced.

Those who still advocate maintaining the wild bird trade at a "sustainable" level should look more closely at the track record. The reality is that traders are expert at avoiding any regulations, and there will never exist proper resources to police such a far-flung business. We need to eliminate demand for wild-caught birds as pets through education and enforceable legislation and look to captive breeding to supply any birds for the pet trade. The mass trade in wild-caught birds for the pet trade will always result in unacceptable cruelty and has a built-in tendency to drive species towards extinction.

On my last overseas trip to research the bird trade in Ghana in 1994, I received two new perspectives on the trade. While attempting to film wild African grey parrots (*Psittacus erithacus*) in a beautiful raffia palm swamp in Côte d'Ivoire, a young man out hunting bush meat approached me. I remarked there were markedly less parrots than I had seen in the swamp two years before. He told me there were once clouds and clouds of parrots there and that while some of the local villagers had wanted to set up a park in the swamp to protect the parrots and receive tourists, some of the local boys had trapped the birds heavily. When I asked the reason for the parrots' decline, he dourly replied, "The whites like parrots."

Later in the trip, I was privileged to meet the President of Ghana, Flight Lieutenant Gerry Rawlings. President Rawlings is a keen advocate of environmental protection in Ghana, despite the financial pressures faced by the country. He shared my misgivings towards the parrot trade. In addition to his concern for Ghana's wild birds, he was concerned with how the trade affected human beings. He appealed to people in the West who buy parrots not to put trappers through the degradation of having to trap and abuse animals because of their poverty.

Notes

1. Vriends, M.M., *The Macdonald Encyclopedia of Cage and Aviary Birds*, Macdonald and Co., Ltd., London, England, 1985.

2. Banks, R.C., "Wildlife Importation into the United States 1900-1972," Bureau of Sports Fisheries and Wildlife, Fish and Wildlife Service, U.S. Department of the Interior, Washington, DC, 1976.

3. Michels, Ann, "Petition to Suspend Trade with Indonesia under the Wild Bird Conservation Act," Environmental Investigation Agency, London, 1994.

4. Wirth, R., "Indonesia," in *PsittaScene*, Vol. 3, No. 4, November 1991, World Parrot Trust.

5. Thomsen, J., Edwards, S. and Mulliken, T. (eds.), "Perceptions, Conservation and Management of Wild Birds in Trade," TRAFFIC International, Cambridge, 1992.

6. Wirth, "Indonesia."

7. Nash, Stephen V., "Concern About Trade in Red-and-Blue Lories," *TRAFFIC Bulletin*, Vol. 13, No. 3, 1993.

8. Ibid.

9. Carter, Nick and Currey, Dave, *The Trade in Live Wildlife, Mortality and Transport Conditions*, Environmental Investigation Agency, London, 1987.

10. Melville, D., "Bird Conservation in Hong Kong," paper presented at the ICBP Asian Section and Asian Bird Protection Conference, Bangkok, Thailand, 1989.

11. Nash, Stephen V., "Sold for a Song, TRAFFIC Southeast Asia, The Trade in Southeast Asian Non-CITES Birds," 1993.

12. Knights, Peter, "Wild Bird Imports for the Pet Trade, An EEC Overview," Environmental Investigation Agency, London, 1990.

13. Ibid.

14. Nilsson, Greta, *Importation of Birds into the United States in 1985*, Animal Welfare Institute, Washington, DC, 1989.

15. Taylor, John B., "A Status Survey of Seram's Endemic Avifauna," 1990.

16. Baker, N., personal communication, ICBP, Tanzania, 11-1-92.

17. Michels, "Petition."

18. Ibid.

19. Ibid.

20. Anon., "The Wild Bird Trade, Investigative Reports from Africa, South America, South-East Asia," compiled by Royal Society for the Prevention of Cruelty to Animals/Royal Society for the Protection of Birds/Environmental Investigation Agency, London, 1991.

21. Department of the Interior press release, February 1994.

22. Linden, E., "Can animals think?" *Time*, March 22, 1993.

23. "Implementation of Tanzania's New Policy on Trade in Live Birds," *TRAFFIC Bulletin*, 15(2):83-89, March 1995.

24. "Congress urged to halt import of exotic birds," *USA Today*, June 5, 1993.

25. Nilsson, Greta, *Importation of Birds into the United States, 1989*, Defenders of Wildlife, Washington, DC, 1992.

26. U.S. Department of Justice press release, January 30, 1995.

27. David Lyons, "Importer admits guilt in parrot scheme," *The Miami Herald*, 30 April 1997.

28. Ibid.

29. U.S. Department of Justice, Indictment of Richard Furzer, February 7, 1992.

30. "An End to the Wild Bird Trade Draws Closer, Transport Deaths Remain High," *The Animal Welfare Institute Quarterly*, Vol. 40, No. 3, Fall 1991, p. 5, Animal Welfare Institute, Washington, DC.

31. "Six booked in drug ring: Police linked," *Miami Herald*, December 17, 1987.

32. Ibid.

33. Ibid.

34. Ibid.

35. Ibid.

36. Nilsson, *Importation of Birds... 1989*.

37. *Los Angeles Times*, San Diego edition, November 18, 1989.

38. *Los Angeles Times*, July 3, 1987.

39. Nilsson, *Importation of Birds... 1989.*

40. *TRAFFIC Bulletin*, Vol. 13, No. 2, August 1994.

41. *Foothill Leader*, Glendale, CA, December 21, 1988.

42. Michels, Ann, "A Deadly Trip for Wild-Caught Birds," *The Animal Welfare Institute Quarterly*, Vol. 41, No. 2, Spring 1992, p. 4, Animal Welfare Institute, Washington, DC.

43. "'OPERATION RENEGADE,' U.S. Fish and Wildlife Service Undercover Investigation," *AWI Quarterly*, Vol. 43, No. 2, Spring 1994, p. 13, Animal Welfare Institute, Washington, DC.

44. O'Connor, Matt, "U.S. says bird expert a smuggler," *Chicago Tribune*, December 14, 1994.

Chapter 14

The Shelf Life of Reptiles

by Clifford Warwick

Introduction

Picture a sea turtle swimming through the tropical waters of Indonesia. Next, it is harpooned through its shell, then hauled on board a boat, turned onto its back and left to the full heat of the day. Struggling in fear at its vulnerability and in pain from its injuries, the creature becomes one of up to two hundred that may be collected and stored thus for two weeks as the trawler gathers its harvest. Dehydration, hyperthermia and capture-related damage will result in some deaths, but, perhaps regrettably, many will survive to endure the next stage in their story.

Arriving at the water's edge, pierced through their flippers and bound with leather straps, the turtles — many weighing 200-300 pounds — are thrown two to three meters from the boat to the beach below. The giant reptiles are suspended on poles placed under their tethered limbs and carried to the coastal markets. This *arribada* seems as close as possible to testudinian hell. Upside-down they stay until buyers turn up for their flesh, but not all at once! Meat is carved off the bone — and the live animal — to the amount required. To kill the turtles would risk having their carcasses deteriorate in the warm climate. Reptilian metabolism being what it is, the effects of blood loss and general trauma are slower, but no less stressful, and the animal "goes on living." Purchasers wanting eggs or meat from inside the turtle wait as the plastron (its underside) is cut away. The panicking reptile struggles yet more. Of course, all is hopeless. When the plastron is removed, the internal organs, including the beating heart and the turtle's own investment in the future — its clutch of eggs — are exposed. Eggs are pulled out and yet more muscle is sliced away, but things will not end here. There is still more animal to sell, and the living turtle will offer testimony to the freshness of its meat. Often, what remains is a gasping head attached to a completely scooped-out shell. Death will probably come within the hour.

So ends their encounter with man.

Now, if you have not already done so, you might ask yourself what all this has to do with international trade in reptiles as pets? It all has to do with perceptions of suffering and injustice. As hard to believe as it may be, the turtle story is a true one, and its misery is realized thousands of times every year. In fact, this account understates the extent of the suffering sustained by these animals. It would, of course, be impossible to understand just what torment really occurs. Anyway, unless you happen to be a turtle slaughterer yourself (in which case you might just shrug your shoulders), or happen to be a government bureaucrat (in which case you defend the practice immediately while stating your neutrality), you will understandably frown somewhat, wince and shake your head in dismay. If you actually witnessed the brutalities themselves, you may feel stricken with grief or anger or both. But be dispassionate? Almost certainly not.

The chances of causing a similar emotional response in a reader by reciting the life of a caged reptile, especially if that animal is a lizard or a snake, are typically rather slim. Apart from the sheer blood and guts aspect with the sea turtle scenario, the routine brutality involved seems worse than anything normally thought associated with the pet animal trade. But this perception is quite wrong. Unfortunately, save for the occasional media expose depicting consignments of dead animals, the relatively benign appearance of the exotic animal market is one of the greatest obstacles faced by those trying to gain support for reptile protection. No doubt the pet keepers would be as disturbed as others when hearing of the fate of many marine chelonians. It may, though, be hard to convince the same people that they are guilty of imposing comparable inhumanities their own charges. Possibly unthinkable even! A reasonable appreciation of reptilian biology and behavior, and of their special sensitivity to abuse, might allow otherwise cold observers to develop a chill in the spine should they witness and understand the suffering inherent in the pet trade.

It would be rather simple to collate a tomb of statistics on reptile trade. It would also be rather redundant. Such data can all too easily detract from the most important focus — the individual. Therefore, "numbers" will receive little attention here. The aims of this chapter are to attempt to provide some insights into the market system in which reptiles are forced and the way in which species and ecology conservation are always compromised by trade. Also, an attempt is made to refute the erroneous claims perpetuated by the live animal industry. Most importantly, this chapter will show why the inhumanities reptiles endure in the pet industry warrant no less sympathy than the tortured turtles of Indonesia.

National and international "controls": legitimizing fraud

If international legislation such as the Convention on International Trade in Endangered Species (CITES) were actually enforced properly, a great deal more protection would be afforded wildlife. As it stands, CITES is arguably as much a millstone around the necks of wildlife protectionists as it is a tool for wildlife protection.

Basically, under the current system, responsibility for protection is up to wildlife organizations or concerned individuals which happen to receive or stray onto a lead implying trade-related take of wildlife. Next, research for confirmation must be started, locations established, field investigations made and reports written, produced and disseminated. Months or years usually elapse between the time an issue is discovered and the time you have the data to show there is a problem. Frequently, this is just the beginning. Ahead lie the daunting tasks of making representations to governments and their formal advisors. Often a proposal to protect wildlife is received with a response such as, "Oh, not another one." Commonly, evaluation of data is conducted by a panel of "experts" with little or no direct experience in the subjects at stake.

After "careful consideration" of the proponent's hard-won material, the "scientific" authority of the respective nation brushes aside the findings and frequently requests more data. Then follows a few more months of study and another report. A second proposal is made two years later at the next conference of the parties; this proposal may well receive the same treatment as the first. It seems most likely to happen where the trade is at its biggest and where money is at stake! For poorly qualified government officials, handing out wildlife trade licenses is much easier than reading scientific reports. Thus, the whole system is weighted against the proposer of protection and in favor of the trader. It might not be so bad if the other legislative systems were more effective.

Even if a nation accepts the proposal, it may not be voted on for inclusion in the appendices. Also, getting a species listed will in no way ensure that it will receive tough protection. In many instances, it is a protection on paper only. If placed on the premiere list, general trade is prohibited, but it goes on anyway.

There is no government mechanism for routine monitoring of trade, so it will again be up to the concerned group or individual to chase up the whole matter when the violations start. With less than 5% of consignments being inspected through customs of the more ambitious nations, it is a near certainty that dealers can say what they want on declaration forms with little risk of the shipment even being inspected, let alone questioned. The diversity of species in trade makes proper identification of legal and illegal species difficult even for experienced individuals—border inspectors can hardly be expected to carry out a thorough check. In most cases of proven violations, local or central governments fail to take legal action, so the species' inclusion in the legislation is far from satisfactory. Enforcement is more a case of chance than anything else. Species put on secondary lists of "regulated" trade fare no better, since, in reality, "regulated" trade amounts to free trade.

All this time, however, wildlife traders are in full swing, swallowing up as much of nature as possible, knowing the government mechanisms for wildlife conservation will be giving the real animal protectionists a hard time. Often, by the time the conservationist's report is produced, the situation has changed and the work is out-of-date, or the traders have already decimated the species and ecology and have moved on to something else—starting the whole dubious system once more.

At every stage, wildlife protection is dependent on conservation and animal welfare groups and individuals. These sources are, of course, primarily dependent on public donations for their work. Money and time are often in short supply, but these groups must somehow stretch themselves still more to accomplish their goals. So, charities and well-meaning individuals carry both the responsibility and costs for trade regulation that should be borne by commerce and government, while animal dealers get a completely free ride. Indeed, some years ago I interviewed a notorious animal trader who told me that the best protection he had to guarantee his continued dealing in illegal and endangered species was the U.K.'s Department of the Environment. At the time, the statement seemed curious. It now seems correct.

An illustrative example is offered by the case of the red-eared turtle, or slider. Of course, as almost any American knows, the red-eared trade was banned in the U.S. in 1975 following the discovery of turtle-related salmonellosis in humans, estimated to affect 270,000-plus people per year. Although import of turtles into the States was banned, export wasn't, even though there is no scientific evidence to show that non-Americans are immune to the consequences of Salmonella bacteria!

At this point a minor digression is warranted, because the human health risks from the exotic pet trade are worth considering. Actually, "foreigners" do suffer from the same "pet" associated diseases that Americans suffer from. Several countries have instituted turtle import bans of their own to safeguard human health.

In the UK, a rather peculiar situation emerged on the "Salmonella-in-turtles" front. There are scientific reports of people developing turtle-related salmonellosis, and one might think this would be enough for action from a nation with such pride in its health service, but realists know better. These realists, incidentally, include the government's own scientific advisors at the Public Health Laboratory Service, who stated they were worried about the threats to humans from turtles and wanted the trade banned. Needless to say, the Department of Health (DoH) ignored, and continues to ignore, the warnings. Perhaps the formal scientific recommendations were too unequivocal for the British government's liking. It is difficult to know precisely because, when pressed strongly, the DoH decided to call a halt to correspondence by simply not answering it.

This subtle tactic was perhaps learned from the UK's Department of the Environment, especially notorious for its incompetence in protecting any form of life other than its work force—assuming they are alive! Finally, recent evidence has shown that threats to human health are greater from lizards and snakes than from turtles. This issue may yet prove to cause a few political upsets, let alone many seriously upset digestive systems.

Digression over! Red-eared sliders have been a heavily traded species of reptile in the pet market for decades—even since the U.S. ban. Around 6-7 million are exported from the States annually to over 30 countries. The animals sold are actually babies, produced on ranches in the southern U.S. from captive adults. For years, the system was presumed to be closed-cycle, and thus self-sustaining.

In the early 1980s, however, it was discovered that the adult breeder stock was actually being supplemented continually from wild populations. At this time, the collection of wild turtles was estimated at around 100,000 animals per year. Disturbing news for various reasons, but particularly so from a conservation standpoint, because the fact that the trade targets adults—here, mainly females—means that humans are preying on the species' most ecologically important group of individuals. Reports from biologists, traders and hunters were clear: the species was now scarce in many areas, very scarce in others, and some populations were no longer viable.

With concern about the slider's status gaining momentum, the International Wildlife Coalition prepared a proposal, including numerous opinions from experts, and submitted it to the Fish and Wildlife Service (FWS), the U.S.'s scientific authority for CITES, in 1986. The case was actually a strong one, but the proposal was rejected for lack of evidence, despite the same evidence having been sufficiently credible for publication in a scientific journal. Two more years of unabated trade ensued while other leads indicating existence of a large additional trade in the turtles as food for humans were followed. An Asian-American population on the U.S. West Coast and an export market to the Far East had been identified by, of all people, U.S. Customs officials who were regularly seeing the shipments — bound for the Orient to be boiled alive.

Another investigation was conducted by Southeastern Louisiana University, which studied several known exploited and non-exploited populations and interviewed turtle ranchers about their production practices. The report confirmed earlier accounts of altered populations and concluded that 33% of ranch breeder stock was replaced annually with wild individuals to compensate for losses. Poor housing, bacterial infections and disease were suggested as major causes of mortalities, giving rise to the collection of free-roaming animals. The 33% figure was particularly worrying because the previous estimate of 100,000 turtles coming from the wild each year was based on a 10% supplementation from nature.

This implied that potentially 300,000 prime breeder turtles were leaving nature for the dirty, crowded ponds of the farms. An obligatory "call for comments" was announced by the U.S. Department of the Interior in the Federal Register, whereby all interested parties can record their views on the worthiness of proposals. Two hundred and thirty-seven comments were received. Of these, 235, originating mainly from herpetologists, biologists and conservationists, were in support of the red-ear receiving CITES status. Many of the respondents presented yet more convincing accounts and data showing the seriousness of the threat to the turtles. Just two individuals wanted the proposal turned down, neither of whom offered any data to support their positions. Surely, all this new and respectable evidence, substantial anecdotal material and general support would do the trick for the second presentation in 1988.

This time the proposal was twofold: one in the U.K. and the other in the U.S. Pessimism about having any luck with the U.K. authorities was on target as always. An officer at the (then) Nature Conservancy Council in Britain once told me that he had just a week to read 80 CITES proposals so probably could not give the red-ear turtle issue much time. Not surprisingly, the U.K. did not accept the red-ear case. Nice to know it received a fair hearing! Things now rested with the American attempt.

After initial (perhaps artificial) enthusiasm from the Fish and Wildlife Service, the proposal was rejected, and so never reached the conference to receive a vote. Why? It emerged that the FWS made a series of late communications to individuals and organizations to seek "confirmation" of the proposal's standing. This it received from its contacts, except for the World-Wide Fund for Nature's "Traffic" office, which, after consultation with colleagues in one Asian location, was unable to confirm the food trade to that area. After much effort, the FWS had found one source that happened to possess no data to support the proposal, an insignificant item in anyone's book, but quite sufficient for the Service to excuse its way out of adopting the proposal. All along, FWS had given the impression that it would most likely accept the proposal, which led to a false sense of security within the conservation community. What's more, the International Wildlife Coalition learned the proposal had been turned down only two days before the closure date for submissions, far too late to contest FWS' position. One could smell the fish in Fish and Wildlife.

The red-eared turtle example is by no means an anomaly. It is really rather typical. The whole problem lies in the fact that, no matter what the rhetoric, so-called conservation legislation has endemic to its operation the presumption of trade, and any benefits of doubt are given to marketeers, not wildlife. This is echoed in the jumped-up nonsense that is otherwise known as "sustainable utilization" (S.U.). Clearly, the term here offers an impression that wildlife trade is never-ending and therefore presents no threat to the structure and stability of the target species in its ecological system. However, generally heard references to S.U. roughly regard it to mean the take of a species in a manner compatible with its survival. Here "survival" implies a greatly reduced, and effectively severely harmed, population. In practice, so long as a government bureaucrat is willing to believe that enough individuals of a species are "out there somewhere" to reproduce, things aren't all that bad! Wrong.

For a start, any human predation (wildlife collection in this case) from outside a long-established ecological rhythm involving indigenous "man" is already an extra stress on population status. Biological populations are known for their delicate sensitivities and for their fluctuations in densities and structure, as well as for the natural controls that enable a population to remain stable.

An outline of the diverse and interrelated factors that regulate ecology would be optimistic for this chapter, but a couple of examples might at least convey the necessary message. Few people realize just how dramatically even a minor disturbance can affect wildlife. For example, during a study of lizard behavior in Costa Rica, it was noted that eye contact alone between the iguanas and observers was sufficiently alarming to dissuade the reptiles from returning to their normally prized arboreal perches for the remaining several days of the research. Because these lizards develop social structures and such a congregation site may be important to breeding arrangements, it is conceivable that a seemingly minute event could alter the former organization in the population. If such a site was a favorite, perhaps this is partly because it allows better avoidance of predators? In which case, have members of the population been pressured into facing greater threats of being killed? Certainly, these concerns lean toward fearing the worst, but they are not unrealistic.

It is becoming increasingly clear that the stability and genetic integrity of a population can be dependent on only one or two individuals among several hundred. Consequently, it is simply not possible to even enter a species' natural habitat, let alone remove a single individual, and have reason to believe that no harm is being done.

Disturbingly, when asked to produce any scientific data whatsoever to demonstrate that sustainable utilization, even as they see it, can work and is reliable in the exotic pet trade, governments consistently fail to do so. In fact, both the U.S. Fish and Wildlife Service and the U.K.'s Department of the Environment have been unable to cite a single successful example. Worse, this thoroughly shameful situation contrasts dramatically with the fact that thousands of examples exist of S.U. not only failing to materialize, but resulting in definite species and ecological damage. The sustainable utilization principle just doesn't work. It is a cover for resource exhaustion in a commercial world, and rather than save wildlife, S.U. merely saves it for dealers.

Captive breeding: better for whom?

Contrary to the claims and expectations of a naive few that "home-grown" stocks would decrease pressures on natural populations, the trade in wild-caught animals has actually increased since captive breeding has become more successful. This is no surprise to those who are familiar with the effects of trade on wildlife, but is, no doubt, an unpleasant discovery to those who genuinely believed they could reduce harm.

Captive breeding reptiles to improve supply sustainability or help conserve free-roaming populations has a variety of detrimental effects. Producing animals in large numbers from a repeatable source should mean that capture, handling, transport and like stresses from nature to captivity are avoided, and direct pressure on natural populations is reduced. Despite the superficial appeal of captive breeding, it falls flat on its face at every turn. For a start, the "We do it for conservation" claim is a little overplayed, because many dealers simply prefer the convenience and, at least initially, perceive better health of commercially reared animals. Popularization of the industry does more than extend the market in captive-bred animals. Increased trade activity refines routes for traffic generally in wild-caught animals, as well as in illegal and endangered species. Wildlife trade is merely masked by captive breeding, not replaced by it.

Often dealers state that animals are captive-bred either to hide the fact that it is a species for which being wild-caught would constitute an offense, or because a local authority refuses to permit any wild-caught animals in its jurisdiction. In many cases, the legal obligation is on the claimants to prove the origin of their stock. Such testimony can be checked in several ways, including requesting detailed documentary evidence of a generic tree or a genetic fingerprint examination. However, claims that animals are captive-bred are rarely challenged and almost never tested — and traders know it. So, what carries a captive-bred label may easily be wild-caught.

Apart from making "off-the-shelf" animals even more readily available and less respected, captive breeding is bad for a variety of additional reasons. Mass-production methods involve highly restrictive facilities. Production practices also result in many developmental anomalies. Experimental incubation techniques frequently lead to the birth of animals who are afflicted with grotesque physical malformations. Often it is incidental — still nasty if you happen to be the animal — but frequently it is a deliberate creation of curiosities, and hybrids occur, commonly with pathetic results. Individuals are not the only ones at risk either.

The diversity of crossbreeds, popular genetic lines and many of those other results of "artificial selection" means that an enormous number of "unnatural" reptiles are "out there." Both through intentional sales and exchanges between private enthusiasts and formal zoological collections, these animals have worked their way into probably many, if not all, establishments that are contemplating releasing animals back to nature. The scientific and ethical credibility of species reintroduction programs has to be seriously questioned during the best of times, but more so when it is not at all clear exactly what one could be releasing. Pet keepers who become bored with their charges or just can't manage them anymore commonly don't even think about such things.

And the "control" answer?

Predictably, what governments are always looking for are compromises. This is the image that wildlife trade "agreements" (don't forget, the utilized "resource" has no direct voice) want to foster. CITES and other legislation can tap popular acceptance by appearing to be reasonable compromises between commerce and nature. Compromises generally suggest that all parties will benefit fairly. Not in the wildlife market, though. Here, "compromises" among governments, protectionists (quite a few actually trying to protect wildlife properly) and wildlife traders amount to no more than the exploiters being offered less than they planned to take anyway. And that's being generous, so to speak! Dictionaries the world over should clarify the definition of "compromise" and state, "except where commercial exploitation of nature occurs." Compromises compromise wildlife.

Well, there is always the decent and correct thing. Banning all animal commerce for the speculative markets would be a good start. Short of this, what mechanism should appeal to governments, permit trade and offer seemingly infinitely improved assurances for wildlife protection—wild-caught or captive-bred? Simple, it is called the "reverse-" or "green-list" principle. Under this system, absolutely no trade of any kind is permitted until it has been proven safe.

First, this would mean that any commercial interest with a target resource in mind would be required to apply to a central body for permission to research trade viability—before there's even a hint of trade. No more chasing around rumors and contacts to track but a fraction of trade.

Second, automatically a record is obtained on who is even contemplating doing what, and where. No more guesswork on who the "movers" are behind a particular sector of the market.

Third, if research is allowed, dealers must fund, from their own pockets, truly independent research into the status and potential exploitability of a species or population. The investigators would be composed of proper specialists, whose work, whatever their findings, then adds to our overall knowledge of ecology—and often needs financial support anyway! No more struggling to compile reports with little time and little money.

Fourth, a report stating that trade would be harmful would be the end of the matter. Trade prospectors will have lost their investment. No different from drilling for oil, or carrying out product research in the high street. No more trade!

Fifth, where trade is approved, it can be predetermined and continuously monitored by the inspectors. Should any doubts occur later, the investigators can call a halt. No more cursing the lack of any scrutiny and immediate "on the ground" action.

Sixth, if there are serious disputes—not that animal dealers are in any way qualified to counter scientists—appeals can be made. Of course, the inspectors' costs during such a contest (or if on any occasion government fails to take the experts' recommendations and the inspectors' wish to appeal) should originate from administration resources. This way, the "good guys" are not without the resources to act, and the bad guys are dissuaded from making routine, deliberately troublesome appeals—it will cost them either way. No more being given the run-around by government departments.

Seventh, money from trade subscribers also could be used to provide strict oversight of the "captive breeding" side of the business. All those planning to trade would have to demonstrate conclusively that their stocks are entirely captive-derived. No more slipping through the nets to freedom for traders here.

All this refinement in monitoring brings with it the mechanism for actually doing something about animal welfare. At all points and through all procedures, animal health and welfare can be watched closely by specialists who know what they are looking for. Welfare officers, like the inspecting ecologists, can authorize immediate cessation of activities when concern arises for both wild-caught and captive-bred animals.

As indicated earlier, the entire system would be paid for through lump-sum fees for initial viability studies, general levies on trade, and importer/exporter and pet shop licenses. Because about half of all wildlife trade may be illegal, the industry can hardly claim to be composed of "honest, tax-paying citizens entitled to all this for free." No more charities and decent folk picking up the burdens and bills for environmentally destructive, inhumane, unethical and illegal businesses.

All these gains for simply saying, "Sorry, no trade until you show us it's safe, and pay for the work," is hardly radical. None of this affects genuine scientific (non-trade-related) wildlife research. If at any point a violation occurs, a criminal investigation should be mandatory, and penalties that are comparable to those involving serious drug-running should be imposed.

A few more misconceptions

Popular misconceptions about reptiles are historical problems that seem to be slowly diminishing. However, through poor education or downright charlatanism, animal dealers perpetuate misinterpretations, mistakes and outright lies about their industry. Unfortunately, "A lie is half-way round the world before the truth has got its boots on"! Misunderstandings result in people comforting themselves with convenient excuses when their consciences challenge them over their participation in the live-animal market. Among the nonsense brought up by the pet trade with tedious inevitability are the following:

"Being caught from the wild is no different than being caught by a predator."

There is a big difference between a reptile being captured by a human and being taken by a natural predator. While humans can be considered predators to a point, in fact, at the point of seizure, a prey reptile will be killed quickly. The period from threat perception to death will be quite quick. A trade-caught reptile will commonly be handled (often abusively), deposited into a sack, box or other container, carted around for some time (even days), stored in sheds under metal sheeting, face more handling and be transported to and stored in different facilities—without food, water or shelter from climatic extremes. This assumes the reptile has not languished for some time already in a net or trap. That is just a sample.

It is becoming increasingly clear from scientific analyses (and some common sense) that even a single, gentle handling experience with a familiar keeper can cause a serious stress response in reptiles. Now, try to compare a natural predator-prey capture sequence with an animal collector's, which must effectively seem like a lifetime in fear of safety to the caught animal. Very often a lifetime is what it proves to be, because many deteriorate and die "on-site."

"It's a cruel world; a life in captivity is better than one of predation and deprivation in the wild."

The apparently gruesome, "cruel" attacks of predators on their prey are not what they seem. For some years, data have been emerging that outline biological systems in nature that actually block the prey's psychological stress and physical pain as the attack occurs. In captivity, this mechanism is frequently compromised or rendered ineffective. The "concern" for those reptiles being caught by predators is a little rich to swallow when the same dealers advise placing a live rat or rabbit in with the python!

Also, captivity stress is very different from stress in nature. Even if one considers the scenario of a reptile facing a period of drought and starvation in the wild, the animal is in an environment with which it has evolved and is biologically equipped to cope. Being on home ground, the animal has around it a diversity of normal mind- and behavior-occupying stimuli that undoubtedly add an extremely important dimension to life quality. In captivity, animals typically are bombarded with stressors, including imposed drought and starvation through inadequate husbandry, but have few or none of the essential psychological and behavioral "distractions" and safeguards integral to the natural world. Given the choice, would a human die at home of natural causes, or in a death camp of unnatural ones. Anyway, you had the choice!

"Few reptiles die in shipping."

Perhaps surprisingly, this is not exactly inaccurate inasmuch as some observers have concluded that the great majority of reptiles tend to arrive alive after 24- to 48-hour shipping routes. Birds and mammals may commonly end up with 30-100% shipping mortalities for the same journeys.

That said, 50-100% mortalities from dehydration, malnutrition, and severe parasite infestations, as well as crushing injuries leading to internal damage, blood-loss, and even the bones of animals piercing through their shells from the extreme compression of being piled on top of each other, among many other things, still arise during storage and transport and are by no means rare. That comparatively more reptiles than some other animals might survive particular journeys is, then, only part of the story.

However, the reason for this apparent resilience in reptiles is not that they enjoy foreign travel or that they are unaffected by the same traumas that cause the downfall of so many other animals. It is because their low metabolic rate results in the slow development of disease. Indeed, their particular metabolism means that in some respects, due to the thermal changes that are imposed during shipping, including the poorly regulated cargo holds of aircraft, they face special stresses that likely will add to their already considerable trauma burden. Follow a consignment of reptiles for a few months after their arrival, and you will see their abnormal behavior and watch their injuries fester and the diseases rampage through their bodies. You will then see them die in droves. What is more, diseases in captivity are almost invariably diseases of captivity. The multitude of latent stresses will surface somewhere.

"Animals live longer in captivity than in nature."

People often say that reptiles live longer in captivity than in the wild. But this cannot honestly be said either. First, we don't know just how long reptiles actually live in nature; very few studies have been made in this area. Where they have been made, data are very varied. For the red-eared turtle, some studies suggest a life span of 15 years in the wild, others 75 years. Both conceivably are correct because longevity may be "localized" to specific ecologies. Second, the belief that reptiles live longer in captivity fails to take account of the heavy mortalities from unnatural causes known in captivity. A glance through the now many glossily illustrated pathology books and at the horrendous morbidities contained therein should offer an appropriate glimpse at the common end result of captivity.

"If reptiles were not content with captivity they would not breed, feed or grow."

Not true. Plenty of evidence is freely available to show that reptiles who are reproductively active, "good" feeders, and "good" growers suffer a catalogue of disease and trauma, regularly fatally so. Not only that, but many diseases are directly related to the reproductive, feeding and growth tendencies the animal managers so cherish.

"Reptiles do not notice their captivity anyway."

For some years, studies have been accumulating evidence of environmental awareness in reptiles. A reptile's recognition of surroundings is not really that different from any other animal's, including human's. Indeed, reptiles demonstrate remarkable sensitivities towards alterations in their world. Reptilian senses identify, for instance, even subtle chemical, seismic, tactile and visual changes with great precision.

Sensory and psychological perception is not the only way that reptiles notice they are not where they should be. Physical differences between nature and captivity, such as amount and rhythm of temperature, light and humidity and environments that do not permit normal behaviors, or environments lacking appropriate stimuli, among others, all present stressors that are either psychologically or biologically noticed. For example, studies have shown an enormous, highly naturalistic environment will surely lead to more positive environmental and co-occupant interaction and far greater health.

The problem, then, is that observers do not notice reptiles noticing captivity.

"Reptiles do not need much space or diversity."

Range studies of reptiles in nature have made clear that these animals are by no means inactive. In fact, not by a long way. Turtles, tortoises, lizards and snakes frequently wander distances measured in hundreds of meters or kilometers per day. Another surprise is that the small species and baby animals often are as active as large species and adults, and sometimes more so. A reptile in a cage, no matter how spacious and environmentally diverse the cage may be, will still notice it and will be adversely affected by it. So, imagine then what the tiny tanks of pet keepers do, and fail to do, for their prisoners trapped inside. Worse, many dealers promote the use of margarine-tub-sized containers for convenience of storage — for life.

Reptile keepers need to ask themselves an important question: Would they confine their dog, cat or child in the same restrictive cages as they do reptiles? Sensible people will answer "No." For reptiles, though, the cages are no better for them than they would be for the dog, cat or human, and in some respects even worse.

"Pet-keeping encourages respect for animals and creates naturalists."

It does not take long to realize that this statement is troubled to the point of absurdity. For this idea to have any sense of balance, it would require proof that for the tens of millions of reptiles entering, suffering and dying in the pet trade each year, a stabilizing team of productive (i.e. planet protecting) naturalists emerges. These individuals would then need to prove that they would not have become naturalists quite independent of their pet-keeping days. The fact is that the numbers of people who could be regarded as real "protectionists," who are actually doing something, are small, and their numbers are hardly surging forward. So much so that a sizeable proportion of effective activists working for ecology and animal welfare actually know each other.

Anyway, if there was but a fraction of such new blood entering the good guys' army, the work force would be so great that there should be no conservation or welfare problems left to tackle. And we all know how accurate that is.

Maybe some anthropologists might like to keep a few pygmy humans in their basements for "pets," in order to further studies or foster respect! Even so, and with as much generosity as there is inaccuracy in the issue, if it were all true, that still would not make it right.

The blind leading the blind

The exotic pet trade is littered with people who seem really not to care at all about whether an animal lives or dies. A few who "study" reptile husbandry typically cite a "certain type" of information source. Often this starts with "Well, whats-his-name round the corner said I should do this." Those that do "read-up" practices nearly always refer to the constant stream of dubious "How to keep reptiles" publications, mostly originating from the U.S. These not only frequently offer ill-informed and inaccurate information that can actually cause long-term harm to captive reptiles, but also help greatly to exacerbate trade by giving the false impression that these animals can be kept in captivity with no ill effects. Authors of life-care publications, along with other semi- or total proponents of trade, should first demonstrate that their statements and husbandry "methods" live up to their optimistic titles and claims.

A little knowledge is . . . well, normal

There are probably only a few hundred people in the world who can conscientiously and honestly say that they have an understanding of reptilian biology sufficient to allow them to guesstimate a fair number of important animal needs. Only a very small number of these probably have a sufficiently "holistic" appreciation of the diverse welfare factors that truly are needed to attempt to safeguard an individual's state of mind and body. What chance, then, does the average biologist, zookeeper or veterinarian have of getting it right for reptiles? For example, few professionals such as veterinarians and zoo animal keepers have sufficient knowledge and experience to enable them to recognize and interpret the often highly subtle signs of stress in reptiles.

As indicated earlier, scraping the barrel of knowledge is the typical pet dealer, who commonly possesses no relevant qualifications or experience in animal husbandry and who tends to gather advice from other low-grade sources of information within the trade and amateurs' groups. And if this wasn't bad enough, these people are often the first source the animal buyer turns to for "reliable" advice. Thus, private animal keepers buy this information in both senses of the word, and frequently it is disastrous. In the pet trade, typically the blind lead the blind all the way to the end.

Another problem here is that those individuals who are responsible for enforcing both conservation and welfare legislation frequently possess an extremely limited amount of expertise. Indeed, almost without exception, official veterinary and other inspectors lack elementary, let alone advanced, reptile species identification and husbandry skills. The way out of this mess for government authorities is to issue licenses to pet dealers anyway. Once more, trade benefits from doubt.

Unwanted animals

Yet another disaster area is that of unwanted animals. Ask almost any zookeeper, sanctuary worker, animal enthusiast or do-gooder you care to, and you will hear him talk of the many requests he receives to take onboard animals. Frequently, these caretakers are already stocked with cast-out or escaped reptiles. Often keepers have tried the usual, and highly doubtful, routes of advertising in the press or approaching a pet shop and have gotten nowhere. A few very concerned individuals offer to fund their pets' return to the wild. Once out of nature, though, an animal cannot go back to the wild for risk of transmitting unnatural diseases and introducing undesirable genetic lines, among other considerations. Desperation and frustration often lead individuals to visit their local waterway, or whatever, and dump the "nuisance." Prospects for the animal when let loose will depend on many things, from climate to local persecution.

Unfortunately, if the animal survives, it becomes an additional threat to indigenous wildlife. In some warm countries, deliberate and accidental releases of unwanted reptiles have resulted in them breeding and infiltrating the local wildlife. Animals removed from the native ecology cause problems, and their transportation to another may do the same.

Suffering in silence

Inhumanities permeate every aspect of the exotic pet trade so deeply that it is necessary to discuss them separately so as to avoid repetition. For this reason, reptile welfare has this section all to itself, but its associations with subjects mentioned elsewhere will become clear.

What is it about reptiles (except giant testudines) that earn them the cool reception of so many observers? A number of things. The traditional "love-to-hate" approach, especially for snakes and crocodiles, long perceived as slimy, aggressive and dangerous creatures, is a major culprit in fashioning peoples' perceptions from an early age. However, misconceptions about all these things are only part of the problem. We can probably fast-forward somewhat in this book and assume that readers will not belong to the category outlined above. That said, it is a fair bet that many will still believe reptiles to be stoic, rather non-sentient animals who simply do not need as much from life or suffer in the same ways as other animals. Big mistake. Given human history, this is an understandable situation, although it really must go. Reptiles may be cold-blooded, but *you* don't have to be — and here's why.

First, a few biological facts. In humans and very many non-human mammals, eye contact and subtle changes in facial aspect are often the first ports of call for an evaluation of one another's emotional state. An alert or depressed dog or cat is spotted at ten paces. Reptiles, on the other hand, do not possess the flexible facial muscles found in mammals, so they cannot display the same clear expressions of feelings in the place humans are accustomed to looking.

To the uninformed observer, then, they can present no obvious and "appealing" signs of distress. Few people would look "into the eyes" of a lizard and see its misery. Humans are also accustomed to hearing responses, or "vocalizations," such as whining in dogs and screeching in rats, or for that matter, birds, which indicate emotional states. Almost all reptiles, though, are "anatomically" non-vocal; they are more or less mute. Some will hiss (not unlike a cat's hiss) when provoked, but an ill, hurt or chronically stressed reptile commonly makes no sound. Its suffering will likely be done in silence.

Indeed, a great many factors can be identified that warrant special concern for reptile health and welfare in captivity. For instance, their ectothermic biology (what people commonly think of as being "cold-blooded") puts great constraints on their abilities to deal with changes in environmental temperature. Furthermore, even a temporary alteration beyond what the animal would naturally expect, or perhaps even differences out of the normal thermal context, could cause stress, disease and even death. Also, keeping a reptile at a constant "perceived" appropriate temperature, as routinely done in most areas of the pet store, can result in stress and ill-health. Not only that, but stressed, compromised and sick animals need to adjust their body temperatures to precise levels to attempt to compensate for their challenges.

From body temperature one could turn to body structure. Snakes, for example, have extremely delicate muscles and skeletons that can be easily bruised or broken during handling, even after such seemingly non-harmful acts as supporting a snake's weight at one place rather than distributing it over at least two good points. The circulatory system of snakes is also organized to cope with its largely horizontal lifestyle. Consequently, holding snakes vertically, as often done by pet keepers, can cause severe displacement of body fluids and become a serious problem. Many lizards have long tails which can become entangled during transport, pull on the animals' spinal columns and lead to paralysis. General healing will also be affected by temperature. This only hints at a minute number of examples of everyday occurrences.

Many people assume that reptiles are relatively unintelligent when compared with other animals, that their "instinctive" nature means they are less affected by captivity. More mistakes. Not only have scientific evaluations blown away the notion that reptiles are stupid, they have revealed that their mental states in captivity may be made worse by their "innateness," because they biologically "expect" the natural world for which they have been very thoroughly programmed. Anyway, apart from the fact that research has shown there is no more reason to suspect reptiles of being any less sensitive than other animals, we now know there is a whole additional area of psychological- and behavioral-based considerations, and that reptiles are psychologically stressed and behaviorally compromised by captivity in ways comparable with their endothermic (warm-blooded) relatives.

None of this means that there are no signs of physical discomfort or mental anguish, only that observers need alter their expectations of signals. Some signs are obvious enough, others require specialist evaluation. Fortunately, a few biologists have begun to research and write about reptilian "sensitivities" and signs of problems. Emerging from this attention is an expanding appreciation of, and, to some, surprise at, the "complexity" of reptilian life and needs. This is making it increasingly obvious that no specialists, not even the strongly welfare-oriented ones, can correctly state they can keep captive reptiles alive and in good physical and mental condition all at one time for very long. Anyone claiming otherwise will have an impossible task proving their case.

With this unpopular truth comes an even more uncomfortable question. How can anyone feel justified keeping animals for their own personal fun and curiosity knowing the suffering to which they are party? With this in mind, imagine what unqualified, inexperienced and often uncaring individuals can do to sensitive, exotic animals when they get to them!

You may already be familiar with the pet trade system, but have you really seen and "felt" the tormented life of an organism that just wasn't where it should be, and understood why? If not, then tracking the most important thing, the individual, on a real-life journey may go some way towards achieving this understanding.

From a memory bank of innumerable individual reptiles' life histories, one needs to be very selective to offer just one example. The story of a soft-shelled turtle called Gemima is one such example. I have chosen her not for her individualism, nor because of her battle with captivity, but because she is representative of so many.

The Loss of Gemima

It is impossible to be exact, but Gemima was probably born between July and September, 1981. Some fairly precise guesswork can track her first few months like this: After about 60 days of forming a body that was a near perfect, but diminutive, replica of her parents, the time was right and she slowly broke through the plastic-like shell of her first home. Gemima emerged to darkness. She was not alone. Moving rather scrappily around her were about 175 others, most in various stages of hatching. Soon she and the rest of the clutch felt the need to scrabble to the surface, where they would make an often described run for the water. Things were not quite right, and the surface seemed ever illusive. She was not in a turtles' nest. Instead, it was a plastic box half the size of a briefcase, situated in a small, dark room on a turtle ranch in Louisiana. This environment was Gemima's first "taste" of biological confusion.

Had Gemima been born a red-eared slider on the same ranch, she might have been left locked up in the box for more than a year, even until she used up all her inherited nutritional reserves and starved, because there can be such a flood of sliders sometimes that one just can't shift 'em! But she was part of a smaller-scale market and would sell more quickly. Gemima and her co-occupants could "find" themselves seeing artificial daylight after a few weeks of fighting to escape. A number did not make it that far and live to see the artificial light of that artificial day.

Through a system of handling, storage, packaging and transport, perhaps several times over, Gemima finally arrived in a warehouse in England following a long journey over land and in the air. Further transport and handling preceded her eventual deposition into an aquarium crowded with other turtles. Illness and deaths in Gemima's cagemates surfaced all the time. A few weeks later the wholesaler received an order from a pet shop for some "soft-shells," and Gemima entered the shipping system once more. Within weeks of her deposition in yet another alien world, a human being walked into the shop during the early summer of 1982, handed over some paper, and strolled out with a life — her life. For her, the journey through the hands of dealers was over. Now all she had to face was her buyer.

Informed speculation is over. We have arrived at the point where Gemima's life story hereinafter is clear.

During their first week, Gemima's latest captors noticed patches of what appeared to them to be eroded skin on her delicate (soft, of course) shell and along her side. She was eating nothing. Inquiries with the pet shop in the Midlands of England received a bored response and the advice that she was shedding her skin. Her keepers insisted something was wrong, and were then told that Gemima had probably "picked something up" in their house. Both answers were incorrect. Skin shedding can look like this problem, but the disease had actually started long before Gemima reached the private home.

She was taken to a local veterinarian. A little puzzled at what to do with this flattish, grey creature measuring just an inch in diameter, he prescribed a vitamin injection (a very small one, of course) and all left. Nothing changed, though, except that the affected areas of skin grew larger, so, courtesy of her perceived predators (her "owners"), Gemima paid another visit to another perceived predator for another examination. Rather than go on experimenting, this clinician opted to make a telephone call for a herpetologist's opinion. From here on, I was to become inextricably aware of yet another case where establishment safeguards had failed the individual.

Gemima was referred to me the same day. The veterinarian's treatment had been a fair attempt in an uncertain situation, but the problem here needed different attention. Nearly all soft-shells "look angry," and many are notoriously "bad-tempered." She was very weak. Gemima, though, was a feisty individual, and unlike many other turtles of her size and age who tend to withdraw their heads into the relative safety of their shells, she would slowly extend her long neck, press her head against a finger, open her mouth and inflict what nip perhaps she thought would get rid of you and then withdraw. Weighing in at about the same as a smallish coin, the amount of damage she could do was rather limited.

Examination revealed her to be affected by malnutrition and a series of lesions – her main symptoms – that had penetrated deep into her skin and shell. In addition, she had numerous other injuries from trade-related practices. For obvious reasons, the evaluation could not have recorded her state of mind with similar clarity. Fungal infection was suspected as causing the primary signs, and precautionary treatment was administered (laboratory analysis of a material specimen later confirmed the diagnosis).

New regimes of treatment, a special diet (administered via, sadly, probably quite stressful forced-feeding) and husbandry brought improvements in her condition within the week, and soon after she began feeding voluntarily. Were it not for the rapid intervention she received, the malnutrition and illness would likely already have killed her. She was, though, permanently scarred by the disease.

It was more than a year until I next saw Gemima. Her keepers came to me directly when they had been shocked at the sight of injuries early one morning. She had clearly been attacked by something. Her limbs were badly bitten and the tips of several toes missing, her neck showed a large bite-site that had torn the skin and muscles and caused her to lose a lot of blood. Her windpipe had narrowly been missed. Had it not, she almost certainly would have died.

Feeling her to be lonely, her caretakers had bought a cagemate for her from a different pet shop the previous day. The newcomer had set about Gemima with all the natural aggressiveness of the species in adverse situations. Captivity frequently results in hyperaggression in many animals who just can't cope with the unnatural lives they endure. Sedated, sutured, smartened-up and to some extent soothed, Gemima went "home." Her associate was separated, because the keepers did not have enough space to construct an enclosure large enough to permit them the seclusion and independence they would have needed if they were to cohabit well. By this time she had grown somewhat, but could still nestle in the palm of a hand. She was as fiery as ever and, like most soft-shells, could administer what one might take to be a piercing stare of disgust at everything—and everyone— she saw.

Her keepers enthusiastically recounted her dietary preferences, dislikes, quirks, moods, and general characteristics that they knew would enable them to pick her from a thousand others in a second. Many incidents I recognized as actually very distressing aspects of psychological and physical trauma hidden from Gemima's "owners" by misinterpretation of the signs. Other impressions, though, were clearly "on the mark." Some seemed very special indeed, in the few times when Gemima was not obviously "depressed," frightened or aggressive.

One such example involved Gemima quickly surfacing from her pool, biting gently any finger that pointed straight at her, then diving under the floating bark, all the time keeping a watchful eye on her keeper. Over and over again it would be repeated until finally she had had enough. "She is a bit of a mischievous puppy sometimes," they recalled. Gemima appeared to be "playing." Accounts like this can provoke a storm of criticisms blaming "anthropomorphism" for the picture of Gemima her captors had created. However, many scientists today working in proper "critical anthropomorphism" would not be so dismissive. Behaviors compatible with definitions of play have indeed been observed in several species of reptile, so there is some ground to believe this "subjective" impression.

During a few weeks in summer, Gemima could be transferred to an outdoor enclosure with an inch or two of mud for her to bury into, as recommended to her keepers. As they often stated, when Gemima was outside she was a different animal. Her repeated sores and abrasions caused by poor fixtures in her cage healed, her behavior calmed, her investigation of the environment increased, and there was all that sediment to dig around in and search out food. Inevitably, though, climate and supervision needs would return her inside. Gemima would again enter her "sulks" for months.

Gemima had to cope with several more injuries and diseases over the next two years. Most of these were managed through telephone consultations between myself and her veterinarian. Some needed direct care and were major battles for both Gemima and those treating her. On a few occasions, Gemima nearly lost her life.

The next winter brought with it the most difficult time of all. I received a call saying that she was in a bad way. The symptoms sounded worrying, and I made the usual arrangement for them to visit their local veterinarian, where down-the-line consultations could be arranged. However, a gut feeling had brought me to call on Gemima and her keepers to see things for myself; I was nearby at the time. On top of a cabinet in a little-used exit hall cluttered with household junk stood a small glass aquarium barely three feet long. An externally placed water filtration mechanism had spared Gemima the stronger disturbance of a noisy internal one; the lighting and heating systems were all "standard" designs. A few pieces of imitation pond-weed floated around, and a large piece of cork bark positioned half-in and half-out of the water. In the corner of the tank, stretched out across the bark, gasping periodically and sporadically twitching, lay Gemima.

She was exhibiting some of the obvious and some of the highly subtle behaviors that one learns, after seeing so many cases, are indicative of imminent death — short of the rare revival successes. The "off-the-peg" life-support system in which she was confined was one of the things that was killing her.

Where was the enclosure I had devised for her years before, which offered at least some facilities with "turtle appeal" within her keepers' budgets? When Gemima's keepers moved, the purpose-built, but still obviously "compromise-style," housing didn't fit. It was broken up and discarded. The latest tank was given to them by a friend whose collection of fish had died. It was free and fitted their house better, but, quite apart from being ridiculously small, it contained not even the sediment that they knew she readily used in her previous facilities. They were hoping at some stage in the future to build another, much better environment for Gemima, and really meant it.

Antibiotics were administered and a constantly warm environment was recommended, among other plans. This was what all the veterinary and textbook advice suggested at the time. She was still strong, albeit occasionally, but progressively breathing more heavily. I advised an environment with far greater diversity in order to offer some potentially important general stimuli. Being very cold outside, all that was available was to let her loose on the floor of the house with a heat source positioned nearby. With this change in conditions, Gemima began a search of her surroundings. This was a better sign — her interest in life was "up." However, it became clear that Gemima was desperately seeking cooler areas in the lounge. Certain treatments require particular temperatures. Warmth could not be maintained like this, so she was immediately intercepted and placed back in the heated area. She still had the strength to administer a bite, this time hard, on the hand of one of her keepers.

As the day progressed, matters became worse. Gemima weakened still more, and her breathing grew heavier. We clung to the hope that the antibiotics, sometimes very effective, would pull her from all this. Secretly, though, I was contemplating suggesting euthanasia by injection, as more and more she appeared to be tired of it all, and one cannot help but think of the future she would face anyway. As this thought was being nurtured increasingly strongly, Gemima became tensed, then collapsed, although her muscles were still twitching a little. The "angry-looking" stare she had blasted us with so many times before would turn out to be the last apparently conscious and coordinated act of her life. No life signs existed beyond the hour.

Perhaps as always, it is not possible to describe the grief that absorbed those present. Nor when she is remembered. Surprisingly, her last captors seemed to really love her; they just couldn't find it in their own characters to put themselves in her position and understand life as she might see it.

I requested a completely independent postmortem. As the phrase, "Oh, the poor animal" was released several times in the room, it became clear that Gemima really was forced into a very hopeless situation. A massive peritonitis, inflamed organs and an inconceivably sore throat overshadowed all else. She had probably endured great pain for a long time in this, the last of her illnesses.

Several things might have caused her downfall, and we could not be really sure which. The water filter had acted as a breeding station for harmful strains of bacteria, bacteria that presented an atypical challenge to her immune system — an immune system probably already compromised by the multitude of captivity-stresses.

Indeed, the development of the disease likely attacked her in ways she was biologically ill-equipped to deal with or able to relieve herself from. The relative humaneness of the natural world was not here to help protect her from the extreme physical and psychological insults of captivity.

Some years later, it emerged that reptiles may on occasion voluntarily lower their temperature when an infection occurs. Distress from the illness might cause the animal to try to "shut down" biologically, which may permit some relief from painful and stressful symptoms. Such "disease-associated voluntary hypothermia" seems a serious occurrence, though, happening when all else has failed. Thus, if this was what Gemima's strategy had actually been, then even our last-ditch endeavors to save her might have added to her suffering and accelerated her death. That said, Gemima's dreadful condition on necropsy strongly suggested that she was unsaveable.

Whatever, captivity thwarted her natural protective biology and behavioral strategies at almost every turn.

Perhaps one important difference does exist between Gemima's story and the average pet trade victim. Her caretakers were unlike the majority in that these people clearly grieved as a result of this entirely human-made disaster. This contrasts dramatically, drastically even, with very many people who may dispose of an animal carcass down the lavatory or via a cardboard box in the garden and then console themselves by going out and buying yet another animal, starting the whole tragic tale once more. Gemima's "family" had been party to a chapter of horror that became increasingly distressing the more it was reflected upon. There would be no repetitions of this situation for her last captors. A most valuable lesson had been learned, but at such a cost.

I requested Gemima's body and later buried her in my own garden. She was about four years of age, one foot long, nose to tail, and about two pounds in weight. She may have lived 30 or more years in nature and developed into a large, majestic creature, in many ways not dissimilar from her relatives, the sea turtles. The main point is that she hadn't really lived at all in captivity.

Conclusions

A decree issued by the Italian government in October 1996 specifically bans the keeping of snakes, alligators and crocodiles as household pets. Other wild animals are also included in the decree, which states that they can no longer be purchased by private individuals. Although the motivation for this action is protection of the public from potentially dangerous animals, its effects are expected to be beneficial to the animals by preventing their exploitation by the commercial trade. Humane societies have long argued against the purchase of exotic pets. Laws like the new Italian decree could go a long way in preventing the needless suffering and death of these animals. Yet far more needs to be done to make clear the scale and severity of species and environmental disruption and animal suffering inherent in the exotic pet market, and far less excused. Such educational work requires that the story be told like it is.

The United States Department of the Interior has recognized the necessity of regulating the transport of these sensitive beings. On June 6, 1997 the U.S. Fish and Wildlife Service published a proposal to amend regulations pertaining to the humane and healthful transport of wild mammals and birds into the U.S. under the 1981 Lacey Act Amendments. The proposed rule extends the transport regulations to include reptiles and amphibians. "The Service possesses substantial evidence showing that current practices of some shippers for transporting reptiles and amphibians are detrimental to the animals," stated FWS in its proposal. If adopted in its current form, the rule will require shippers to comply with regulations governing veterinary certification, temperature range, enclosure structure and size and proper handling.

The burdens of detecting, studying, lobbying for protection, monitoring and enforcing issues in the reptile and amphibian trade, as well as for husbandry advice, re-homing, care of unwanted animals and many other factors, have rested with animal welfare charities, zoos and others. Certainly the pet industry has been shown to be sufficiently untrustworthy to manage any of these important aspects, but that it should evade the costs involved — all the costs, including the hidden "clean-up" bills for the many disasters — is a fault of government.

When one considers the "chance" aspect of whether or not exploitation even gets discovered, the over-stretched resources of charities in investigating the matter, the often outrageous up-hill struggle with ignorant bureaucrats and their arrogant rejections, coupled with the near zero back-up monitoring and enforcement, it becomes apparent that the trade in reptiles and amphibians is simply not being controlled by government at all.

Burdens of proof, at every stage, should rest squarely with dealers, and the benefit of any doubt should be overwhelmingly on the side of wildlife and the individual animals. In effect, there are far less safeguards for live animals in the "curiosity" market and for the members of the public who eventually buy the survivors than there are for inanimate domestic goods. It should always be up to the proponents to prove their practices are safe. Anything less than this is unscientific, unethical and inexcusable.

We must urge governments to continue to expand their protection of amphibians and reptiles especially in light of the unprecedented decline in their numbers throughout the world.

Dedicated to the Gemimas of this world and the millions even more unfortunate.

Background Reading

Arena, P.C. and Richardson, K.C. (1990) The relief of pain in cold-blooded vertebrates, *A.C.C.A.R.T. News*, 3:1-4.

Arena, P.C. and Warwick, C. (1994) Miscellaneous factors affecting health and welfare. In: *Health and Welfare of Captive Reptiles* (eds. C. Warwick, F.L. Frye and J.B. Murphy) Chapman and Hall, London.

Bowers, B.B. and Burghardt, G.M. (1992) The scientist and the snake: relationships with reptiles. In: *The Inevitable Bond, Examining Scientist-Animal Interactions* (eds. H. Davies and D.

Balfour) Cambridge University Press, pp. 250-263.

Burger, J. and Gochfield, M. (1993) The importance of the human face in risk perception by black iguanas, Ctenosaura similis. *Journal of Herpetology*, 27:426-430.

Burghardt, G.M. (1988) Precocity, play, and the ectotherm-endotherm transition: profound reorganisation or superficial adaptation. In: *Handbook of Behavioral Neurobiology* (ed. E.M. Blass) Plenum Publishing Corporation, pp. 107-147.

Burghardt, G.M. and Layne, D. (1994) Effects of ontogenetic processes and rearing conditions on ethology. In: *Health and Welfare of Captive Reptiles* (eds. C. Warwick, F.L. Frye and J.B. Murphy) Chapman and Hall, London.

Carstens, E.E. (1987) Endogenous pain suppression mechanisms. In: Colloquium on Recognition and Alleviation of Animal Pain and Distress. *Journal of the American Veterinary Medical Association*, 191:1203-1206.

Chiszar, D., Tomlinson, W.T., Smith, H.M., Murphy, J.B. and Radcliffe, C.W. (1994) Behavioural consequences of husbandry manipulations: indicators of arousal quiescence, and environmental awareness. In: *Health and Welfare of Captive Reptiles* (eds. C. Warwick, F.L. Frye and J.B. Murphy) Chapman and Hall, London.

Cooper, J.E., Ewbank, R., Platt, C. and Warwick, C. (1989) *Euthanasia of Amphibians and Reptiles*, Universities Federation for Animal Welfare/World Society for the Protection of Animals, 35 pp.

Cooper, J.E. and Williams, D.L. (1994) Veterinary perspectives and techniques in husbandry and research. In: *Health and Welfare of Captive Reptiles* (eds. C. Warwick, F.L. Frye and J.B. Murphy) Chapman and Hall, London.

Cowan, D.F. (1980) Adaptation, maladaptation and disease, in S.S.A.R. Contributions to Herpetology number 1, *Reproductive Biology and Diseases in Captive Reptiles* (eds. J.B. Murphy and J.T. Collins) Society for the Study of Amphibians and Reptiles.

Frye, F.L. (1991) *Biomedical and Surgical Aspects of Captive Reptile Husbandry*, Krieger Publishing Co., Inc., Malabar, Florida.

Frye, F.L. (1994) Nutritional considerations. In: *Health and Welfare of Captive Reptiles* (eds. C. Warwick, F.L. Frye and J.B. Murphy) Chapman and Hall, London.

Gillingham, J.C. (1994) Normal behaviour. In: *Health and Welfare of Captive Reptiles* (eds. C. Warwick, F.L. Frye and J.B. Murphy) Chapman and Hall, London.

Greenberg, G. (1994) Ethologically informed design in husbandry and research. In: *Health and Welfare of Captive Reptiles* (eds. C. Warwick, F.L. Frye and J.B. Murphy) Chapman and Hall, London.

Guillette, Jr., L.J., Cree, A. and Rooney, A. (1994) Biology of stress: interactions with reproduction, immunology and intermediary metabolism. In: *Health and Welfare of Captive Reptiles* (eds. C. Warwick, F.L. Frye and J.B. Murphy) Chapman and Hall, London.

Honnegger, R.E. (1993) Undesirable trends in the captive management and conservation of reptiles. *International Zoo News*, 246:11-17.

Jacobson, E.R., Gaskin, J.M., Brown, M.B., Harris, R.K., Gardiner, C.H., LaPointe, J.L., Adams, H.P. and Reggiardo, C. (1991) Chronic upper respiratory tract disease of free-ranging desert tortoises (Xerobates agassizi). *Journal of Wildlife Diseases*, 27:296-316.

Kreger, M.D. (1993) The psychological well-being of reptiles. *Humane innovations and alternatives*, 7:519-523.

Lance, V.A. (1990) Stress in reptiles. *Progress in Comparative Endocrinology*, 46:1-6.

Lance, V.A. (1992) Evaluating pain and stress in reptiles. In: *The Care and Use of Amphibians, Reptiles and Fish in Research* (eds. D.O. Schaeffer, K.M. Kleinow and L. Krulisch) Scientists

Center for Animal Welfare, p. 196.

Lillywhite, H.L. and Gatten, Jr., R.E. (1994) Physiology and functional anatomy. In: *Health and Welfare of Captive Reptiles* (eds. C. Warwick, F.L. Frye and J.B. Murphy) Chapman and Hall, London.

Warwick, C. (1986) Red-eared terrapin farms and conservation. *Oryx*, 20:37-40.

Warwick, C. (1987) The decline of North American box turtles. *Animals International*, 23:6-7.

Warwick, C. (1990) Reptilian ethology in captivity: observations of some problems and an evaluation of their aetiology. *Applied Animal Behaviour Science*, 26:1-13.

Warwick, C. (1990) Important ethological considerations of the study and maintenance of reptiles in captivity. *Applied Animal Behaviour Science*, 27:363-366.

Warwick, C. (1990) *Reptiles – Misunderstood, Mistreated and Mass-marketed*. Reptile Protection Trust, 46 pp.

Warwick, C. (1991) Tender-age moribund endangered terrapins. *BBC Wildlife* Magazine, 9:630-632.

Warwick, C. (1991) Observations on disease-associated preferred body temperatures in reptiles. *Applied Animal Behaviour Science*, 28:375-380.

Warwick, C. (1992) Conservation of red-eared terrapins (Trachemys scripta elegans): threats from international pet and culinary markets. *Testudo*, 3:34-44.

Warwick, C. and Steedman, C. (1994) Naturalistic versus clinical conditions in husbandry and research. In: *Health and Welfare of Captive Reptiles* (eds. C. Warwick, F.L. Frye and J.B. Murphy) Chapman and Hall, London.

Warwick, C. (1994) Psychological and behavioural principles and problems. In: *Health and Welfare of Captive Reptiles* (eds. C. Warwick, F.L. Frye and J.B. Murphy) Chapman and Hall, London.

Warwick, C., Frye, F.L., and Murphy, J.B. (eds.) (1994) Introduction: Health and welfare of captive reptiles. In: *Health and Welfare of Captive Reptiles*, Chapman and Hall, London and New York, pp. 300.

Warwick, C., Steedman, C. and Holford, T. (1990) Ecological implications of the red-eared turtle trade. *Texas Journal of Science*, 42:419-422.

Appendix A

List of Currently Licensed Class B Dealers Supplying Dogs and Cats for Research

Name	License #	City
Alabama		
Marlin Pesnell	#64-B-044	Arab
Lem Miller	#64-B-053	Estillfork
Arkansas		
C.C. Baird (Martin Creek Kennels)	#71-B-108	Williford
Connecticut		
Glenn Lawton (Team Associates)	#16-B-003	Dayville
Illinois		
Bill and Peggy Woodward	#33-B-269	Mulberry Grove
Indiana		
Gene Clark (Salt Creek Kennel)	#32-B-035	Trafalgar
Alvie Fields	#32-B-008	Portland
Mark and John Lynch (LBL Kennel)	#32-B-045	Reelsville
David Wilson (Wilson's Small Animal Farm)	#32-B-001	Vincennes
Iowa		
Kenneth Bige	#42-B-011	Clear Lake
Dick Garner (Country Canines)	#42-B-031	Osceola
Donna Zieman (D-N Kennels)	#42-B-081	Luana
Kansas		
Charles Brink (Brink Kennel)	#48-B-086	Paola
Kentucky		
Clifford Ball (Laurel Fork Kennels)	#61-B-109	Elkfork
Douglas Grubb (Skyline Kennels)	#61-B-102	London
M.E. Northcutt (Goodwill Kennels)	#61-B-001	Cynthiana
Wayne Pierce (Bill Chain Kennels)	#61-B-0103	Garrison
Dennis Silcox (Regency Research Enterprises)	#61-B-105	Lexington

Massachusetts
Charles River Laboratories, Inc.   #14-B-013   Wilmington

Michigan
Fred Hodgins (Hodgins Kennel, Inc.)	#34-B-002	Howell
International Animal Exchange	#34-B-004	Ferndale
Mary Ulrich (Cheri-Hill Kennel & Supply)	#34-B-006	Stanwood
Roberta & James Woudenberg (R & R Research)	#34-B-001	Howard City

Minnesota
Kenneth Schroeder   #41-B-017   Wells

Missouri
Kent and Debbie Embry	#43-B-264	Clarksburg
Danny Schachtele(Middlefork Kennels)	#43-B-032	Salisbury

Nebraska
Jean Packer   #47-B-011   Wood River

North Carolina
Max Gravitt (Baux Mt. Beagle Farm)	#55-B-033	Germantown
Bob Perry (S.E. Lab Animal Farm, Inc.)	#55-B-076	Raleigh
Barbara Phillips (Pearcroft Cattery)	#55-B-106	Beaufort
John Wise	#55-B-101	Dunn
Eva Wise (Hillside Kennel)	#55-B-081	Four Oaks

Ohio
Andy Ball (Kiser Lake Kennels)   #31-B-001   St. Paris

Oklahoma
Henry Lee Cooper (C&C Kennels)   #73-B-130   Wewoka

Oregon
Betty Davis   #92-B-183   Azalea

Pennsylvania
Buckshire Corporation	#23-B-002	Perkasie
Forest Ridge Stable & Kennel	#23-B-0026	Paradise
Hazelton Research Products, Inc.	#23-B-053	Denver
Mike Kredovski (Bio-Medical Association, Inc.)	#23-B-006	Friedensburg
Eugene Peachey	#23-B-013	Huntingdon
Bruce Rotz	#23-B-004	Shippensburg

Tennessee
Johnnie Hargove (Bio Research Supply)   #63-B-119   Medina

Texas
Larry Wells (Texas Kennels)   #74-B-202   Rockdale

Washington
H.D. Cowan (Showline Beagles)   #91-B-006   Renton
Marvin and Joye Dart   #91-B-045   Eatonville

West Virginia
Mona Hill   #54-B-002   Huntington
Robert Seekman   #54-B-019   Omega

Wisconsin
Walter and Hildegard Peuschel   #35-B-008   Mequon

Appendix B

USDA-APHIS-AC Headquarters and Regional Offices

Headquarters Office
USDA-APHIS-AC
4700 River Road, Unit 84
Riverdale, MD 20737-1234
(301) 734-4981

Eastern Region — Alabama, Connecticut, Delaware, District of Columbia, Florida, Georgia, Kentucky, Illinois, Indiana, Maine, Maryland, Massachusetts, Michigan, Minnesota, Mississippi, New Hampshire, New Jersey, New York, North Carolina, Ohio, Pennsylvania, Puerto Rico, Rhode Island, South Carolina, Tennessee, U.S. Virgin Islands, Vermont, Virginia, West Virginia, Wisconsin

USDA-APHIS-AC
2568-A Riva Road, Suite 302
Annapolis, MD 21401
Telephone: (410) 571-8692

Central Region — Arkansas, Iowa, Kansas, Louisiana, Missouri, Nebraska, North Dakota, Oklahoma, South Dakota, Texas

USDA-APHIS-AC
P.O. Box 6258
Fort Worth Federal Center, Bldg. #11
Fort Worth, TX 76115
Telephone: (817) 885-6923

Western Region—Alaska, Arizona, California, Colorado Hawaii, Idaho, Montana, Nevada, New Mexico, Oregon, Utah, Washington, Wyoming

USDA-APHIS-AC

9580 Micron Avenue, Suite J

Sacramento, CA 95827

Telephone: (916) 857-6205

Appendix C

Glossary of Terms

Administrative hearing: Most USDA enforcement proceedings are carried out in administrative hearings. Hearings are formal in nature and presided over by an administrative law judge who hears sworn testimony subject to cross-examination and reviews exhibits received in evidence. Individuals charged with violating the Animal Welfare Act can appear pro se (representing themselves) or be represented by an attorney. They can specifically admit, deny, or explain each allegation, or set forth any defense in their answer. Failure to respond to USDA charges constitutes an admission of guilt.

Alleged violation: A violation of Animal Welfare Act regulations or standards that has been documented as existing, as on an inspection, but has not been legally concluded.

Animal Welfare Act: Adopted in 1966 as the Laboratory Animal Welfare Act (Public Law 89-544) to regulate dealers who handle dogs and cats, as well as laboratories that use dogs, cats, hamsters, guinea pigs, rabbits, and nonhuman primates in research. Amended in 1970, when the name was changed to "Animal Welfare Act." Further amended in 1976, 1985 and 1990.

Animal and Plant Health Inspection Service (APHIS): An agency within the U.S. Department of Agriculture (USDA) that is responsible for developing and implementing regulations to enforce the Animal Welfare Act. Within APHIS, the Animal Care (AC) program has direct responsibility to administer and enforce the Animal Welfare Act, including licensing, registration, inspection and investigation of complaints. Investigative and Enforcement Services (IES) performs investigative and enforcement functions for all APHIS programs. IES investigates violations of Animal Care regulations and reviews and processes violation cases referred for formal administative action.

Buncher: An individual who engages in the unlicensed and unregulated acquisition of dogs and cats from random sources for resale to USDA-licensed dealers or other bunchers. Typically, dealers pay a buncher between $5 and $35 per animal.

Carrier: The operator of any airline, motor freight line, ground freight transport, railroad or shipping line that is engaged in the business of transporting any animals for hire. Intermediate handlers provide services for animals between consignor and carrier and from carrier to consignee. In 1996, there were 725 registered carrier sites and 417 intermediate handler sites.

CFR: Code of Federal Regulations

Class A licensee: Anyone meeting the definition of "dealer" who sells animals bred and raised on his or her own premises in a closed or stable colony and buys animals for the sole purpose of maintaining or enhancing the breeding colony. The vast majority of these licensees supply animals for the pet trade. In 1996, there were 2,976 Class A licensees (with a total of 3,043 sites).

Class B licensee: Anyone meeting the definition of "dealer" who buys and resells animals not raised or bred on the dealer's own premises. Class B licenses are required for brokers and operators of auction sales. In 1996, there were 1,099 Class B licensees (with a total of 1,222 sites). According to USDA, there are currently less than 40 Class B dealers who supply dogs and cats for research.

Complaint: Informs an alleged violator of the AWA about the charges brought against him or her.

Compliance: Indicates that a facility meets all of the regulatory requirements set forth in the AWA regulations and standards.

Consent Decision: A settlement agreement made by an individual charged with violating the AWA to pay a civil penalty, in which he or she neither admits nor denies the charges brought against him or her.

Dealer: Any person who, for profit, buys, sells or negotiates the purchase or sale of any dog or other animal, whether alive or dead, for research, testing, experimentation, exhibition or for use as a pet; or any dog for hunting, security, or breeding purposes.

Dog Exercise Program: The 1985 Improved Standards for Laboratory Animals amendment to the Animal Welfare Act required the Secretary of Agriculture to promulgate standards for the exercise of dogs under the care and custody of licensed dealers and registered research facilities.

Enforcement: Actions taken to ensure compliance with Animal Welfare Act regulations and standards, including developing alleged violation cases and taking action in the form of Letters of Warning, warning tickets (not issued until 1987), stipulations, administrative complaints, hearings, trials, and other legal procedures or methods necessary to achieve compliance.

Exhibitors: Any individuals exhibiting animals including operators of animal acts, carnivals, circuses, public zoos, roadside zoos, marine mammal displays and educational exhibits. A licensed exhibitor (Class C licensee) either obtains or sells animals in commerce or exhibits them for profit. A registered exhibitor does not buy, sell or transport animals and does not accept compensation. In 1996, there were 2,073 licensed exhibitors (with a total of 2,422 sites) and 25 registered exhibitors (with a total of 31 sites).

Inspection: After a license is granted, APHIS performs inspections to ensure compliance with the Animal Welfare Act. Compliance inspections are unannounced. APHIS will also perform an inspection in response to complaints from the public about a facility. If the inspector observes that a facility is not in full compliance with Animal Welfare Act standards and regulations, he or she will give the facility owner a deadline for correcting the deficiencies. The inspector will return to reinspect the facility. If conditions remain uncorrected, the inspector carefully documents them for possible enforcement action. A prelicensing inspection is an announced inspection made after application for licensure to ascertain compliance with the regulations before the facility receives a license.

Licensing: Individuals who sell 1) regulated animals for research or teaching, 2) wild or exotic animals in retail channels for exhibition, or for pets, or 3) domestic pet animals at the wholesale level must be licensed by USDA. The sale for research purposes of any dog or cat not born and raised on the premises requires a license. An individual who sells fewer than 25 dogs and/or cats per year which were born and raised on his or her premises, for research, teaching or testing purposes or to any research facility is not required to obtain a license.

Office of the General Counsel (OGC): USDA's Office of the General Counsel reviews case reports and documentation of apparent violations submitted by the IES staff and determines if there is a legally sound basis to pursue enforcement action. OGC prosecutes cases on behalf of APHIS.

Pet Theft Act Amendment to the AWA: Passed by Congress as part of the Food, Agriculture, Conservation and Trade Act of 1990, the Pet Theft Act sets forth specific holding periods for animals in public or private pounds or shelters and requires certification that the holding period has been met.

Random source dogs and cats: Dogs and cats obtained from pounds, shelters, auctions, sales, or from any person who did not breed or raise them on his or her premises.

Research facility: Any school (other than elementary or secondary), institution, organization, or person that uses or intends to use live animals in research, tests, or experiments, and that; 1) purchases or transports live animals in commerce or, 2) receives funds under a grant, award, loan, or contract from a department, agency or instrumentality of the United States for the purpose of carrying out research, tests or experiments. All research facilities are required to comply with the AWA's regulations. Although Federal research facilities are not registered or inspected under the AWA, they are responsible for maintaining compliance with the AWA's regulations and standards. The AWA requires that non-Federal research facilities receive at least one unannounced inspection per year to determine compliance. In 1996, there were 2,506 registered research facility sites.

Site: A physical location where animals are used, housed, or held by a licensed or registered facility; a site can be a room, building, outdoor run area or similar facility.

Specific pathogen free: An organism rendered devoid of a specific disease-causing bacterium, virus, or other microorganism.

Stipulation: Instituted by APHIS in 1992, the stipulation procedure offers an alleged violator the opportunity to waive a formal administrative hearing and accept assessment of a civil penalty, license suspension, or a combination thereof in its place. If the offer is not accepted, the case is referred to the Office of the General Counsel for prosecution through administrative procedures.

Traceback: A method of auditing sales and/or purchase records to determine the chain of acquisition (origin and ownership) of an animal. It is useful in uncovering incorrect or fraudulent record-keeping, which is sometimes used to obscure improper acquisition methods and sources.

Violation: Any area or item that is alleged as not being in compliance with Animal Welfare Act regulations or standards.

(Primary source: USDA-APHIS "Animal Welfare Enforcement, Fiscal Year 1996")

Appendix D: Affidavit of Mark Yardley

Privacy Act Notice on Reverse

AFFIDAVIT

Before me _Marshall G. Smith_ _____, an employee of the United
States Department of Agriculture designated by the Secretary of Agriculture under authority of section 1
of the Act of Congress approved January 31, 1925 (43 Stat. 803; 7 U.S.C. 2217), personally appeared
Mark A. Yardley, 449 SE 80th Ln. Lamar, MO 64759 , who deposes and says:

I, Mark A. Yardley, make the following voluntary statement to Marshall G. Smith who has identified himself as an investigator for the USDA.

This statement pertains to dogs/cats that I sold to Mr. C.C. Baird during this year (1994) using family members names. I've used the following names: Cindy Knight - sister-in-law, Larry Yardley - brother, Josh Watkins - step son, Magie Watkins - wife (C.L.), Alma Young - mother-in-law, Delbert & Laura Frezell - Cindy's brothers, And Dustin Roach - brother-in-law. I used these names since I'd already sold 25 dogs/cats during my business year. Most of these dogs/cats were random source but I did raise some. I believe that all of my relatives listed above knew that I was going to use their names for these sales to Mr. Baird. Mr. Baird usually meets me somewhere halfway to pick up dogs. I am an independent supplier and am not Mr. Baird's employee or agent. Nor am I an agent for any other USDA brokers. I have sold dogs/cats to Mr. Waterbury and maybe one dog to Kenny S. (at Salsbury, MO) I have been in this business about 10 years from.

I am in the process of getting my U.S.D.A. license. My inspector was here for a pre-license inspection on September 26, 1994. He left U.S.D.A. forms so that I could record my purchases from random sources. I haven't kept records for my past sales.

I have read this statement and I affirm that it is accurate and complete, to the best of my knowledge and ability. This is given freely without promise or reward.

_____
SIGNATURE OF AFFIANT

Subscribed and sworn to before me at _449 SE 80th Ln, Lamar, MO 64759_
on this _8th_ day of _November_ 19_94_.

Marshall G. Smith
DESIGNATED PURSUANT TO LAW TO
ADMINISTER OATHS, AFFIDAVITS,
AND AFFIRMATIONS, AUTHORITY NO. _2604_

VS FORM 3-59G   Previous editions obsolete.
(MAY 77)

Appendix E: USDA Inspection Report Form

U.S. DEPARTMENT OF AGRICULTURE ANIMAL AND PLANT HEALTH INSPECTION SERVICE	1. LICENSE NO. OR REGISTRATION NO.		2. PAGE 1 OF ___
ANIMAL CARE INSPECTION REPORT	3. DATE OF INSPECTION		4. TIME
☐ Routine ☐ Reinspection ☐ Pre-license ☐ Attempted ☐ Other	5. DATE OF LAST INSPECTION		6. TIME
7. NAME AND MAILING ADDRESS OF LICENSEE OR REGISTRANT	8. ADDRESS OF PREMISES AT TIME OF INSPECTION *(If different than Item 7)*		

STANDARDS AND REGULATIONS	DOGS	CATS	GUINEA PIGS	HAMSTERS	RABBITS	PRIMATES	MARINE MAMMALS	OTHER			
9. NO. OF ANIMALS INSPECTED	A		B		C	D	E	F			

"X" If in compliance; CIRCLE Non-compliant items *(explain on APHIS FORM 7100, Continuation Sheet)*; NA If not applicable; NS If not seen.

			DOGS	CATS	GUINEA PIGS	HAMSTERS	RABBITS	PRIMATES	MARINE MAMMALS	OTHER			
FACILITIES	GENERAL	10. Structure and Construction	3.1	3.1	3.25	3.25	3.50	3.75	3.101	3.125			
		11. Condition and Site	3.1	3.1				3.75	3.101	3.125			
		12. Surfaces & Cleaning	3.1	3.1				3.75	3.101				
		13. Utilities/Washrooms/Storage	3.1	3.1	3.25	3.25	3.50	3.75	3.101	3.125			
		14. Drainage and Waste Disposal	3.1	3.1	3.25	3.25	3.50	3.75	3.101	3.125			
	INDOOR	15. Temperature/Ventilation/Lighting	3.2	3.2	3.26	3.26	3.51	3.76	3.102	3.126			
		16. Interior Surfaces	3.2	3.2	3.26	3.26	3.51		3.101				
		17. Drainage							3.101	3.126			
	SHELTERED	18. Temperature/Ventilation/Lighting	3.3	3.3				3.77					
		19. Shelter from elements	3.3	3.3				3.77					
		20. Surfaces	3.3	3.3				3.77					
		21. Capacity/Perimeter fence/Barrier						3.77					
	OUTDOOR	22. Restrictions or Acclimation	3.4	3.4	3.27	3.27		3.78	3.103				
		23. Shelter from elements	3.4	3.4	3.27		3.52	3.78	3.103	3.127			
		24. Drainage			3.27		3.52			3.127			
		25. Construction	3.4	3.4	3.27			3.78	3.101				
		26. Capacity/Perimeter fence/Barrier						3.78	3.101	3.125			
	MOBILE	27. Temperature/Ventilation/ Lighting	3.5	3.5				3.79					
		28. Public Barrier						3.79					
PRIMARY ENCLOSURE		29. General Requirements	3.6	3.6	3.28	3.28	3.53	3.80	3.104	3.125			
		30. Space & Additional Requirements	3.6	3.6	3.28	3.28	3.53	3.80	3.104	3.128			
		31. Protection from Predators	3.6	3.6	3.25	3.25	3.52	3.80	3.101	3.125			
ANIMAL HEALTH AND HUSBANDRY		32. Exercise and Socialization	3.8	3.8									
		33. Environment Enhancement						3.81					
		34. Feeding	3.9	3.9	3.29	3.29	3.54	3.82	3.105	3.129			
		35. Watering	3.10	3.10	3.30	3.30	3.55	3.83	3.106	3.130			
		36. Cleaning and Sanitation	3.11	3.11	3.31	3.31	3.56	3.84	3.107	3.131			
		37. Housekeeping and Pest Control	3.11	3.11	3.31	3.31	3.56	3.84	3.107	3.131			
		38. Employees	3.12	3.12	3.32	3.32	3.57	3.85	3.108	3.132			
		39. Social Grouping and Separation	3.7	3.7	3.33	3.33	3.58		3.109	3.133			
TRANSPORTATION		40. Primary Enclosure	3.14	3.14	3.36	3.36	3.61	3.87	3.113	3.137			
		41. Primary Conveyance	3.15	3.15	3.37	3.37	3.62	3.88	3.114	3.138			
		42. Food and Water	3.16	3.16	3.38	3.38	3.63	3.89	3.115	3.139			
		43. Care in Transit	3.17	3.17	3.39	3.39	3.64	3.90	3.116	3.140			
		44. Handling during Transportation	3.19	3.19	3.41	3.41	3.66	3.92	3.118	3.142			

45. Identification - 2.38 & 2.50	52. PREPARED BY *(Signature and title)*		53. DATE
46. Records & Holding Period - 2.35, 2.75, 2.76, 2.77, & 2.38, 2.101			
47. Handling - 2.38, 2.131, 3.111, & 3.135	54. COPY RECEIVED BY *(Signature and title)*		55. DATE
48. Veterinary Care - 2.33, 2.40, & 3.110			
49. IACUC - 2.31			
50. Personnel Qualifications - 2.32	56. REVIEWED BY *(Signature and title)*		57. DATE
51. Other items? YES *(If yes, see continuation sheet)* NO			

APHIS FORM 7008 (AUG 91)   (Replaces APHIS FORM 7008 (APR 90), which is obsolete.)   PART 3 - INSPECTOR

*U.S.GPO:1991-0-526-504/40250

Appendix F: Application for License

FORM APPROVED OMB NO. 0579-0036

No license may be issued unless a completed application has been received (7 U.S.C. 2133-2143), and the applicant is in compliance with the standards and regulations Section 2133.

U.S. DEPARTMENT OF AGRICULTURE
ANIMAL AND PLANT HEALTH INSPECTION SERVICE

APPLICATION FOR LICENSE
(TYPE OR PRINT)

☐ RENEWAL

DO NOT USE THIS SPACE - OFFICIAL USE ONLY

SEND THE COMPLETED FORM TO;

LICENSE NO.	RENEWAL DATE	FEES	
		AMOUNT	DATE RECEIVED

1. NAME(S) OF OWNER(S) AND MAILING ADDRESS

COUNTY: TELEPHONE (   )

2. ALL BUSINESS NAMES, LOCATIONS, AND ALL SITES HOUSING ANIMALS *(P.O. Box not acceptable)*

COUNTY: TELEPHONE (   )

3. IF PREVIOUSLY LICENSED - NAME AND ADDRESS

PREVIOUS LICENSE NO.:

4. NAME AND ADDRESS OF OTHER BUSINESS(S) HANDLING ANIMALS IN WHICH APPLICANT/LICENSEE HAS AN INTEREST

5. TYPE OF LICENSE

☐ A - Dealer *(Breeder)*   ☐ B - Dealer   ☐ C - Exhibitor

6. DATE OF LAST BUSINESS YEAR

FROM			TO		
MO	DAY	YEAR	MO	DAY	YEAR

7. NATURE OF BUSINESS *(Check item that describes nature of your business)*

☐ A - Zoo   ☐ B - Aquariums   ☐ C - Auction
☐ D - Breeder   ☐ E - Pets   ☐ F - Roadside Zoo
☐ G - Circus   ☐ H - Animal Acts   ☐ I - Carnival
☐ J - Drive thru Zoo ☐ K - Pet Store   ☐ L - Broker

8. TYPE OF ORGANIZATION

☐ Partnership   ☐ Corporation   ☐ Individual
☐ Other (Specify) _____

9. LIST OWNERS, PARTNERS, AND OFFICERS

NAME AND TITLE	ADDRESS

10. DEALER ONLY		**11. EXHIBITOR ONLY** *(No. of animals holding now or held during the last business year, whichever is greater.)*		
TOTAL NO. OF ANIMALS PURCHASED IN THE LAST BUSINESS YEAR		DOGS		RABBITS
TOTAL NO. OF ANIMALS SOLD IN THE LAST BUSINESS YEAR		CATS		NONHUMAN PRIMATES
TOTAL GROSS AMOUNT DERIVED FROM THE SALE OF ANIMALS		GUINEA PIGS		MARINE MAMMALS
		HAMSTERS		WILD OR EXOTIC MAMMALS
DOLLAR AMOUNT ON WHICH FEE IS BASED *(Sections 2.6 and 2.7)*		OTHER (i.e., farm animals) *(List Species and No.)*		

CERTIFICATION

I hereby make application for a license under the Animal Welfare Act 7 U.S.C. 2131 et seq. I certify that the information provided herein is true and correct to the best of my knowledge. I hereby acknowledge receipt of and certify to the best of my knowledge I am in compliance with all the regulations and standards in 9 CFR, Subpart A, Parts 1, 2 and 3. I certify that I am over 18 years of age.

12. SIGNATURE	13. NAME AND TITLE *(Type or Print)*	14. DATE

APHIS FORM 7003   *(Previous editions are obsolete)*   **PART 1 - SECTOR OFFICE**
(JAN 95)

Appendix G: Acquisition and Disposition Forms

This record is required by law (7 USC 2131-2156). (9 CFR, Subchapter A, Parts 1, 2 and 3). Failure to maintain this record can result in a suspension or revocation of license and/or imprisonment for not more than 1 year, or a fine of not more than $1,000, or both.

FORM APPROVED
OMB NO. 0579-0036

U.S. DEPARTMENT OF AGRICULTURE
ANIMAL AND PLANT HEALTH INSPECTION SERVICE

See reverse side for OMB information

RECORD OF ACQUISITION AND DOGS AND CATS ON HAND

1. RECORD FOR ("X")
- [ ] Dealer
- [ ] Holding Facility (Submit copy to Dealer)
- [ ] Other
- [ ] Exhibitor (Dogs and Cats only)

2. NAME AND ADDRESS OF LICENSEE, REGISTRANT, OR HOLDING FACILITY

USDA LICENSE OR REGISTRATION NO.

3. BUSINESS YEAR
FROM (Mo. Day, Yr.) TO (Mo. Day, Yr.)

4. PAGE NO.

IDENTIFICATION OF EACH ANIMAL BEING DELIVERED (See reverse for Breed Abbreviations)

A. TATTOO OR USDA TAG NO.	B. DOG	C. CAT "X" M or F	D. AGE OR DATE OF BIRTH	E. WT.	F. BREED OR TYPE (If mixed breed, last 2 dominant breeds)	G. DESCRIPTION OF ANIMAL (Color, Distinctive Marks, Hair, Tail Tattoos, etc.)	ACQUIRED FROM			DISPOSITION	
							H. DATE ACQUIRED	I. NAME AND ADDRESS USDA LICENSE OR REGISTRATION NUMBER, OR DRIVER'S LICENSE NUMBER AND STATE, VEHICLE LICENSE NUMBER AND STATE,		J. Date Removed or Sold	K. Date Died or Euthanized (Specify)
	M F	M F									
	M F	M F									
	M F	M F									
	M F	M F									
	M F	M F									
	M F	M F									
	M F	M F									

APHIS FORM 7005 (JUN 95)	INSPECTOR USE ONLY	LAST INSPECTION (Date)	TOTAL NO. ANIMALS ENTERED SINCE LAST INSPECTION	COUNT TOTAL NO. ANIMALS ACTUALLY ON PREMISES	DIFFERENCE (+ OR -)	DATE	INITIALS

(Replaces VS Form 18-5 which may be used.)

This record is required by law (7 USC 2131-2156). (9 CFR, Subchapter A, Parts 1, 2 and 3). Failure to maintain this record can result in a suspension or revocation of license and/or imprisonment for not more than 1 year, or a fine of not more than $1,000, or both.

See reverse side for additional information

U.S. DEPARTMENT OF AGRICULTURE
ANIMAL AND PLANT HEALTH INSPECTION SERVICE

RECORD OF DISPOSITION OF DOGS AND CATS

☐ SALE   ☐ EXCHANGE OR TRANSFER   ☐ DONATION

FORM APPROVED OMB NO. 0579-0036

1. DATE OF DISPOSITION

2. PAGE

1   OF

INSTRUCTIONS: Complete applicable items 1 through 8, Original and USDA Copy to be retained by seller.
Buyer's Copy to accompany shipment. It must be retained by Buyer.

3. SELLER OR DONOR *(Name & Address)*

4. BUYER OR RECEIVER *(Name)*

3A. DEALER'S LICENSE NO. OR RESEARCH FACILITY REGISTRATION NO. *(Seller)*

4A. USDA LICENSE NO. OR RESEARCH FACILITY REGISTRATION NO *(if any)*

5. IDENTIFICATION OF EACH ANIMAL BEING DELIVERED *(See reverse for Breed Abbreviations for Dogs and Cats)*   * If mixed breed, list 2 dominant breeds

COMPLETE ITEMS A THRU G FOR EACH ANIMAL

IDENTIFICATION NUMBER	DOG "X" M OR F	CAT	AGE OR DATE OF BIRTH	WT.	BREED OR TYPE *	DESCRIPTION OF ANIMAL *(Color, Distinctive Marks, Hair, Tail, Tattoos, etc.)*
A	B	C	D	E	F	G
	M / F	M / F				
	M / F	M / F				
	M / F	M / F				
	M / F	M / F				
	M / F	M / F				
	M / F	M / F				
	M / F	M / F				
	M / F	M / F				
	M / F	M / F				
	M / F	M / F				
	M / F	M / F				
	M / F	M / F				
	M / F	M / F				

6. DELIVERY BY *(Check one and complete applicable Items 7 and 8.)*

☐ COMMERCIAL SHIPPER   ☐ BUYER'S VEHICLE   ☐ SELLER'S VEHICLE

7. NAME AND ADDRESS OF COMPANY OR FIRM *(Include Zip Code)*

8. NAME AND BUSINESS ADDRESS OF TRUCK DRIVER *(Include Zip Code)*

9. RECEIVED BY

10. SIGNATURE

11. TITLE

12. DATE

APHIS FORM 7006   (Previous edition may be used.)
(JUN 95)

ORIGINAL - Seller's Record

Appendix H: Maps

DESTINATIONS OF DOGS SOLD BY A MISSOURI CLASS B DEALER

USDA's 1990 Stolen Dog Task Force audit of this dealer's records revealed that he had illegally acquired dogs and cats from at least three unlicensed individuals. This dealer also acquired animals from another dealer who was investigated by both USDA and the Missouri State Attorney General for acquiring dogs under false pretenses.

SOURCES OF DOGS AND CATS PURCHASED BY A PENNSYLVANIA CLASS B DEALER

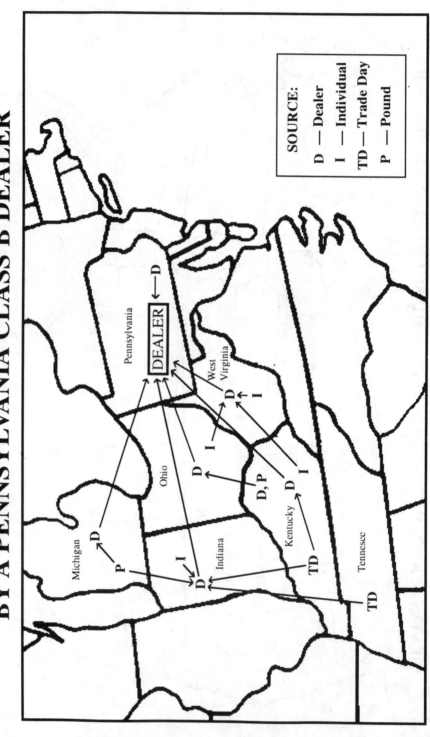

SOURCE:

D — Dealer
I — Individual
TD — Trade Day
P — Pound

Appendix I

Excerpts from U.S. Department of Agriculture Animal Welfare Act Regulations Governing Licensed Dealers and Exhibitors

TITLE 9 CODE OF FEDERAL REGULATIONS

CHAPTER 1

9 CFR Ch. I (1994 Edition)
Animal and Plant Health Inspection Service, USDA
SUBCHAPTER A - ANIMAL WELFARE
****

PART 2 - REGULATIONS Subpart A - Licensing
§ 2.1 Requirements and application.

(a)(1) Any person operating or desiring to operate as a dealer, exhibitor, or operator of an auction sale, except persons who are exempted from the licensing requirements under paragraph (a)(3) of this section, must have a valid license. A person must be 18 years of age or older to obtain a license. A person seeking a license shall apply on a form which will be furnished by the APHIS, REAC Sector Supervisor in the State in which that person operates or intends to operate. The applicant shall provide the information requested on the application form, including a valid mailing address through which the licensee or applicant can be reached at all times, and a valid premises address where animals, animal facilities, equipment, and records may be inspected for compliance. The applicant shall file the completed application form with the APHIS, REAC Sector Supervisor.

(2) If an applicant for a license or license renewal operates in more than one State, he or she shall apply in the State in which he or she has his or her principal place of business. All premises, facilities, or sites where such person operates or keeps animals shall be indicated on the application form or on a separate sheet attached to it. The completed application form, along with the application fee indicated in paragraph (d) of this section, and the annual license fee indicated in table 1 or 2 of § 2.6 shall be filed with the APHIS, REAC Sector Supervisor.

(3) The following persons are exempt from the licensing requirements under section 2 or section 3 of the Act:

(i) Retail pet stores which sell nondangerous, pet-type animals, such as dogs, cats, birds, rabbits, hamsters, guinea pigs, gophers, domestic ferrets, chinchilla, rats, and mice, for pets, at retail only: Provided, That, Anyone wholesaling any animals, selling any animals for research or exhibition, or selling any wild, exotic, or nonpet animals retail, must have a license;

(ii) Any person who sells or negotiates the sale or purchase of any animal except wild or exotic animals, dogs, or cats, and who derives no more than $500 gross income from the sale of such animals to a research facility, an exhibitor, a dealer, or a pet store during any calendar year and is not otherwise required to obtain a license;

(iii) Any person who maintains a total of three (3) or fewer breeding female dogs and/or cats and who sells only the offspring of these dogs or cats, which were born and raised on his or her premises, for pets or exhibition, and is not otherwise required to obtain a license;

(iv) Any person who sells fewer than 25 dogs and/or cats per year which were born and raised on his or her premises, for research, teaching, or testing purposes or to any research facility and is not otherwise required to obtain a license. The sale of any dog or cat not born and raised on the premises for research purposes requires a license;

(v) Any person who arranges for transportation or transports animals solely for the purpose of breeding, exhibiting in purebred shows, boarding (not in association with commercial transportation), grooming, or medical treatment, and is not otherwise required to obtain a license;

(vi) Any person who buys, sells, transports, or negotiates the sale, purchase, or transportation of any animals used only for the purposes of food or fiber (including fur);

(vii) Any person who breeds and raises domestic pet animals for direct retail sales to another person for the buyer's own use and who buys no animals for resale and who sells no animals to a research facility, an exhibitor, a dealer, or a pet store (e.g., a purebred dog or cat fancier) and is not otherwise required to obtain a license;

(viii) Any person who buys animals solely for his or her own use or enjoyment and does not sell or exhibit animals, or is not otherwise required to obtain a license;

(b) Any person who sells fewer than 25 dogs or cats per year for research or teaching purposes and who is not otherwise required to obtain a license may obtain a voluntary license, provided the animals were born and raised on his or her premises. A voluntary licensee shall comply with the requirements for dealers set forth in this part and the Specifications for the Humane Handling, Care, Treatment, and Transportation of Dogs and Cats set forth in part 3 of this subchapter and shall agree in writing on a form furnished by APHIS to comply with all the requirements of the Act and this subchapter. Voluntary licenses will not be issued to any other persons. To obtain a voluntary license the applicant shall submit to the APHIS, REAC Sector Supervisor the application fee of $10 plus an annual license fee. The class of license issued and the fee for a voluntary license shall be that of a Class "A" licensee (breeder). Voluntary licenses will not be issued to any other persons or for any other class of license.

(c) No person shall have more than one license.

(d) A license will be issued to any applicant, except as provided in §§ 2.10 and 2.11, when the applicant:

(1) Has met the requirements of this section and of §§ 2.2 and 2.3; and

(2) Has paid the application fee of $10 and the annual license fee indicated in § 2.6 to the APHIS, REAC Sector Supervisor and the payment has cleared normal banking procedures.

(e)(1) On or before the expiration date of the license, a licensee who wishes a renewal shall submit to the APHIS, REAC Sector Supervisor a completed application form and the application fee of $10, plus the annual license fee indicated in § 2.6 by certified check, cashier's check, personal check, or money order. A voluntary licensee who wishes a renewal shall also submit the $10 application fee plus an annual license fee. An applicant whose check is returned by the bank will be charged a fee of $15 for each returned check. One returned check will be deemed nonpayment of fees and will result in denial of license. Payment of fees must then be made by certified check, cashier's check, or money order. An applicant will not be licensed until his or her payment has cleared normal banking procedures.

(2) The $10 application fee must also be paid if an applicant is applying for a changed class of license. The applicant may pay such fees by certified check, cashier's check, personal check, or money order. An applicant whose check is returned by a bank will be charged a fee of $15 for each returned check and will be required to pay all subsequent fees by certified check, money order, or cashier's check. A license will not be issued until payment has cleared normal banking procedures.

(f) The failure of any person to comply with any provision of the Act, or any of the provisions of the regulations or standards in this subchapter, shall constitute grounds for denial of a license; or for its suspension or revocation by the Secretary, as provided in the Act.

****

Subpart D - Attending Veterinarian and Adequate Veterinary Care

§ 2.40 Attending veterinarian and adequate veterinary care (dealers and exhibitors).

(a) Each dealer or exhibitor shall have an attending veterinarian who shall provide adequate veterinary care to its animals in compliance with this section.

(1) Each dealer and exhibitor shall employ an attending veterinarian under formal arrangements. In the case of a part-time attending veterinarian or consultant arrangements, the formal arrangements shall include a written program of veterinary care and regularly scheduled visits to the premises of the dealer or exhibitor; and

(2) Each dealer and exhibitor shall assure that the attending veterinarian has appropriate authority to ensure the provision of adequate veterinary care and to oversee the adequacy of other aspects of animal care and use.

(b) Each dealer or exhibitor shall establish and maintain programs of adequate veterinary care that include:

(1) The availability of appropriate facilities, personnel, equipment, and services to comply with the provisions of this subchapter;

(2) The use of appropriate methods to prevent, control, diagnose, and treat diseases and injuries, and the availability of emergency, weekend, and holiday care;

(3) Daily observation of all animals to assess their health and well-being; Provided, however, That daily observation of animals may be accomplished by someone other than the attending veterinarian; and Provided, further, That a mechanism of direct and frequent communication is required so that timely and accurate information on problems of animal health, behavior, and well-being is conveyed to the attending veterinarian;

(4) Adequate guidance to personnel involved in the care and use of animals regarding handling, immobilization, anesthesia, analgesia, tranquilization, and euthanasia; and

(5) Adequate pre-procedural and post-procedural care in accordance with established veterinary medical and nursing procedures.

Subpart E - Identification of Animals

§ 2.50 Time and method of identification.

(a) A class "A" dealer (breeder) shall identify all live dogs and cats on the premises as follows:

(1) All live dogs and cats held on the premises, purchased, or otherwise acquired, sold or otherwise disposed of, or removed from the premises for delivery to a research facility or exhibitor or to another dealer, or for sale, through an auction sale or to any person for use as a pet, shall be identified by an official tag of the type

described in § 2.51 affixed to the animal's neck by means of a collar made of material generally considered acceptable to pet owners as a means of identifying their pet dogs or cats, or shall be identified by a distinctive and legible tattoo marking acceptable to and approved by the Administrator.

(2) Live puppies or kittens, less than 16 weeks of age, shall be identified by:

(i) An official tag as described in § 2.51;

(ii) A distinctive and legible tattoo marking approved by the Administrator; or

(iii) A plastic-type collar acceptable to the Administrator which has legibly placed thereon the information required for an official tag pursuant to § 2.51.

(b) A class "B" dealer shall identify all live dogs and cats under his or her control or on his or her premises as follows:

(1) When live dogs or cats are held, purchased, or otherwise acquired, they shall be immediately identified:

(i) By affixing to the animal's neck an official tag as set forth in § 2.51 by means of a collar made of material generally acceptable to pet owners as a means of identifying their pet dogs or cats; or

(ii) By a distinctive and legible tattoo marking approved by the Administrator.

(2) If any live dog or cat is already identified by an official tag or tattoo which has been applied by another dealer or exhibitor, the dealer or exhibitor who purchases or otherwise acquires the animal may continue identifying the dog or cat by the previous identification number, or may replace the previous tag with his own official tag or approved tattoo. In either case, the class B dealer or class C exhibitor shall correctly list all old and new official tag numbers or tattoos in his or her records of purchase which shall be maintained in accordance with §§ 2.75 and 2.77. Any new official tag or tattoo number shall be used on all records of any subsequent sales by the dealer or exhibitor, of any dog or cat.

(3) Live puppies or kittens less than 16 weeks of age, shall be identified by:

(i) An official tag as described in § 2.51;

(ii) A distinctive and legible tattoo marking approved by the Administrator; or

(iii) A plastic-type collar acceptable to the Administrator which has legibly placed thereon the information required for an official tag pursuant to § 2.51.

(4) When any dealer has made a reasonable effort to affix an official tag to a cat, as set forth in paragraphs (a) and (b) of this section, and has been unable to do so, or when the cat exhibits serious distress from the attachment of a collar and tag, the dealer shall attach the collar and tag to the door of the primary enclosure containing the cat and take measures adequate to maintain the identity of the cat in relation to the tag. Each primary enclosure shall contain no more than one weaned cat without an affixed collar and official tag, unless the cats are identified by a distinctive and legible tattoo or plastic-type collar approved by the Administrator.

(c) A class "C" exhibitor shall identify all live dogs and cats under his or her control or on his or her premises, whether held, purchased, or otherwise acquired:

(1) As set forth in paragraph (b)(1) or (b)(3) of this section, or

(2) By identifying each dog or cat with:

(i) An official USDA sequentially numbered tag that is kept on the door of the animal's cage or run;

(ii) A record book containing each animal's tag number, a written description of each animal, the data required by § 2.75(a), and a clear photograph of each animal; and

(iii) A duplicate tag that accompanies each dog or cat whenever it leaves the compound or premises.

(d) Unweaned puppies or kittens need not be individually identified as required by paragraphs (a) and (b) of this section while they are maintained as a litter with their dam in the same primary enclosure, provided the dam has been individually identified.

(e)(1) All animals, except dogs and cats, delivered for transportation, transported, purchased, sold, or otherwise acquired or disposed of by any dealer or exhibitor shall be identified by the dealer or exhibitor at the time of delivery for transportation, purchase, sale, acquisition or disposal, as provided for in this paragraph and in records maintained as required in § § 2.75 and 2.77.

(2) When one or more animals, other than dogs or cats, are confined in a primary enclosure, the animal(s) shall be identified by:

(i) A label attached to the primary enclosure which shall bear a description of the animals in the primary enclosure, including:

(A) The number of animals;

(B) The species of the animals;

(C) Any distinctive physical features of the animals; and

(D) Any identifying marks, tattoos, or tags attached to the animals;

(ii) Marking the primary enclosure with a painted or stenciled number which shall be recorded in the records of the dealer or exhibitor together with:

(A) A description of the animal(s);

(B) The species of the animal(s); and

(C) Any distinctive physical features of the animal(s); or

(iii) A tag or tattoo applied to each animal in the primary enclosure by the dealer or exhibitor which individually identifies each animal by description or number.

(3) When any animal, other than a dog or cat, is not confined in a primary enclosure, it shall be identified on a record, as required by § 2.75, which shall accompany the animal at the time it is delivered for transportation, transported, purchased, or sold, and shall be kept and maintained by the dealer or exhibitor as part of his or her records.

****

Subpart F - Stolen Animals

§ 2.60 Prohibition on the purchase, sale, use, or transportation of stolen animals. No person shall buy, sell, exhibit, use for research, transport, or offer for transportation, any stolen animal.

Subpart G - Records

§ 2.75 Records: Dealers and exhibitors.

(a)(1) Each dealer, other than operators of auction sales and brokers to whom animals are consigned, and each exhibitor shall make, keep, and maintain records or forms which fully and correctly disclose the following information concerning each dog or cat purchased or otherwise acquired, owned, held, or otherwise in his or her possession or under his or her control, or which is transported, euthanized, sold, or otherwise disposed of by that dealer or exhibitor. The records shall include any offspring born of any animal while in his or her possession or under his or her control.

(i) The name and address of the person from whom a dog or cat was purchased or otherwise acquired whether or not the person is required to be licensed or registered under the Act;

(ii) The USDA license or registration number of the person if he or she is licensed or registered under the Act;

(iii) The vehicle license number and state, and the driver's license number and state of the person, if he or she is not licensed or registered under the Act;

(iv) The name and address of the person to whom a dog or cat was sold or given and that person's license or registration number if he or she is licensed or registered under the Act;

(v) The date a dog or cat was acquired or disposed of, including by euthanasia;

(vi) The official USDA tag number or tattoo assigned to a dog or cat under § § 2.50 and 2.54;

(vii) A description of each dog or cat which shall include:

(A) The species and breed or type;

(B) The sex;

(C) The date of birth or approximate age; and

(D) The color and any distinctive markings;

(viii) The method of transportation including the name of the initial carrier or intermediate handler or, if a privately owned vehicle is used to transport a dog or cat, the name of the owner of the privately owned vehicle;

(ix) The date and method of disposition of a dog or cat, e.g., sale, death, euthanasia, or donation.

(2) Record of Dogs and Cats on Hand (VS Form 18-5) and Record of Disposition of Dogs and Cats (VS Form 18-6) are forms which may be used by dealers and exhibitors to make, keep, and maintain the information required by paragraph (a)(1) of this section.

(3) The USDA Interstate and International Certificate of Health Examination for Small Animals (VS Form 18-1) may be used by dealers and exhibitors to make, keep, and maintain the information required by paragraph (a)(1) of this section and § 2.79.

(4) One copy of the record containing the information required by paragraph (a)(1) of this section shall accompany each shipment of any dog or cat purchased or otherwise acquired by a dealer or exhibitor. One copy of the record containing the information required by paragraph (a)(1) of this section shall accompany each shipment of any dog or cat sold or otherwise disposed of by a dealer or exhibitor: Provided, however, that, except as provided in section 2.133(b) of this part for dealers, information that indicates the source and date of acquisition of a dog or cat need not appear on the copy of the record accompanying the shipment. One copy of the record containing the information required by paragraph (a)(1) of this section shall be retained by the dealer or exhibitor.

(b)(1) Every dealer other than operators of auction sales and brokers to whom animals are consigned, and exhibitor shall make, keep, and maintain records or forms which fully and correctly disclose the following information concerning animals other than dogs and cats, purchased or otherwise acquired, owned, held, leased, or otherwise in his or her possession or under his or her control, or which is transported, sold, euthanized, or otherwise disposed of by that dealer or exhibitor. The records shall include any offspring born of any animal while in his or her possession or under his or her control.

(i) The name and address of the person from whom the animals were purchased or otherwise acquired;

(ii) The USDA license or registration number of the person if he or she is licensed or registered under the Act;

(iii) The vehicle license number and state, and the driver's license number and state of the person, if he or she is not licensed or registered under the Act;

(iv) The name and address of the person to whom an animal was sold or given;

(v) The date of purchase, acquisition, sale, or disposal of the animal(s);

(vi) The species of the animal(s); and

(vii) The number of animals in the shipment.

(2) Record of Animals on Hand (other than dogs and cats) (VS Form 18-19) and Record of Acquisition, Disposition, or Transport of Animals (other than dogs and cats)

(VS Form 18-20) are forms which may be used by dealers and exhibitors to keep and maintain the information required by paragraph (b)(1) of this section concerning animals other than dogs and cats except as provided in § 2.79.

(3) One copy of the record containing the information required by paragraph (b)(1) of this section shall accompany each shipment of any animal(s) other than a dog or cat purchased or otherwise acquired by a dealer or exhibitor. One copy of the record containing the information required by paragraph (b)(1) of this section shall accompany each shipment of any animal other than a dog or cat sold or otherwise disposed of by a dealer or exhibitor; Provided, however, That information which indicates the source and date of acquisition of any animal other than a dog or cat need not appear on the copy of the record accompanying the shipment. The dealer or exhibitor shall retain one copy of the record containing the information required by paragraph

(b)(1) of this section.

****

Subpart H - Compliance With Standards and Holding Period

§ 2.101 Holding period.

(a) Any live dog or cat acquired by a dealer or exhibitor shall be held by him or her, under his or her supervision and control, for a period of not less than 5 full days, not including the day of acquisition, after acquiring the animal, excluding time in transit: Provided, however:

(FOOTNOTE) \5\ An operator of an auction sale is not considered to have acquired a dog or cat which is sold through the auction sale.

(1) That any live dog or cat acquired by a dealer or exhibitor from any private or contract animal pound or shelter shall be held by that dealer or exhibitor under his or her supervision and control for a period of not less than 10 full days, not including the day of acquisition, after acquiring the animal, excluding time in transit;

(2) Live dogs or cats which have completed a 5-day holding period with another dealer or exhibitor, or a 10-day holding period with another dealer or exhibitor if obtained from a private or contract shelter or pound, may be sold or otherwise disposed of by subsequent dealers or exhibitors after a minimum holding period of 24 hours by each subsequent dealer or exhibitor excluding time in transit;

(3) Any dog or cat suffering from disease, emaciation, or injury may be destroyed by euthanasia prior to the completion of the holding period required by this section; and

(4) Any live dog or cat, 120 days of age or less, that was obtained from the person that bred and raised such dog or cat, may be exempted from the 5-day holding requirement and may be disposed of by dealers or exhibitors after a minimum holding period of 24 hours, excluding time in transit. Each subsequent dealer or exhibitor must also hold each such dog or cat for a 24-hour period excluding time in transit.

(b) During the period in which any dog or cat is being held as required by this section, the dog or cat shall be unloaded from any means of conveyance in which it was received, for food, water, and rest, and shall be handled, cared for, and treated in accordance with the standards set forth in part 3, subpart A, of this subchapter and § 2.131.

****

§ 2.126 Access and inspection of records and property.

(a) Each dealer, exhibitor, intermediate handler, or carrier, shall, during business hours, allow APHIS officials:

(1) To enter its place of business;

(2) To examine records required to be kept by the Act and the regulations in this part;

(3) To make copies of the records;

(4) To inspect and photograph the facilities, property and animals, as the APHIS officials consider necessary to enforce the provisions of the Act, the regulations and the standards in this subchapter; and

(5) To document, by the taking of photographs and other means, conditions and areas of noncompliance.

(b) The use of a room, table, or other facilities necessary for the proper examination of the records and inspection of the property or animals shall be extended to APHIS officials by the dealer, exhibitor, intermediate handler or carrier.

****

§ 2.128 Inspection for missing animals. Each dealer, exhibitor, intermediate handler and carrier shall allow, upon request and during business hours, police or officers of other law enforcement agencies with general law enforcement authority (not those agencies whose duties are limited to enforcement of local animal regulations) to enter his or her place of business to inspect animals and records for the purpose of seeking animals that are missing, under the following conditions:

(a) The police or other law officer shall furnish to the dealer, exhibitor, intermediate handler or carrier a written description of the missing animal and the name and address of its owner before making a search.

(b) The police or other law officer shall abide by all security measures required by the dealer, exhibitor, intermediate handler or carrier to prevent the spread of disease, including the use of sterile clothing, footwear, and masks where required, or to prevent the escape of an animal.

§ 2.129 Confiscation and destruction of animals.

(a) If an animal being held by a dealer, exhibitor, intermediate handler, or by a carrier is found by an APHIS official to be suffering as a result of the failure of the dealer, exhibitor, intermediate handler, or carrier to comply with any provision of the regulations or the standards set forth in this subchapter, the APHIS official shall make a reasonable effort to notify the dealer, exhibitor, intermediate handler, or carrier of the condition of the animal(s) and request that the condition be corrected and that adequate care be given to alleviate the animal's suffering or distress, or that the animal(s) be destroyed by euthanasia. In the event that the dealer, exhibitor, intermediate handler, or carrier refuses to comply with this request, the APHIS official may confiscate the animal(s) for care, treatment, or disposal as indicated in paragraph (b) of this section, if, in the opinion of the Administrator, the circumstances indicate the animal's health is in danger.

(b) In the event that the APHIS official is unable to locate or notify the dealer, exhibitor, intermediate handler, or carrier as required in this section, the APHIS official shall contact a local police or other law officer to accompany him to the premises and shall provide for adequate care when necessary to alleviate the animal's suffering. If in the opinion of the Administrator, the condition of the animal(s) cannot be corrected by this temporary care, the APHIS official shall confiscate the animals.

(c) Confiscated animals may be placed, by sale or donation, with other licensees or registrants which comply with the standards and regulations and can provide proper care, or they may be euthanized. The dealer, exhibitor, intermediate handler, or carrier from whom the animals were confiscated shall bear all costs incurred in performing the placement or euthanasia activities authorized by this section.

****

§ 2.132 Procurement of random source dogs and cats, dealers.

(a) A class "B" dealer may obtain live random source dogs and cats only from:

(1) Other dealers who are licensed under the Act and in accordance with the regulations in part 2;

(2) State, county, or city owned and operated animal pounds or shelters; and

(3) A legal entity organized and operated under the laws of the State in which it is located as an animal pound or shelter, such as a humane shelter or contract pound.

(b) A class "B" dealer shall not obtain live random source dogs and cats from individuals who have not bred and raised the dogs and cats on their own premises.

(c) Live nonrandom source dogs and cats may be obtained from persons who have bred and raised the dogs and cats on their own premises, such as hobby breeders.

(d) No person shall obtain live random source dogs or cats by use of false pretenses, misrepresentation, or deception.

(e) Any dealer, exhibitor, research facility, carrier, or intermediate handler who also operates a private or contract animal pound or shelter shall comply with the following:

(1) The animal pound or shelter shall be located on premises that are physically separated from the licensed or registered facility. The animal housing facility of the pound or shelter shall not be adjacent to the licensed or registered facility.

(2) Accurate and complete records shall be separately maintained by the licensee or registrant and by the pound or shelter. The records shall be in accordance with § § 2.75 and 2.76, unless the animals are lost or stray. If the animals are lost or stray, the pound or shelter records shall provide:

(i) An accurate description of the animal;

(ii) How, where, from whom, and when the dog or cat was obtained;

(iii) How long the dog or cat was held by the pound or shelter before being transferred to the dealer; and

(iv) The date the dog or cat was transferred to the dealer.

(3) Any dealer who obtains or acquires a live random source dog or cat from a private or contract pound or shelter, including a pound or shelter he or she operates, shall hold the dog or cat for a period of at least 10 full days, not including the day of acquisition, excluding time in transit, after acquiring the animal, and otherwise in accordance with § 2.101.

§ 2.133. Certification for Random Source Dogs and Cats

(a) Each of the entities listed in paragraphs (a)(1) through

(a)(3) of this section that acquire any live dog or cat shall, before selling or providing the live dog or cat to a dealer, hold and care for the dog or cat for a period of not less than 5 full days after acquiring the animal, not including the date of acquisition and excluding time in transit. This holding period shall include at least one Saturday. The provisions of this paragraph apply to:

(1) Each pound or shelter owned and operated by a State, county, or city;

(2) Each private pound or shelter established for the purpose of caring for animals, such as a humane society, or other organization that is under contract with a State, county, or city, that operates as a pound or shelter, and that releases animals on a voluntary basis; and

(3) Each research facility licensed by USDA as a dealer.

(b) A dealer shall not sell, provide, or make available to any person a live random source dog or cat unless the dealer provides the recipient of the dog or cat with certification that contains the following information:

(1) The name, address, USDA license number, and signature of the dealer;

(2) The name, address, USDA license or registration number, if such number exists, and signature of the recipient of the dog or cat;

(3) A description of each dog or cat being sold, provided, or made available that shall include:

(i) The species and breed or type (for mixed breeds, estimate the two dominant breeds or types);

(ii) The sex;

(iii) The date of birth or, if unknown, then the approximate age;

(iv) The color and any distinctive markings; and

(v) The Official USDA-approved identification number of the animal. However, if the certification is attached to a certificate provided by a prior dealer which contains the required description, then only the official identification numbers are required;

(4) The name and address of the person, pound, or shelter from which the dog or cat was acquired by the dealer, and an assurance that the person, pound, or shelter was notified that the cat or dog might be used for research or educational purposes;

(5) The date the dealer acquired the dog or cat from the person, pound, or shelter referred to in paragraph (b)(4) of this section; and

(6) If the dealer acquired the dog or cat from a pound or shelter, a signed statement by the pound or shelter that it met the requirements of paragraph (a) of this section. This statement must at least describe the animals by their official USDA identification numbers. It may be incorporated within the certification if the dealer makes the certification at the time that the animals are acquired from the pound or shelter or it may be made separately and attached to the certification later. If made separately, it must include the same information describing each animal as is required in the certification. A photocopy of the statement will be regarded as a duplicate original.

(c) The original certification required under paragraph (b) of this section shall accompany the shipment of a live dog or cat to be sold, provided, or otherwise made available by the dealer.

(d) A dealer who acquires a live dog or cat from another dealer must obtain from that dealer the certification required by paragraph (b) of this section and must attach that certification (including any previously attached certification) to the certification which he or she provides pursuant to paragraph (b) of this section (a photocopy of the original certification will be deemed a duplicate original if the dealer does not dispose of all of the dogs or cats in a single transaction).

(e) A dealer who completes, provides, or receives a certification required under paragraph (b) of this section shall keep, maintain, and make available for APHIS inspection a copy of the certification for at least 1 year following disposition.

(f) A research facility which acquires any live random source dog or cat from a dealer must obtain the certification required under paragraph (b) of this section and shall keep, maintain, and make available for APHIS inspection the original for at least 3 years following disposition.

(g) In instances where a research facility transfers ownership of a live random source dog or cat acquired from a dealer to another research facility, a copy of the certification required by paragraph (b) of this section must accompany the dog or cat transferred. The research facility to which the dog or cat is transferred shall keep, maintain, and make available for APHIS inspection the copy of the certification for at least 3 years following disposition.

****

Note: for a complete copy of the Animal Welfare Act Regulations, contact the Animal and Plant Health Inspection Service's publications office at (301) 734-7255. Or, on the World Wide Web, go to

http://www.aphis.usda.gov/reac/awaregs.html

Appendix J

Animal Welfare Act
as amended

(7 U.S.C. §§ 2131 et. seq.)

Section 1. (a) This Act may be cited as the "Animal Welfare Act".

(b) The Congress finds that animals and activities which are regulated under this Act are either in interstate or foreign commerce or substantially affect such commerce or the free flow thereof, and that regulation of animals and activities as provided in this Act is necessary to prevent and eliminate burdens upon such commerce and to effectively regulate such commerce, in order—

(1) to insure that animals intended for use in research facilities or for exhibition purposes or for use as pets are provided humane care and treatment;

(2) to assure the humane treatment of animals during transportation in commerce; and

(3) to protect the owners of animals from the theft of their animals by preventing the sale or use of animals which have been stolen. The Congress further finds that it is essential to regulate, as provided in this Act, the transportation, purchase, sale, housing, care, handling, and treatment of animals by carriers or by persons or organizations engaged in using them for research or experimental purposes or for exhibition purposes or holding them for sale as pets or for any such purpose or use. The Congress further finds that—

(1) the use of animals is instrumental in certain research and education for advancing knowledge of cures and treatment for diseases and injuries which afflict both humans and animals;

(2) methods of testing that do not use animals are being and continue to be developed which are faster, less expensive, and more accurate than traditional animal experiments for some purposes and further opportunities exist for the development of these methods of testing;

(3) measures which eliminate or minimize the unnecessary duplication of experiments on animals can result in more productive use of Federal funds; and

(4) measures which help meet the public concern for laboratory animal care and treatment are important in assuring that research will continue to progress.

(7 U.S.C. § 2131) (P.L. 89-544, § 1, Aug. 24, 1966, 80 Stat. 350; P.L. 91-579, § 2, Dec. 24, 1970, 84 Stat. 1560; renumbered and amended by P.L. 94-279, § 2, Apr. 22, 1976, 90 Stat. 417)

Section 2. When used in this Act—

(a) The term "Person" includes any individual, partnership, firm, joint stock company, corporation. association, trust, estate, or other legal entity;

(b) The term "Secretary" means the Secretary of Agriculture of the United States or his representative who shall be an employee of the United States Department of Agriculture;

(c) The term "commerce" means trade, traffic, transportation, or other commerce

(1) between a place in a State and any place outside of such State, or between points within the same State but through any place outside thereof, or within any territory, possession, or the District of Columbia;

(2) which affects trade, traffic, transportation, or other commerce described in paragraph (1),

(d) The term "State" means a State of the United States, the District of Columbia, the Commonwealth of Puerto Rico, the Virgin Islands, Guam, American Samoa, or any other territory or possession of the United States;

(e) The term "research facility" means any school (except an elementary or secondary school), institution, organization, or person that uses or intends to use live animals in research, tests, or experiments, and that

(1) purchases or transports live animals in commerce, or (2) receives funds under a grant, award, loan, or contract from a department, agency, or instrumentality of the United States for the purpose of carrying out research, tests, or experiments: Provided, That the Secretary may exempt, by regulation, any such school, institution, organization, or person that does not use or intend to use live dogs or cats, except those schools, institutions, organizations, or persons, which use substantial numbers (as determined by the Secretary) or live animals the principal function of which schools, institutions, organizations, or persons, is biomedical research or testing, when in the judgment of the Secretary, any such exemption does not vitiate the purpose of this Act;

(f) The term "dealer" means any person who, in commerce, for compensation or profit, delivers for transportation, or transports, except as a carrier, buys, or sells, or negotiates the purchase or sale of, (1) any dog or other animal whether alive or dead for research, teaching, exhibition, or use as a pet, or (2) any dog for hunting, security, or breeding purposes, except that this term does not include

(i) a retail pet store except such store which sells any animals to a research facility, an exhibitor, or a dealer; or

(ii) any person who does not sell, or negotiate the purchase or sale or any wild animal, dog, or cat and who derives no more than $500 gross income from the sale of other animals during any calendar year;

(g) The term "animal" means any live or dead dog, cat, monkey (nonhuman primate mammal), guinea pig, hamster, rabbit, or such other warm-blooded animal, as the Secretary may determine is being used, or is intended for use, for research, testing, experimentation, or exhibition purposes or as a pet; but such term excludes horses not used for research purposes and other farm animals, such as, but not limited to livestock or poultry, used or intended for use as food or fiber, or livestock or poultry used or intended for improving animal nutrition, breeding, management or production efficiency, or for improving the quality of food or fiber. With respect to a dog the term means all dogs including those used for hunting, security, or breeding purposes;

(h) The term "exhibitor" means any person (public or private) exhibiting any animals, which were purchased in commerce or the intended distribution of which affects commerce, or will affect commerce, to the public for compensation, as determined by the Secretary, and such term includes carnivals, circuses, and zoos exhibiting such animals whether operated for profit or not; but such term excludes retail pet stores, organizations sponsoring and all persons participating in State and country fairs, livestock shows, rodeos, purebred dog and cat shows, and any other fairs or exhibitions intended to advance agricultural arts and sciences, as may be determined by the Secretary;

(i) The term "intermediate handler" means any person including a department, agency, or instrumentality of the United States or of any State or local government (other than a dealer, research facility, exhibitor, any person excluded from the definition of a dealer, research facility, or exhibitor, an operator of an auction sale, or a carrier) who is engaged in any business in which he receives custody of animals in connection with their transportation in commerce; and

(j) The term "carrier" means the operator of any airline, railroad, motor carrier, shipping line, or other enterprise, which is engaged in the business or transporting any animals for hire.

(k) The term "Federal agency" means an Executive agency as such term is defined in section 105 of Title 5, United States Code, and with respect to any research facility means the agency from which the research facility means the agency from which the research facility receives a Federal award for the conduct of research, experimentation, or testing, involving the use of animals;

(l) The term "Federal award for the conduct of research, experimentation, or testing, involving the use of animals" means any mechanism (including a grant, award, loan, contract, or cooperative agreement) under which Federal funds are provided to support the conduct of such research;

(m) The term "quorum" means a majority of the Committee members;

(n) The term "Committee" means the Institutional Animal Committee established under section 13(b); and

(o) The term "Federal research facility" means each department, agency, or instrumentality of the United States which uses live animals for research of experimentation.

(7 U.S.C. § 2132) (P.L. 89-544, § 2, Aug. 24. 1966, 80 Stat. 350; P.L. 91-579, § 3, Dec. 24, 1970, 84 Stat. 1560; P.L. 94-279 §§ 3, 4, Apr. 22, 1976, 90 Stat. 417, 418; P.L. 99-198, Title XVII, § 1756(a), Dec. 23, 1985,, 99 Stat. 1650)

Section 3. The Secretary shall issue licenses to dealers and exhibitors upon application therefor in such form and manner as he may prescribe and upon payment of such fee established pursuant to section 23 of this Act: Provided, That no such license shall be issued until the dealer or exhibitor shall have demonstrated that his facilities comply with the standards promulgated by the Secretary pursuant to section 13 of this Act: Provided, however, That any retail pet store or other person who derives less than a substantial portion of his income (as determined by the Secretary) from the breeding and raising of dogs or cats on his own premises and sells any such dog or cat to a dealer or research facility shall not be required to obtain a license as a dealer or exhibitor under this Act. The Secretary is further authorized to license, as dealers or exhibitors persons who do not qualify as dealers or exhibitors within the meaning of this Act upon such persons complying with the requirements specified above and agreeing, in writing, to comply with all the requirements of this Act and the regulations promulgated by the Secretary hereunder.

(7 U.S.C. § 2133) (P.L. 89-544, § 3, Aug. 24, 1966, 80 Stat. 351; P.L. 91-579, § 4, Dec. 24, 1970, 84 Stat. 1561)

Section 4. No dealer or exhibitor shall sell or offer to sell or transport or offer for transportation, in commerce, to any research facility or for exhibition or for use as a pet any animal, or buy, sell, offer to buy or sell, transport or offer for transportation, in commerce, to or from another dealer or exhibitor under this Act any animal, unless and until such dealer or exhibitor shall have obtained a license from the Secretary and such license shall not have been amended or revoked.

(7 U.S.C. § 2134) (P.L. 89-544, § 4, Aug. 24. 1966, 80 Stat. 351; P.L. 91-579, § 5, Dec. 24, 1970, 84 Stat. 1561; P.L. 94-279, § 5, Apr. 22, 1976, 90 Stat. 418)

Section 5. No dealer or exhibitor shall sell or dispose of any dog or cat within a period of 5 business days after the acquisition of such animal or within such other period as way be specified by the Secretary: Provided, that operators of auction sales subject to section 12 of this Act shall not be required to comply with the provisions of this section.

(7 U.S.C. § 2135) (P.L. 89-544, § 5, Aug. 24, 1966, 80 Stat. 351; P.L. 91-579. § 6, Dec. 24, 1970, 84 Stat. 1561)

Section 6. Every research facility, every intermediate handler, every carrier, and every exhibitor not licensed under section 3 of this Act shall register with the Secretary in accordance with such rules and regulations as he may prescribe.

(7 U.S.C. § 2136) (P.L. 89-544, § 6, Aug. 24, 1966, 80 Stat. 351; P.L. 91-579, § 7, Dec. 24, 1970, 84 Stat. 1561; P.L. 94-279, § 6, Apr. 22, 1976, 90 Stat. 418)

Section 7. It shall be unlawful for any research facility to purchase any dog or cat from any person except an operator of an auction sale subject to section 12 of this Act or a person holding a valid license as a dealer or exhibitor issued by the Secretary pursuant to this Act unless such person is exempted from obtaining such license under section 3 of this Act.

(7 U.S.C. § 2137) (P.L. 89-544, § 7, Aug. 24, 1966, 80 Stat. 351; P.L. 91-579. § 8, Dec. 24, 1970. 84 Stat. 1561)

Section 8. No department, agency, or instrumentality of the United States which uses animals for research or experimentation or exhibition shall purchase or otherwise acquire any dog or cat for such purposes from any person except an operator of an auction sale subject to section 12 of this Act or a person holding a valid license as a dealer or exhibitor issued by the Secretary pursuant to this Act unless such person is exempted from obtaining such license under section 3 of this Act.

(7 U.S.C. § 2138) (P.L. 89-544, § 8, Aug. 24, 1966, 80 Stat. 351; P.L. 91-579, § 9, Dec. 24, 1970, 84 Stat. 1562)

Section 9. When construing or enforcing the provisions of this Act, the act, omission, or failure of any person acting for or employed by a research facility, a dealer, or an exhibitor or a person licensed as a dealer or an exhibitor pursuant to the second sentence of section 3, or an operator of an auction sale subject to section 12 of this Act, or an intermediate handler or a carrier, within the scope of his employment or office, shall be deemed the act, omission, or failure of such research facility, dealer, exhibitor, licensee, operator of an auction sale, intermediate handler, or carrier, as well of such person.

(7 U.S.C. § 2139) (P.L. 89-544, § 9, Aug. 24, 1966, 80 Stat. 351; P.L. 91-579, § 10, Dec. 24, 1970, 84 Stat. 1562; P.L. 94-279, § 7, Apr. 22, 1976, 90 Stat. 418)

Section 10. Dealers and exhibitors shall make and retain for such reasonable period of time as the Secretary may prescribe, such records with respect to the purchase, sale, transportation, identification, and previous ownership of animals as the Secretary may prescribe. Research facilities shall make and retain such records only with respect to the purchase, sale, transportation, identification, and previous ownership of live dogs and cats. At the request of the Secretary, any regulatory agency of the Federal Government which requires records to be maintained by intermediate handlers and carriers with respect to the transportation, receiving, handling, and delivery of animals on forms prescribed by the agency, shall require there to be included in such forms, and intermediate handlers and carriers shall include in such forms, such information as the Secretary may require for the effective administration of this Act. Such information shall be retained for such reasonable period of time as the Secretary may prescribe. If regulatory agencies of the Federal Government do not prescribe requirements for any such forms, intermediate handlers and carriers shall make and retain for such reasonable period as the Secretary may prescribe such records with respect to the transportation, receiving, handling, and delivery of animals as the Secretary may prescribe. Such records shall be made available at all reasonable times for inspection and copying by the Secretary.

(7 U.S.C. § 2140) (P.L. 89-544, § 10, Aug. 24, 1966, 80 Stat. 351; P.L. 91-579, § 11, Dec. 24, 1970, 84 Stat. 1562; P.L. 94-279, § 8, Apr. 22, 1976, 90 Stat. 418)

Section 11. All animals delivered for transportation, transported, purchased, or sold, in commerce, by a dealer or exhibitor shall be marked or identified at such time and in such humane manner as the Secretary may prescribe: Provided, That only live dogs and cats need be so marked or identified by a research facility.

(7 U.S.C. § 2141) (P.L. 89-544, § 11, Aug. 24, 1966, 80 Stat. 351; P.L. 91-579, § 12, Dec. 24. 1970, 84 Stat. 1562; P.L. 94-279, § 5. Apr. 22, 1976, 90 Stat. 418)

Section 12. The Secretary is authorized to promulgate humane standards and recordkeeping requirements governing the purchase, handling, or sale of animals, in commerce, by dealers, research facilities, and exhibitors at auction sales and by the operators of such auction sales. The Secretary is also authorized to require the licensing of operators of auction sales where any dogs or cats are sold, in commerce, trader such conditions as he may prescribe, and upon payment of such fee as prescribed by the Secretary under section 23 of this Act.

(7 U.S.C. § 2142) (P.L. 89-544, § 12, Aug. 24, 1966, 80 Stat. 351; P.L. 91-579, § 13, Dec. 24, 1970, 84 Stat. 1562; P.L. 94-279, § 5, Apr. 22, 1976, 90 Stat. 418.)

Section 13. (a)(1) The Secretary shall promulgate standards to govern the humane handling, care, treatment, and transportation of animals by dealers, research facilities, and exhibitors.

(2) The standards described in paragraph (1) shall include minimum requirements —

(A) for handling, housing, feeding, watering, sanitation, ventilation, shelter from extremes of weather and temperatures, adequate veterinary care, and separation by species where the Secretary finds necessary for humane handling, care, or treatment of animals; and

(B) for exercise of dogs, as determined by an attending veterinarian in accordance with the general standards promulgated by the Secretary, and for a physical environment adequate to promote the psychological well-being of primates.

(3) In addition to the requirements under paragraph (2), the standards described

in paragraph (1) shall, with respect ot animals in research facilities, include requirements—

(A) for animal care, treatment, and practices in experimental procedures to ensure that animal pain and distress are minimized, including adequate veterinary care with the appropriate use of anesthetic, analgesic or tranquilizing drugs, or euthanasia;

(B) that the principal investigator considers alternatives to any procedure likely to produce pain or distress in an experimental animal;

(C) in any practice which could cause pain to animals-

(i) that a doctor of veterinary medicine is consulted in the planning of such procedures;

(ii) for the use of tranquilizers, analgesics, and anesthetics;

(iii) for presurgical and postsurgical care by laboratory workers in accordance with established veterinary medical and nursing procedures;

(iv) against the use of paralytics without anesthesia; and

(v) that the withholding of tranquilizers, anesthesia, analgesia, or euthanasia when scientifically necessary shall continue for only the necessary period of time;

(D) that no animal is used in more than one major operative experimenta from which it is allowed to recover except in cases of—

(i) scientific necessity; or

(ii) other special circumstances as determined by the Secretary; and

(E) that exceptions to such standards may be made only when specified by research protocol and that any such exception shall be detailed and explained in a report outlined under paragraph (7) and filed with the Institutional Animal Committee.

(4) The Secretary shall also promulgate standards to govern the transportation in commerce to govern the transportation in commerce, and the handling, care, and treatment in connection therewith, by intermediate handlers, air carriers, or other carriers, of animals consigned by a dealer, research facility, exhibitor, operator of an auction sale, or other person, or any department, agency, or instrumentality of the United States or of any State or local government, for transportation in commerce. The Secretary shall have authority to promulgate such rules and regulations as he determines necessary to assure humane treatment of animals in the course of their transportation in commerce including requirements such as those with respect to containers, feed, water, rest, ventilation, temperature, and handling.

(5) In promulgating and enforcing standards established pursuant to this section, the Secretary is authorized and directed to consult experts, including outside consultants where indicated.

(6)(A) Nothing in this Act—

(i) except as provided in paragraph (7) of this subsection, shall be construed as authorizing the Secretary to promulgate rules, regulations, or orders with regard to design, outlines, guidelines or performance of actual research or experimentation by a research facility as determined by such research facility;

(ii) except as provided in subparagraphs (A) and (C)(ii) through (v) of paragraph (3) and paragraph (7) of this subsection, shall be construed as authorizing the Secretary to promulgate rules, regulations, or orders with regard to the performance of actual research or experimentation by a research facility as determined by such research facility; and

(iii) shall authorize the Secretary, during inspection, to interrupt the conduct of actual research or experimentation.

(B) No rule, regulation, order, or part of this Act shall be construed to require a research facility to disclose publicly or to the Institutional Animal Committee during its inspection, trade secrets or commercial or financial information which is privileged or confidential.

(7)(A) The Secretary shall require each research research facility to show upon inspection, and to report at least annually, that the provisions of this Act are being followed and that professionally acceptable standards governing the care, treatment, and use of animals are being followed by the research facility during actual research or experimentation.

(B) In complying with subparagraph (A), such research facilities shall provide—

(i) information on procedures likely to produce pain or distress in any animal and assurances demonstrating that the principal investigator considered alternatives to those procedures;

(ii) assurances satisfactory to the Secretary that such facility is adhering to the standards described in this section; and

(iii) an explanation for any deviation from the standards promulgated under this section.

(8) Paragraph (1) shall not prohibit any State (or a political subdivision of such State) from promulgating standards in addition to those standards promulgated by the Secretary under paragraph (1).

(b)(1) The Secretary shall require that each research facility establish at least one Committee. Each Committee shall be appointed by the chief executive officer of each such research facility and shall be composed of not fewer than three members. Such members shall possess sufficient ability to assess animal care, treatment, and practices in experimental research as determined by the needs of the research facility and shall represent society's concerns regarding the welfare of animal subjects used at such facility. Of the members of the Committee—

(A) at least one member shall be a doctor of veterinary medicine;

(B) at least one member—

(i) shall not be affiliated in any way with such facility other than as a member of the Committee—

(ii) shall not be a member of the immediate family of a person who is affiliated with such facility; and

(iii) is intended to provide representation for generaly community interests in the proper care and treatment of animals; and

(C) in those cases where the Committee consists of more than three members, not more than three members shall be from the same administrative unit of such facility.

(2) A quorum shall be required for all formal actions of the Committee, including inspections under paragraph (3).

(3) The Committee shall inspect at least semiannually all animal study areas and animal facilities of such research facility and review as part of the inspection—

(A) practices involving pain to animals, and

(B) the condition of animals, to ensure compliance with the provisions of this Act to minimize pain and distress to animals. Exceptions to the requirement of inspection of such study areas may be made by the Secretary if animals are studied in their natural environment and the study area is prohibitive to easy access.

(4)(A) The Committee shall file an inspection certification report of each inspection at the research facility. Such report shall—

(i) be signed by a majority of the Committee members involved in the inspection;

(ii) include reports of any violation of the standards promulgated, or assurances required, by the Secretary, including any deficient conditions of animal care or treatment, any deviations of research practices from originally approved proposals that adversely affect animal welfare, any notification to the facility regarding such conditions and any corrections made thereafter;

(iii) include any minority views of the Committee; and

(iv) include any other information pertinent to the activities of the Committee.

(B) Such report shall remain on file for at least 3 years at the research facility and shall be available for inspection by the Animal and Plant Health Inspection Service and any funding Federal agency.

(C) In order to give the research facility an opportunity to correct any deficiencies or deviations discovered by reason of paragraph (3), the Committee shall notify the administrative representative of the research facility of any deficiencies or deviations from the provisions of this Act. If, after notification and an opportunity for correction, such deficiencies or deviations remain uncorrected, the Committee shall notify (in writing) the Animal and Plant Health Inspection Service and the funding Federal Agency of such deficiencies or deviations.

(5) The inspection results shall be available to Department of Agriculture inspectors for review during inspections. Department of Agriculture inspectors shall forward any Committee inspection records which include reports of uncorrected deficiencies or deviations to the Animal and Plant Health inspection Service and any funding Federal agency of the project with respect to which such uncorrected deficiencies and deviations occurred.

(c) In the case of Federal research facilities, a Federal Committee shall be established and shall have the same composition and responsibilities provided in subsection (b) of this section, except that the Federal Committee shall report deficiencies or deviations to the head of the Federal agency conducting the research rather than to the Animal and Plant Health Inspection Service. The head of the Federal agency conducting the research shall be responsible for —

(1) all corrective action to be taken at the facility; and

(2) the granting of all exceptions to inspection protocol.

(d) Each research facility shall provide for the training of scientists, animal technicians, and other personnel involved with animal care and treatment in such facility as required by the Secretary. Such training shall include instruction on —

(1) the humane practice of animal maintenance and experimentation;

(2) research or testing methods that minimize or eliminate the use of animals or limit animal pain or distress;

(3) utilization of the information service at the National Agricultural Library, established under subsection (e) of this section; and

(4) methods whereby deficiencies in animal care and treatment should be reported.

(e) The Secretary shall establish an information service at the National Agricultural Library. Such service shall, in cooperation with the National Library of Medicine, provide information —

(1) pertinent to employee training;

(2) which could prevent unintended duplication of animal experimentation as determined by the needs of the research facility; and

(3) on improved methods of animal experimentation, including methods which

could—

(A) reduce or replace animal use; and

(B) minimize pain and distress to animals, such as anesthetic and analgesic procedures.

(f)1(See footnote on last page) In any case in which a Federal agency funding a research project determines that conditions of animal care, treatment, or practice in a particular project have not been in compliance with standards promulgated under this Act, despite notification by the Secretary or such Federal agency to the research facility and an opportunity for correction, such agency shall suspend or revoke Federal support of the project. Any research facility losing Federal support as a result of actions taken under the preceding sentence shall have the right of appeal as provided in sections 701 through 706 of Title 5, United States Code.

(f)2 No dogs or cats, or additional kinds or classes of animals designated by regulation of the Secretary, shall be delivered by any dealer, research facility, exhibitor, operator of an auction sale, or department, agency, or instrumentality of tile United States or of any State or local government, to any intermediate handler or carrier for transportation in commerce or received by any such handler or carrier for such transportation from any such person, department, agency, or instrumentality, unless the animal is accompanied by a certificate issued by a veterinarian licensed to practice veterinary medicine, certifying that he inspected the animal on a specified date, which shall not be more than 10 days before such delivery, and, when so inspected, the animal appeared free of any infectious disease or physical abnormality which would endanger the animal or animals or other animals or endanger public health: Provided, however, That the Secretary may by regulation provide exceptions to this certification requirement, under such conditions as he may prescribe in the regulations, for animals shipped to research facilities for purposes of research, testing or experimentation requiring animals not eligible for such certification. Such certificates received by the intermediate handlers and the carriers shall be retained by them, as provided by regulations of the Secretary, in accordance with section 10 of this Act.

(g) No dogs or cats, or additional kinds or classes of animals designated by regulation of the Secretary, shall be delivered by any person to any intermediate handler or carrier for transportation in commerce except to registered research facilities if they are less than such age as the Secretary may by regulation prescribe. The Secretary shall designate additional kinds and classes of animals and may prescribe different ages for particular kinds or classes of dogs, cats, or designated animals, for the purposes of this section, when he determines that such action is necessary or adequate to assure their humane treatment in connection with their transportation in commerce.

(h) No intermediate handler or carrier involved in the transportation of any animal in commerce shall participate in any arrangement or engage in any practice under which the cost of such animal or the cost of the transportation of such animal is to be paid and collected upon delivery of the animal to the consignee, unless the consignor guarantees in writing the payment of transportation charges for any animal not claimed within a period of 48 hours after notice to the consignee of arrival of the animal, including, where necessary, both the return transportation charges and an amount sufficient to reimburse the carrier for all out-of-pocket expenses incurred for the care, feeding, and storage of such animals.

(7 U.S.C. 2143) (P.L. 89-544, §13, Aug.24, 1966, 80 STAT. 352; P.L. 91-579, §14, Dec. 24, 1970, 84 Stat- 1562; P-L94-279, §§9, 10, April 22, 1976, 90 Stat- 418; P.L. 99-198, Title XVII, § 1752, Dec. 23, 1985, 99 Stat- 1645)

Section 14. Any department, agency or instrumentality of the United States having laboratory animal facilities shall comply with the standards and other requirements promulgated by the Secretary for a research facility under section 13 (a), (f), (g), and (h). Any department, agency, or instrumentality of the United States exhibiting animals shall comply with the standards promulgated by the Secretary under section 13 (a), (f), (g), and (h).

(7 U.S.C. 2144) (P.L. 89-544, §14, Aug. 24, 1966, 80 Stat. 352; P.L- 91-579, § 15, Dec. 24, 1970, 84 Stat. 1563; P-L 94-279, § 19, April 22, 1976, 90 Stat. 423; P.L. 99-198, Title XVII, § 1758, Dec. 23, 1985, 99 Stat. 1650)

Section 15. (a) The Secretary shall consult and cooperate with other Federal departments, agencies, or instrumentalities concerned with the welfare of animals used for research, experimentation or exhibition, or administration of statutes regulating the transportation in commerce or handling in connection therewith of any animals when establishing standards pursuant to section 13 and in carrying out the purposes of this Act. The Secretary shall consult with the Secretary of Health and Human Services prior to issuance of regulations. Before promulgating any standard governing the air transportation and handling in connection therewith, of animals, the Secretary shall consult with the Secretary of Transportation who shall have the authority to disapprove any such standard if he notifies the Secretary, within 30 days after such consultation, that changes in its provisions are necessary in the interest of flight safety. The Interstate Commerce Commission, the Secretary of Transportation, and the Federal Maritime Commission, to the extent of their respective lawful authorities, shall take such action as is appropriate to implement any standard established by the Secretary with respect to a person subject to regulation by it.

(b) The Secretary is authorized to cooperate with the officials of the various States or political subdivisions thereof in carrying out the purposes of this Act and of any State, local, or municipal legislation or ordinance on the same subject.

(7 U.S.C. 2145) (P.L. 89-544, § 15, Aug. 24, 1966, 80 Stat. 352; P.L. 91-579, § 16, Dec. 24, 1970, 84 Stat. 1563; P.L. 94-279, § 11, April 22, 1976, 90 Stat. 419; P.L. 98-443 § 9(i) Oct. 4, 1984, 98 Stat. 1708; P.L- 99-198, Title XVII, § 1757, Dec. 23, 1985, 99 Stat. 1650).

Section 16.

(a) The Secretary shall make such investigations or inspections as he deems necessary to determine whether any dealer, exhibitor, intermediate handler, carrier, research facility, or operator of an auction sale subject to section 12 of this Act, has violated or is violating any provision of this Act or any regulation or standard issued thereunder, and for such purposes, the Secretary shall, at all reasonable times, have access to the places of business and the facilities, animals, and those records required to kept pursuant to section 10 of any such dealer, exhibitor, intermediate handler, carrier, research facility, operator of an auction sale. The Secretary shall inspect each research facility at least once each year and, in the case of deficiencies or deviations from the standards promulgated under this Act, shall conduct such follow-up inspections as may be necessary until all deficiencies or deviations from such standards are corrected. The Secretary shall promulgate such rules and regulations as he deems necessary to permit inspectors to confiscate or destroy in a humane manner any animal found to be suffering as a result of a failure to comply with any provision of this Act or any regulation or standard issued thereunder if (1) such animal is held by a dealer, (2) such animal is held by an exhibitor, (3) such animal is held by a research facility and is no longer required by such research facility to carry out the research, test or experiment for which such animal has been utilized, (4) such animal is held by an operator of an auction sale, or (5) such animal is held by an intermediate handler or a carrier.

(b) Any person who forcibly assaults, resists, opposes, impedes, intimidates, or interferes with any person while engaged in or on account of the performance of his official duties under this Act shall be fined not more than $5,000, or imprisoned not more than 3 years, or both. Whoever, in the commission of such acts, uses a deadly or dangerous weapon shall be fined not more than $10,000, or imprisoned not more than 10 years, or both. Whoever kills any person while engaged in or on account of the performance of his official duties under this Act shall be punished as provided under sections 1111 and 1114 of Title 18, United States Code.

(c) For the efficient administration and enforcement of this Act and the regulations and standards promulgated under this Act, the provisions

(including penalties) of sections 6, 8, 9, and 10 of the Act entitled "An Act to create a Federal Trade Commission, to define its powers and duties, and for other purposes," (15 U.S.C. 46, and 48-50; 38 Stat. 721-723, as amended) (except paragraph (c) through (h) of section 6 and the last paragraph of section 9, and the provisions of Title II of the "Organized Crime Control Act of 1970" (18 U.S.C. 60001 et. seq., 62 Stat, 856), are made applicable to the jurisdiction, powers, and duties of the Secretary in administering and enforcing the provisions of this Act and to any person, firm, or corporation with respect to whom such authority is exercised. The Secretary may prosecute any inquiry necessary to his duties under this Act in any part of the United States, including any territory, or possession thereof, the District of Columbia, or the Commonwealth of Puerto Rico. The powers conferred by said sections 9 and 10 of the Act of September 26, 1914, as amended, on the district courts of the United States may be exercised for the purposes of this Act by any district court of the United States. The United States district courts, the District Court of Guam, the District Court to the Virgin Islands, the highest court of American Samoa, and the United States courts of the other territories, are vested with jurisdiction specifically to enforce, and to prevent and restrain violations of this Act, and shall have jurisdiction in all other kinds of cases arising under this Act, except as provided in section 19(c) of this Act.

(7 U.S.C. 2146) (P.L. 89-544, § 16, Aug. 24, 1966, 80 Stat. 352; P.L- 91-579, § 17, Dec. 24, 1970, 84 Stat. 1563; P.L94-279, § 12, April 22, 1976, 90 Stat. 420; P.L. 99-198, Title XVII, § 1753, Dec. 23, 1985, 99 Stat. 1649)

Section 17. The Secretary shall promulgate rules and regulations requiring dealers, exhibitors, research facilities, and operators of auction sales subject to section 12 of this Act to permit inspection of their animals and records at reasonable hours upon request by legally constituted law enforcement agencies in search of lost animals.

(7 U.S.C. 2147) (P.L. 89-544, § 17, Aug. 24, 1966, 80 Stat. 352; P.L. 91-579, § 18, Dec. 24, 1970, 84 Stat. 1564)

Section 18. Repealed. Pub. L. 91579. Similar provisions incorporated in section 13 by P.L. 91-579, SS 19, Dec. 24, 1970, 84 Stat.

(7 U.S.C. 2148)

Section 19. (a) If the Secretary has reason to believe that any person licensed as a dealer, exhibitor, or operator of an auction sale subject to section 12 of this Act, has violated or is violating any provision of this Act, or any of the rules or regulations or standards promulgated by the Secretary hereunder, he may suspend such person's license temporarily, but not to exceed 21 days, and after notice and opportunity for hearing, may suspend for such additional period as he may specify, or revoke such license, if such violation is determined to have occurred.

(b) Any dealer, exhibitor, research facility, intermediate tion sale subject to section 12 of this Act, that violates any provision of this Act, or any rule, regulation, or standard promulgated by the Secretary thereunder, may be assessed a civil penalty by the Secretary of not more than $2,500 for each such violation, and the Secretary may also make an order that such person shall cease and desist from continuing such violation. Each violation and each day during which a violation continues shall be a separate offense. No penalty shall be assessed or cease and desist order issued unless such person is given notice and opportunity for a hearing with respect to the alleged violation, and the order of the Secretary assessing a penalty and making a cease and desist order shall be final and conclusive unless the affected person files an appeal from the Secretary's order with the appropriate United States Court of Appeals. The Secretary shall give due consideration to the appropriateness of the penalty with respect to the size of the business of the person involved, the gravity of the violation, the person's good faith, and the history of previous violations. Any such civil penalty may be compromised by the Secretary. Upon any failure to pay the penalty assessed by a final order under this section, the Secretary shall request the Attorney General to institute a civil action in a district court of the United States or other United States court for any district in which such person is found or resides or transacts business, to collect the penalty, and such court shall have jurisdiction to hear and decide any such action. Any person who knowingly fails to obey a cease and desist order made by the Secretary under this section shall be subject to a civil penalty of $1,500 for each offense, and each day during which such failure continues shall be deemed a separate offense.

(c) Any dealer, exhibitor, research facility, intermediate handler, carrier, or operator of an auction sale subject to section 12 of this Act, aggrieved by a final order of the Secretary issued pursuant to this section may, within 60 days after entry of such an order, seek review of such order in the appropriate United States Court of Appeals in accordance with the provisions of section 2341, 2343 through 2350 of Title 28, United States Code, and such court shall have exclusive jurisdiction to enjoin, set aside, suspend (in whole or in part), or to determine the validity of the Secretary's order.

(d) Any dealer, exhibitor, or operator of an auction sale subject to section 12 of this Act, who knowingly violates any provision of this Act shall, on conviction thereof, be subject to imprisonment for not more than 1 year, or a fine of not more than $2,500, or both. Prosecution of such violations shall, to the maximum extent practicable, be brought initially before United States magistrates as provided in section 636 of Title 28, United States Code, and sections 3401 and 3402 of Title 18, United States Code, and, with the consent of the Attorney General, may be conducted, at both trial and upon appeal to district court, by attorneys of the United States Department of Agriculture.

(7 U.S.C. 2149) (P.L.- 89-544, § 19, Aug. 24, 1966, 80 Stat. 352; P.L. 91-579, § 20, Dec. 24, 1970, 84 Stat. 1564; P.L. 94-279, § 13, April 22, 1976, 90 Stat. 420; P.L. 99-198, Title XVII, § 1755, Dec. 23, 1985, 99 Stat. 1650)

Section 20. Repealed. Similar provisions incorporated in section 19 by P.L. 94-279, § 14, April 22, 1976, 90 Stat. 421.

(7 U.S.C. § 2150)

Section 21. The Secretary is authorized to promulgate such rules, regulations, and orders as he may deem necessary in order to effectuate the purposes of this Act.

(7 U.S.C. 2151)(P.L. 89-544, § 21, Aug. 24, 1966, 80 Stat. 353)

Section 22. If any provision of this Act or the application of any such provision to any person or circumstances shall be held invalid, the remainder of this Act and the application of any such provision to persons or circumstances other than those as to which it is held invalid shall not be affected thereby.

(7 U.S.C. 2152) (P.L. 89-544, § 22, Aug. 24, 1966, 80 Stat. 353)

Section 23. The Secretary shall charge, assess, and cause to be collected reasonable fees for licenses issued. Such fees shall be adjusted on an equitable basis taking into consideration the type and nature of the operations to be licensed and shall be deposited and covered into the Treasury as miscellaneous receipts. There are hereby authorized to be appropriated such funds as Congress may from time to time provide: Provided, That there is authorized to be appropriated to the Secretary of Agriculture for enforcement by the Department of Agriculture of the provisions of section 26 of this Act an amount not to exceed $100,000 for the transition quarter ending September 30, 1976, and not to exceed $400,000 for each fiscal year thereafter.

(7 U.S.C. 2153) (P.L.- 89-544, § 23, Aug. 24, 1966, 80 Stat. 353; P.L. 94-279, § 18, April 22, 1976, 90 Stat. 423)

Section 24. The regulations referred to in section 10 and section 13 shall be prescribed by the Secretary as soon as reasonable but not later than 6 months, from the date of enactment of this Act. Additions and amendments thereto may be prescribed from time to time as may be necessary or advisable. Compliance by dealers with the provisions of this Act and such regulations shall commence 90 days after the promulgation of such regulations. Compliance by research facilities with the provisions of this Act and such regulations shall commence ,6 months after the promulgation of such regulations (August 24, 1966), except that the Secretary may grant extensions of time to research facilities which do not comply with the standards prescribed by the Secretary pursuant to section 13 of this Act provided that the Secretary determines that there is evidence that the research facilities will meet such standards within a reasonable time. Notwithstanding the other provisions of this section, compliance by intermediate handlers, and carriers, and other persons with those provisions of this Act, as amended by the Animal Welfare Act Amendments of 1976, and those regulations promulgated thereunder, which relate to actions of intermediate handlers and carriers, shall commence 90 days after promulgation of regulations under section 13 of this Act, as amended, with respect to intermediate handlers and carriers, and such regulations shall be promulgated no later than 9 months after April 22, 1976; and compliance by dealers, exhibitors, operators of auction sales and research facilities with other provisions of this Act, as so amended, and the regulations thereunder, shall commence upon the expiration of 90 days after April 22, 1976: Provided, however, That compliance by all persons with paragraphs (f), (g), and (h) of section 13 and with section 26 of this Act, as so amended, shall commence upon the expiration of said 90-day period. In all other respects, said amendments shall become effective upon April 22, 1976.

(7 U.S.C. 2154) (P.L. 89-544, § 24, Aug. 24, 1966, 80 Stat. 353; P.L. 94-279, § 15, April 22, 1976, 90 Stat. 421)

Section 25. Not later than March of each year the Secretary shall submit to the President of the Senate and the Speaker of the House of Representatives a comprehensive and detailed written report with respect to—

(1) the identification of all research facilities, exhibitors, and other persons and establishments licensed by the Secretary under section 3 and section 12 of this Act;

(2) the nature and place of all investigations and inspections conducted by the Secretary under section 16 of this Act, and all reports received by the Secretary under section 13 of this Act;

(3) recommendations for legislation to improve the administration of this Act or any provision thereof; and

(4) recommendations and conclusions concerning the aircraft environment as it relates to the carriage of live animals in air transportation. This report as well as any supporting documents, data, or findings shall not be released to any other persons, non-Federal agencies, or organizations unless and until it has been made public by an appropriate committee of the Senate or the House of Representatives.

(7 U.S.C. 2155) (P.L. 89-544, § 25, as added by P.L. 91-579, § 22, Dec. 24, 1970, 84 Stat. 1565; P.L. 94-279, § 16, April 22, 1976, 90 Stat. 421)

Section 26. (a) It shall be unlawful for any person to knowingly sponsor or exhibit an animal in any animal fighting venture to which any animal was moved in interstate or foreign commerce.

(b) It shall be unlawful for any person to knowingly sell, buy, transport, or deliver to another person or receive from another person for purposes of transportation, in interstate or foreign commerce, any dog or other animal for purposes of having the dog or other animal participate in an animal fighting venture.

(c) It shall be unlawful for any person to knowingly use the mail service of the United States Postal Service or any interstate instrumentality for purposes of promoting or in any other manner furthering an animal fighting venture except as performed outside the limits of the States of the United States.

(d) Notwithstanding the provisions of subsection (a), (b), or (c) of this section, the activities prohibited by such subsections shall be unlawful with respect to fighting ventures involving live birds only if the fight is to take place in a State where it would be in violation of the laws thereof.

(e) Any person who violates subsection (a), (b), or (c) shall be fined not more than $5,000 or imprisoned for not more than 1 year, or both, for each such violation.

(f) The Secretary or any other person authorized by him shall make such investigations as the Secretary deems necessary to determine whether any person has violated or is violating any provision of this section, and the Secretary may obtain the assistance of the Federal Bureau of Investigation, the Department of the Treasury, or other law enforcement agencies of the United States, and State and local governmental agencies, in the conduct of such investigations, under cooperative agreements with such agencies. A warrant to search for and seize any animal which there is probable cause to believe was involved in any violation of this section may be issued by any judge of the United States or of a State court of record or by a United States magistrate within the district wherein the animal sought is located. Any United States marshal or any person authorized under this section to conduct investigations may apply for and execute any such warrant, and any animal seized under such a warrant shall be held by the United States marshal or other authorized person pending disposition thereof by the court in accordance with this subsection. Necessary care including veterinary treatment shall be provided while the animals are so held in custody. Any animal involved in any violation of this section shall be liable to be proceeded against and forfeited to the United States at any time on complaint filed in any United States district court or other court of the United States for any jurisdiction in which the animal is found and upon a judgment of forfeiture shall be disposed of by sale for lawful purposes or by other humane means, as the court may direct. Costs incurred by the United States for care of animals seized and forfeited under this section shall be recoverable from the owner of the animals if he appears in such forfeiture proceeding or in a separate civil action brought in the jurisdiction in which the owner is found, resides, or transacts business.

(g) for purposes of this section-

(1) the term "animal fighting venture" means any event which involves a fight between at least two animals and is conducted for purposes of sport, wagering, or entertainment except that the term "animal fighting venture" shall not be deemed to include any activity the primary purpose of which involves the use of one or more animals in hunting another animal or animals, such as waterfowl, bird, raccoon, or fox hunting;

(2) the term "interstate or foreign commerce" means—

(A) any movement between any place in a State to any place in another State or between places in the same State through another State; or (B) any movement from a foreign country into any State;

(3) the term "interstate instrumentality" means telegraph, telephone, radio, or television operating in interstate or foreign commerce;

(4) the term "State" means any State of the United States, the District of Columbia, the Commonwealth of Puerto Rico, and any territory or possession of the United States;

(5) the term "animal" means any live bird, or any live dog or other mammal, except man; and

(6) the conduct by any person of any activity prohibited by this section shall not render such person subject to the other sections of this Act as a dealer, exhibitor, or otherwise.

(h)(1) The provisions of this section shall not supersede or otherwise invalidate any such State, local, or municipal legislation or ordinance relating to animal fighting ventures except in case of a direct and irreconcilable conflict between any requirements thereunder and this section or any rule, regulation, or standard hereunder.

(7 U.S.C. 2156)(P.L- 89-544, § 26(a)-(h)(1), as added by P.L- 94-279, § 17, April 22, 1976, 90 Stat. 421)Note: P.L. 94-279 also amended 39 U.S.C. 3001(a) on material that may not be mailed.

Section 27. (a) It shall be unlawful for any member of an Institutional Animal Committee to release any confidential information of the research facility including any information that concerns or relates to—

(1) the trade secrets, processes, operations, style of work, or apparatus; or

(2) the identity, confidential statistical data, amount or source of any income, profits, losses, or expenditures, of the research facility.

(b) It shall be unlawful for any member of such Committee—

(1) to use or attempt to use to his advantages; or

(2) to reveal to any other person, any information which is entitled to protection as confidential information under subsection (a) of this section.

(c) A violation of subsection (a) or (b) of this section is punishable by—

(1) removal from such Committee; and

(2)(A) a fine of not more than $1,000 and imprisonment of not more that I year; or

(B) if such violation is willful, a fine of not more than $10,000 and imprisonment of not more than 3 years.

(d) Any person, including any research facility, injured in its business or property by reason of a violation of this section may recover all actual and consequential damages sustained by such person and the cost of the suit including a reasonable attorney's fee.

(e) Nothing in this section shall be construed to affect any other rights of a person injured in its business or property by reason of a violation of this section. Subsection (d) shall not be construed to limit the exercise of any such rights arising out of or relating to a violation of subsections (a) and (b) of this section.

(7 U.S.C. 2157) (P.L. 89-544, § 27, as added by P.L. 99-198, Title XVII, § 1754, Dec. 23, 1985, 99 Stat. 1649)

Section 28. Protection of Pets

(a) Holding Period. —

(1) Requirement.- In the case of each dog or cat acquired by an entity described in paragraph (2), such entity shall hold and care for such dog or cat for a period of not less than five days to enable such dog or cat to be recovered by its original owner or adopted by other individuals before such entity sells such dog or cat to a dealer.

(2) Entities Described. An entity subject to paragraph (1) is-

(A) each State, county, or city owned and operated pound or shelter;

(B) each private entity established for the purpose of caring for animals, such as a humane society, or other organization that is under contract with a State, county, or city that operates as a pound or shelter and that releases animals on a voluntary basis; and

(C) each research facility licensed by the Department of Agriculture.

(b) Certification. —

(1) In General — A dealer may not sell, provide, or make available to any individual or entity a random source dog or cat unless such dealer provides the recipient with a valid certification that meets the requirements of paragraph (2) and indicates compliance with subsection (a).

(2) Requirements. — A valid certification shall contain

(A) the name, address, and Department of Agriculture license or registration number (if such number exists) of the dealer;

(B) the name, address, and Department of Agriculture license or registration number (if such number exists), and the signature of the recipient of the dog or cat,

(C) a description of the dog or cat being provided that shall include —

(i) the species and breed or type of such;

(ii) the sex of such;

(iii) the date of birth (if known) of such,

(iv) the color and any distinctive marking of such- and

(v) any other information that the Secretary by regulation shall determine to be appropriate;

(D) the name and address of the person, pound, or shelter from which the dog or cat was purchased or otherwise acquired by the dealer, and an assurance that such person, pound, or shelter was notified that such dog or cat may be used for research or education (E) the date of the purchase or acquisition referred to in subparagraph (D);

(F) a statement by the pound or shelter (if the dealer acquired the dog or cat from such) that it satisfied the requirements of subsection (a) and

(G) any other information that the Secretary of Agriculture by regulation shall determine appropriate.

(3) Records. — The original certification required under paragraph (1) shall accompany the shipment o[a dog or cat to be sold, provided, or otherwise made available by the dealer, and shall be kept and maintained by the research facility for a period of at least one year for enforcement purposes. The dealer shall retain one copy of the certification provided under this paragraph for a period of at least one year for enforcement purposes.

(4) Transfers. — In instances where one research facility transfers animals to another research facility, a copy of the certificate must accompany such transfer.

(5) Modification. — Certification requirements may be modified to reflect technological advances in identification techniques, such as microchip technology, if the Secretary determines that adequate information such as described in this section, will be collected, transferred, and maintained through such technology.

(c) Enforcement. —

(1) In General — Dealers who fail to act according to the requirements of this section or who include false information in the certification required under subsection (b) shall be subject to the penalties provided for under section 19.

(2) Subsequent Violations Any dealer who violates this section more than one time shall be subject to a fine of $5,000 per dog or cat acquired or sold in violation of this section.

(3) Permanent Revocations.-Any dealer who violates this section three or more times shall have such dealer's license permanently revoked.

(d) Regulation. — Not later than 180 days after the date of enactment of this section, the Secretary shall promulgate regulations to carry out this section.

Section 29. Authority to Apply for Injunctions. —

(a) Request. — Whenever the Secretary has reason to believe that any dealer, carrier, exhibitor, or intermediate handler is dealing in stolen animals, or is placing the health of any animal in serious danger in violation of this Act or the regulations or standards promulgated thereunder, the Secretary shall notify the Attorney General who may apply to the United States district court in which such dealer, carrier, exhibitor, or intermediate handler resides or conducts business for a temporary restraining order or injunction to prevent any such person from operating in violation of this Act or the regulations and standards prescribed under this Act.

(b) Issuance. The court shall, upon a proper showing, issue a temporary restraining order or injunction under subsection (a) without bond. Such injunction or order shall remain in effect until a complaint pursuant to section 19 is issued and dismissed by the Secretary or until an order to cease and desist made thereon by the Secretary has become final and effective or is set aside on appellate review. Attorneys of the Department of Agriculture may, with the approval of the Attorney General, appear in the United States district court representing the Secretary in any action brought under this section.

Appendix K

Note: the following statements in support of H.R. 3398, the Pet Safety and Protection Act, were submitted to the U.S. House of Representatives Subcommittee on Livestock, Dairy and Poultry following the subcommittee's August 1, 1996 hearing on the bill. Even though the statements were submitted within the ten-day comment period set by the subcommittee, they were excluded from the hearing record.

August 8, 1996

FROM: Norman T. Flint
           P.O. Box 26
           Eastsound, WA 98245

TO: Subcommittee on Livestock, Dairy & Poultry
           Steve Gunderson
           Fax (202) 225-0917

RE: Bill HR3398

Dear Mr. Gunderson:

For the record, my name is Norman T. Flint. I am a victim of criminal behavior regarding Class B Dealers, Barbara Ann Ruggiero and Frederick "Rick" Spero and "Buncher" Associate, Ralf Jacobsen.

In 1988, I owned four Labrador mix dogs. Los Angeles County, in which I lived, did not allow any single residence more than three dogs. After repeated fines, I was forced to put one of my much loved pets up for adoption. I chose not to break up the two brothers that had been raised together. I put an ad in the paper "free to good home". After literally a dozen plus interviews, I selected the couple (Ralf Jacobsen and Barbara Ruggiero) I believed to be the best candidates to love and care for my beloved dogs. I was assured I would be able to visit them frequently, and that they would provide a loving home.

Words cannot describe my feelings when I found that approximately one week after I handed my dogs over to Ralf Jacobsen, my dog "Bear" underwent experiments where heart attacks were induced, repeatedly, for three days by Chief Veterinarian, Dr. John Young at Los Angeles Cedars Sinai Research Hospital. My dog "Wiggles" was nearly starved to death over a three month period at "Budget Boarding Kennels," a Class B Dealer Facility owned and operated by Barbara Ruggerio. He was fed only dry bread. The condition Wiggles was in, when he was rescued, was deplorable. My heartfelt gratitude goes out for the Department of Animal Regulations and Last Chance for Animals (in Los Angeles) for their limitless effort in animal welfare.

In the past eight years, I have:

Testified in court which led to convictions of Class B Dealers Barbara Ann Reggiero, Frederick "Rick Spero and "Buncher" Ralf Jacobsen.

Given interviews for text in a book bringing to light this issue.

Appeared on nationwide and local daily news programs.

Appeared on Eye to Eye, with Connie Chung, the Phil Donahue Show and used in reference on other media coverage of this issue.

Made it possible for King 5 Television (NBC-Seattle) photographer Ken Jones to obtain footage which won a Golden Globe Award. The footage for the "Other Times" TV Investigative News Magazine was shot at the compound of Class B Dealer "Dave Knight". Dave Knight has since had his license suspended. However, all fines have been suspended as long as he complies with court orders.

As you can see, my exposure to this issue is extensive. I have talked with, mourned with and consoled other victims. I feel my first-hand experience is proof that:

Fraudulently obtaining animals and pet theft runs rampant and unchecked.

Forged and fraudulent documents are used to mollify those obtaining animals for laboratory research. This was proven in my case when Cedars Sinai received documents with my "forged" signature releasing two Lab mix dogs for the purpose of research. Not only were the documents Number 92 and 93 forged, but the animals described in these documents did not match up with the actual animals received.

Some laboratories turn a blind eye to these crimes and continue to provide the "BIG BUCKS" ($500 per dog in my case) to motivate this continuing atrocity. This is proven in the statement made by Chief Veterinarian, Dr. John Young, "We don't have any other alternative".

This is not an issue about animals being used in research. The opposition to this bill attempted to confuse the issue of the "need for animal use in research vs pet theft". Much time was allowed them in their efforts to confuse these separate issues. Bill HR3398 is the best solution to date to prevent fraudulently obtained animals and family pets from finding their way into laboratories. The opposition to this bill would have you believe that the number of family pets disappearing from back yards is minimal, but my personal experiences have shown differently. What has gone overlooked is the fact that for every one pet that reaches the laboratories, many, many suffer in the death camps of some fifty Class B Dealers.

There are big money incentives to Class B Dealers, no enforcement, virtually no prosection, resulting in penalty. This is confirmed by Mike Dunn of the U.S.D.A., who expressed his frustration in the enormous amount of time and the cost to prosecute these crimes. With all the loop holes, justice is rarely served. I think it makes Mike Dunns' job very ungratifying when people like Dave Knight only receive a "slap on the hands". The doctors, veterinarians and technicians need to feel the impact of these crimes also. Ignorance is no excuse. It is their responsibility to be aware of how their animals are obtained. For each Class B Dealer put out of business, another one comes forward to take their place earning a quick profit from family pets.

It appears all parties agree that, out of thousands of Class B Dealers, approximately fifty sell dogs to be used in science research. Of these, fifty two percent of tracebacks are not in compliance. Only twenty five percent of animals used in research come from these Class B Dealers. With other sources for dogs, what could possibly detour Congress from passing this bill (HR3398) that will end the greedy financial opportunity that motivates these Class B Dealers.

I would like to take this time to thank you for the opportunity to speak out in favor of this Bill and to share my personal experience. I would like to think that "Bear's" death would not be in vain. I thank you for your consideration on this issue and would be happy to answer any questions regarding my experiences and how important they are to this issue.

I can be reached by telephone at (360) 376-4088 or (360) 376-5433 or fax at (360) 376-2994.

By mail to: Norman T. Flint
                P.O. Box 26
                Eastsound, WA 98245

                        Sincerely,

                        Norman Flint 8·9·96

                        Norman T. Flint

(202) 337-2334

August 9, 1996

Steve Gunderson, Chairman
House Subcommittee on Livestock, Dairy and Poultry
1301 Longworth House Office Building
Washington, DC 20515

Dear Mr. Chairman:

The Society for Animal Protective Legislation appreciates the opportunity to submit the following statement and attachments for the record of the August 1, 1996 hearing on H.R. 3398 and H.R. 3393.

We are writing in support of H.R. 3398, the Pet Safety and Protection Act of 1996. The notebook prepared by the Animal Welfare Institute and submitted at the hearing provides extensive documentation regarding the sale of pet dogs and cats to random source, Class B dealers who sell animals for experimentation. The notebook also outlines the many failures of random source dealers to comply with the Animal Welfare Act. The Society believes that H.R. 3398 offers a sound solution that will stop pets from being sold for experimentation, reduce USDA's regulatory burden, and permit research on dogs and cats to continue.

The legislation was carefully drafted to ensure that it would not pose an impediment to the acquisition of dogs and cats for research purposes. In response to statements made by advocates of random source dealers, we wish to point out their failure to identify how the legislation would prevent them from acquiring animals for experimentation.

The holdouts in the research industry who still use random source dealers seem intent on attempting to paint us as radical extremists. This is simply not the case. We are not anti-vivisectionist. We do not have a secret agenda to stop the use of dogs and cats in research. The Society for Animal Protective Legislation supports the position of the Animal Welfare Institute regarding the use of animals in research; a copy of the position statement is attached. The decision by so many individuals conducting research on dogs and cats not to use

1

random source dealers reveals how mainstream our position is.

Our review of USDA inspection reports of dealers who sell dogs and cats for research reveals widespread failure to comply with existing law. Therefore we were curious regarding the random source dealers whom opponents of the legislation rely on to supply them dogs and cats. Following the hearing we requested the names of the USDA licensed Class B dealers who supply Wayne State University and the Rush Arthritis and Orthopedic Institute/Rush Medical College/University of Illinois. Despite discussions with numerous individuals at both research facilities, they have yet to provide us with a single name.

A few animal experimenters stated that they will not be able to purchase the large or older dogs that they need without Class B dealers. This is hard for us to understand since random source dealers are simply middlemen. The researchers should be able to go directly to the source of the animals--providing it is a legal source--rather than through Class B dealers . These middlemen, who significantly mark up the price of the animals, typically fail to comply with many of the minimum requirements under the Animal Welfare Act, and have been proven to trade in stolen and fraudulently obtained animals.

Breeders, licensed by USDA as Class A dealers, are currently supplying approximately half of the dogs and cats used in research. We contacted a number of these companies, and they stated they will gladly increase the numbers of animals they breed in response to demand. As long as institutions turn to random source dealers as a cheap source of animals and don't ask questions about where the animals they get come from, breeders will not move to increase their inventory. The breeders are carefully watching the legislation in anticipation of a demand for more animals.

We understand that a number of Institutional Animal Care and Use Committees (bodies mandated by federal law to oversee the use of animals for experimentation at each research facility) are adopting policies not to conduct business with random source dealers. Class A dealers are already showing an increase in the number of dogs and cats they sell, and they are expanding their facilities in response. The breeders do not foresee a problem making large dogs available in the future. They also have older dogs, ex-breeders, that are sold for research once they are no longer used for breeding.

Under the proposed legislation, the research industry does have a number of other sources for dogs and cats in addition to Class A dealers. One such option is public pounds. Millions of animals are euthanized in public pounds each year,

2

and approximately half of these animals, who have been turned in by their owners, will be available for research purposes. A significant number of these animals are older, and many of the dogs turned in to pounds are large-framed.

One example of a facility that does not use Class B dealers is the University of California at San Diego. In 1990 the University purchased approximately 325 dogs and cats for research purposes from the county animal control department. That same year, the county received more than 10,000 animals that were brought in by their owners.

Under H.R. 3398, there should be no additional expenses or additional recordkeeping for public pounds that supply dogs and cats for experimentation. The responsibilities for pounds will be to: 1) hold the animals for 5 days (this is already required under existing law), 2) maintain data regarding the owner who turns in an animal to the pound (this, too, is already required under existing law), and 3) not provide stray animals for research purposes. Pounds which supply animals for research purposes must provide notice that this is the case. Pounds will be registered by USDA, which will permit them access to confirm that the above requirements are being met. We are pleased that Assistant Secretary of Agriculture Dunn testified that the agency supports these requirements.

Research facilities can also breed dogs and cats themselves, and individuals can donate animals for experimental purposes, a common practice in veterinary schools.

STRENGTHENED ENFORCEMENT OF EXISTING LAW WILL NOT SOLVE THE PROBLEM OF PET THEFT

Preventing the theft of pet dogs and cats for sale to laboratories was one of the major concerns prompting passage of the federal Animal Welfare Act in 1966. Decades after the Act was passed, evidence that stolen pets were still being sold to laboratories prompted Congress to amend the original legislation with the intent of closing loopholes that allowed unscrupulous random source dealers to continue funnelling stolen pets into the research trade. In 1988, Senator Wendell Ford introduced the Pet Theft Act, which would have prohibited Class B dealers from obtaining animals from sources other than municipal pounds or individuals who had bred and raised the animals on their own premises. This legislation was vigorously opposed by the research industry, which claimed it would cut off the supply of animals available for research. As a result, a weakened version of Senator Ford's bill was finally passed in 1990. The amendment added a five-day holding period for pounds selling animals to Class B dealers and set forth certification requirements for sales of dogs and cats by dealers. In response to the failure of even this amendment to solve the problem, USDA has made every effort through its own rulemaking process to ensure that stolen and fraudulently obtained dogs and cats are not entering the research trade. These efforts continue to be inadequate despite strengthened regulations and increased enforcement actions at taxpayer expense.

For example, in 1987 USDA proposed to strengthen its regulations governing the acquisition of random source dogs and cats by Class B dealers. At the time, USDA acknowledged that theft of pets for sale to research was a recurring problem. In its proposed rules, the agency stated: "In the past few years there have been several instances of licensed dealers obtaining dogs and cats by fraudulent means and apparently knowingly purchasing stolen animals." Like Senator Ford's bill, the proposed rules would have limited the sources of dog and cats for Class B dealers to municipally owned and operated pounds and to people who had bred and raised the animals on their own property. One of the loopholes the rules were intended to close was the sale of dogs and cats at auctions and trade days. The proposed rules stated: "The Department has also noted an increase in licensed dealers buying dogs and cats at flea markets or trade-day type sales. These animals are purchased from anyone and are usually purchased one, two or three dogs or cats at a time .... The net effect of the above types of activity is to encourage animal theft for profit."

The proposed rules were also designed to eliminate what USDA called "the indiscriminate impoundment of 'lost' animals by contract pound operators who are also licensed dealers." Well aware of the conflict of interest inherent in such arrangements, USDA stated it had received an increasing number of complaints that contract pound operators who also held Class B licenses had been 'overzealous' in impounding cats and dogs and that the impounded animals were not always stray or lost. The proposed rule would have prevented pound operators with Class B licenses from "intermingling animals and selling those dogs and cats that must be held ... for the requisite holding period pending identification and return to their owner, with those that have completed the requisite holding period and may be sold to research facilities."

USDA's proposed rules were met with strong opposition from the research industry, which claimed, once again, that the new provisions would severely limit the availability of animals for research. The industry also argued that the proposed rules would exceed USDA's statutory authority. As a result, USDA removed the provision restricting the sources of dogs and cats for Class B dealers to pounds and individuals who bred and raised the animals themselves. It did,

4

however, enact a provision prohibiting the acquisition of random source dogs and cats by use of false pretenses, misrepresentation or deception. Contrary to the assertions of the research industry, this provision has not solved the problem of pets being sold to laboratories. Since its implementation in 1989, there have been numerous documented cases of Class B dealers selling stolen and fraudulently obtained pets to laboratories.

One of the ways in which USDA attempts to ensure that stolen pets are not being sold to laboratories is by requiring dealers to keep accurate records regarding the acquisition of random source dogs and cats. Despite increased frequency of inspections and tracebacks of sources listed on dealer records, inaccurate and fraudulent recordkeeping by Class B dealers continues to be a serious problem. USDA has stated that the percentage of inaccurate or fraudulent dealer records (based on random tracebacks) is approximately 50 percent. However great the incidence of inaccurate or falsified records, the number of animals involved in each documented case of fraudulent or inaccurate records is significant: in January 1996, USDA charged one Indiana dealer with falsely claiming to have acquired a total of 357 dogs from a pound that USDA investigators discovered was nonexistent. In 1994, another dealer in Indiana failed to record the required information for approximately 1,162 dogs and cats acquired from random sources, and between 1990 and 1991, a dealer in Iowa failed to record the required information for the acquisition of at least 1,600 dogs and cats.

During its 1993 Random Source Dog Traceback project (report attached), USDA discovered that many dealers were illegally purchasing animals from unlicensed dealers. These unregulatable individuals, otherwise known as bunchers, provide licensed dealers with a great opportunity to "launder" illegally acquired dogs and cats. An unlicensed dealer in Missouri, who has allegedly been selling animals to dealers for 20 years, admitted selling animals from various sources to an Arkansas dealer and giving the dealer false names to list in his acquisition records (affidavit attached). This individual admitted to selling animals to at least two other licensed dealers on a regular basis. It is simply not possible for USDA to keep track of the comings and goings of all of the unlicensed individuals who are selling animals to Class B dealers. Thus, there is no way to ensure that the animals these individuals are selling have been acquired legitimately. Since they are interested in acquiring as many animals as possible, dealers frequently "turn a blind eye" to the activities of their suppliers. Within the last several years, there have been a number of instances of bunchers stealing pets and then selling them to licensed dealers. Just last year in Ohio, a buncher stole Karyl Parks' dog, Danny, from her truck and sold him to a Class B dealer in

5

Indiana, who in turn sold him to a laboratory. Parks was lucky enough to recover Danny before he was experimented on. (See attached photo).

USDA's 1993 traceback effort remains the most extensive and thorough checking of random source dealer's acquisition records. Records were tracked from the B dealers to the original owners of the animals, and affidavits were taken from individuals who supplied animals to the random source dealers. A large sample of each dealer's records were checked.

USDA's current approach to tracebacks can only be described as shoddy. The traceback is only done on a couple of animals at each dealer's facility, even though a number of dealers provide more than 800 animals a year to research. Of the few animals that are traced back, the check only goes one step back in the acquisition process, though many animals are traded from one individual to another and another. Thus the traceback is unlikely to extend back to the original owner of each animal. A number of Class B dealers buy only from other Class B dealers. In this case, the check confirms that one Class B dealer sold an animal to another Class B dealer--and the traceback goes no further!

The traceback is conducted by telephone, rather than by affidavit, making it easy to provide fraudulent information. Further, because so few records are checked at each dealer's premises, it will be virtually impossible to identify bunchers. Dealers are adept at finding loopholes in USDA's attempts to seek compliance with the Animal Welfare Act; the current traceback effort is full of them.

Efforts by USDA to bring Class B dealers into compliance with both recordkeeping requirements and minimum standards of animal care have been grossly inadequate. Many dealers have long histories of violating the Animal Welfare Act. When finally assessed, fines are typically so low as to be considered merely as the cost of doing business. Enforcement actions against dealers who are violating the Act can take up to three years or longer, and the dealers are allowed to remain in business throughout the administrative process. In 1991, USDA referred a case to its Office of General Counsel (OGC) because the individual involved, a Class B dealer in Indiana, had failed to maintain accurate acquisition records and was suspected of operating a facility that had not been registered. The case was with OGC for almost three years before any action was taken. During this time, the dealer refused a USDA inspector access to his facility on 29 separate occasions. On the few occasions when the inspector was able to conduct inspections, he documented continuing recordkeeping and animal care violations. Finally, in June 1994, USDA filed a complaint against the dealer. A hearing on the charges did not take place until May 1996, nearly two years later. A decision is not expected until this fall. This dealer, against whom there is an outstanding arrest warrant for violation of a state cruelty to animals statute, is still in business. He supplies animals to other Class B dealers and directly to research facilities.

In the few instances that USDA has been able to suspend or permanently revoke a dealer's license, family members or employees have stepped in to carry on with the business, simply obtaining their own Class B licenses. Typically, the violations continue under the new licensee's management. In other cases, the dealers are able to stay in business under other people's licenses. One California dealer who had been charged with obtaining animals under false pretenses simply moved her business to another town and continued operating under a friend's USDA license number.

The history of complete disregard for the provisions of Animal Welfare Act by dealer after dealer makes clear the need for a profound change in the law governing the acquisition of dogs and cats for research. As long as random source dealers are licensed to sell animals, family pets will continue ending up in laboratories.

Sincerely,

Cathy Liss
Senior Research Associate

ANIMAL WELFARE INSTITUTE POLICY
on the use of Vertebrate Animals for Experimentation and Testing

Abstract: Animals should be used for experimentation only 1) when there is no known feasible alternative; 2) after review of a carefully designed experiment based on knowledge of existing literature on the subject; 3) using the smallest possible number of animals 4) of the most suitable species, 5) maintained in an optimum environment, 6) under the care of trained, sympathetic personnel, and 7) preventing pain, fear, and anxiety by judicious experimental design and generous use of anesthetic, analgesic and tranquilizing drugs. 8) Endangered species should not be used; 9) threatened species should only be used for experiments conforming with requirements for human experimentation.

Animals should not be subjected to any pain, fear or anxiety which can be avoided. This means:

1) If other equally effective methods of experimentation or testing are known to be available they should be used in preference to any experiment likely to cause pain or fear to an animal.

2) If the experiment or test can be conducted on a fully anesthetized animal it should be, and, if injury is caused, the animal should be destroyed without regaining consciousness, OR:

3) If it is imperative that the animal survive the injury inflicted, sufficient pain-relieving drugs must be administered to prevent each animal from feeling pain.

4) Nursing care must be provided to all animals following surgery or other injurious interventions.

5) Competent staff should be available at all times, day and night, weekends and holidays to care for experimental animals. They must make rounds for the purpose of ascertaining the state of the animals' health and well-being. They must be authorized to dispense pain-relieving or tranquilizing drugs or, where specified, to phone the investigator or director for such authorization with regard to specific animals at any time.

6) Before undertaking any experiment involving animals, the experimental design must be reviewed by a committee including a senior scientist in the discipline involved, a veterinarian familiar with the treatment, care and management of the species of animal involved, and a person primarily concerned with the welfare of animals. Purpose of the review is to ensure 1) that it is not feasible to substitute for the use of animals, 2) that the least possible distress and injury is caused, 3) that excessive numbers of animals are not used, and 4) that appropriate anesthetics, analgesics and tranquilizers are employed if needed. In those special circumstances in which the investigator feels his research would be marred by general anesthesia or use of narcotic alkaloids, this should be given special scrutiny by the review committee, and, if necessary, by a further impartial authority. The committee must also ensure that no experiment is undertaken by a person untrained in the methods to be employed and that the kind of animals selected are the ones most likely to develop the new knowledge or test result being sought.

If a disagreement between the investigator and

the institutional committee cannot be resolved, and the design of the experiment is questioned either 1) on the basis of inadequate preparation and review of the literature and sound scientific conception, or 2) on the basis of the humane considerations listed above, the proposal should be submitted to an objective committee or arbitrator who is not associated with the institution and a decision taken based on evidence requested or submitted to the committee or arbitrator.

7) No endangered species should be used for experimental purposes. Threatened species should only be used under constraints which prevent risk of death or serious injury as required in human experimentation. Capture and transportation of wildlife for laboratory use must be subject to regulation and inspection both nationally and internationally.

8) The great majority of experimental animals are bred for the purpose. This is the preferred method of acquiring animals. They should be raised in facilities whose standards of housing and care are equal to those described in this statement for animals under experiment. Dogs and cats, for use in experiments under full anesthesia from which they are not allowed to recover but pass directly into death, may be obtained from among animals already condemned to death in pounds because no homes can be found for them. This simply constitutes a change in the place where euthanasia is conducted. Transportation and handling of these and all other animals must be humane, providing the same high standards of sanitation, ventilation and temperature control as for animal quarters. Transportation should be conducted by the most rapid means feasible. The size of the cage must permit normal postural adjustments for any animal.

9) Euthanasia must be considered a major responsibility. Animals should be killed by anesthetic overdose and their inability to recover ensured by surgical means. No animal should be discarded without holding it long enough after death to observe rigor mortis.

Housing of experimental animals must be so constructed and maintained as to provide for the activities natural to the species. Enclosures or cages must be sufficiently large and well constructed to permit burrowing, climbing, perching, swinging, walking, stretching, rolling, or other normal actions ordinarily seen in the species when not confined. Any exceptions to such basic rules for housing for purposes of a particular experiment must be considered as part of the experimental design and reviewed as outlined above.

If funds are not available for housing any particular species comfortably, providing a diet which will maintain optimum health, providing veterinary and nursing care following surgical or other adverse experimental intervention and providing high standards of sanitation, ventilation and temperature control at all times, the experimentation should not be undertaken.

Well trained staff who like animals and sympathize with their feelings are essential. They must be observant and make their observations known to the director of the laboratory or other person with authority to act in all cases. For example, moribund animals should be euthanized. Suffering animals should be, depending on the situation and the nature of the work, euthanized, anesthetized, sedated or otherwise treated to prevent suffering.

Experimental animals, sacrificed for human benefit, should be provided optimum living conditions before, during, and after their use. This is a minimum repayment for their services—the only one which can be made.

Painful animal experiments should not be conducted for any frivolous or non-essential purpose; therefore, new products should be tested to the greatest extent possible using substitutes for living, conscious vertebrates; and where known substances are being evaluated, safe and painless human testing should be substituted, as, for example, in the way that new soaps, creams, and other cosmetics are tested by leading manufacturers. Where obviously harmful effects can be predicted by the chemical or physical properties of a new product, for example a strong acid, it should be automatically given a warning label without requiring further animal testing.

All institutions that use research or test animals should make an active effort to develop means of replacing animals wherever possible. Funds saved by adoption of substitute methods should be applied to improving the quality of food, care, and housing for animals used.

Tests of products in different countries should be coordinated to eliminate useless duplication. Experiments or tests should not be carelessly repeated merely because it is easier to use animals than to search the literature or because a competitor will not release his test data. Duplication of an experiment or test should be undertaken only for a genuine scientific reason.

Appendix L: Newspaper Editorials in Support of the Laboratory Animal Welfare Act

THE LIGHT

SAN ANTONIO   TEXAS

A Constructive Force in the Community

WEDNESDAY, JUNE 15, 1966   PAGE **40**

Protecting Pets

RECENT letters from readers, on this page, have drawn attention to the ill treatment and abandonment of pets.

The work of the local Humane Society is handicapped by lack of funds and the fact that the organization is not even tax-exempt.

It is encouraging, therefore, to see that efforts on the national level are gaining ground.

The Senate Commerce Committee has approved Sen. Magnuson's bill to require the humane care and housing of animals inside laboratories as well as on dealers' premises, and in transit.

The bill is much stronger than the House-approved version of the Poage bill, HR 13881.

In the Senate version of HR 13881, dogs, cats, primates, rabbits, hamsters and guinea pigs would come under the protection of the Secretary of Agriculture.

It provides humane standards with respect to housing, feeding, watering, sanitation, ventilation, shelter from extremes of weather and temperature, separation by species and veterinary care.

Supplying laboratories with animals for testing is now a big business.

Some shocking pictorial evidence of ill treatment has been collected by the Humane Society of the United States and the Society for Animal Protective Legislation, Washington, D.C.

Reform is sure to come if the American public is made aware of the need.

The Washington Post

AN INDEPENDENT NEWSPAPER   MONDAY, JUNE 13, 1966

Animal Protection

The Senate Commerce Committee has, in a humane way, taken the bull by the horns so to speak and put the brand of its approval on a solid, sensible bill to protect research animals from needless, wanton cruelty. Its bill, introduced by Senator Magnuson and measurably strengthened by Senator Monroney's amendment, is markedly superior to the animal care measure passed by the House. We hope that the Senate will give it speedy endorsement and that the House will accede to its wise humaneness.

The Senate Commerce Committee bill would require laboratories, animal dealers and persons transporting animals to be used in scientific research to observe certain elementary standards to be set by the Secretary of Agriculture for the handling of these creatures before they are used for experimentation. The standards would be designed to deter the stealing of pets for sale to laboratories and to require giving them decent shelter, ventilation, sanitation, food and water. The legislation would not limit or affect actual use of the animals for scientific experimentation in any way.

There is not a syllable in this bill that can be said to impair or impede research. It is not antivivisectionist, or antimedical or antiscientific or anti-anything save senseless neglect and brutality. It amounts to no more than a simple expression of humanity.

Tasha, shortly after her rescue from a Pennsylvania Class B dealer who had failed to maintain accurate records on her and provide her with needed veterinary care.

NOTES

NOTES

NOTES